PUBLIC ADMINISTRATION
VALUES, POLICY, and CHANGE

ALFRED PUBLISHING CO., INC.

PUBLIC ADMINISTRATION

VALUES, POLICY, and CHANGE

ROBERT H. SIMMONS
California State University at Los Angeles

EUGENE P. DVORIN
California State University at Los Angeles

Published by Alfred Publishing Co., Inc.
75 Channel Drive, Port Washington, N.Y. 11050

Copyright © 1977 by Alfred Publishing Co., Inc.
All rights reserved.

Printed in the United States of America

Library of Congress Cataloging in Publication Data

Simmons, Robert Harrison.
    Public administration.

    Bibliography: p.
    Includes index.
    1. Public administration. I. Dvorin, Eugene P.,
joint author. II. Title.
JF1351.S49   350   76-7966
ISBN 0-88284-042-8

to

George A. Shipman

    for his contributions to administrative theory

and

Arthur J. Misner

    for his contributions to administrative practice

CONTENTS

PART II – CONFLICTING VALUES

"Now, of course, ideologies are human creations, and all human creations are liable to error. Presumably, there is no body of doctrine in which every statement is true. Now, error is disconnection from reality and loss of possible control over it. There is therefore a duty to correct errors of doctrine and it will be a loyal act in leaders and members to remove false statements from the organization's ideology and to replace them with true ones . . .

There are thus tremendous reasons for being a rebel. Nothing less can save mankind."

Barrows Dunham
Ethics Dead and Alive

PREFACE

The problems of organizing and teaching the introductory course in Public Administration are legion and need not be recounted here. The agency experience and maturity level of students, their backgrounds in understanding the governmental system and their expectations as they enter class are factors that will affect their perceptions of the course. No single text can be designed to meet all their variant needs. The background and professional interests of the professor, his or her value framework and the type of student "product" regarded as the desirable goal of the course are other variables that shape the success, or otherwise, of the course.

This volume will meet the needs of those who are discontent with the value-free neutrality approach so long and so assiduously cultivated within public administration. We feel that public administration is not value-free but, to the contrary, "value-full." Any other assumptions we regard as out of touch with the value-conflicts of the broader society. We, ourselves, are not value-free nor are we neutral on many of the issues requiring resolution within the discipline. Consequently, we choose not to hide behind the guises of "scientific objectivity" or scholarly remoteness traditionally associated with the scientific management movement or the early behavioral approaches. However, we do not denigrate them. We regard them as crucial to understanding the administrative processes because, despite the protestations of their most ardent supporters, they do reflect values.

Having accepted the validity of value-full or value-laden public administration we then, at an earlier time, had to work back to the sources and nature of our own discontent with administrative orthodoxy. These were briefly expressed in our previous volume, *From Amoral to Humane Bureaucracy.* Once we had become aware of our own value "first principles" the intellectual unease within public administration assumed new importance and, we believe, we were able to view it with a new clarity.

In presuming the need for yet another text for the introductory course we were guided by the belief that the very real contributions of the more traditional "value-free" approaches could be successfully wedded to the newer "value concerned" approaches. Especially did we feel the need for this symbiosis at the introductory level—that crucial stage where the student's vista and interests may be immeasurably expanded and the environment provided for continuing further to other administrative courses and experiences.

Once these tentative conclusions were reached the strategies for accomplishing our goal were shaped by a number of value assumptions. We feel that previous texts for the introductory course erred in emphasizing the national administrative system when in fact much of the "action" and the bulk of public employees are at the state and local levels. Therefore, we have endeavored to redress the balance by devoting more attention to administrative developments below the national level. Also, we have used a "macro" rather than a "micro" approach based upon our belief that introductory students should gain a wide perspective, a sense of proportion and relationship among the components of the public administrative process. We also believe that despite the tenacity of the traditional approaches in most public agencies, it would be a disservice to the student to ignore the serious challenges to orthodoxy. Conversely, we have rejected the notion of a text reflecting only the non-orthodox approaches as constituting an equal disservice to the student. The balance we have sought is to allow the student to appreciate the traditional processes of the ongoing agency while being aware of the refreshing air of non-conformity and intellectual discontent these processes have produced in their wake.

Part I describes public administration within the broader

environmental setting and suggests the range of problems to which it must respond. Also, the "problem" of dealing with these problems is emphasized by exposing the student to the highly diverse, and sometimes conflicting, perspectives or "spectacles" through which the administrative processes may be viewed.

Parts II and III reflect our belief in the richness of the past. We refute the notion that purely behavioral approaches adequately explain or describe public administration. Modern administration is modern only because it follows from an administrative past. No student should be deprived of a sense of historical development nor of philosophic tradition. The seeds of contemporary discontent have sprouted from the soil of orthodoxy. To merely water and pick the leaves is insufficient; the host soil must also be reexamined and nurtured. The evolution of administrative law with its potential for freedom or constraint and the development of intergovernmental administrative and fiscal relationships reveal the intricate procedural networks linking agency and client, administrator and judge, government and government.

Part IV focuses upon the new horizons of public administration. It encompasses developments in policy-making, program action systems, organization theory and decision theory. The dynamics of interpersonal interaction within organizational processes reveal yet another layer of intervening network. The transition from the centrality of hierarchy to more open systems of administration is described.

Part V reflects our fundamental belief that the humaneness of bureaucracy is the acid test of its appropriateness to a democratic society; and all change should be channeled to achieve this goal.

In a volume of this breadth and within the boundaries of our own values we had, of necessity, to be highly selective. Breadth precludes depth and one set of value assumptions precludes others. We hope the end product of our efforts will be of sufficient merit to encourage the use of readily available supplementary materials for those who may wish their students to delve more deeply into specific subjects they feel not given their "full due" here.

R. H. S.
E. P. D.
Los Angeles, California

ACKNOWLEDGMENTS

Several people were helpful in the evolution of this book. Our wives, Audrey and Estelle, were a source of constant support and sound judgement and we thank them for their patience and help. John Crow of the University of Arizona, John Ballard of San Jose State University, and Morley Segal of The American University all read the manuscript and provided useful and insightful criticism; and we are grateful to them for their valuable comments. Benjamin Smith and Daniel Sager of California State University, Los Angeles provided useful and valuable suggestions at strategic points in the development of the manuscript; and George Littke and Virgil Stevens of California State University made special contributions in the chapters on policy making and public management. Kathleen Callanan provided important and insightful contributions, particularly in Chapter 16 on humane bureaucracy. Francis Dickinson and Carol Gee did an excellent typing job on the manuscript. And finally, we thank Bill Knowles for suggesting the project to us initially and John Stout of Alfred for seeing the project through with us.

PUBLIC ADMINISTRATION
VALUES, POLICY, and CHANGE

PART I

LOST HORIZONS

1

INTRODUCTION: CHALLENGES TO PUBLIC ADMINISTRATION

People working in public administration today perform a vast array of activities and functions within the framework of massive bureaucratic structures. Public administrative efforts can create an environment as idyllic, dignified and humane as the campus and redwoods environs of the University of California, Santa Cruz. Likewise, it is capable of creating an environment as dark as an Arkansas prison farm which deprecates, dehumanizes and denigrates the person. Tyranny frequently appears in our technological times in the guise of administrative rules, orders, regulations and services. Marcus Raskin has observed:

> Modern tyranny is the maintenance of organized power in the hands of the state, its military and bureaucratic apparatus, and its corporate system. The corporate forms seek the death of politics, favoring instead hierarchic and administrative processes through which human concerns are transformed into matters of interest, ideological pretension, or quantitative measurement.[1]

The excesses of My Lai, the pervasive immorality of Watergate, the riot at New York's Attica Prison and the tragedy of Kent State point up how easily we can abuse our fellow human beings through the tidy and orderly processes of administration. Each day within the complex networks of administrative activity, thousands of practicing administrators make significant value-laden choices which affect the lives of millions. It is vitally important that the administrator become aware of and concerned with the value context surrounding his administrative tasks. To do this, each administrator must become conscious not only of his own values, but also of those proffered to him as he determines courses of action to carry out his tasks. The excitement and meaning of our very existence—indeed, the future of life itself on this planet—is linked to the administrative process. Theory, values and practice are inexorably interwoven and enmeshed. It is this complex net which is the center of attention in the study of public administration.

Public administration is responsible for a vast array of social, political, economic and military activities often characterized by contradictory missions; yet all have some apparent semblance of political legitimacy. Within the United States there are sometimes wide gaps between the administrative mission and administrative practice. These gaps point up serious contradictions between values sought and services delivered. Thus, within the myriad responsibilities of public administration are many significant and unresolved ambiguities and conflicts, the resolution of which is also in the center of public administrative attention.

THE IMPORTANCE OF PUBLIC ADMINISTRATION

It is important to identify the special strengths and contributions of public administration within the United States. These make it a unique field and highlight the vast promise it offers for the future.

The development, at the close of the nineteenth century, of the civil service concept, based upon honest and competent professional performance and the separation of the administrative concern from political leadership, encouraged a commitment to "getting the job done" at the federal, state and local levels. This reflected the pragmatic spirit which permeated American life during the westward expansion. The closing of the frontier brought growing settlements and greater demands for more honest and effective performance by public officials. This demand for excellence by the public generated a commitment to excellence by the increasingly professionalized public servants. The development of a competent and professional public service spawned a new concern for the "public interest" which, by definition, should transcend private and special interest. The failure to fully develop an effective theory of the public interest by those in the field of public administration has contributed to the contradictions between theory and practice.

The Civil Service Act of 1883, often referred to as the Pendleton Act, signaled the transition of the public service from political patronage and spoils to professional excellence and honesty. It was a giant step toward freeing the public service from a vile corruption of the spirit. This act established a bipartisan three-member Civil Service Commission, appointed by the president and confirmed by the Senate, each serving an indefinite term subject to removal by the president. It gave the commission authority to establish benchmark standards as well as rules of operation and procedure. These included the requirement of open competitive examinations, appointment from among those earning the highest grades, a probationary period and protection of the classified service from political coercion or the necessity of enforced contributions to party treasuries.

A public service thus came into being at the federal level which was destined to become a model for state and local administration. It was committed to a high degree of excellence, oriented to solving very immediate and practical problems and generally supportive of democratic ideals. These standards were gradually achieved, in greater or less degree, in a large number of the hundreds of political jurisdictions in the ensuing decades. As these operational values took hold, they served the public servant well. The growing strength and competence of the administrative arm of government helped greatly in the transition from a predominantly rural base to a predominantly industrial one; from a nation of small villages to a nation of large urban centers; and later, from an industrial to a "post-industrial" society. Administrative integrity and efficiency as publicly proclaimed goals provided much of the cement needed in a highly diverse and heterogeneous society undergoing severe strains of transition. It responded further by developing those specialized skills and services demanded by a growing and articulate population committed to technological, scientific and industrial leadership.

Today the public service is broad, diverse and multifaceted. It is now steeped in the tradition of open recruitment and demonstrated competence. Its inner processes are constantly being modified to sustain high levels of competence and to develop expertise in newly emergent fields. It has avoided authoritarian unification and remains today multifunctional, politically diverse and service-oriented. Yet, in the wake of Watergate, this great promise has once again been tarnished by the shabby behavior of men in high administrative office. The public service today faces another challenge: that of restoring integrity to its own procedures, restoring public confidence in its capacities and reinvigorating its commitment to democratic ideals.

ABUSES OF ADMINISTRATIVE POWER

The American people are reeling, not only from the daily exposure of corruption, but also from the long-term economic and psychological effects of an unpopular and divisive war and severe domestic economic troubles. Any positive, hopeful or optimistic pronouncements from within the public service are literally overwhelmed by the overabundance of pessimistic forecasts and negative alternatives.

Americans were alternately incredulous, stunned, and outraged as the abuses of power at the highest levels of the federal government were exposed in the summer of 1973. The Senate Select Committee on Presidential Campaign Activities, chaired by Senator Sam Ervin of North Carolina, held its hearings over national television. The events which followed the burglarizing of the Democratic campaign headquarters at the Watergate complex in Washington, D.C., during the darkness of the early morning of June 17, 1972, revealed extraordinary abuses of power. Senator Ervin, a recognized authority on the Constitution, concluded in his report to the Senate that "Watergate was unprecedented in the political annals of America in respect to the scope and intensity of its unethical and illegal actions."[2] A president, cabinet officers, presidential counsels, highest level White House staffers and a host of lesser officials and Republican Party functionaries betrayed their public trust by participating in activities far beyond the traditionally accepted values which are basic to a free society.

The misuses and abuses of federal agencies such as the Internal Revenue Service, the Federal Bureau of Investigation and the Federal Communications Commission are well chronicled and confirmed. Some executive departments, such as Commerce and Justice, were subjected to serious manipulation by their own political leadership as well as by top presidential staff. The story is lengthy, complex and sordid. Proceeding undiscovered and unchecked, the abuses could have brought our political democracy to its knees. The unconscionable may have profited greatly from the mistakes of Watergate. Discovery and ultimate exposure in any future corruption may be compounded in difficulty, for corruption may be exquisitely sophisticated as well as bumbling and gross. In the face of the overwhelming possibility of an impeachment conviction and after an historic vote in support of three articles of impeachment by the Judiciary Committee of the House of Representatives, President Richard Nixon resigned his office effective August 9, 1974. Though not tried by the Senate nor indicted by a federal grand jury, the ex-president accepted a full and complete pardon by his successor, President Gerald Ford. Many others involved received public trials and prison terms.

One of the more ominous developments of recent years was the covert expansion of the Central Intelligence Agency into the domestic political arena. There were serious violations by the C.I.A. of its legislative charter in matters related to the Watergate break-in, as suggested in a special addendum to the Watergate Committee report by Senator Howard Baker, Vice-Chairman and ranking Republican member on the committee.[3] Much later, Seymour Hersch, in a lead article in the *New York Times,* December 22, 1974, noted other direct violations of the agency's statutory charter when it conducted massive illegal domestic intelligence. Later confirmation came from C.I.A.

Director William E. Colby. Three resignations by high-level C.I.A. officials followed and the developments brought into question the veracity of sworn testimony given months earlier to a Senate committee by C.I.A. personnel.[4]

Presidential misuse of the C.I.A. may have reached its highest point under the Nixon administration, yet as long ago as 1963, the changing role of the C.I.A. was so disturbing to former President Harry S Truman that he felt it necessary to speak out, especially since it was an agency which had been established during his presidency. It was originally conceived as a means to coordinate the diverse intelligence-gathering activities of the military. Former president Truman vigorously opposed injecting the C.I.A. into peacetime domestic and overseas "cloak and dagger" operations.

> We have grown up as a nation respected for our free institutions and our ability to maintain a free and open society. There is something about the way the C.I.A. has been functioning that is casting a shadow over our historic position and I feel we need to correct.[5]

He went on to state the need for the agency to return solely to its information-gathering and analysis function. The nation failed to heed his warning. He could not have known then that the C.I.A. would later spend over $8 million between 1970 and 1973 to "destabilize" a Marxist, yet democratically elected, regime in Chile. The bloody coup occurred in 1973 and established in power one of the most onerous dictatorships in the modern world. Nor could he have known then of the incipient use of police state tactics of infiltration and surveillance at home, yet he clearly warned of the dangerous trend.

Particularly odious was the use of authoritarian police state techniques of infiltration, surveillance, political subversion and corruption of the election process. Mass arrests on an unprecedented scale took place in May, 1971, when over 12,000 Viet Nam war protesters gathered in Washington, D.C. These citizens were listening to Congressman Ronald Dellums on the steps of the Capitol when the District of Columbia police converged on them and in great sweeps arrested and detained the prisoners in

Oliphant, The Denver Post

"Hi, Ferguson, FBI" . . . "Oh, Hi, Kelley, CIA . . . Meet Wilson, Phone Company" . . . "Hi."

THE NATION/*February 22, 1975*

a football stadium. These arrests were encouraged and applauded by Attorney General John Mitchell, who was later convicted for his part in covering up the burglary of Democratic headquarters at the Watergate on June 17, 1972. This use of "realpolitik" domestically is a serious threat to democratic institutions. This threat was recognized by the courts, for the protesters have since won a spectacular legal victory that provides over $12 million in compensatory damages for illegal arrest, detention and violation of the civil rights of free speech and peaceful assembly.

The present situation is marked by the absence of inspirational and effective administrative leadership. Traditional philosophical orientations no longer provide helpful guidance. The failure to develop a comprehensive measure and definition of the *public interest* has left the public servant nearly defenseless against those who would capture the concept by defining it as synonymous with their own private interests. The admonition by Woodrow Wilson to separate *policy* from *administration*, leaving policy-making to the political side and administration to those professionally trained and specialized, was suitable for its time.[6]   But when the public service is faced with a lack of effective political leadership and with corrupt leadership as well, the civil servant appears bereft of adequate defenses against misuses of the awesome power of political directives.

Even so, morally corrupt political leaders issuing unlawful orders do not always hold sway. There were men such as Elliot Richardson, former Attorney General, and William Ruckelshaus, former Deputy Attorney General, who could not be bought or intimidated. These men resigned rather than carry out what they considered a breach of the agreement between Attorney General Richardson and Special Prosecutor Archibald Cox by which Cox had come to assume office.

Even under the impact of these harrowing events the vast administrative structure continued to perform daily administrative tasks in an orderly and competent manner. Much of the stability in the American system during the difficult days of civil turmoil in the late sixties and the failure of political leadership and growing disillusionment in the early seventies may be traced to the professional attitudes and competence of millions of dedicated federal, state and local public employees.

The underlying strength of the administrative system was clearly demonstrated. Yet, it is disturbing that some of the trained civil service did follow immoral and unlawful orders from top executives. They acted in ways that were consistent with a perception of their task as simply carrying out policy in a professional and efficient manner. Internal Revenue Service employees responded to a request from the White House to provide tax information and begin tax harassment for some "enemies" of the president.   The C.I.A. investigated thousands of United States citizens within the continental United States in direct violation of its legislative mandate.   The Federal Bureau of Investigation released raw files to the press and generally abused its information and investigative functions. Although no federal civil servant has gone to prison or been fined for criminal or civil violations of the law growing out of Watergate, a serious identity crisis for the public employee has shaken public confidence. The Nuremberg Principle does apply. This is the guiding rule established in international law when the Nazi war criminals were tried for their crimes. Stated simply: Following orders from a higher authority is no defense against criminal prosecution for an unlawful act.

The professional civil servant is placed in a particularly difficult position under these conditions. If he refuses to follow orders, he might be disciplined in any number of ways, including reassignment, demotion, a "tainted" career or even loss of his position. Each daily act of the public employee may be significantly related to a value-laden moral and legal choice. The teaching and practice of public administration has not in the past emphasized this very real, yet very difficult, dimension of public employment. This does present the value dimension in the context of theory and application.

PROBLEMS OF ADMINISTRATION

Public administration contains a vast reservoir of information and expertise centering on an infinite number of daily problems. It provides alternative routes of action to public policy choices. Political deliberative bodies such as independent regulatory agencies, boards, commissions, legislatures and city councils are dependent upon administrative advice and expertise. Yet, public administration has not effectively marshaled its potential strengths and capacities to resolve the immense problems of the post-industrial state. Technology runs amuck, threatening the life support systems of the planet. Effective responses to these abuses are delayed, thwarted and rendered ineffective. The past has demonstrated that many highly efficient and specialized societies rapidly collapsed when conditions drastically changed. Complex and highly specialized societies are rarely adaptable. Social regimentation and the cultural homogenization resulting from the increasing monotony of technological civilization, its standardized educational patterns and mass communications make it more difficult to establish varied and flexible responses to the survival needs of our civilization.[7]

Today progress has become an end in itself and the captains of industry seem to dominate social and economic vision. The work ethic provides an industrious and unquestioning employee.

The inefficiencies of raw competition in the private sector have resulted in a shift to cooperation with the federal executive. Federal authority now provides the function of overseer. Interchangeability in the top leadership of big industry and big government raises serious questions as to what is really in the best interests of the nation. A large military establishment maintains a Pax Americana internationally at the same time that multinational corporations increasingly challenge the dominance of the nation-state system.[8]

These profound changes do violence to our traditional values. They have spawned a military-industrial technology with unanticipated consequences, including a very real threat to human existence. The concept of production efficiency and its value context is a distinctive American contribution to the development of technology. Under contemporary conditions, however, efficiency in its traditional role can become a threat to survival. As one scientist has stated:

> The inefficient society is the goal of the post-technological society. Efficiency is for robots and those who would master the earth though it hasten the end of their petty lives. Efficiency jeopardizes human survival and all life on earth. The humane society, not efficiency, is a fitting goal for man.[9]

The assumption that the earth provides infinite resources and unending property to use and own as one will has given way to the realization that earth's resources are finite and expendable and, for an alarming number of resources, in short supply. "Growthmania" has had a catastrophic impact on the planet's resources. The view is emerging that the planet and its life support system needs to be held in trust and shared by the generation of the living to be preserved and replenished for the yet unborn. Perhaps not surprisingly, new legal doctrine may be developed which thinks about the unthinkable—vesting natural objects in nature (such as trees) with legal rights.[10]

The contemporary urban and industrial environment with its high-rise, right-angled towers amidst the squalor of ghetto poverty thrusts nature aside with little heed to the consequences. Indeed, the closest the urban dweller may ever come to nature is the cemetery. He lives in an environment of polluted air, estranged human relationships, rising crime, overcrowded and inadequate public transportation and distortion of the life cycles of the nearby waters (streams, lakes or oceans), bringing them to the point of death until, finally, they are unable to sustain any biological life or serve human needs. Public administration, although not charged with the full responsibility for the identification and resolution of these problems, has not responded as creatively and effectively as its potential suggests. The responses, when made, have often been safe, uncertain and uncreative. The administrative awareness and expertise required to resolve these problems have not been adequate. The potential administrative energies have often been inhibited by effective clientele interference with agency mission and tasks. In many instances, they have been held in check by a failure of legislative commitment. Scientific and technological development within the industrial, corporate and bureaucratic world has led to an exponential increase in the number of problems demanding definition and solution. Value contradictions and competitive games of power within the arena of public decision-making paralyze effective public action. Ill-designed and conflicting administrative structures are oriented to pursue conflicting goals. This exponential expansion of problems places its own special brand of pressures on administrative processes and immensely complicates their tasks.

The traditional housekeeping functions of public administration have expanded and changed. The early functions included such tasks as the collection of taxes and the distribution of revenue, building and maintaining roads and bridges, recording vital statistics, public lands management and public safety. These were generally state governmental functions. At the federal level administrative tasks were concerned with foreign affairs, war, post roads, and mail service, and, as in the states, matters concerned with the administration of justice. Today, public functions have been drastically altered and expanded. All levels of government are concerned with the accumulation, evaluation and publication of data and information crucial to informed decision-making. Regulation and intervention in all phases of

13

human life, together with active and positive pursuit of programs serving human needs, increasingly characterize the responsibilities of modern public administration.

Public Safety

One area of increasing community concern is the establishment, maintenance and restoration of public safety. Public administration is central to this concern, from the prevention of crime to the ultimate return to society of those who are subjects of the criminal justice system. No area is more replete with value contradictions. The "law and order" orientation simply assumes that the punishment swiftly applied will automatically effect behavioral reform. The rehabilitation approach assumes that behavior is quite complicated and to prepare a person for healthy participation in a social system requires attention and action related to the complex causes of behavior and misbehavior.

Prisons are variously viewed in the following ways: 1) Prisons are meant to punish social offenders. 2) Prisons are disastrous instruments of oppression and tribal vengeance. 3) Prisons are quite necessary but should be less punitive and more humane. 4) Prisons are necessary but should be oriented toward reform and rehabilitation. 5) Prisons should be replaced with more effective social institutions which attack the causes of crime and are directed toward restoring the violator of the social order back into healthy and effective participation within that order.[11] Modern correctional programs are a maze of these conflicting value orientations in which representatives of these perspectives are found in innumerable combinations. Within these perplexing and inconsistent approaches stands the public administrator. He attempts to fulfill daily tasks involved in maintaining prisons and making sense of the social mission he is assigned to carry out. Indeed, the prison official must operate out of one of these value orientations. This adds to the contradictions in the entire process and contributes to the growing problems within prisons and increasing rates of crime generally.

Leadership within the planning processes which will alter public policy in this area requires the public administrator to be deeply immersed in the definition of the problem and the selection of the values guiding the choices and to be a crucial participant in the solution. Here there are important challenges and there is much to be done where public administration must take the lead. On the law enforcement side of public safety, creative and innovative approaches and responses by the professionals are required.

Educational Administration

The great American experiment in educating the masses, an historic first for any people, is threatened today by declining resources, institutional rigidity and paralyzing value conflicts. This is compounded by a growing ambivalence in public commitment. Compulsory school education was instituted primarily to shrink the labor market, curb child labor abuses, educate children for skilled labor, and only minimally because education is a good thing for the young. As its liberating power was demonstrated, other values began to dominate choices concerning the utilization of educational resources. Education for life, preparation for the exercise of intelligent participatory citizenship within a democratic system, self-fulfillment (among others) became goals of the public educational systems paralleling the broadening of the franchise and the growth of the industrial system.

Conventional wisdom sees society as open and free, where any citizen can achieve his full potential and rise from the log cabin to garner the highest rewards attainable. Others blame the ills of modern society on permissive education, which ill-prepares children for the work-a-day world. Yet others note our schools have evolved to meet the employment needs of our industrial society. They see industry as needing a disciplined and skilled labor force. The society also requires a mechanism for social control and political stability.

Today, schools are effectively segregated, unequally financed, and have imposed class stratification, specialization, boredom, order, rigidity and stultifying routine on our nation's elementary and secondary students. Educational administrators are now faced with court-ordered desegregation and are required to abide by equal financing regulations. Uncertainty, confusion and chaos now reign in many school districts. Conflict and violence on the campus increase, while reading, writing and arithmetic skills decline. In California, usually a harbinger of things to come elsewhere in the land, the scores of high school seniors continue to decline seriously in reading and English grammar and usage.

In New York City, efforts by some local groups to bring about decentralized control over public schools reflect a wide spectrum of conflicting values. The struggle to achieve local control pits layman against professional, ethnic group against ethnic group, religious group against ethnic group and established power centers against new challengers for power. The conflict, and similar ones elsewhere, reflects the fact that American government has often excluded or ignored public involvement in policy-making. In New York the alienated and previously powerless black community demanded more responsiveness to their needs.

The black community's attempt to establish even one experimental, decentralized, locally controlled school district was bitterly fought, and when an experimental district was established, opposition continued to deter its success. Although the people of the Ocean Hill–Brownsville community lost the major battle for local control of schools, the total effort did result in their becoming a viable and cohesive community with greatly enhanced political "savvy" and power.

American federalism, although essentially decentralized in appearance, has shown a countervailing increased preference for centralized control. One study by Fantini and Gittel of the New York City experience found that:

> ... on the action level, decentralization (defined ... as redistributing power for decision-making to community representatives, limiting professional controls) ... has been tried and harshly resisted and constrained by coalitions of professionals, labor and political leaders. . . .[12]

The conflict reached great emotional heights among all concerned. It occurred because those within the centralized educational system viewed the emerging demands for participation and decentralization as a serious threat to their own well-being. This resulted in heightened tensions between the insiders in the sprawling big-city school bureaucracy (professional educators, administrators and teachers) and those seeking participation, reform and a significant degree of control (parents, community residents and students). In 1969 a misleading decentralization plan passed by the New York State legislature establishing "decentralized school control" actually avoided the transfer of effective power to the local community and, instead, strengthened the school system's central machinery. Yet the decentralization effort was not a total failure. The local community school boards succeeded in enlisting new participants, such as blacks and Puerto Ricans dedicated to school reform. Also, more minority school supervisors were appointed. This new leadership created a highly motivated educational élan. The schools, which were previously fortresses, became more open and better able to effectively service community needs. Finally, the great majority of the parents felt they had more influence and thought the schools were better for such changes as had occurred. Fantini and Gittel concluded their study by observing that social change could come only through "confrontation with the system and displacement of the established interests."[13]

Effective alternatives to traditional rigid and routine education are proving workable and useful in fulfilling the educational mission. Yet the overarching educational system seems moribund and stultifying or, in some instances, consumed by the chaos of social change. Thus, education generally seems locked in a crisis not only at the secondary and elementary levels, but at the university and college levels as well. The underfinancing which reflects among other problems the loss of public faith in the educational system now threatens higher education. University enrollments are declining and alternative modes and forms of post-secondary education are being sought by college-age young people. Major shifts by students to career programs and away from the social sciences and humanities distort the funding base of public colleges and universities. This, along with the application of narrow, efficiency-oriented budgetary criteria and modern management techniques, challenges the traditional

17

perceptions concerning curriculum and college governance. It also raises serious questions about value assumptions concerning the role and function of higher education in the modern world. Within this value-conflicted milieu stands the public administrator charged with meeting the public needs, yet remaining mystified as to what the demands of his mission require. As in the area of public safety, the conflict of values inhibits effective policy responses to the growing crises at all levels of our educational system. Here again the public administrator will be at the center of the effort if effective definitions of the problems are to be developed, helpful policy choices made, values and their consequences identified and effective action taken.

Transportation

In the United States the automobile and the airplane dominate private and public choices concerning transportation priorities. The automobile has spawned a vast national interstate highway system that has required immense investment in planning, design and construction. Within the great American urban centers, comprehensive freeway systems move autos carrying mostly single drivers from suburban home or urban fringe to and from central city jobs. The journey each way should be swift and comfortable. Yet, at the rush hour freeways are jammed and autos, often barely able to creep along, contribute their noxious portion to putrid, polluted air. More often than not, public transportation is archaic and inadequate to meet commuter needs. In Los Angeles it is virtually nonexistent. In that city after World War II powerful oil, rubber and auto manufacturers aided in dismantling one of the nation's most effective fixed guideway systems. Throughout the nation, the auto has become king. All choices, state and local, affecting transportation needs have been shaped by its dominance. Freeways are built by subsidies from gasoline sales and federal interstate highway monies. Rail lines have been ripped up and extremely valuable public rights of way sold off or lost. The rapid transit district, which uses rubber and gasoline and buses built by the auto industry, operates on routes which are hard to learn, infrequently serviced and insufficient.

Cities want fixed guideway systems such as subways, trolley lines, commuter railroads or elevated automatic "people movers." The federal government's response to these needs is to tell the cities that budgetary limitations and high costs of building subways and other fixed transit systems require that they will have to get by with the use of buses. Unless, of course, the cities can provide large amounts of capital from local taxes. Such taxing sources are already overburdened. Other tax sources are dominated by the federal government. The best example is the federal tax on gasoline, which is dedicated to highway construction. Commuter needs, industry demands, vested interests in cement, oil, autos, gasoline, rubber and previously established priorities in established public agencies vie for control over the expenditures of scarce public dollars for public transport. The result is failure to meet growing public transit needs.

This story is the same when the problems of the public national passenger railway system are examined. Inadequate and deteriorating trackage, insufficient routes, schedules designed to serve only the high population areas—these are some of the most obvious deficiencies. Amtrak is working valiantly against great odds with obsolescent stations and equipment. The tight operational strictures and the conflicted value context assure that it cannot operate profitably, provide a high-quality service or satisfactorily meet the needs of interurban transportation. Early in 1975 federal planners concluded that it is impossible to establish profitable rail systems in parts of the midwest and the northeast. Extensive trackage must be rehabilitated and maintenance qualities upgraded. Nationalization of trackage has thus been suggested, with the rail companies leasing the trackage they use. As in the highway system, the road on which the wheels roll would be federally subsidized.

The queens of public transportation, the private airline passenger carriers, are likewise facing difficulties. They are burdened with the compound increases in the cost of oil. This overriding fact permeates all phases of transportation from planning and construction to scheduling and flying. Great public airports are located in or near the nation's urban centers. High-density air traffic is increasingly difficult to control. Automobile access and exit lanes are choked with traffic. The aircraft produce both air and noise pollution. These and many other hazards are acute problems related to this facet of the public transport system.

Ground travel by auto or rail, public or private, or air travel by commercial airline or by private plane, are dependent upon public administrators who have planned, built and supervised the roadways and runways and who maintain the railways. They also operate the air traffic control systems and are responsible for the maintenance of airline safety. Public administrators regulate routing, fares and determine rates and tariffs under guidelines designed to meet the public interest.

The role of the public administrator is absolutely crucial to the effective functioning of public and private transportation. The resolution of the complex problems presently facing the transportation industry cannot even be begun without significant participation and contributions from the public sector. Here, too, value conflicts and contradictions contribute to the worsening of problems and inhibit their eventual solution. The public administrator must become aware of the conflicted value context, the power centers dominating decisions, seek to identify overriding public needs, envision the possibilities for resolution of conflict and provide problem-solving assistance.

Health Care

The delivery of effective health care to a majority of citizens remains a fundamental national concern. There has been political and administrative failure to confront the value conflicts inherent in the situation. The well-organized and politically strong medical profession appears unresponsive to nationwide public and personal health needs. It is nearly always successful in paralyzing appropriate responses in this area.

Health care is the nation's third largest industry, employing over four and one-half million persons. The nation's health bill approaches 100 billion dollars annually. It is important to note that nearly 50 percent of the total bill is paid by tax dollars. In 1974 Caspar W. Weinberger, former Secretary of Health, Education and Welfare, suggested that health care costs could increase at a rate of 15 percent or more a year (see Figure 1-1). The public is searching for relief from staggering health costs. Effective health care for the young, the poor and the aging is often only partial or completely lacking. Often what is delivered is inadequate, untimely and undignified in application. There is growing pressure for national health insurance. Many powerful forces have conflicting values and expectations about a national health insurance program. Health providers, Congress and consumers

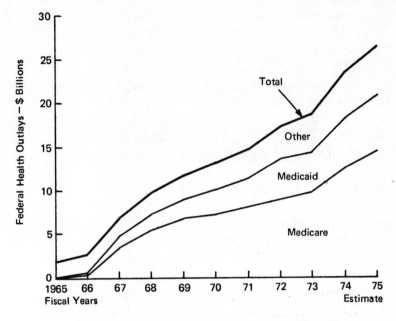

SOURCE: *Federal Budget in Brief, Fiscal Year, 1975, p. 20.*

Figure 1-1. FEDERAL HEALTH OUTLAYS

make differing demands and have differing perceptions of what interests should be given the greatest weight.

A national health insurance program symbolizes to the public a refuge from the anxieties of ill health or medical disaster, which can bankrupt and destroy a family or individual. Physicians fear that the regulations that will inevitably accompany such a program will restrict their professional duties and invade their professional responsibilities. Still others see self-enrichment as a possibility, especially in the extended care field.

Congress, as well as the planners of health care, fears that a national health insurance program could enormously increase the total health bill by lifting the financial barrier now keeping many people from seeking adequate health care for themselves. This is what happened after the passage of Medicare and Medicaid. In California in 1965 15 percent of the population became qualified for these programs and many millions of the poor received needed medical attention that they previously had been unable to obtain and for which they could not pay. Yet, these important programs placed great pressure on already limited facilities. This situation, repeated in other states, helped produce a cost spiral which doubled health costs nationally between 1965 and 1972.

Immediate access by the American public to more effective and more adequate health care would undoubtedly swamp doctors' offices with patients and reduce the amount of time for physician-patient contact. There would be pressures for increasing the number of doctors and trained support staff. Quality and extent of training, hospital construction and care, extended care facilities, hospital charges, physicians' fee schedules, professional excellence and quality of care, preventive medicine, quota systems on specializations are a few of the areas where public regulation, sanctions and reviews might be introduced. The question remains who will dominate the regulation and enforcement of those areas designated for review and control. The professions? Government professionals? Consumer groups? In 1972 Congress rejected voluntary medical audits and utilization review committees supported by the American Medical Association. Congress instead chose a method still heavily weighted in favor of the physician but, nevertheless, resisted by their professional organization.

Local PSRO's (Professional Standards Review Organization) review the medical necessity of every service performed for the 35 million Americans on Medicare and Medicaid. Under this program, PSRO boards appointed by local physicians or by the Secretary of Health, Education and Welfare establish norms for the treatment of every kind of major illness, tests to be given, therapies that are appropriate, and normal lengths of hospitalization.

Canadians, it appears, are exceptionally satisfied with their government's medical insurance program. Even the physicians who originally opposed their inclusion into the plan are generally satisfied and making more money than ever. Having satisfied basic Canadian health care needs, that country's health care planners are focusing upon the need to change people's most basic attitudes about health care *per se:* what it comprises, who is responsible for it, and how it should be delivered, with special emphasis upon preventive medicine. The goal is now to redesign the health care system so that unnecessary medical procedures and duplicative hospital or clinic facilities are discouraged. The public plays a larger role in running the system and patients have more responsibility for maintaining their own good health. Reduction of self-imposed health risks, such as smoking, drinking and overeating, is being encouraged. Active reduction of environmental risks in the public and private sectors, such as air and water pollution, is being pursued.

Combined local services are being encouraged. The idea supporting these centers is based upon an awareness that many health programs have social causes at their root. Thus, where social and medical services are combined, reciprocal programs would emerge and be encouraged. When a person is chronically ill with colds and the flu, adequate diet and nutrition education could be suggested. In Canada, an entire population has been relieved of the threat of financial ruin by a very successful public health care program.[14]

Top quality surgery is of no avail if postoperative care is inadequate and the patient dies. The finest medicine available is meaningless if a nation's infant mortality rate continues to climb. The United States is now sixteenth among nations in infant deaths. The myth of good medicine and adequate health delivery fades when American health care is measured against Canada's. Effective responses to the American situation will come only with public awareness of the paralyzing effects of the value contradictions which fully inhibit adequate understanding and resolution of the problem. It is no longer enough to scoff at public medicine when president, senator, congressman and Supreme Court justice seek medical treatment at two of the nation's finest hospitals which are publicly owned and operated by the United States Army (Walter Reed) and Navy (Bethesda Naval Hospital). Veterans' Administration hospitals, county general hospitals and other medical facilities such as mental hospitals range across the United States, providing widely varying levels and quality of medical care.

Public administration and the public administrator have significant roles to play and fundamental tasks to perform in contributing to the resolution of the value conflicts and developing a program of effective and adequate health care for all citizens, as has been accomplished in Canada and Great Britain.

Effective health care delivery can occur within publicly financed hospitals. The great teaching and research centers located in many states and associated with the great public universities in each state are a source of valuable research, expertise and knowledge. The resources and skills necessary for resolution of our health needs are available. The public administrator specializing in this area has a tremendous role to play. His skills, training, knowledge and energy are vitally needed for the task. This is one area where expansion, growth, problem-solving, program development and increasing involvement by the public administrator will continue and even expand.

Energy

The oil crisis of 1973 was a glaring demonstration of the failure of public administration to define and respond effectively to emerging energy needs. It marked a failure to define a total national effort protecting users, providing for environmental safeguards and responding to the needs of future users. Figure 1-2 indicates the United States uses more energy than any other nation in the world. Although the nations of the world consume varying amounts of energy per capita, energy consumption correlates fairly well with the total GNP per capita. The American energy shortage was clearly predictable as early as 1972, when domestic supplies of fuel began to lag sharply behind the rising total demand for energy. At present the United States has an elaborate and effective energy provisioning system involving fossil fuels, natural gas, hydroelectric resources and nuclear fission. Yet to be developed are nuclear fusion

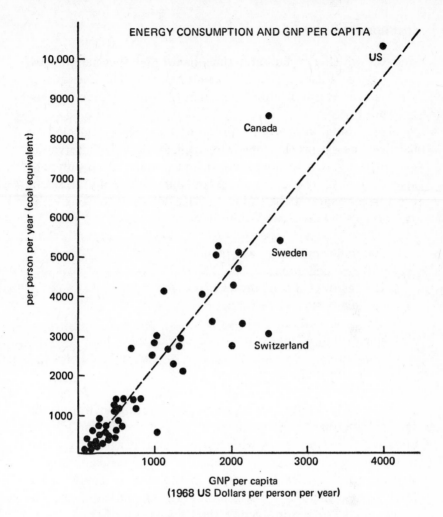

Although the nations of the world consume greatly varying amounts of energy per capita, energy consumption correlates fairly well with total output per capita (GNP per capita). The relationship is generally linear, with the scattering of points due to differences in climate, local fuel prices, and emphasis on heavy industry.

SOURCES: Energy consumption from UN Department of Economic and Social Affairs, Statistical Yearbook 1969 (New York: United Nations, 1970). GNP per capita from World Bank Atlas (Washington, DC: International Bank for Reconstruction and Development. 1970).

Figure 1–2. D. H. Meadows, D. L. Meadows, J. Randers, W. W. Behrens, *The Limits to Growth,* A. Potomic Associates Book, Universe, N.Y. (1707 L. Street, N.W., Wash., D.C.). 1972, p. 70.

sources, which are far safer than fission, geothermal sources, solar energy sources, tide and wind sources. The energy supplied serves transportation, commercial, domestic and industrial needs.

The United States, on the other hand, has neglected to balance energy provisioning with utilization and conservation measures oriented to its more efficient use and as an unrenewable resource. The energy program put forward by President Ford in his State of the Union message delivered to Congress in January, 1975, envisions within the next decade:

200 major nuclear power plants
250 new coal mines
150 major coal-fired power plants
 30 major new oil refineries
 20 new synthetic fuel plants
The drilling of many thousands of new oil wells
Construction of millions of new trucks, automobiles and
    buses that use much less fuel

Very little attention was given to eliminating environmental threats, altering consumption activity and developing equally effective power resources with less potential hazards, e.g., solar energy and nuclear fusion.[15] National, state and local administration agencies are deeply involved in the nation's energy problems. These include the Atomic Energy Commission, the Environmental Protection Agency, the Department of the Interior, the Department of Health, Education and Welfare, the Tennessee Valley Authority, the Bonneville Power Authority, local utility districts, city gas and electric companies and private utilities. Problems of shortages, environmental protection and conservation require urgent resolution. The public administrator will necessarily provide an essential contribution to such resolution. The energy field is replete with value conflicts that often paralyze and distort responsible action. The public administrator must be prepared to be both responsive to these problems and to play a positive role in the development of a more effective energy program. That program must rest firmly on values which reflect the needs of the country as a whole, national security, costs, environmental protection and replenishment, and the present and future quality of life. Here again the public administrator will be involved at all stages of planning, operations and delivery.

THE LIFE SUPPORT SYSTEM

There are 4 billion people on earth. Today there are 200,000 more than yesterday. By the year 2000, there will be 2.4 billion more than there are today. April 1, 1975, was an anniversary of sorts, for on that date the world's population exceeded 4 billion. The estimated population in the mid-1970's is slightly higher than the projection in Figure 1–3. If industrial growth and food production keep pace or even approach keeping pace with meeting the demands of an explosive population growth that maintains pollution output and resource depletion at present rates, the limits to growth on the planet will very probably be reached, according to some scientists, within 100 years. When this point is reached, unless these trends are seriously and swiftly altered, the probable result will be a sudden, catastrophic and unmanageable decline in population and industrial capacity accompanied by the Four Horsemen of the Apocalypse: war, famine, pestilence and death.

Experts aver that one of two kinds of response may avert this impending catastrophe. It is possible to alter these trends and reestablish an economic and ecological equilibrium that can be maintained far into the future. This global equilibrium is needed if each person is to approach the full development of his human potential as well as meet his basic material needs. Others feel that there are no substantial limits to raw materials or energy and that through the effective use of science exploration, technology, planning and good management, the collapse of the life support system on the planet can be avoided.[16] Life on the planet is precarious at best. Yet the delicate and intricate interdependencies of life are seriously threatened by how humans utilize technology and resolve the existing conflicts.

WORLD POPULATION

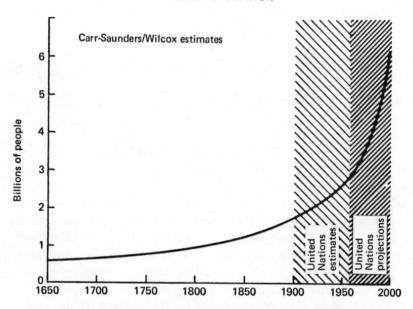

World population since 1650 has been growing exponentially at an increasing rate. Estimated population in 1970 is already slightly higher than the projection illustrated here (which was made in 1958). The present world population growth rate is about 2.1 percent per year, corresponding to a doubling time of 33 years.

SOURCE: Donald J. Bogue, Principles of Demography (New York: John Wiley and Sons, 1969).

Figure 1-3. WORLD POPULATION

Whatever alternatives are selected to avert these grim projections, the energy, knowledge and skills of the public administrator will be an integral part of the planning, problem-solving and programming used to respond and, hopefully, alter these patterns. Resource management, curbing pollution, food production and delivery are fundamental concerns of modern public administration in a highly developed nation.

The oil crisis of 1973 emphasized the stresses and needs surrounding essential, nonrenewable resources. There are over twenty of these mineral and fuel resources, including aluminum, chromium, manganese, molybdenum, natural gas, nickel, oil, platinum, tin and tungsten. The first annual report of the Council on Environmental Quality observed that given decreasing availability and increasing prices, the present supplies of platinum, gold, zinc and lead are not adequate to meet demands. Also given the present rate of demand, silver, tin and uranium could be in short supply by the turn of the century. The Council's report also noted that by the year 2050 several more minerals may well be exhausted.[17]

Each day the news accounts detail the growing impact of pollution on the life support system of the planet. Bulletins range from the mercury contamination of fish, from fertilizers and industrial wastes to air contamination alerts, from oil spills from supertankers and off-shore oil rigs to threats to the ozone shield around the planet from SST's, nuclear testing above ground and aerosol sprays. In addition, there is a rapid reduction of ocean fish crops through overfishing. Dolphins and whales, important links in the Pacific Ocean life cycle, are seriously threatened and may soon join the list of endangered species. These are only a few in a list of environmental dangers which are resultant side effects of industrial outputs and man's neglect. Not only are they a direct threat to the environmental production of food, but they are also an ever-increasing threat to human health. There is but a small delay in time as pollutants pass through air, rivers or soil into the food chain and finally into human ingestion or absorption to the point where clinical symptoms of related diseases appear.

Famine is a fact of modern life in Africa, India and parts of Latin America. Malnutrition at the edge of famine is a fact of life for many in the United States. The Food for Peace Program begun after World War II has ended. The plentiful granaries of the United States have given way to precarious surpluses between growing seasons.

Shortages appear with ever greater frequency on American supermarket shelves. Despite increasing expenditures to 5 billion federal dollars on food stamps malnutrition and other hunger-related problems are on the increase. There is hard evidence that millions of Americans are hungry a portion of their lives, many suffer from malnutrition and many children in the United States suffer resultant permanent mental and physical damage.[18]

In the United States, according to the Federal Trade Commission staff, seventeen food and food-related industries are able to overcharge consumers by more than $2.5 billion annually. A quarter of all food production in the United States is vertically integrated. This means that large corporations control production from the farm to the retail market and, therefore, can manipulate supplies and costs to consumers at will. Oligopolies have control of a number of American food industries. Four firms control 90 percent of the sales in breakfast cereals; four firms control 75 percent of the sales in the bread and prepared flour industry; similarly, in baking, 65 percent; in fluid milk, 60 percent; in dairy products, 70 percent; four companies, too, control 56 percent of the processed meat sales; four control 65 percent of the sugar sales; one firm controls 90 percent of the soup market.[19]

Public administration is intimately involved in exploring and defining these problems and will be intimately involved in their solution. Land planning and land use are just two areas where such reevaluation and resolution must take place. This area of human endeavor is fraught with value contradiction and conflict. Today, vast national, state, provincial, regional and local parks as well as special districts, public forests, prairies, deserts, waterways and recreational areas are dotted across the land in Canada, Australia, New Zealand and the United States. In the United States the National Forest Service, the National Park Service, the Bureau of Land Management, the United States Geological Survey, state park systems, state forests, fish and wildlife services and departments, state departments of natural resources are only a few of the agencies having some impact on public and private land use and management.

Each of these agencies reflects a variety of settled and conflicting value orientations. Public policy-making in these areas is a battleground for the resolution of power struggles between conservationist and profit-oriented or industrial-use-oriented groups. Generally, profit-oriented groups have had more success in dominating land use choices. For example, during the Nixon administration, with little attention and generally in contradiction to good environmental land use and management practice, the administration ordered a 20 percent increase in the cutting of timber on United States Forest Service lands. This was combined with a piece of aberrant legislation (since corrected) which eliminated a modest use fee on Forest Service campgrounds. Federal responses to recreational needs were cut back and personnel were assigned away from the recreational function to supervise the increased cutting. Public administrators charged with the care and protection of the nation's public forests found their efforts to carry out their mission impeded and hampered. Not an unusual story in agencies concerned with land use and planning where special interests are constantly making, and succeeding in, efforts to shape public policy to their own advantage.

The great land grant and homesteading programs which opened up the western United States in the last century provided tremendous advantages for larger corporate interests, particularly such railroads as the Southern Pacific, Santa Fe, Union Pacific and the Burlington Northern. Later special legislative treatment gave exploration and tax advantages to oil and mineral companies.

Today, corporate farming is rapidly replacing the family farm, which is barely economically viable. The "green revolution" spawned by major chemical companies, such as E. I. Du Pont, and agribusinesses have created new superstrains of wheat, corn and rice. These strains show some vulnerability to disease and all the evidence is not yet in concerning their impact upon nutrition and fertilizer use. The technological promise is great, but the utilization and environmental impacts are not yet fully assessed. In any event, it is another link in the chain that is being forged tying food production to the larger agribusinesses. Land ownership patterns within the United States may be characterized by rapidly receding individual ownership and swiftly increasing corporate holdings of vast land tracts on and below the earth's surface. Accompanying this are attempts to manipulate, control, persuade, invade the public land management and use sector for their own special purposes.

Serious problems of public policy exist and demand resolution in the areas of resource management, pollution and food production and delivery. Public administration is vitally linked to their effective resolution. With the family farm giving way to agribusiness, the New Deal dream of self-supporting 160-acre farms turns to ashes as the engine of technology fundamentally alters our system. Higher prices, shortages, malnutrition and inordinately high profits for the middleman are outcomes which indicate serious value conflicts. The public administrator who functions within these program areas will be deeply immersed in the resolution of these value conflicts and participate dramatically in the administration of programs designed to rectify these awesome problems.

THE ADMINISTERED WORLD

Increasingly, power is shifting away from the nation-state to public and private international institutions. The most remarkable phenomenon is the growth of world corporations. These multinational enterprises are collections of corporations of diverse nationality joined together by common bonds of ownership and mutual responsiveness to a common management strategy. The majority of these corporations are based in the United States. Of the 500 largest corporations in the world, 306 are American with 74 others based within the EEC (European Economic Community) nations. The top 500 corporations in America have increased their share of all United States manufacturing and mining assets from 40 percent to 70 percent within a fifteen-year period. They are virtually global, with interlocking directorates tying them to the top dozen banks, which are also world-wide.

The very largest of the corporate giants are not merely more wealthy than many countries, but have their own foreign policies, such as ITT (International Telephone and Telegraph), which helped to overthrow the Allende presidency in Chile. In 1974 General Motors' yearly operating revenues exceeded those of all but a dozen nation-states with about 127 plants at home

★ Los Angeles Times   Sun., Jan. 5, 1975—Part VIII 3

"I pledge allegiance to the flag of the country
that gives me the best deal . . ."

and 43 abroad.[20]   Although the order would vary somewhat today, Figure 1–4 illustrates that (based on dollars) some multinationals have evolved into power complexes more formidable than many nation-states.

These corporations play a crucial role in the world's economy.   They have specialized international languages, international staffs, international funding and international com-

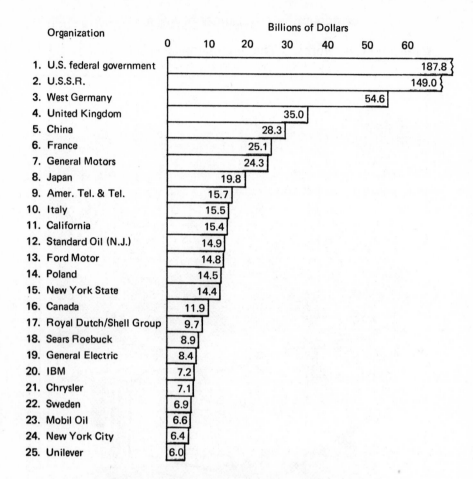

Organization	Billions of Dollars
1. U.S. federal government	187.8
2. U.S.S.R.	149.0
3. West Germany	54.6
4. United Kingdom	35.0
5. China	28.3
6. France	25.1
7. General Motors	24.3
8. Japan	19.8
9. Amer. Tel. & Tel.	15.7
10. Italy	15.5
11. California	15.4
12. Standard Oil (N.J.)	14.9
13. Ford Motor	14.8
14. Poland	14.5
15. New York State	14.4
16. Canada	11.9
17. Royal Dutch/Shell Group	9.7
18. Sears Roebuck	8.9
19. General Electric	8.4
20. IBM	7.2
21. Chrysler	7.1
22. Sweden	6.9
23. Mobil Oil	6.6
24. New York City	6.4
25. Unilever	6.0

SOURCE: *Robert D. Lee, Jr., and Ronald W. Johnson, Public Budgeting Systems, University Park Press, Baltimore, 1973, p. 32.*

Figure 1-4. Twenty-five largest organizations in the world, by receipts or revenues, 1968-1969. *Sources:* U.S. Department of Commerce, Bureau of the Census, *City Government Finances in 1968-69* (Washington: U.S. Government Printing Office, August, 1970); U.S. Department of Commerce, Bureau of the Census, *Governmental Finances in 1968-69* (Washington: U.S. Government Printing Office, September, 1970); Statistical Office of the United Nations, Department of Economic and Social Affairs, *U.N. Statistical Yearbook, 1969,* 21st issue (New York: United Nations, 1970). "The 500 Biggest Corporations by Revenues," *Forbes,* 105 (May, 1970): 75-76; "The 200 Largest Industrial Companies Outside the U.S.," *Fortune,* 82 (May, 1970): 143-46. Financial data for the Catholic Church, which probably would rank in this list of organizations, are unavailable.

munication networks. The international corporation is the instrument of no government. It is responsive to the laws of the lands where it operates and to its own board of directors.[21]

These corporations frequently develop foreign policies conceived in their own self-interest. Very often such policies may directly contradict the policies of those countries from which they originate or in which they do business. During the Arab oil boycott of the United States in 1973, the Philippine subsidiary of Exxon refused to sell oil to the United States Navy at Subic Bay because its overall interest was to help enforce the world-wide boycott of the United States.

The United States Senate Subcommittee on Multinational Corporations under Senator Frank Church investigated Aramco and its four American stockholders—Exxon, Mobil, Standard Oil of California and Texaco—and their impact on foreign policy. The committee disclosed in its findings that these oil companies acted under instructions from King Faisal of Saudi Arabia. These companies, the committee found, undertook in May, 1973, extensive lobbying and propaganda campaigns designed to dilute support of Israel by the United States.[22] Two oil companies, Mobil and Gulf, according to Senator Henry Jackson, implicitly threatened to cut off the supply of oil for United States activities in Antarctica and in Turkey unless they were exempted from a law requiring them to justify their prices.[23] Exxon, in an attempt to respond to the growing awareness of these abuses, on one occasion noted the importance of business in achieving national goals, but in the attempt made it, instead, an appeal against government interference and limitations on the size and profits of big companies.[24]

A consultant report prepared by a public interest law firm for the Federal Energy Administration evaluated the options of the national government in its relationships with domestic firms dealing in international petroleum affairs. The report stated, "The performance of the large U.S. multinational firms during the (Arab) embargo ... emphasized that the United States cannot rely upon those companies to favor its interests. ..." The report added:

It is difficult to examine the issue without concluding that the existing incentives for the companies do not assure their behavior will be consistent with the national interests of the United States.[25]

In examining a number of alternatives which might be utilized to develop more effective monitoring and control of these companies, the report recommended establishment of a regulatory body similar to the Federal Reserve Board. Once again the use of public administrative responses is viewed as necessary to solve a critical national problem.

"The process of tapping high-level foreign policy officials from business," concludes Professor Dennis Ray, "biases the structure of decision-making towards business, for government is not just conscripting the talents of the businessman; it is buying his ideology, his values, and his orientation towards the world."[26] In addition, Professor William Domhoff has observed the impact of the corporation on American foreign policy-making

... through participation in key government positions, through serving on specially appointed committees and task forces, and through financing and leading major non-governmental policy-planning, opinion-forming, and opinion-disseminating organizations.[27]

Major financial contributions (both legal and illegal) by corporations to political candidates and political parties does affect, in both gross and subtle ways, the judgments of public officials entrusted with the public interest.

The nation itself has been persuaded, seemingly in its own self-interest, to dilute its monopoly of force and through the contract mechanism, which we shall discuss in full later, transfer its power to corporate entities. In one instance the Pentagon has contracted with a private corporation to train foreign troops on American soil. Ironically the training was to be given to Saudi Arabian soldiers for the explicit protection of Saudi oil fields at a time shortly after Secretary of State Kissinger, with the support of President Ford, indicated that under certain contingencies it was conceivable that American forces could be used to seize Arabian oil fields.[28] The implications of equipping world corporations with the power and know-how of the nation-state in military and foreign affairs are staggering. Similarly, some relatively autonomous agencies, such as the C.I.A., established profit-making proprietary businesses whose funds are treated as virtually exempt from presidential or legislative control and remain exclusively under agency control. The implications for the accountability process are grave. Activities funded in such a manner are rarely scrutinized and then only perfunctorily.

An "administered world" is emerging in which human existence will be dominated by vast managerial systems including not only private domestic and multinational corporate entities, local, regional and national bureaucracies, but also vast international administrative agencies. The latter exercise the functions of maintaining stability, order and rationality. The World Bank, the European Economic Community and the United Nations Economic and Social Council are just a few of these supranational public agencies. Today, within nations and on the international scene, vast economies operate under managed conditions in which public and private interests are frequently viewed as identical. National and international licensing, cooperative exploration and productive enterprises, marketing agreements and a wide plethora of regulatory compacts combine nation with nation, and nation with public and private bureaucracies.

To restore confidence and effective leadership in the public sector and respond to the interests of the general public presents yet another challenge to public administration. Public administration has responded successfully to equally awesome challenges in the past. After World War II, two defeated nations, Germany and Japan, were nurtured back to economic health under the European Recovery Act, popularly termed the Marshall Plan. Vast conquests of nature were undertaken to benefit mankind, including protection of environmental needs such as the establishment of the Tennessee Valley Authority and the Bonneville power project in the Grand Coulee of the mighty Columbia River in the Pacific Northwest. Notable also are the establishment and development of vast national and state parks and exceptional public colleges and universities. More recently, great numbers of civil servants in the classified service have resisted becoming politicized by illegal fiscal and procedural use of their powers in order to keep an incumbent administration in office.

Yet danger is constant, for there always exists the temptation for those holding power to persuade themselves that what they want coincides with what society needs done for its own good. This comfortable illusion is shared as much by strong leaders of private enterprise as by strong leaders of government. The rise of the strong presidency in the United States has overshadowed the abdication on the part of the public administrator of his creative and self-conscious participation in emerging public policy. Today he has remained an onlooker, a reactor, content to be less a participant in policy-making than more simply a vehicle for the expression of public policy. This situation conduces to his being vulnerable and he becomes easy prey for those who would assault and rape the public interest. Nor has he sufficiently attended to the necessary task of defining that interest or of determining what comprises the public and humane components of his responsibilities. All actions and decisions by public administrators are implicitly or explicitly value-laden. To administer without aiming toward moral imperatives is to exercise power without moral responsibility. The public bureaucracy must accept a major responsibility in reordering those values that otherwise may lead to planetary disaster. Such reordering must enthrone those fundamental values contributing most to human dignity.

NOTES

1. Marcus Raskin, *Notes on the Old System.* New York: David McKay Company, Inc., 1974, p. 5.

2. *The Final Report of the Select Committee on Presidential Campaign Activities,* Volume 1. New York: Dell Publishing Co., Inc., 1974, p. 8.

3. *Ibid.,* pp. 733–761.

4. *New York Times,* December 22, 1974, p. 1. See also *Report* to the President by the Commission on CIA Within the United States, N. Rockefeller, Chairman. Washington, D.C.: Government Printing Office, 1975.

5. Reprinted in the *Los Angeles Times,* Friday, January 24, 1974, Part II, p. 7.

6. Woodrow Wilson, *The Study of Public Administration* (reprint). Washington, D.C.: Public Affairs Press, 1955.

7. Eugene S. Schwartz, *Overskill.* Chicago: Quadrangle Books, 1971, pp. 246-309.

8. See Abdul A. Said and Luiz R. Simmons, eds., *The New Sovereigns: Multinational Corporations as World Powers.* Englewood Cliffs, N.J.: Prentice-Hall, Inc., 1975, and Richard J. Barnett and Ronald E. Müller, *Global Reach: The Power of Multinational Corporations.* New York: Simon and Schuster, 1974.

9. Schwartz, *op. cit.,* p. 293.

10. See Christopher D. Stone, "Should Trees Have Legal Standing?— Toward Legal Rights for Natural Objects," 45 *So. Cal. Law Review,* 450-501.

11. Robert Martinson, "The Paradox of Prison Reform," *The New Republic,* April 1, 1972, pp. 23-25.

12. Mario Fantini and Marilyn Gittel, *Decentralization: Achieving Reform.* New York: Praeger Publishers, 1973, p. 20.

13. *Ibid.,* p. 121.

14. Marc Lalonde (Minister of National Health and Welfare), Governor of Canada, *A New Perspective on the Health of Canadians.* Ottawa, April, 1974. *Los Angeles Times,* November 29, 1974.

15. D. J. Rose, "Energy Policy in the U.S.," *Scientific American,* January, 1974, pp. 21-28.

16. Doneila H. Meadows, Dennis L. Meadows, Jorgan Randers, William W. Behrens III, *The Limits to Growth* (A report for the Club of Rome's Project on the Predicament of Mankind). New York: Universe Books, 1972.

17. *Ibid.,* pp. 45-87.

18. *New York Times,* October 29, 1974, p. 35.

19. William Robbins, *The American Food Scandal.* New York: William Morrow Company, 1974.

20. "The Fortune Directory of the 300 Largest Corporations Outside the U.S.," *Fortune,* August, 1974, p. 174, and Richard J. Barnett and

Ronald E. Muller, *Global Reach: The Power of Multinational Corporations.* New York: Simon and Schuster, 1974.

21. John Kenneth Galbraith, "What Comes After General Motors?" *The New Republic,* November 2, 1974, pp. 13-17.

22. *Los Angeles Times,* August 7, 1974, p. 7; byline, Morton Mintz from the *Washington Post.*

23. *Los Angeles Times,* January 3, 1975, p. 2.

24. Randall Meyer (Pres., Exxon), "The Role of Big Business in Achieving National Goals," President's Lecture Series, Florida State University, Tallahassee, Florida, November 26, 1974.

25. Robert B. Krueger, Project Director, with Bruce G. Merritt, Paul R. Alanis and Thomas J. Weiss, *Summary, An Evaluation of the U.S. Government in its Relationship to U.S. Firms in International Petroleum Affairs.* A Report prepared for the Federal Energy Administration by the law firm of Nossaman, Waters, Krueger, Marsh & Riordan, Los Angeles, California, January 10, 1975, p. 119.

26. Dennis M. Ray, "Corporations and American Foreign Relations," *The Annals of the American Academy of Political and Social Science,* Philadelphia, September, 1972, p. 92.

27. G. William Domhoff, *The Higher Circles.* New York: Random House, 1970, p. 154.

28. *Los Angeles Times,* February 9, 1975, p. 1; byline, Peter Arnett. See also the *New York Times,* September 11, 1974, p. 18.

2

FRAGMENTATION, RESPONSIBILITY AND ACCOUNTABILITY

Governmental administration is vast, complex and often bewildering. The complexities of size, behavior and purpose together with the large number of administrative units make comprehension and analysis quite difficult. Growth of administrative and executive power is a global phenomenon. This development is especially significant for Americans as our political institutions and public philosophy are based upon assumptions of diffused power through fragmentation among competing power centers. Resting upon formal constitutional powers and informal accretions which have emerged over the years, these traditional arrangements were presumed to assure continuance of responsible and accountable government.

Executive power in America may be conceptualized as follows: (a) separated from the legislative and judicial functions at the federal and state levels, (b) divided among the federal, state and local governments, and (c) fragmented among multiple elected and independently appointed boards and commissions at all levels of government.

Where traditionally we had assumed that fragmented government would be an obstacle to the growth of executive and administrative power, the reality of today is quite different. We have both. To attempt to lay bare the dynamics of this far-reaching development is hazardous and difficult; yet it is necessary to focus upon its highlights. The alternative is to proceed largely unaware of the nature of the transitional period through which we are presently passing. Consequently, to clutch tenaciously to traditional theory in light of significant and emergent changes could be catastrophic, for where our theory of government does not reflect reality, illusion becomes the master of our fates.

We are witnessing the initial stages in the dissolution of the notion of three equal and coordinate branches of government. At the same time other traditionally perceived countervailing centers of power regarded as obstacles to the growth of unchecked governmental authority are weakened or have simply disappeared. The theory of diffusing power among competing power centers in order to assure individual liberty was appropriate to the agricultural, rural, craft-oriented society with a modest commercial establishment reflected in America's past. It is unworkable in a society whose recent history has been dominated by wars and increasing resource shortages. Modern wars are "managed" as well as fought, with perhaps skillful management more important in the long run than the numbers of troops that can be thrown into the conflict. Dwindling natural resources require systematic coordination of what is available with increasing regulation of extractors, producers and distributors. Further, the nation's industrial, scientific, technological and urban base is dependent upon large public, commercial and manufacturing bureaucracies.

Neither written constitutions, legislatures nor courts have been able to check the inexorably aggressive and expansionist executive power required by modern societies. Parliamentary systems such as those in England and Canada have also witnessed the increase of the executive and administrative power. The power of the cabinet within the legislature and the power of the prime minister within the cabinet, both essential components of the parliamentary executive, have steadily advanced. The power to select his cabinet and the power to dissolve the legislature enables the prime minister to dominate cabinet and Parliament. Parliamentary systems have also been marked by an extensive increase in autonomous and semiautonomous governmental agencies. The nationalization of important distributive and energy industries, as in the case of steel, coal and railroad sectors of the British economy, has been followed with the establishment of quasi-public corporations and commissions for the conduct of those activities. A number of these measures have been suggested as applicable to the United States, where a function essential to the public interest is necessary but no longer profitable for private enterprise.

The ascendency of the executive function is due in part to the increased size and expanding public expectations concerning the public executive. While public administration has a distinctive and unique mission, all too often it approaches its tasks with a negative spirit: static, veto-producing, crisis-ridden and paralyzed. The administered system is not unified; it is incredibly diverse, fragmented and frequently autonomous. It is a paradox of our time that executive power and administrative practice, seen historically as the primary source of tyranny, is now perceived also as the source for restraint and resolution of tyranny stemming from private corporate abuses and for the alleviation of social and economic ills. This contradiction of values parallels the value contradictions observed in the previous chapter. Size provides the setting and context for these contradictions. Amidst these contradictions the public administrator is charged with performing conflicted functions.

PUBLIC ADMINISTRATION: SIZE AND SCOPE

The scope of public administration virtually defies comprehension. Size and complexity are only partially revealed by examination of statistics. One helpful measure is to compare government finances with the total output of all the goods and services produced by the nation's economy. The figure representing the total market value of the output of all goods and services produced by the nation's economy is called the *Gross National Product* (GNP). In 1974 the Gross National Product exceeded $1,289 billions. The federal, state and local government share of that output was about 33 percent.[1] Administering this governmental output in 1974 were over 14.5 million employees: 2.8 million in the federal service, 3 million in state government, 8.3 million in local government. One in every four jobs developed within the last decade was government sponsored and most of the growth occurred at the local and state levels. Today one in every six civilian employees in the United States works in public administration.[2]   The fastest growing areas of public employment are education, health and welfare (see Figure 2-1). The

WHERE THE BIG SURGE IS COMING

	Number of State and Local Employees		
	1963	1973	Change
Education	3,437,000	5,901,000	Up 72%
Through high School	2,781,000	4,371,000	Up 57%
Higher education	623,000	1,445,000	Up 132%
Welfare	151,000	311,000	Up 106%
Health	89,000	180,000	Up 102%
Correction	102,000	178,000	Up 75%
Parks and recreation	113,000	191,000	Up 69%
Police protection	368,000	581,000	Up 58%
Hospitals	664,000	975,000	Up 47%
Others	2,264,000	3,036,000	Up 34%

SOURCE: U.S. News and World Report, Special Report, Washington Bureaucrats: Real Rulers of America, "Nov. 1974, p.47.

Figure 2-1

rapid growth of public employment at the state and local levels of government is indicated in Figure 2-2. The largest factor in public employment growth was a 72 percent increase in the number of public education employees: from 3.4 million in 1963 to 5.9 million in 1973. This rise is due to the post-World War II crop of babies passing through the schools and also the demise of many Catholic parochial schools and the consequent entry of their students into the public school system.

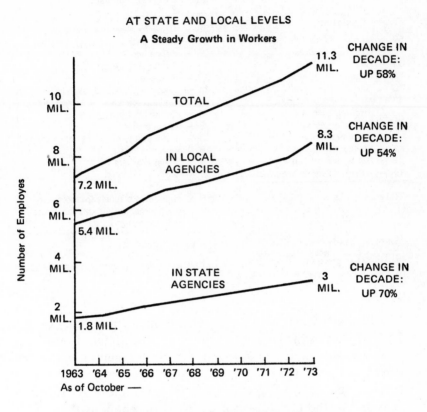

SOURCE: *U.S. News and World Report, Special Report, Washington Bureaucrats: Real Rulers of America,"* Nov. 24, 1974, p. 47.

Figure 2-2.

The present size of the public payroll may be appreciated by considering the hypothetical example (Figure 2-3) of a town comprising 10,000 persons with its public employment distribution and numbers proportional to national employment statistics. Out of this population 133 would be federal employees, 107 members of the armed forces and 456 would work for state and local governments.

10,000 INHABITANTS*

Federal Employees

50 — Non-uniformed assigned
to armed services
33 — Postal
11 — Federal hospitals
10 — Agricultural, forestry,
mining and other natural
resource agencies
5 — Financial clerks
2 — Administrators
1 — FBI agent
1 — Aerospace official
19 — Assorted federal agencies

TOTAL = 133

*Statistics from
Los Angeles Times
(December 19, 1974)

State and Local Employees

119 — Teachers
58 — Other local school employees
27 — Street and highway workers
25 — Policemen
14 — Public welfare workers
10 — Firemen
11 — Clerks in state and local
finance agencies
8 — Public health workers
8 — Jail guards
6 — Trash collectors and street sweepers
6 — Park workers
3-4 — Sewer workers
3 — Library workers
(+)
15 — High level officials (mayors, city
councilmen, city managers, state
legislators, etc.)

TOTAL = 456

(+) Others in various agencies and categories

Figure 2-3.

General civilian government employment now accounts for 14.6 percent of the labor force in the United States. Four-fifths of this employment is in state and local governments. During the period between 1955–1973 employment at the state and local levels increased by 119.5 percent, at the federal level by 17.1 percent and in the private sector by 38.5 percent.[3] Although the demand for teachers has diminished, there are increased demands for policemen, firemen and many other specialized state and municipal employees. If a national health plan eventually is adopted, this too will increase the ranks of the public service.

Revenue, expenditures, employee numbers and payroll statistics indicate the extent and variety of public programs; they tell an important story. Yet the fragmentation of administrative functions is shown no more dramatically than in the number and diversity of governmental administrative units. In 1972 there were over 78,000 distinctive units at all levels of government. Local governmental units fall within categories which may be identified as counties, townships and towns, municipalities, school districts and special districts. Each of these has its own unique origin, history, powers and administrative mission. Except for the special districts, each carries on a multiplicity of functions within its political boundaries. In the case of special districts their function is a specific purpose or task, i.e., flood control or mosquito abatement. Of the 78,000 units, 3,000 are counties; 18,000 are municipalities; nearly 17,000 are towns and townships; more than 15,000 are school districts; and more than 23,000 are nonschool special districts.[4]

SIGNIFICANT TRENDS

In this century a fundamental change has taken place in the relationship between state and local governments and the federal system. In 1913, one year prior to the introduction of the federal income tax, state and local governments enjoyed more than twice the revenues generated by the federal government. In the same year state and local expenditures accounted for more than twice the federal expenditures.[5] By 1974 a dramatic alteration had occurred. The federal government now generated and expended more than all state and local governments. At the same time the relative financial autonomy of state and local governments had declined precipitously.[6]

Expenditures at the federal level are distributed among national defense, international relations, commerce, transportation, labor affairs, income security, public health, agriculture, natural resources and space, among others. State governments spend a greater part of their funds upon highways, higher education, public welfare, corrections and public safety, parks, recreation and regulation activities. Local governments contribute the bulk of money dedicated to public education but they also expend considerable funds upon public safety, health and hospitals and roads.

These trends reflect a picture of vast change. It is also important to consider the data about population changes. During the period from 1901 to 1973, the American population increased from 77.5 million persons to nearly 210 million.

Population projections for 1985 are as high as 251 million persons. It is estimated that the largest single category, containing over 93 million people, will comprise the age group between 20 and 44 and will be, as now, concentrated in the urban centers.

These social changes have created unique problems. The public administrator within this exceptionally rapid social transition must be able to utilize complex technological "know-how" in a highly skilled manner. Today the size, complexity and diversity of public agencies contrast with their early beginnings. A large degree of hostility and mistrust characterized the historic attitude of the citizen toward the public executive. This attitude was well expressed by Thomas Jefferson when he observed, that government is best which governs least. Much has been altered today, although a latent suspicion of bureaucracy is indeed an integral portion of the American psyche. Still, in the face of such size and diversity, it is well to keep in mind the words of Alexander Pope, who wrote in his *Essay on Man:*

> For forms of government let fools contest;
> What e'er is best administered is best.

How to achieve effective administration that is both responsive and responsible is one of the key problems facing our democratic society.

ACCOUNTABILITY

Executive power and administrative practice have been viewed historically as a primary source of tyranny. Yet, paradoxically, today governmental administration is a gigantic, expanding enterprise and viewed as a necessity to implement programs aimed at the alleviation of social-economic ills and to attain economic well-being. The roots and development of these contradictory trends are reviewed in Part II.

The Federalist elaborates an original conception of how tyranny and executive abuse are to be avoided. Three aspects of these early constitutional arrangements were designed to provide a defense of freedom against arbitrary abuse. First, the establishment of a system of representation which would provide

". . . in the society so many separate descriptions of citizens as will render an unjust combination of a majority of the whole very improbable. . . ." Thus, ". . . society itself will be broken into so many parts, interests and classes of citizens that the rights of individuals, or of the minority, will be in little danger from interested combinations of the majority. . . ."[7] Accordingly, the legislative arrangement establishing two separate houses chosen by differing methods was justified.

Second, authority was to derive from the people. Delegated responsibility for the exercise of the people's authority was to be through periodic election.[8] Third, liberty was to be secured in part from the functional separation of power into legislative, executive and judicial branches; and in part from the division of power between two levels of government, i.e., state and national.[9] Finally, liberty and freedom from arbitrary executive power were to be secured through reliance upon guaranteed civil rights. Some of these rights operate to restrain majorities; in addition, some were designed, too, as a check upon the powers of central government.[10] There is little need to dwell upon these well-known aspects of the early constitutional arrangements. The separation of powers was a specific design to diffuse authority and achieve an approximate *balance* of competing forces assuring stability.

History amply demonstrates that at various times persons exercising legislative, executive and judicial functions have usurped power and abused its practice. Suspicion of a strong executive was a widespread attitude in the colonies. Yet it is helpful to note that Madison cautioned against legislative usurpation as well. He notes that the founders of republics, ". . . seem never to have recollected the danger from legislative usurpations . . ."[11] and, ". . . it is against the enterprising ambition of this department that the people ought to indulge all their jealousy and exhaust all their precautions. . . ."[12] Legislative abuse was to be resisted by dividing ". . . the legislature into different branches; and to render them, by different modes of election . . . as little connected with each other as the nature of their own common dependence upon society will admit. . . ."[13]

The separation of power among the branches of government with the addition of countervailing checks and balances and a bicameral legislature provided the setting and rationale for a strengthened executive.[14] Hamilton stated the rationale for a strong executive:

> A feeble Executive implies a feeble execution of the government . . . and a government ill-executed, whatever it may in theory must be, in practice, a bad government. . . .[15]

He advanced a strong case for a ". . . single Executive and a numerous legislature . . .", as ". . . it tends to conceal faults and destroy responsibility. . . ." In elaboration, he wrote:

> . . . the plurality of the Executive tends to deprive the people of the two greatest securities they can give for the faithful exercise of any delegated power, *first,* the restraints of public opinion, which lose their efficacy, as well as bad measures among a number, as on account of the uncertainty on whom it ought to fall; and *secondly,* the opportunity of discovering with facility and clearness the misconduct of the persons they trust, in order either of their removal from office, or to their actual punishment. . . .[16]

The events surrounding former President Nixon's resignation and the convictions of his top aides might be seen to validate Hamilton's vigorous support of a strong executive, since those whose actions constituted misconduct in office were clearly identified and removed or forced to resign from their positions of power and trust. A unified executive was included in the constitutional design envisioned by the Founders and explained by the writers of *The Federalist*.

Today this frame of reference clouds our perceptions. The legislature is assumed to make public policy and the executive is assumed to carry it out actively and with dispatch. The legislature is presumed to be the primary source of substantive legislation, financial authorization and performance review, i.e., accountability. The proper executive is seen as a single and unified office responsible for the effective and immediate response to legislative command.

THE FRAGMENTED EXECUTIVE

The emergence of the fragmented executive began during Andrew Jackson's presidency. The executive underwent three phases of development in this period. In the first phase state executive functions were carried out by legislative committees. In the second phase executive functions were carried out through a number of executive officials chosen by the legislature. The final phase witnessed the development of independently elected officials as the primary instrument for performing executive functions.[17]

Most states entering the union or undergoing constitutional reform at this time established executive branches with large numbers of officials elected to perform special functions alongside the governor. State executive patterns today have been profoundly influenced by the Jacksonian period. The modern, powerful presidency exists alongside many highly fragmented state executive systems—the heritage of Jacksonian beliefs. Political scientist Robert Dahl has noted:

> Jackson developed a new pattern of relationships, a new constitutional system, and since his day that system has largely prevailed.[18]

The implications for public administration are clear. Dahl focused upon a facet of the accountability problem when he observed that bureaucratic organizations ". . . must also be responsive to their own specialized clientele. . . ." He observed that the ". . . most effective clientele . . . is one like the farmers, that is also well represented in Congress and even in the executive branch; sometimes bureaucracy and clientele become so intertwined that one cannot easily determine who is responsive to whom. . . ." This, then, is yet another way the fragmented bureaucracy is encouraged and the accountability problem magnified. Thus he observed that, ". . . the vast apparatus that grew up to administer the affairs of the American welfare state is decentralized bargaining bureaucracy. . . ."[19]

Today at the state and federal levels of government the single unified executive checked by legislative and judicial power as conceived by the Founders has been fundamentally altered. The development of independently elected executive officials under President Jackson and the tendency of agencies to heed the needs of particular constituencies did meet certain problems, but they also served to fragment and frustrate accountability of the administrative function. Most states, in addition to the federal government, submitted to the trend and established innumerable elected officials to perform a wide variety of administrative functions. Later, independently elected boards and commissions appeared; so, too, did independent boards with staggered terms of office. Thus, the trend established in the Jacksonian period was continued, widened and deepened throughout the nation. The elected executives, viz., the president and the governor, have their responsibilities split away and distributed to administrative agencies and other elected officials.

THE LEGISLATIVE TIE

Legislatures within the United States function on the basis of well-established standing committees. In general, these committees parallel the functional arrangement of the fragmented executive and consider substantive and financial matters of their executive counterparts. Members of legislative bodies seek to obtain membership on those committees which are involved in determining matters affecting their individual districts or their perceived constituency.[20] To be reelected it is necessary to serve those groups well that assure reelection. Masters, in his study *Committee Assignments in the House of Representatives,* observes:

> Although a number of factors enter into committee assignments — geography, groups support, professional background, etc. — the most important single consideration — unless it can be taken for granted — is to provide each member with an assignment that helps assure his reelection. Stated differently, the most impressive argument in any applicant's favor is that the assignment he seeks will give

him an opportunity to provide the kind of service to his constituents that will sustain and attract voter interest and support. . . .[21]

These and other legislative mechanisms support the varying needs of particular clientele and legislative groups. They include: funding the administrative effort, budget review, administrative reorganization and consideration of substantive matters which concern the affected agency or clientele groups.[22]

Some scholars studying the legislative process concluded: "The House Agriculture Committee is organized to allow a maximum of constituency-oriented representation."[23] Other investigations of the functions of informal legislative groups concluded: "The constituencies of the members are essentially similar and the electoral party organizations and interest groups upon which they rely are either the same or have similar views, and expectations."[24] One scholar of the "congressional committee" observed:

> The members of this Committee (the Senate Committee on Banking and Currency) did not sit as legislative judges to discover an abstract general interest, nor did they seem concerned with presenting a balanced debate for public consideration. On the contrary most of them did take sides. The Committee hearings clearly were used as a public platform for opposing groups with which the Senators identified. . . .[25]

Subject-matter committees are also crucial in state legislatures. An outstanding demonstration of this centers on the relationship of the Washington State Joint Interim Committee on Highways, Streets, and Bridges and the Highway Department. This committee not only provides the determinative legislative leadership on highway matters, it also plays a definitive role in some very important administrative decisions. For example, it participates in the planning and operation of joint research programs from funds allocated to the Highway Department. Such research may be conducted by the personnel of the department or by consultants usually retained for that purpose by the

Interim Committee. The Joint Interim Committee participated in the periodic reallocation of gasoline tax receipts to local jurisdictions which is primarily the administrative application of a statutory formula previously written into law by the committee.

The key membership on this Interim Committee is provided by the leaders of the standing committees concerned with highway matters in the regular legislative session. Effective access for interested clientele groups which seek to have an impact upon decisions affecting highway matters is through active participation in a wide range of advisory committees established by the Joint Interim Committee. No significant clientele advisory group is directly attached to the Highway Department. Although one is provided by statute, it has seldom—if ever—met. The highway budget is written, for all intents and purposes, under the guidance of this committee. When considered in the legislature, it is the only departmental budget which is reviewed by the subject-matter committee and escapes review by the appropriations and finance committees of both legislative houses in Washington State. The governor has no access or impact upon the Highway Department budget, although it is not officially excepted statute from his quarterly and biennial review. Thus the committee effectively dominates Highway Department policy-making, program development *and* administration.[26]

The traditional view of legislative-executive relations have to be seriously modified if the fragmented executive is considered within these legislative developments. The legislative role is not merely initiating laws, passing appropriations bills and supervising and reviewing the executive. The executive role is not unified; neither does the executive passively await instructions from the legislature to be carried out with speed and dispatch.

INDEPENDENT ADMINISTRATIVE UNITS

Independence for American bureaucracy is not as it seems to be. The appearance of independence results from apparent freedom from supervision by the chief executive; yet the reciprocal supports provided by legislative groups, constituents' groups and the concerned administrative groups operate at varying stages of autonomy and within a relatively self-contained system of administrative activity. These self-contained administrative units seek freedom from centralized supervision. They also seek "ear-marked" or protected revenues, control over definition of their programs and pursue a variety of other devices which reinforce their seeming autonomy. A closer glance will reveal significant trade-offs with legislative subject-matter committees and affected clientele groups. These groups support their resistance to presidential or gubernatorial supervision, but the result is often a dependency upon those groups. Interdependence more accurately describes the relationship. The *independence* refers to independence from the governor or president, not from politics.

This, of course, was not the legislative intention. It was to get these agencies "out of politics." Yet they are very much "in politics," which often involves very particular and very specialized interests. What seems apparent is a far different arrangement of internal relationships than was conceived by the Founders and described in *The Federalist*. George Shipman, an early proponent of the use of social theory in administrative practice, posited the predominant characteristics of the modern American executive system when he said:

> The broad view is one of gradual emergence of several states within each state. Education, public welfare, highways, labor, agriculture and other closely-knit interest clusters tend to develop their own bodies politic, their own legislative mechanisms, their own administrative establishments, and their own special means for enforcing official responsibility to their special points of view.
>
> The state as such is really a loose confederation of these "functional states." Various devices are used to avoid destructive collisions—dedicated revenues, self-financing debt, nonpartisan elections and often, special personnel systems. . . .[27]

These specialized administrative systems that Shipman describes as "closely-knit interest clusters" involve ties with legislative and clientele groups which are, in fact, an important diversion from the traditional view of executive-legislative relations. In addition, the state chief executive, the governor, is restrained by a variety of devices from "interfering" in these settled arrangements. Thus the state executive function and state administrative activities are often not amenable to clear delineation but rather are a collection of fragmented units.

A similar phenomenon occurs at the federal level. Ernest Griffith writes of a similar situation emerging at the national level which he identifies as "government by whirlpools." He elaborates:

> The spokesmen of the group are not only those paid to speak . . . . Spokesmen are also found among the people whose own prosperity, whose standing in their local community, are at least indirectly determined by the . . . groups in question. They are also the government officials whose clientele these groups are. They are members of Congress from the states and districts whose experience and attitudes are woven from the same fabric and who truly "represent" their district, by experience and conviction as well as by election. . . .[28]

The steady creation of the federal independent regulatory commissions, beginning with the Interstate Commerce Commission in 1887, indicates that in the economic history of the United States the creation of each commission was, in effect, a response by Congress to public demands for regulation of a portion of the American economy. Three of the commissions regulate public transportation: Commerce, Maritime and Civil Aeronautics. Two regulate utilities: Power and Communications. Finance and credit are regulated by the Securities and Exchange Commission and the Federal Reserve Board. The Federal Trade Commission, among other things, monitors marketing practices for quality, fraud and threats to public and personal health. The National Labor Relations Board mediates labor-management disputes and facilitates communication between management and labor. The Atomic Energy Commission controls the development and utilization of fissionable nuclear energy. There are at the federal level thirty-nine of these autonomous boards, commissions and public corporations.

Each of these agencies makes policies, defines standards of usage and conduct, and hears and adjudicates cases arising under its jurisdiction. The independent regulatory commissions are often termed headless, unaccountable and in the service of special interests. They develop policy determinations which may conflict with presidential intent. They were created in the sweep of progressive reform and were intended to shield the public from excessive business exploitation and unfair business practices. Some of these agencies are dominated by the industries and sectors of the economy they were mandated to regulate and may promote these external interests. Furthermore, they frustrate the efforts of president and Congress to reform them or even hold them effectively accountable.[29]

York Willbern, in his study of the Texas Railroad Commission, found that the commission conducted its business by "cooperating" with the "dominant" portion of the regulated industry.[30] He has called attention to the special district as "... the most extreme manifestation of the almost universal desire for separateness and autonomy on the part of special constituency and clientele groups. . . ."[31] Aaron Wildavsky has called attention to the crucial role of clientele groups within the budgetary process. He observes that budgetary strategy by government agencies includes those actions which are intended to maintain or increase the money available to them. One of the crucial strategies is to find, expand and serve the concerned clientele.[32]

It is also important to devote attention to the legislative tie. Legislative relations play a supportive and defensive role, protecting existing arrangements and supporting development of legal bases and operational programs furthering agency survival. They enable clientele groups to prosper and supply the concerned legislative officials with some resources necessary for reelection. In addition, the legislature plays an accommodative role; i.e., if there are conflicts between two or more clientele groups or between the agency and its clientele, the legislature will be among the first points of appeal after all internal efforts to resolve the conflict have been exhausted. Other points of appeal may be to the political party or the chief executive.

Finally, the legislative role may involve drastic action when faced with a variety of crises. Such a crisis may occur when effective clientele or constituent support is lacking or extensive misfeasance or malfeasance has been exposed in administrative activity. Withdrawal or neutralization of effective constituent supports may be followed by a consequent reduction of support in the legislature. This is often followed by implementing major revisions in substantive legislation or severe budgetary reductions. Thus, separate executive or administrative units play a reciprocal role with concerned legislative and constituent groups which supports and reinforces the administrative unit.

What emerges is a pattern of autonomous functional areas of administrative activity. Each of these areas is often relatively self-contained and characterized by ear-marked funding, budgetary independence and an isolated, protected *independent* or *nonpartisan* executive in the concerned agency. Effective and strong constituent groups which have been coopted into the administrative decision-making processes are necessary to agency well-being. The existence of adequate support and protection within the legislative process may also serve to establish, sustain and reinforce autonomous administrative activity. The greater the intensity of these elements seems to be, the greater the degree of agency self-sufficiency.

THE ROLE OF THE CHIEF EXECUTIVE

Presidential or gubernatorial leadership, in relation to these semi-autonomous units, presents a special problem. The chief executive is a negotiator, who by the nature of his position is drawn toward these self-contained units if there is conflict within that remains unresolved or cannot be contained. He is primarily a negotiator or a bargainer with considerable advantage. Neustadt has observed, "Presidential power is the power to persuade."[33] As we have learned from Watergate, he can also effectively cajole, pressure, manipulate and threaten. This is a primary role of the governor as well.[34] Second, the national or state chief executive is drawn into any area of national or state life that threatens the stability of the existent arrangements. These issues may transcend the fragmented executive and at times threaten the entire system with catastrophe. John Gaus observes the chief executive is required by his position to develop programs which will avoid such anticipated catastrophe or respond to catastrophe that has occurred.[35] The content of public policy considered by Congress or state legis-

58

latures is usually forwarded by the chief executives. Where legislation or policy involves specific areas of administrative activity, the chief executive reflects what the plural executive or administrative units wish after the important bargains have been struck.[36] He assumes the lead in thwarting threats both internal and external and leads also in providing programs necessary to remedy areas of crucial concern which, if left unattended, would threaten deterioration or disintegration of the system.[37]

Representativeness has long been considered to be a basic component in the responsiveness of government to public needs. Norton Long and others have found modern bureaucracy to be possibly more "representative" than the legislative function. Long observed.

> ... the bureaucracy now has a very real claim to be con-
> sidered much more representative of the American people
> in its composition than Congress. This is not merely the
> case with respect to the class structure ... but equally ...
> with respect to the learned groups, skills, economic in-
> terest, races, nationalities and religions. . . .[38]

Peter Woll focuses upon these new arrangements as ". . . add-ing an important dimension to our government...," which in effect adds a fourth branch that operates within the traditional separation of powers system. Instead of recognizing a funda-mental modification of the internal system of checks and bal-ances, Woll envisages the changes as simply an elaboration of the separation of powers system.[39] Long observes the separate bureaucracies are much more representative of the American people than Congress; and the decentralized bureaucracies, Woll submits, are an extension of the checks and balances system. Each of these is a profound departure from the classical separa-tion of powers concept. Yet the fragmented decentralized units of administrative activity cannot be conceded to be an equal partner with president, Congress and courts, nor can the inde-pendently elected officials in state governments be conceded to be equal partners with a state governor, state legislature or state court system. There is not a single American bureaucracy—only American bureaucracies of varying degrees of power and autonomy. The fundamental problems of responsibility and accountability remain.

CHECKS AND CONTROLS

Separation of powers and checks and balances are so much a part of our mental equipment in thinking about modern American government that often developments are tortuously made to conform with these preconceived notions. Americans have such faith in the "mechanics" of their system it has been assumed that virtue, accountability and good government simply flow "automatically" from its processes. Earlier misgivings aside, Watergate has now cast grave doubt on these assumptions. Can so subtle and complex an equilibrium, presumably resulting from our unique pluralism, be relied upon as an instrument for the maintenance of our stability and assure accountability? Can it do this any more than the *invisible hand* of Adam Smith, which was then thought to be the guardian of the good life at the marketplace? Is there any guarantee that one of these decentralized, self-contained centers of power might not maximize its power to the extent that it may ultimately dominate the whole of society?

In theory at least, the technological proficiency of the public agency is its source of power and the guarantee of agency *independence,* which is presumed to automatically produce responsibility and accountability. Congress has found no effective way to hold these agencies accountable. They are, as yet, isolated from the president. Yet they are subject to effective influence by specialized interests through the activity of interested senators and congressmen and, as revealed by Watergate, by the president or his agents. As suggested, each agency develops its own constituency, which is drawn from the industry or economic sector that is supposed to come under its control and regulation.[40]

In the face of this, the public servant charged with implementing the *public interest* faces nearly overwhelming barriers. Powerful corporate entities seek to affect his judgment and his actions. Clientele-oriented administrative units equate public interest values as consistent with the narrow clientele interests. Legislative committees and chief executives, such as the president or governors, seek to influence administrative judgment. These are compounded often by inadequate information, meagre resources and insufficient staff, and also the resulting external special interests. Conflicted self-perceptions about the role and function of the administrator exist among the administrators themselves.

There continues among the scholars studying public administration a long-standing dispute concerning the most effective way of holding administrative power accountable and checking its growth as well. Some believe that the expertise, professionalism and role perception of the individual bureaucrat constitute a substantial check upon the extravagant use of bureaucratic power. Yet the problem here is that the deference to citizen preference may have contributed to the predominance of the private interests within many public policy-making jurisdictions. Francis Rourke observes that reliance upon these purely "psychological inner checks" depends upon the inculcation of a code of ethics or conscientious beliefs and are tenuous at best. Herman Finer has emphatically asserted that "The political and administrative history of all ages . . . has demonstrated without the shadow of a doubt that sooner or later there is an abuse of power when external punitive controls are lacking."[41]

There are extensive internal and external controls and accountability devices aimed at checking bureaucracy. Many of them are ineffectual. Well-grounded fears regarding the uses of power by administrative officials still properly exist. To initiate, identify and defend the public interest is the constant duty of the public administrator. One of the great failures of modern bureaucracy is not dealing creatively, imaginatively and vigorously with the problems of immediate public concern. Yet where an agency is not properly responsible nor effectively accountable, serious abuses may occur.

Not only does funding support for the C.I.A. come from regularly apportioned congressional appropriations but also from the Pentagon budget and from the various private corporations it has established and *owns*. Two observers of the intelligence activities in the United States have commented on the accountability problem in regard to this agency:

Fully aware of these additional sources of revenue the C.I.A.'s Chief of Planning and Programming . . . observed a few years ago that the director does not operate a mere multi-million dollar agency but actually runs a multibillion dollar conglomerate—with virtually no outside oversight.[42]

This agency presents distinct difficulties concerning the problems of accountability. Traditional checks have not proved sufficient and secrecy concerning its operations seems to have contributed to its irresponsible behavior both domestically in violation of its statutory charter and internationally in over-zealous pursuit of its clandestine missions.

COMPARING BUSINESS AND PUBLIC AFFAIRS

Public administration and business administration exhibit numerous similarities. There is little difference, for example, between the daily tasks of accountants, clerk-typists or office managers. The similarity is not too surprising as a recurrent theme of governmental reform has been to operate government like an efficient business, i.e., to incorporate business values of efficiency and economy into governmental management. Yet the differences are fundamental.

It is important to notice how the differences relate to their political/social environments with special attention to the sources of authority upon which the administrative organization rests. In public administration, mission, financing and organizational structure and operation are all established by statute. The public administrator may have to follow rigid contracting and purchasing regulations prescribed in statute. Larger private organizations may also have rules and regulations as elaborate as those in public statutes. However, they often have a flexibility of change generally not available to the public jurisdiction.

Private administration may be licensed, i.e., given permission by a legislature to operate or granted a charter by an executive agency. Yet it may not have its mission defined, funding sources identified or organizational structure prescribed by either legislative or administrative fiat. In some cases, however, governmental supervision of private administration may lead to a publicly determined mission and pattern of funding and to a prescribed organizational structure. Examples are public utilities engaged in water, gas and electrical production and distribution where the agency funding rests upon payment for services or goods and is not a tax-supported agency.

Similarly, the public-private distinction is seriously undermined in cases where the Department of Defense is the sole source of income for private operations. Here the government is in a more favorable position to closely direct the affairs of the dependent private administrative establishment. In some instances, private prime contractors with the government agencies are utilized to perform functions which the government could perform more cheaply.

Often similar functions are being performed by government workers and by workers in private administration, yet the latter will be remunerated at considerably higher rates. A government attorney, accountant or engineer may well be performing a similar function to his counterpart in a private organization under the terms of a prime contract, but he may receive less pay. Recently great strides have been made to alleviate these kinds of differences. These differentials have been justified on the basis that government service is more secure and the risk of job displacement or unemployment is higher in private administration. Even this distinction disappears in the case of those employed by a prime contractor who exists solely on government contracts. Conversely, extensive public fiscal rescue operations of Lockheed and the Penn Central rail system provide the conditions for the perpetuation of private employment. Paradoxically, it is public employment which becomes tenuous when the federal government fails or delays support for public jurisdictions facing bankruptcy, such as New York City, while preventing bankruptcy of major corporations in the private sector.

Another difference lies in the source of supervision, i.e., accountability. In public administration supervision theoretically occurs through legislative review of administrative budget requests, programs and activities. Also, legislatures may investigate for malfeasance and misfeasance or to effect substantive social change.

The quality and nature of the legislative tie is distinctly different from supervision to which the private administrative organization is subject. Supervision emerges from a board of

63

directors or, more remotely and usually perfunctorily, from the stockholders. On occasion, a legislative investigation of private administration may occur and, as in the case of public administration, it may reveal unethical and illegal practices. Thus legislative investigation cannot be regarded as a distinguishing characteristic between public and private administration. The extent of legislative investigation will vary according to the network of defenses and supports available within the legislature itself to the public or private organization. The C.I.A., the F.B.I. and the I.R.S., as well as the multinational corporations (including the oil interests), Penn Central and Lockheed, have recently felt the investigative lash of the legislature.

Perhaps the most valid distinction between public and private organizations is their ultimate purpose. Public administration is expected to carry out public policy. The primary task of the public administrator is to facilitate this end. The private organization is most often expected to produce profit. The non-profit private organization is a special and distinct instrument of its owners, primarily to fulfill special purposes defined by those owners. Social impact is only derivative.

The private administrator is to facilitate the production of profit, i.e., to produce dollars over and above the total resources expended. Public administration is most often required to expend resources without anticipated or expected financial returns. The goal sought is to produce a difference in the environment or in social or economic relations or to maintain the system against actual or threatened external force. The expenditure of funds to maintain the armed forces in war or peace is one instance of the expenditure of funds without anticipated returns upon such expenditures. Other examples are the distribution of surplus commodities to economically deprived areas or the maintenance of public recreation facilities, fire and police protection, and economic regulatory activities. An exception to this observation on the private side may be noted in the case of non-profit organizations such as private foundations and schools or private charities. Here neither the mission nor the ultimate purpose may explain the distinction between public and private organizations.

Government today is in the investment business, the insurance business, the public utility business, the liquor business and the fertilizer business among others. In these instances, one must examine the sources of authority and the statutory mission of the agency to determine those public values to be implemented through administrative action.

In theory, every act of a public administrator is in some fashion accountable under some provision of law. One function of a legislature has been the raising of and supervision of the expenditure of monies through levies and taxations to support the activities of government. The ultimate form of legislative control over the executive and the administrative structure has been the authorization or withholding of funding for administrative purposes. Other forms of control have included impeachment and removal from office of the offending executive incumbent, but use of this method has been rare.

The concept of accountability to the public is another distinctive characteristic of public administration. Business administration, on the other hand, has a more limited responsibility to a small non-public population, identified as owners or stockholders who are often managers of such businesses as well. In addition, public administration is not expected to yield a direct monetary profit on its activities.

Profit maximization is the compelling force which renders a clear and immediate criterion for effectiveness and is the viable motivational force in the private organization. Public administration lacks the criterion of profit maximization; yet there still remain some areas where monetary returns have a significant impact on administrative activity. For example, the continuation of the archaic fee judge and sheriff in some remote parts of the United States is an indication of the use of governmental power in the direct pursuit of private profit. In the fee system the judge and sheriff obtain their incomes from the fines levied upon lawbreakers. The system was originally devised for lightly populated rural areas which saw no use for full-time salaried positions for those purposes. Typically, those archaic systems tend toward abuses and corruption under the impact of modernization and industrialization. Happily, they may be listed among the "endangered species."

The concept of public accountability through a political process is the main point of difference between the two major forms of administration. Public administrative power in its most fundamental aspects derives from a grant of power from a publicly accountable governing body. Business or private administration springs from a voluntary association in the expectation of profit return from funds invested.

In summary, the difference between public and private administration (profit maximization and accountability) centers upon their relationship to the political system of which public administration is an integral part and a determinant as well. Public administration is essentially political in its nature. Private interests do invade and influence public agencies; yet their role is *not* one of being authorized to act only on behalf of the state and the broader "public interest." This is the unique role of public administration.

PUBLIC AFFAIRS BY CONTRACT

Public administration has turned more and more frequently to the use of the "contract" to achieve performance in novel programs as well as traditional administrative functions. The contract device may be used in conjunction with private organizations but also with other public jurisdictions. For example, there were over three hundred American corporations in Saigon, South Viet Nam, performing many of the functions that were performed there in the 1960's when we had a large military presence. These corporations performed their functions through contracting arrangements negotiated with the Pentagon. Many services in local government today are contracted services provided by other governmental jurisdictions. For example, many smaller cities in the County of Los Angeles, California, contract with the county sheriff to have their public safety needs fulfilled by deputies of the county sheriff. Power from the Tennessee Valley Authority is delivered to private and public electric utilities via the contract device. The goal in utilizing this mechanism is to obtain requisite staff, flexibility and efficiency of operations and a more conducive work atmosphere. In addition, the corporation may be more likely and faster than an agency to attempt to develop its own competence; and it may, indeed, be cheaper. Under these circumstances accountability versus independence becomes a key concern.

The accountability process must assure that public funds are spent for the purposes specified. The compensation for services must be just and fair, and a fair value must be rendered to the contracting government agency requiring the services or the goods. Policy-making should remain within the public sector. Yet independence and freedom to do a good job are also vitally important. The contractor may not be able to render effective service if the government's supervision is ineffective and heavy-handed. The key problem in this arrangement is to achieve a satisfactory balance between the need for legislative oversight and, at the same time, avoid self-defeating intrusion into the internal management of the contractor's operations.

The corporation itself is an awesome focus of power with tendencies in its private form toward amorality or even irresponsibility. At times it may even be immoral. It is generally self-serving. There have not been up to the present time any effective political means developed to hold the corporation responsible and accountable either for the manner in which it uses its power or the consequences flowing from that power. Much has been tried, some with a little success, yet the problem of corporate abuses remains more virulent now than ever.

Its source of power stems from its legal setting and the financial and technical resources it can command. The corporation is characterized by "perpetual succession"—it is legally immortal until dissolved under the law. It is legally a "person" in the courts, a kind of "third sex" at law. It is able to, within its terms of reference, legislate and execute policy. It coordinates science and technology for productive effort and is a powerful instrument which is gaining more and more dominance in industrial societies. It may be public, quasi-public or private. It is generally an arrangement of power pyramidal in form, with power, prestige and wealth distributed in ever diminishing amounts downward through its hierarchy. Its outputs may be profit, implementation of a defined social value or the achievement of an environmental change. It is this collectivity of skills, resources and energy which, when specialized, coordinated and integrated toward ends the management deems desirable, is aiding in the conduct of government today.

The nexus of the relationship between government and corporation is the *contract*. Basically, a contract is an agreement between a government agency and another governmental agency, public or private corporation to purchase goods or services or carry out an assignment for which the government pays remuneration. Such a contract can be a letter of understanding or a complex legal document. Sometimes primary contractors to a government agency will *subcontract* part of their assignments to other firms. Such a contract may arrange for payment to occur upon a cost-plus-fixed-fee, cost-plus-incentive-fee, fixed-price or some other cost-plus arrangement.

At the federal level expenditures for the past several years via the contract mechanism, which includes grants-in-aid, have been ranging around one-third of the total federal budget. It may therefore be appreciated that this device for the conduct of the public's business is an extremely important one and the problems surrounding contractual accountability and responsibility are also extremely important. Old-line agencies tend to use the payroll and direct operations for the bulk of their expenditures. The newer agencies generally use the contract device and set goals, establish policy and guidelines and oversee their performance. The Department of Health, Education and Welfare spends only about 6 percent of its total budget on payroll. The National Aeronautics and Space Administration spends over 90 percent of its budget on contracts with industrial firms, private research firms and major universities.

Under these conditions the traditional methods of democratic accountability reviewed earlier, namely, legislative oversight, external and internal audits, the electoral process, in addition to scrutiny by the mass media seem inadequate to the task required. With an administered system traditional accountability goes upward to the highest levels with the highest executive levels accountable to the parliament or legislature. The legislature is generally assisted in its review by a special audit arm responsible to it. With the growth in the use of the contract these traditional devices become considerably diluted. One authority on contracts warns:

> Government has grown too big and complex for the minister or department head, and still less the chief executive, to know in detail all that happens within the agency or the

government on a given program. Under the circumstances the doctrine of accountability may be seen as a polite function. . . . The citizen's doubt that the responsible officials are firmly in charge becomes compounded when extensive contract operations are added to the equation.[43]

One helpful approach to the problem is to focus upon a proper balance among three different perspectives on accountability, viz., fiscal, programs and process.[44] Fiscal responsibility is concerned with regularity and legality of public expenditures. Program accountability is concerned with whether the government is actually obtaining the results sought from a particular program. Accountability by process refers to the operations and procedures by which an assignment is carried out. Thus it focuses upon the integrity of the process and tasks rather than upon objectives and mission.

There are many difficult problems which have not been successfully solved as yet: the relationship of creativity or risk-taking to conformity, professional standards versus nonprofessional standards, whether the standards should be those external to the agency or agency standards, program goals versus cost-effectiveness audits—to identify merely a few.

The use of the contract mechanism in public administration does not diminish the need for managerial competence; rather the need for effective public management is enhanced. If public policy and the integrity of the governmental process is to be maintained and improved, government must keep a steady and guiding hand on the entire process. If this is not maintained, policy formulation will tend to gravitate toward the satellite contractors, and the diffusion and dispersal of governmental power will continue until there is no effective governmental cadre capable or powerful enough to integrate the disparate segments into a responsible and accountable whole.

Basic values and fundamental problems of social policy are deeply embedded in the administrative process and range above and beyond questions of efficiency and operational integrity. These larger issues are the rightful province of public officials and should necessarily be linked to mechanisms of social control. Serious problems surround the uses of private institutions to accomplish public purposes. When these share in the use of public power for profit-making purposes, there is always the danger they will pursue their own goals with little check or effective control by the public sector. Their emphasis upon privacy in their operations and control over selected or unique areas of information are powerful resources against effective public accountability.

The sheer volume of the financial transactions makes it impossible for traditional audit agencies to check each one. In most respects it is the prime contractor's responsibility to determine who gets hired, fired, how the work is scheduled, and this generally lies outside the provinces of public accountability. Occasionally, they may be subject to public audit to insure that standards involved in such public programs as "affirmative action" and fair labor practices are adhered to. The temptation of the corporate professional staff to deal directly with counterpart governmental officials without review from prime contractor supervisors is also generally present. The question of how to create a good mix of independence for the prime contractor and the extent of public agency monitoring is a difficult one.

Public agencies, too, contracting for their services with other public agencies tend to develop problems. The agency offering the contractual services may feel the contract as a means of power enhancement and ultimate survival. In addition, they sometimes suffer from a tendency to become moribund and ritualized and the goals originally contracted will give way to organizational maintenance and survival.

The whole fabric of democratic responsibility and accountability is strained as the scope of public responsibility has broadened to include these new performers. Old concepts and understandings are changed and altered. In the delegation of power to the private sector, the lines between public and private become dim, at times even indistinguishable. Independent executive agencies and public corporations are formed, industries are nationalized or supported in a complex variety of ways, extensive contracting with the private sector or with diverse segments of the public sector form new and mixed activities, alliances and decision-making networks. Often these are arranged *independently* without adequate public-interest questions being raised beforehand. Sometimes there is a complete absence of a special public panel or board of experts to define or respond to important public interest issues raised by the contracts.

Accountability and responsibility must be related to the ends to be sought as determined by public policy-making. These considerations range far beyond organizational issues alone. Organizational recruitment, training and budgetary priorities have always been regarded as susceptible to publicly determined value choices. Beyond this, the development of an overarching theory of public interest is essential to guide decision-making in novel and experimental areas. It is the prerequisite for the development of an internal discipline and commitment to goals which will enhance democracy.

Where new ways of delivering publicly desirable services are intermingled with the private sector, the public servant must be a major participant in developing both operational and value constraints. There is a distinctive public interest concern aside from organizational maintenance and operational efficiency. The public interest must always be tempered with considerations about human dignity.

NOTES

1. U.S. Bureau of the Census, *Statistical Abstract of the United States: 1974* (95th ed.), Washington, D.C.: Government Printing Office, 1974, p. 374; see also *Facts and Figures on Government Finance* (17th ed.), New York: Tax Foundation, 1973, p. 33; ACIR Report M-86, *Trends in Fiscal Federalism 1954-1974,* Advisory Commission on Intergovernmental Relations, Washington, D.C.: Government Printing Office, February, 1975, p. 1-3.

2. "Washington Bureaucrats: Real Powers of America," *U.S. News and World Report,* November 4, 1974, pp. 38-48; see also U.S. Bureau of the Census, *Statistical Abstract, op. cit.,* pp. 265-267.

3. U.S. Bureau of the Census, *Statistical Abstract, op. cit.,* pp. 256-266; ACIR Report, *Trends in Fiscal Federalism, 1954-1974, op. cit.,* pp. 11-23.

4. U.S. Bureau of the Census, *Statistical Abstract, op. cit.,* p. 244.

5. *Ibid.*, p. 264, and U.S. Bureau of the Census, *Historical Statistics of the United States, Colonial Times to 1957,* Washington, D.C., Government Printing Office, 1960, pp. 718-730.

6. U.S. Bureau of the Census, *Statistical Abstract, 1974, op. cit.,* p. 248; ACIR Report, *Trends in Fiscal Federalism, 1954-1974, op. cit.,* pp. 11-21; U.S. Bureau of the Census, *Historical Statistics, op. cit.,* p. 726; and U.S. Bureau of the Census, *Statistical Abstract, 1974, op. cit.,* pp. XV, 250-252; ACIR Report, *Trends in Fiscal Federalism, 1954-1974, op. cit.,* p. 15.

7. Alexander Hamilton, John Jay, and James Madison, *The Federalist,* New York: Modern Library, No. 51, p. 339; see also No. 10, p. 53, for a similar perspective.

8. *Ibid.*, No. 39, p. 247.

9. *Ibid.*, No. 51, pp. 338-339.

10. *Ibid.*, No. 43, pp. 280-281.

11. *Ibid.*, No. 48, p. 322.

12. *Ibid.*, pp. 322-323.

13. *Ibid.*, No. 51, p. 338.

14. *Ibid.*, pp. 338-339.

15. *Ibid.*, No. 70, p. 455.

16. *Ibid.*, pp. 459, 460-461.

17. It has, however, been only since World War I that the multiple executive has come into its own. See Leslie Lipson, *The American Governor,* Chicago: University of Chicago Press, 1939, pp. 9-30; York Willbern, "Administration in State Government," American Assembly, *The Forty-Eight States: Their Tasks as Policy Makers and Administrators,* New York: Columbia University Press, 1955, pp. 11-137; Robert H. Simmons, "American State Executive Studies: A Suggested New Departure," *Western Political Quarterly,* Dec. 1964, pp. 777-783. For insight into the fluctuating vicissitudes in relations among Congress, president and administration, see Leonard D. White, *The Republican Era: 1869—1901,* New York: Macmillan, 1963, pp. 20-67; and Woodrow Wilson, *Congressional Government* (originally published in 1885, republished by World Publishing Co., Cleveland, Ohio, 1956), *passim,* but especially the "Preface to Fifteenth Printing."

18. Robert A. Dahl, *A Preface to Democratic Theory,* Chicago: University of Chicago Press, Phoenix Books, 1956, p. 144.

19. *Ibid.;* all preceding material is found between pp. 144-148.

20. For the court's position on unrepresentative congressional districts, see *Westberry vs. Sanders,* 11 L ed. 481 (1964); for its position on unrepresentative state legislatures, see *Baker vs. Carr,* 369 U.S. 186 (1962).

21. Nicholas A. Masters, "House Committee Assignments," *American Political Science Review,* Vol. LV, No. 2, June 1961, p. 357.

22. For a very useful but somewhat dated collection of materials which probes aspects of this evolving role in the U.S. House of Representatives, see Robert L. Peabody and Nelson W. Polsby (eds.)., *New Perspectives on the House of Representatives,* Chicago: Rand McNally, 1963, *passim.*

23. Charles Jones, in Peabody and Polsby, *op. cit.,* p. 125.

24. Alan Fiellin, in Peabody and Polsby, *op. cit.,* p. 66.

25. Ralph K. Huitt, "The Congressional Committee: A Case Study," *American Political Science Review,* Vol. XLVIII, No. 2, June 1954, p. 365.

26. For further discussion see Robert H. Simmons, "The Washington State Plural Executive: An Initial Effort in Interaction Analysis," *Western Political Quarterly,* Vol. XVIII, No. 2, June 1965.

27. George A. Shipman, "The Pacific Northwest States," *The States of the Pacific Northwest,* American Assembly, The Washington Research Council, Seattle, 1957, pp. 12-13.

28. Ernest S. Griffith, *Congress: Its Contemporary Role,* New York: New York University Press, 1961, p. 158; see also pp. 51, 59, 123, and 158ff.

29. Louis M. Kohlmeier, Jr., *The Regulators: Watchdog Agencies and the Public Interest,* New York: Harper and Row, 1969, see generally; see also Emmette S. Redford, *The Regulation Process,* Austin: University of Texas Press, 1969; and John F. Winslow, *Conglomerates Unlimited: The Failure of Regulation,* Bloomington, Ind.: Indiana University Press, 1973.

30. York Willbern, "Administrative Control of Petroleum Production in Texas," in Emmette S. Redford (ed.), *Public Administration and Policy Formation,* Austin: University of Texas Press, 1956, pp. 3-50; see also James W. Fesler, *The Independence of State Regulatory Agencies,* Chicago: Public Administration Service, 1942, *passim;* cf. Emmette S. Redford, "Administrative Regulation: Protection of the Public Interest," *American Political Science Review,* Vol. XLVIII, No. 4, Dec. 1954, pp. 1103-1113.

31. York Willbern, *The Withering Away of the City,* Birmingham: University of Alabama Press, 1964, p. 41.

32. Aaron Wildavsky, *The Politics of the Budgetary Process,* Boston: Little Brown & Company, 1964, pp. 63-74.

33. Richard E. Neustadt, *Presidential Power,* New York: John Wiley & Sons, Inc., 1960, p. 10.

34. Simmons, "The Washington State Plural Executive: An Initial Effort in Interaction Analysis." Of course, these administrative units usually have their own access to the legislature.

35. John Gaus, *Reflections on Public Administration,* University, Alabama: University of Alabama Press, 1974, pp. 16-18.

36. Simmons, "The Washington State Plural Executive: An Initial Effort in Interaction Analysis," *passim.*

37. Clinton Rossiter, *The American Presidency* (rev. ed.), New York: Harcourt Brace and World, Harvest Book, 1960, pp. 251-261.

38. Norton E. Long, *The Polity,* Chicago: Rand McNally, 1962, pp. 71-72; see also same article in *American Political Science Review,* Vol. XLII, Sept. 1952, p. 814; see also Charles M. Wiltse, "The Representative Function of Bureaucracy," *American Political Science Review,* Vol. XXXV, June 1941, pp. 510-516; Emmette S. Redford, *Ideal and Practice in Public Administration,* University, Alabama: University of Alabama Press, 1958, chap. 5; and Herbert Kaufman, "Emerging Conflicts in the Doctrines of Public Administration," *American Political Science Review,* Vol. L, Dec. 1956, p. 1070 *et seq.*

39. Peter Woll, *American Bureaucracy,* New York: Norton, 1962, p. 177.

40. Kohlmeier, *The Regulators: Watchdog Agencies and the Public Interest,* pp. 3-16.

41. Herman Finer, "Administrative Responsibility in Democratic Government," *Public Administration Review,* Vol. I, Summer, 1941, pp. 336-337; see also Carl J. Friedrich, "Public Policy and the Nature of Administrative Responsibility," in C. J. Friedrich and Edward S. Mason (eds.),*Public Policy,* Cambridge: Harvard University Press, 1940, pp. 3-24. For a summary of these varying positions see Francis E. Rourke, *Bureaucracy, Politics and Public Policy,* Boston: Little Brown & Company, 1969, pp. 125-153.

42. Victor Marchetti and John D. Marks, *The C.I.A. and the Cult of Intelligence,* New York: Alfred A. Knopf, Inc., 1974, p. 62.

43. Bruce L. R. Smith, "Accountability and Independence in the Contract State," in *The Dilemma of Accountability in Modern Government,* Bruce L. R. Smith and D. C. Hague (eds.), London: Macmillan, 1971, p. 27.

44. David Z. Robinson, "Government Contracting for Academic Research: Accountability in the American Experience," in Smith and Hague, *op. cit.,* pp. 103-117.

3

THEORIES OF PUBLIC ADMINISTRATION

The broad range of issues challenging public administration and the complexity and depth of the crises facing the nation give rise to a bewildering array of approaches by those who practice or observe the governmental process. These perspectives emerge from diverse social and historical settings that reflect both settled and unresolved issues. Especially in the study of public administration both doctrinal disputations and controversies over those strategies which might best meet societal needs assure that the student need not "chew over old bones." Rather, students of public administration today, more than at any time in the past, are dipping their toes into swirling waters of unease, discontent and self-searching that characterize a discipline at odds with itself.

A large part of this current restlessness arises from a lack of agreement as to the type and nature of data to be utilized in understanding administration. The many divergent approaches are not necessarily mutually exclusive. Many, if not most, of these approaches overlap to some degree, though a few are quite distinctive, even conflictive with others. Imagine that you as a student are at the center of the diagram below (Figure 3-1) so that no matter in what direction you turn you will see a different approach to the subject, each with its distinct perspective.

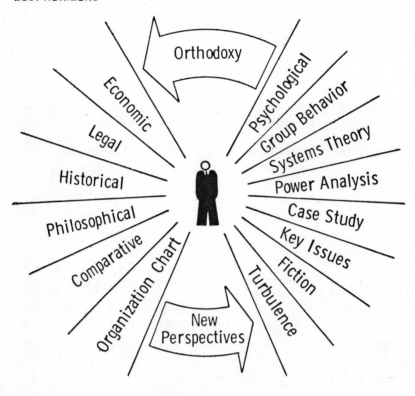

Diverse Approaches to the Study
of Public Administration

Figure 3-1

As you read this chapter you will become aware of the wide variety of perspectives through which you may view public administration. The validity of no particular approach is advocated, for each has made a unique contribution. There is no one true path to "truth" in public administration. Each approach has a set of implicit operative values. As you begin to comprehend the strengths and weaknesses of these differing paths you will appreciate the many contributions each has made. Their influences are found both in texts and classroom materials as well as in daily practice of administration in the thousands of public agencies. Today the literature and practice of public administration reflect turbulence and discontent. The diversity of these approaches is representative of the state of the art in our time.

ORTHODOX APPROACHES

There are two main approaches to public administration: the orthodox and the new. Most of the orthodox approaches utilize tangible data and as a group they dominated the practice and theory of public administration through World War II. Their intellectual *bona fides* are well established. Within this category are the philosophical, legal, historical, organization chart, comparative and economic approaches. The philosophical approach to public administration is crucial to an understanding of the discipline's present state of affairs. Accordingly, two of the chapters which follow are devoted exclusively to philosophical issues which have so greatly shaped the study and practice of administration.

The Legal Approach

One of the earliest and still one of the most pervasive approaches to public administration emphasizes the "legalisms" of the public administration process. This is, of course, the logical consequence of the crucial roles played by written constitutions and charters as supreme and fundamental sources of law in the American governmental system. The need for interpretation of constitutional phraseology and the peculiar nature of American judicial review, embracing legislative and executive acts, have imparted a heavily legalistic flavor to all aspects of governmental responsibility. It is one of several areas where value conflicts in the administrative processes may be effectively resolved.

The three constitutional branches of American government base their powers upon external sources of authority whether constitutional, historical (custom and tradition) or "political" (public opinion). The concept of limited government itself gives rise to the significance of legalism, for the central question in such a system, as observed in Chapter 2, is the legitimacy of the decisions and actions of public officials. The issue of legitimacy must often, perhaps always, be resolved by reference to constitutional articles and clauses, statutory enactments, executive orders, administrative agency rules and regulations and judicial decisions. Often the past will provide a guideline to the "legitimacy" or "illegitimacy" of public decisions and actions. Frequently, however unprecedented problems involving value conflicts emerge which call for new policies—untried, controversial and highly experimental. Nevertheless, in either instance the question of legality and the scope of legitimate authority will be raised sooner or later if, indeed, they had not been of central concern in the earliest stages of policy formulation.

The admonition of the United States Constitution's second article that the president "shall take care that the laws be faithfully executed" is paralleled by similar provisions in state constitutions and local charters applicable to governors and mayors. At all levels in the American system the link between law and execution is direct and explicit—it's not to be implied. In short, it is a "given" from which much else follows. The legal approach is consequently not only central to much of the past study of public administration but dates from the earliest exercises of executive authority.

The legal approach to understanding the administrative process does not center exclusively upon the executive branch but focuses also upon the products of the two coordinate branches of government—the legislature and the judiciary. The legislative branch, through its statutory enactments or resolutions, provides the "trigger" for much executive action. Laws are passed in order to be put into force—the "execute" portion of the "executive" process. The intent of the legislature when specific and unambiguous is to provide a legal source of authority for executive policy-making and action. Where the intent is not clear, then Congressional committee hearing transcripts and reports, debates recorded in the *Congressional Record* and other sources of extrinsic data must be utilized to establish legal parameters which, in turn, invest executive decisions and actions with "legitimacy." One current example of this relationship is the controversy over the "domestic spying" activities of the Central Intelligence Agency. Here the terminology of that agency's legislative charter is crucial in evaluating the legitimacy or illegitimacy of its actions. Yet even specific language, as in this case, may be interpreted in terms of other "overriding" standards such as a sudden crisis or a claim of "national defense."

The C.I.A.'s legislative charter includes the following provisions:

> ... it shall be the duty of the Agency, under direction of the National Security Council—
>
> (1) to advise the National Security Council in matters concerning such intelligence activities of the Government departments as relate to national security;
>
> (2) to make recommendations to the National Security Council for the coordination of such intelligence activities of the departments and agencies of the Government as relate to national security;
>
> (3) to correlate and evaluate intelligence relating to the national security, and provide for the appropriate dissemination of such intelligence within the Government using where appropriate existing agencies and facilities: *Provided*, that the Agency shall have *no police, subpoena, law-enforcement powers or internal security functions*; ... (Italics supplied)
>
> (4) to perform for the benefit of the existing intelligence agencies such additional services of common concern as the National Security Council determines can be more efficiently accomplished centrally;
>
> (5) to perform such other functions and duties related to intelligence affecting the national security as the National Security Council may from time to time direct.[1]

The domestic turmoil which resulted from the opposition to the Viet Nam War led the National Security Council to override the specific prohibitions in paragraph 3 against internal security functions in favor of such C.I.A. practices as opening the mail of private citizens, including that of members of Congress. The "catch-all" wording found in paragraphs 4 and 5 seems to provide the avenue for escaping the prohibition in paragraph 3. The clash of values occurred behind the closed doors of the National Security Council and the consequent decision to override traditional democratic values protected in paragraph 4 in the interests of national security was secretly determined. The knotty problem of accountability emerges. Legislative oversight of the uses put to the charter it had enacted was seriously inadequate. The impact of external developments may, indeed, cause even the most specific legislative enactment or constitutional clause to be "suspended." For example, limits on executive power reflected in the acts of Congress are set aside or greatly weakened during a war—especially a war declared by Congress. The same is also true of the limitations expressed in the Constitution's Bill of Rights.

The legal approach to public administration extends far beyond concern for semantic construction in determining legislative intent as a guide for executive action. The study of judicial decisions is equally important. For many years the study of "public law" comprised the only approach to the study of public administration. The recognition of issues of legal authority as paramount to executive concerns resulted in the detailed study and analysis of court cases by students of public administration. Today many public administration programs still require a foundation in constitutional law and/or administrative law.

Through the study of judicial decisions final resolutions of ambiguous constitutional or legislative phraseology are made where other means have proved futile. Challenges to the legitimacy of executive actions are carried out in large measure through the judicial process. Judicial decisions are important reference points for the shaping and execution of public policy by administrators. In a sense, they may be looked upon as "buoys" marking the safe channels through a hazardous harbor entrance. Conflicts concerning agency mission, agency power and services are often resolved through judicial procedures which become important agency lessons defining legally "appropriate responses." Only at great peril to one's safety, or the safety and well-being of one's agency, are these "safe channel" reference points ignored.

The "legal rights" and prerogatives of public agencies are just one side of the concern with legalism in public administration. The other side is concern for the legal rights of those affected by agency decisions and actions. Frequently, in determining individual rights and status under existing laws, the courts will, in effect, cause a shift in agency policies or practices.

The executive branch itself may be a source of its own legal authority under limited conditions. So-called "executive orders" have the force of law. Although often directed to executive agencies—reorganization of internal management, for example— they sometimes have tremendous implications beyond the executive branch. Executive orders declaring natural disaster emergencies; for the allocation of scarce resources; for the imposition of tariffs on imported goods or raw materials; or the declaration of an embargo, may affect many businesses, thousands or millions of citizens or even our relations with foreign nations. There are important legal, policy and administrative implications.

Individual executive agencies themselves issue thousands upon thousands of rules and regulations on hundreds of different subjects ranging from garbage collection schedules at the municipal level to the prohibition of dispensing certain types of medicines and drugs without prescription at the national level. Legal rights are affected. Advertising agencies must be aware of how far they may go in describing the virtues of their clients' products and toymakers may have to modify the design of toys or even abandon certain models in order to conform with administratively determined safety standards. Challenges by affected persons or corporations may be made through a complex process of administrative "adjudication" comprising quasi-judicial and highly specialized procedures outside of the regular courts. Quasi-judicial proceedings are administrative proceedings which use the judicial format to arrive at their determinations. These adjudicatory procedures may involve prosecution and defense counsel, oral and written evidence, and final determination by a hearing officer or examiner of the relative rights of agency and citizen. Administrative adjudication takes place at the national, state and local levels of government. The administrative process is permeated with legal issues, guidelines and procedures which are critical in determining values and choices in the public sector. These choices and values often have considerable impact on individuals and on the total society.

There are several distinct advantages to approaching public administration from a legal perspective. The legal approach is compatible with democratic theory, i.e., the coercive aspects of government are limited by a complex system of legal restraints. These prohibitions are expressed through constitutional and charter provisions, legislative enactments, judicial decisions and administrative adjudication. This array of democratic safeguards provides accessible data not just to administrators but to citizens, lawyers, students, corporate executives and anyone else interested in determining what can "be expected" of government. The "positive" conferral of power or the "negative" denial of power are both subjects of concern in the legal approach. The courts are one of the important avenues for resolution and settling of administrative conflict inherent in the struggle to implement and define public values. The legal approach, therefore, may be summarized as being concerned with the imperatives, both positive and negative, which shape administrative decisions and actions.

The elements of permanence and stability are also characteristics of the legal system. The longevity of the national Constitution and many state constitutions (most of which were adopted prior to the twentieth century) provide continuity of legal principles and processes. Change requires a formal amendment and in some constitutions this may be difficult to attain. While much statute law is either temporary or transitional, the vast bulk tends to remain largely as originally intended and the many volumes of codified public laws at all levels reflect continuity of principle. Judicial emphasis upon *stare decisis* ("let the previous decision stand") and the judicial presumption of the constitutionality of legislative and executive acts further contribute to legal stability. The student is able to follow the "unfolding" of the law and relate this to the evolution of administrative practice. Both are inexorably intertwined and change is viewed as possible or sometimes necessary. However, more often than not it is regarded as undesirable.

The weaknesses of the legal approach to public administration are emphasized by those not sympathetic to it. Their central criticism is that the legal approach may present a distorted and excessively narrow view of the administrative processes. Legal guidelines are deceptive. While appearing to offer preciseness and tangible data—guidelines by which to shape administrative power and discretion—they frequently fail to provide either "positive" or "negative" standards of any degree of usefulness. Constitutional and legislative phraseology is often vague—sometimes purposely so—and the resulting ambiguity leads to conflicts of interpretation. The Supreme Court obscenity ruling on movies is one example. Even judicial resolution of interpretative issues may be unsatisfactory, as witness the possibilities of separate written decisions by different judges in the same case, reversals on appeal, overrulings of previous judicial decisions and "split" decisions. The "5–4" majority decision reflects an unsatisfactory state of the law as does the "4–4" split decision.

Much legislation is never challenged in the courts despite vagueness or ambiguity and much remains on the statute books long after its usefulness is past. Legislative authority or limitations as the determinative factors in understanding the administrative processes may consequently be misleading. Often the law does not reflect reality, i.e., it is antiquated or ill-conceived. Administrative requirements are sometimes ignored in the passage of legislation or legislation is passed which is desired by administrators but adequate funding or the proper agency facilities and personnel to carry out the tasks do not necessarily follow. Problems concerning difficulty of enforcement are sometimes not a major factor in legislative considerations, while they are of prime importance in administrative considerations so that the "gap" between legal authority and effective administrative authority may be a fatal flaw to accurate perceptions of public administration.

Criticism also centers around the inability of the legal approach to take into account the inherent dynamism of the administrative process. It is felt that a concentration upon legal principle and authority emphasizes formal structure and lacks an appreciation for human dynamics in the administered organization. In the legal approach it is assumed the administrator will react predictably in accordance with higher legal authority and, consequently, his role is not a creative one. The significance of human behavior is therefore minimized. The study of administration is reduced to description of the legal attributes of public agencies. Too much is consequently ignored. The student utilizing only the legal approach is doomed to looking at the vast field of public administration through blinders—he might just as usefully attempt to study the heavens through a drinking straw.

Despite such alleged shortcomings, the legal approach does raise certain fundamental questions that are central to understanding the relationships between administrative power and the concept of limited government:

1. What legitimate means are available in executing the law?
2. Under what conditions may an administrator exercise discretion in interpreting statutes? What standards are to be utilized?
3. What is the intent of the law?
4. What are the legitimate penalties that public agencies may impose for violation of laws or administrative rules and regulations?
5. What is the nature of "administrative justice"?
6. What is the proper role for appeals from administrative decisions?
7. What are the sources of administrative authority?
8. What are the proper safeguards to prevent abuses in the issuance of executive orders?
9. What are the minimal standards for the drafting of agency rules and regulations?
10. What are the most significant changes in the laws that affect administrative agencies?

Adequate answers to these questions are still to come within the discipline. These are difficult yet crucial questions for those charged with formulating and implementing public policy.

The Historical Approach

The historical approach is an effort to understand the development of administrative systems within the context of specific times past. To this extent it overlaps the legal approach, as the bulk of Anglo-Saxon law has emerged over long periods of time on the basis of evolving case law. Just as the data of the legal framework is tangible in the form of written judicial decisions, constitutional and charter provisions, statutes, executive orders, rules and regulations, so also much historical evidence is based on visual, tangible data. While a great deal of ancient history is conjectural, more recent data concerning the evolution of administrative systems is confirmable with only the implications of specific developments subject to differing interpretations.

Historical writings on bureaucratic organization embrace the most ancient civilizations. The early Sumerian, Egyptian, Indian and Chinese civilizations had significant administrative institutions. The establishment of communications, collection of taxes, building of massive public works, the maintenance of temple accounts, the storage of food for emergencies, the establishment of diplomatic relations with other states, the necessity for the crafts of espionage and intelligence gathering, and the waging of wars required the setting of priorities, the allocation of human and material resources, the development of strategies to reach specific goals and the designing of particular organizational structures.[2]

The global administrative system of the Catholic Church developed in medieval and more recent times remains one of the administrative wonders of the world. The activities of church administration rival and, in fact, exceed those of many nations in the international community. Historical studies abound on the role of rationally directed and hierarchically organized bureaucracies. They have been central in shaping society's institutions in the far past as well as in contemporary life.

The historical approach embraces many foci of interest. Many studies have concentrated on particular civilizations or specific historical epochs. Others have concentrated on administrative accomplishments of individual leaders or specific political regimes. Some studies emphasize the administrative philosophies of political parties, while the more contemporary deal with the background and underlying forces leading to the scientific management movement and the industrial organization of modern technologically oriented societies.

The underlying assumption of the historical approach is that past and present events are interconnected in innumerably diverse ways and patterns. A better understanding of the past may, therefore, aid in more effectively dealing with the problems of the present. Consequently, human existence at any period is never isolated but is inescapably connected with its past. Some historical schools of thought stress the "circular" nature of human existence. Here the commonality of the basic problems facing mankind, such as allocation of resources, war and peace, disease, love and hate, and social upheaval merely confirm there is really "nothing new under the sun." Whether or not history really does repeat itself there is much in the past to enrich man's life in the present. The contributions of the great classical works of former civilizations aid in evaluating our own levels of cultural and moral dilemma.

The historical approach to American public administration is marked by a number of outstanding contributions. Leonard D. White's volumes, *The Federalists, The Jeffersonians, The Jacksonians,* and *The Republican Era 1869–1901,* mark a high point in scholarly research and writing by the late distinguished professor of public administration.[3] White uncovered the interrelationships between earlier American administrative systems and the contemporary political and social institutions of those times.

No account of the historical approach to administration would be complete without reference to Dwight Waldo's *The Administrative State.* The publication of this work was the culmination of a pioneering effort by Professor Waldo to lay bare the value bases of American public administration through interpretation of a wide range of historical data.[4] Add to this small representative sampling the wide array of presidential biographies and autobiographies so popular in recent years and it becomes apparent that the historical approach is one of the most fully developed and established paths to understanding the administrative process.

Some of the basic questions implied by the historical approach are:

1. What institutions and administrative practices in the past are applicable to the contemporary scene?
2. What "seeds" of the past are found in new administrative movements?
3. What are the conditions under which societies will make radical breaks with their past and seek to establish new institutions and administrative patterns?
4. What is the nature of the "public trust" as exemplified by past practices and experience?
5. What roles have citizens played in the past vis-à-vis administrative authority?

Administration which has been shaped by history in turn shapes the future, which is to become history. Such questions aid us in understanding that process. The next chapter is devoted to examination and interpretation of those historical forces influencing the evolution of American public administration and its distinctive characteristics.

The Organization Chart Approach

"Charting the organization" has traditionally been a major preoccupation of both practitioners and academics. Begun as a technique for describing both legal authority and vertical and horizontal relationships within administrative structures, it emerged as virtually an end in itself. This final development was the consequence of the belief that the organization chart reflected reality and that administrative phenomena not reflected by the lines and squares were of secondary importance. While the organization chart today is recognized as of more limited usefulness, the significance of this approach has left an indelible imprint upon the practice and study of public administration. The high point of the organization chart approach paralleled the dominant period of scientific management. The organization chart (see Figure 3-2) and flow-process chart were two of the indispensable tools of "scientific" managers and "efficiency" engineers.

The organization chart approach is visual and based on the belief that the key characteristics and interrelationships within administrative structures can be "pictured." The principle of hierarchy, comprising the division of the organization into superior and subordinate levels of authority, describes the "flow of authority" downward. Further, it assumes such authority is legal in nature: in other words, authority at all levels and the interrelationships between levels is legally sanctioned and, therefore, legitimate. In addition, it is assumed that legal authority is effective authority. If these assumptions are valid, then the organization chart is an accurate visualization of the decision-making processes.

The advantages of the organization chart approach are many. In assuming the validity of the pyramidal organizational structure, legal responsibility can be pinpointed at the top of the hierarchy. Top management can, therefore, be held accountable for the efficiency and effectiveness of the organization. Each level can also be held responsible to the next highest level. In this manner, the organization is "self-contained" in terms of responsibilities and prerogatives. Another advantage is that both responsibilities and prerogatives can be empirically confirmed and precisely delineated by reference (on the chart) to position held, superiors responsible to and subordinates responsible for. All legal and effective power is assigned power; there are no "loose ends." Stated in another way, the "situs" or resting place of power can be depicted. Power is definable and the occupant of each position can legally exercise only that authority assigned to him. There is no "independent" power or power that is not legally assigned. A third advantage of this visual approach is the impression of "unity" of the total organization regardless of complexities at any given level or the devolution of authority between central headquarters, regional field offices and subregional units. The "whole" is bound together by lines of authority and advisory relationships into a unified organization. Another advantage is that complex formal-legal relationships can be depicted on a single sheet of paper. In this manner, any agency or person can be made aware of his relationship to the "whole" or to any other agency or person.

The organization chart in Figure 3-2 is illustrative of their utility:

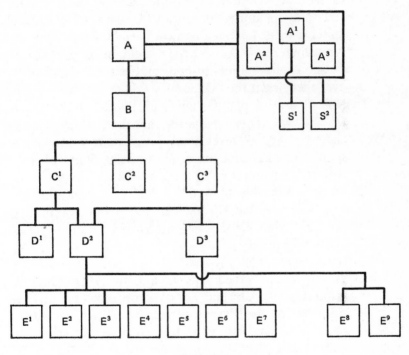

Figure 3-2.

The official relationships depicted by the chart may be described as follows:

1. The Chief Executive (A) of the organization is served by an advisory board or commission.
2. The advisory board or commission comprises three members (A^1, the chairman, with A^2 and A^3 as members).

89

3. A^1, the chairman of the advisory board, is served by a "staff" official (S^1); note the "by-pass" device to depict direct responsibility to A^1. Another staff official (S^2) serves the entire board.

4. B is the "second in command" under A and has direct responsibility for level "C" and all other subordinate levels.

5. However, it is apparent that A chooses to maintain some direct relationship with agencies at the "C" level and that, in limited instances, "C" level officials deal directly with A. For the most part, however, they are subordinate to and under the direct control of B.

6. C^1 and C^3 have direct responsibilities for and authority over agencies at the "D" level.

7. Note that D^1 is placed slightly higher on the chart than D^2 and D^3. This depicts the fact that, while all agencies at the "D" level have approximately similar responsibilities, D^1 does exercise some significantly higher authority or functions not delegated to D^2 or D^3.

8. D^2 is responsible to both C^1 and C^3. However, the lines indicate that C^1 exercise most of the authority over D^2, while D^2 is responsible to C^3 for only certain limited purposes.

9. D^3 is responsible only to C^3.

10. "E" level units (perhaps field offices) are directly responsible to D^2 and D^3. An organization manual will describe the division of responsibilities. However, E^8 and E^9 are (note the by-pass device) responsible only to D^2.

The close relationship between the legal approach and the organization chart approach is one of the weaknesses of the latter. Critics assert that legal power may not necessarily be effective power. Consequently, problems of ambiguity and interpretation of legal sources of authority and directives are not always valid guidelines for administrative action. In addition, the organization chart approach cannot depict the differences in effective influence due to personal qualities that individuals may exert aside from their formal allocation of legal authority. Numerous studies have concluded that informal or group norms often conflict with the formal patterns of authority depicted by organization charts. Under a variety of conditions the informal and uncharted personal relationships may dilute and avoid the normal channels of authority and emerge as the determinative forces in administrative decision-making.

A final weakness of organization charts is their emphasis upon rationality, logic and symmetry. It is *assumed* that organization members will react according to their position on the chart. More recent approaches to public administration stress the non-visual and non-quantifiable nature of authority and leadership in organizations and the irrational and emotional nature of much administrative behavior. The organization chart is, therefore, accorded a quite limited role and those who place too much stock upon them as accurate descriptions of the administrative process do so at the peril of dangerous distortions and misconceptions. Although they may be of some help in locating formal authority in an administrative hierarchy, undue reliance on these charts is little more than an invitation to unreality.

The Comparative Approach

The underlying assumption of the comparative approach to public administration is that the administrative process transcends the political boundaries that separate nation from nation, nation from state, state from state, state from local governments and local governments from each other. Rather than emphasizing the separateness of different political units, the interdependence of all upon the processes of administration makes it necessary to study and understand those processes which transcend political boundaries. The intent is, therefore, to observe and evaluate commonalities of administration independent of their peculiar national backgrounds as well as dissimilarities attributable to such backgrounds. Where differences in administration do exist in institutional structures, techniques or value assumptions, the comparative approach seeks to relate them to their causal factors, be they psychological, historical, political, cultural, religious, economic or constitutional.

Comparative administration regards the total environment as of extreme significance in shaping administrative processes and values. Cross-cultural and cross-national studies will, it is hoped, shed new knowledge on those fundamental propositions inherent in administration. The search for such knowledge goes beyond knowledge for its own sake, but rather it is assumed it may be fruitfully utilized by other governments. Even if the administrative practices of other governments are not susceptible to adoption, the understanding of other systems contributes towards better understanding of one's own. Comparative analysis of observable and often quantifiable data tends to have an aura of scientism and many comparative studies are exceedingly sophisticated in both conceptualization and application, as their theoretical foundations are based upon systems theory.

The comparative approach overlaps the legal approach to the degree that differences in legal systems may be significant. It also overlaps the economic approach to the degree that national resources (human, fiscal, material, etc.) aid in explaining differences. Also, to the extent that governments differ in the degree of national regulatory planning, the comparative and economic approaches tend to overlap. The comparative and power-analysis approaches to administration also have much in common. Studies of political parties, the many shades of governmental authoritarianism, tutelage, or the broad spectrum of "democratic" variations are directed toward the end of understanding the nature of power in differing environmental contexts and their relevance for the exercise of administrative power. The philosophic approach is also relevant to the comparative approach when differences in national outlook, cultural and religious differences produce dissimilar value frameworks that dominate differing societies. The comparative approach may, therefore, be a useful adjunct to several other approaches to understanding administration.

Students of comparative government may either develop "models" or conceptualizations prior to the gathering of specific data and thereby hope to confirm or disprove those hypotheses or theories advanced beforehand. Conversely, many studies are begun with the gathering and analysis of data in the expectation that this approach will lead to the later development of theories. In either event, "theory building" is central to comparative administration.

There are many difficulties inherent in the comparative approach. It is often difficult for observers of foreign systems to rid themselves of their own cultural biases and values. Even assuming this can be accomplished, the "weighting" of the myriad factors affecting other administrative systems is a difficult task, especially when those factors may be unique to non-Western societies.

The comparative approach has a long history, but it was especially influential in the late 1940's, '50's and '60's. The immediate post-Second World War era spurred America's interest in the "underdeveloped" countries, many of which were emerging from colonial status to independence. American technical assistance programs on a global scale provided the means by which many Americans developed considerable knowledge and skills in delivering technical aid to other nations. The crucial problem was to shape these programs to the peculiar and, for Americans, often strange institutions and values of other societies. Sometimes aid was given with the expectation that American institutions and values might be adopted. Frequently, however, these expectations were not realized and some aid programs were consequently viewed as "suspect" by the recipients. Many American aid administrators returned eventually to the classroom and were instrumental in the development of academic programs in comparative administration.

In 1963 the American Political Science Association established a committee on comparative administration and several years later a similar comparative administration group was formed within the American Society for Public Administration. While comparative administration is generally understood to embrace the study of foreign administrative systems, the comparative approach is of great consequence within the United States. Wherever administrative processes between our numerous governmental jurisdictions are compared, the comparative approach is utilized. Even studies comparing the administrative problems of central city minority areas with other areas of our metropolitan complexes may be considered within the field of comparative administration and the possibilities for its use are legion.

The Economic Approach

In few ages of the past have economic relationships shaped the directions and priorities of domestic and foreign policies of nations more than today. Karl Marx's nineteenth century insistence that the means of production and economic class warfare are the determinants of man's future is paralleled today by the insistence of middle Eastern oil monarchs that the economics of a single resource can cause a fundamental shift in the distribution of global wealth and resources. On a more modest scale, the most significant domestic decisions of governments of modern industrialized nations may well be those in the economic realm. Regulation of business practices by regulatory commissions, raising or lowering of tariffs or excises, manipulation of interest rates for the nation's banking system, devaluation of currency and governmental aid and subsidies to private enterprise and individual citizens merely suggest a few of the interlocking relationships between public policy and the economy.

With the breaking down of previous barriers between public authority and private enterprise, administrative decision-making is increasingly based primarily on economic considerations, or the economic consequences of alternative public policies are projected and evaluated. Still, public and private roles in the economy may be differentiated. Traditional differences between the two may be described as follows:

1. The administrative agency and private enterprise may be competitive or even conflictive with one another. For example, public utilities may compete with private utilities for customers. Or, alternatively, a publicly-owned power project may provide a "yardstick" to determine the validity of private power rates.

2. Public agencies may set broad guidelines comprising "rules of the game" within which private enterprise will be allowed to exercise its discretion. Such guidelines may comprise quality-safety standards, pricing, degrees of competition and regulation of stock-bond issues.
3. Private enterprise may have to affirmatively seek customers while public agencies may serve "captive" clienteles who have no choice in seeking services elsewhere. Economists view government as a monopoly.
4. Private enterprise may justify decision-making in terms of its own self-interests, while public enterprises must justify, despite frequent lapses, their decision-making on the basis of the "public interest."
5. Private entrepreneurs will generally be able to exercise more freedom of discretion and assume more risks than public administrators.
6. The concept of "economic man" is based upon the assumptions of his acting in his own "self-interest" in choosing between economic alternatives and of his seeking to maximize his own satisfactions. The economic approach to the study of public administration views "administrative man" as acting on equally rational bases but his "self-interest" is perceived to be the interests of his agency.
7. While payments for goods and services in private enterprises are voluntary, the unique nature of public financing derives from coercive contributions, through taxation, and the power to create and establish the value of money.

Bureaucrats, therefore, operate within a unique framework. Their behavioral pattern will consequently differ widely from members of private enterprises. Where decision-making in private enterprise will be oriented toward maximization of profit, economists view "administrative man" in a public bureaucracy as acting to assure a maximized budget. The public bureaucracy, consequently, is a unique economic phenomenon. Public bureaucratic decision-making will be oriented to the ends of proliferation of programs and reluctance to reduce or eliminate existing programs. Rational public agency decision-making also will reject or tend to avoid support of those programs liable to produce powerful political enemies.

Yet the economic consequences of agency decision-making often force the bureaucrat to cater to those groups and, consequently, support their programs and goals, which, as suggested in Chapter 2, will maximize political support for the agency, resulting in increased budgets. In such a situation the weaknesses and liabilities of certain key programs will be "swept under the rug" while their virtues will be magnified and extolled far beyond deserved merits. Consequently, the budgetary process becomes the focal point of study in attempting to understand the nature of the administrative process.

The political economist does not view the bureaucrat as a neutral automaton. He is regarded instead as a dispenser of privileges and prerogatives in the form of licenses, franchises and contracts while, at the same time, as capable of exacting penalties backed by the full coercive power of government. In the economic approach to public administration, the student studies the full interaction of external forces seeking maximization of private satisfactions as well as the rationalized, calculating processes by which bureaucrats seek to satisfy their "own," i.e., agency, satisfactions. The economic role of the bureaucrat is, therefore, unique insofar as he acts as an agent of the state even while he helps shape the redistribution of power in the society.[5]

NEW PERSPECTIVES

Within this category are a broad range of divergent approaches to the administrative process which have emerged, in more recent times, as largely "reactive" to orthodoxy. It must be emphasized that no hard-and-fast line between these two groups exists, although for analytic purposes their assumptions and concerns do differ. As a group these approaches have gained prominence in the post-World War II period and may be described as generally sympathetic with the "new public administration" described later in this volume.

The Power-Analysis Approach

Where the philosophical approach is concerned with the justice or morality of the ends of public policy, the power-analysis approach accepts power as an end in itself. Indeed, to the degree it assures agency well-being and survival, it is the only justifiable end of public policy. The power-analysis approach is essentially amoral; it views power as a "given." It is the crucial element in agency survival, which is regarded as the highest good. Whether other consequences of such survival have moral or immoral implications is regarded as quite irrelevant. Rather, power is studied in all its ramifications and especially important are the techniques by which power is attained, maintained and expanded. Once attained, power is utilized for whatever purpose its possessor intends.

The power-analysis approach also conflicts with the legal approach. The basic assumption of the legal approach, that legal power is effective power, is challenged. Rather, the power approach recognizes that legal power may or may not be effective power. For that reason it assumes that dependence upon legal authorization or directives may not accurately depict the actual exercise of power within an administrative organization. Thus, while agencies may exercise authority from common legal sources, some may be far more powerful and influential than others. The reasons cannot, therefore, be traced to legal sanction. On the contrary, power is to be studied for its own sake, for it frequently establishes its own terms and conditions, irrespective of legal theory.

The power-analysis approach is, by its nature, in conflict with the organization-chart approach. It rejects the usefulness of organization charts in understanding the administrative process. The square boxes and lines depict only "formal" patterns of power and authority and graphically portray only their legally sanctioned fragmentation and distribution. On the other hand, the "informal" patterns and networks of power may conflict with those that are charted.

The power-analysis approach is concerned with the means by which power is actually exercised and the conditions under which agencies will hold or lose power. In this approach power is never constant and fluctuates widely. Consequently, administrative agencies must continually readjust their goals and strategies in order to build up a power "surplus" over a power "drainage." Especially important are the links between public agencies and those external power centers that may serve to supplement and reinforce agency power and influence. Studies oriented to the power approach may, therefore, describe and analyze power configurations internal to the public organization, external to it, or the interrelationships between the two.

This approach may also emphasize the coercive techniques by which public power is exercised. The wide range of monetary and non-monetary sanctions in the arsenal of public administration are within its purview.[6] These are particularly significant, as even in a democratic society the vast bulk of administrative decisions at any level of government are not reviewed by the courts of law.

The Psychological Approach

The psychological approach is concerned with human behavior in organizations. It assumes, like the power-analysis approach, that bureaucrats will behave in ways that are not describable on organization charts or in a reading of legal directives. In the psychological approach the focus of attention is upon the "hidden agenda" of the bureaucrat and the attempt is made to understand and analyze those factors that influence his decision-making. Such factors may be external but, for the most part, will be internal to the bureaucrat himself. Thus, both conscious and subconscious decision-making processes are concerns of this approach. The main emphasis, however, is on those factors that cannot be explained by reference to external criteria. This approach is, therefore, non-visual, insofar as it focuses on and attempts to understand the "internal" determinants of bureaucratic behavior.

Those sympathetic to the psychological approach feel that to properly understand public administration is to observe and study the behavior of the individual as an individual and, again, as a member of a much larger total organization with declared priorities of values and goals. Causes of variations in behavior on the individual-individual level, the individual-group level and the individual-organization level are of great significance as the combined impact and influence of numerous individuals on organizational goals and values may be so great as to modify or even displace them.

The psychological approach gives very little credence to the outward image bureaucrats present to others in their organization or to the organization's clientele. Instead, there is much evidence that the naive observer views only a bureaucratic mask and that organizations that might appear placid are, in fact, arenas of conflict, competition and ruthless decision-making. Not only is much concealed, but the "hidden agendas" of networks of cliques often are at odds with broader organizational purposes. Both public and private organizations are worlds of warfare and characterized by internal intellectual dishonesty where the "true" personality diverges so much from the "mask." In the words of two close observers of bureaucratic behavior:

> In the back corners and interstices of the organization there are informal agreements, plots, cabals, and so on, in which, depending on the relationships between the parties, only the manifest content of the intention is revealed even within these groups themselves. Only occasionally, in drinking bouts and in office parties, and sometimes in satire and humor, are the undercurrents revealed. Insofar as the bureaucratic *form* has come to permeate all areas of modern life, it can be expected that its accompanying psychological *consequences* will be expressed in all areas. Thus, in its psychological overtones, life in business bureaucracies is not much different from life in political, educational, or religious bureaucracies.[7]

A large number of studies depict the member of the organization as sublimating his own restlessness, uniqueness and creativity in favor of conformity to the organization's dominant norms, modes of dress, behavior, attitudes and values. Here "getting ahead" is rationally calculated to require complete absorption into the "sameness" of organizational orthodoxy. Other studies reveal a psychological unwillingness to surrender one's "real" self to the "other" self demanded by others. Instead, an uneasy reconciliation is attempted in which the bureaucrat, during the working hours, affects to being "as one" with organizational orthodoxy in order to hold his job. However, outside of regular working hours he reverts to his "real self" in terms of dress, attitudes, behavior and values. The conclusions reached by such studies document various degrees of alienation and instances of psychological breakdown in the inability of the bureaucrat to live over prolonged periods as "two" persons.

Much of the psychological approach to public administration is concerned with the development of techniques to "screen out" individuals from public service who are, or may become, organizational malcontents. Attempts to develop ideal "personality profiles" by which to compare candidates for the public service have been widely discussed. Especially sensitive agencies, such as law enforcement and intelligence agencies, have developed highly sophisticated techniques by which to reveal the "inner" man. In some instances the attempt may be not so much to assure a high probability or organizational conformity as to discover undesirable traits which might be potentially dangerous for the society. For example, many large urban police departments with large racial minorities within their jurisdiction are extremely concerned to discover any latent or consciously hidden racial or religious hatreds or animosities in candidates for employment. Many agencies employ, on either full-time or part-time bases, qualified psychologists and/or psychiatrists to advise personnel officers.

The possibility of "undemocratic" attitudes on the part of bureaucrats, particularly in defense agencies, has also been raised. The evidence would seem to suggest that there are psychological factors in different agencies with widely variant missions that tend to dispose the bureaucrat toward or away from democratic ideals. Through the process of acculturation to agency beliefs, democratic principles may be reinforced or squelched.[8]

The psychological approach to public administration is concerned with the attitudes and self-perceptions of bureaucrats as well as the attitudes and perceptions of clientele. Agency stability or instability is explained by reference to the psychological make-up of the participants in agency decision-making. The focus is upon the internal processes of individual participants and there is, consequently, less attention to the unity and overall structure of the organization. The psychological approach has some element of science insofar as the predictability of human behavior in organizations is a major concern. To the extent that human behavior, however, remains unpredictable this approach must be based, in large measure, on faith. The psychological approach does imply an interdisciplinary cooperation in the study of public administration since many political scientists, sociologists and cultural anthropologists also regard human behavior and its causative factors to be of crucial importance. The subject is not the preserve of any one field of knowledge.

The Group-Theory Approach

This approach is concerned with the roles played by organized groups in the shaping of administrative policy. The group-theory approach overlaps the psychological approach insofar as it emphasizes the behavior of groups, their attitudes and actions, and the influence of groups on individual behavior within administrative organizations.

Externally, special interest groups or pressure groups are the focus of attention. The basic assumption is that society is highly pluralistic and that one group seldom completely dominates the shaping of public and administrative policy. Instead, the broader contours of public policy and the more limited area of administrative policy are the product, in large measure, of accommodation between competing special-interest groups. Thus, "incremental" policy-making emerges which is kept from being too radical by the "mutual vetoes" these groups have upon each other. In a sense no one group really wins everything and, consequently, most groups obtain some benefits from public policy but not all that they originally sought. A "no win–no lose" system emerges.[9]

Within this context, public agencies are viewed as reflective of the compromises necessary in order to keep such a pluralistic

101

system from disintegrating into serious conflict. Administrative values largely confirm the existing power structure. Policy advances are short-term rather than long-term and administrative contributions to such policy are minimal. To the discontented of society this smacks of administrative capitulation to special interests. Cynicism, frustration and a jaundiced view of bureaucracy are frequent by-products. Much alienation may be traced to such a system. On this basis, the group-theory approach appears to be in conflict with the philosophical approach, where ultimate moral values are regarded as the only justifiable criteria for the exercise of administrative power. In the group-theory approach, democracy is understood to be based on compromise and this, in turn, prevents the great ideological leap forward. As a result, startling changes or radical innovations in public and administrative policy are precluded.

One offshoot of this approach may be described as "elitist." It is based on the belief that the spirit and reality of compromise are largely illusory and that only a few key groups really control public and administrative policy. In short, there is a hierarchy among special-interest groups external to public agencies and, at the very apex of power, are the true "power-movers" of society. Perhaps the most popularly held recognition of this elitism or "multiple elitism" is the military-industrial complex identified by President Dwight Eisenhower, where extremely powerful agencies with defense-oriented missions find common cause with industrial groups. Banking and insurance corporations, oil companies and politicians are also described as crucial elitist groups holding the destiny of the nation in their hands. Critics of these "alliances" stress the furtherance of self-interest with a consequent neglect of the broader public interest. The power of such alliances is compounded by the fact that the elitist network extends into the legislative branch and certain key administrative agencies. This finally results in the "cooptation" or capture of such agencies by external elites so that agency values and choices become those determined by such elites.

Yale psychologist Irving Janis carried out a very important study of small-group decision-making within administrative agencies in the shaping of American foreign policy. He con-

SOURCE: *Los Angeles Times, July 6, 1975.*

cluded that the individual tends to be coerced into group norms, that critical faculties which ordinarily would challenge the strategies and goals give way to group "solidarity" and that loyalty to the group often causes an inability to properly appraise alternative courses of action. What emerges is "soft-headed" thinking in which the morality of goals and individual conscience give way to group decisions that become, in themselves, the highest morality. In short, the deficiencies in decision-making are in the collective judgments of members of small cohesive groups. The more cohesive the group originally and the greater its *esprit de corps,* the more it is able to "domesticate" the dissenter through subtle, small-group dynamics. Not wishing to be excluded from "the club," the individual member harboring doubts about group strategies or goals is made aware of the very limited area in which he may safely tread. Beyond these borders he may be excluded from the group or, at the least, gain the reputation among his organizational peers and superiors of having lost his "effectiveness."[10]

Through such studies our knowledge of group dynamics in the development of agency policy has reached new levels of sophistication. Increasing pressures for "participative management" and earlier assumptions of the inherent strengths of the small-team or -group decision-making may now be appraised more realistically.[11]

The Turbulence Approach

Perhaps the approach differing most radically from orthodoxy is that which views society as being in ceaseless flux. The turbulent environment will lead to new forms of social, political and economic institutions bearing little resemblance to those of the past. It is felt that history, consequently, can provide few guidelines appropriate to societal needs. Instead, radically new ways of viewing societal problems and especially new ways of designing administrative organizations are urgently required. The notion of permanent or even stable administrative institutions must, in this approach, give way to new experimental modes, including temporary or "disposable" organizations. A society in the throes of unprecedented fundamental change is felt to be ill-served by traditional approaches to the administrative process.

The irrelevance of not only the historical approach but also the legal and organization-chart approaches is quite obvious. The turbulence approach is highly sociological and views society as hosting a large number of differing and turbulent environments. Each of these must be served by highly flexible and transitory administrative institutions and organizational patterns. These administrative processes and patterns, in turn, are to be shaped by the unique requirements demanded by the unstable and highly conflictive societies in which traditional values and assumptions can no longer serve as effective guidelines. Any search for the "one best" administrative form of organization is, therefore, doomed to be an exercise in futility. Effective administrative patterns are those which best reflect the uniqueness of a given environment. Administrative effectiveness is consequently to be measured only on the basis of a particular situation. The end result is rejection of any concept of a universal administrative "good" or "bad" and the emergence in its place of a "situational ethic."

The Systems Approach

The systems and turbulence approaches have much in common. Both are based upon the assumption of ceaseless change. The two approaches, therefore, overlap insofar as they both reject the notion of a static society or static institutions to serve that society. Where they differ is in their view of the change process itself. The systems approach views societal change as not turbulent but more systematic and developmental. In either case, there is an increased need for students of public administration to study and attempt to understand change processes.

In the systems approach the change processes can be conceptualized into four interrelated phases (see Figure 3–3): input-conversion-output-feedback. The administrative agency in this approach is subjected to stimuli from the external environment ("input"). The stimuli force administrative change and response. The stimuli triggering administrative change and response are modified in turn and converted into "output" in the form of modified administrative behavior, attitudes or processes which impinge upon the external environment, including agency clientele. As the environment is affected by the modified administrative processes it "feedsback" new stimuli which affect the agency. Then, once again, the agency is triggered into reaction to the now modified environment. This four-phase process continues unceasingly. A simplified graphic of the process appears below.

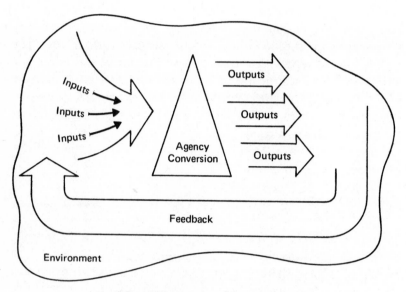

A Simplified Graphic of the Systems
Approach to the Public Administrative Process

Figure 3-3.

All four phases are interconnected and only have meaning in relation to inputs and outputs. The assumption is that the "system" is all-embracing, with no significant element contributing to change left unaccounted for. It may be, in effect, a "closed system" in which every stimulus for change contributes to more change. Or it may be a tentative heuristic conception which is only a hunch about how a particular system works. For the student of administration the key concern is that the organization is viewed as both receiving stimulation and, through the conversion process, causing stimulation. Hence, administration is creative rather than static. The administrative organization does not merely react to external stimuli but becomes a source of stimuli itself. In a broader context, it does not merely react to policy made elsewhere but helps shape policy.

Systems analysis is a conceptual technique for identifying and describing an interrelated system of causes and effects.[12] There are no fixed actors or activities. On the contrary, everything is in the process of becoming something else and, therefore, affecting everything else. This approach assumes that public agencies cannot be considered apart from their environments but are affected by and do, in turn, affect those environments. There is a mutuality or reciprocity of influences between agency and surrounding environment. The field of public administration is, therefore, involved in a constant unfolding of policy.

A variation of the systems approach might be to divide an administrative problem or issue into its basic component parts and to study them in some systematic manner (see Figure 3–4). Thus, the first phase might be devoted to defining the problem. Here concern would be to assess the values and theoretical notions and identify the component parts of the problem. A second phase would focus upon developing a plan to resolve the conditions leading to the problem. In this phase priorities would be assessed, crucial controlling values identified and alternative policies considered. A third phase would be concerned with identifying the most desirable policy. A final phase would focus upon the programs necessary to carry out the policy. An important linkage in the whole process might be the budget. On the basis of these processes a particular problem or issue might be broken down and graphically portrayed as follows:

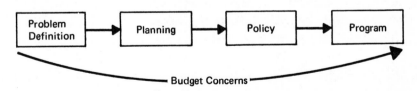

Figure 3–4. A PROBLEM-SOLVING SEQUENCE

The systems approach views administrative agencies as converting input stimuli into specific outputs. The implications about human nature are quite clear within the systems-analysis context; man is capable of adapting to changing conditions. Human nature is not "fixed" but rather is indeterminate. Man has the potential "to become" something other than what he is. What "is" at any given moment will depend upon the stimuli he received and the nature of his adaptation. Humans cannot be considered apart from the total environment and, instead, are intimately related to it. The first task in understanding "administrative man" is, consequently, to attempt to understand the nature of the environment and the change processes which are operative and available. Unlike the psychological approach, man is considered in relation to the externalities rather than his internalities. Much of the material discussed in Part III is rooted in the systems approach to public administration.

The Issues Approach

This approach differs from the others in that it focuses upon a specific issue or problem facing contemporary society. In seeking a better understanding of the issue and in considering available alternatives in public policy toward its resolution, any of the previous approaches or any combination of them may be utilized. The issue itself serves as a means or, in effect, may be regarded as a sort of "spectacles" by which to view and analyze the administrative process.

One of the advantages of the issue approach is the absence of any preconceived assumptions which typify each of the other previous approaches. Rather, the issues approach may utilize those other approaches regarded as most potentially fruitful in attacking the problems selected. An example of the issues approach might be the problem centering around the issue of "resource allocation"—certainly a key issue in view of increasing scarcities. Who gets what and why? Who gets the least and why? What are the means by which allocations are determined? What are the crucial values involved? How should the interests of utilization be balanced with the needs for conservation? Are the allocations "just" or "unjust"? Are allocation decisions final? Are there appeals procedures? Are there exemptions from the rules and regulations of the allocating authority? Are there "gaps" between the "promise" of an allocation program and the amount-pattern of final distribution? What are the administrative consequences of resource scarcity? Are existing agencies adequate or should new agencies be established? Does resource allocation require unique patterns of administrative organization? Should public agency decisions be centralized or "regionalized" or decentralized to local agencies in order to reflect diversities of needs? What roles, if any, should community-based citizens' groups play? What roles should private business groups play? Should regulatory authority be delegated from the national level to state or local public agencies? How does administrative structure and process within a framework of resource scarcity differ from administrative structure and process within a framework of abundance? How can the society, used to abundance, readjust to a future characterized by scarcity? How can public administration ease the necessary transition?

These and half a hundred other vital questions are implicit in the problem of resource allocation. In selecting the problem a means has been provided by which to study public administration within the confines of a specific issue. Community organizers and the politically active tend to be particularly attentive to this approach. Perhaps the significance of the conclusions will go far beyond the original problem. It might lead to a particular kind of administrative action which is needed. It is obvious that in this one problem—resource allocation—several of the previously discussed approaches will be relevant. The legal, philosophical, economic, group theory, psychological and systems approaches each have appropriate contributions to make.

The Case Approach

The case approach centers attention upon an actual controversy or event that becomes a primary source of data. The case approach, when used in public administration, need not be restricted to court decisions. Instead, actual episodes in some phase of the administrative process may be utilized. Usually such cases lay out the broad framework of the problems, dilemmas or controversies involved, the persons or agencies concerned and the solutions sought or found. Through this method the student is encouraged to consider a number of crucial questions. Were the decisions the only ones that could be made or were there viable alternatives? How did the administrator evaluate and choose between available policy alternatives? What values were involved? What centers of power existed? How were the decisions made? Were his choices sound? What lessons are to be learned? What of significance was learned from the case that has broader implications for the administrative process?

One advantage of this approach is the infinite choice of "cases" that might be utilized. Cases can center upon problems involving federal, state or local administrative systems. Alternatively, cases might center on a particular position and its attendant problems, i.e., a federal meat inspector in a local slaughterhouse and packing plant who must face overt and subtle influences and pressures for a "higher" grading of meat.[13] Or case studies of decisions by city managers in small and medium-sized cities present a far different administrative environment with unique problems. The list of possibilities is endless. A number of case books and individual case studies have been published during the past two decades and have proven useful in innumerable classes in the administrative process.[14] The case approach to public administration parallels the case approach in the training of potential lawyers in the law schools of the nation. It brings an air of reality into the study of administration. It is a highly pragmatic approach in which hypotheses or tentative theoretical constructs may emerge as a consequence of case study.

The Fiction Approach

In contrast to the case approach based upon real incidents, the fiction approach utilizes imaginary episodes and characterizations to further understanding of the administrative process. Many of the best-known contemporary novels are useful devices and a significant departure from orthodoxy in administrative enlightenment. Few will argue against the merits of Herman Wouk's *The Caine Mutiny,* Mary McCarthy's *The Groves of Academe* or Cameron Hawley's *Executive Suite* in laying bare some of the conflicts, dilemmas and psychological factors in administrative decision-making. Whether the story centers on decision-making in a single warship trying to ride out a violent storm, in the narrower context of university administration under political siege or in a struggle for power for the presidency of a furniture company, the "administrative novel" may reveal rare insights into the forces underlying organizational dynamics as they clash head-on with established administrative tradition.

The student of comparative administration may also find a number of novels dealing with decision-making in foreign systems. An excellent example is C. P. Snow's *The Corridors of Power,* which centers on the intricate network of decision-making in Britain's parliamentary system. Few written works have equaled the power with which the author sensitively describes the relationships between elected and permanent officials. Eugene Burdick's and William Lederer's *The Ugly American* remains perhaps the classic administrative novel depicting the conflicts involved in the administration of an overseas technical assistance program, based on American values, in an "underdeveloped" Asian nation with its own unique culture and traditions. In a slightly different vein, Vern Schneider's *Teahouse of the August Moon* raises the issue of "nonbureaucratic" methods as perhaps the best means for effective occupation administration overseas—in this case, Okinawa. John Masters' *Bhowani Junction* centers on problems of military and railroad administration in India as that nation approached independence. Nicholas Monsarrat's *The Tribe That Lost Its Head* involves conflicting political, administrative and anti-colonial forces in Africa.

Science fiction may be utilized to raise administrative issues. George Orwell's *1984* reveals the emergence of an all-knowing and all-embracing administrative system that raises crucial issues of public power vis-à-vis personal liberty and privacy. Aldous Huxley's *Brave New World* is of a similar genre and no less valuable. Equally penetrating science fiction volumes raise

111

significant administrative questions. As one apologist of the science fiction approach has commented:

> It is precisely because our political times are so turbulent that science fiction can teach us something about politics. We can't believe in the orderly and predictably slow development of events anymore; we have learned to expect the unlikely.
>
> Science fiction (or at least good science fiction) is the literature of the possible. . . .
>
> What we call "reality" is only one special case of the sequences of events which are possible: That is, the sequence that happens to come true. But we have no way of knowing in advance which sequence will come true, and it is only in science fiction that we can contemplate a wide spectrum of possible events and circumstances—and hopefully, with that sort of advance warning guard against at least some of the disasters.[15]

The foregoing listing and description of approaches to the study of public administration is not all-inclusive but does cover major variations on the theme. Part of the richness of public administration is its susceptibility to being approached from so many diverse directions with such widely variant assumptions. To be aware of this diversity is to recognize that public administration is a multi-faceted subject with interests fully as broad as the society it serves.

NOTES

1. U.S. Code annotated, Title 50, War and National Defense, chap. 15, Sect. 403.

2. See S. N. Eisenstadt, *The Political Systems of Empires*, New York: The Free Press, 1963, especially "The Historical Bureaucratic Politics," pp. 3–50 and "The Place of Bureaucracy in the Political Process," pp. 273–300.

3. Leonard D. White, *The Federalists: A Study in Administrative History* (1961); *The Jeffersonians: A Study in Administrative History 1801-1829* (1961); *The Jacksonians: A Study in Administrative History 1829-1861* (1963); *The Republican Era 1869-1901* (1963), New York: Macmillan Publishing Company.

4. Dwight Waldo, *The Administrative State: A Study of the Political Theory of American Public Administration*, New York: The Ronald Press, 1948. Other significant and representative historical works include Paul van Riper, *History of the United States Civil Service*, Evanston, Illinois: Row, Peterson, 1958; Frank Mann Stewart, *The National Civil Service Reform League–History, Activities and Problems*, Austin: University of Texas Press, 1929; Barry Dean Karl, *Executive Reorganization and Reform in the New Deal. The Genesis of Administrative Management, 1900-1939*, Cambridge: Harvard University Press, 1963.

5. J. A. Stockfish, *The Political Economy of Bureaucracy*, New York: General Learning Press, 1972.

6. For a useful classification and description of such techniques, see Dalmas Nelson, *Administrative Agencies of the U.S.A., Their Decisions and Authority*, Detroit: Wayne State University Press, 1964.

7. Joseph Bensman and Arthur J. Vidich, *The New American Society. The Revolution of the Middle Class*, Chicago: Quadrangle Books, 1971, p. 52.

8. See Bob L. Wynia, "Federal Bureaucrats' Attitudes Toward a Democratic Ideology," *Public Administration Review*, Vol. 34, No. 2 (March-April 1974), pp. 156-162.

9. See Duane Lockard, *The Perverted Priorities of American Politics*, New York: Macmillan Publishing Company, 1971, especially chaps. 1-2, 8.

10. Irving Janis, *Victims of Group Think*, Boston: Houghton Mifflin, 1972.

11. See W. R. Bion, *Experiences in Groups*, London: Tavistock Publications, 1961.

12. David Easton, "An Approach to the Analysis of Political Systems," *World Politics*, Vol. IX, April 1957; see also his *A Systems Analysis of Political Life*, New York: John Wiley & Sons, Inc., 1965 and *A Framework for Political Analysis*, Englewood Cliffs, N.J.: Prentice-Hall, 1965.

13. Peter Schuck, "The Curious Case of the Indicted Meat Inspectors," *Harper's Magazine*, Spetember 1972, reprinted for classroom case use by Warner Modular Publications, Andover, Mass., Reprint 79 (1973), pp. 1-8.

14. A useful legal case approach to administrative problems that tends to bridge the "gap" between the legal and case approaches discussed in

this chapter is Daniel R. Mandelker, *Managing Our Urban Environment: Cases, Text and Problems,* Indianapolis: Bobbs-Merril, 1971. More representative of the event-incident approach are Robert T. Golembiewski and Michael White, *Cases in Public Management,* Chicago: Rand, McNally, 1973; Warner E. Mills, Jr. and Harry R. Davis, *Small City Government. Seven Cases in Decision Making,* New York: Random House, 1962; Richard T. Frost, *Cases in State and Local Government,* Englewood Cliffs, N.J.: Prentice-Hall, 1962.

15. Frederik Pohl in the foreword to Joseph D. Olander, Martin H. Greenberg and Patricia Warrick, *American Government Through Science Fiction,* Chicago: Rand, McNally, 1974, p. x.

PART II

CONFLICTING VALUES

4

HISTORICAL PERSPECTIVES: BUREAUCRACIES TO THE 1930'S

The American administrative system reflects a lack of a sense of tradition. The pragmatism of Americans is generally recognized as perhaps their most distinguishable attribute, combined, somewhat paradoxically, with a generous amount of idealism. Neither American pragmatism nor idealism, however, is related to a strong commitment to the past as a guideline to the future. American pragmatism centers on the resolution of practical problems and issues in the most direct and effective manner. The society tends to elevate the significance of the contemporary and those groups seeking the preservation of the contributions of the past as a heritage for future generations are required to engage in an uphill endeavor. American idealism is related more to a deep feeling of "justice" and "fair play" than to the impact of well-defined historical processes.

American public administration has developed with a strong commitment to action and an absence of administrative tradition. Consequently, the historical roots of the administrative system are often dimly perceived even by those who have devoted their careers to the public service. Nevertheless, it is important to recognize that the interaction of conflicting historical forces, including conflicts of value, at various periods in America's past has left a number of indelible imprints upon contemporary public service.

THE EISENSTADT FRAMEWORK

Professor S. N. Eisenstadt, a sociologist-historian at Hebrew University of Jerusalem, in his seminal *The Political Systems of Empires,*[1] provides a useful conceptual framework within which to consider the evolution of American bureaucracy. Professor Eisenstadt examined the most important centralized bureaucratic empires or polities that mankind had developed. These consisted of civilizations in the Near East, Egypt, Ancient America (the Incas and Aztecs), the Byzantine world, Persia, China, India, the Moslem world (including the Ottoman Empire) and Europe in the Age of Absolutism (the 1700's). In comparing the political systems of these polities Professor Eisenstadt developed a conceptual model of roles played by bureaucracies throughout history. His model comprises four types of political orientation that could be developed by a bureaucracy. Keeping in mind Professor Eisenstadt's insistence that there were, in fact, many gradations, the four types do provide a useful analytical reference point in considering administration in an historical perspective.

These four types of political orientation developed by historical bureaucracies are:

1. A Service Orientation.
2. Subjugation of the Bureaucracy by Rulers.
3. Bureaucratic Self-aggrandizement or Usurpation of Power.
4. Combining Self-Aggrandizement with a Service Orientation to Rulers.

A Service Orientation

In a service-oriented bureaucracy there was no alienation between the bureaucracy and other strata of society. Often quite close links were maintained with the aristocracy, upper and middle classes or upper peasant groups from which the bureaucrats might be recruited. The rulers were usually successful in retaining control over service-oriented bureaucracies by means of strong budgetary controls, controlling entrance to office or participating in the decision-making at upper echelon bureaucratic levels.

Within the bureaucracy itself there was an emphasis upon serving both rulers and the major strata of society. Explicit rules of service or usage existed, systems of appointment and promotion were maintained. Internal colleagueship, responsibility and strong professional orientations emerged. Supervision, standards of discipline and service were maintained by internal bodies. Hence the bureaucracy maintained a degree of internal organizational autonomy despite its own internal tensions and conflicts or quarrels between the bureaucracy and the rulers.

Subjugation by Rulers

In this type of political orientation the bureaucracy has little internal autonomy and evolves as a passive tool of rulers. A service orientation is absent or minimized, comprising only some minor technical services to the major strata of the society. On the contrary, emphasis is upon power and services to the rulers. The bureaucracy derives its status and powers from its relationship with the rulers. Rulers maintain their subjugation over the bureaucracy by rotation of officials from place-to-place or office-to-office without any fixed patterns or rules; by destruction of any career patterns; by strong discipline that is often arbitrary and not based on any general criteria. Any professional *esprit de corps* is undercut as a matter of policy and the rulers insist that bureaucrats are "personal" servants to both rulers and state. The bureaucracy becomes an efficient means by which to mobilize resources, unify the country and suppress opposition. A monolithic hierarchical pattern of administration emerges. However, bureaucracy could not usually develop into a cohesive or separate group. The regulative authority of the bureaucracy is emphasized while its technical aspects are minimized.

Yet, according to Professor Eisenstadt, the efficiency of the bureaucracy was often diminished by the strong hand of the rulers insofar as bureaucratic initiative was quashed, an excessive formalism developed and the bureaucrats often engaged in activities aimed at avoiding control of the rulers. These included attempts to find allies in the other strata of society, especially among the aristocrats. In short, the efforts of the rulers became counterproductive, with the result often being both a growing rapacity and self-assertion by the bureaucrats.

Self-aggrandizement/Usurpation of Power

In this type of political orientation the goals of service to the polity and to the various strata are displaced in favor of the goals of bureaucratic self-interest. This self-interest is manifested by bureaucratic estrangement to some extent from the rulers and closer ties to groups with which the bureaucracy closely identifies. Consequently, the bureaucracy seeks a weakening of political supervision from above. The upper echelons of the bureaucracy minimize their political and service responsibilities and tend toward political and social autonomy. Professional ideology is weakened, as is the concept of the bureaucrat as the servant of the nation. The bureaucracy works to maximize its own benefits and becomes a self-seeking group. Internally, bureaucracy is relatively inefficient. Some other internal characteristics are recruitment through nepotism; offices regarded as an hereditary possession and as a private sinecure; numbers of personnel increase far beyond needs; an increasing proliferation of departments leading to problems of coordination; and increasing formalization and ritualism in bureaucratic processes. In Professor Eisenstadt's words, an "aristocratized bureaucracy" emerges.[2]

Combining Self-aggrandizement and Service to Rulers

This political orientation is characterized by a strong bureaucratic self-interest in social, economic and political matters, together with a service commitment to the rulers but not to the other strata of society. Here the bureaucracy has reached a working arrangement with the rulers in which it is neither totally subservient nor totally aristocratized. The bureaucracy may be described as "semi-usurpatory." It remains a relatively closed group with membership restricted to the upper social groups. A relatively efficient administrative system is operative together with some internal supervision. The bureaucracy is able to further policies and political goals of benefit to it while, at the same time, a certain level of professional or service ideology and a status image are maintained. This type of political orientation could emerge as a consequence of a reform movement from a prior period of self-aggrandizement, where the rulers, in alliance with other social groups, attempt to reestablish control over the bureaucracy.

After analyzing these four types of political orientation in historical bureaucratic societies, Professor Eisenstadt suggests a number of significant conclusions:

1. The orientation of bureaucracy was closely related to its societal standing—especially its relationships with the rulers and the various strata in society. Hence its position (status and function) in the social structure was crucial.

2. The four types of orientation did not exist as wholly pure types. Rather, "... the bureaucracy in each of the historical bureaucratic polities usually exhibited a mixture or overlapping of all these tendencies toward orientations. However, as a rule, a particular tendency preponderated for at least part, if not the whole, of each polity's history."[3]

3. The conditions which play a role in shaping bureaucratic orientations are not fixed. Hence bureaucracies are subject to change during the course of the history of any society.

4. The relative strengths of the major social strata, vis-à-vis rulers and each other, are the most important determinants affecting the political orientations of the bureaucracy. Therefore, bureaucracy can only be understood within the context of political struggles and their outcomes.

5. Bureaucracies, for their part, are very consequential in the historical development of polities. The bureaucracy's position is often crucial to the outcomes of political struggles, i.e., it may cause changes in the constellation of forces in any society.

6. Where the bureaucracy has maintained its basic service orientation to the rulers and the major strata, it has contributed to the continuity and stability of centralized bureaucratic regimes.
7. To the extent that bureaucracy was not effectively controlled in the political field it could become an omnivorous consumer of resources and impede the autonomy of the different groups and strata in society.
8. The scope of the regulative activities of the bureaucracy was inversely proportional to the social and political strength of the different strata in society.[4]

The significance of bureaucracies in the histories of major civilizations and empires is due, in large measure, to the varieties of roles they could play. As Professor Eisenstadt concludes:

The bureaucracy was both a functional group performing relatively specific functions, and a group closely related to the bases of power, and thus able to monopolize power positions and evolve into an independent social stratum that could impede the continuity of these political systems.[5]

The broad brush of Eisenstadt's conceptual framework provides a background to the emergence of an American New World, a noncentralized bureaucratic system in the shoestring of former British colonies scattered along the Atlantic seaboard. The emergence of the uniquely noncentralized American bureaucratic system took place within a sociopolitical laboratory geographically far enough removed from England and Europe to allow experimentation with unprecedented patterns of political doctrine and organization. Some immediate implications of Professor Eisenstadt's framework for an examination of American administrative history are:

1. The roles a bureaucracy may assume vary from society to society, depending upon the interactions of a range of major variables.
2. The conditions giving rise to a unique sociopolitical environment might be expected to give rise also to unique bureaucratic orientations.

3. As American civilization advanced and matured the roles played by the bureaucracy would be expected to be modified.

4. Consideration of administrative history may be a significant means to a better understanding of the American system of government and society in its broader contexts.

5. Under certain conditions American bureaucracy might be expected to play an increasingly crucial role in the social-economic-political system.

6. The roots of administrative activity are implanted as far back as man's recorded history. Consequently, the emergence of the American administrative system within an historical time frame has yet to proceed beyond the lusty infancy stage.

EARLY DEVELOPMENT
OF AMERICAN BUREAUCRACY

Every effort must be made to avoid the common tendency to describe the historical development of American bureaucracy only in terms of the federal government. The bulk of governmental responsibilities in the period from 1789 to 1829 was not federal in nature but was carried out by executives at the state and local levels of government.

Mistrust of the Executive

Executive power below the federal level was in a particularly weak condition. Administration within the states was felt to be a function subservient to that of the legislative function. There was a universal mistrust of state governors—no doubt a holdover from the widespread mistrust of the British Colonial governors who acted as agents of the Crown in the colonies. As the prestige of state governors waned the glorification of state legislatures gained new heights. The underlying mistrust of executives found its full flowering in the early state constitutions, which were often drafted by legislators and, consequently, with an eye to assuring their own dominance in the governmental system. Governors were "chief executives" in name only—in practice their powers were minimal and frequently shared with legislative committees.

The Weak Executive

From 1789 to the Civil War, chief executives in America's towns and municipalities inherited the seeds of mistrust and suspicion visited upon state executives. The concept of the chief executive as being "representative of the people" had not been widely accepted. If democracy as a belief had any institutional manifestations, they were to be found in the existence of written constitutional documents and elected legislative bodies—somehow overlooking the fact that American chief executives were also the products of popular choice and not of hereditary monarchical systems.

The rural villages and towns lacked governments that provided for the exercise of executive leadership. The public policies of the outlying village and town governments were determined largely by direct participatory democracy at "town meetings." The people consequently served as the legislative body when convened for the purposes of enacting ordinances and resolutions and adopting budgets. The actions were taken by public vote following deliberation by the total assemblage. An interim citizen group of "selectmen" was responsible for the administration of policies once they were adopted by the town meeting. Executive decision-making and the management of local affairs by the elected selectmen was "collegial" (as a body) in nature and there was no single executive on whom the community could pinpoint responsibility. In addition, many township officials were elected. In a very real sense, it was a "no executive" type of government.

Outside the rural areas in the urban concentrations comprising America's cities ("municipalities" is the more technical term) suspicion of centralized power was likewise reflected in the "weak mayor–council" form of local government. While there are only a few vestiges of the town meeting–selectman form of local government in existence today, the weak mayor–council form is still in wide use.

The weak mayor–council form of local government (Figure 4–1) was, with numerous variations, virtually universal in urban areas prior to the Civil War. Dominant city councils paralleled dominant legislative power at the state level. Yet even the

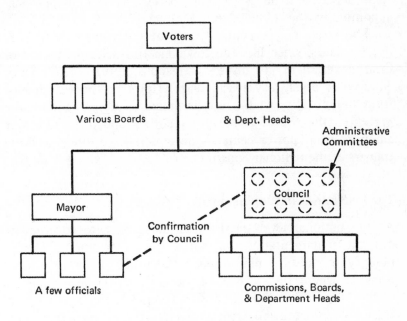

Figure 4–1. WEAK MAYOR-COUNCIL FORM OF LOCAL GOVERNMENT

councils were limited by the popular election of large numbers of local officials in addition to the mayor and the council itself. Like governors, mayors had few significant administrative powers and lacked even a limited veto power. They lacked power over municipal personnel (including hiring and firing) and were authorized to appoint only a few local officials (and often these required the consent of the council). The budget was legislative in nature in initial formulation and responsibility for administration of the budget was frequently vested in the council. Some early mayors enjoyed no popular base, as they were selected by members of the council. The executive authority of the mayor was further weakened by the practice of some councils of dividing into administrative committees and assuming responsibility for the operations of municipal departments even to the extent of appointing department heads and holding them accountable to the council. Further fragmentation of public decision-making resulted from the popular election of members of various local boards and commissions as well as some department heads. Other boards and commissions were appointed by the council.

The weak mayor–council form of government had many disadvantages, since like the town meeting–selectman form of local government, it dispersed responsibility. The mayor emerged as largely a symbolic figure. However, the weak mayor form did exactly what it was intended to do. It effectually prevented the rise of powerful executives and diffused power among several power centers—the underlying rationale of the framers of the national Constitution.

The Federalists and Jeffersonians

At the national level the Federalist approach to government differed fundamentally from that of the Jeffersonians. The bipolarity in political philosophy rested upon differing perceptions of where the "center of gravity" of the governmental system lay. For the nationalists, represented by President George Washington and Treasury Secretary Alexander Hamilton, the new central government was to provide national leadership. In addition, Hamilton stressed the need for executive leadership within the central government rather than reliance upon leadership by Congress or the courts. Indeed, for the Federalists and, especially for Hamilton, the terms "executive" and "energy" were synonymous, for executive power was to be exercised with vigor and in an energetic manner. Consequently, a feeble exercise of executive power was regarded as ill-suited to the needs of the new nation.

Washington's patrician views were reflected in his approach to establishing the federal public service. While the administrative systems of Britain and France were in considerably low estate because of a series of scandals, deep corruption and widespread ineptitude, Washington succeeded in laying the foundations of a small public service that soon attracted the envy of British and French observers.

Washington's insistence upon quality of character assured a high exclusivity in the ranks of the fledgling federal service. Even veterans of the Revolutionary War were required to produce evidence of fitness of character and community respect. In addition, competence and education were weighed heavily. One's loyalty not merely to the new nation but to Federalist beliefs was an additional factor taken into consideration for public employees. Washington also followed the policy of distributing public employment on a geographical basis. With no precedent to guide him and wishing to avoid perceived deficiencies in the British civil service, Washington contributed greatly to a system of administration by the most qualified in terms of quality of character, learning and contributions to the community; in short, administration by an élite.

When Thomas Jefferson assumed the presidency, it was widely believed he might reverse many of the policies and institutional practices of the Federalists, for his political views reflected wide variations from their themes. Jefferson viewed the new national government with suspicion and, as a result, favored a strict interpretation of national powers in the Constitution. Further, the Congress, being viewed as more representative of people than the executive branch, was assumed to be the agency to provide leadership to the country.

Jefferson felt the center of gravity in society should be in the smaller local governments closer to the people.[6] During his presidency, however, Thomas Jefferson found that theory was not always compatible with the exigencies of practice. Federal authority not only did not diminish during his administration but was successful in acquiring vast new territories for the United States. Upon assuming his duties as chief executive in 1801, Jefferson largely continued the pattern of Federal public service recruitment inaugurated by Washington. Despite Jeffersonian suspicions of public servants, the administrative corps expanded in response to a growing population and territorial acquisition. Jefferson's recruitment practices continued the early emphasis upon élitism represented by fitness of character and standing in the community. Likewise, geographical distribution of appointments was continued. While there was no wholesale displacement of Federalist appointees, there were enough

127

removals with replacement by Republican loyalists to give some credence to the view that patronage had found fertile soil for tender roots during Jefferson's tenure. Nevertheless, Jefferson had not dismantled the administrative structure he had inherited from the Federalists. Though nonpartisanship had been considerably eroded, the federal public service was still recognized as reflecting a high degree of efficiency, competency and moral integrity.

On the eve of Andrew Jackson's assumption of the presidency the administrative élitism of both Federalists and Jeffersonian Republicans had provided stability and continuity and few significant innovations. This approach had well-served an embryonic nation facing the newer problems of internal development to the West and finding its proper role in international affairs. It was essentially a period of consolidation and the intervening administrations of presidents John Adams, James Madison, James Monroe and John Quincy Adams did little to modify the policies and courses of action that had already been set into motion.[7]

Jacksonian Administration, the Doctrine of "Happy Versatility"

By the time Andrew Jackson was inaugurated in 1829 the spoils system, based upon partisan removal and appointment to the public service, was already well-established in New York, Pennsylvania and Massachusetts. At the national level conditions were ripe for overt partisanship and political party participation in filling governmental offices. Although a spoils system had not yet been adopted wholesale at the federal level, the merit system of Washington had been under incessant attack by those who believed democracy could be best served through the control of public office by the victorious political party. The Tenure of Office Act of 1820 had already limited certain classes of public officers to a period of four years. In addition, the egalitarianism of the Western frontier conflicted with the importance accorded to the "gentlemanly qualities" regarded as requisite to official station under Washington and Jefferson.

In his first annual message to Congress President Jackson rejected the concept, which he held was rampant among federal office holders, of public office as a species of private property. Fearing that continuation of administrative élitism would produce an un-American bureaucratic aristocracy, possibly following along family lines, Jackson attacked the notion that one person had more right to official station than any other. Hence, no individual wrong was done when the "public benefits" required removal of office holders. The duties of all public officers are, Jackson declared, so "plain and simple" that any man of intelligence can perform them. Consequently, a system of rotation would "give healthy action to the system."

While acting in what he felt to be the interests of the nation in democratizing democracy, Jackson attempted to purify the processes of personnel selection and retention. The result, however, was to undermine the high ethical standards of the federal service and to virtually destroy the career concept that was emerging. The impact of Jackson's approach broadened during the next several decades as the political hack gained entry into the public service as his reward for service to the victorious political party. The patronage system, with public office regarded as merely a part of the booty or spoils of political war, was dominant at all levels of the American governmental system until well past the Civil War.

There is little doubt, however, that the Jacksonian approach to administration had wide support and did, in fact, reflect much of the unique credo of American democracy. It also has much in common with Western man's first attempt at democracy—the political processes of the Greek city–state of Athens.

Both ancient Athenian and American political thought extolled the virtues of wide participation by members of society in the processes of government. Athenian democracy was limited to the "citizen" class and it should be kept in mind that on the federal level of American government the franchise had, until the twentieth century, been quite restricted. It was not until 1913 that the United States Senate became elective and not until 1920 that the franchise was extended to women.

Even today there is no recall, no referendum or initiative process (constitutional or legislative) at the national level nor are amendments to the United States Constitution subject to popular vote. Both Athenian and American democracy may be described as "qualified democracy."

The essence of Athenian democracy was the concept of "happy versatility," i.e., the idea that rotation in office, rather than tenure, encouraged maximum participation in the holding of public office and that citizens could be selected who had little experience or expertise. Office holding in ancient Athens was determined by lot—a citizen could be selected as chorus master, military leader or keeper of temple accounts. Upon rotation at a later time another type of office might be the citizen's responsibility. Therefore, the proper functioning of this early democracy was based upon the versatility of citizen-incumbents in office. Jackson's belief that there were but few public offices that could not be successfully administered by common sense reflects much the same belief in the underlying versatility of the average citizen and in the need for rotation in office and maximization of participation in the civic affairs of a properly functioning democracy. Jackson's approach was to be faulted for its eventual consequences: the decline of morality, competence and integrity in the public service. It cannot, however, be faulted on democratic grounds. For Jackson, as for the Athenians in ancient Greece, a system of administrative élitism ran counter to even the most rudimentary forms of democratic government. The movement inaugurated by Jacksonian democracy might be well termed "government by the common man."

Jacksonian Equalitarianism

The states were profoundly influenced by Jacksonian equalitarianism derived from the frontier experience and also by maximized citizen participation in the weak mayor–council form of local government. From 1830 to about 1910 state systems of government were based upon a diffusion of authority to the people.

The techniques for the diffusion of authority were primarily the increase in the number of elected offices and the establishment of limited periods of tenure in office in preference to lengthy terms. This was the era of the "bed sheet" ballot at both state and local levels in which maximum citizen participation in holding of office was encouraged and maximum turnover assured. Further, it was felt that the affairs of state could be best carried out by multiple centers of decision-making and this represented a fundamental shift away from reliance on the legislature as the single dominant center.

The notion of fragmented state government was, in part, a manifestation of the growing movement for grass-roots equalitarianism. It was also a reaction to growing legislative abuses— the legislature was no longer to be totally trusted as reflecting the public interest. Many state constitutions were amended to increase gubernatorial power vis-à-vis state legislative power. A check-and-balance was emerging in embryonic form. Still, at the same time, governors were themselves kept in check by heading fragmented executive branches. Large numbers of independently elected state officials, boards and commissions were made responsible to the voters rather than to the governors. While the governors enjoyed more prestige and respect, they were still denied means to effectively direct the activities and policies of the elected executive officials and board members.

Prior to the Civil War the governors were not effective coordinators of the dispersed governmental agencies and independent officials and they lacked the authority to even attempt playing such a role. A managerial vacuum existed in most states and most American towns and cities.

THE POST-CIVIL WAR ERA: 1865–1883

In the background post-Civil War American society was undergoing fundamental changes and consequently faced new needs. With westward expansion communities proliferated and the need for public services increased at a prodigious rate. Protection of persons and property, the laying of streets, sewerage facilities, the administration of justice, the prevention of contagion and epidemics, the reporting of vital statistics, public education, free libraries and half a hundred other local pressures reflected new priorities to serve rapidly expanding populations.

Post-Civil War industrial and commercial expansion, including the rapidly proliferating railway network, produced sporadic but frequently intense pressures for the public regulation of selected business enterprises. Yet effective public regulation demands expertise, whether in rate-making, the inspection of industrial safety devices, or in testing food products for their purity. From 1865 to the early 1880's public administration was part of the world of politics. Although state and local public services expanded to meet the needs of a growing and highly mobile westward moving population, there was a significant postwar administrative retrenchment at the national level. At neither national, state nor local levels of government was there any real appreciation of the administrative requirements of a modern industrialized nation.

Reform of the patronage-spoils system could gain only a portion of citizen attention and concern at either national, state or local levels. It had to compete with other pressures for recognition in the public policy of a nation in the turmoil of reevaluating its postwar public policies. By the early 1870's, however, the problems of a dispirited, considerably corrupt, inefficient and politically inspired public service at all levels did emerge for the first time as a major issue of public policy.

A succession of scandals involving U. S. Treasury officials and diplomatic personnel, as well as state administrators, and widespread local corruption (personified by the machinations of "Boss" Tweed in New York) had impressed themselves upon the national conscience and a temper of public repugnance was emerging.

Beginnings of Reform

In the 1870's there were sporadic attempts at the national level to introduce limited reform in the selection procedures for entry into the federal service. In 1871, under prodding from President Ulysses S. Grant, Congress passed a "rider" to an appropriations bill allowing the president to prescribe rules and regulations for entry into the federal service in order to "best promote the efficiency" of the service and to determine the "fitness" of each candidate as to "age, health, character, knowledge, and ability for the branch of service into which he seeks to enter."[8] Under authority of this law, President Grant appointed the first U. S. Civil Service Commission, comprising seven members, three of whom were full-time federal employees. The following year, 1872, the commission conducted the first competitive examination for entry positions. In 1873 Congress refused to fund the commission's work and it was abandoned in 1875. Despite its brief existence, a number of "firsts" had been established which served later as foundations for the modern federal service. Among other things the law of 1871:

1. established the first Civil Service Commission;
2. established the principle of competitive examinations;
3. provided for a trial of administrative reform;
4. laid the groundwork for the later patterns of federal personnel administration;
5. provided the federal government for the first time with a centralized personnel agency;
6. provided the president with staff assistants in the personnel field.

Paul Van Riper, in his *History of the United States Civil Service*, accords to the law of 1871 a crucial position in the evolution of governmental reform.

> ... while the rider ... was extremely brief and general and was not then pressed far in terms of implementation, it gave the President powers over the personnel of the executive branch which he had never possessed unchallenged before. *This early legislation is still in force* and is yet considered a primary source of presidential authority in federal personnel management.[9]

Nevertheless, the momentum for reform was lost. The enterprise broke down and, according to one authority, "The distribution of spoils under Grant was as great as under any of his predecessors."[10]

In the decade after 1871 no further civil service legislation passed through Congress despite a number of proposals for reform. The great controversy continued unabated. The major arguments for and against reform in the years prior to 1883 are summarized below.[11]

Against Reform

Patronage is "natural" to the American system and has prevailed in Washington, the federal field services, the states and the cities.

Patronage is essential to the well-being and support of political parties. Without strong parties democracy is weakened. Thus reform could eventually destroy democracy.

Patronage is supported by democratic theory. Life tenure in office is antidemocratic and subversive of elected government.

Life tenure in office would beget aristocracy and a caste system in opposition to American custom and traditions.

Democracy must be based upon maximum citizen participation. Every citizen with political experience who conducts himself well should be able to aspire to public office.

The people should not be deprived of their rights to maintain their supremacy.

Examinations in grammar or arithmetic are inadequate tests of competency or efficiency.

"Custom" should not lightly be legislated away.

For Reform

The political process is weakened by the struggle for "plunder" between the "ins" and the "outs."

To the degree that parties are weakened public policy makers evade responsibility.

Participation in public life is made more attractive for those lacking influence in party activities. Young persons of promise will find civic affairs more "open" to their influence.

Efficiency, economy and honesty should be the ends of public policy. These, in turn, depend upon competency, integrity and fidelity as the criteria for fitness for public office.

National executive leadership will be enhanced as Congressional pressures and recommendations for public appointments decrease.

Public offices as "plunder" or "prizes" degrade the national character and lower the moral standards of the nation.

Political parties will be responsible to public opinion rather than to behind-the-scenes manipulators.

New needs of an expanding nation necessitate changes in methods of appointment to public office.

Following the death of President Garfield, the initiative shifted to the reformers. Now buttressed by an outraged public as well as by support from leading magazines, journals, newspapers and businessmen, a new momentum rolled over opposition arguments and moral indignation replaced the apathy of many. In 1880 Senator George H. Pendleton had introduced a bill for civil service reform. Despite some delaying tactics in Congress, the bill passed both Houses and was signed into law by President Arthur in 1883.

The Civil Service (Pendleton) Act of 1883

Passage of the Civil Service Act of 1883 represented the high point of the governmental reform movement. Although a wide range of other reforms would be accomplished in later decades, the passage of this law represents the "high water" mark of reform effort. In a very real sense the act is based upon a philosophy of administrative élitism but an élitism founded upon competition, qualification and experience—not upon property holding or family ties. Fitness, however, is less a product of community respect than of impartial evaluation. In reporting out the bill a Congressional committee stated:

> The single, simple, fundamental, pivotal idea of the whole bill is that whenever a new appointment or promotion shall be made in the subordinate civil service in the larger departments or larger offices, such appointments shall be given to the man who is best fitted to discharge the duties of the position and that such fitness shall be ascertained by open, fair, honest, impartial, competitive examination. The impartiality of these examinations is to be secured by every possible safeguard. They are to be opened to all who choose to present themselves. They will be tests of the fitness of the applicant for the particular place to which he aspires.[12]

While the act was simple in principle its provisions were quite comprehensive. It provided for presidential leadership and placed the Civil Service Commission within the executive branch. Further, the act enabled the president, with the aid of the commission, to make rules governing the filling of positions and it required that they be filled from among those graded "highest" in examinations. The commission itself comprised three members, not more than two of whom might be members of the same political party. The commissioners were to be appointed by the president with the advice and consent of the Senate. The act also provided for a probationary period prior to permanent appointment or employment. Political assessments were prohibited. Noncompetitive examinations in "proper cases" were authorized under certain conditions. Certain investigatory powers were delegated to the commission. Promotions, as well as initial appointments, came under the jurisdiction of the commission.

In 1883 only about one-tenth of the 110,000 federal employees were classified as permanent. By 1927, forty-five years later, more than three-fourths of all employees in the executive civil service were classified employees, that is, permanent and selected through a competitive process under Civil Service Commission jurisdiction. Over a period of time the activities of the commission centered upon recruitment, examination, certification of eligibles to appointing officers, maintenance of entry records and some service records, and post-appointment activities including training and promotional examinations.

The establishment of Civil Service systems in state and local governments followed passage of the act of 1883. The quality and effectiveness of these systems vary widely, with some matching the reputation of the federal system. The New York, Michigan and California Civil Service systems are outstanding examples. Patronage, however, is rampant in a large number of state and local governments with merit systems applicable to relatively few agencies—often only those using federal funds.

From the beginning the United States Civil Service Commission faced certain difficulties. The problem of adequate appropriations was a perennial issue and a number of authorities feel the commission could have played a much more vigorous and creative role had more funds been forthcoming in the formative years. Another problem centered around the "negative policeman" role of the commission. The elimination of widespread partisan abuses gave the commission the image of the traffic cop holding up the "bad guys" and allowing only the "good guys" to proceed along the road to federal employment. Over the years, the commission was hardly popular with other federal agencies, many of which had to abandon longstanding but now proscribed personnel policies. The very aloofness of the commission itself and its bipartisan nature conflicted with the political leadership of the major executive departments.

THE PROGRESSIVE MOVEMENT

While one major goal of the reformers had been accomplished with the passage of the Civil Service Act of 1883, others lay ahead. Failure by the states to effectively control the interstate railway system led to federal regulation with the passage of the

Interstate Commerce Act of 1887 and the establishment of the Interstate Commerce Commission. This pattern of federal regulation through so-called "independent" agencies was in line with reformist sentiment to halt abuses and regulate the activities of vast areas of the American economy. In the last decades of the nineteenth century and the early decades of the twentieth century additional regulatory commissions and boards reflected the widespread agitation for improvement in the conditions of the economic marketplace and the quality of American life.

Much of the reform-oriented legislation emerged as a result of the "Progressive" movement. The "Progressives" aimed to weaken both political parties and gigantic corporations which they regarded as corrupt and acting contrary to the public interest.

Through the Progressive-inspired device of the "initiative" voters could circulate petitions to gain a certain percentage of signatures for the purpose of putting selected issues of public policy to the direct vote of the people. In some states a bill that had failed to pass the state legislature or a city council or a county board could still be enacted into law by popular vote, i.e., people could "initiate" legislation themselves. The "referendum," another Progressive device, allowed voters to decide on a "yes" or "no" basis the outcome of policy issues, thereby circumventing the politicians and the legislature. The referendum was extended to amendment of state constitutions and local charters, even though not applicable to amending the national Constitution. The "recall" was adopted at state and local levels of government under Progressive pressures and permitted the removal, through popular vote, of an elected official prior to the official expiration of his term of office. In fact, the introduction of state and local civil service systems in the late nineteenth and early twentieth centuries can be traced to agitation by Progressive "muckrakers" who, through their tireless activities and startling exposés of corruption, succeeded in capturing the nation's attention.

Each of these developments weakened political bosses and politicians holding public office. In a few states the Progressive device of "cross-filing" weakened allegiance to party platforms and philosophy by allowing candidates to file in the primaries of other political parties in addition to their own. The intended result was to break the backs of political parties or at least to weaken their influence so that party labels became meaningless and the voters would be free to "vote the best man—not the party."

The implications for public administration were clear. The center of gravity of the American system had to be gradually shifted from corrupt legislatures, controlled by giant corporations, labor leaders and other special interests, to reinvigorated executives. Belief in the virtues of fragmented government had steadily been eroded in the post-Civil War era. Power, however, cannot exist in a vacuum—it must rest somewhere, i.e., have a "situs." The Progressives envisaged that the center of gravity of governmental power should be located in the executive branch. They regarded the enhancement of executive power as the surest means to provide clear and responsible leadership. The gradual tendency toward forceful presidential leadership at the national level and increased presidential authority spilled over to the state and local levels.

The Strong Executive

At the state level of government the governors evolved from figureheads to real leaders and public managers. Previously independent state boards and commissions were either abolished or consolidated into the executive branch under direct gubernatorial control. "Good government" was now equated with the "doctrine of energy" advanced earlier by Alexander Hamilton and the Federalists. The terms of governors were extended from two to four years and many state constitutions were amended to provide that governors be allowed to succeed themselves. A "short ballot" movement led to a reduction in the number of elected officials outside of the effective authority of the governor at the same time that gubernatorial powers were broadened. The power to exercise the "item veto" on budget bills, authority to convene special sessions of the legislature and determine its agenda, making the governor the commander-in-chief of state military forces and the power to introduce legislation were new tools for executive leadership.

A parallel movement was launched at the local level of government. Here reformers centered their attention on the creation of strong mayors (Figure 4–2) to counterbalance the role played by traditionally weak mayors. His Honor was to do much more than cut ribbons at the opening of the new pickle factory or confer the key to the city upon

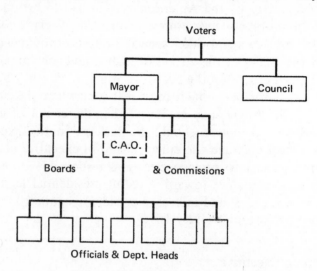

Figure 4-2. STRONG MAYOR–COUNCIL FORM
OF LOCAL GOVERNMENT

visiting dignitaries on the steps of city hall. The enhancement of executive mayoralty power was to be accomplished by a drastic diminution of councilmanic authority and the shifting of much of this power to the mayor in order to provide him with the basic tools necessary for the assumption of effective municipal leadership. From the 1880's to the 1920's the strong mayor–council form of local government was a key factor in many local governments being able to accommodate the vast influx from the rural areas and the absorption of large numbers of foreign immigrants from abroad. In addition, it helped to provide more responsible municipal services under unified direction and control.

The new administrative requirements were met in a number of ways.

In replacing the long ballot of the weak mayor–council form of government with a short ballot, responsibility for administrative performance could be pinpointed upon the mayor. He was now responsible for appointing local authorities, a wide range of high-level officials and the members of municipal boards and commissions. The personnel function was integrated rather than diffused and was centered in the executive branch under direct mayoral authority.

The mayor's relationships, vis-à-vis the council, were fundamentally altered. Large numbers of appointments no longer required confirmation by the council. He was able to exercise a veto over councilmanic legislation. The budget considered by the council was that initially formulated by the mayor and presented by him to the council. The execution of the budget in the post-appropriation stage was the responsibility of the mayor and of his chief fiscal advisers. He was authorized to present a legislative program to the council, thereby assuming policy leadership. In addition, he was made an *ex officio* member of the most important municipal boards and commissions.

Largely divested of any significant administrative powers, the city council was able to concentrate upon legislative proposals, broad policies and revenue-taxation matters. In addition, it would hold public hearings on the mayor's budget and, after due deliberation, fix its final approval upon the budget, albeit with perhaps some modifications.

Day-to-day administrative operations were the responsibility of the mayor. In a few of the larger cities the mayors utilized a "C.A.O." or city (sometimes "chief") administrative officer, a professional and trained public manager to be responsible for coordination of the various municipal agencies, to aid in formulating the budget, administer the personnel system and to represent the mayor in the daily business of running a city. This C.A.O. did not operate under his own independent authority but acted more as an "agent of the mayor" and remained responsible to him. More simply, he was the chief administrative adviser to the mayor and worked to assure that mayoralty policies and municipal programs and services were administered effectively and efficiently. What the mayor as a "political animal" lacked in administrative competence, the C.A.O. provided. This was a significant development along the road to increased professionalization of municipal administration.

The overall advantage of the strong mayor–council form of government from the citizen's perspective was its utter simplicity when contrasted to the weak mayor-council form. The shortened ballot, the clear differentiation between executive and legislative functions and the pinpointing of responsibility in one office, the mayor's, greatly simplified the mysteries of municipal government.

In spite of its many advantages and the fact that it was part of a larger reform movement to increase executive power, the strong mayor–council form frequently brought other problems in its wake. Strong mayors often had strong personalities and tended to dominate municipal affairs. With their independent political bases buttressed by wide appointing and removal powers, powerful and influential political machines based on patronage and spoils emerged, especially in those cities with partisan (political party labels) elections. Consequently, councilmen often viewed mayoralty "machine power" with apprehension and feared (often correctly) a diminution of their influence and prerogatives. Occasional policy stalemates between mayor and council might weaken municipal efficiency and the provision of public services and create community divisiveness. Further, despite enhanced mayoral authority, His Honor was still a product of political campaigning and was elected on the basis of political attractiveness, with little weight accorded to administrative experience or managerial competence. Without a C.A.O. or the benefit of sound administrative advice, high-level decision-making on matters of public management might be based on inadequate knowledge, nonprofessional intuition or partisan political advantage. Yet, despite shortcomings the strong mayor–council form of government did resolve to a large degree the mounting problems of fragmented municipal power—a problem-plagued heritage from the earliest days of the nation.

Another reformist approach to fragmented power resulted from a natural disaster. A tidal wave and flood struck Galveston, Texas, in 1901. The existing weak mayor–council form of municipal government was inadequate to cope with the problems of immediate rescue and later reconstruction. No one center of recognized authority existed to provide overall direction and leadership. Determined to reorient their municipal government from its self-inflicted paralysis and borrowing from what they conceived to be the methods of business corporations, leading businessmen convinced the citizens of Galveston that a "commission" form of government (Figure 4–3) was necessary. Soon after the disaster Galveston adopted their recommendation.

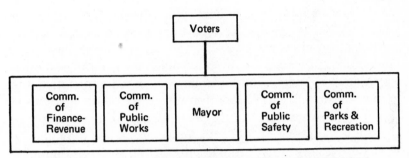

Figure 4-3. THE COMMISSION FORM OF LOCAL GOVERNMENT

The central feature of the so-called "Galveston plan" is the commission of five members, including the mayor, to exercise combined administrative and legislative authority. There are no other local officials elected. Consequently, a very short ballot serves to fix responsibility upon the small commission. One of the commissioners is designated as mayor and the remaining four exercise joint legislative responsibilities with their colleagues while, at the same time, each has individual administrative responsibility over specific municipal functions. The mayor presides over commission meetings, but his functions are largely ceremonial rather than administrative, as he heads no department providing municipal services. He does, however, exercise a vote like the other commissioners, but he has no significant legislative powers beyond those of his colleagues.

Advantages of the commission form of government are alleged economy, the fusion of legislative and executive responsibilities and the simplicity of its pattern of organization. Responsibility for municipal affairs is held "collegially" by the entire commission, while responsibility for the administration of individual departments is focused upon individual commissioners.

By 1917 almost five hundred cities had adopted the commission form of government. However, due to certain inherent defects, it is gradually disappearing from the governmental scene. The lack of a single source of effective leadership within the commission and the absence of any external executive review left no counterbalance to commission decisions. For example, the same body that formulates the budget, considers the budget, adopts the budget and, finally, administers the budget. Also, the small size of the commission made it unsuitable for larger cities, where a wide variety of interests have to be represented. In addition, most commissioners lacked administrative experience. The combination of administrative and legislative responsibilities therefore fell to part-time amateurs at a period in American history when the growing problems of cities and the provision of a wide range of services were increasingly of a technical nature. Despite the decline in the number of cities with the commission form of government, the combined legislative-executive-collegial approach is still utilized on a large scale in county governments in the United States.

The emergence of the council–manager plan of municipal organization (Figure 4–4) in 1912 in Sumter, South Carolina, marked the high point of the inexorable movement toward the integration of administrative responsibility. Today more than

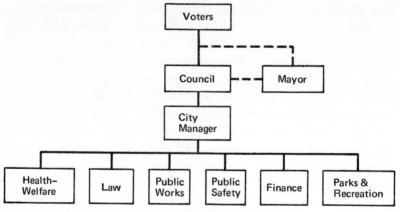

Figure 4–4. THE COUNCIL-MANAGER FORM OF
LOCAL GOVERNMENT

half of the medium-sized cities, between 25,000 and 250,000 population, have adopted it.

The council-manager form of local government centers upon the city manager, an experienced administrator who undertakes full-time responsibility for the supervision of municipal affairs. Though appointed by the elected council and responsible to it, the manager is the ultimate authority in administrative matters and the council does not intervene. The manager holds his position at the discretion of the council. His is a nonpolitical position in that he does not run for office, campaign for any incumbent councilman or for any candidate for a council position. He does, however, greatly influence policy matters before the council, as he is a "professional expert" and his advice to the council is given great weight. The efficiency of the city's administrative operations is his responsibility, for which he will be held accountable by the council. Unlike both weak mayor-council and strong mayor-council forms of government, the mayor under the manager system plays a public relations role and presides over the council. He does not, in the classic pattern of council-manager government, exercise administrative responsibility, nor does the mayor interfere in the manager's administrative area. About half of the mayors are selected by their council colleagues and the other half are elected by the voters. A cardinal feature of the council-manager plan is that neither council nor mayor competes with the manager in the administration of city affairs, nor do they exercise any administrative functions. Within a period of five years a number of local governments had adopted the council-manager plan and it spread rapidly westward to the shores of the Pacific.

By 1915 local government had undergone many basic changes and the wide variety of administrative patterns reflected the fact that innovation and experimentation in totally new approaches proceeded much further at the local level than they had at the state and national levels. The small size of municipal governments in comparison to gargantuan state and national governments is undoubtedly a factor in innovation, as experimentation on a small scale could more easily take place. Further, the formation of new cities often encourages experimentation with infinite variations of the several patterns in order to meet unique community needs. Many municipal governments today reflect adaptations from more than one of the forms described here.

Executive power in the second decade of the twentieth century was on the ascendency at all levels of American government. Later, two World Wars and a number of major "police actions" produced the conditions in which it is problematic as to what degree and in what manner ascending executive power can be held fully accountable.

THE RISE OF SCIENTIFIC MANAGEMENT

The movement toward integration of administrative power from the 1880's to the 1920's must be considered along with the growth of the scientific management movement, which likewise arose and reached a high point in roughly the same period. The governmental reform movement and scientific management were closely interlinked in action as well as spirit. Although both movements emerged quite independently of each other, the two merged later as federal, state and local public administration fully embraced the doctrines and many of the techniques of scientific management.

Scientific management is based upon the application of the scientific techniques of careful observation and the compilation of measurement data derived from experience (as opposed to introspection). Its underlying assumption is that man lives in a world governed by physical laws and that through experimentation and the application of these laws to his existence, man may achieve a better life. This doctrine of man's potential and unrelenting progress is conditioned upon the application of scientific observation, measurement and experimentation to the production of physical goods and the design of machinery to produce those goods.

Scientific management is more than the perfectability of machines; it embraces the physical placement of men and materials in relation to those machines. Through precision studies of the time and motion expended by workmen in industrial operations, a mechanical engineer, Frederick W. Taylor,

146

with stopwatch and tape, measured the distances traversed by both men and materials. He gradually evolved the theory that a large percentage of both labor and materials was needlessly wasted by improper coordination and supervision of machines, men and materials. Through detailed comparisons of data gained from differing physical placements of the three factors, significant economies could be effected. Savings were expressed in terms of productivity in relation to input-resources.

"Taylorism" was exported abroad and American industry and scientific management became virtually synonymous. Scientific management was America's contribution to the burgeoning industrial age. Taylor's work began around 1885 and by 1911 his general principles of management had been highly refined. Although he was the major figure in scientific management, others had laid down a tentative new approach to industrial management in the 1870's. Long before Taylor had perfected his doctrine, Woodrow Wilson was well aware of the governmental significance of scientific management. In his essay "The Study of Administration," published in 1887, Wilson describes a science of administration. He observed:

> The object of administrative study is to rescue executive methods from the confusion and costliness of empirical experiment and set them upon foundations laid deep in stable principle. . . . We are now rectifying methods of appointments; we must go on to adjust executive functions more fitly and to prescribe better methods of executive organization and action.[13]

For Wilson, the study of public administration centered upon two objects: First, "To discover . . . what government can properly and successfully do." Second, to determine "how it can do these proper things with the utmost possible efficiency and at the least possible cost either of money or of energy."[14]

Wilson and the scientific managers of private industry fundamentally agreed that administration, whether public or private, was really one all-pervading technical process. Wherever workers were assigned tasks, whether at lathes or in governmental bureaus, the "one best way" existed—it merely had to be dis-

147

covered. Where the industrial plant foreman might be concerned with the assembly line production and the time-distance-materials coordination required for maximum productivity, a postal supervisor might be concerned with the proper location of the sacks of incoming mail in relation to the sorting tables, the weighing scales, stamping devices, forwarding bins and transportation vehicles together with the locations of postal employees so as to minimize their physical movements, duplicative motions and intersecting mailroom traffic.

In 1910 the major railroads of the eastern portion of the nation had requested rate increases before the Interstate Commerce Commission. The shippers who would be affected by a rise in rates hired a young attorney, Louis D. Brandeis, as their legal counsel. Brandeis was later to gain fame as a distinguished member of the United States Supreme Court. In the rate hearing Brandeis called upon Frederick W. Taylor to testify as to the savings the railroads might enjoy (estimated to be one million dollars a day) if only they applied the principles of scientific management to their operations. While the railway executives were outraged at the compendious and convincing data Brandeis and Taylor laid before the commission, the nation was exposed to the methodology of scientific management—especially time-and-motion studies. The dramatic disclosures caused the scientific management movement to sweep the country.

SCIENTIFIC MANAGEMENT IN GOVERNMENT

Reform was in the air! The muckrakers had exposed political corruption and the proponents of scientific management were exposing inefficient production processes. Soon scientific management advanced far beyond the quantitative analyses of Taylor and his disciples. The movement evolved with a moral orientation equating the principles of scientific management with the visions and spirit of the Christian ethic. It reflected all of the impulses of a true Messianic fervor.

America's laboring men were not so convinced that their interests were necessarily tied to the application of scientific management to every nook and cranny of the work-a-day world. On the contrary, they viewed these efforts as an attempt to squeeze more productivity out of the working classes so as to satisfy the investigations of production spies armed with stop-watches, tape measures and cameras. In 1911 an attempt was made to apply scientific management to a federal arsenal. But the workers' union objected to time-and-motion studies on the grounds that the stepped-up pace might be injurious to the health of the workers. A committee of the House of Repre-sentatives found no evidence of such an injurious pace. How-ever, there was considerable sentiment in support of the workers.

In 1912 the House of Representatives attached a rider to an appropriations bill which prohibited the use of time-and-motion studies in governmental arsenals and post offices. The early strength of public unions is evidenced by the fact that identical provisions were attached to all succeeding appropriation meas-ures until 1948. Yet the intrusion of scientific management in governmental bureaus could not be quelled.

In the background a significant event had taken place—the establishment of the New York Bureau of Municipal Research in 1906. The Bureau was instrumental in applying the methods of scientific management to municipal government. Only later was scientific management adopted at the federal and state levels. Once again pioneering innovativeness and receptivity to untried administrative techniques marked the municipal level of government. The New York Bureau inaugurated the munici-pal research movement in the United States. Over a period of years many research bureaus in other cities throughout the nation were established as were bureaus of municipal research and institutes of governmental research at major colleges and universities. Virtually all could trace their lineage in one way or another to the New York Bureau of Municipal Research.

Professor Jane Dahlberg has written the definitive history of the New York Bureau. She comments:

> The Bureau came along simultaneously with a period of tremendous ferment in business and industry. Henry Ford had developed the assembly line, offering the best example at the time of efficient management, time-keeping, and the analysis of work into its component parts. Fred-erick Taylor wrote of the discoveries in industry . . . .

149

With the industrial development in the United States, the closing of the Frontier, and the concentration of population in large urban areas, the philosophic concern with the proper functions of government acquired new dimensions. The spoils system, the inadequacy of performance, the neglected areas of government service, the interdependencies of society, and the need for new regulations and service were all spotlighted in the changing cities . . . .

Periodic housecleaning through elections did not provide the panacea promised by the muckrakers. As the Bureau recorded in subsequent years, "The muckraker had nothing to offer of *constructive* criticism."[15]

The role of constructive critic was assumed by the New York Bureau. The work of the Bureau was carried out under the direction of leading private citizens, independent of government or of political party, rather than by governmental effort. They believed that the citizens, in an era of rising public expenditures and taxation, wanted—and were entitled to—efficiency in governmental operations. Also, the men who formed the Bureau believed that the overhauling of governmental machinery to bring it in line with the practices of business and the methods of science was overdue. They were convinced that a private, nonpartisan agency equipped with professional staff and knowledgeable and sympathetic to the principles of scientific management was the best device to apply the criterion of efficiency to the public service. In time the Bureau not only engaged in detailed studies and recommendations for the improvement of New York's government, but was widely utilized for similar studies in other cities and other states.

Philosophically, the Bureau men were part of the Progressive movement, while in methodology they were fundamentally committed to an objective, empirical scientific method. The Bureau reflected, in fact, the joining of the democratic ethos and the new pragmatism. Professor Dahlberg describes the Bureau approach:

The new social science was pragmatic, a function of experience requiring empirical fact and proof in observation. The founders of the Bureau, influenced by this practice, did not attempt to deal with government in its entirety, but rather they chose to break the total into its constituent parts and to focus on these. They studied health department estimates, financial reports, milk distribution; from these and other studies they began to observe a similarity of methods and procedures affecting any department regardless of subject matter. Certain techniques of administration began to be established in their minds as principles, based on their experience rather than on the type of *a priori* rationalism of the nineteenth century; the principles they evolved were not axioms of right but rather results of concrete fact—what they could observe. . . .

A fairly frequent criticism of the Bureau was that it overlooked the fiery issues of the times and measured success of administration in terms of efficiency.[16]

The Taft Commission

If the Bureau had its way, Jackson's "democratic America" would be joined by scientific management's "efficient America." The occasion for the wedding of the two was the establishment of the Taft Commission, officially known as the President's Commission on Economy and Efficiency, authorized by Congress in 1910 after prodding by the president. The Commission's work was the first instance of the vast organization of the federal government being studied as one piece of administrative mechanism and with a view to integrating all the agencies of the government for the most economical and efficient dispatch of public business. President Taft appointed Dr. Frederick A. Cleveland, one of the founding organizers of the New York Bureau of Municipal Research, to the chairmanship of the presidential commission and upon completion of his duties in 1914, Dr. Cleveland returned to the Bureau as its director. In his work with the commission Cleveland utilized the investigative methodology of the Bureau and, through Cleveland and others serving on the commission who were sympathetic to the Bureau approach, the federal enterprise was evaluated through the perspective of scientific management.

The commission prepared a number of reports recommending readjustment and reorganization of different bureaus and agencies. An important part of the data presented to the president and Congress by the commission was recommendations for agency consolidation and abolishment of other agencies. Cost studies were also a key factor in their outline of governmental administrative problems. The commission concluded that waste in the various federal offices varied from 10 to 50 percent. The commission studied the existing procedures in the personnel, record-keeping, finance and retirement fields. Due to the strong links between federal bureaus and committees of Congress, many of the recommendations were not acted upon, although many, especially those concerned with records management and labor-saving techniques, were affected.[17]

Within a few years, by the 1920's, scientific management was the mainstay of American public administration and had somewhat belatedly followed the path of American business and industrial management. Both public and private spheres, whatever their differences, accepted the necessity for administration to center around the techniques of scientific management. The scientific management approach always emphasized the role of management and supervision—the worker *per se* was beyond its concern. This assumption that efficiency was largely a function of management, especially at the higher levels, was not challenged until after World War II, when attention shifted to the crucial roles played by the workers themselves.

ADMINISTRATIVE CONSOLIDATION: THE '20's AND '30's

The next decade was largely one of the consolidation of scientific management and administrative processes at all levels of government. The decade is perhaps best described from an administrative perspective as the era of the "businessman-scientist-engineer." Not only had scientific management brought a businesslike orientation into government bureaus but the concept of efficiency brought engineers into new posts of public responsibility. Indeed, it appeared during the booming economy of the '20's that government's main need was for a hand at the throttle that would, as one administrative historian noted, "exercise only efficient guidance."[18] At both local and national levels there was dramatic evidence of the new role of the engineer in society.

> One of the heroes of the new concept of efficiency was the city manager, the first of whom were engineers who understood street construction, railways, and bridges—the old plum of the grafters. . . . Technical knowledge could save money and provide service. The new profession could command high salaries and, as each manager proudly sought to prove, save the city not only the cost of the salary but impressive additional sums in the first year of his service.[19]

In the 1922 meeting of the City Managers Association, forty of the forty-five members of that organization were engineers. Up to the mid-1940's, the overwhelming majority of city managers were graduate engineers—some being representative of the finest engineering schools in the nation—or men who had advanced over the years into high-level positions in public works departments by dint of hard work, experience and some night school courses from which they were appointed as city managers. Indeed, one engineer with an international reputation became president of the United States in 1928. "Herbert Hoover, respected as an engineer, famed as food administrator of World War I, beloved symbol of household efficiency and management, became the public model of the new era man."[20]

The manifestations of the engineering approach to public administration were many. Work-flow analysis, physical layout studies, and development of scientific cost-accounting techniques were a few of the more important emphases traceable to the engineer-efficiency influence. The position of "administrative analyst" took its place alongside that of personnel, finance and legal specialties. The essence of administrative analysis centered upon some key questions:

> *Why* is the activity necessary?
> *What* does the activity really accomplish?
> *When* is it done and when should it be done?
> *How* is it done and how should it be done?
> *Where* is it done and where is the best place to do it?
> *Who* is doing it and who could do it most conveniently?

The answers to many of these questions were based upon the use of "flow-process" charts at all levels of government. In fact, administrative analysis based upon these charts centered on the three variable factors of distance, time and type of operation involved. By analyzing the flow of materials or paper work, by breaking it up into separate steps or phases of the "flow" ("operation," "transportation," "delay," "storage," and "inspection"), together with descriptions of what is done and by whom, a quantitative graphing based upon distance and time would emerge that proved to be of great usefulness in workflow analysis and physical layout planning. Once the flow-process chart was completed for a specific process the total number of steps, operations, transportation, delays, storages and inspections could be computed. In addition, the total distance traveled and manhours or minutes involved could be totalled. Finally, the average time per distance in each step could be computed. A flow-process chart of office or production processes could then be utilized to improve those processes by diminishing the number of separate operations, minimizing the distance traveled and also minimizing the time spent.

When the differences between the existing and proposed methods led to "more efficiency" (i.e., a quantitative reduction in physical energy, resources and time), the new process could be put into effect. In this manner by observation, measurement, timing and calculation, individual job performance was to be improved and the most economical sequences, routing and layout (location) and handling were to be realized. These "scientific" techniques are still in wide use today at all levels of government in certain phases of administrative analysis. Comparison of the flow-process charts utilized by the United States Foreign Service (Figure 4–5) and the County of Los Angeles (Figure 4–6) confirms this point.

Form T-412
5-27-48

Date _____

FOREIGN SERVICE OF THE UNITED STATES OF AMERICA
PROCESS CHART

Process Charted _____

Service, Division, etc. _____ Unit _____

(For use in the work simplification program)

O In Feet	△ Time In Min.	Operation	Transport	Storage	Inspect.	Step No.	DESCRIPTION OF EACH STEP (Show WHAT is done—WHO does it)
		◯	○	△	☐		
		◯	○	△	☐		
		◯	○	△	☐		
		◯	○	△	☐		
		◯	○	△	☐		
		◯	○	△	☐		
		◯	○	△	☐		
		◯	○	△	☐		
		◯	○	△	☐		
		◯	○	△	☐		
		◯	○	△	☐		
		◯	○	△	☐		
		◯	○	△	☐		
		◯	○	△	☐		
		◯	○	△	☐		
		◯	○	△	☐		
		◯	○	△	☐		
		◯	○	△	☐		
		◯	○	△	☐		
		◯	○	△	☐		

Figure 4-5. SAMPLE FLOW PROCESS CHART

Chief Administrative Office – County of Los Angeles PROCESS CHART							Summary		
							Present	Proposed	Difference
Date		Page	of	Pages	Total No. of Steps				
Procedure Charted					No. of Operations				
Office, Division, etc.					No. of Transportations				
Subject Charted					No. of Delays				
Chart Begins					No. of Storages				
Chart Ends					No. of Inspections				
Charted By					Man Hours or Minutes				
☐ Present Method ☐ Proposed Method					Distance Traveled				

Distance in Feet	Time in Min.	Operation	Transport.	Delay	Storage	Inspection	Description of Each Step (show WHAT is done—WHO does it)	Remarks
1		◯	○	D	△	☐		
2		◯	○	D	△	☐		
3		◯	○	D	△	☐		
4		◯	○	D	△	☐		
5		◯	○	D	△	☐		
6		◯	○	D	△	☐		
7		◯	○	D	△	☐		
8		◯	○	D	△	☐		
9		◯	○	D	△	☐		
10		◯	○	D	△	☐		
11		◯	○	D	△	☐		
12		◯	○	D	△	☐		
13		◯	○	D	△	☐		
14		◯	○	D	△	☐		
15		◯	○	D	△	☐		
16		◯	○	D	△	☐		
17		◯	○	D	△	☐		
18		◯	○	D	△	☐		

Figure 4-6. SAMPLE FLOW PROCESS CHART

The 20's were not seminal years in the evolution of the American administrative system but were primarily years of consolidation. In the words of Dwight Waldo:

> The period of more than a decade following the peace [after World War I] witnessed such advances as the multiplication of organizations of public servants, the extension of research in many fields, and the appearance of the first textbooks on public administration. Progressivism's spirit of high civic endeavor had all but vanished. But in breadth and depth of administrative thought the period as a whole must be characterized as stagnant in comparison with the Progressive and War periods that preceded it, and the Depression period that followed. Neither the disillusionment and cynicism which followed the War nor the spirit of "get and spend" which dominated the twenties were conducive to the spread of governmental activity or to the study of administration as a high civic endeavor.[21]

The 30's, however, were marked by significant developments in economic affairs, foreign affairs and military policy. Their impact upon administration was destined to be direct and far-reaching.

NOTES

1. S. N. Eisenstadt, *The Political Systems of Empires*, New York: The Free Press, 1963.

2. *Ibid.*, p. 287.

3. *Ibid.*, p. 276.

4. *Ibid.*, Chapter 10, "The Place of the Bureaucracy in the Political Process," *passim.*

5. *Ibid.*, p. 299.

6. For an excellent discussion, see Anwar Syed, *The Political Theory of American Local Government*, New York: Random House, 1966, chap. 1, "Introduction" and chap. 2, "The Popular Theory."

7. Indispensable to the study of administration during this period are Leonard D. White's *The Federalists: A Study in Administrative History,* New York: Macmillan, 1961, and *The Jeffersonians: A Study in Administrative History 1801-1829,* New York: Macmillan, 1961. (See also Paul P. Van Riper, *History of the United States Civil Service,* Evanston: Row, Peterson, 1958, chap. 2, "Bureaucratic Beginnings 1789-1829.")

8. U. S. Statutes 514 (1871).

9. Van Riper, *op. cit.,* p. 70.

10. William Dudley Foulke, *Fighting the Spoilsmen, Reminiscences of the Civil Service Reform Movement,* New York and London: G. P. Putnam's Sons, 1919, p. 7.

11. Based upon Leonard D. White, *The Republican Era: 1869-1901 A Study in Administrative History,* New York: Macmillan, 1963.

12. As quoted in Darrell Hevenor Smith, *The United States Civil Service Commission. Its History, Activities and Organization,* Baltimore: The Johns Hopkins Press, 1928, pp. 13-14.

13. Woodrow Wilson, "The Study of Administration" (reprint), *Political Science Quarterly,* Vol. LVI, No. 4 (December 1941), p. 482.

14. *Ibid.,* p. 481.

15. Jane S. Dahlberg, *The New York Bureau of Municipal Research. Pioneer in Government Administration,* New York: New York University Press, 1966, pp. 3-4.

16. *Ibid.,* p. 40.

17. *Ibid.,* chap. 5, "The Taft Commission," pp. 81-91.

18. Barry Dean Karl, *Executive Reorganization and Reform in the New Deal. The Genesis of Administrative Management, 1900-1939,* Cambridge: Harvard University Press, 1963, p. 22.

19. *Ibid.,* p. 20.

20. *Ibid.,* p. 22.

21. Dwight Waldo, *The Administrative State. A Study of the Political Theory of American Public Administration,* New York: Ronald Press, 1948, p. 11.

HISTORICAL PERSPECTIVES: THE 1930'S TO 1970'S

A STRENGTHENED PRESIDENT, DEPRESSION & WAR: THE '30's & '40's

The decades of the '30's and '40's were crisis decades—the '30's dominated by the domestic ramifications of global economic depression and the '40's by the American war effort and the problems of conversion to a peacetime society. The immediate impact of the depression upon public administration was the enhancement of executive leadership as the nation, including Congress, looked to presidential direction and policies for guidance out of the morass of economic devastation. Despite some serious scrimmages with Congress and a long-simmering dispute with the Supreme Court over invalidation of some major New Deal legislation, the presidency at the end of the decade of the '30's was immeasurably strengthened. Franklin D. Roosevelt had often circumvented Congressional obstructionism by appealing directly to the people in his "fireside chats" via radio. Congressmen, upon hearing from their constituents within a few days after each "chat," generally managed to circumvent the obstacles and give the president approximately what he wanted.

The report of the President's Committee on Administrative Management, under the direction of Louis Brownlow, led to the establishment by Congress of the Executive Office of the

President "with functions and duties so prescribed that the President will have adequate machinery for the administrative management of the executive branch of the government." Key managerial offices were brought within the Executive Office: the Bureau of the Budget, the National Resources Planning Board, the Liaison Office for Personnel Management (to serve as a conduit between the Chief Executive and the Civil Service Commission) and the Office for Emergency Management. In the words of the Chairman of the Committee:

> ... as the responsibilities of government increased, the legislature lost its ability to take a coherent view of the state of the nation, because it had not permitted the executive to develop its management controls over the departments of government. The President was overburdened on the one hand with a mass of petty detail, and on the other hand he was denied the assistance that he needed if he was to control the actions of his subordinates; thus he could not delegate the work he should have delegated, and he let slip from his hands the essential controls of administrative management.
>
> To remedy this situation, it was not necessary to give the President any powers that the Constitution did not originally give him. It was necessary only to create in the Executive Office the physical and organizational facilities that any Chief Executive must have under modern conditions if he is to discharge his responsibilities.[1]

At the state level the governors were also strengthened by the widespread rise of executive staff agencies (fiscal, personnel, management) under direct gubernatorial control. The parallel between the rise of presidential and gubernatorial managerial power is quite clear. In fact, the link between the two offices was really direct. President Franklin Roosevelt had not only served as governor of New York but had developed many of his strong leadership techniques in Albany prior to his departure for the White House. During his presidency a number of governors adopted his more successful techniques for the assumption of administrative and political leadership. By the early 1940's strong executive leadership was the dominant theme in the capital of the nation, in a large number of state capitals and in many municipal civic centers.

The position of the president as Chief Executive was greatly strengthened by the Reorganization Act of 1939. Traditionally, the president did not have full and continuing authority over the organization or reorganization of the Executive branch—he had never been delegated such powers by Congress. For a two-year period, 1933 to 1935, President Roosevelt had been granted by Congress, under the pressures of the economic emergency, temporary authority for minor reorganization provided that executive orders to that effect were laid before Congress and that Congress did not act adversely upon them. In 1937 his Committee on Administrative Management proposed that such power to reorganize executive agencies again be conferred upon the president. In 1939 Congress recognized a permanent shift in authority by allowing the president to submit reorganization plans to Congress and these were to be effective unless Congress by concurrent resolution disapproved the plans in their entirety. Congress, in restraining its own power by defeating a motion to not allow any reorganization plan to become effective unless *approved* by Congress and in not permitting itself to modify any organization plan, greatly improved the possibility that presidential plans would become effective. In the period from April 1939 to December 1940, the President submitted five reorganization plans to Congress and all became effective.[2]

The economic crisis contributed not only to a growing tendency to strengthen executive leadership but also to a modification of the views of students of public administration toward the business community in general. According to Waldo:

> The period of economic depression inaugurated by the market crash in 1929 affected the thinking of students of public administration in a number of ways. Perhaps the most important was the changed attitude toward business. Much as American students owed to business practice and business thinking, hardly any of them are longer content with the simple objective of "more business in government." Allied to this is a general shift in sentiment toward greater

government participation in economic life. The Depression's general stimulation of social conscience caused doubts to be raised as to whether "economy and efficiency" provide the ultimate criteria for judging administration, and attempts have been made either to broaden their connotations to include "social" values or to cast them into outer darkness.[3]

Closer intergovernmental administrative relations emerged as a permanent legacy of the Depression. Many local governments were increasingly dependent upon state governments for financial sustenance as well as broadened legal authority to provide relief of the hungry and the destitute and more flexibility in revenue-raising authorization. Administrative linkages between cities and the federal government multiplied as many state governments were themselves financially needy and unable to meet the needs of cities attempting to provide traditional services, maintain law and order and provide relief. By the middle 1930's vast federal relief programs were being administered with the cooperation of local officials. Today many of the civic center buildings, libraries, recreational facilities and other permanent structures of America's urban areas are those built by federal relief work programs. Rural America likewise developed closer administrative ties with federal agencies as emergency programs for electrification, reclamation, conservation, road building and the prevention of foreclosures were put into effect.

The decade of the '40's centered upon the conduct of World War II and the later problems of winding down the war effort as peace emerged in 1945. Both the crises of depression and war had greatly expanded public payrolls at all levels. Also, both crises had seen the rise of hundreds of temporary administrative agencies purposely kept outside existing departments so as to encourage maximum administrative flexibility and the spirit of experimentation and innovation without the "dead hands" of established procedures, precedents, habits and inertia. Consequently, hundreds of thousands of citizens who might otherwise never have sat behind a government-issue desk were given the opportunity to serve their government, in the Jacksonian sense, in some administrative capacity.

The administration of the nation's global war effort was a Herculean task that literally defies the imagination in its complexity. In addition to the establishment of overall central direction and management of the war production effort, including establishment of communications with various temporary state and local agencies relevant to war production, was the need for reorganization of national agencies necessary for conversion to a war economy. Personnel had to be recruited and trained to manage new government offices, corporations and boards to handle selective needs such as food, fuel and gasoline rationing and civil defense. Stockpiles of strategic materials, especially those in short domestic supply, had to be bolstered. The letting of airplane, ship, tank and amunitions contracts on the widest scale ever experienced by the nation had to go hand in hand with governmental supervision of quality control and private plant expansion to meet defense needs. In addition, manpower and materiel priorities for defense plants had to be established. The problem of maintaining an adequate labor supply for essential industries and agriculture had to be balanced with the needs for military manpower. Price controls in the economy and the establishment of ceilings for rent, fuel, food and other commodities created the need for a new and vast bureaucratic network. The expansion of the transportation system, especially the railways and trucking, had to be co-ordinated with increased production and military movements of troops and supplies. All of this had to contribute in an unequivocal manner to the expansion, training and deployment of the nation's military forces at home and overseas.[4]

Even before the attack on Pearl Harbor by Japanese forces the United States government, while technically at peace, was ideologically committed to the Allied cause. It was evident that authorities were preparing for a larger role despite the various prevailing theories of the nation's neutrality.

Bureaucracies are designed to operate in normal, not abnormal, circumstances. Consequently, once normalcy was abandoned as the basis of national policy then normalcy in the administrative branch became abnormal. As Herbert Emmerich, the Secretary to the Office of Production Management, observed in the period of preparation for war:

> The time is short; we must root out every vestige of administrative normalcy which is at the moment impeding and may defeat our program of national defense . . . . Such a change in approach is now taking place and it must proceed at an even faster tempo to set aside outworn general attitudes and to retool our administrative habits and attitudes. . . . In federal administration particularly but also in state and local governments there are habits of mind which we should make especial efforts to change.[5]

In this vein administrative re-orientation required the reduction of jurisdictional jealousies among public agencies; increasing the liaison between permanent agencies and emergency bodies; abandoning uniform procedures in favor of flexibility and freedom of action whenever possible. One key problem was the need for new techniques for determining what had priority under the new conditions. Another problem was the influx of inexperienced and untrained newcomers to government service.

CONTINUITY, SKEPTICISM AND LOYALTY: THE '50's

Outwardly government offices changed little after the postwar conversion to a peacetime society. Temporary emergency agencies were disbanded and permanent agencies reverted to the needs of a civilian rather than a quasi-military environment. To the average citizen the conversion was smooth and uneventful— public services continued and national attention could now be devoted to easing the problems of millions of returning G.I.'s. State and local government agencies faced increased pressures of a different nature. The rural areas gained back but a small percentage of those who had left to join the armed forces or to work in defense industries in the industrialized urban areas. City populations skyrocketed and the postwar exodus to the cheaper land and G.I. housing tracts began—a development which was to greatly alter the nature of American life. Within a decade "suburbia" became the subject of weighty sociological tomes, involved political analyses by political commentators, and was the subject of numerous novels and motion pictures. For state and local officials suburbia was miscast—in place of barbeques, white picket fences and neat rows of similar looking homes, they saw problems in providing adequate sewage, intelligent tract subdivision patterns, facilities and services for electricity, road construction and other daily requirements for survival. Pressures of the suburban exodus made many local "master plans" largely irrelevant as issues of incorporation and annexation dominated community affairs. Many communities just grew under conditions of minimal public standards and within very few years the "baby boom" created its own pressures for park, recreational and school facilities.

At the federal level some of the outfall from the war was of a positive nature. For example, many of the most significant advances in meteorology were of great value to the weather services and the army's development of sophisticated, mass testing techniques (particularly its "Alpha" and "Beta" tests) were applicable to the work of the U.S. Civil Service Commission, which adopted some of the methods. In addition, the decentralization of the Civil Service Commission, which had taken place under emergency conditions in order to meet the manpower requirements dictated by war, continued into the postwar era as the commission delegated vast powers in the recruitment, examination and promotional areas.

The upheavals of the two decades of depression, war and conversion to peace, however, made a complete return to administrative normalcy highly problematical. The apparent continuity of public services experienced by citizens was at odds with the growing intellectual unease within the academic sphere of public administration. There was new interest in the non-rational aspects of administrative decision-making and less deference to efficiency as a valid end of the administrative process. The traditional lack of concern with ethical or "value" considerations was viewed as a serious problem. Hence the concepts of scientific management were put on the defensive.

The 1950's were shaped by the rejection of administrative orthodoxy. First was the rise of professionalization in the public service at all levels of government and the mushrooming of public employee associations—many with a union orientation. This burgeoning movement—unabated in the '60's and '70's—

raises a number of vexatious issues ranging from the possibilities of an unwelcome fragmentation of public administration into rigid specialties each with its own organizational base to the problem of whether such associations should reflect the interests of their members or the broader "public interest" or whether, in fact, the two may be approximately congruent.[6]

The reorganization movement, exemplified by the first (1949) and second (1955) Hoover Commissions, realized quite limited changes. At the national level those recommendations of the commissions calling for internal reorganization enjoyed a high percentage (75%) of approval by Congress and the president. Those more significant and consequently more controversial proposals, involving agency consolidation, transfer of functions, or agency dissolution met congressional opposition and fewer than half of those enjoying presidential support were ever passed by that body. Also, many of the most far-reaching proposals were never submitted by the president to the Congress. The significance of the Hoover Commission approach, however, transcends any statistical scoreboard. In contrast to the appointment of three political scientists by Franklin D. Roosevelt to comprise his Committee on Administrative Management, the Hoover Commissions represented a cross-section of many powerful interests with representatives of the public, the legislature, and executive agencies as well as of the majority party and the minority party. Where the president's committee had submitted a unanimous report, the series of Hoover Commission reports were often marked by majority and minority statements and sometimes by several minority statements.

The Hoover Commission approach did have a significant "spillover" effect at state and local levels of government. By the late 1950's many "little Hoover Commissions" were investigating state and local processes of government with perhaps the greatest degree of citizen participation in civic affairs since the days of the muckrackers.

The 1950's were marked at the federal, state and local levels by a growing interest in regional planning. The concept of "planning," aside from military planning, had traditionally been suspect in the United States due to the unpopularity of economic planning and the feeling that planning was a key tool of "socialistic centralizers." The emergence of physical city planning as a growing and respected professional discipline overbalanced much of the earlier suspicion of the planning process. With the growth of America's great metropolitan areas and even the emergence of the "megalopolis" (the convergence of several metropolitan regions) trained city planners were in short supply during the '50's. The growth of academic graduate planning curricula in major universities reflected the inescapable fact that planning had become a part of modern government and administration.

A growing economic, developmental and even social interdependence among the many units of American state and local governments led in the 1950's to the creation of overall and coordinative planning agencies devoted to comprehensive development of "regions" combining otherwise politically independent governmental jurisdictions. Where these regions had been served previously by a confusing array of public agencies representing federal, state and local authorities, the planners attempted to develop coordinative techniques in order to further common endeavors toward similar goals as well as to minimize the inevitable frictions and conflicts of policies among divergent jurisdictions operating within the same general geographic region. Comprehensive river basin planning (for the best utilization of resources in a particular area) created the framework for joint federal-state task forces and commissions and the establishment of permanent federal-interstate planning agencies—sometimes by presidential appointment and Congressional authorization and also by the technique of federal-interstate compacts.

The '50's were also years of public shock and chagrin at some noteworthy lapses in administrative ethics. Cheating on examinations at the U.S. Military Academy at West Point in violation of the Honor Code and the exposure of serious irregularities among agents of the Internal Revenue Service brought out the fact that even those perceived to be most immune from corruption were, indeed, subject to its enticements.

A far more serious matter was the impact of the "cold war" between the Soviet Union and the West. This bipolar ideological confrontation and military standoff created conditions approximating the "Red Scare" following World War I. Through

167

the late 1940's and the '50's the issue of loyalty dominated much of the administrative landscape. Loyalty oaths, reminiscent of the oaths of loyalty of the Middle Ages, were requisite rituals for employment or retention of positions in federal, state and local governments, including public school systems and public institutions of higher learning. Many, probably most, of these requirements are still in existence today. That the public employee sector of society would be so pinpointed lay bare a latent and very real native American suspicion of the role of the bureaucracy within the framework of "Americanism." Essentially a nonproducer in a system that elevates the morality of production, profit and work, and politically suspect, the bureaucrat during this period was subjected to rituals appropriate to pariahs. Probably at no time since the height of patronage and the spoils system had the public perception of the bureaucrat reached such a low point.

THE CONFLICTIVE SOCIETY: THE 1960's

Outside the frosted panes of governmental offices racial tensions, urban riots and anti-Vietnam demonstrations racked the nation during the conflictive decade of the '60's and frequently pitted American against American. For many of the young in the vanguard of much of the unrest, the symbol of bureaucracy was the policeman with his club, helmet and plexiglas face shield and his tear gas canister. The rioting cut across ethnic lines and created unprecedented problems of riot control and the administration of justice when hundreds had been arrested. For many the unrest signaled an attempt to topple the basic institutions of the nation itself.

Continuation of racial discrimination, the rise of large and impersonal government, the widespread use of computers and the reduction of the individual to a number or a notch on a "do not fold—do not spindle—do not mutilate" card, together with the apparent irrelevance of much of education for a world in transition to a post-industrial society, were factors that, when combined with the unpopularity of the Vietnam conflict, lit the fuse of underlying popular discontent.

The public bureaucracy became the target of both extremes of the political spectrum. The attacks on public administration from Left and Right centered upon the increasingly centralized power of government, the size of government and an alleged loss of control of the people over their own institutions. Bureaucracy also became the target of attack by the conservationist-ecology movement which, somewhat parallel to the allegations of Ralph Nader in his consumerism movement, held that public administrative agencies were too closely linked to special and narrow interests, i.e., real estate developers, oil interests and other fuel and energy interests, and speculator-investors.

The "new public administration" emerged within this environment as a movement of young scholars largely sympathetic to many of the decade's discontents. Placing much of the blame for the ills of society upon unresponsive and non-participative, inward-oriented and value-neutral bureaucratic systems, the "new public administrationists" favored non-hierarchical, participative and temporary forms of organization which would lead, hopefully, to the maximum fulfillment of each man's potential. The movement, although not clearly demarcated, tends to favor decentralization of decision-making in preference to centralization of authority and the goal of "social justice" in place of the more traditional "due process" as that to which the citizen is entitled in his relations with bureaucracy.

One of the most significant developments of the '60's in the background of the more publicized conflicts was the increasingly technological orientation of the federal government. Since World War II the federal government's involvement with and support of scientific research and advanced technology had increased steadily. By the late 1960's the growth rate in federal employment for scientific professional personnel (engineers, scientists and health professionals) exceeded that of any other category. The growth for aeronautical and electronic engineers in the federal service for the years 1957–1967 increased over 150 percent; for mathematicians and physicists in the same period the increase was over 100 percent; chemists increased by nearly 60 percent; biological scientists by nearly 40 percent; and social scientists (primarily in the departments of State and Labor) increased by nearly 50 percent. Non-professional scientific and technical personnel utilized in support of scientific, engineering and health professionals increased by 50 percent in the Department of Defense and by 13 percent in the Department of Agriculture. The largest number of non-professional personnel were in the engineering and mechanics fields, followed in order by the biological sciences, mathematics-statistics, psychology and social science.

The three-point pivot of federal administration during the '60's comprised persons trained in the professions (medicine, veterinary medicine, dentistry, law, nursing, etc.), scientists, and those trained in university and college programs in the administrative and managerial arts (generally business or public administration).

The days of the clerks and the chief clerks with their high school educations as the public figures most representative of the federal service had come to an end in the early 1900's. This was followed by a period of several decades to the 1940's when the fiscal officers tended to symbolize the federal service and the methods of fiscal management were accorded a high place in the federal administrative processes. By the close of the 1960's the requirements for higher education degrees and advanced technological training merely reflected the reality of a remarkable change in the character of governmental operations.

ADMINISTRATIVE MORALITY AND
EQUAL OPPORTUNITY: THE 1970's

The decade of the '70's has brought into prominence three key issues that will be of continued central concern: administrative morality and public morale, public labor relations and equal opportunity. The successful resolution of these complex issues may be crucial to the future quality of life in America.

Richard Nixon's second term in office was highlighted by the events of "Watergate"—the sordid and disheartening episode of political and moral corruption that led to his own resignation under the immediate threat of impeachment and to the prosecution and conviction of his key staff aides as well as his former

Attorney General. Earlier Vice-President Spiro Agnew had resigned from his office after pleading *nolo contendere* (no contest) to a charge of income tax evasion. The copious literature of Watergate fully chronicles the moral debacle leading to the nation's being governed, in the year of its Bicentennial, by an unelected president and unelected vice-president—the first such occasion in its history. Another shock to public sensibilities occurred when Gerald Ford, Nixon's appointee as Vice-President, succeeded him as president and soon granted Nixon a full, absolute and unconditional pardon for any and all crimes that might have been committed. The pardon, not subject to any appeal, effectively foreclosed any prosecution of the former president and, for many Americans, appeared to place Richard Nixon above the rule of law and the processes of justice.

The litany of abuses of Constitutional and executive power continued unrelenting and 1975 might well be regarded by future historians as the post-Watergate year of startling agency abuses of power. The Central Intelligence Agency, the Federal Bureau of Investigation, Army Intelligence and the Internal Revenue Service were revealed, upon Congressional investigation, to have engaged in activities that were either blatantly illegal or contrary to the spirit of a democratic society and reflective of the tactics of a police state. Some evidence emerged tentatively linking some abuses with previous presidential administrations. The remainder of the decade of the '70's may well be devoted in large measure to the task of developing new techniques of control over executive agencies.

These depressing events, combined with the nature of the American withdrawal from Vietnam (a hasty evacuation following the collapse of South Vietnamese military forces), a serious economic depression, double-digit inflation and a national unemployment rate approaching 10 percent, have produced an erosion of faith in the quality of America's public leadership and the effectiveness of its governmental institutions. The apparent inability of any nation to control the power of multinational corporations and the reality that Americans may look forward to a society of scarcities rather than perpetual abundance have all contributed to the 1970's being marked as a decade of disillusionment.

Election statistics at all levels reflect a massive disengagement from civic affairs and participation. The sense of unease is compounded by the growing phenomenon of strikes and slow-downs by public employees—teachers, bus drivers, postal workers, policemen, prison guards, firemen, sanitation workers, public hospital personnel and air traffic controllers.

The turbulence of the '60's has been transformed into the confusing '70's. Long-range creative solutions and innovative approaches to public issues are conspicuously absent—a curious phenomenon in a nation with the highest percentage of college and university graduates in the world.

The nation's future will be determined by the degree to which public confidence is restored in the quality of its leadership and the operations of its basic institutions, including the bureaucracy. New approaches must be developed in the remaining years of the '70's to prevent errant agencies from prostituting the spirit and practice of administration appropriate to a democratic society.

Employee-management relations in the '70's are undergoing rapid change. Images of the public servant as a "servant"—complacent, docile and conservative—with less than adequate compensation balanced by the job security of the merit system and providing uninterrupted delivery of services are now little more than wistful visions of a once relatively idyllic state of affairs. Today's public employee is increasingly characterized by labor militancy, organizational power and the ability (not necessarily legal) and determination to bring about complete work stoppages or "slowdowns." Public work stoppage in the '70's increased to twenty times the rate of the '50's and the rate of increase of public employees being either unionized or represented in labor negotiations by employee associations is greater than in the private sector. The American Federation of State, County, and Municipal Employees is generally recognized as the largest and fastest growing industrial-type union.

The emergence of collective bargaining for specific groups of public employees and its growth in the '70's contrasts vividly with the traditional concept of "privilege" in public employ-ment. The latter is based upon the notion that determination of the conditions of such employment is the sole prerogative of the sovereign government. By 1970 governmental recognition of unions was official federal policy as it was for many state and local governments. The politics of unionism emerges as an increasingly important aspect of governmental operations and many public government bodies and administrative agencies have had to modify their personnel policies in order to bring them in line with the changed conditions surrounding public employee-management relations.

One of the most complex and confusing issues of the '70's in public administration will be the effort to balance the merit principles of public employment with the needs of an enlightened program of employee-management relations, including the growing tendencies toward collective bargaining. In 1974 the President's Advisory Council on Intergovernmental Personnel Policy dealt with some of the major issues in labor-management relations in the public service. The Council felt that merit systems and collective bargaining can and should co-exist though both may have to accept some modification in purpose and procedure. The Council rejected uniform nation-wide personnel standards in labor relations, preferring to allow the states to determine their own policies rather than having them follow federal policy. Employee-management relations laws should, the Council noted, be administered by special, impartial and independent boards and public jurisdictions should be required to recognize employee organizations which meet basic criteria. Further, the framework for collective negotiations should be clearly and specifically established by law. The Council gave special emphasis to the lack of sufficient training for public supervisors and managers who must negotiate with experienced leaders of employee organizations. The Council noted that certain public policy areas should be outside the boundaries of negotiation (i.e., the mission of the agency, standards of service to the public, etc.) while the negotiating table should be used as a problem-solving device on conditions of employment. Strikes by public employees should be prohibited by law with adequate machinery to resolve impasses. Strike penalties, according to the Council, should be flexible and workable.[7]

The sensitive and complex nature of labor relations was evidenced by divisions within the council itself, especially by the vigor of some of the dissenting views expressed. Among dissenting positions were those in favor of national standardization in place of widely varying state labor laws and those who expressed opinions opposed to the complete outlawing of strikes. There is little doubt that the '70's will continue to be a decade of significant developments in public employee-management relations.[8]

The roles of women and racial minorities in the public service have, within the decade of the '70's, come under increasingly intensive reevaluation. At the beginning of the decade the U.S. Civil Service Commission published statistics on the fulltime employment of women in the federal government that revealed that:

1. The total number of white collar women employed fulltime represented about one-third of the total white collar working force.
2. Where about 55 percent of all federal white collar employment was in positions in Civil Service grades 1 through 6, women comprised about 46 percent of this grade range.
3. Where 35 percent of the white collar work force was in the intermediate grades 7 through 12, women comprised 20.7 percent of this grade range.
4. The remaining 10 percent occupy the upper-level grades 13 and above with women comprising only 1.7 percent of this grade range.
5. The general administrative, clerical and office services continued to be dominated by women, who comprised 69 percent of this group. Within this group about 86 percent of all women were in grades 1 through 6.
6. Average salaries for women were significantly lower than for men—$7,727 compared with $10,981.[9]

The statistics speak for themselves. Aside from wage differentials women predominated in the lower Civil Service grade ranges and at the intermediate and especially at the upper grades their percentages declined significantly.

Federal employment policy for the racial minorities, especially Blacks, prior to World War II was highly restrictive. From the establishment of the nation it was assumed that the federal service would be largely limited to whites. It was not until the post-Civil War Reconstruction era that significant appointments of Blacks occurred, mostly as compensatory measures. Eventually, however, the number of Black appointees in the South diminished as the reaction to Reconstruction emerged. Thus appointments of Blacks to positions of managerial responsibility and to postmasterships declined despite their numbers in the population.

Patronage did not ease the lot of the Black or expand his opportunity for public employment. But the emergence of the Civil Service system did greatly expand Black participation. As Van Riper points out:

> The federal public service in 1881 contained only 0.57 percent Negro employees. However, this rose to about 5.86 percent under Taft in 1910. Though the Civil Service rules did not explicitly forbid racial discrimination . . . the generally impersonal nature of the examination system encouraged Negro employment, particularly in the city of Washington, and the effective entry of the Negro into federal public service must be dated from 1883.[10]

From this point on the gains of Blacks become quite spotty. Segregation of Blacks existed in the Navy prior to World War I and the requirement that photographs, possibly for the determination of color, be attached to federal job applications was ordered by the Civil Service Commission in 1914. Considerable Black gains occurred during World War I. According to one study the percentage of Blacks in federal service almost doubled from 1921 to 1928, when the figure was estimated at nearly 10 percent.[11]

Black gains in the federal service were relatively slight under the New Deal of the 1930's. Nevertheless in the later years of the New Deal the proportion of Blacks in the federal service reached the proportion of nonwhites in the general population. At the local level, however, the position of Blacks was conspicuously weakened and as portions of the New Deal were decentralized from Washington to local authorities the impact upon Blacks was quite disadvantageous.

The decade of the '40's, dominated by World War II, provided the conditions for an upsurge in opportunities for Blacks in the federal service. In 1940 racial discrimination became illegal in federal employment and promotions. During the 1950's and '60's steady gains were made through actions of the Civil Service Commission, presidential Executive Orders and congressional enactments.[12] In 1972 Congress passed the Equal Opportunity Act to insure that all federal applicants and employees would be accorded fair treatment in all aspects of personnel administration without regard to sex, race, color, national origin, religious creed or political affiliation. The most effective method to put this policy into effect has caused some controversy in the mid-'70's.

The President's Advisory Council on Intergovernmental Personnel Policy issued a statement in 1973 supporting an "affirmative action" approach.

> It takes more than lip service to make equal employment opportunity a reality. It is important now and in the years ahead for American government to reach out to assure the opportunity for full participation in our public workforce, as well as in policy making. This can be accomplished only through vigorous, affirmative action. Entrenched customs, while not overtly discriminatory, have served in many cases to screen out women and minority group members from employment and advancement. These include inadequate publicity about openings, unrealistic job requirements, adherence to traditional exclusionary practices, invalid tests, and closed doors to upward movement.

The report added:

> The principle of equal opportunity requires positive and aggressive action. . . . it requires administrators to reach out to all possible sources of applicants to assure that individuals in every segment of society have a fair chance to obtain employment on the basis of relative ability. The principle also means that selection methods, job requirements, personnel practices, and the working environment itself

must be reexamined to see that they afford fair and equal treatment.[13]

One member of the Council raised perhaps the central issue of an evolving controversy of the '70's: the problem of numerical goals, their impact on a merit system and the spectre of "reverse discrimination." In arguing that the Council's report did not go far enough in furthering the concept of an affirmative action, he declared:

> Vigorous affirmative action programs which use numerical goals and targets as measurements and which are wisely and fairly administered are not incompatible with merit principles and do not represent a lowering of standards or qualifications for the public service. . . .
> Of course, public personnel experts should be wary of over-reliance on goals and on methods of affirmative action which short-cut or denigrate merit standards, principles, and procedures for merit system administration, thus resulting in reverse discrimination.[14]

This statement probably raises more issues than it resolves. It does, nevertheless, attempt a balance—though it is quite devoid of tangible guidelines. Professor Samuel Krislov in his study, *The Negro in Federal Employment,* lays bare the dilemma of the administrator in the current situation:

> A federal executive attempting to implement the Equal Employment Program, who conscientiously examines implications, is forced into an awareness of a long trail, with many possible detours. He may begin by merely taking a lordly position that he will evaluate objectively applicants who present themselves before him, but if he is truly conscientious he will go on to examine recruitment policies in order to make sure that they give more than lip service to the quest for equality. He may decide to do what many fellow executives have done: dispatch recruiters to Negro colleges in the South, once so infrequently visited by government recruiters. . . . Recruitment through gossip can

be supplemented by initial posting of notices of vacancies in places where potential Negro applicants will see them. Positive publicity can be channeled to the Negro press, and so on.

Further soul searching may result in reopening the question of proper definition of qualifications in terms of their actual application to performance on the job as well as in terms of possible racial discrimination in the testing process. An executive who recognizes that the opportunities for gaining the necessary qualifications may themselves be imbedded in discriminatory patterns may even delve into remote aspects of social relationships.

A truly sensitive administrator thus tackling the apparently simple problem of expanding opportunity for employment can find himself driven to constant examination of the whole network of selection and the entire philosophical problem of merit. In practice he must draw the line somewhere, decide that total redress of the balance of social wrongs is beyond his power. The subjectivity of that line—along with the sheer human necessity for drawing it—constitutes the justification and rationalization for any level of authority or inactivity on the part of the administrator.[15]

The national government's affirmative action program has had a significant impact on state and local administration in the '70's. For some administrators things will never be quite the same again. Some implications for city managers are described below:

Equal employment opportunity and its attendant affirmative action requirements, fair labor standards, and citizen involvement, for example, all represent deep and permanent incursions into the formation and execution of public policy on the local level. When these national policy goals are added as conditions to grants-in-aid and revenue sharing blocks, the trade-off becomes the exchange of sorely needed fiscal resources in return for the implementation of national policy goals. Furthermore, whatever the city does in support of these goals will to some degree become a demand for similar action in the private affairs of the community. The appointed executive is involved in this process of change whether he likes it or not, and the policy choices he assists in making will have serious consequences for the future of the city he serves and the profession to which he belongs. Involvement is no longer a matter of choice, even if a community is able for the moment to avoid reliance on federal sources.[16]

A survey of American cities published in the 1975 edition of *The Municipal Yearbook* revealed:

1. The management of cities is overwhelmingly in the hands of male Caucasians.
2. Whether the cities are classified by geographical region, population or type (suburban, central or independent) male Caucasians are predominant (between 93 percent and 95 percent) in all classifications.
3. One percent of council-manager cities are headed by women.
4. Of the 1,663 cities participating in the survey 54 percent reported no action to improve employment opportunities for women and 45 percent reported no action with regard to minorities.[17]

The reactions by city managers or C.A.O.'s to temporary relaxation of civil service requirements in order to increase minority employment are (of 1,653 cities participating) reported below: [18]

Form of Government	No. of Cities Reporting	% Favor	% Somewhat Favor	% Neutral	% Somewhat Oppose	% Oppose
Council–Manager	1516	6.1	10.9	17.8	20.6	44.6
Mayor–Council	128	6.3	11.7	18.8	19.5	43.8
Commission	5	0	0	40.0	20.0	40.0
Town Meeting	3	0	0	0	66.7	33.0
Representative Town Meeting	1	0	0	0	0	100.0

Figure 5-1. REACTIONS TO SUGGESTIONS TO RELAY CIVIL SERVICE REQUIREMENTS

On the other hand, the survey did reveal that city manager or C.A.O. reactions were favorable to the establishment of future employment goals and objectives for women and minorities in local services.[19] This position, of course, does not derogate from the principles of equal opportunity advanced by federal authorities but does assure their implementation at a more leisurely pace in the broader society. These and other data from the survey led the investigators to conclude:

> Quite obviously, much remains to be done to encourage the entry of minority persons and women into the field of public management. Because elective office appears a more open avenue, minorities may not see professional management as a particularly effective way to enter a public career. Cities utilizing appointed executives tend still to be middle class and nonindustrial. Minority group municipal employees in such places have often been held to blue collar occupations—or, in the case of women, to clerical duties. Federal policies embodied in grant programs, through requirements for affirmative action plans broadening equal employment opportunity, are having an effect, but it will take at least a decade for such policies to become visibly effective in the managerial ranks through up-from-the-bottom career progression.[20]

Despite the obvious reluctance of local governments to set aside existing Civil Service requirements city and county attorneys are increasingly advising their respective legislative bodies and officials of policies that could be construed as discriminatory. The guidelines are based upon federal policy as well as a number of federal and state judicial decisions. Discrimination might be assumed to exist if no "outreach" efforts are made to direct recruitment to those sources most likely to attract minorities and women; if in the selection and promotion process a standard or a test has a disparate effect on minorities or women unless the employer can clearly demonstrate that the standard or test is job-related. Discrimination might be assumed if members of minorities or female employees seem to be "clustered" in specific job classifications, assignments or locations.

State and local governments as well as educational institutions have been frequently confused by vague and conflicting federal guidelines. It is difficult in some instances to reconcile and coordinate the mass of variant regulations and data imposed by the U.S. Department of Labor, the Department of Health, Education and Welfare, the Equal Employment Opportunity Commission and the U.S. Civil Service Commission.

In 1975 the U.S. Commission on Civil Rights called for the creation of a superagency to lay down uniform guidelines rather than have them dispersed among numerous federal agencies. The commission's report was also critical of the methods and agencies responsible for enforcing existing laws. Especially singled out for harsh criticism was the U.S. Civil Service Commission, accused of using discriminatory promotional examinations and of being less than enthusiastic about opening up federal jobs to minorities. In reply the Civil Service Commission proclaimed the belief that the Civil Rights Commission's endorsement of a federal bureaucracy "reflective and representative of all race, ethnic and sex groups" comprised, in reality, a "quota system" incompatible with the Civil Service Commission's emphasis upon merit.

There is little doubt that the last half of the decade of the '70's will be devoted in considerable degree to the problems of public employment opportunities for *both* minority and non-minority persons. Both seek "justice" in public recruitment processes, promotional opportunities and retention. Especially in a time of social unease, economic uncertainty and high unemployment, attempts to utilize "quotas" or other compensatory devices in public employment to redress history will create crucial problems affecting millions of Americans.

CONTRIBUTIONS TO BUREAUCRATIC HISTORY

The scope and longevity of America's noncentralized administrative system is unique in the world today. It has served a highly pluralistic and regionally oriented society with admirable continuity in normal times as well as in crises and wars. Administration at all levels of American government has demonstrated its ability to adjust to major alterations in public policy and is a force increasingly recognized to have influenced the shaping of that policy. Throughout the various periods of American history the bureaucracy, by and large, has mirrored the dominant societal values as well as its own self-interests.

Viewed alongside Professor Eisenstadt's conceptual framework the evolution of America's bureaucracy may be interpreted in a wide variety of roles not unlike those of the historical centralized bureaucracies ranging from the dominant service orientation to self-aggrandizement. Like many of the historical bureaucracies described by Eisenstadt, American bureaucratic systems have also maintained close links with external "ruling" groups and various strata of society. The nature of this linkage network will be more fully explored in later chapters.

Unlike the historical centralized bureaucracies, American public administration cannot be understood by mere reference to the national administrative system. On the contrary, American bureaucratic history is just that—*bureaucratic*—not national or state or local history. It is bureaucratic evolution at *all* levels of government. This is, by all odds, its most distinguishing characteristic.

NOTES

1. Louis Brownlow, "A General View in The Executive Office of the President: A Symposium," *Public Administration Review*, Vol. I, No. 2 (Winter 1941), pp. 103-104.

2. See John D. Millet and Lindsay Rogers, "The Legislative Veto and the Reorganization Act of 1939," *Public Administration Review*, Vol. I, No. 2 (Winter 1941), pp. 176-189.

3. Dwight Waldo, *The Administrative State: A Study of the Political Theory of American Public Administration*, New York: Ronald Press, 1948, p. 11.

4. See Joseph P. Harris, "The Emergency National Defense Organizarion," *Public Administration Review*, Vol. I, No. 1 (Autumn 1940), p. 21, and William D. Carey, "Central Field Relationships in the War Production Board," *Public Administration Review*, Vol. 4, No. 1 (Winter 1944), p. 21.

5. Herbert Emmerich, "Administrative Normalcy Impedes Defense," *Public Administration Review*, Vol. I, No. 4 (Summer 1941), p. 318.

6. See York Wilbern, "Professionalization in the Public Service: Too Little or Too Much?," *Public Administration Review,* Vol. XIV, No. 1, (Winter 1954), pp. 13-21; *Public Service Professional Associations and the Public Interest.* Monograph 15. Philadelphia: The American Academy of Political and Social Science, 1973.

7. *More Effective Public Service Supplementary Report to the President and the Congress.* Prepared by the Advisory Council of Intergovernmental Personnel Policy — July 1974. Subcommittee on Intergovernmental Relations of the Committee on Government Operations, U.S. Senate, 93rd Congress, 2nd Session, October 1974.

8. For a background to the issues of public employee-management relations, see "Symposium on Collective Bargaining in the Public Service: A Reappraisal," *Public Administration Review,* Vol. XXXII, No. 2 (March, April 1972); *Collective Bargaining in Public Employment and the Merit System.* Washington D.C.: Labor-Management Services Administration, Office of Labor — Management Development, April 1972; *State-Local Employee Relations.* Iron Works Pike, Lexington, Kentucky: Council of State Governments, 1970, Arvid Anderson and Hugh D. Jascourt, editors, *Trends in Public Sector Labor Relations. An Information and Reference Guide for the Future,* Vol. I, 1972-73. Chicago: International Personnel Management Association and the Public Employment Relations Research Institute, 1975.

9. *Study of Women in the Federal Government 1970.* Prepared for The Federal Women's Program. Washington, D.C.: U.S. Civil Service Commission, Manpower Statistics Division, December 1971, p. 7.

10. Paul P. Van Riper, *History of the United States Civil Service,* Evanston: Row, Peterson, 1958, pp. 161-162.

11. Samuel Krislov, *The Negro in Federal Employment. The Quest for Equal Opportunity,* Minneapolis: University of Minnesota Press, 1967, p. 22.

12. *Ibid.,* chap. 2, "The Negro and the Federal Service in an Era of Change," pp. 28-45, examines developments from 1940 to 1965.

13. *More Effective Public Service. The First Report to the President and the Congress by the Advisory Council on Intergovernmental Personnel Policy — January 1973.* Subcommittee on Intergovernmental Relations of the Committee on Government Operations, U.S. Senate, 93rd Congress, 2nd Session, March 1974, pp. 19-20.

14. *Ibid.,* pp. 45-46.

15. Krislov, *op. cit.,* pp. 75-76.

16. Robert J. Huntley and Robert J. Macdonald, "Urban Managers: Organizational Preferences, Managerial Styles and Social Policy Roles,"

The Municipal Yearbook 1975, Washington, D.C.: International City Management Association, 1975, p. 155.

17. *Ibid.*, p. 156 and Table 2/11, p. 157.
18. *Ibid.*, Table 2/13, p. 158.
19. *Ibid.*, Table 2/12, p. 158.
20. *Ibid.*, p. 156.

6

PHILOSOPHICAL PERSPECTIVES: WEBER AND WILSON

Public administration, approached from a philosophical perspective, emphasizes the centrality of issues of value, including problems of value-conflict and the relevance of moral dilemmas. This approach is especially appropriate to a governmental system operating within a democratic framework. Democracy is regarded as emerging from a number of value propositions resting primarily upon faith, rather than demonstrated truth. Basic to belief in democracy are the notions of both limited government and government empowered to accomplish morally justifiable ends.

A democratic philosophy, as an interrelated series of values, is compatible with and supplements other approaches to the administrative process. In fact, the implementation of a particular philosophy, whether of libertarian or authoritarian bent, will be dependent upon at least several of the approaches previously described. For example, legal edicts are necessary to give practical form or "utility" to the philosophical values sought to be implemented and effective power (both symbolic and real) to enforce the legal edicts must be available. Hopefully, also, the techniques and processes of administering that philosophy will be compatible with the psychological needs and perceptions of the people.

Is there *a* philosophy of public administration? The answer is an unqualified "no." No administrative philosopher or theoretician has yet succeeded in synthesizing in the grand Aristotelian manner the vast content of administrative thought into a unified and systematic framework. Some theoreticians have attempted, with varying degrees of success, to strengthen the conceptual basis of the administrative process. However, the materials are found across the wide spectrum of separate fields of knowledge and are scattered far and wide in numerous books and professional journals; no sense of unity has been achieved.

Nothing in administrative theory today approaches the general unity of thought or the consensus professors of political theory held as to the content of their subject matter during the late nineteenth and the first half of the twentieth centuries. A syllabus on the philosophy of public administration today in all probability would reflect few commonalities either in major figures and their works or even the strategy of approaching the subject.

This situation is both a strength and a weakness. It is a strength to the extent that intellectual ferment and experimentation are maximized. The disadvantage is that the student seeking a predigested and unified field of study may be frustrated and question both the content and boundaries of the field of public administration itself.

It is doubtful that many of the major writers whose works are described in these chapters would themselves answer to the "roll call" of "philosophers." They represent various fields of knowledge—sociology, law, political science, psychiatry, economics and philosophy. Nevertheless, they have made fruitful contributions to a better understanding of the value bases of American public administration. In a very real sense, therefore, they are a representative group of "pioneers" in the newly emerging field of administrative philosophy. The philosophical approach to public administration may perhaps be the most difficult of all to master because of the intangible nature of its key concern: the moral justification for the exercise of public power and coercion in a democratic society.

MAX WEBER: THE CLASSICAL MODEL

The German sociologist Max Weber literally stands astride the conjunction of the nineteenth and twentieth centuries as a giant among scholars. A man of prodigious scholarly production, he combined keen powers of observation with painstaking research. His analytic abilities culminated in a series of theoretical conceptualizations or "ideal" types applicable to economics, law and public administration. With the translation of his major works into English during the 1920's, '30's, and '40's, two generations of American scholars and students have been given access to his wide-ranging observations and original analyses.

Weber's focus upon the interrelationships of race, history, law, economics and politics was based upon his belief that no single dominant force shaped man's existence. In contrast to Karl Marx's insistence that the major institutions and socio-economic process were determined by class struggle, Max Weber's works stand as cosmopolitan contributions to the understanding of man's social existence. Weber's technique centered upon the development of theoretical constructs to explain the myriad interrelationships underlying societal development. These "ideal types" remained as classic benchmarks in the evolution of economic, legal, social and administrative theory. His "ideal bureaucrat" who staffs his "ideal bureaucracy" must serve as a beginning or reference point requisite to understanding competing concepts of bureaucracy.

One caveat is, however, in order. He was not attempting to describe reality in the sense of flesh and blood bureaucrats or of any existing public bureaucracy. The Prussian civil service of the nineteenth century had been widely recognized as the model of efficient and professionalized bureaucracy and Weber's idealized bureaucracy does reflect many of the attributes of the Prussian system. Still, his descriptions of the bureaucrat and the bureaucratic process are not actual descriptions, nor are they in any sense recommendations of what should be developed. Rather, as Professor Max Rheinstein has observed in his introduction to one of Weber's major works:

Situations of such pure type have never existed in history. They're artificial constructs similar to the pure constructs of geometry. No pure triangle, cube, or sphere has ever existed. But never could reality have penetrated scientifically without the use of the artificial concepts of geometry . . . .

The "ideal types" of Weber's sociology are simply mental constructs to serve as categories of thought, the use of which will help us to catch the infinite manifoldness of reality by comparing its phenomena with those "pure" types which are used, so to speak, to serve as guides in a filing system.[1]

With an "ideal type" in one's mind's eye a reference point is provided by which variations or deviations become meaningful. In other words, comparative analysis between theory and practice as well as between differing theoretical constructs is not only possible but difficult to avoid. To Weber, this was the most fruitful approach to divining the true relationships between those vast forces underlying all social phenomena.

The Politician versus the Civil Servant

The foundations of Weber's political philosophy and his ideal bureaucratic construct are found in his "Politics as a Vocation," delivered in a speech in 1918 at the University of Munich.[2] Beginning with the concept of "the state," Weber views it through its means, for, in his view, it cannot be defined in terms of ends. The primary means of the state is its legitimized and monopolistic use of physical force. Consequently, the state reflects the legitimate domination of men over men. The state may delegate its use of force. Therefore, it remains the sole source of "legitimized violence."

"Politics," for Weber, is directly connected to the state as the reservoir of coercive power. His approach to politics was, no doubt, the foundation for a much later commonly held description of politics as "who gets what, when and how." For Weber, politics is the striving to share power or influence between states (nations) and among groups within the state.

The politician exercises through this power the leadership of a political association, i.e., the state. The unique attributes of the politician are important, for they set him conspicuously apart from the modern official or bureaucrat.

> To take a stand, to be passionate . . . is the politician's element, and above all, the element of the political leader. His conduct is subject to quite a different, indeed, exactly the opposite principle of responsibility from that of the civil servant. The honor of the civil servant is vested in his ability to execute conscientiously the order of the superior authorities, exactly as if the order agreed with his own conviction. This holds even if it appears wrong to him and if, despite the civil servant's remonstrances, the authority insists on the order. Without this moral discipline and self-denial, in the highest sense, the whole apparatus would fall to pieces. The honor of the political leader, of the leading statesman, however, lies precisely in an exclusive personal responsibility for what he does, a responsibility he cannot and must not reject or transfer . . . .

The "passion" of the politician is, for Weber, the passion of a cause believed in.

> . . . the serving of a cause must not be absent if action is to have inner strength. Exactly what the cause, in the service of which the politician strives for power and uses power, looks like is a matter of faith. The politician may serve national, humanitarian, social, ethical, cultural, worldly, or religious ends. The politician may be sustained by a strong belief in progress . . . or he may coolly reject this kind of belief. He may claim to stand in the service of an "idea" or rejecting this in principle, he may want to serve external ends of everyday life. However, some kind of faith must always exist.[3]

In short, the politician is to be a man of faith regardless of just what that faith comprises. Hopefully, according to Weber, he would not seek personal self-intoxication in the exercise of the state's power. To the contrary, the politician must be aware of the consequences of his policies and conduct—while the civil servant must avoid concern with consequences. In Weber's analysis the tragedy of the politician is the eternal dilemma of means versus ends. Ultimately, the politician must resolve this inherent conflict in specific instances. The politician is, therefore, a man of conscience.

> ... somewhere he reaches the point where he says: "Here I stand; I can do no other." That is something genuinely human and moving . . . .[4]

The politician, whether he gains power legally (by statute or rationally created rules), by habitual obedience (the authority of eternal yesterday) or by charisma (qualities of individual leadership) seeks to *maintain* continuous domination. This, in turn, is dependent upon "continuous *administration*." Weber describes the politician in quasi-democratic terms: Subject to transfer at will, dismissed or temporarily withdrawn. In contrast, only the administrative officials can provide the continuity requisite to unbroken domination by the power of the state. The long-range consequences are clear: Politically dominant leaders are dependent upon stable, continuous and efficient administration. While the politician is to be a man of faith, emotion and conscience, the career civil servant is to engage in "impartial administration"—one might even regard him as faithless in the sense of his lack of concern for values, ends or consequences. In fact, as Weber describes the civil servant, he ideally has little in common with the politician. Weber's speech remains, perhaps, the classic justification for the separation of policy and administration.

Weber's detailed presentation of his "ideal" bureaucratic organization appear in his other works, especially his famed essay, "Bureaucracy." Although evidently unfinished at the time of his death in 1920, it was published in 1922 and is an indispensable reference point in the evolution of modern administrative philosophy. Here the bureaucrat emerges as the key figure who ultimately wields decisive power in all societies, whether capitalistic or socialistic, democratic or authoritarian.

For Weber, the question is merely one of timing. In France and the Germanic states of Europe, the process of bureaucratization had already been well established and made all the firmer by a gradual evolutionary development spanning several centuries.

Politician	Civil Servant
• "Faith"; passion; emotion • Conscience • Personal responsibility for policies • Transitory	• "Faithless"; passionless; emotionless • No conscience • No personal responsibility for policies executed • Career

Figure 6–1. SIMPLE COMPARISON OF POLITICIAN AND CIVIL SERVANT CHARACTERISTICS

Cameralism

The earmarks of bureaucratic ascendency were evident everywhere. They included centralization of decision-making, obsessive concern with obedience to legal authority, the development of compendious legal "codes" and regulations to govern virtually all aspects of life in the state. Individual citizens were required to carry official "papers" or documents on their persons recording date and place of birth, residence, occupation and arrest record, together with other relevant data. Restrictions on freedom of movement, the emergence of governmental systems of licensure and the imposition of ever more detailed marketing, trade and labor regulations, together with the compilation of "dossiers" (files) for individual citizens, provided the background to Weber's bureaucratic model.

In addition, the essay "Bureaucracy" reflects the influence of the Germanic-Austrian "cameralist" tradition. Cameralism was a system of political science and public administration designed to aid those absolute monarchs of the middle 1700's who were replacing the disappearing feudal relationships with their own central authority. The rise of cameralism, therefore, paralleled the rise of the absolute monarch. Cameralism was primarily concerned with developing administrative techniques for managing highly centralized states. It represented a shift from legal training to training for governmental "action" (the "what" and "how" of administration). Philosophically, the cameralists believed in freeing trade from its many limitations and fetters under feudalism while, at the same time, they believed in increasing state activity and regulatory power vis-a-vis the individual citizen. The cameralists attempted to develop a "science of administration" through detailed and rigid managerial training of public functionaries to serve as the basis for managing the royal domain and broadening civil regulation. As political economists, the cameralists wrote widely on the needs for a systematic approach to public administration and eventually chairs in cameralism were established at leading universities, the first being at the University of Halle in Prussia in 1727. The occupants of these academic posts sometimes held concurrent positions in the public service. Aside from its economic doctrine, based on free flow of commerce, the public administration component of cameralism stressed the development of administrative skills. University cameralist courses included formal studies in finance administration and accountancy, police science and agricultural administration. They also included the compilation of vast bibliographies that would be helpful in synthesizing data and knowledge and would provide valuable library resources for administrative students. While the writings of the cameralists were not widely read outside of Germany and Austria, their impact within those states was quite significant. The cameralists laid the groundwork for the academic study of public administration and gave impetus both to its professional status and the high prestige enjoyed by the career civil servant in the central European states.

Weber's belief in the inevitability of increasing bureaucratization was the logical consequence of his basic assumptions on the nature of bureaucratic power. These assumptions may be briefly described:

1. *Administrative power is based on law.* The administrative process is heavily legalistic. The authority to give commands and to issue commands is distributed in a stable manner and is strictly limited according to

fixed rules and regulations. This "calculability of rules" assures the "calculability of consequences."

2. *Bureaucracies (public and private) operate on a hierarchical basis.* Bureaucracy is divided into levels. Each level is graded according to its legal authority.

3. *The most effective bureaucracies culminate in a single (monocratic) head.* Decisions made on a "collegial" basis (by group, commission or board) are wasteful of energy, encourage frictions and conflicts. Consequently, "collegial" decisions fragment responsibility.

4. *The "general rules" of management can be learned.* Public administration is a field of specialized knowledge. The rules or principles of public management are detailed and exhaustive, and they are necessary for proper office management.

5. *The "applicable rules" are to be applied in an impartial and objective manner without regard to persons.* The more bureaucracy is "dehumanized" the more virtuous it becomes. Bureaucracy becomes detached—"professionals" (experts) are removed from personal sympathy, favor, grace or gratitude. Proper administrative decisions are based on rationality, not upon emotions.

6. *Once established, the bureaucracy is permanent.* Bureaucracy is one of the most difficult of all social institutions to destroy. There is no chance of revolution from within and a mature bureaucracy remains virtually immune from external attack.

7. *Despite the overall power of bureaucracy, the individual bureaucrat is in a fixed position from which he cannot escape.* The bureaucrat's duties are fixed by legal authority attached to the specific position he occupies. He cannot influence or deflect from within the bureaucracy the predetermined path of the organization once its goals have been set by higher authority.

8. *As societies become more highly developed, the greater is their dependence upon permanent bureaucracy.* Bureaucracies are socially indispensable, for without their functional specialties and expertise, their mastery of the "coordinative function," chaos would result.

Bureaucracy is, therefore, the most highly developed power in the hands of man.

9. *Bureaucrats are highly disciplined.* Precise and habitual obedience to legal authority and rules is the most important responsibility of the professional bureaucrat. In this manner, a mature bureaucracy can be made to work for anybody or any group, including an enemy who succeeds in gaining control over it. The only possibility of capture is consequently "from the top." Paradoxically, the so-called "Achilles heel" of bureaucracy is at the very apex of the organization.

10. *Every bureaucracy keeps its knowledge (the "files") and its intentions secret.* As bureaucracies mature the inherent tendency towards secrecy (the "official secret") increases. This is, in fact, the real leverage of the bureaucrat. Both popularly elected parliaments and absolute monarchs alike are dependent for information upon the bureaucrat and they are consequently powerless in the face of his superior knowledge. In this manner, the "political master" emerges, in reality, as the subordinate.

Weber versus Marx

Weber's ideal bureaucracy literally rides the waves of historical determinism to ultimate societal dominance. This inevitability is akin to the rise of the proletarian masses to final power in Marxian theory. Yet, Weber and Marx viewed bureaucracy from opposing assumptions. For Marx the inevitability of bureaucratic dominance follows from the proletarian revolution in some countries where bureaucratic power must remain the key to prevention of counterrevolutionary movements. Only when the proletarian revolution succeeds on a *global* scale will bureaucracy as an instrument of the state wither away. The state for Marx was the key coercive instrument of oppression utilized by the capitalistic class to continue its dominance over the proletariat. The bureaucratic-police functions were viewed by Marx as little more than manifestations of man's inhumanity to man and as extensions of state authority. With the global destruction of capitalism the victorious proletariat would have no need for the oppressive instruments of the capitalist, i.e., the state and its coercive and oppressive bureaucracy. This "final stage" of the Marxian dialectic process with its classless, stateless and "bureaucratless" society was an anathema to Weber whose writings attack Marxian "theology" on several points:

1. Instead of the "withering away" of the state as foreseen by Marx, state nationalism will remain as one of man's basic institutions for organizing his societal relations.

2. The state bureaucracy will continue as the dominant institutional feature of state authority. Man in modern society can no more exist without the crucial services provided by the bureaucracy than he can exist without food.

3. Capitalism, far from being destroyed in a "proletarian revolution," will dominate the relations of production and commerce.

4. Weber viewed capitalism as the only counterfoil or balance to the power of bureaucracy. Philosophically, capitalists contributed to the "public interest," interpreted as the well-being of society, by virtue of their efficient production of goods and the fact that they operated in an identical manner to the bureaucrats. Capitalistic enterprises were hierarchically organized, exerted discipline over their employees, exercised secrecy (the "company secret"), withheld data from both competitors and public. Capitalism, being bureaucratically organized itself, was the only force that Weber conceived as capable of successfully providing a counterweight to public bureaucracy. Thus man is destined to live under a "condominium" or dual role of both capitalism and bureaucracy; not, as in Marxian thought in the final stage of the dialectic, in some fanciful paradise without any vestiges of capitalism or bureaucracy. As Weber observed, "The idea of eliminating these [public and private] organizations becomes more and more utopian."[5]

5. Weber regarded bureaucracy as impervious to the

influences of the external environment. With the possible exception of having to exercise public authority within a capitalistic framework, the bureaucracy itself was literally not capable of being successfully shaped or attacked from the outside and internal revolution was quite out of the question. For Marx, the role and future of bureaucracy was directly shaped by the global contest between economic classes. In a world environment of destroyed capitalism its hand-maidens of oppression and coercion, the state and its bureaucracy, would disappear.

Figure 6-2 graphically portrays some of the key characteristics of Weber's ideal-construct.

Meanings for Democracy

Overall, Weber's writings on bureaucracy give rise to a profound philosophical pessimism. Philosophies of determinism, whether based on proletarian or bureaucratic-capitalistic inevitability, provide few, if any, alternatives or options for human choice. It is the inability to deflect these overwhelming forces from their predestined courses that makes human will so irrelevant. There is a further penalty in Weber's bureaucratic construct—the bureaucrat is asked, indeed is required, to divest himself of his conscience; in short, he must negate his own will. Emotionless rationalism emerges dominant over moral concern with the consequences of administrative action. That countless human tragedies may ensue as the effect of such a doctrine is the price that man in modern society must pay to avoid chaos. The democratic techniques of referendum, election and representation are of decreasing utility as the bureaucratic phenomenon advances along its path to dominance. As Daniel Bell observes, "For Weber . . . a single ethic and style begins to pervade all society."[6] Implicit is the universalism of conformity, impersonality and rational calculation in order to achieve the ultimate ends of man: efficiency, preciseness and obedience. A diverse world is to find diversity a sin and, instead, the universalism of bureaucratic method becomes a moral virtue.

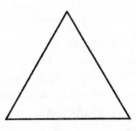

I.

Bureaucratic relationships are hierarchical. The bulk of bureaucrats occupy the lower and middle levels. Ultimate legal authority is vested in a single head at the apex.

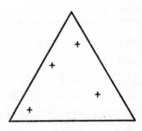

II.

By locating one's "fixed" position in the hierarchy (the "latitude" and "longitude" of a position) the role and authority of the occupant of that position is known. Consequently his behavior and decisions are calculable.

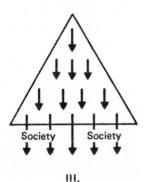

III.

Legal authority (therefore effective authority and power) flows downward through the levels of hierarchy. In the final stage it is exerted outward to be imposed upon society.

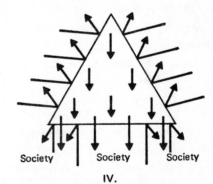

IV.

The bureaucracy is impervious to external attack or internal revolution. Hence power continues to flow downward according to legal directives and out into the society. The bureaucracy affects the environment but the environment does not affect the bureaucracy.

Figure 6-2. CHARACTERISTICS OF WEBER'S IDEAL-CONSTRUCT

Was Max Weber aware of the possibility of a "democratic" system of administration? While he rejected the possibilities for effective administration within a democratic context, he did outline a "pure form" of "immediate democratic administration." In essence, the conditions for democratic administration were applicable only in "small associations resting upon neighborly or personal relationships." Weber observes on this crucial point:

> Democracy becomes alienated from its purity where the group grows beyond a certain size or where the administrative function becomes too difficult to be taken care of by anyone whom rotation, the lot, or election may happen to designate. . . . As soon as mass administration is involved, the meaning of democracy changes . . . .[7]

There is much evidence that Weber was essentially correct. The seemingly inexorable rise of bureaucratic power in all modern states today appears to give credence to this thesis. The late distinguished British political scientist Harold J. Laski, in his article "Bureaucracy" published in the 1930 edition of the *Encyclopedia of the Social Sciences,* wrote as a close observer of the governmental processes within Great Britain— possibly the most democratic of all modern nations. Yet Laski begins with the admonition that:

> Bureaucracy is the term usually applied to a system of government, the control of which is so completely in the hands of officials that their power jeopardizes the liberties of ordinary citizens. The characteristics of such a regime are a passion for routine in administration, the sacrifice of flexibility to rule, delay in the making of decisions and a refusal to embark upon experiment.[8]

He continues:

> The scale of the modern state and the vastness of the services it seeks to render make expert administration inevitable. To control the expert in such conditions is no

enviable task. .... In England, for example, the last thirty years have seen the increasing abandonment by Parliament of any effective control over departmental action. Even judicial control has had to surrender to the need for administrative discretion. .... Where the legislative machinery still attempts interference, as in the United States, the result is fatal to expert and adequate administration . . . .

The result is discretion, secrecy, conservatism, and all these minister to the preservation of power.[9]

As if mirroring Weber's own words, Laski writes:

It should be pointed out that these undesirable characteristics of bureaucracy are not in the least confined to the service of the state; they operate wherever there is large scale organization. Trade unions, churches, institutions for social work, great industrial corporations, all these are compelled by the very size of the interest they represent and by their complexity to take on the same habits of bureaucracy.[10]

This same argument was immeasurably strengthened by the publication of European sociologist Robert Michels' classic volume *Political Parties,* in which he advances the notion of the "iron law of oligarchy." This "iron law" describes the inexorable tendency to bureaucracy in all forms of human organization, no matter how democratically conceived. Both authoritarian political parties and mass democratic parties become increasingly dependent upon a careerist, professionally oriented inner core of bureaucrats.

One might argue that the United States, with its official fragmentation of power and its multiple governmental centers of authority, would be the exceptional case disputing the general rule. However Weber, while recognizing the United States as one of the least regulated and administered of all nations, nevertheless concludes with a rare prescience:

The United States still bears the character of a policy which, at least in the technical sense, is not fully bureaucratized. But the greater the zones of friction with the outside and the more urgent needs for administrative unity at home become, the more this character is inevitably and gradually giving way formally to the bureaucratic structures.[11]

There is little argument that events in the United States do support rather than undercut Weber's forecast. The legacy of the economic depression of the 1930's, two world wars, the Korean "police action," the Vietnam war, the attempts to contain domestic dissent in the United States in the late '60's, and the economic-energy problems of the early to mid-'70's have all given impetus to increasing governmental regulation and ascending bureaucratic power. The newer schools of administrative philosophy do not deny this tendency. The data and evidence are too overwhelming. Instead, they do attempt to modify the nature of bureaucratic behavior and to direct administrative decision-making toward morally compelling, rather than amoral ends. They reject the assumption that the consequences of an administrative action should be of little consequence to the bureaucrat.

WOODROW WILSON AND
THE DEMOCRATIZATION OF BUREAUCRACY

Both Woodrow Wilson and Max Weber bridge the nineteenth and twentieth centuries. They were contemporaries, not only in terms of overlapping life spans, but because of their intersecting interests. Weber remained professor, lecturer and writer to the end of his life. Wilson gained early academic distinction as a political scientist but spent the latter portion of his life assuming the burdens of the highest public offices of state governor and president of the United States.

Wilson and Weber made valuable contributions to administrative philosophy. Yet neither was exclusively or even primarily concerned with public administration *per se*. Rather, their interests were far broader. For Weber, man's social, economic and legal history, as reflected in his widely differing cultures, provided the basic data for much needed sociological analysis. All of man's institutions, familial, social, as well as governmental, were significant and their interrelationships were the focus of his concern. Wilson's interests were considerably more limited to the study of governmental processes, especially in the United States and Great Britain. At the same time, Wilson was also a keen student of European governments, notably those of France and Germany. He was thus able to compare and relate America's unique governmental and political processes with those of the most advanced nations of the West. He sought to evaluate both the strengths and the deficiencies of American government. Wilson regarded administration as the most glaring deficiency in the nation's governmental system.

Wilson's essay, "The Study of Administration" remains one of the most crucial writings in the vast literature of American public administration. It is a "benchmark" to understanding the basic assumptions and values of traditional or classical American public administration. The "newer" approaches to administration gain added significance to the degree that they are compared to Wilson's bureaucratic model.

The Need for Reform

Originally given as a speech, Wilson's paper on administration was later published in the *Political Science Quarterly* in 1887.[12] The essay appeared at a critical juncture in American governmental history. A number of state governments had already entered the regulatory field in order to curb abuses by banking corporations and railroads. In 1886 the first federal regulatory commission, the Interstate Commerce Commission, was established to regulate activities of commerce beyond state jurisdiction. The trend toward regulation was recognition of the society's transition from an agriculture-pastoral society to increasing industrialization and technology. More and more the "laissez faire" philosophy of the classical economists was giving way to application of the "police power"—the authority of American governments at all levels to regulate the private use of property in order to protect the overriding "health, morals, welfare, and safety of society." The belief in a higher "public good" that outweighed the traditional freedom to use one's property as one desired implied an increasing dependence of citizen upon citizen. This dependence was paralleled by an increasing dependence of each citizen upon his government, for only public agencies could regulate in the name of a community-wide or society-wide "public interest." The growth of "scientific management" in industrial production and the application of science and research in agriculture, as only two examples of the increasing technological orientation of the society, would, Wilson realized, require competence, specialization and proper training within the agencies of government. A scientific-technologically based nation could neither be served nor regulated by a government lacking knowledge, functional skills and respect.

The westward population movement beyond the Mississippi by wagon and rail also required increasing competence at the local level as new mountain, prairie and coastal communities required pure water, straight streets, properly engineered electrical works and sewage disposal facilities. Wilson, as he examined the governmental systems overseas, was particularly impressed by the emergence of highly respected, trained and career-oriented civil services which contrasted with the dominance of "political hacks" in American public agencies at all levels. The emerging American republic required administrative skills and knowledge and would only be ill-served by continued reliance upon the "by guess and by golly" approach to administrative services. Although the Civil Service Act had been passed by Congress several years earlier in 1883, Wilson was aware that this legislation was only the opening salvo in a long and uphill battle with the entrenched systems of patronage and political allegiance that held sway for a full half century.

Wilson was philosophically as one with the civil service reform movement and savored its initial victories. The problem as he viewed it, however, was that the establishment of a trained career public service required more than a single victory and a single piece of legislation. It required nothing less than a shift in the value priorities of the American people. In the past, Wilson wrote, political philosophy had centered attention upon issues of diminishing significance such as "the nature of the state, the essence and seat of sovereignty, popular power and kingly prerogative." According to Wilson:

The central field of controversy was that great field of theory in which monarchy rode tilt against democracy, in which oligarchy would have built for itself strongholds of privilege, and in which tyranny sought opportunity to make good its claim to receive submission from all competitors. Amidst this high warfare of principles, administration could command no pause for its own consideration. The question was always: Who shall make law, and what shall the law be? The other question, how law should be administered with enlightenment, with equity, with speed, and without friction, was put aside as "practical detail" which clerks could arrange after doctors had agreed upon principles.[13]

A Science of Administration

Wilson's essay was published exactly one hundred years after the drafting of the American Constitution. The Civil War had been fought and won a generation before. For Wilson, the great questions of "who rules" and "what should the laws be" were already well settled in the nation. The constitution had endured despite all the travails of the infant nation. The country was on the threshold of industrialization, expansion from sea to sea, and was destined to take its place among the ranks of the great powers of the world. The time was now at hand to shift priorities from issues of political philosophy and constitutional "tinkering" to questions of administration. As Wilson observed, "It is getting harder to *run* a constitution than to frame one."

The proper "running" of the Constitution could be best accomplished, in Wilson's views, by the development of a "science of administration." Wilson's use of the term "science of administration" at several points in his essay reflected his belief that administration was a distinctive field of knowledge characterized by many of the attributes of scientific investigation. Wilson felt that a scientific-systematic approach to public service would assure impartiality in the administration of public policy. Based upon "stable principle" and removed from the strife of politics it was worthy of academic study in America's colleges and universities. A "science of administration" also implied quantification—of fundamental importance to a public service dedicated to "utmost possible efficiency." To Wilson "efficiency" was understood as "the least possible cost either of money or of energy." Yet, in the development of such a science Wilson lamented that his own countrymen had been sadly negligent.

> Where has this science grown up? Surely not on this side of the sea ... No; American writers have hitherto taken no very important part in the advancement of this science. It has found its doctors in Europe. It is not of our making; it is a foreign science, speaking only foreign tongues. . . . It has been developed by French and German professors . . . .[14]

Clearly an admirer of the efficiency and professionalism of European civil services, Wilson also recognized that they served governments whose values were alien to the American system. He, therefore, advocated a selective incorporation of the principles of European administrative science into the unique environment of the United States.

> It [the European science of administration] is consequently in all parts adapted to the needs of a compact state, and made to fit highly centralized forms of government; whereas, to answer our purposes it must be adapted, not to a simple and compact, but to a complex and highly multi-formed state, and made to fit highly decentralized forms of government. If we would employ it, we must Americanize it ... in thought, principle and aim ... it must learn our constitutions by heart; must get the bureaucratic fever out of its veins; must inhale much American free air. . . .
>
> We can scrutinize the anatomy of foreign governments without fear of getting any of their diseases into our veins; dissect alien systems without apprehension of blood poisoning.[15]

This is the central thesis of Wilson's essay—and, in long-range perspective, its most important. Democracy as well as absolutism can be served only by efficient public services whose members are properly trained, competent and impartial in executing the laws. Americans, according to Wilson, need not give up their birthright in the movement to reform and upgrade their public service. Nevertheless, in Wilson's view, democracy is immeasurably strengthened to the degree it is able to take advantage of tested practices and conclusive experiences elsewhere. Still, advance may not be spectacular due to the fact that in the United States, unlike other systems, "the sovereign's mind has no definite locality, but is contained in a voting majority of several million heads."[16] Wilson notes:

> Wherever regard for public opinion is the first principle of government, practical reform must be slow and all reform must be full of compromises. For wherever public opinion exists it must rule.[17]

Public opinion, while ultimate master, still had best not interfere in the internalities of administration. Thus, for Wilson:

> The problem is to make public opinion efficient without suffering it to be meddlesome. Directly exercised, in the oversight of daily details and in the choice of the daily means of government, public criticism is, of course, a clumsy nuisance, a rustic handling of delicate machinery. But as superintending the greater forces of formative policy alike in politics and administration, public criticism is altogether safe and beneficent, altogether indispensable.[18]

What role then for the career bureaucrat?

> The administrator should and does have a will of his own in the choice of means for accomplishing his work: He is not and ought not to be a mere passive instrument. The distinction is between general plans and special means. . . . The cook must be trusted with a large discretion to the management of the fires and the ovens.[19]

Wilson was aware of the advances of scientific management in the American business sector where impartial quantitative investigation and experimentation had greatly increased worker efficiency and productivity. His goal was to make the public service "business like" and more systematic. Its methodology was to be that of business where, in Wilson's view, ultimate managerial truth had already been discovered and needed only to be transferred to the public sector.

> The field of administration is a field of business. It is removed from the hurry and strife of politics . . . even from the debatable ground of constitutional study. It is part of political life only as the methods of the counting-house are part of the life of society. Only as machinery is part of the manufactured product . . . .
>
> The object of administrative study is to rescue executive methods from the confusion and costliness of empirical experiment and set them upon foundations laid deep in stable principle.
>
> . . . We must go on to adjust executive functions more fitly and to prescribe better methods of executive organization and action.[20]

Here Wilson, in his search for stable principles of administration, foresaw the importance of organization and management ("O and M") studies and techniques. He laid the groundwork for a static approach to American public administration—an approach that dominated the field for three-quarters of a century through the mid-1960's.

The proper preparation of civil servants was, for Wilson, to be based upon proper training in the nation's institutions of higher education. The core of such training would be the study and application of already self-evident truths of administrative principle and technique. It is essential to note that proficiency and technique were, for Wilson, the *sine qua non* for qualification to entry into the career civil service. A technically proficient, rather than a philosophically value-oriented, civil service would best serve the interests of the United States. According to Wilson:

> It will be necessary to organize democracy by sending up to the competitive examinations for civil service men

definitely prepared for standing liberal tests as to technical knowledge. A technically schooled civil service will presently become indispensable.[21]

Wilson believed that all modern governments reflected a commonality irrespective of their peculiar forms of government. "Monarchies and democracies, radically different as they are in other respects, have in reality much the same business to look to."[22] Still, Wilson insisted that the bureaucrat in a democratic society differed fundamentally from his counterparts in other systems. In perhaps the best definition of bureaucracy within a democratic society Wilson summarized:

> The ideal for us is a civil service cultured and self-sufficient enough to act with sense and vigor, and yet so intimately connected with the popular thought, by means of election and constant public counsel, as to find arbitrariness or class spirit quite out of the question.[23]

Wilson's essay is a clarion call for the blending of the Germanic administrative tradition with American scientific management and the value framework of American democracy. Wilson had little use for administrative theory or philosophy favoring American "how-to-do-it."[24] Nevertheless, perhaps unwittingly, his greatest contribution was to administrative philosophy, i.e., the belief that bureaucratic power was a limited power, albeit efficient and technically proficient. Further, bureaucratic power was limited by values reflected through a diffused external sovereign to which the bureaucracy was subordinate, namely, the "many masters"—public opinion as exemplified in its elective representatives. Wilson noted that public opinion should be both informed and educated by those most knowledgeable in the techniques of public administration. Still this marked the very outer limits of allowable bureaucratic discretion. "Good behavior" was to be the fundamental condition for a continued career in the public service. Wilson defined such behavior as:

> Steady, hearty allegiance to the policy of the government they serve. . . . It will not be the creation of permanent

officials but of statesmen whose responsibility to public opinion will be direct and inevitable.[25]

Wilson and Weber Compared

Although later commentators and administrative scholars would fault portions of Wilson's essay in light of much later developments in the American governmental system, it remains still an amazingly accurate projection of the future direction of the American civil service. If one could juxtapose Wilson's and Weber's bureaucratic models, there would be much more similarity and congruence than dissimilarities.

The similarities may be identified as:

1. Belief in the rationality of man.
2. Man can learn and be trained in administrative principles and techniques.
3. The principles and techniques themselves are static and, therefore, applicable to all situations and exigencies.
4. There are administrative processes and techniques that are common to all modern governments.
5. The tasks of administration are nonpartisan, detailed, systematic and businesslike.
6. Administration is a field of knowledge worthy of study in colleges and universities.
7. Administration is separate from politics and broad policy-making. Policy (politicians) set(s) the task of administration.
8. The best administration of policy is that which is speedy, frictionless, impartially administered and efficient (least cost in effort and energy).
9. There is little creativity in administration.
10. Administration is a career.
11. Administrators bear no responsibility for the consequences of policy executed.
12. Administration may best be described as a "science."
13. Administration will become increasingly important to the well-being of society.

14. Administrative study should include data and experiences from other governmental systems and cultures.
15. Administrative study should focus upon the internalities of organization rather than upon externalities.
16. Administrative authority is based upon legal authority.
17. The behavior of bureaucrats is calculable (neither Wilson nor Weber had developed any notion of informal organization).

Despite their many similarities of viewpoints, Wilson and Weber do disagree upon certain important propositions. These may be identified as:

1. The ultimate dominance of bureaucratic power. For Weber, society was inexorably and ultimately subjected to it; for Wilson, public opinion in a democratic society is "master"—not merely tolerated but enthroned.
2. The issue of sovereignty: Weber believed the state *per se* is sovereign while Wilson believed the people to be sovereign.
3. The issue of secrecy. Weber emphasized bureaucratic secrecy, while for Wilson administration must be characterized by openness.
4. The role of compromise in the shaping of public policy. Subjecting administrative policy to compromise is foreign to Weber's model, while for Wilson all administrative reforms and policies have to be based upon compromise.
5. The role of environment. Weber's model does not take environment into account. For Wilson the unique constitutional and fragmented nature of American government would shape a distinctive American administrative system.
6. The unassailability of bureaucracy. For Weber the bureaucracy is virtually immune from any type of attack from the outside and not subject to revolution from the inside. For Wilson the machinery of demo-

cratic government when functioning properly will be sufficient to restrict or reduce administrative power where conditions warrant.

7. Pessimism versus optimism. Weber's model reflects the belief that democratic processes designed to serve mass societies will prove ineffective in attempting to limit bureaucratic power. Wilson's model of bureaucracy reflects a deep belief in the possibilities of developing a vigorous yet responsible administrative system operational within the value constructs of democratic society.

The timing of Wilson's essay on administration was crucial to its later influence. His model of the ideal American civil service reflected growing popular sentiment for a competent civil service. His insistence upon the application of scientific method—highly rational, based upon quantification and stable principle, was reiteration of the idea of unlimited human progress if society would only embrace scientism without reservation.

The limiting of administrative, discretion to choice of means—excluding the "ends" of policy from such discretion—seemed to answer American democracy's need for continued faith in the effectiveness of responsible, popularly elected representatives. Dr. Wilson had accurately diagnosed the governmental ills of a nation in the throes of fundamental transition. His administrative prescriptions suggested remedies derived from practical experiments and experiences abroad and at home; they were commonsensical and devoid of involved theoretical analyses. His essay marked the beginning of the "self-consciousness" of public administration both as an indispensable ingredient to the proper functioning of American government and as a subject worthy of our best student and academic minds. No single figure has since dominated the field to an equal degree. Woodrow Wilson, with considerable justification, may be regarded as the founding father of American public administration.

NOTES

1. Max Rheinstein, "Introduction," in *Max Weber on Law in Economy and Society,* edited and annotated by Max Rheinstein, New York: Simon and Schuster/Clarion Books, 1954, pp. xxix-xxx.

2. The complete essay is found in H. H. Gerth and C. Wright Mills, translators and editors, *From Max Weber: Essays in Sociology,* New York: Oxford University Press, 1958, pp. 77-128. Also Max Weber, *Politics as a Vocation,* Philadelphia: Fortress Press, 1965.

3. Max Weber, *Politics as a Vocation,* Philadelphia: Fortress Press, 1965, p. 20.

4. *Ibid.,* p. 43.

5. *Ibid.,* p. 54.

6. Daniel Bell. *The Coming of Post-Industrial Society: A Venture in Social Forecasting,* New York: Basic Books, 1973, p. 75.

7. *Max Weber on Law in Economy and Society,* p. 334.

8. *Encyclopedia of the Social Sciences,* New York: Macmillan, 1930, Vol. 3, p. 70.

9. *Ibid.,* p. 72.

10. *Loc. cit.*

11. As quoted in Bell, *op. cit.,* p. 8.

12. Vol. 2 (June 1887), pp. 197-222. Wilson's essay was reprinted in the *Political Science Quarterly,* Vol. LVI, No. 4 (December 1941), pp. 481-506. The essay was reprinted separately by the Public Affairs Press in 1955.

13. "The Study of Administration," *Political Science Quarterly* (1941 reprint), pp. 482-483.

14. *Ibid.,* p. 485-486.

15. *Ibid.,* p. 486, p. 504.

16. *Ibid.,* p. 492.

17. *Loc. cit.*

18. *Ibid.,* p. 499.

19. *Ibid.,* pp. 496-497, p. 498.

20. *Ibid.,* pp. 493-494.

21. *Ibid.,* p. 500.

22. *Ibid.,* p. 502.

23. *Ibid.,* p. 501.

24. For an excellent background to Wilson's essay see Richard J. Stillman II, "Woodrow Wilson and the Study of Administration: A New Look at an Old Essay," *The American Political Science Review,* Vol. 67, No. 2 (June, 1973), pp. 582-588.

25. "The Study of Administration" (1941 reprint), p. 500.

7

PHILOSOPHICAL PERSPECTIVES: FROM SCIENTIFIC MANAGEMENT TO THE "INEFFICIENT SOCIETY"

SCIENTIFIC MANAGEMENT

American public administration emerged as an amalgam of Wilson's model of bureaucracy and private industry's scientific management. The fusion of the two dominated from the 1920's through the 1950's and early 1960's. Emphasis upon methods or technique rather than upon the value implications of the consequences of administrative policy was the most significant characteristic of this "age of management." A mechanistic view of the administrative process resulted—with focus upon the "proper running" of the machine rather than concern with its direction. Agency practice and classroom lectures minimized bureaucratic creativity. Experimental data and careful observation of working processes had resulted, it was believed, in the discovery of basic principles whose stability or "truth" led logically to their application. The "one best way" was to establish or correct, as the case might require, agency organization in light of these principles. Man's important discoveries of natural laws in the physical sciences were now paralleled by equally significant "natural laws" based largely upon the assumptions and methods of scientific management for the organization of the governments of modern man.

As the "best organization" would result in increased productivity in relation to resources committed (efficiency), the achievement of the better life was inevitable. Stopwatches, slide rules, graphs, charts and statistical analyses were highly visual appurtenances of this approach.

Each employee was regarded as a "unit"—quantifiable, predictable, rational, and each "unit" was viewed as identical to all the others. The individual's role was therefore dependent upon his location in the organization and the formal legal authority attached to that specific position. The whole approach exuded a heavy Platonic foundation. "Justice" was interpreted, in the Platonic manner, as the welfare of society being totally dependent upon each individual finding his proper niche as determined by his abilities. Once accomplished on an organization-wide scale, "automatic administration" resulted; that is, the organization was set upon its proper course to achieve its predetermined objective. Little wonder that personnel management developed at a rate far beyond that of other managerial functions.

In order to assure the proper Platonic symbiosis of the candidate for public service and the vacant position, an imposing array of personnel techniques was developed. These included the perfecting of examination procedures and statistical methods appropriate to mass examination and tests of competency. "Position classification" emerged as the key to the proper merging of the man and the position. The identification of positions and the relationships between the positions themselves gave added impetus to the construction of highly complex organizational charts which supposedly mirrored the real and effective interrelationships of the administrative process. These charts also proved useful in the proper allocating of technological equipment and processes to the appropriate administrative units. The focus of management was internal, that is, internal within the organization, which was assumed to be a self-contained entity subject to a range of controls emanating from the Constitution, the Congress and the courts. However, it was recognized that these were to be only infrequently brought into play.

The administrator's role was to ensure the efficiency of agency operations and to coordinate the specialists within the organization. This was to be done in a harmonious manner so that each was orchestrated into a symphony whose score had been written in popular elections and the committees of Congress. The period is therefore characterized by the rise of nonspecialist "managers" responsible for the coordinative function and whose occupational status was becoming increasingly "professionalized." Public management had come "of age" and the managers took their places in the public service alongside other professionals such as physicians, veterinarians, engineers, accountants, nurses and social workers.

The questions around which managerial responsibility centered focused upon the internalities of both large and small organizational structures. The central questions were:

1. How should activities be divided into groups for purposes of administration?
2. What organizational relationships between individuals with differing responsibilities should be formally established?
3. How may authority and duties be delegated from one position to another?
4. What organizational forms would best link separate agencies required to carry out common goals?
5. What relationships should exist between central headquarters and field offices?

Organization was viewed as a technical problem. Consequently, associations of employees originally centered upon technical specialization: a few examples are the establishment of the American Water Works Association in 1871; the American Public Health Association in 1872; the American Association of State Highway Officials in 1914; the American City Manager's Association in that same year; the American Institute of Planners in 1917; the National Association of State Budget Officers in 1945; and the National Association of State Purchasing Officials in 1947. Specialist was linked to specialist through these and close to 100 other professional and technical public service organizations. In many cases membership cut across political jurisdictional lines as municipal specialists met with county specialists; state specialists with national specialists;

national specialists with state, county and municipal specialists.

These professional interrelationships, going far beyond the traditional notions of political jurisdictions, had tremendous consequences for American federalism. Common administrative experiences were shared irrespective of jurisdictional affiliation, and the rigidities of political boundary lines were eased by a newfound sense of administrative camaraderie and "oneness." In addition, these myriad public service organizations tended to confirm the age of specialization, and few challenged the assumption that the proper role of management was to refine methodology in the search for the "one best way" to carry out work assignments.

On the private side, counterpart associations proliferated. The American Society for Mechanical Engineers, the Society for the Advancement of Management, the American Management Association and a host of others were dedicated to the same ends. The methods—the "how to's"—were refined and honed. The "efficiency engineer" and the "administrative analyst" were the men of the hour and of the age in large and intricate administrative structures. Physical layout surveys, resource-allocation studies, product quality control, cost control, fiscal audit, work simplification through "flow-process" charting and forms (paperwork) management were the stuff of which administration was made. Little reason to doubt that as long as the earth revolved around the sun, the work of administration would remain basically the same.

It would have been surprising to find many "scientific managers" who thought of themselves as philosophers. Indeed, the opposite was true; scientific managers regarded themselves as part of a "hard-nosed" fraternity of objective realists. Yet, despite this attitude and despite the uncreative role of the bureaucrat within his structured administrative confines, scientific management did reflect a philosophy. Though not concerned with the value implications of agency goals and the broad external controversies swirling around the content of the "public interest," the managers of bureaucracies did what philosophers do. They forwarded an abstraction—the "ideal" pattern of management—and allotted to it positive values.

Scientific management was homocentric—man centered—insofar as its essential attributes were human rationality and the ability to measure. In short, rational quantitative analysis was the required condition to bring about salvation of modern man. The "goodness" or "badness" of a particular organizational pattern was a mathematical relationship of "inputs" to "outputs." Where the latter was maximized and the former minimized, a moral "good" resulted. Where the situation was reversed, a moral "bad" resulted. Virtue or "goodness" was therefore equated with the relationship of these two factors, that is, "efficiency" or "inefficiency." Mathematics was transformed into ethics. As "good" and "bad" were now subject to measurement, a true "moral calculus" emerged to guide the destiny of modern man. Scientific management had found the "Rosetta Stone" to its happiness.

Even as scientific management thrived and emerged as an international movement with serious philosophical overtones, its pretensions were being eroded by developments in the field of psychiatry. Central to the value framework of the Weberian-Wilsonian-Scientific Management models of bureaucracy was the unchallenged assumption that man was rational. Once the "ideal" organization—the "one best way"—had been set before them, the members would react predictably within specifically designated guidelines set by that form of organization. The members were therefore uncreative in varying degrees—ranging from the required "harnessing" and "dehumanization" of Weber's bureaucrat to the quite limited creativity of Wilson's bureaucrat. They were allowed discretion only in the choice of means. Bureaucracy was incapable of being shaped from within. Certain attributes followed logically: the bureaucracy was staffed by persons of predictable behavior acting without emotion and devoid of moral dilemmas. Their actions and reactions were shaped by organizational needs; the needs of the latter determined the behavior of the former. Rationality was the crucial element linking organizational requirements and bureaucratic responses.

However, if man by nature was not rational or rational only in varying degree, then his "predictability" had to be suspect. If his "predictability" was suspect, then *all* the elements shaping

217

organization have not been accounted for. Man's irrationality would be the missing factor in the design of the ideal organization. To the extent that this missing factor remained unaccounted for, the notions of "ideal organization" or the "one best way" were, in fact, unrealized.

SIGMUND FREUD: THE "INTERNAL MAN"

The work of psychiatrist Sigmund Freud marked a turning point in man's understanding of man. In his research into human personality, Freud laid bare the dynamics of those subconscious internal forces that determined human behavior patterns and values. Through the technique of "free association"—the talking out of what a patient feels and thinks at a particular moment—and the study of dreams, Freud discovered certain critical linkages between an individual's subconscious processes and his behavior.

Freudian psychology emphasized that man's behavior was the product of the interplay of unconscious forces with the external world. The dynamics of this highly complex process take place in man's subconscious. This emphasized, for Freud, the basic irrationality of man and, consequently, of society. Man, far from being a predictable rational individual, was in truth, ignorant of the roots of his own behavior. All men are virtually at war internally with themselves. Each individual's behavior is shaped by the interplay of three basically conflicting forces—the "id," the "ego" and the "superego." The "id" seeks to maximize pleasure and minimize tension and pain and has no moral or ethical implication. The "superego," or the moral component of man's subconscious conflicts, seeks to regulate or control the "id" and does so according to the ideals of the society which have been transmitted to the individual through the socialization process. The "superego" acts as a brake on the otherwise unrestrained "id" which, if not so restrained, would produce lawlessness and social upheaval, even chaos. The third force, the "ego," reflects "reality" and, according to the manner in which it perceives the external world, seeks to balance in a harmonious way the relationship between the "id" and the "superego."

Human personality, for Freud, in specific instances is the culmination of the blending of interactions of id, superego and ego. There are infinite permutations and relationships among the three subconscious forces during the course of a lifetime. Each individual's subconscious is the arena for this ceaseless interplay.[1] Not only is man ignorant of his own personality dynamics, but only skillful probing through intensive psychoanalysis will lay bare the roots of his behavior and values.

The broader implications of Freud's findings are apparent. If rationality assumes knowledge, then man is not rational since he cannot, except in a few rare instances with great insight and professional psychiatric skills, know himself. Man is not viewed as acting on a reasoned and logical basis, rather he is, in Freudian terms, the unwitting product of his emotions. Further, the values a man professes are no more determined by rational or logical thought processes than is his behavior. Consequently, external man can only be understood through insight into man internally—the "true man."

HAROLD LASSWELL: THE "INTERNAL BUREAUCRAT"

The direct application of Freudian psychology to public administration occurred in 1930 with the publication of Harold Lasswell's *Psychopathology and Politics*.[2] Though Lasswell's work was widely read at the time, its full impact was not apparent until several decades later. Lasswell's study was a direct frontal assault upon the value underpinnings of the Weberian-Wilsonian-Scientific Management school of thought. Lasswell's primary objective was to understand the personality traits of "politicians" (persons in political authority) and to categorize the different types. He was aware that "normal" persons were those whose internal behavior dynamics had enabled them to relate effectively to their environments. Others, who were mentally ill (either permanently, cyclically or occasionally), had behavior patterns affected by imbalances, rather than harmonious interplay, between the internalized psychological forces identified by Freud. Through the study of psychiatric case histories and life histories of those ill persons who were exercising or had exercised public authority, Lasswell hoped to be able to identify those "critical experiences" that had shaped their later attitudes and behavior while occupying public positions.

Lasswell was highly critical of what he termed the "institutional mechanics" approach of political science. This approach had ignored what he regarded as central to a realistic understanding of political processes, namely, personality-behavioral traits of individuals. For Lasswell, the actual "outpourings of the human mind" through free association and the interpretation of dreams would provide the observer with a "window on society." Those who exercised public authority would give unrestrained accounts of themselves—a source of data that political science had overlooked. Consequently, the conflicts between "social self" and the "unaware self" would produce unconventional data of primary importance. For Lasswell, scientific management and the Weberian-Wilsonian assumptions of predictable behavior within organizations were unscientific, despite pretensions to the contrary.

A truly scientific political science had to be based upon information that was not visual but hidden in the human psyche. For Lasswell, a truly scientific approach could not therefore be logical or rational because behavior was frequently not logically or rationally induced. He attacked previous beliefs that men could be trained to use their minds wisely through disciplined intellectual exercises designed to help them become logical, detached and unprejudiced in outlook and behavior. Lasswell viewed logic as a mental process bereft of human impulse. Like Freud, he decried the orthodox faith placed in logical thinking as not reflective of reality. To the contrary, free fantasy and dream interpretation would be the crucial means by which man's mind would be unfettered from its "logical binders." In short, no science of politics could be based upon approaches that denied the significance of the self; "directed thinking" had to be replaced by "self-understanding."

Academic programs aiming at the development of future men of authority had to center around the significance of "self-knowledge," whereas traditionally they had been trained in "self-deception." In short, a study of politics would have to shift from the study of institutions external to man to the study of man "within." Only one chapter in Lasswell's book deals specifically with "political administrators"; yet, it does provide a turning point in understanding bureaucratic processes.

Where obedience to legal authority and "dehumanization" had characterized the bureaucrat previously, Lasswell raised a number of questions the implications of which were truly revolutionary. What personality types are drawn into bureaucracies? What are the crucial elements in determining whether a bureaucrat will neglect details for general policy or have a passion for details, accuracy and a delight in routine? Which bureaucrats will gain influence over subordinates? What are the relationships between legal authority of position and authority of personality? What are the bases of prejudices, preferences and creeds? How do bureaucrats react in crisis-stress situations? What are the real patterns of power in "hierarchical" organizations? Do we have the best information necessary to perpetuate democracy and prevent authoritarian movements?

Laswell, in the delineation of these previously unasked questions, implied a number of radical propositions: Appearances are deceiving. The bureaucrat may exercise power on the basis of an internal "hidden agenda." Formal patterns of organization as described by organization charts are unrealistic as human dispositions may be unpredictable. Further, the "setting" of an organization is not determined by preconceived logical-rational design but by the reactions of differing personality types to each other and to the overall "social setting."

Bureaucratic man is merely one type of political actor. He must be studied alongside other political types because administration is a *part* of politics—not separable from it. Lasswell's work also implied that public administration is not necessarily visual. Consequently, a study of public administration should center on the processes of the individual mind. "Nonrational" data are requisite for an accurate understanding of administrative processes.

Each individual in a public organization is not to be counted as a unit as each may vary in his degree of rationality. Each does not exert the same degree of rationality. Each does not exert the same degree of influence nor does each play an equal role in the complex process of decision-making.

221

"Informal" organization may be more significant than formal organization. Also, the bureaucratic processes cannot be described through legal authority and directives since these take into account only external behavior and not internal dynamics of the human mind.

Lasswell's work further implied a theory of values far removed from the traditional emphasis upon input-output efficiency as the value goal of administration. Bureaucrats view agency goals through "psychological spectacles," and their administrative decisions in relation to these goals would reflect the outcome of contending internal forces based upon conscious or unconscious perceptions of the "self." For example, one's self-perceptions could be "pro-self" or "anti-self" or "pro-others" or "anti-others." In addition, man's morality is a consequence of the degree of socialization impressed upon him by history and his culture as well as the interchange of the id, ego and superego. Therefore, the highest values of man may not be quantifiable nor related to the most "efficient" productivity. The potential, if not real, conflict in values between "man the individual" and "man the bureaucrat" was a theme destined to become of primary importance in later developments in administrative philosophy.

THE HAWTHORNE EXPERIMENT

In 1927 the Western Electric Company at its Hawthorne plant began a series of far-reaching experiments. Company officials were aware that their policies with respect to machines and materials were based upon experiment and knowledge, but that their human policies were based only upon executive perceptions and traditional practice. The objective was to assess human behavior under differing working conditions. Data from the Hawthorne studies, derived over a period of several years, revealed a number of significant conclusions.

It was the organization of human relations, rather than organization on a technical basis, that increased work production. On the other hand, a spontaneous social organization or group could adversely affect production not on the basis of careful consideration or logical processes but by "just happening"; hence, informal organization of workers' groups could defeat official plans.

Insofar as output was found to be a form of social behavior, the logic of technical organization was undercut and had failed. Therefore, organizations must take into account "nonlogical social routines." In sum, any group of people working together will sooner or later develop a social system apart from that based on technical authority and rationalization. The electrifying message conveyed to the world of management was that organization could be spontaneous and unplanned.[3]

In 1938 Chester Barnard, in his *Functions of the Executive*, advanced the thesis that informal organizations were not only significant but that formal and informal organizations were both dependent upon each other—and each gave rise to the other.[4] What had taken place were a number of successive shifts in administrative thought: from (a) early recognition of formal structure only to (b) recognition of the existence of nonformal forces shaping organizations to (c) the later hypothesis that informal organizations were of equal importance to the formal. In the early 1970's a "new" public administration school of thought would arrive at a fourth stage. That stage would be marked by the conclusion that, far from being equal, the human aspects of administration were of overwhelming preeminence and that, in fact, formal organization had to be derived from the human—not the technical—setting.

By the eve of World War II, the underpinnings of administrative orthodoxy derived from the value assumptions of Weber, Wilson and Scientific Management had been challenged intellectually by the use of new types of data. Intellectual challenge is, however, not necessarily effective challenge. Academic students of the administrative process as well as practitioners had been trained either in public law (analyzing judicial decisions and legal principles in order to gain insight into the administrative processes) or in the methodology of scientific management. Upon America's entry into the conflict, professor and administrative practitioner alike left their accustomed routines to enter military service or service in expanded governmental agencies of a new or peculiarly war-emergency nature. A large number of temporary agencies were established by government to circumvent the sluggishness of existing organizations. Governments at all levels entered into the planning and execution of nonfamiliar functions and activities at home and abroad.

In this highly fluid milieu the constraints and values of administrative orthodoxy simply gave way to the exigencies of improvisation and the new spirit to "try the untried." The intellectual attack on traditional administrative approaches was now reinforced by a more effective attack—that of trial-and-error. The results often served to break down confidence in the immutability and validity of that which had long been assumed.

With the advent of peace scholars and practitioners went back to more familiar routines as the nation's life returned to normal. However, the seeds of discontent with administrative philosophical thought were planted, and public administration was destined to face a future of marked ideological unease.

HERBERT SIMON: "NONRATIONAL" DECISION MAKING

Building upon a Lasswellian base, political scientist Herbert Simon in his *Administrative Behavior*[5] (1948) advanced the philosophical revolution in public administration during the immediate postwar years. For Simon decision making is the heart of administration. Since decision making is a process within the mind, he focuses upon those factors which have a direct or indirect impact upon the mental choice of alternative actions rather than upon "doing." In a radical departure from orthodoxy, Simon forwards the belief that decision making by rank-and-file workers in an organization is of no less importance than decision making at the managerial levels. Simon observes that the operative employee will determine the success or failure of the organization despite the fact that the managerial levels had previously been regarded as the most important; consequently, decision making is a group activity and not the exclusive preserve of any particular level in the hierarchy. In effect, Simon reverses the traditional notion of hierarchy, that is, if the "higher levels" are those with the most influence, then the rank-and-file workers should be at the levels formerly occupied by managers who themselves are placed at the bottom (Figure 7-1).

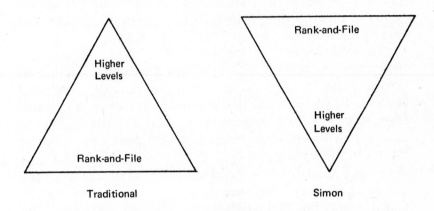

Figure 7-1   DECISION-MAKING IN ORGANIZATIONS

Simon notes also that authority and influence can operate in any direction, not exclusively downward. Later movements toward "participative management" find an early apologist in Simon.

No man in the organization is wholly rational. Instead man may react by unconscious reflex, and complete and absolute knowledge of all the data in a given situation is seldom available. The usefulness of facts is limited because of their inaccessibility and because they have been shaped by those in the earlier stages of the decision making process. In addition, one cannot know all possible alternative courses of action nor all possible consequences of different paths to action. Further, past decisions will frequently limit available alternative courses, and the organizational environment, including the informal relationships, provides a framework of "givens." Consequently, man cannot hope to be rational to any degree if this implies complete and attainable knowledge free of the distortion of all possible alternatives and their consequences. Simon concludes, therefore, that "real behavior" is based upon compromise and cannot be "ideal."

In such an approach, decision making, in part, must be based on faith, and Simon introduces the unprecedented notion that

225

man's imagination must be a part of the decision making process. Hence, the bureaucrat is not a neutral compliant individual but rather one whose own personal values enter into his decisions to a greater or lesser degree. There is much here that reflects the "creative expert." Any "science" of administration must therefore be based upon an analysis of human behavior.

The philosophical contributions of his volume follow from these views. As decision making is a selecting among alternatives ("what ought?"), each decision does have an ethical or value content. However, from the beginning, due to man's limited rationality, the value-judgement of each decision cannot be described as "correct" or "incorrect," but merely as "good" or "bad." In short, decisions can only be evaluated in a situational sense, that is, relative to such criteria as the organization's goals, community values, subjective human values, the information available and the time available for reaching a decision. This concept of an administrative "ethics of relativism" looms large in ideological developments in the late 1960's and early 1970's.

NORTON LONG: THE PHILOSOPHY OF ADMINISTRATIVE SURVIVAL

Another distinctive development in the postwar intellectual ferment was the publication of Norton Long's essay "Power and Administration" in a 1949 issue of *Public Administration Review*.[6] He rejected the Weberian-Wilsonian enthronement of legal power as the essential ingredient in administration. Long, a political scientist who had served in temporary war-time agencies, denied that executive orders, statutes, judicial decisions or other instruments of legal authority reflected the reality of administration. Power, the life blood of administration, can never, he noted, be delegated or bestowed. To the contrary, power must be earned.

Critical of traditional notions of the administrative process emphasizing techniques for making organizations more efficient and frictionless, Long introduced the need to develop theories and techniques of gaining, holding and expanding power. Like Simon, Long rejected the idea that power merely flowed from the apex of the hierarchy downward or that it could be gained exclusively from superiors. To the contrary, due to weaknesses inherent in the presidency as a source of vigorous administrative leadership, together with undisciplined and weak political parties and a fragmented legislative branch, the executive agencies were left largely to fend for themselves in order to supplement resources coming down from the chain-of-command.

Long introduced a new type of administrative rationality. He forwarded a Machiavellian calculability that measured agency success against the criterion of "survival" rather than upon efficiency or economy. Failing to obtain, maintain and expand its extrahierarchical sources of power, the agency will eventually wither and atrophy regardless of its legal bases. Necessary for the acquisition of such power is the establishment of agency links with external interest and pressure groups. Previous theories had not viewed administrative agencies as consciously representative of external interests in a manner similar to that of legislatures. For Long, such agencies would even rival Congress as a major channel for representation of external interest groups.

The influence and strength of the interest groups are requisite resources for the agencies if they are to increase their political support in the halls of Congress and with the chief executive. Each agency must secure the maximum of "customer acceptance" as a necessary precondition for survival, as well as develop and carry out a program for fostering objectives that will attract the support of external groups. The power of these external groups will then be transmitted into the agency and flow *upward* to enhance the limited resources of both agency and president.

Long's hierarchy differs from Weber's in several critical respects. Power flows not only downward within the organization but also *into* the organization from external sources and then *upward*. Also, formal or legal power may not reflect effective power. In Long's model bureaucrats do not merely react to directives, they must also be creative, that is, calculate and carry out strategies to gain alliances with external groups. Consequently, the role of bureaucracy is not exclusively "to

227

execute" but to become representative of external interests.

A bureaucracy is not placid or frictionless; instead it is internally competitive as each agency seeks to maximize its "power budget." Agency survival is precarious rather than assured; with little inherent permanence, it must fight for survival.

The chain-of-command is of secondary importance. Actual power configurations may differ radically from formal organizational charts. Thus, the chief executive may be dependent upon his subordinate agencies as sources of his own power and influence—vis-à-vis Congress, for example. Finally, there is little commonage in bureaucratic agencies. Each must develop its own patterns for maximization of power. Because of this, administrative agencies are involved in the "politics" of the external world.

Where Woodrow Wilson had observed that bureaucracy was subject to the "many masters," Long would interpret these many masters to be the special interest and pressure groups rather than individual voters in the Wilsonian sense. The bureaucracy is dependent upon external "masters" who are themselves effectively organized to seek their own maximum privilege and prerogative. In this pluralistic society, agencies must carry out a dual role: they must receive the consensus of the more important external groups and then represent these interests. A graphic representation of Long's model would reveal power exerted downward within the hierarchy and also upward as well as entering in a lateral direction. Where Weber's idealized bureaucracy is impervious to external influences, Long's bureaucracy must constantly adjust to the changing dynamics of power in the external environment (Figure 7-2).

It is perhaps in its philosophical impact that Long's thesis takes on its greatest significance since it raises a dilemma that strikes at the very heart of "democratic" government. Any doctrine placing survival as the highest value for bureaucratic decision making may be incompatible with democratic philosophy. What emerges is an administrative Machiavellianism void of any concept of the "public interest." To the contrary, the "public interest" is interpreted as "agency interest." If agency survival is the highest value in the agenda of bureaucracy, then all other values are, by definition, subordinate and subject to sacrifice. It would indeed be a tortured definition of democracy that could embrace such a value priority. While democracy is admittedly difficult to precisely define, any reasonable definition would seem to exclude agency survival as its ultimate moral commitment. Few citizens would be willing to devote their lives, liberty or property to such a cause.

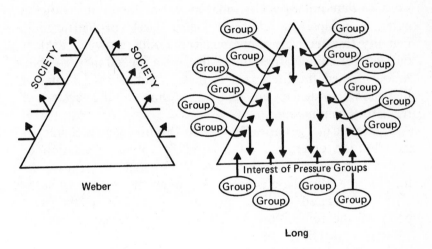

Figure 7-2. POWER FLOW IN BUREAUCRACIES

THE LAW OF ADMINISTRATIVE SENILITY

Agency strategies to maintain a "power budget," that is, a preponderance of external political support over political opposition, led to consequences that were investigated by others. The results have a direct relevance for questions of the "public interest" in a democratic society. Professors Marver Bernstein and Samuel P. Huntington of Princeton and Harvard respectively had, in the 1950's, investigated the nation's oldest regulatory commission, the Interstate Commerce Commission.

Both arrived at the conclusion that the commission, which had originally been established by Congress to administer national transportation policy and to regulate those groups coming within its jurisdiction, had emerged as largely ineffective and decreasingly able to carry out its responsibilities.[7] Later accounts of other federal regulatory commissions revealed a similar lack of vigor. Each of these studies concluded that in rough proportion as their alliances and growing dependence on the external groups to be regulated increased, the more difficult, if not impossible, it became for the regulatory commissions to determine policies independent of the interests of the external groups. In addition, higher levels of inefficiency, inability to effectively apply managerial skills, growing backlogs of cases for adjudication and review and a general inertia-debilitation marked the life spans of these commissions.[8] Professor Bernstein's evidence led him to outline a "life cycle" of regulatory commissions.

The first or "gestation" phase of this life cycle is characterized by the emergence of a need for public regulation of external industries. This is followed by agitation for a regulatory statute; the phase is concluded when the regulatory authority is delegated to a commission. This represents the highpoint of the reform movement for corrective action against industry abuses of the public interest.

The second or "youth" phase is marked by problems of interpretation of commission power and the gaining of experience in the face of well-organized industrial groups. This phase begins with a firm resolve to regulate in order to further the public interest. At the same time public support erodes, and "trial by legal combat" favors the industrial groups as commission policy that is still tentative is challenged. The commission ends this phase in "splendid isolation"—ignored by a Congress concerned with other pressing issues and a public which assumes that the initial legislation assured continued and effective reform.

The third phase, the phase of "maturity," is characterized by a process of continuing commission devitalization. Seeking political support, the commission begins to identify with the need for "healthy" regulated industrial groups. Passivity and apathy become discernible, and it takes a narrower view of its mandate. Its procedures become highly technical, and a spirit of internal "professionalism" emerges. A regulatory status quo represents the basic strategy of the commission as its ability to interpret the public interest wanes.

The fourth phase is marked by debility and decline. The commission has little creative force to exercise vis-á-vis the regulated groups. Doubts arise within the commission concerning its regulatory responsibilities. Consequently it becomes unable to keep abreast of public sentiment or needs for changes in the economy. Case loads increase and professional staff becomes bogged down in sluggish procedures and technical minutiae. In the end its initial objectives are rejected as the primary mission of the commission is equated with business-as-usual. A stance as defender-protector of the regulated industries is adopted, and industry policy, in effect, is reflected in commission decisions.

Professor Bernstein provides little hope that even a new agency will be able, in the long run, to accomplish what the commission has failed to do. For once again, the same inevitable process will take place. Thus, an "iron law of administrative senility" emerges in which the "public interest" is eventually defined as "private interest," and the regulatory agency becomes an apologist for the ostensibly regulated industries. There is massive evidence to support the inadequacies of regulation by "independent" regulatory commissions.[9]

The same "life cycle" emerging from alliances with external clientele groups may be descriptive of other types of public agencies. Professor Philip Selznick in his *TVA and the Grass Roots*[10] describes the process of "cooptation." The Tennessee Valley Authority, in order to build a stronger base and to strengthen local public and private agencies, to avoid duplication of effort and to encourage democratic grass-roots participation and decision making in authority policies adopted the strategy of minimizing federal administrative machinery and policy-discretion. The end result was "cooptation" (an informal but real involvement of local agencies in TVA processes of policy determination) resulting in "status-quoisin" and the favoring of groups already "in power" at the local level.

With TVA, as with the regulatory commissions, the building of a strong constituency base assuring public agency support and survival resulted in a heavy price being paid, that is, weakening of agency independence as well as the sacrifice of its original raison d'être—to encourage experimentation and change in regional public policies.

The common thread through a long list of studies of regulatory commissions centers upon an apparent inevitability, under certain conditions, of "goal" or "value displacement." In more philosophical terms the displacement of values dearly held by the public seeking reform are metamorphosed by the regulatory commissions into often contradictory and conflicting values more reflective of special interests. The scope of the problem is significantly broadened as other studies have revealed similar tendencies for regulatory agencies located within the executive branch of government. In such a situation the criterion of the "public interest" becomes a friction and is literally thrust aside as a basis for agency decision making.[11]

The life-cycle theory underlying the law of administrative senility and the theory of value displacement also gives rise to a biological interpretation of public administration. The central values of survival and adaptation to the external environment suggest biological imperatives. Failing to adjust to the external environment, administrative agencies, like the dinosaur and the dodo bird, are doomed to pass from the scene. The administrative process is viewed as dangerous, turbulent and competitive for limited available resources so that only the "fittest" survive—and, just as surely, other agencies are doomed. Some agencies may consequently be described in biological terms: as embryonic, adolescent, mature, torpid, senile or decaying.[12] This approach also suggests that imperialism—the expansion of one power center at the expense of another or others—is necessary to assure survival in the bureaucratic world.[13]

In such an environment, rationality is limited in its usefulness by internal pathologies and organizational weaknesses. An operative and healthy mind, for example, is dependent for its existence upon the continued health of the host body. Survival may then depend upon nonrational rather than rational factors. To the extent that public administration reflects the biological analogy, organizations may well justify the "highest interest" as their maintenance of a satisfactory equilibrium with their immediate surroundings. Under such conditions, other values become irrelevant. Survival must be earned and thus can be accomplished only through a "cult of power"—not morality.

DANIEL BELL: THE "POST-INDUSTRIAL SOCIETY"

The concept of the "post-industrial society" marks a turning point in administrative philosophy. The "new public administration," which has attracted much attention in the decade of the seventies, is directly related to the post-industrial society and may, perhaps at the risk of oversimplification, be described as administrative response to such a societal forecast.

Its initial abstract formulation in 1962 and subsequent refinements are found in the studies of Daniel Bell, noted Harvard sociologist. In a major work, *The Coming of Post-Industrial Society*,[14] Bell forecasts the future of advanced industrial societies—those of Japan, the Soviet Union, Western Europe and the United States.

The post-industrial society will, in Bell's projection, be a major feature of the twenty-first century and reflects primarily a change in social structure. Bell believes that the United States will provide the best example of post-industrial society because its processes of change are so pronounced and advanced.[15] He describes the next thirty to fifty years, marking the emergence of the post-industrial society, as characterized by increasing tension between two axes of social conflict. These axes are the historic American drive for equality and the process of increasing bureaucratization of society's institutions. Bell notes that contemporary manifestations of the quest for equality are evidenced in movements for greater participation by individuals in decisions by public and private organizations that affect them. The increasing bureaucratization of mankind, foreseen by Max Weber, is due, according to Bell, to the requirements for more technical knowledge and is evidenced by a rising professionalism and "meritocracy."

233

The nature of knowledge itself will shift. Its previous foundation of empiricism (observation and practical experimentation) will yield to the primacy of theoretical or abstract knowledge as central to policy formulation and innovation. The techniques of scientific management in assembly-line production will give way in the post-industrial society to the centrality of man's intellectual organizations, research institutes and universities. A new "intellectual technology" will emerge. Intellectual activities will increasingly utilize mathematical formulas, statistical analyses and computers. Because of this Bell projects the "end of ideology" based upon intuition or emotion. Ideology will be replaced by systems analysis. In the post-industrial society man will be faced with systems of such complexity that his intuition will have diminished utility.

Bell projects a post-industrial society that will be conflictive rather than placid, as a dominant technical elite rises to power over the literary, value-oriented, emotionally inspired intellectuals. Not only will a system based on an educational elitism and education-based "meritocracy" conflict with the irresistible human drive for equality,[16] but underlying populist sentiment reflecting an antiorganizational value system will also revolt against the "organizational harness" of increased bureaucratization.

For Bell the conflict may already have been joined, though its apex will be reached in the post-industrial future beyond the twentieth century. He notes that the student revolts of the 1960's were a reaction against a growing science-based society and may mark the first stages of sociological resistance in an emerging adversary culture. Not without reason, the university was the main battleground.

Bell's forecast of the post-industrial society is a significant conceptual contribution to administrative philosophy. It stands in the evolution of American administrative thought as the dividing line between the "traditional" and the "new" public administration. Like Weber's model, Bell's abstraction reflects the certainty of a society dominated by an emotionless rationalism. No less than Weber, Wilson and the scientific managers, Bell's post-industrial world is dominated by technique. The computer is the key to making up for the deficiencies of the human mind in solving the problems arising from highly variable relationships in ultracomplex systems. Methodology is to be the fundamental tool of the post-industrial society.

Bell's conceptualization of the post-industrial society also mirrors much that is explicit and implicit in the new public administration. For Bell man is, by nature, an intuitive creature whose behavior and emotions cannot be reduced to mathematical formulas, abstract economic constructs or "bits" of information punched onto computer tapes. Man, being expressive, seeks maximum freedom for that expression toward his own self-fulfillment. Bell and the new public administrators are also in agreement in their appraisal of societal trends and the nature and dimensions of the conflict that is developing.

THE NEW PUBLIC ADMINISTRATION

Those writings most reflective of the new public administration are the product of a few advanced thinkers who have made important contributions to administrative philosophy in a period of less than a decade. Although this group tends, comparatively speaking, to be younger than most of the leading figures in public administration, a number of established scholars have expressed sympathy with many of the values undergirding this school of administrative radicalism.

The new public administration is not easily defined and any single description is apt to produce disagreement. Nevertheless, in attempting a distillation of the "new" writings, certain value themes do pervade the views of many of its proponents.[17]

The new public administration is a philosophical movement with its first principles moral propositions. Consequently, it is at war with every model or abstraction of the administrative process that attempts to elevate technique over values.

The radicalism of the new public administration is reflected in the belief that administrative decision making is based upon value choice and that the effects of administrative decision making have value consequences. This being the case, the only legitimate exercises of administrative power in a democratic society are those toward morally compelling ends. These ultimate ends are individual "human dignity" and "social justice." Social justice, however, is relative to specific environments. This implies an "ethic of relativism."

Human emotions, intuition and interrelationships are crucial factors in the shaping of administrative organizations, and a transitional and turbulent society may be best served by flexible organizational structures of limited duration. The focus of the new public administration is outward from the organization to its surrounding environment and inward toward the "inner man." A cardinal assumption is that clientele should participate in administrative decisions affecting them. The broader "public interest" takes precedence over any other conflicting interest.

These assumptions make one point very clear: there is little to be salvaged from traditional public administration. In fact, there is general agreement that public administration in both thought and practice has tended toward repression.

Traditional administration, its critics allege, favors the dominant power-wielding groups in society while disfavoring those outside existing power structures at all levels of government. Not being concerned with the ends or consequences of power, traditional administration merely assumes the virtue of those able to monopolize power. Lacking a bureaucratic ethic, public agencies execute the law in a manner to assure their own survival. Conflicts of conscience and moral dilemmas are regarded as concerns both external to and inimical to the efficient execution of public policy. These are "political" problems not any more appropriate to the administrative mandate than the shaping of administrative policy or the determination of policy goals. The end result is an alliance with society's dominant institutions.

The repressive nature of traditional administration is also reflected in the required dehumanization that the individual bureaucrat must undergo. To the degree that the bureaucrat divests himself of conscience, he will apply the coercive power of government in defense of the ideological status quo.

The result is a marked decline of confidence in public agencies. Now regarding his own government with suspicion, man is increasingly alienated from those who, in democratic theory at least, are supposed to serve and not repress him. Traditional public administration has centered its attention upon organizations-institutions. It assumes that the well-being of all men will be determined by the well-being of these structures. The new public administration centers its attention on man per se and assumes that the requirements of his well-being should *precede* and finally shape all organizations-institutions that claim to be in his service. The new public administration consequently exposes a glaring schism between democratic philosophy and traditional administrative thought and practice.

The centrality of man pervades the literature of the new public administration. Values which men hold dear and necessary for their well-being and self-fulfillment become operative rather than ignored. These may be summarized as those values most conducive to "human dignity." References to "humane administration" and "human dignity" may be traced in the public organizational context to the earliest postwar years.[18]

With the positing of human dignity as the highest operational value and the ultimate goal of bureaucratic decision making, the human conscience replaces the rules, regulations and stable principles so assiduously studied in the classroom. In its more radical manifestations the call is for a moral or philosophical reorientation of public administration's academic programs. The moral relevance of administrative power in a democratic society should be separated from operational needs. The latter is to be the concern of training units within governmental agencies, while concern with value choices and their consequent moral dilemmas will be the foci of academic programs. Public administration will become unified in its theory and practice only when practice becomes subservient to the morality of the ends of public power.[19]

The relationship between human dignity and social justice is viewed as one of mutual interdependence. That which contributes to the fulfillment of the dignity and highest potential of each man will also contribute to the well-being of the total community. Conversely, that which, under the guise of public policy, arbitrarily favors some groups of men over others or causes the dominance of some men over others will ultimately

237

reduce the dignity and sense of worth of all men. The ambiguity of these terms does not appear as a major problem in advocacy of the new public administration. Rather, the new approach emphasizes the value of ambiguity in contrast to its distrust of the specificity inherent in traditional administrative thought and practice.

The specific meanings and content of human dignity and social justice are not detailed. Like the evolution of the common law in early English political history, human dignity will evolve as a series of understandings over a prolonged period of time. In the interim the meanings of these terms are to be worked out in practice in specific situations and will be related to differing environments. Hence, the necessary conditions for the dignity of man will be determined in relation to the unceasing processes of social change. Different community settings within differing societies are therefore best served by a bureaucratic "situational ethic." The traditional belief in a common administrative process is therefore rejected in the new public administration. Administrative process is, instead, reflective of a diversity of values and, no less important, of the diverse means by which such values are realized. It is easy to appreciate the futuristic orientation of the new public administration which stands in stark contrast to the "here and now" orientation of traditional public administration.

The significance of technique gives way in the new public administration to the dominance of human emotion and belief in the primacy of certain values. If, indeed, there are techniques at all, they are the techniques of innovation and experimentation. These require a spirit of "not knowing" and a "yearning to learn" that differs fundamentally from the "it is known—now learn it" approach of the traditionalists. Even here, however, it must be pointed out that innovation and experimentation are as much states of mind as techniques.

Innovation and experimentation will revolve around the application of intuition and emotion to organizational design. Man's intuitive senses and his feelings are to be trusted, rather than mistrusted, since they are basic to man himself. Hopefully, therefore, the restraints of hierarchy and its attendant superior-subordinate relationships (vertical) will give way to new relationships that may be described as "free form." Once legal authority is rejected as the fundamental criterion for organizational design, other factors, such as encouragement of maximum participation within the organization as well as between the bureaucrats and their external clienteles, should produce new patterns of organization. Here the emphasis is upon the transitory nature of all organizations, as the needs of society in turbulent and conflictive times undergo profound changes.

Daniel Bell's forecast of a future of technological complexity and environmental instability would appear to require such an administrative response. This would especially seem to be the case where the central conflict is that of increasing bureaucratization versus individual self-expression and equalitarianism.

The new public administration not only rejects administrative survival as a morally indefensible guideline for decision making, but new organizational forms may have to be designed with built-in "self-destructive" features. In this manner maximum flexibility in administrative organization is assured. Risk taking, rather than being penalized, as in traditional public administration, is to be encouraged with "disposable" organizations. Consequently, failure of one pattern of organizational response to societal needs is not catastrophic, but merely the occasion for the testing of alternative strategies for action.

The dominance of emotion and intuition over logic and rationalism give promise of myriad unorthodox and untested nonsymmetrical patterns of organization. Their effectiveness will be determined by their relationships to a large number of interacting environmental variables. Little wonder that one group of new public administrators centers their hopes for a revitalized discipline upon existential phenomenology—the ultimate philosophy of relativism.

EXISTENTIAL PHENOMENOLOGY

This philosophical movement is based upon the belief that the nature of the universe is unpredictable and no rational scheme can fully explain it. Despite the advances of science and physics, the universe is not "ordered." Therefore, no matter of fact can be stated as absolute truth, for any relationship between things is subject to change at any moment. Man's existence is not capable of exhaustive description in scientific terms. Much that science posits as truth is therefore illusory. Phenomena—the subject of phenomenology—are not describable as empirically verifiable facts; however, this does not affect their truthfulness or falsity. Science and mathematical measurement have only very limited applicability for understanding reality. Existential phenomenology is consequently based upon recognition that belief is always belief and cannot be anything more.

Causal explanations of human behavior are suspect and a scientific-mechanistic view of the universe is rejected. The error of the scientific approach has been its insistence that man the "observer" can be impartial and removed from the world which he "observes." Instead, existential phenomenology regards the phenomenal universe as approachable only through man's consciousness. His consciousness consists of what he is conscious of. Consequently, to impose a split between observer and the object he observes merely produces an "artificial reality" which alienates man from the world he is attempting to understand. There are no unconscious acts of man.

Existential phenomenology rejects Freudian psychology and biological determinism. In both cases man's future is determined by forces he is unable to consciously modify or deflect. As a result, man plays a minor role in shaping his own future, and the role of individual choice is minimized. This situation combined with the growth of technology and bureaucracy have produced men who are conformist by nature, mediocre in terms of accomplishment, and who have lost their individuality. The real nature of man, however, is his importance as a choice-making individual. These choices can only be understood in relation to specific situations: the values underlying these choices are the "true reality" and can be evaluated only in relation to the broad contextual environment of the situation itself. Consequently, for each man his own experiences are the bases for his own choices. The individual is therefore central to his own existence.

The "facts" of natural science are not unadulterated reality for they are the product of a very restricted human experience. Scientific facts are therefore no more true than the speculations of the philosophers. Truth lies only in situations where the human element is taken into account and is therefore subject to man's emotions, his presuppositions and his limitations. The nonrational subjective factors in any situation are irreducible truths insofar as they are integral parts of the whole situation. The experience of the subject is therefore crucial to the true understanding of his observation. Ultimately, each man helps to create the situation that he perceives.

Existential man exists in a universe of random unfolding so that rationalized schemes for controlling it are doomed to futility. Existence cannot be reasoned or contained within any conceptual scheme. Man's choices are the essence of man himself and there is no escape from making choices. Existentialism reflects a limited role for reason. Because of this, man's freedom is dependent upon his being aware of his unlimited potential for freedom. Man is, in the final analysis, both free and unfree. He is free insofar as he is not restricted by natural or biological determinism; this is the basis of human freedom. He is not free, however, insofar as he is part of every situation he perceives. His freedom is therefore in relation to a given situation. Man is capable of understanding himself only in a relational context. The world as it unfolds is therefore shaped by man, but he is also shaped by it. Freedom in this context is not absolute nor unlimited; it is freedom based on possibilities which themselves are shaped by man's choices.

Existential phenomenology regards experience as an intensely human event, and situations in which men find themselves are intensely human phenomena. The essence of human situations are the humans involved. Human relationships are the key to man's destiny. One can become distinctively human and reach one's highest fulfillment only in relation to others; reality cannot be described in terms of the individual but only in terms of his relationship to others. The essence of man is feeling and emotion, not physical empiricism or intellectualism. This requires identification with the feelings, values and emotions of others. Man coexists with other men. His existence is therefore a duality. The existential nature of man is ultimately to live in a loving coexistence.[20]

The bureaucratic implications of this philosophical movement are quite profound. Rational-intellectual conceptualizations of administrative organization lead only to predetermined structures in conflict with man's unstable and unpredictable environment. Such conceptualizations, accorded the status of "ideal forms," have succeeded only in alienating man from those institutions supposed to serve him. They have also created mutual suspicions and hostilities between the bureaucracies and their external clienteles. Such predetermined organizational structures prevent an "open-ended" approach to organizational forms. The possibilities of boundless change and ceaseless organizational "unfolding" are foreclosed. No organization of humans can ever be a "finished product."

The rationalistic-mechanistic approach typified by Weber, Wilson and the scientific-managers emphasizes "boundaries" separating man from man. Divided by levels of authority within organizational structures, bureaucrats are also separated from the external society. An intentional structure is placed in both instances between persons. This elevates the misguided concept of "me" and "thee" and prevents the arising of an existential transcendence.

The most important "direction" of human relationships is not vertical but horizontal. The enforced distinction between subject (bureaucrat) and object (clienteles) is contrary to the nature of human experience which, to reach its highest creativity and fulfillment, requires an interpenetrating or melding of subject and object. Consequently, the dysfunctional aspects of rationalistic organizational forms must be eliminated by better understanding of human dynamics.

Organizational forms can only be the product of open communication, the harmonization and duality of all men (to oneself and to each other). Freedom, being corporate rather than individual, is consonant with organization but such organization must be based upon the new humanism.

For the existentialist, administration is not visual (organization charts and other "tools") but emotional. Public administration must redirect itself to abandon its prejudices against emotion and feelings. The intellectual-rationalization of the head must give way to the feelings of the heart.

Notions of a supreme and universal ethic are no more appropriate to the conditions of man's existence than are notions of "one best" form of organization. Human potential is constrained by the input-output criterion of morality. The true freedom of man is the recognition that he is free to make choices. Organizational "virtue" is consequently meaningful only in relation to each situation in a universe of ceaseless change and infinite situations.

The scope or size of organizations must be proportional to the needs of the situation. Existential phenomenology implies a sympathy for decentralization rather than centralization as the former will be conducive to maximum interpersonal encounters. Existential phenomenology reflects an "administrative optimism" based on a future of manifold and unbounded possibilities in contrast to the administrative pessimism that has dominated much of traditional administrative thought. Man's future need not be competition with other men and alienation from man's own institutions. With a redirection of the approach to the conditions and nature of human existence, man is capable of living in a free and fulfilling communion with all other men.

Man's organizational needs as he faces an unknown future must be based upon the reality of the present and not upon administrative prescriptions emanating from an irrelevant past. Futuristic bureaucracy will bear few if any earmarks of its bureaucratic antecedents.

The value premises of the new public administration comprise an antibureaucratic philosophy of bureaucracy. The existentialist approach raises a crucial question, "Is public administration possible?" One observer notes, "Not only is the future manifold and unbounded, but P.A. would cease to have any boundary whatever."[21]

VINCENT OSTROM: THE ETHICS OF POLYCENTRISM

With the publication of Vincent Ostrom's *The Intellectual Crisis in American Public Administration,*[22] administrative philosophy took a new turn. The approach of Professor Ostrom to the problem of organizational design places him within the broad value framework of the new public administration. However, much of his argument is based upon the works of political economists rather than psychologists or philosophers.

Ostrom, sympathetic to the rejection of traditional public administration, believes the underlying problem of contemporary public administration is its failure to develop a new "paradigm" or model. He forwards the notion that the current "crisis" in the field is an amalgam of an emerging identity crisis, increasing doubts about bureaucratic rationality and the fact that bureaucratic anomalies and dysfunctions contradict the promises of orthodox administrative theories. The true nature of the crisis, however, is "paradigmatic." Ostrom feels a radically new intellectual approach is needed to replace the technical solutions traditionally offered by administrative experts. The contemporary doubts concerning the ability of public administration to meet future challenges and to remain in the service of a "democratic" society can be counterbalanced only by new experimentation and the questioning of the traditional paradigm. "It is even faintly possible," he observes, "that the beauties of yesteryear may be revealed as ugly illusions."[23]

The contributions and insights of political economists should be applied, according to Ostrom, to the design of public administrative organizations. Unlike Weber and Wilson, contemporary political economists reject the notion that a single administrative process pervades both public and private administrative enterprises. Rather, the lack of a free competitive market in relation to governmental functions and services results in the absence of free citizen choices. This situation requires radically different decision making arrangements. The ends of public administration are therefore not the greatest efficiency (input versus output) or adoption of businesslike practices by public organizations. Instead a much more complex set of values, requiring a much more complex total organizational system for democratic society, must be developed. Such a system must eschew traditional simplistic solutions and meet the diverse needs of innumerable communities of men with widely variant preferences making widely variant choices.

Ostrom holds that administrative efficiency is meaningless except within the context of large numbers of communities, comprising the clienteles of public agencies, being given the opportunities for expression of consumer values and preferences. These opportunities can only be provided by a departure from outdated criteria. Hierarchical forms of organization are no longer ideal. Also the assumption that a single large organization with broad jurisdiction is necessarily superior to a multiplicity of smaller organizations, playing more limited roles and serving more limited clienteles, cannot be substantiated. Ostrom, rejecting the belief that the sovereignty of the state can be located at only one point, attacks the Hobbesian notion of an absolute ruler. Ostrom likewise attacks Woodrow Wilson's assumption, expressed in his book *Congressional Government*,[24] that power in the American system cannot be effectively fragmented but ultimately will find its situs in a dominant power center: the Congress. This assumption, in conjunction with Wilson's belief that there is only one ideal form of organization, causes Ostrom to describe the Wilsonian theory of administration as a "counterrevolutionary doctrine."[25]

Thrusting aside any possible recognition of Wilson as contributing to the democratization of administration, expressed in Chapter 6, Ostrom develops the theme that Wilson's approach to public administration is basically counter to the values of American democracy as expressed by the framers of the Constitution. In Ostrom's view the framers imparted an ethical content to federalism since they believed man's freedom to be dependent upon a system of fragmented power as well as upon the existence of many governments serving differing communities in different ways. The inherent values of many diverse governments must become the foundation for any system of "democratic administration." By definition, this excludes the Wilsonian model of "bureaucratic administration." The values underlying the two models of administration are, for Ostrom, philosophically at odds with each other. The "monocentricity" of Hobbes, Weber and Wilson cannot serve as the value framework for the democracy envisaged by the nation's founders.

The needs of man in a democratic society can only be served by large numbers and varieties of governments with differing scopes and differing responsibilities existing concurrently with each other and counterbalancing each other. The abandonment of existing governmental "polycentrism" in favor of a supposedly ideal monocentrism is a matter not to be taken lightly. Scoring those consultants and commissions that have uncritically assumed the validity of Wilson's "one best" form of organization, Ostrom attacks the supposed rationality of such an approach. Heterogeneity, rather than being a pathological condition within a governmental system, is the basic requirement for a healthy and functioning system of democratic administration. In contrast, the pathologies of large-scale, all-embracing bureaucracies are apparent: cumbersome procedures, dis-economic scales of operations, declining output, risk avoidance, inability to adapt to changing conditions, error proneness and goal displacement.

For Ostrom the ideal situation would be large-scale and small-scale organizations existing side-by-side, each playing its most effective role in accordance with its particular scope of operation. Potential conflicts of jurisdiction and the rigid limitations of geographical boundaries would be minimized by the wide use of interorganizational and interjurisdictional techniques, including contractual agreements between governments.

Ostrom's volume is a noteworthy supplement to the new public administration; it provides a morality for the existence of multiple and diverse governments serving diverse clienteles with differing needs and preferences. This contrasts sharply with the view of some leading commentators on federalism who merely describe it as a process or technique devoid of any philosophical base.[26] The new public administration evidences a sympathy for governmental decentralization. Ostrom's book gives that decentralization an ethical justification. Polycentrism and humanism are, for Ostrom, inseparable.[27]

"THE INEFFICIENT SOCIETY"

The rejection of technological rationalism, with its emphasis upon technique rather than ends and upon efficiency rather than human needs, has led to a movement toward the "inefficient society." It has much in common with the values expressed in the new public administration and Ostrom's plea for administrative diversity. The underlying theme of the "inefficient society" is that of post-technological man freed from the "monoculture" and the restrictive standardization of life everywhere. Emphasis upon ever-increasing production and consumption of the earth's limited resources has led, in this view, to a depleted world with great ecological damage and a declining quality of life.

Both Marxism and capitalism are scored for having promised man freedom and having led him only to increasing degrees of "unfreedom" as the major crises he faces grow in depth and complexity. The thesis is simply that the most efficient and technique-oriented societies are those closest to self-destruction, as they become less and less humane and more distant from nature than ever.

Jacques Ellul in his *Technological Society* chronicles the interplay of those forces which assure the inevitability of technique's dominance over humane values. He concludes:

> It is vanity to pretend the monolithic technical world can be checked or guided. Indeed, the human race is beginning confusedly to understand at last it is living in a new and unfamiliar universe ... enclosed within his artificial creation, man finds there is "no exit"; that he cannot pierce the shell of technology to find again the ancient milieu to which he was adapted for hundreds of thousands of years.[28]

Scientist Eugene Schwartz, in his *Overskill: The Decline of Technology in Modern Civilization*,[29] differs from Ellul's conclusion. Science and technology, he holds are still subject to counteraction and resistance by man. The sole hope, however, is rejection of production efficiency as the measure of economic and public policy.

Man, in order to survive, must get off his great "growth kick" and return from a robotized consumer to being a creative, erotic and sensate human. The production process must be reoriented to a "rollback" based on the earth's diminishing

247

resources. Hopefully, the post-technological society will allow man to regroup his production processes to a more limited, but more creative scale. Recognizing that there is no "one best way," small-scale "creatories" of designers, artisans and craftsmen are envisioned as replacing the huge impersonal and gigantic production collectives that modern factories have become.

Though Schwartz is anything but optimistic, he does cite some evidence of decline of technology due to its own destructive tendencies. Still, the issue is in doubt. The key is the preservation of diversity among different communities of man. Although diversity implies a freedom of choice from among a multitude of alternatives, Schwartz emphasizes that this will, in fact, produce stability rather than societal conflict.

> Revolt and dissent are necessary stabilizing forces in the steps leading towards the future.... Dialectically, the disorder stemming from freedom and diversity beget order, while planned order can beget disorder. A leaven of disorder is the pathway to a free and human society .... A stable community in nature is one that is diverse and complex; an unstable community is homogeneous and ordered.[30]

The post-technological society for Schwartz will consequently be one which will survive only because it has become "inefficient" in traditional terms: reflecting differing values, diversities of scale and an overriding concern for the humane ends of man. It is evident that the administrative requirements of Schwartz's "inefficient society" will be best met within the framework of the new public administration.

By the mid-1970's administrative thought had come full-circle. Where once man's progress was assured by his embracing production efficiency, now his survival is questionable and possible only if he embraces inefficiency. Consequently, the morality of efficiency so characteristic of scientific management is transformed into immorality in the "inefficient society." Obviously, the same administrative values cannot serve both worlds.

Figure 7-3 below summarizes some of the key terms and characteristics reflecting the continuing value bipolarity in the field of administrative thought.

Traditional Administration	The "New" Public Administration
• Survival-Oriented — — — — — — — — •	Client-Oriented
• "One best" Administrative — — — — •	Multiplicity of Administrative
Pattern	Patterns
• Practioner-Oriented — — — — — — — •	Philosophically-Oriented
• Quantification - — — — — — — — — — •	Humanism
• Experiential — — — — — — — — — — •	Conceptual
• Rationalistic - — — — — — — — — — •	Emotions; Intuition; Irrational
• Man's Knowledge — — — — — — — — •	Man's Ignorance
• Management-Oriented — — — — — •	Policy-Oriented
• Efficiency - — — — — — — — — — — •	Inefficiency
• Preciseness - — — — — — — — — — — •	Ambiguity
• Hierarchical — — — — — — — — — — •	Non-hierarchical
• Internalities of Organizations — — — •	Externalities of Organizations
• Minimal Environmental Impact — — •	Maximal Environmental Impact
• Does not question — — — — — — — •	Questions
• Amorality — — — — — — — — — — — •	Morality
• Standardization — — — — — — — — •	Diversity
• Process-techniques — — — — — — — •	Goals-ends
• Non-participatory — — — — — — — •	Participatory
• Non-innovative - — — — — — — — — •	Innovative
• Institutional-programmatic - — — — •	Ad hoc; temporary; transitional
permanence	Institutions-programs

Figure 7-3. CHARACTERISTICS OF TRADITIONAL AND "NEW" PUBLIC ADMINISTRATIVE THOUGHT

A few concluding observations are in order. There are no hard-and-fast boundaries separating "traditional" and "new" public administration. In fact, much of the literature is concerned with this specific point. Despite the bipolarity of administrative thought, there are many halfway points along the "traditional"-"new" continuum. Some of the scholars of the administrative process who are supportive of the newer approach nevertheless are careful to emphasize that the two approaches need not be mutually exclusive. Some situations may best be served by traditional hierarchical forms of organization, while others may be more appropriate candidates for "free-form" patterns. In fact, the same agency may have some units organized along traditional hierarchical lines with other units, serving a different clientele with unique needs, patterned along radically different lines.

Some of the writings in the field of administrative thought have reflected a "mid-position"—supportive of the humanistic goals of the new public administration but still emphasizing the importance of procedures. Emmette Redford's *Democracy in the Administrative State*[31] is perhaps the outstanding example of this "middle-of-the-road" position. Redford has been accurately described as a "practical idealist," and his volume reflects his stance. Redford's theme is that the "ideal" and "fact" can exist only in a basic duality in administration and that each must adjust to the other. Arguing that "democratic morality" based on "individual realization" is not attainable in its pure form, Redford forwards "workable democracy" which, though less than ideal, is still attainable.

"Workable democracy" as applied to the "administrative state," where men are subject to the decisions of other men, is based upon "due process." For Redford "due process" embraces the representation of all interests affected by administrative decisions plus opportunities to present evidence before fair and unbiased tribunals. In this procedural approach administrators are to exercise minimal discretion—which places Redford at some distance from the "creative" administrative proclivities of the "new" public administrators.

Redford's work implies that once representativeness and the objectivity of procedural safeguards are attained, the results, whether just or unjust, are legitimatized. The new public administration, in contrast, does not emphasize procedures but rather the *results* of those procedures. That which is unjust can never be legitimatized regardless of procedures. In short, only values can be the highest value. Procedures are techniques whose only legitimacy is in the "justness" of the final decision.

NOTES

1. For a brief and easily read introduction to the work of Freud, see Calvin S. Hall, *A Primer of Freudian Psychology*, New York: Mentor Books, 1960.

2. Harold D. Lasswell, *Psychopathology and Politics*, Chicago: University of Chicago Press, 1930.

3. See L. J. Henderson, T. N. Whitehead, and Elton Mayo, "The Effects of Social Environment," in *Papers on the Science of Administration*, eds. Luther Gulick and L. Urwick, New York: Institute of Public Administration, 1937, p. 158.

4. Chester I. Barnard, *The Functions of the Executive*, Cambridge: Harvard University Press, 1938, chap. IX, "Informal Organizations and their Relation to Formal Organizations."

5. Herbert A. Simon, *Administrative Behavior: A Study of Decision-Making Processes in Administrative Organization*, New York: Macmillan, 1948.

6. Norton E. Long, "Power and Administration," *Public Administration Review*, 9, no. 4 (Autumn 1949): 257-64.

7. See Marver Bernstein, *Regulating Business by Independent Commission*, Princeton: Princeton University Press, 1955, pp. 74-95; and Samuel P. Huntington, "The Marasmus of the I.C.C.," *Yale Law Journal*: 61, 467-509.

8. See Bernard Schwartz, *The Professor and the Commissions*, New York: Knopf, 1959; Edward F. Cox, Robert C. Fellmuth, and John E. Schulz, *The Nader Report on the Federal Trade Commission*, New York: Grove Press, 1969.

9. For a general overview of the problems and performances of federal regulatory agencies, see Louis M. Kolhmeier, Jr., *The Regulators: Watchdog Agencies and the Public Interest*, New York: Harper & Row, 1969; Paul W. MacAvoy, *The Crisis of the Regulatory Commissions: An Introduction to a Current Issue of Public Policy*, New York: W. W. Norton, 1970; Roger G. Noll, *Reforming Regulation. An Evaluation of the Ash Council Proposals. A Staff Paper*, Washington, D.C.: The Brookings Institution, 1971. Significant earlier studies include U.S. Congress, Committee on the Judiciary, *Report on the Regulatory Agencies to the President-Elect*, 86th Cong., 2d sess. (December 1960), and Henry J. Friendly, *The Federal Administrative Agencies: The Need for Better Definition of Standards*, Cambridge: Harvard University Press, 1962.

10. Philip Selznick, *TVA and the Grass Roots*, Berkeley: University of California Press, 1949.

11. For an extended treatment of the "public interest" by a number of commentators, see Carl J. Friederich, ed., *Nomos v. The Public Interest*, New York: Atherton Press, 1962.

12. See Herbert Kaufman, "Organization Theory and Political Theory," *American Political Science Review*, 58, no. 1 (March 1964): especially 11-14.

13. See Matthew Holden, Jr., "Imperialism in Bureaucracy," *American Political Science Review*, 60, no. 4 (December 1966): 943-51.

14. Daniel Bell, *The Coming of Post-Industrial Society: A Venture in Social Forecasting*, New York: Basic Books, 1973.

15. American society as the vanguard of future societal "revolutions" is also the theme of Jean-Francois Revel's *Without Marx or Jesus: The New American Revolution Has Begun*, New York: Delta Publishing Co., 1972

16. Frederick Mosher describes this emerging conflict in contemporary terms in his *Democracy and the Public Service*, New York: Oxford University Press, 1968, chaps. 4-6, especially chap. 7.

17. See Frank Marini, ed., *Toward a New Public Administration: The Minnowbrook Perspective*, Scranton: Chandler Publishing Co., 1971; Dwight Waldo, ed., *Public Administration in a Time of Turbulence*, Scranton: Chandler Publishing Co., 1971. While not all contributors to these volumes would identify themselves as new public administrators, both collections do reflect the major concerns and propositions of this approach.

18. See, for example, C. Spencer Platt, "Humanizing Public Administration," *Public Administration Review*, 7, no. 3 (Summer 1947): 193-99.

19. See Eugene P. Dvorin and Robert H. Simmons, *From Amoral to Humane Bureaucracy*, San Francisco: Canfield Press, 1972, chap. 6.

20. See Alastair MacIntyre, "Existentialism," *Encyclopedia of Philosophy*, vol. 3, New York: Macmillan, The Free Press, 1972, pp. 147-54; William A. Sadler, *Existence and Love. A New Approach in Existential Phenomenology*, New York: Charles Scribner's Sons, 1969.

21. Professor John Crow, Univ. of Arizona, in his written review of this manuscript (Tucson, 1975).

22. Vincent Ostrom, *The Intellectual Crisis in American Public Administration*, Birmingham, Alabama: University of Alabama Press, 1973.

23. *Ibid.*, p. 17.

24. Woodrow Wilson, *Congressional Government: A Study in American Politics*, New York: Meridian Books, 1965.

25. Ostrom, *op. cit.*, p. 133.

26. See, for example, Richard H. Leach, *American Federalism*, New York: W. W. Norton, 1970. Leach forwards the belief that the framers, given a choice today, would probably not adopt a federal form of government.

27. For an unusually perceptive essay on these issues from the viewpoint of an economist, see Procter Thompson, "Size and Effectiveness in the Federal System: A Theoretical Introduction" in *Essays in Federalism,* Claremont, Calif.: Institute for Studies in Federalism, 1961, chap. 5.

28. Jacques Ellul, *The Technological Society,* New York: Vintage Books, 1964, p. 428.

29. Eugene S. Schwartz, *Overskill: The Decline in Technology in Modern Civilization,* Chicago: Quadrangle Books, 1971.

30. *Ibid.,* p. 305.

31. Emmette S. Redford, *Democracy in the Administrative State,* New York: Oxford University Press, 1969.

PART III

THE PROCEDURAL NETWORK

8

ADMINISTRATIVE LAW: FREEDOM AND CONSTRAINT

The field of administrative law is that portion of the legal system embracing those administrative agencies that, apart from legislature or judiciary, determine private rights and obligations of individuals, organizations or corporations.[1] The administrative determination of private rights differs from that of the legislature insofar as legislative enactments (statutes) do not deal, except in rare instances, with single individuals, organizations or corporations but deal instead with large segments of society. Legislation is virtually always of general applicability save an occasional "private bill" to provide relief to a single individual where otherwise an injustice may result. Many state constitutions are very precise on this point: a "special act," one aimed at a single city or county, is prohibited if a general act embracing all cities and counties or groups of cities and counties is applicable. In contrast, administrative agencies hand down thousands, indeed hundreds of thousands, of decisions each year affecting specific individuals, organizations or corporations.

ADMINISTRATIVE AGENCIES AND PRIVATE RIGHTS

The determination of private rights under administrative law also differs from that portion of the legal system which embraces the regular courts of law. The federal courts may also determine private rights in specific "cases and controversies" according to Article III of the U.S. Constitution. This has been interpreted to restrict judicial proceedings to cases involving actual adverse litigants where substantial interests, that is, "damages" have resulted. However, the courts cannot determine rates, charges or prices allowable under public regulation, and legislatures are ill-equipped to attempt this task. Administrative agencies, however, acting under legal authority, not only may determine "how much" the traffic should bear but also the conditions under which businesses and other activities affected with the public interest may operate.

Administrative agencies, in determining private rights and obligations, exercise their legal powers under constitutional, statutory or executive authority, the latter generally by the issuance of "executive orders." On the federal level, administrative agencies, whether the so-called "independent regulatory commissions," authorities, boards or those units within executive departments, act primarily under delegations of power from Congress since Article II of the Constitution, the executive article, neither establishes nor empowers specific administrative agencies. Article II establishes the presidency and sets forth the powers of that office, though often in undefined and ambiguous terms. The establishment of executive agencies is by implication a legislative responsibility, together with determination of agency size and mission.

On state and local levels, state constitutions and county and city charters frequently do establish administrative agencies with sometimes detailed provisions of organization and powers. Other agencies are established by legislative bodies and they, as on the federal level, operate under a legislative delegation of power.

The range of administrative agencies that determine private rights and obligations is truly mind-boggling. At the local level of government are planning and zoning boards, property tax assessment appeals boards and legislative bodies such as county boards of supervisors or county commissioners that are empowered to exercise both legislative and executive responsibilities. On the state level of government are public utility commissions, state licensure boards (medicine, law, architecture, optometry, real estate, general contracting, etc.), parole boards and state civil service commissions. These represent both at local and state levels a minute sampling of administrative agencies granting privileges, determining rates for charges, holding hearings or appeals, and issuing rules and regulations with the force of law. On the federal level the great regulatory boards and commissions (Interstate Commerce, Securities and Exchange, Federal Power, Federal Trade, Civil Aeronautics, National Labor Relations, etc.), the Atomic Energy Commission and U.S. Civil Service Commission operate outside the executive departments. Examples of administrative agencies that determine private rights and obligations within executive departments are the Federal Maritime Board responsible to the secretary of commerce, the Coast Guard under the Department of Transportation, the Pure Food and Drug Administration under the Department of Health, Education and Welfare. The General Accounting Office, under the comptroller general, responsible to Congress, exercises some administrative adjudicating powers especially when it hands down legal opinions.

In all, hundreds of boards, commissions, authorities, administrations, and departments exercise powers of investigation, prosecution, hearing, adjudication and licensure. Despite popular perceptions to the contrary, the overwhelming bulk of administrative law agencies and tribunals exist at state and local levels rather than at the federal level of government. To cite some examples: The federal government issues very few occupational licenses (airline pilot, merchant marine officer and radio operator) while virtually all occupational licensing including the professions and the teaching field occurs at the state level of government. The federal government inspects and certifies very few businesses (mines, airworthiness of aircraft, seagoing vessels under American registry, atomic energy power plants, trains in interstate commerce). In contrast, dairies, dry-cleaning establishments, private investigation agencies, the liquor industry, insurance companies, private educational institutions, restaurants, theaters, food processing plants, steel mills, and laundries are merely a small cross section of businesses that come under state and/or local licensing inspection laws. In the licensing of automobile drivers alone, the states overwhelm all the licensure activities of federal authorities.

In each of the areas of federal, state or local regulation, administrative agencies wield great power: to investigate complaints or initiate investigations, to order the elimination of practices prohibited by law, to set standards, to prosecute flagrant violations of law or administrative regulations, to set forth rules and regulations, to hold hearings prior to issuance of rules and regulations, to hold adjudicatory hearings (to determine negligence or guilt or innocence for alleged infractions of the law), to issue licenses, to withhold licenses, to revoke licenses, to provide appeal procedures, to order permanent or temporary suspension of an activity, to seize property, to impose fines or penalties. It is evident that the techniques of administrative coercion constitute an impressive arsenal to assure citizen compliance with public policy. Little wonder that administrative law has been one of the most controversial and contentious areas where citizen and governmental interests so frequently appear to collide.

The Early Setting

Administrative agencies with powers to dispense privileges and franchises, issue rules and regulations, and determine private rights and responsibilities outside the regular courts under congressional delegations of power characterized the new government of the United States. From the beginning the emergence of such agencies was a highly pragmatic response to specific problems and not due to any dominant or favored political philosophy. Indeed, the history of administrative law reflects theories following, rather than preceding, the facts. Response to the dynamics of American society and especially the economy over long periods of time, rather than adherence to dogma, best describes the empirical growth of administrative law.

By 1865 significant administrative authority had been invested in those agencies responsible for veterans' affairs, Indian affairs, revenue, interior affairs, patents, passports, marine inspection and customs. From the end of the Civil War to 1900, administrative agencies dealing with fisheries and animal husbandry, the mails and interstate commerce were granted extensive regulatory powers. The Interstate Commerce Commission, the grandfather of all the federal regulatory commissions, established in 1887, was the most important and novel administrative agency established in this period. The first two decades of the twentieth century were marked by the establishment of the Federal Reserve System, the Federal Trade Commission, the Pure Food and Drug Administration and the Agricultural Marketing Service.

The decade of the 1920's saw the establishment of the Federal Power Commission, the Federal Communications Commission, the National Mediation Board, the Civil Aeronautics Administration and the Board of Tax Appeals. Among the most important federal administrative agencies established in the 1930's were the Securities and Exchange Commission, the National Labor Relations Board, the Federal Deposit Insurance Corporation, the Social Security Board, the Selective Service Administration and the Wage and Hour Division of the Department of Labor.

The report of the attorney general's Committee on Administrative Procedure, published in 1941, estimated that nine executive agencies under the authority of the president and eighteen independent agencies possessed significant administrative powers to issue rules and regulations and determine private rights and obligations.[2]   State and local administrative agencies also increased at a prodigious rate.

The Early Conflicts

Many of the most important administrative agencies had neither a painless birth nor a happy "maturity." The rapidity of their growth and the significance of their powers, indeed, the very implications of their existence, conflicted with a number of long held assumptions and values centering on the role of government in American society.

The first major conflict was the post–Civil War movement for governmental regulation. At state and local levels in particular, the emerging doctrine of the "police power"—the power of government to protect the health, morals, welfare and safety of society—was based upon the notion of a higher community or "societal good" that overrode the traditional rights of the citizen to use both his skills and his property as he pleased. The drive for increased governmental regulation was evident in large numbers of areas: zoning, health, quarantine control, nuisance abatement, business and occupational licensing, rates and safety standards for common carriers, food inspection, child labor, hours of labor, minimum wages and dangerous occupations. Many of the more progressive states, such as Oregon and Wisconsin, paved the way for the growth of administrative regulation, and their legislation became models for other states and, at a later time, for Congress.

On the other hand the administrative regulation of property rights, as more activities were vested with a "public interest," met increasing opposition from those who regarded government as best limited to its traditional functions. The heat and emotions generated by this fundamental conflict between a dominant *laissez faire* philosophy and the movement for regulation was intense and prolonged, with the controversy escalating until it reached its peak in the 1930's and 1940's. American society was destined to become the bitter battleground for the irresistible force—administrative regulation—meeting head-on with the nearly immovable body of law centering on the sanctity of private property rights.

The second conflict was the consequence of the establishment by Congress of the Interstate Commerce Commission in 1887. Earlier state regulatory efforts in the field of railway rates and the prevention of discriminatory economic practices had foundered. State railway commissions only had jurisdiction within their respective borders and the states varied widely in both their commitment to regulation and their strategies to realize that goal. Because of its interstate nature, it eventually became apparent that anything less than national regulation of the railroad transportation system would not be effective. When Congress did finally pass the Interstate Commerce Act, the commission it established to administer that act departed fundamentally from existing assumptions of American government.

The Interstate Commerce Commission was based upon a *fusion* rather than a separation of legislative, executive and judicial powers. Congress had empowered the commission to exercise "quasi–legislative" powers (the making of "rules" and "regulations" enforceable in law), "quasi–executive" powers (investigation and prosecution) and "quasi–judicial" powers (adjudication via formal hearings of disputes involving commission rules and regulations). Thus, what the framers of the Constitution had so assiduously separated, in the belief that liberties were thereby best preserved, Congress had joined together in one regulatory agency. Not only were the powers of the Interstate Commerce Commission expanded over the years, but the pattern of the quasi–legislative, quasi–executive and quasi–judicial agency were followed in the later establishment of other federal administrative commissions, boards and authorities.

The opposition of the propertied and business interests against governmental regulation expanded to a new battleground—those administrative agencies whose functions embraced the powers of all three branches of government. As the nation entered the twentieth century, the competing claims of industry and democracy were the focal point of combative thrust and counterthrust in the popular press, the rostrum, the Congress and the courts.

The third conflict centered on the role of judicial review by the regular courts of law established under Article III of the Constitution. The detractors of administrative regulation opposed the notion that emergent "administrative law" was to have any degree of finality. Rather, they envisioned that appeals to the regular courts would not be foreclosed and that decisions lost in the administrative arena would find more favorable reception from a judiciary traditionally extrasensitive to vested private property rights. Opponents of such a position stressed that administrative agencies, for the most part, dealt with unique problems no more appropriate for judicial than for legislative determination and that the judicial processes were ill-adapted for their resolution.

The fourth conflict involved the legal profession. Defendants appearing before administrative agencies for alleged violations of statute law or agency rules and regulations usually retained legal counsel to represent their interests. The rules of evidence and procedures in administrative hearings differed for a variety of reasons from those applicable to the regular courts. Attorneys often felt that these departures from traditional practice adversely affected the interests of their clients and, equally important, necessitated their own detailed knowledge of the unique procedures. The agency hearing room was consequently regarded as the scene of suspicious proceedings in an unfamiliar environment; yet, enough legal procedure and terminology was retained to give an unwarranted "aura" of legal legitimacy.

The fifth conflict or controversy in which administrative agencies have been embroiled raises a different type of issue. A number of consumer groups, some congressmen, scholars and investigative reporters have forwarded the belief that a fundamental reorganization or even abolition of many of the so-called independent regulatory agencies should take place with their functions parcelled out and transferred to purely executive agencies and/or to a separate system of administrative courts. The general argument is that these agencies have been poorly managed, have built up almost insurmountable backlogs of cases and have too often developed policies departing from the interests of the broader public in favor of specific industries they are supposed to regulate. Questionable ethical practices, blatant conflicts of interest and poor appointments of those who shape agency policies have all contributed to a feeling by many who are essentially sympathetic to the regulatory function that all is not well. Hence mere modification of the existing procedures or internal reorganization is just not adequate to counterbalance an increasing lack of confidence. The "sell-out" of some regulatory agencies to industry blandishments and pressures is often allegedly confirmed by the fact that the "regulated" industries comprise the greatest block of opposition to abolition or drastic overhaul of the existing agencies and their procedures.

Some of the conflicts surfacing over the years have been more or less resolved, while others present challenges that are capable of resolution only in the future. The battle over broadened governmental regulation and enhanced use of the police power has now been reduced to little more than a skirmish.

Whereas the courts through the 1920's continued to favor property rights over administrative regulation, they have, since the late 1930's tended to confirm and reinforce public power, to condition the use of private property and to regulate commercial activities at all levels of government. One of the leading factors was the increasing interdependence of all men in a highly urbanized and industrial society where the liberty to use one's property as before did often result in adverse consequences for other men. Also, the magnitude and depths of the Great Depression of the 1930's and the state of public opinion simply would not allow continued judicial invalidation of congressional regulatory schemes to bring more business activities under public control. About midway into President Franklin D. Roosevelt's administration, the United States Supreme Court, for all intents and purposes, abandoned much of its previous doctrine and gave its stamp of approval to a number of novel experiments to combat the depression. The trend was irrevocable and, despite occasional lapses reflective of concern for private property rights, the courts have laid such a strong foundation for administrative regulation that it is no longer subject to challenge per se.

The conflict concerning the combination of quasi–legislative, quasi–executive and quasi–judicial functions had steadily built up until it reached its peak in the late 1930's and early 1940's. Involved were lawyers, judges, administrators, businessmen and laymen. At issue was the question of whether the "rule of law" had been violated by administrative justice. According to the "rule of law," as developed in England, no man should be deprived of private property rights except in a court of law according to established judicial procedure. To many persons the spirit of the "rule of law" had been violated by making administrative agencies the "judges in their own cases" through the combining of investigatory, prosecuting and adjudicatory powers. Not only were private rights determined outside the regular courts, but the volume of administrative cases made any extensive review by the courts extremely unlikely.

The issue was put to rest by Congress's passage of the Administrative Procedure Act in 1946. The act, described in detail at a later point, set forth the fundamental proposition that the combination of functions was not contrary to the rule of law provided that certain procedural protections were accorded those persons affected by agency decisions. Despite some continuing criticism, this approach is central to agency decision making today.

Another conflict involving the question of the finality of administrative decisions has been more or less resolved by both congressional action and the courts themselves. In numerous statutes Congress has limited judicial review of administrative actions and, over a period of years, the courts have tended to passivity rather than activism in the administrative area. In a long line of decisions, the United States Supreme Court has recognized the unique nature and requirements of administrative decision making and has preferred not to substitute its own judgment for that of responsible administrative officials. Consequently, few administrative cases and controversies reach the appellate courts when considered in relation to the vast numbers decided within administrative agencies. The scope of judicial review has been drastically limited though not completely precluded.

Yet another type of conflict is a continuing one and will not be finally resolved at any one point in time. Legal counsel representing those individuals, organizations or corporations affected by administrative decisions will always seek to improve procedural processes, protect client interests and strive for more of a traditional legal atmosphere in administrative proceedings. For example, the legal profession has consistently exerted pressures for legal training for officials vested with decision making responsibilities. Most law school programs do now include a course in administrative law and some attorneys specialize in cases involving administrative adjudication. It is a highly specialized field of legal practice.

Finally, one conflict characterizing administrative law centers around different perceptions of the inherent ability of many administrative agencies to represent the "public interest" rather than private interests. Despite numerous studies and congressional hearings, little has been accomplished to meet head-on the problem of ethical lapses and conflicts of interest. The malady of "goal displacement"—the increasing irrelevance of originally mandated agency goals in favor of goals serving special private interest—has not yet had a proper prescription for its cure.

Overall, the battle over fundamentals between so-called "administrative absolutists" and the champions of unfettered private rights in property has been brought to a lower level of conflict. The outcome, largely in the nature of compromise, made administrative decision making less absolute by enhanced procedural safeguards while rights to the use of one's property have been considerably diluted. A balance of sorts has been struck, with Congress and the courts favoring one side or the other on specific issues. The important point to note is that administrative departure from the traditional "triadic" fragmentation of powers into legislative, executive and judicial functions has been upheld by the courts and, in fact, in 1935 the Supreme Court recognized the independent regulatory commissions with their combination of functions as a "fourth branch of government."[3]

THE ADMINISTRATIVE REGULATORY PROCESS

The regulatory functions of administrative agencies with powers to determine private rights and obligations and to issue rules and regulations should not be regarded as necessarily negative or constraining. True, regulation does imply potential or real limitation of freedom and discretion. However, regulation broadly construed also implies the authority to shape policy in "positive" directions, that is, to authorize action or discretion where they were previously limited and to influence policy toward beneficial and morally compelling ends. Consequently, the regulatory power is more of a tool, rather than an end in itself, to be utilized for either restrictive or freedom-enhancing purposes.

The negative or restrictive potential of regulatory authority must always be a cause for concern in a democratic society. The arsenal of punitive measures with which administrative agencies are endowed makes it imperative that the regulatory process, especially its negative or restrictive component, be carefully circumscribed by safeguards to ensure the exercise of authority only within a framework of democratic values.

The many hundreds of governmental jurisdictions with thousands of administrative agencies exercising regulatory powers make it difficult to prescribe precisely a "common" regulatory process. The following description of the process does however suggest the basic essentials that characterize a "composite" model (Figure 8–1). Containing elements of federal as well as state and local regulatory procedures, it should prove useful as a simplified introduction to a very complex field of public law and is not meant to accurately describe any single jurisdiction or level of government.

Phase I: Legal Authority

The regulatory process carried out by administrative agencies must commence with a source of power. The initial authority is traced to the legislative act establishing the agency. Such legislation will describe in detail, but sometimes in rather generalized or vague terms, the purposes and mission of the agency. This legislation, in effect, becomes its "charter" and, despite later amendments which may modify initial authority, the legitimatizing of the agency is accomplished by the earlier legislative enactment.

Alternatively, new programs or objectives sought by the legislature may best be accomplished through existing agencies. In this situation, a legislative act will add to existing agency authority. Such legislation may utilize existing machinery and resources within the agency or, occasionally, a new internal subunit may be authorized along with newly assigned resources—fiscal, manpower or facilities-equipment. In either case the agency operates under a delegation of power from the legislature. By its nature a delegated power may be abrogated or modified.

Where an agency is established in the state constitution or at the local level in its basic fundamental document (likewise termed "charter"), that agency is immune from abolition by legislative fiat although its budgetary and personnel resources

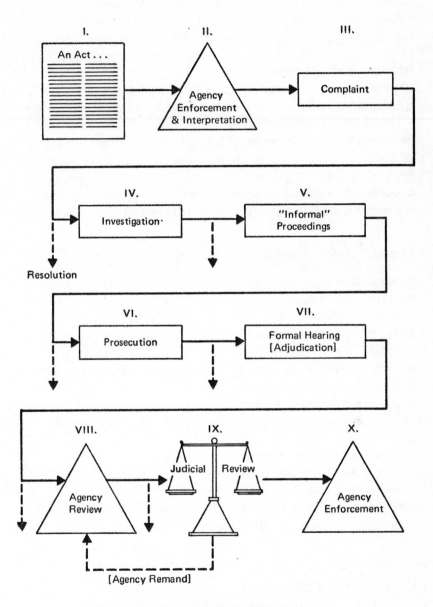

I.

An Act . . .

II.

Agency
Enforcement
& Interpretation

III.

Complaint

IV.

Investigation·

V.

"Informal"
Proceedings

Resolution

VI.

Prosecution

VII.

Formal Hearing
[Adjudication]

VIII.

Agency
Review

IX.

Judicial   Review

X.

Agency
Enforcement

[Agency Remand]

Figure 8-1. THE ADMINISTRATIVE
REGULATORY PROCESS

may be affected by legislative action. Where the mission of the agency is included in the fundamental document comprising either state constitution or local charter, it is not subject to drastic revision by the legislature. Constitutionally delegated power is consequently on a firmer foundation than is legislatively delegated power.

The issuance of agency rules and regulations, enforceable in law and affecting private rights and obligations, also becomes a source of agency authority. This authority, however, must be traceable to an earlier delegated power—either legislative or constitutional. The point to be made is that by whatever method—legislative, constitutional or rule making—a legitimate basis for the exercise of agency power has been established by a separate institution of government external to that agency.

Phase II: Enforcement and Interpretation

Agency mandates, whether legislative, constitutional or based on rules and regulations, must be enforced. In addition, the specific provisions have to be interpreted in practice as they are applied to those persons or organizations subject to agency authority. Here semantics or grammatical construction is extremely important. Where the written provisos are precise, there will be little room for administrative discretion. On the other hand, when agency authority is mandated, either intentionally or unintentionally, in ambiguous phraseology, then administrative discretion in determining the terms, conditions and content of policy to be enforced is maximized. Whether or not the agency's interpretation of its own powers is valid, its authorized powers may become a subject of dispute. The issue may be resolved either by a legislative enactment more precisely delineating legislative intent or by formal legal challenge to either the agency's legality or the constitutionality of its actions.

Phase III: Complaint

In the normal course of events, administrative agencies enforce and interpret the laws and their own rules and regulations with relatively few challenges. Thousands of decisions are made each day affecting private rights and obligations with minimal points of contention. Inevitably, however, some persons or organizations will feel adversely affected, perhaps unjustly, by agency policy or some bureaucratic decision or action. A challenge to agency policies and/or procedures may result. Conversely, agencies may take the initiative themselves in filing charges alleging violations of the law by persons or organizations subject to their jurisdiction.

A third and quite frequent possibility is that of Citizen A being adversely affected by the actions or practices of Citizen B or of a corporate entity. Where Citizen A feels that such actions or practices violate laws, rules or regulations that the agency is responsible for administering, then a complaint (an allegation of legal wrongdoing) may be filed with that agency by this citizen. The agency may therefore be perceived as a potential protector of liberty and well-being by Citizen A as well as a potentially oppressive agency by Citizen B or the corporation whose activities are at issue. Examples are legion: a citizen may be charged an exorbitant rate by a common carrier under public regulation, a homeowner may find his neighbor engaged in a prohibited and incompatible commercial or manufacturing activity in an area zoned for single-family residential use only; a consumer may find he has been "short-weighted" in the product packaged in a container contrary to the specifications on the label. Examples of agency initiative in complaints may emerge from local health department inspections of nursing or convalescent homes or homes for the elderly where inadequate facilities, improper sanitation, adulterated food or evidence of physical abuses are uncovered. At a higher level the state real estate agency may discover fraudulent land promotional schemes or, at the national level, the public sale of unregistered stocks or bonds may trigger the issuance of an agency complaint.

The point is that the administrative agency here acts as protector of the community, and the burdens of taking remedial action, which might prove beyond the means and abilities of the ordinary citizen, are assumed by the agency as representative of the total society. Administrative relief therefore precludes the necessity of individual suits being filed in the regular courts—a process few citizens can sustain, especially against corporate entities with superior fiscal resources and their own legal staffs.

Phase IV: Investigation

Agency investigation may either precede or follow a complaint. When a citizen or corporation complains to an administrative agency about an alleged violation of law by another citizen or corporation, the administrative agency has two alternatives. The first is to determine whether or not the alleged violation is within the agency's jurisdiction. If not, the matter is dropped or the complaint is referred to the appropriate agency for proper relief. The second alternative is to determine whether or not the alleged misdeed or practice, if within agency jurisdiction, is of sufficient severity to warrant further agency action. If the matter does not warrant agency action, the complaint is "dropped," that is, no further action is taken. Note on the chart that the vertical arrow shows that a significant number of private complaints requesting agency action never proceed beyond this point. Some alleged violations may not, in fact, constitute violations within the strict meaning of the law as interpreted by the agency. Others may not, as earlier suggested, be under agency jurisdiction. Some complaints may be dropped because of insufficient evidence of wrongdoing. For whatever reason, this is the end of the road for large numbers of complaints.

Those private complaints which do merit agency action continue in an active status as agency investigative powers come into play. Frequently, as in the case of routine agency inspections or audits, violations are uncovered as further and more detailed investigation takes place. In these instances investigation may precede the issuance of a formal complaint or "order" by the agency itself.

The investigatory stage is highly specialized and outside public scrutiny. Many administrative agencies have a common plea: higher budgets for support of more investigatory staff in the face of heavier case loads. Some investigations involving interstate or even international activities may extend over several years; other investigations may be quite perfunctory and limited in scope. Following investigative reports, agency officials must determine on the basis of the record whether or not to pursue the matter further. Here investigative evidence, agency resources (both fiscal and personnel), value priorities and external political pressures must be taken into account. At some point an internalized agency decision will be made to proceed to the next stage or, as in many cases, not to pursue the matter further. As the chart indicates, some cases progress to the informal proceeding state while others are relegated to the "inactive" file.

Phase V: Informal Proceedings

An "informal" administrative proceeding varies from agency to agency and even at different levels of government. In general, however, it is best described as an agency attempt to resolve the issue of alleged wrongdoing by action short of formal prosecution. The latter would necessitate a formal "quasi-judicial" hearing. Informal proceedings may comprise little more than a requested conference between agency officials and persons alleged to have violated the law or agency rules or regulations. Here the original complaint and the investigatory evidence will be presented by the agency with opportunity for rejoinder by the persons accused. Frequently, this is culminated by a warning that further violations may be dealt with more severely. If the accused recognizes the "errors" of his ways, the case proceeds no further.

If the violation is one of a more significant nature, the accused may be asked to sign a "cease and desist" order. This constitutes an admission of guilt, but further prosecution of a formal nature may not be undertaken provided that no similar violations occur in the future. The "cease and desist" order is, as its name implies, an agency order to refrain from the questionable activity. By signing the order, the accused, in effect, enters into a contractual relationship that is legally binding. In some jurisdictions violation of a previously signed cease and desist order is prima facie evidence of criminal contempt of court and, as such, prosecutable by appropriate authorities before the regular courts.

Once again, as the vertical arrow indicates on the chart, a large number of cases terminate at the stage of informal proceedings. The accused may find the cessation of illegal activities or practices a relatively small price to pay in order to avoid formal prosecution. Knowing that the case can be renewed if further violations occur, few will view this as a viable alternative to simply ceasing and desisting. Conversely, other accused parties may on their own and on the advice of legal counsel challenge agency jurisdiction, dispute agency interpretations of existing applicable laws or challenge either the validity or the sufficiency of the investigative evidence. In short, a virtual admission of guilt and an agreement to cease and desist is rejected, and further agency action is regarded as an acceptable risk.

Phase VI: Prosecution

The bulk of pending cases are successfully resolved at the informal stage—often in the agency's favor but sometimes on the basis of compromise. Those cases for which informal proceedings are not adequate will be forwarded to the prosecuting staff within the larger agencies or, in the case of some smaller jurisdictions, to appropriate prosecuting authorities outside the agency, that is, a state attorney general, a county district attorney or a city attorney. The stage is now set for formal notice of "adjudicatory" hearing as detailed specifications of the alleged wrongdoing are drawn up by responsible officials. The accused and his legal counsel likewise prepare their defense and their "answers" to the formal allegations. Once again the possibility of the case being "dropped" remains, as last-minute compromise agreement may forestall a formal hearing of the dispute.

Phase VII: Adjudication

On a given date at a designated time, assuming the lack of a "last-minute" agreement, a formal administrative tribunal or hearing within the agency is held. Such hearings are "quasi-

judicial" in nature, that is, having some characteristics of proceedings in the regular courts but with different rules of evidence
and procedures. Evidence of both prosecution and defense is
presented before a single officer who may be identified as a
"hearing officer," "hearing examiner," "administrative referee,"
"administrative commissioner" or "administrative law judge."
There are no juries and the public is usually excluded since only
the regular courts are required to conduct trials open to the
public. The hearing officer or examiner, in recent years, has
been required to be a member of the Bar with specified minimum years of practice in adjudicatory proceedings before administrative agencies.

The role of the hearing officer is to evaluate the evidence of
both sides to the dispute and arrive at a conclusion based upon
such evidence. His discretion varies with the law applicable to
his agency. He should attempt to weigh countervailing public
and private interests in the light of evidence presented. His decision determines guilt or innocence for the accused. If the
allegations of wrongdoing are not upheld by the hearing officer,
the case is terminated. If, on the other hand, some degree of
guilt or liability is established, the hearing officer may assign an
appropriate penalty within the power of the administrative
agency to impose. They include required reimbursements for
overcharges, permanent or temporary suspension of licenses,
withholding of certain governmental benefits, deportation in
immigration and naturalization hearings, denial of the use of
governmental facilities including the mails, cancellation of a
government contract, ineligibility to bid on a government contract, financial penalties, withholding of governmental certification (airworthiness or seaworthiness, for example) necessary for
common carriers or refusal to certify a product for sale. Jail
terms are not included in the arsenal of administrative
"remedies" and may only be imposed after trial in the regular
courts on the basis of a criminal conviction.

Phase VIII: Agency Review

The bulk of hearing officer decisions are final and few cases
proceed beyond this point. However, because of quite limited

opportunities for review by the regular courts, most governments do provide for appellate procedures within the agency itself. The highly complex conditions and techniques of agency review need not be detailed here. Suffice it to note that agency review of the hearing officer's decision may be mandatory or, in some cases, may have to be triggered by appeal on specific points by the adversely affected party. In some agencies appeals can be made only on technical points and the review is restricted to these issues. In other agencies or for certain categories of cases, the review process may be quite sweeping and not limited merely to technical points. The larger administrative agencies may have intermediate reviewing boards whose members are endowed with the power to reverse or modify the decision or penalty imposed by the hearing officer.[4] In some instances final appeal may be made to the agency's highest authority, that is, its head or the board or commission ultimately responsible for agency policy.[5] Where agency review is quite extensive, issues of fundamental policy may be considered by the intermediate legal reviewing officers. Other issues may relate to questions of sufficiency of evidence, mitigating circumstances, interpretation of existing laws, alleged denial of certain procedural rights preceding or during the formal hearing and potential conflicts of interest by hearing officers. Modification of the hearing officer's decisions is final, provided there are no further grounds for appeals to the regular courts.

Phase IX: Judicial Review

Relatively few cases proceed to judicial review by the regular courts. Most of the disputes, as the chart indicates, are resolved prior ro regular adjudicatory hearing and the majority of those adjudicated are finalized upon agency review. Judicial review of administrative adjudicatory decisions is therefore based upon highly selective criteria. The sheer volume of administrative disputes assures that, without a separate system of specialized administrative courts, only a small number of select cases can be realistically reviewed by the nation's regular courts of law.

Certain fundamental propositions govern the selection of administrative cases for judicial review:

1. The role of the courts is not primarily to substitute judicial values for administrative values; rather it is to redress or counterbalance abuses of administrative power and agency decision making.

2. Where a "privilege" rather than a "right" is involved (granting or revoking a license, refusal or award of a franchise or contract, application for public employment or dismissal from public employment, etc.), the courts are reluctant to interfere unless specifically empowered by applicable law.

3. When the adequacy of the "process" by which the administrative agency reached its decision is evident, the courts are unlikely to seek to reverse that decision. However, a prejudicial error in the procedure itself or the withholding of certain procedural rights may "trigger" judicial review.

4. Where the administrative agency has based its decision on "substantial evidence" (or in some types of cases in some jurisdictions on the basis of "any evidence"), the courts will not interfere.

5. "Findings of material facts" in administrative hearings are not subject to challenge in the courts unless there is considerable evidence of an error, that is, a finding is erroneous. However, once a finding of fact is made, the burden of proof to refute that finding is upon the person or organization to be regulated.

6. Where administrative decision making is legally "discretionary" rather than "ministerial" (an absolute duty with no discretion), the courts view this as an attribute of valid power and will not set aside such decisions. In such instances, unless the party regulated can challenge the discretionary decision on the basis of conflict of interest, arbitrary vindictiveness or some similar ground, the decision will be allowed to stand.

7. Where there is evidence of administrative agencies hav-

ing exceeded their constitutional or statutory authority or the authority of previous judicial holdings, the courts may review the case.

8. Where administrative agencies have initially interpreted the law and that interpretation is challenged, the courts may grant judicial review. In matters of constitutional or statutory interpretation, the courts do insist on having the "final" word. This is regarded as the very essence of judicial duty.

9. Judicial review is most likely where there are few, if any, governing judicial precedents in case law.

10. Judicial review is likely where administrative interpretation of the law departs from established agency policy and rules.

11. Judicial review will not be granted unless all available administrative remedies have been exhausted.

In addition to potential judicial review of administrative decisions, the courts have traditionally been vested with the authority to issue "writs" or orders that are directed toward administrative officials. Most frequently used are:

Writ of Mandamus: an order of the court that the official carry out certain mandatory duties (ministerial) vested in him by law.

Writ of Prohibition: An order of the court that the official cease activities that are beyond his legal authority.

Writ of Quo Warranto: An order of the court forcing the official and/or agency to set forth the legal authority by which claim to office is held or by which activities are conducted.

Writ of Injunction: An order of the court to prevent a threatened harm. It may be applicable to an administrative official or a private citizen or organization where the public interest may be adversely affected by such action.

It must be remembered that internal administrative decision making and procedures are not subject to judicial review or the

reach of judicial "writs." Examples are fiscal or physical facilities planning, internal management reorganization, executive
rules or regulations directed to internal procedures, technical-
scientific-engineering decisions in which the courts have little
expertise and newly emerging fields of administrative activities in which widely accepted standards have not yet been
established.

Despite the limitations surrounding judicial review of administrative decisions, the impact of court scrutiny should not
be minimized. Occasionally, the courts not only exert jurisdiction where administrative actions are challenged, but some of
these decisions become basic reference points in the endless interactions of administrative agency and private citizen.
Sometimes the judges themselves exercise judicial "self-restraint"
and choose not to enter into certain types of controversies—for
example, the "legality" of undeclared wars carried out under
presidential authority. In other matters, despite judicial inclination to intervene, the role of the judiciary in reviewing administrative decisions may be severely limited by law. One of the
most common congressionally imposed limitations is that which
provides that administrative findings based on "substantial evidence" shall be conclusive.

Administrative cases reviewed by the federal courts may be
upheld, substantially modified, "remanded" back to the administrative agency for further action or modification in line
with a judicial decision or the administrative decision may be
reversed (that is, the court arrives at an opposite and final conclusion thereby invalidating the administrative decision). Following judicial review, the agency has final responsibility to
execute the decision of the court under such specific terms and
conditions as may be laid down by proper judicial authority.
This, in effect, is the final stage of the administrative regulatory
process. It must be kept in mind, however, that the courts are
not able to execute their own decisions so that the effectiveness
of judicial policy making will depend, in large measure, upon
the vigor, or conversely, lack of commitment of administrative
agencies in executing the law as propounded by the judiciary.
In theory, the law as finally interpreted by the courts is to be
enforced vigorously and with dispatch. In practice, however,

there may be considerable "foot-dragging," especially if agency values and judicial values conflict.

The administrative regulatory process provides the means for conflict resolution at numerous points along a lengthy continuum. From the enactment of legislation or the issuance of agency rules and regulations to the many points at which administrative decisions are finalized or compromised, conflicts of values, goals and interpretation of the law are evident. Even the final stage of judicial review may reflect differing views as evidenced by "split" (separate majority and minority) decisions.

THE ADMINISTRATIVE PROCEDURE ACT

The passage of the Administrative Procedure Act by Congress in 1946 was a very consequential event in the development of the regulatory process. The act has run the spectrum of praise as well as damning criticism. One fact does stand out, however: the act represents the first comprehensive legislative attempt to improve the administrative process. It is a remedial legislative approach to regulatory problems.

Prior to passage of the act, the most controversial and emotional issue was that of the "rule of law." As administrative agencies with regulatory powers multiplied during the 1930's, opponents of the administrative process, ignoring any constructive programs that the agencies might be carrying out, viewed them as symbolic of an obnoxious political philosophy that was rapidly destroying freedom. The social legislation of the Roosevelt administration brought the issue of the proper form of administrative procedure into the open, and a multitude of proposals for administrative reform were forwarded both by apologists and opponents of the regulatory process. By 1937 the Supreme Court had been sufficiently influenced by presidential threats and cajoling and the mood of the public to reverse its traditional conservative stance and outlook and to vest experimental social programs and their administrative agencies with an aura of constitutional legitimacy. Administrative agencies were no longer regarded as "alien intruders," as their regulatory powers were now sanctified.[6] The courts were beginning the process of giving great weight to administrative decisions despite departure from the hallowed separation of powers principle. Still, in the minds of many, the issue of injustice was raised—indeed the issue of whether or not any agency could be investigator, prosecutor and judge of its own authority and power.

The problem had perhaps best been summarized by Chief Justice Charles Evans Hughes when he warned:

> ... if these multiplying agencies deemed to be necessary to our complex society are to serve the purposes for which they are created and endowed with vast powers, they must accredit themselves by acting in accordance with the cherished judicial tradition embodying the basic concepts of fair play.[7]

Upon its enactment in 1946, one authority described the Administrative Procedure Act as "one of the most dramatic legal developments of the past century."[8] Despite many evident weaknesses, the act did attempt to balance administrative authority with concepts of fair play by laying down guidelines that emphasized procedural protections rather than substantive policy to be followed by agencies. In effect, the concept of "due process" was viewed as the key to holding administrative agencies responsible under a system of laws rather than of men.[9]

The act provides for internal separation of adjudicatory functions from the investigatory and prosecuting ones. Barriers between the functions were established without removing the hearing examiners from the agencies themselves. In addition, hearing examiners under the Administrative Procedure Act are no longer agents of their respective administrative agencies but are accorded more of the status of judicial officers. In fact, at a later date their title was changed from "hearing examiners" to "administrative law judges."

The U.S. Civil Service Commission was given jurisdiction over the hearing examiners. They are appointed under established Civil Service procedures with their tenure, ratings, promotions and compensation set by the commission rather than by the agency. The examiners may not be subject to direction or supervision of any person engaged in the investigative or prosecuting functions of an agency. The act provides that no hearing examiner shall consult any person or party on any fact in issue unless upon notice and full opportunity of all parties in the case to participate.

Hearing examiners may be removed only after good cause after trial before the Civil Service Commission with the decision subject to judicial review. Lastly, hearing examiners are to have rotating assignments as far as practicable.

Further, the act provides that no officer, employee or agent performing investigating or prosecuting functions for any agency in any case shall participate or advise in the decision, recommended decision or agency review of that case. Decisions shall be based upon "reliable, probative and substantial evidence," and all parties must be afforded reasonable opportunity to submit written briefs for consideration of the hearing examiner.

The act went far beyond providing procedural safeguards for persons or organizations during hearings. Significant provisions outside the adjudicatory stage include the requirement that descriptions of agency organization in both central and field offices and procedures by which subsequent agency rules and regulations are made shall be published in the *Federal Register*. All final adjudicatory decisions as well as orders shall be available for public inspection (except in military, naval or foreign affairs or agency management or personnel matters). General notice of proposed agency rule making shall be published in the *Federal Register*.

After notice, interested persons shall be given an opportunity to participate in the rule making through submissions of written data, views or arguments with or without the opportunity of oral presentation. Further, except as provided by statute, the proponent of a rule or order has the burden of proof.

Agency action made reviewable by statute and final agency action for which there is no adequate remedy in a court are subject to judicial review. The reviewing court may compel agency action unlawfully withheld or unreasonably delayed. The reviewing court may hold unlawful and set aside agency action, findings and conclusions which are arbitrary, contrary to constitutional right, in excess of statutory jurisdiction, or without observance of procedure required by law. Exempt from provisions of the Administrative Procedure Act are Congress, the courts, military courts martial and military commissions.

The federal Administrative Procedure Act was followed in rapid succession by a large number of state procedure acts that roughly approximated the federal provisions. The legislative approach to reform and strengthening of the regulatory process has therefore been a dominant theme since passage of the original act itself. The courts for their part have tended to interpret these administrative procedure acts broadly rather than narrowly so that the internal separation of investigatory prosecuting and adjudicatory functions is now well-established.

Despite some criticism, the provisions of most administrative procedure acts do establish fairly rigid standards to be followed and provide statutory protection to some of the basic rights that had previously depended only upon particular circumstances for their existence. At the very least a measure of responsibility has been imposed and the centrifugal tendencies of the multitudinous agencies, boards and commissions have been reduced in the establishment of uniform minimal standards of procedural due process.[10]

CHALLENGES FOR THE FUTURE

Some major problems of administrative regulation remain to be resolved. One of the most significant is the problem of conflicts of interest where boards and commissions are composed of representatives of groups to be regulated. Licensing boards are a prime example as are banking and insurance commissions comprised wholly or in part of representatives of the regulated corporations. A second problem is the "mass program" oriented to serve the needs of millions of individuals. Often unaware of administrative remedies for specific problems or, conversely, not aware of remedies for agency abuse of power, the individual citizen tends to "shrink" before such administrative behemoths. The third problem is the probability of diminished opportunities for judicial review despite authorization of such review by law.   As court congestion and case backlogs increase, the percentages of administrative cases reviewed by the regular courts decreases.[11]

Under federal law the final decisions of administrative agencies and regulatory commissions may, under certain conditions, be appealed to federal courts. Most go directly to the U.S. Court of Appeals while a few (from the Interstate Commerce Commission, for example) are heard by three-judge panels at the district court level.   The United States Supreme Court through "certiorari" (an order to a lower court to send up the full record of a case for review by the Supreme Court) exercises quite limited discretionary review of cases heard in appellate and district courts.

One member of the United States Supreme Court has estimated that only about fifteen to twenty opinions each term involving judicial review of administrative decisions are issued by that court. Further, he observes that today the Supreme Court hears fewer than 10 percent of all cases appealed to it and that the court is fast approaching the limit of its ability to hear and decide cases.

The implications of this trend in judicial review are forcefully set forth by Associate Justice Byron White:

> I do not for a moment question the importance of the work of the Court in connection with the review of administrative agency decisions. Of course, as far as it goes it is very important.   But as case loads in the District Courts and the Courts of Appeals continue to grow and our certiorari docket does likewise, a greater and greater proportion of administrative law decisions in the Courts of Appeals will receive no further review and the number of Supreme Court judgments in this area will decline relative to the total universe of reviewable judgments. The Court's overall participation in the development of administrative law will become increasingly spasmodic and episodic. . . . [D]oes the Supreme Court's growing reject pile contain many cases that by standards of bygone years would have been given further review? The question will be much sharper and more telling if 10 years from now the Court is still writing 150 opinions but has culled those cases not from

4000 but from 8000 certiorari petitions and statements of jurisdiction on appeal. That a constantly increasing proportion of the decisions of the Courts of Appeals on administrative law questions are, as a practical matter, beyond the reach of Supreme Court review is, at the very least, a matter of substantial legal significance.[12]

This is a problem far beyond legal significance since it may have vast political, economic and social ramifications. At the time of increasing public regulatory power, the role of the nation's highest judicial tribunal appears headed for inexorable decline.

Another problem is inevitably a continuing one—that of new areas under regulatory authority. The impact of pressures from conservation–ecology groups upon public policy in recent years has been truly amazing. Federal, state and local legislative enactments to protect the environment, conserve limited or fragile resources and further aesthetic harmony between man and his natural habitat have delegated vast powers to new boards and commissions. Some of these new regulatory policies and agencies have been accorded constitutional status in a number of states and have been approved at statewide referendums. A new societal bipolarity has emerged, pitting development–employment–economic interests against historical–preservation–conservation–ecology–oriented interests. The existing laws and judicial decisions have provided few precedents for this titanic struggle which promises to be of long duration. Not only have vast new powers that are largely untested been delegated to these public agencies under the guise of serving the "public interest," but new tools such as "environmental impact reports" have been required in many jurisdictions before public or private development may take place. The contents and limits of such devices are only now being shaped by hundreds of administrative decisions and sporadic judicial review.

Our transitional society will be the arena for the resolution of many conflicts, the increasing irrelevance of some traditional conflicts and the occasion for the emergence of unprecedented new confrontations based upon widely divergent values. Administrative law, reflecting both freedom and constraint, will remain a crucial element in their peaceful resolution. Democracy is never conflict-free but, on the contrary, is the most conflict-prone of all forms of government. Where wide representation of interests is assured, differences in perception of those interests will inevitably arise. It is the role of law to assure that the resultant tensions do not go beyond those manageable limits that are essential to any civilized polity.

NOTES

1. One of the earlier administrative law texts emphasized this point in its title. See Ernest Freund, *Administrative Powers Over Persons and Property,* Chicago: University of Chicago Press, 1928.

2. U.S. Congress, Senate, Document no. 8, 77th Cong., 1st session. pp. 7-21.

3. *Humphrey's Executor (Rathbun) v. United States,* 295 U.S. 602 (1935).

4. On the subject of agency review boards, see James O. Freedman, "Review Boards in the Administrative Process," 117 *University of Pennsylvania Law Review* 546; "Note: Intermediate Appellate Review Boards for Administrative Agencies," 81 *Harvard Law Review* 1325; Donald J. Berkemeyer, "Agency Review by Intermediate Boards," *Administrative Law Review* vol. 26, p. 61.

5. See Robert J. Corber, "A Practitioner Looks at the Effectiveness of the Agency Review Process," *Administrative Law Review* vol. 26, p. 67.

6. See C. Herman Pritchett, *The Roosevelt Court,* New York: Macmillan, 1948, especially chap. 7.

7. *Morgan v. United States,* 304 U.S. 22.

8. Victor S. Netterville, "The Administrative Procedure Act: A Study in Interpretation," 20 *George Washington Law Review* 1.

9. For a general background, see U.S. Congress, Senate, Document no. 248, *Administrative Procedure Act: Legislative History,* 79th Cong., 2d sess., 1946.

10. A useful, though somewhat dated, presentation of shortcomings and suggested solutions to regulatory problems is "Administrative Regulation," *Law and Contemporary Problems* vol. 26: pp. 179-346.

11. For an up-to-date discussion of the strengths and weaknesses of the regulatory process, see "Symposium: Review of Administrative Adjudication," 26 *Administrative Law Review,* pp. 1-128.

12. Byron K. White, "Supreme Court Review of Agency Decisions," *op. cit.,* p. 109.

9

THE INTERGOVERNMENTAL MAZE: ADMINISTRATIVE FEDERALISM

The term "administrative federalism" is appropriate to describe administrative relations among the many American governments, just as the term "fiscal federalism" is a useful label to describe intergovernmental fiscal relationships. Both subjects are essential to understanding the very complex area of dynamic interchange between public jurisdictions. Although administrative federalism and fiscal federalism are sometimes separate processes, quite often the two are intimately linked together. In some processes of American government, it is difficult to discuss one without reference to the other. Nevertheless, this chapter and Chapter 10 do give separate emphasis to each in order to better understand their differing assumptions, techniques and problems.

FEDERALISM

Perhaps the simplest nontechnical definition of federalism is the fragmentation or division of governmental powers among several centers of authority. The United States, with over 80,000 separate governmental jurisdictions, represents (despite certain discernible centralizing tendencies) the most marked federal system in the world today.[1] This is particularly evident when one considers the multitude of national, state and local constitutions, legislative bodies, executive agencies, courts, elections and political parties. If, as some scholars insist, the concept of federalism includes those powerful and influential quasi-public agencies (such as public utilities and chambers of commerce) as well as private organizations that effectively influence public policy at all levels, then the diffusion of government power in this country has no parellel anywhere.

Professor Richard Leach, a recognized authority on federalism, insists that the framers bequeathed to us an "open-ended" federal system intended to be a process of "action." Professor Leach further insists that our federal system is basically "irrational" insofar as theory played virtually no role in the development of American federalism.[2] While accepting that our fragmented system has emerged from very real pressures and needs unique to specific epochs in our national development, many, your present authors among them, nevertheless do stress that the federal process is indeed closely intertwined, inexorably so, with certain underlying theories or values. In contrast to Professor Leach, therefore, the proposition is put forward that federalism in the American historical context is largely a problem of value priority and value conflict. First, however, it is necessary to describe the underlying value assumptions of American federalism.

The first of these value assumptions is the belief that governmental power may lead to tyranny unless limited. Further, such a limitation may be accomplished in several ways:

1. *By absolute prohibition.* Thus neither national nor state governments, and by implication local governments, shall pass "ex post facto" laws or "bills of attainder."[3]
2. *By conditional prohibition.* For example, neither national nor state governments shall deprive any person of "life, liberty, or property, without due process of law."[4]
3. *By assigning functions to different levels of government.* Foreign affairs, coinage of money and regulation of the value thereof, commerce between the states and the postal functions are a few of the specific powers delegated to the nation. Selection of members

of Congress and of the president and ratification of proposed constitutional amendments are specifically reserved to the states. This pattern does represent choices among competing alternatives to the problem of limiting governmental power.

A second value assumption underlying American federalism is that governmental power is an "evil" that tends to expand unless held in check or counterbalanced by equal or superior centers of power. Hence at the national level and in all fifty states, governmental power is "horizontally" fragmented among legislative, executive and judicial branches. Further, it is "vertically" fragmented among national, state and local levels of government. The combination of both horizontal and vertical fragmentation attests to the weight accorded this assumption.

The third value assumption underlying American federalism is the belief that governmental power is quantifiable and, therefore, measurable. This assumption is absolutely fundamental to the American federal system. Otherwise, there could be no means of assigning power in different gradations for different purposes (3/4 majorities, 2/3 majorities and simple majorities), limiting terms of office (two years, four years and six years) or dividing authority among the nation, the states and the hundreds upon hundreds of local jurisdictions.

A fourth value assumption is that a written constitution is ideally suited to serve as the "contract" by which governmental power is authorized, conditioned, prohibited or fragmented. The supremacy of this "contract" is not left to speculation or implication. In its own words, the United States Constitution is the "supreme law" of the land. Further, unless it conflicts with the national constitution, each state constitution and local "charter" (constitution) is likewise the supreme law within its own political boundaries.

Beyond these fundamental value propositions, several of the more important "beliefs" are subject to disputation. One especially conflictive issue is that of the "proper interpretation" of American federalism, that is, what are the "correct" relationships among the various governments? The United States

Constitution contains provisions that do lead to differing interpretations. Far from the federal system being settled, it is in
ceaseless flux and there is little likelihood of permanent or
static intergovernmental relationships. The differing approaches
to the carving up of the "pie of power" in the federal system
are portrayed below. These are not all-inclusive but do reflect
major variations:

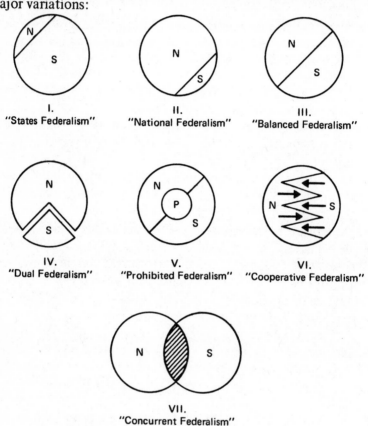

I.
"States Federalism"

II.
"National Federalism"

III.
"Balanced Federalism"

IV.
"Dual Federalism"

V.
"Prohibited Federalism"

VI.
"Cooperative Federalism"

VII.
"Concurrent Federalism"

Figure 9-1. DIFFERING APPROACHES TO FEDERALISM

Advantages of Diversity

Some of the administrative consequences of the American approach to federalism are suggested below.

Since it is a dynamic process, federalism is capable of undergoing frequent adjustment and modification to reflect shifting

societal values and needs. This requires experimentation with administrative patterns that are flexible and capable of reflecting new outlooks. A system of many thousands of separate public jurisdictions provides a unique opportunity for wide-ranging experimentation in administrative organization. The surprising fact is that so little innovative experimentation has taken place at the national and state levels—the bulk of administrative experimentation has occurred among America's local governments. Oftimes a novel administrative pattern tried in one jurisdiction has wide applicability in other jurisdictions. American federalism, therefore, permits administrative experimentation in "laboratories" of limited size that may be undertaken with a minimal commitment of resources.

The large number of administrative systems required to serve the large number of governments provides maximum opportunities for potential participation by clientele and interested citizens. In addition, the diversity of administrative systems allows different approaches to personnel practices in the areas of recruitment, training, salary negotiation and retirement. This would appear to be especially appropriate to a highly pluralistic society with significant regional differences in economic resources, governmental traditions and political practices.

A great many different academic programs to educate students for public service and provide advanced education for those already in public service are required. A fragmented and diverse governmental system served by potentially highly experimental administrative systems should be reflected by academic programs in public administration with widely divergent emphases. Attempts during the past few years to develop a single format for academic public administration programs run the risk of eventually imposing an orthodoxy and commonness not appropriate to the highly pluralistic and heterogeneous administrative tradition of the United States.

Disadvantages of Diversity

Although there are several advantages to diversity, there are also some disadvantages. Large numbers of separate administrative systems produce jurisdictional conflicts and overlapping, leading to duplications of effort. The more numerous jurisdictions are frequently of such limited scope that they are unable to realize those economies of scale identified with much larger jurisdictions. Also, the citizens are faced with a bewildering multitude of public agencies under differing levels of government. They are frequently frustrated in attempting to pinpoint responsibility for service deficiencies.

Furthermore, many governmental agencies are "behind the scenes" insofar as their activities are seldom made public and they may operate as independent "fiefdoms" with little budgetary or personnel accountability. There are also widely differing recruitment, training and public retirement programs which produce a "hodge-podge" of differing standards and fragmented loyalties inimical to the emergence of an understanding of the broader public interest.

The crucial problems that must be resolved are those which embrace many jurisdictions and which overlap the innumerable political boundaries. With excessive fragmentation no single government may be capable of resolving the problems—especially in our politically fragmented metropolitan areas.

National–State–Local Administrative Conflict

A governmental system of multiple power centers can never be free of conflicting values and interests. Fortunately, only once were conflicts resolved on the battlefield. The daily tensions and controversies involving national, state and local administrative systems are resolved by discussion, negotiation and occasionally by resort to the courts. Recent conflicts involve questions of national versus state ownership of subsea resources in tidal waters of the states,[5] the breadth of federal authority to issue leases involving oil production in offshore areas of state coastlines and national governmental liability for coastal pollution and damage to beaches from crude oil leaks. Related to this type of conflict has been state and national litigation concerning liability for bunker oil released by naval ships prior to entering coastal harbors and drydocks for maintenance, inspections and repairs. A different type of issue is involved in state and local challenges to presidential authority to impound funds for state programs allocated by Congress or to reduce congressional allocations by discretion of federal administrators.[6]

Occasionally conflicts between local contending special interest groups bring federal and local governments into the fray. Thus the Federal Bureau of Land Management in one state had granted a permit for an extended recreational motorcycle race involving several hundred entries over a course of hundreds of miles on desert land under federal ownership. Ecology and conservation-oriented groups opposing the race pointed out that the permit was in conflict with a number of existing county ordinances. County officials opposed the granting of the permit on grounds that the projected race not only violated county ordinances but would also create severe traffic problems to and from the race site. In addition, problems of law enforcement by the county sheriff would necessitate special shifts of officers and overtime pay for a large number of county employees—all at county expense. County officials were quite miffed by a federal agency's administrative decision made without consultation or consideration of its impact upon local budgets and availability of personnel.

In 1975, the city of New York, in a suit followed closely by a large number of state governments, won an important legal decision brought against the administrator of the U.S. Environmental Protection Agency, claiming that he had wrongfully failed to allot to the states the full amount authorized by Congress under the Federal Water Pollution Control Act.[7]

The federal government may also bring suit against a state. For example, the United States sued the State Tax Commission of Mississippi for attempting to regulate the sales and delivery of liquor to officers' clubs in military facilities on bases solely within federal jurisdiction.[8]

Occasionally the impact of foreign policy decisions made by executive officials in Washington is adversely felt by their state and local counterparts. In April 1975 both the governor of California and the secretary of the state's Health and Welfare Agency were highly critical of decisions made by the United States Department of State to place thousands of Vietnam refugees in California at a time when unemployment within that state was at an extremely high level and welfare rolls were already swamped. In addition to the anticipated burden on California taxpayers to support the refugees, it was felt that their massive health problems would tax state and local health departments and their already limited resources. The governor noted that California could hardly take care of its own unemployed and needy who must come first. The secretary of the Health and Welfare Agency estimated it would cost $5,000 to care for each refugee for one year and the vast majority of them, it was felt, would probably settle in the Golden State. Not only had no consultations taken place between federal and California or local authorities, but the impact on the state's political institutions and financial and social structures was not taken into account nor were there any indications of federal financial assistance to state and local governments having to bear the brunt of the immigrant wave. A resolution of the Los Angeles County Board of Supervisors added to the criticisms of federal immigration policies concerning the Vietnamese.[9] This small sampling is merely indicative of the broad range of conflicts that may involve national, state and local administrative officials.

FEDERAL AGENCY DELEGATION
TO THE STATES

In contrast to the reality of intergovernmental conflicts are vast areas of cooperation. Under some circumstances a federal administrative agency may directly delegate its powers to state agencies or officials. In the 1960's the Agency for International Development (A.I.D.) within the Department of State entered into a contractual relationship with the state of California, on the basis of earlier discussions between President John F. Kennedy and Governor Edmund Brown. The agreement centered on the state's willingness and ability to provide overseas technical assistance to Chile in furtherance of American foreign policy. In effect, California became a subcontractor to the Agency for International Development to assign its own state public employees overseas in the fields of highway transportation, education, planning, budgeting, agricultural marketing and regional water resources management. The state then sub-contracted for private experts also required by the program. Before congressional disenchantment with foreign aid programs in the late 1960's and early 1970's, no fewer than sixteen other American states were engaged in various Latin American programs under authority delegated by the Agency for International Development and the Department of State.[10]

MULTILEVEL FEDERALISM

Far too often the realities of administrative and fiscal federalism in the United States are ignored. In part, the Constitution is to blame, for it is deceivingly simplistic in its description of the American system. Some provisions are hopelessly antiquated, others reflect reality only slightly while some extremely important characteristics of government are just ignored. Its mention of only national and state governments is simplistic in the extreme and, consequently, this omission of local governments continues to fuel the illusion that American federalism is bipolar, that is, involves only two levels of government. There are probably between eight to fifteen or even as many as twenty different levels of government or authorities in the United States. The number varies with the area in which a citizen may be living. Figure 9–2 gives some indication of the depth of the problem.

Each of the governmental jurisdictions and agencies over the average citizen exercises significant administrative powers including the "police power," that is, authority to regulate citizen behavior and/or his property so as to protect the health, morals, safety and welfare of society. Each jurisdiction and agency also provides either a multitude of services upon which the well-being and survival of Mr. John Q. Citizen depend or, in some instances, a specific service through the device of special districts.

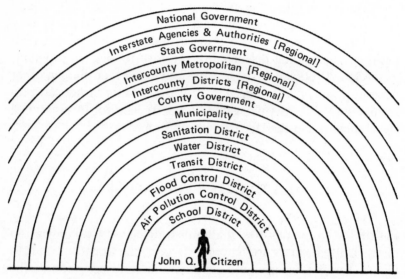

Figure 9-2. LEVELS OF ADMINISTRATIVE INFLUENCE

The complexity of this system is more apparent when the network of intergovernmental administrative linkages is considered:

Nation–State
Nation–County
Nation–Municipality
Nation–Special District
Nation–Interstate (Regional)
Nation–Intercounty Districts (Regional)
Nation–Intercounty–Metropolitian (Regional)

State–National
State–State (Regional)
State–Intercounty Districts (Regional)
State–Intercounty–Metropolitan (Regional)
State–Municipality
State–Special District

County–National
County–State
County–County
County–Municipality
County–Special District

Municipality–National
Municipality–State
Municipality–Intercounty
Municipality–County
Municipality–Municipality
Municipality–Special District

These administrative linkages make the American federal system of government by far the most complex and difficult to understand of any governmental system in the world. Each of the separate governments and authorities must maintain external relationships with a multitude of other public agencies at the same level or at higher or lower levels. There is both separation and interpenetration of the different governments.

In Figure 9-3 some of the most common inter-governmental relationships are suggested:

A. State to state administrative relationships are governed to a significant degree by U. S. constitutional provisions and congressional action. Article IV of the Constitution requires "full faith and credit," "privileges and immunities" and the extradition of fugitives who cross state lines. Article I of the Constitution requires congressional consent to compacts between states.

B. Individual state legislative action follows executive negotiations between states in interstate relations. Without individual state action, state to state relationships are impossible.

297

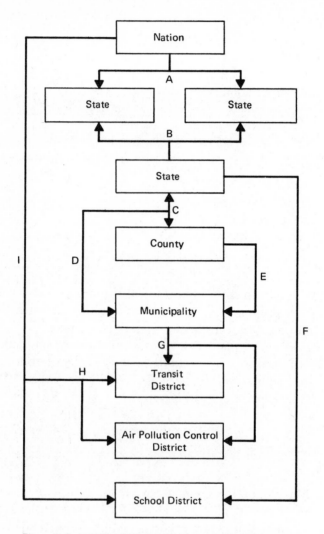

Figure 9-3. INTERGOVERNMENTAL ADMINISTRATIVE
RELATIONSHIPS

C. Counties exist in nearly all of the states as "agents" of
state policy at the local level in addition to providing
local services to unincorporated areas. The state establishes the boundaries of counties and delegates to
them their administrative powers including their patterns of organization.

D. Municipalities (cities) are "incorporated" (given legal recognition and powers) by the state. State legislation creates different classifications of municipalities with differing levels of authority. "Charters" (municipal constitutions) are adopted according to procedures laid down by state law and must be approved by the state.

E. Citizens of municipalities are subject to both municipal and county ordinances. Many county services and responsibilities embracing municipalities are mandated by state law and are not subject to municipal option or discretion. Increasingly counties are offering "contract" services to municipalities.

F. State authority over local school districts is direct. Education is subject to state administrative authority, including facilities, standards for teaching credentials, curriculum requirements and adoption of textbooks.

G. Local special districts (excluding school districts) are usually established under municipal authority to provide specified services to citizens. Composition and size of district governing boards are usually determined by municipalities. District budget, fiscal planning and personnel practices are often subject to municipal supervision and review.

H. Many local special districts also have direct administrative links with national agencies. Transit districts and air pollution control districts are examples of local districts utilizing federal funds and working in conjunction with counterpart agencies at the national level.

I. National interest and authority in public education is increasing. Federal requirements for hiring ("Affirmative Action") of teachers and staff, funding of remedial, experimental and minority programs and for certain types of physical facilities, as well as racial desegregation and sexual antidiscrimination guidelines have greatly influenced policies and services of local school district boards.

If the thousands of private and quasi-public special interest and pressure groups are also considered as significant shapers of governmental administrative decision making in our fragmented system, it is obvious that the complexity of the influence patterns and administrative relationships will truly lay to rest any simplistic approach. Indeed, if the student is temporarily confused, this is perhaps the best indication that he is beginning to understand the true nature of our intergovernmental maze.

ADMINISTRATIVE REGIONALISM.

American federalism is undergoing significant developments and trends. Two of the most important developments are the movements for interstate and substate administrative regionalism. In both instances, the inadequacies of existing political boundaries demarcating the states from each other as well as the political boundaries within the states separating counties, cities and special districts have given rise to administrative agencies and programs that serve to "break down" the rigidity of political boundaries. Traditional boundaries have produced jurisdictions with inadequate resources and/or authority to resolve problems of a multijurisdictional nature. The need for administrative regionalism consequently emerges from the existing deficiencies of the arbitrarily drawn maze of political boundary lines so characteristic of American government.

The movement for interstate administrative regionalism has gained impetus as the usefulness of existing state boundaries has diminished. Dissatisfaction with the necessity of having governmental programs and services under either national or state authority is due to growing recognition that many very real problems are beyond the ability or authority of the separate states to handle and yet are subnational in scope rather than truly national. As a result a number of radical proposals have emerged in recent years forwarding the consolidation of the existing states into fewer and more comprehensive geographical entities or regions. (Figures 9–4, 9–5, 9–6). In this manner, problems of multistate scope may be dealt with directly without the inherent divisiveness of state boundaries and sovereignties.[11]

Procimaps
the New Constitution with
Proposed New States Under
1970 (in millions) Alaska,
Hawaii, and Puerto Rico
not Shown.

Alaska: 295,000
Hawaii: 748,000
Puerto Rico: 2,690,000

SOURCE: Leland D. Baldwin, Reframing the Constitution (1972).

Figure 9–4.

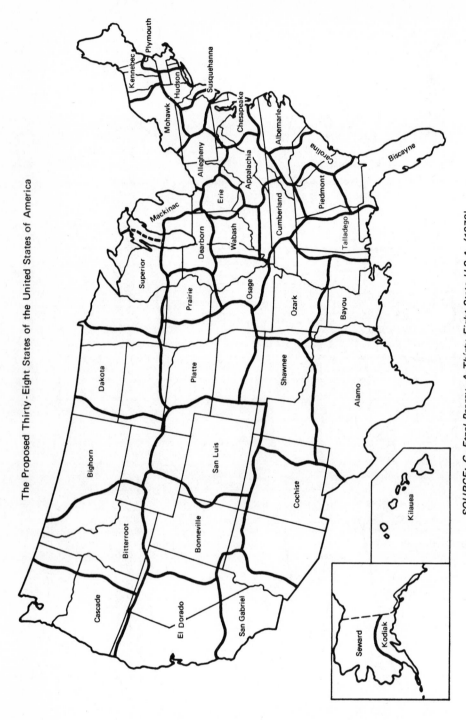

The Proposed Thirty-Eight States of the United States of America

SOURCE: G. Etzel Pearcy, A Thirty Eight State U.S.A. (1973).

Figure 9-5.

A More Perfect Union?

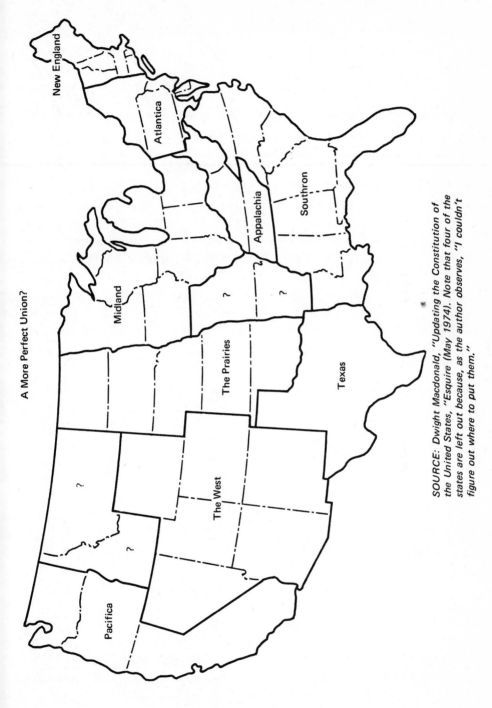

SOURCE: Dwight Macdonald, "Updating the Constitution of the United States," Esquire (May 1974). Note that four of the states are left out because, as the author observes, "I couldn't figure out where to put them."

Figure 9–6.

The dimensions and implications of regionalism are quite broad. Short of drastic consolidation and merging of the states into regions, a prospect with minimal chances of accomplishment, the concept of regionalism is still fraught with problems that must be considered alongside its many alleged advantages. It must be borne in mind that regionalism, in view of the permanence of state political boundaries, requires intergovernmental cooperation. Failing this, the abilities of the many American governments to deal with some of their major problems and issues will be significantly impaired. In addition, regionalism, while it resolves or at least alleviates certain problems, creates others, that is, increases the number of levels of operative governments. Where, for example, a bistate or multistate regional program is developed with a permanent interstate agency to administer its activities, it is evident that a new level of government has emerged. The "horizontal" consolidation consequently results in "vertical" proliferation as illustrated below (Figure 9–7):

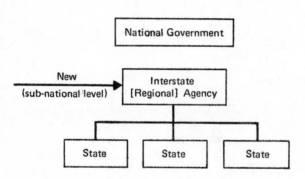

Figure 9–7. VERTICAL PROLIFERATION

The same consequences are evident in substate administrative regionalism (Figure 9–8).

Regionalism may be used to accomplish opposite objectives: either decentralization (Figure 9-9) or centralization (Figure 9-10) of policy and administration. The national government has provided the initiative and leadership to develop interstate regional commissions comprising federal and state representatives

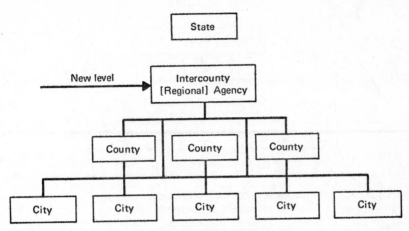

Figure 9-8. SUBSTATE REGIONALISM

in order to carry out functions previously administered exclusively by the national government.

Conversely, the states have often sought to centralize at the interstate regional level those functions previously the responsibilities of the separate states and their executive agencies. Regionalism as a technique to accomplish centralization and decentralization has also been widely used within the individual states.

In its broadest sense, regionalism may be described as geographic, economic, social-psychological, planning, administrative or a combination of these. Geographic regionalism is based on the existence of homogeneous natural factors, such as climate, vegetation and geology, that differentiate the region from others. As such the region has a static quality quite apart from its human groupings and activities. "Natural" regions have been identified and have served as the basis for natural resource development and policies. Economic regionalism is based upon the existence of homogeneous economic characteristics, for example, economic underdevelopment as in Appalachia or a region of separate, smaller cities dominated economically by a large, single city around which they cluster. The latter pattern, in fact, is often referred to as a "metropolitan region." The

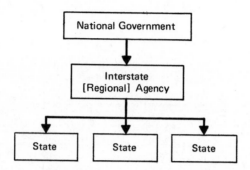

Figure 9-9. DECENTRALIZATION THROUGH
REGIONAL ORGANIZATION

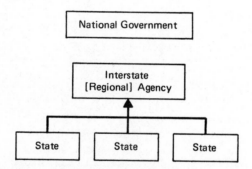

Figure 9-10. CENTRALIZATION THROUGH
REGIONAL ORGANIZATION

economies of the "core" or "mother" city and the surrounding cities may differ. For example, the core or mother city may be highly urbanized and industrialized while the surrounding hinterland may be primarily residential. Yet the economic interdependence of each upon the other creates, in effect, a single web of regional economic relationships.

The "social-psychological" region may be based upon popular loyalties, identification and perceptions, that is, "like-mindedness" in terms of cultural interrelationships and attachments, religion, sectional patriotism, common outlooks toward other regions and their peoples. Such attitudes often serve as the basis for intergovernmental cooperation within the social-psychological region. Mere mention of the "Deep South," the "Far West" or "New England" conjures up highly variant human environments.

"Administrative" regionalism stands apart from the other types of regionalism insofar as it is descriptive of a technique of governmental administration for effective centralization or decentralization. Since it may or may not reflect adherence to geographic, economic or social-psychological regional boundaries, administrative regionalism may, therefore, be regarded as more "artificial," being shaped more by extrinsic than intrinsic factors. In short, it is a useful and significant technique for the redistribution of governmental power. Administrative regionalism also serves as the basis for public regional planning without any connotation of redistributed power; hence, the term "regional planning" in much of the literature of contemporary public administration. Administrative regionalism may be realized in political practice or, as in some phases of planning, merely utilized as a theoretical framework for planning analysis and projections.[12]

Administrative regionalism, to be described further, must consequently be viewed as only one of many approaches to the problems of rigid political boundaries and it may manifest itself in a variety of different patterns reflecting different administrative environments and public needs.

Administrative Commissions

The subject of administrative regionalism is quite complex and its literature is extensive. For the purposes of this chapter, three aspects are emphasized. The first is the establishment of administrative commissions at the initiative of national officials and organized under terms and conditions established by congressional and presidential action for specific and limited purposes. The second is the use of compacts to establish interstate administrative agencies. The former reflects national interest in decentralization of national authority while the latter reflects the goal of a centralization of administrative power and authority. The third is "substate regionalism"—techniques and devices to break down the artificialness of county and municipal boundaries.

U. S. constitutional provisions have long made multistate river basin planning and resource development the prerogative of national authorities. Authority over the nation's navigable waters, combined with the responsibilities of a wide range of federal executive agencies with the important functions for interior regulation and development (Army Engineers, Bureau of Reclamation, Federal Power Commission, Bureau of Land Management), made the national government the most logical government to deal with water and land resources management and development for areas beyond the borders of single states. Occasionally, comprehensive multi-river basin studies within single states were handicapped as state governments were unable to provide the resources or necessary administrative leadership to coordinate their own separate state and local agencies.

Two commissions may serve as examples of federal leadership in multi-river basin planning. (See maps, Figure 9-11.) The U. S.-Southeast Commission was authorized by Congress in 1958 as a temporary interstate agency for purposes of cooperative federal–interstate investigation, surveying, planning and study of the conservation, utilization and development of seventeen principal river basins embracing Georgia, northern Florida, Alabama, South Carolina and a small area in North Carolina. Congress also authorized at the same time the U. S.-Texas Commission for the same purposes but confined it to the study of contiguous river basins within the borders of that state. The reports of both commissions were forwarded to the president in 1962 and 1963. The patterns and experiences of these pioneer commissions served as valuable guidelines for later national efforts to encourage combined federal–state regional administrative cooperation. The chairman of each commission was appointed by the president and was a resident of the study area. The laws further required the remaining members of the commissions to be selected from two sources: federal and state. Members of the Southeast Commission, in addition to the chairman, were appointed by the president with six of the members to be federal representatives of each of the following depart-

Texas Commission Study Area

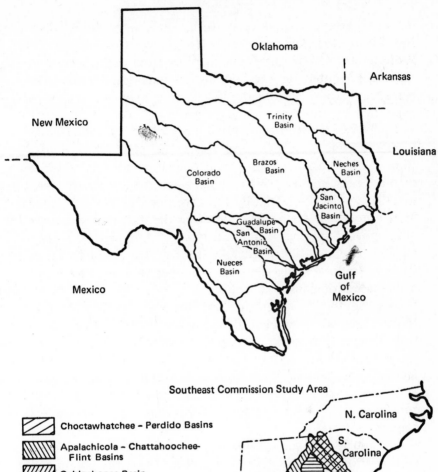

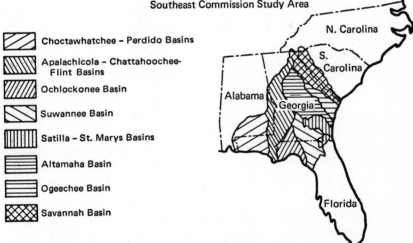

Southeast Commission Study Area

Choctawhatchee – Perdido Basins

Apalachicola – Chattahoochee-
Flint Basins

Ochlockonee Basin

Suwannee Basin

Satilla – St. Marys Basins

Altamaha Basin

Ogeechee Basin

Savannah Basin

SOURCE: Robert H. Pealy, Organization for Comprehensive River Basin Planning: The Texas and Southeast Experiences Institute of Public Administration, University of Michigan.

Figure 9-11. EXAMPLES OF MULTI-RIVER BASIN PLANNING

ments: Army; Commerce; Health, Education and Welfare; Agriculture; Interior; and the Federal Power Commission. In addition, the law required one member from each of the four states represented on the commission (Georgia, Florida, Alabama, and South Carolina). Each state member was to be appointed by the appropriate governor.

The Texas Commission also comprised six federal members from the same agencies in addition to one state representative from each of the river basin areas (eight) plus a representative of the Texas Board of Water Engineers. All the states' representatives were nominated by the governor and then appointed by the president. On both commissions the state representatives outnumbered the federal representatives. Although both commissions operated under federal authority, the intent that they strongly reflect state views and cooperation in river basin planning was obvious.

The Southeast Commission was characteristic of an administrative regionalism directed toward decentralization of planning from federal agencies to a federal-multistate body. In contrast, the Texas Commission reflected a natural interest in the development of more centralized planning by a federal-intrastate body.[13] Since that time a large number of federal–state administrative commissions have been established for comprehensive regional planning.

Although the subject matter of such regional bodies is largely technical, it should be remembered that the nature and course of future basin development, conservation and resource management have tremendous political ramifications and affect different interests in widely different ways. The concluding words of a detailed study of the Southeast and Texas commissions points up the very thin line between administrative decision making and political controversy:

> If major changes in general attitudes about what consitutes "proper" comprehensive river basin planning, at least in a political sense, are to occur in the future, they must arise out of the continuing contest between agencies and their supporting groups, state and local groups, and Congressional forces that determine who gets what in the water

field. Undoubtedly this contest will produce changes, the nature of which cannot be foreseen. Those who wish to change current policies must participate in this contest if they are to influence the future significantly. Technicians at administrative levels and policy-makers at both administrative and political levels can best contribute to the smoother operation of the technical-political process that is comprehensive river basin planning in the United States if they understand the political issues that are at stake in this contest. Those who are in ostensibly neutral or technical positions must realize that many of their actions will have unavoidable political consequences, and that such consequences will not necessarily be evil because they are political.[14]

Interstate Compacts

The use of interstate compacts to establish interstate administrative agencies is an extremely significant movement in the evolution of American federalism and reflects the dynamism of our federal system. Prior to the turn of the century, the use of interstate compacts was quite limited. In fact, between 1789 and 1900 only twenty-one compacts were put into effect. Most dealt with boundary disputes and the compact device was a useful means to allow the states to resolve their differences short of the use of force. In more recent times the use of interstate compacts has multiplied many-fold. The more contemporary emphasis has been upon positive programs rather than eradication of disputes. Since the early 1920's, many compacts have established permanent bistate or multistate administrative agencies with career administrative staffs. This development has led to the evolution of a truly regional level of government providing services, regulatory functions or planning or a combination of these activities.

The Constitution does not limit the subjects of interstate compacts; it merely makes their use conditional upon consent of Congress. The significance of compacts was enhanced when, in 1823, the United States Supreme Court ruled that a compact was a binding contract and that state laws contrary to the terms of a compact are null and void.[15] Further, in 1918, the Supreme Court held that the terms of a compact were enforceable and that once congressional consent is given that legislative body may compel compliance in such manner as it deems most appropriate. Hence, state officials negotiating such agreements are very concerned that the terminology be precise for the compact is, indeed, a binding contract.

Often the plain language of the Constitution is given an interpretation that appears at odds with it. In 1893 in *Virginia v. Tennessee,* the Court announced that congressional consent was not required for "certain types" of compacts.[16] Specifically, said the Court, those matters upon which the states can agree but which are not the concern of the United States are not subject to scrutiny of Congress. Rather, only those agreements tending to increase the political power of the contracting states and which may, consequently, encroach upon or interfere with the "just supremacy" of the United States are subject to the consent requirement. Congressional scrutiny is to be utilized to prevent any potential embarrassment of national power. In recent times, congressional consent was not required for the consolidation of two municipal library systems serving cities divided by a state boundary. In practice, however, interstate compacts are submitted to Congress with Congress itself making the decision as to whether or not the "national interest" requires its action.

Compacts between states generally provide for a statement of the compact's purposes and objectives, the creation of an interstate administrative agency (where appropriate) to carry out the terms of the compact and the size and composition of the policy-making commission, board or authority including the number of members from each of the compacting states. Provision may also be made for the methods of selection of the permanent professional administrative staff to serve the commission, board or authority as well as the procedures for adopting an annual budget and the apportionment among the member states of the operating costs. Often the procedures for termination of the compact or the means, if any, by which a state may voluntarily withdraw will be included. The site or location of the headquarters of the permanent agency to be established is also usually specified.

Where Congress assents to an interstate compact, a "triangular federalism" (Figure 9–12) emerges, linking the national legislature with the legislatures of the states.

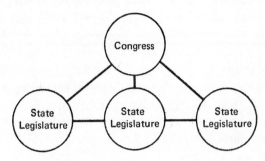

Figure 9-12. TRIANGULAR FEDERALISM

The first permanent interstate administrative agency established by an interstate compact was the Port of New York Authority in 1921. This is one of the best-known and perhaps the largest and most influential of all the interstate administrative agencies. Operating as a body corporate with wide powers to issue rules and regulations, and supervise railroad, truck, bus and truck terminals, tunnels and airports, the authority employs several thousand persons and may borrow money through the issuance of bonds. It does not, however, have taxing powers. The authority was established to bring about uniformity in place of previous conflicting navigational and commercial regulations by New Jersey and New York in the New York port area. Many later compacts also established permanent interstate administrative agencies with regional jurisdiction to administer compact provisions.

Federal–State Compacts

A major development in the use of compacts for regional administration occurred in 1961 when Congress approved the Delaware River Basin Compact involving the states of Delaware,

New Jersey, New York and Pennsylvania. The compact created a regional administrative agency with jurisdiction over the whole Delaware River Basin. The objective of the compact was the multipurpose development of the basin's water resources for the benefit of local, state and national interests in the region. At the time the region had no fewer than nineteen federal, fourteen interstate and forty-three state agencies concerned to some degree with the basin's water resources. For the first time the national government became a full signatory participant in an interstate compact. However, the national government entered on the basis of a special relationship and therefore is not bound in the same way as the other member states. Congressional consent was conditioned by several requirements for national government participation:

1. Congress would not relinquish any existing authority over the basin's navigable waters.
2. The compact does not diminish congressional authority over interstate commerce or commerce with foreign nations.
3. Although the compact was established for an initial period of one hundred years, Congress could withdraw the national government from the compact or modify the conditions for continued national participation.
4. The executive powers of the president to respond to a national emergency were safeguarded.

These provisions made it clear that national authorities are unable to "contract away" their constitutional responsibilities by entering into an interstate compact. According to one authority, the Delaware River Basin Compact reflected "a confluence of two previously separate lines of development—federal aid to the states and interstate cooperation through compacts. . . ." He noted that this new "federal–state" type of compact shifts federal authorities away from a posture of merely "a self-protective interest" to a new posture of "active partnership."[17] In short, the fact of its membership is not just to protect federal administrative interests against multistate encroachment but to positively advance federal interests and development. The constitutional implication is clear: Congress may assent to the national government joining an interstate compact in any field or on any subject on which Congress may legitimately legislate.

Although the compact was the first formal device for interstate negotiation and cooperation, its applicability to contemporary societal needs accounts for the rapid proliferation of compacts between the states. The compact approach to problems beyond individual state borders has its strengths and weaknesses. Often the compact commission, board or authority is immersed in a tug of war between contending interests operating within highly divergent value frameworks. The fact is that compacts have been used to promote broader interests but also to promote special interests. Pressures continue often after the compact itself is established as the special interest group attempts to shape compact agency policies once the compact is operative.[18] Regional compacts should be considered capable of dealing with highly technical problems and of causing value conflict to be acted out on an otherwise nonexistent intermediate level of government.[19]

Another type of interstate administrative regionalism exists which is not multigovernmental but merely consists of a national government agency establishing interstate administrative regions to facilitate its own organizational responsibilities. Examples of this type of regionalism are the "regions" of the Office of Civil Defense(Figure 9-13), the Federal Reserve System and the U. S. Civil Service Commission. This is, in effect, a pattern of administrative decentralization, albeit on a regional basis. It does give added weight to the concept of administrative regionalism.

Substate Administrative Regionalism

The problem of arbitrarily drawn political boundaries ill-suited for the administration of many public services is greatly magnified at those levels of government below the state level. The highly diffused mix of municipal, county and special district boundaries created intricate networks of jurisdictional conflicts, duplication and divided authority at a time when pressing issues

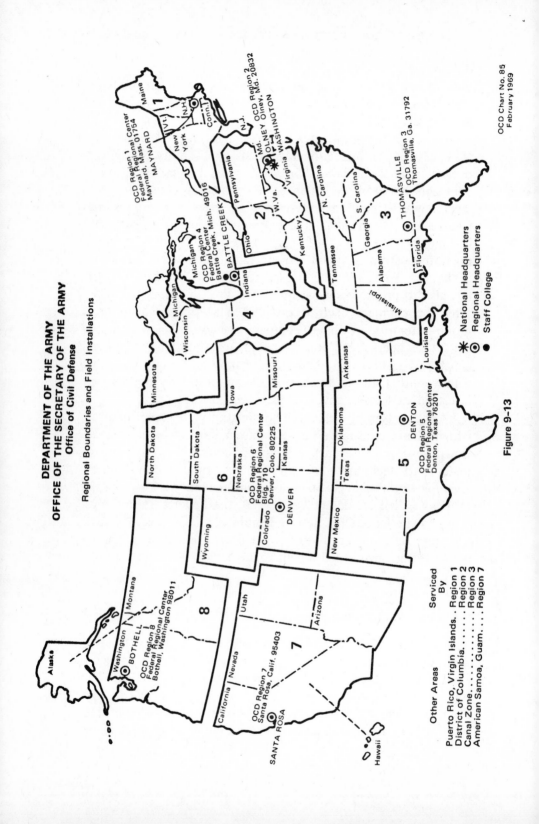

DEPARTMENT OF THE ARMY
OFFICE OF THE SECRETARY OF THE ARMY
Office of Civil Defense

Regional Boundaries and Field Installations

OCD Chart No. 85
February 1969

OCD Region 1
Federal Regional Center
Maynard, Mass. 01754
MAYNARD

OCD Region 2
Olney, Md. 20832

OLNEY
WASHINGTON

OCD Region 3
Thomasville, Ga. 31792
THOMASVILLE

OCD Region 4
Federal Center
Battle Creek, Mich. 49016
BATTLE CREEK

OCD Region 6
Federal Regional Center
Bldg. 710
Denver, Colo. 80225
DENVER

OCD Region 5
Federal Regional Center
Denton, Texas 76201
DENTON

OCD Region 8
Federal Regional Center
Bothell, Washington 98011
BOTHELL

OCD Region 7
Santa Rosa, Calif. 95403
SANTA ROSA

Maine
N.H.
Vt.
New York
Conn.
N.J.
Pennsylvania
Ohio
W.Va.
Virginia
Md.
N. Carolina
Kentucky
Tennessee
S. Carolina
Georgia
Alabama
Mississippi
Florida
Louisiana
Arkansas
Oklahoma
Texas
New Mexico
Missouri
Iowa
Kansas
Nebraska
Colorado
Wyoming
Utah
Arizona
Nevada
California
Montana
Washington
North Dakota
South Dakota
Minnesota
Wisconsin
Michigan
Indiana
Alaska
Hawaii

1
2
3
4
5
6
7
8

National Headquarters
Regional Headquarters
Staff College

Other Areas   Serviced By

Puerto Rico, Virgin Islands . . Region 1
District of Columbia . . . . Region 2
Canal Zone . . . . Region 3
American Samoa, Guam . . . . Region 7

Figure 9–13

Substate Planning and Development Districts, September 1972

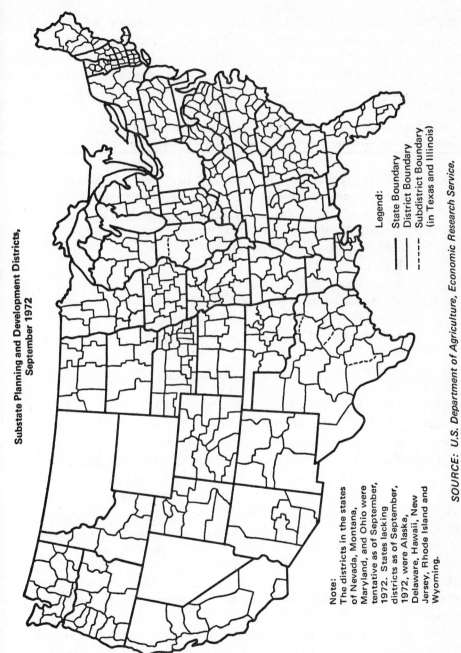

Note:
The districts in the states of Nevada, Montana, Maryland, and Ohio were tentative as of September, 1972. States lacking districts as of September, 1972, were Alaska, Delaware, Hawaii, New Jersey, Rhode Island and Wyoming.

Legend:
State Boundary
District Boundary
Subdistrict Boundary
(in Texas and Illinois)

SOURCE: *U.S. Department of Agriculture, Economic Research Service.*

Figure 9–14.

of local government tend to overlap political boundaries and affect whole regions (Figure 9–14). These regions embrace a wide variety of different governments that lack, any one of them alone, the legal authority or resources to deal adequately with common issues. The problem exists even at the state level, for existing county lines, traditionally used to carry out many state programs and laws at the local level, are themselves frequently reflective of historical circumstance irrelevant to contemporary conditions. Also, their numbers and boundaries are often made more rigid by specification in state constitutions. In recent times, state governments have adopted a number of techniques by which to circumvent existing county, municipal and special district boundaries where the most effective administration would seem to require such action.

Intercounty Administrative Regionalism

A significant number of state governmental agencies have, in a manner similar to many federal agencies, established administrative "regions" for planning purposes or for providing services beyond the boundaries of single counties. While a number of state functions are administered either through the agencies of single counties (courts, election administration, public health, law enforcement, vital statistics, etc.) or by state agencies utilizing existing county boundaries, other state activities are found to be inappropriate for administration by state officials on a single-county basis. Hence, state-initiated regions have been established to operate on an intermediate level between the state and county levels. Many of these substate regional districts were established in response to pressures of the national government which prefers to deal in many of its grant programs (especially those administered by state and local authorities) on a regionwide basis, instead of with a large number of separate county and municipal governments.

On the other hand, many regional district grids were developed on initiative of the governors and often following recommendations by private consultants as well as state and local administrative agencies. Substate regionalism, therefore, has served federal, state and local interests. Such substate districts tend to be utilized by clusters of state agencies—especially those responsible for physical and/or economic planning and economic development. Most of these districts comprise groups of adjacent counties so that district boundaries reflect political tradition, and the necessity of cutting across existing boundaries (leading to more fragmentation) is precluded.

The map of substate districts in South Carolina (Figure 9–15) is illustrative. Note how the grid of ten substate districts is based upon "regional" groupings of adjacent counties. By 1972 all but seven states had established either permanently or tentatively substate regionalism based on administrative districts.[20]

Administration through intercounty districts is a nonradical approach to meeting societal needs for it does not require the abandonment of existing county boundaries, displacing county government or even adversely affecting it in any significant manner. Other nonradical devices are widely used to facilitate more effective administration within fragmented environments at local government levels. Here, again, as with intercounty districting, the aim is to preserve the integrity and continuation of existing governments while emphasizing the inadequacies of present political boundaries to serve as the basis for the provision of many public services.

Extraterritoriality

Many states allow their cities (or "municipalities") to exercise "extraterritorial" powers when administrative service, planning or regulatory requirements make it feasible for local authority to extend beyond political boundaries into territory *not* a part of the municipality. Hence, a municipality may own the land upon which the local airport, located beyond municipal boundaries, stands and may provide services and regulate airport activities through municipal employees. Another municipality may, under its "police powers," inspect dairies beyond its political boundaries as a condition for licensing such dairies to do

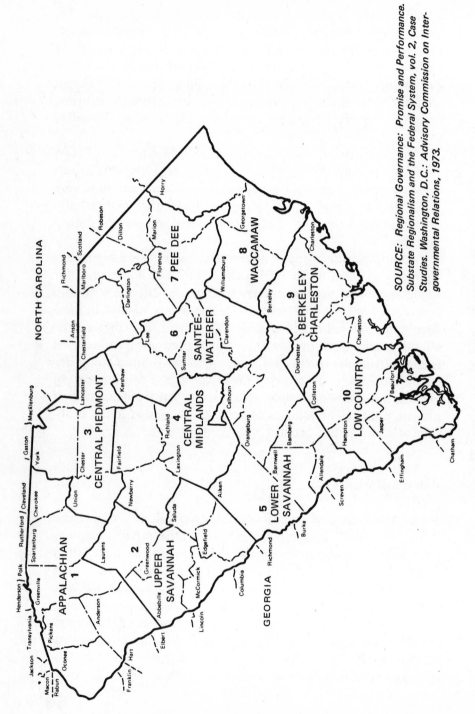

SOURCE: *Regional Governance: Promise and Performance. Substate Regionalism and the Federal System*, vol. 2, *Case Studies.* Washington, D.C.: Advisory Commission on Intergovernmental Relations, 1973.

Figure 9-15. SOUTH CAROLINA SUBSTATE DISTRICTS

business within its borders. Quite frequently, municipal sewage farms and treatment plants are purposely located outside political boundaries. Municipalities dependent on water from distant sources may purchase lakes or construct reservoirs in other counties and staff these facilities with their own engineers and guards. Extraterritoriality may even be interstate in nature. The Los Angeles Department of Water and Power purchased land in Boulder City, Nevada, bought its own building (with the Los Angeles city seal atop) and constructed and maintains through its employees an intricate system of electrical grids extending from Boulder City across vast desert areas to the Southern California metropolitan area. Therefore, with no modification of existing boundaries, extraterritoriality may extend to contiguous or far-distant areas. Where a municipal bus line crosses into and serves an adjacent municipality, it is also exercising extraterritoriality.

Annexation

Through the process of "annexation," a city or municipality legally expands its boundaries outward to encompass adjacent, contiguous territory that is not part of the existing city, that is, the annexed territory is "unincorporated." The legal requirements for annexation are set forth in state law and vary widely from state to state.

The advantages of annexation are expansion of municipal services to embrace a larger region where community needs may require these services without the necessity of incorporating new cities. In this manner, further fragmentation at the municipal level is avoided. One significant administrative consequence is that the county government will have diminished service responsibilities for the former "unincorporated" area since services will now be provided by the annexing city. Annexation does have many geographical limitations. Some states prohibit crosscounty annexation, and the intervening county boundary may, therefore, prevent unification of service functions.

Informal Agreements and Contracts

The use of informal agreements and contracts is widespread among America's local governments, and the popularity of such devices for circumventing rigid jurisdictional boundaries has reached a high point. Their utility is underscored by the fact that, unlike annexation, they allow existing political boundaries to remain intact while the most desirable administrative service areas may be patterned to reflect needs irrespective of politically fragmented jurisdictions. Because of this, structural changes in local governments are not required.

Informal techniques for intergovernmental cooperation include exchanges of information which may lead to "unwritten" understandings. For example, separate fire departments in a single politically fragmented metropolitan area may operate within a framework of a well-understood, yet unwritten, agreement among fire chiefs. This mutual understanding is to respond as requested or to offer "backup assistance" to each other in the event of a major conflagration. Previous exchanges of information may have made it painfully evident that no single fire department could possibly handle the worst potential fire and that fire is no respecter of political boundaries. Where all are potentially affected, the irrelevance of boundaries necessarily leads to such common understandings. Unwritten agreements of this type have stood the tests of time and many emergencies; their inherent strength does not require the formalities or rigidities of written documents.

Informal adjustments to the realities of jurisdictional fragmentation are feasible primarily for short-term situations. Where long-term, interlocal administrative relationships are contemplated, formal contracts may be more appropriate. Such contracts are authorized on the basis of state delegations of power to local governments. Some written agreements have evolved from a long history of previous informal understandings and were merely formalized. Delegations of authority for local intergovernmental cooperation, exchanges of services or even the provision of services are found either in state constitutional provisions or in statutes passed by state legislatures.

Written agreements may embrace joint ownership of physical facilities and joint administration of services. Other agreements may involve the provision of services, on a charge basis, by one government to several adjacent governments. Such agreements may be "horizontal"—between municipalities—or "vertical"— involving county–municipal cooperation. Some formal agreements have even been international in scope. Adjacent American and foreign municipalities divided by an international boundary (Canada and Mexico) have entered into formal contractual agreements.

The Advisory Commission on Intergovernmental Relations, in a detailed study of interlocal agreements and contracts, noted that Milwaukee County, Wisconsin, had over 124 cases of formal cooperative activities. St. Louis County, Missouri, had over 350 service contracts with municipalities. Philadelphia, Detroit, Cleveland and Los Angeles are among the nation's larger cities utilizing the contract device.[21] The "contract system" has probably reached its most sophisticated and widespread use in California with Los Angeles County offering an extremely broad range of single services or a "total package" (the so-called "Lakewood Plan"). The services are provided by county personnel with charges determined by a complex county cost accounting system. Cities, individually, determine whether or not to "contract" and the level of services desired, with costs proportional to the desired level. Such contracts may be terminated by one party upon due notice to the other.

The contract device has been used on higher levels of government; thus, the U.S. Forest Service has contracted for fire protection on federal lands by entering into formal agreements with state fire departments already providing fire protection to adjacent state park and recreational lands. Also, contracts have been negotiated between the federal government and county governments for fire protection and county law enforcement services on Indian reservations. In addition there are numerous instances of contractual leases in which federal offices have been located in municipal civic centers.

Preemption

Occasionally, a service or regulatory responsibility of local governments is legally "preempted" by a higher level of government. This is frequently due to the fact that statewide or even federal standards of uniformity may now be required in place of variant patterns of administration and differing interpretations of the law by local governments. The regulation of obscenity in many states was formerly a local "police power" responsibility. Increasingly, however, the "local community standards" brought problems of such widely divergent criteria for enforcement and prosecution in different local governments that state legislatures have assumed authority by "preemption" statutes followed by statewide guidelines for local officials. Air pollution control originally was a county function, but winds spread pollutants across county lines to such an extent that state authorities established air pollution control boards and commissions with statewide authority. Eventually, as the problem of pollution became interstate, Congress preempted much state authority for air quality control. Today, a state desiring to depart from federal air quality standards must seek a congressional exemption. Sometimes the dividing line is very difficult to draw. For example, the U.S. Supreme Court determined that Congress had preempted the authority of a city council to regulate noise within the city where a local ordinance had prohibited flights into or out of a local airport from 11:00 P.M. to 6:00 A.M.[22] Consequently, federal authorities had preempted a portion of the traditional police power of a municipality.

Transfer of Functions

A local government may voluntarily authorize the transfer of a select function to a higher level of government. Thus, where a municipality finds that the maintenance of its own health department is becoming too expensive (considering current costs of operating hospitals, doctors' salaries, laboratory facilities, etc.) and where the county may be mandated by state law to operate its own health department, the best policy may be to transfer city facilities, staff and responsibilities to the county. Where large airports, some of international caliber, are operated by a municipal government, a number of counties have transferred authority over smaller county-operated airports to the municipal government in deference to a more centralized air space control and the elimination of separate airport systems and duplicate departments.

A large-scale transfer of functions occurred in Dade County, Florida, in 1957, where a reconstituted county government was declared to be "metropolitan" in nature with a large number of previous municipal service functions transferred to the new metropolitan county. At the same time certain guarantees of municipal rights over the remaining services were included in the new charter adopted by referendum.

Councils of Government

Substate adjustment to the rigidities of political boundaries may be accomplished through voluntary associations termed "councils of governments" (COGs). These are substate regional associations composed of representatives of county governments and of municipalities within the counties. The free discussion of common problems with the objective of developing coordinated approaches and policies to meet these problems provides the operating framework for these councils of government. Many of these councils, heavily subsidized by the federal government, are utilized by federal executive agencies to require, through council staff, a "regional certification" for municipal and county applications for federal fiscal grants. Such certification or approval by a council of government is increasingly the prerequisite for federal agency consideration of grant applications. In this manner the federal government is exerting great pressure upon counties and municipalities to adopt a regional approach. But primarily, the federal government is concerned that grant applications by municipalities or counties do not conflict with pending applications from other local governments and that the proposed projects reflect regional needs rather than the unmodified self-interests of local jurisdictions. At the very least, the federal government seeks assurance that local projects for which federal money is sought do not conflict with any regionwide interest.

Regional Special Districts

Special districts (Figure 9–16), the most numerous of all American governments, are identified by a single or "special" service or function in contrast to the multitude of services and functional responsibilities of "multipurpose" or "general" governments, that is, counties and municipalities. Examples are school (the most widely known), air pollution control, flood control, fire protection, public utility, transit, hospital, mosquito abatement, street lighting, reclamation and cemetery districts. The boundaries of special districts are very flexible and may overlap entire municipalities or counties, or only portions of these, unincorporated (nonmunicipal) land and other special districts.

Such overlapping is based upon the legal assumption that a particular district must provide a service not provided by any of the multipurpose governments or any other special district within its boundaries. Hence, there is no conflict of functions. Where intergovernmental cooperation has lagged or the geographical scope of the service area is so extensive that a single agency is preferable, a regionwide special district may be established under state law. Thus a school district may encompass a large number of cities as well as overlap numerous special districts performing other specific functions. Intercounty water districts may bring water great distances into several counties and the cities within those counties. Many water districts embrace significant portions of a state. A simplified graphic example is presented in Figure 9–16.

Consolidation

Each of the above approaches to substate administrative regionalism left the existing governments intact but provided for the adjustment of service boundaries. Other approaches to political fragmentation are more drastic and result in the demise of some general purpose governments in creating larger administrative

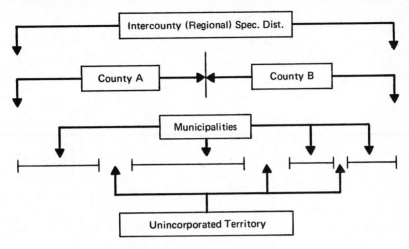

Figure 9-16. SPECIAL DISTRICT

service areas. These approaches may include city–city consolidation, city–county consolidation and county–county consolidation. Such developments are relatively rare since few existing multipurpose governments choose to be the ones to "go out of business" in order to reduce the fragmentation of administrative services.

Decentralization

In contrast to consolidation and the other approaches to substate administrative regionalism is a movement toward a diffusion or decentralization of service responsibility and policy making. The least radical type of decentralization is "agency decentralization," undertaken by the agency itself under its own initiative or in response to external community or clientele pressures. The essence of agency decentralization, however, is the recognition that agency policy will be shaped within the agency itself. Thus, despite the establishment of branch offices to serve different districts within the county or municipality, the pattern of decision making is an agency matter with little or no conse-

quential input from external sources. Some variations in agency
decentralization patterns are in Figure 9–17.

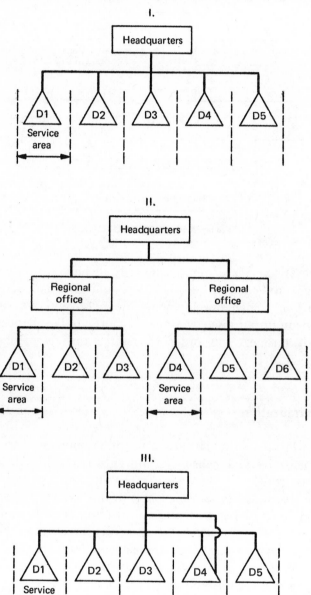

Figure 9–17. VARIATIONS IN AGENCY
DECENTRALIZATION

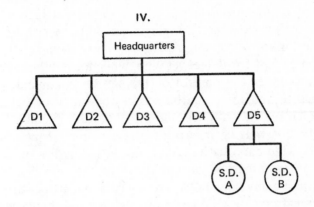

In pattern I the decision has been made to decentralize operations into five districts, each under the control and supervision of a field office directly responsible to agency headquarters. In pattern II field offices are directly responsible to their respective regional offices. Thus, through agency decentralization, a "reverse subagency administrative regionalism" emerges, that is, a new level of operations somewhere between central headquarters and the field offices in each district. The new pattern, however, has emerged due to decentralization rather than to pressures for centralization. The regional office may have final decision-making authority in field operations but may be required to refer some matters (personnel, finance, etc.) to central headquarters for final review, approval or appeal. Note that from the standpoint of officials at agency headquarters, administrative operations may appear to be highly decentralized whereas for agency personnel in the field offices in each of the districts, administrative operations appear to be highly centralized.

In pattern III each field office may be decentralized and the supervisor in charge may exercise wide discretion in personnel assignments and allocation of existing resources to meet the peculiar needs and unforeseen emergencies within his district.

Note, however, that the field office in District 4 has within it one "unit" directly responsible to agency headquarters. This pattern or organization has been widely used in law enforcement. For example, all personnel and operations are the responsibility of the commander in charge of the district police station except for detectives who, while located in each station, are not under the control of the station commander but are subject to the direct authority of the chief of detectives at headquarters. Centralized crime laboratory facilities, coroner facilities, as well as fingerprint files, and the frequent necessity for citywide coordination, city–city coordination or even city–county coordination have resulted in the prevalence of this pattern in many large police and sheriffs' departments.

In pattern IV subdistrict offices may be established in one of the districts where population may be much larger than in other districts or where the clientele may be dispersed over a much greater geographical area.

In a large number of American counties and municipalities, multipurpose "branch civic centers" have been established where the citizen may transact his "civic business" with a variety of different decentralized agencies at the same location. The "mobile civic center" is a newer concept where representatives of key municipal agencies will be housed in a mobile trailer and park according to a regular schedule at strategic locations convenient to citizens for the transaction of minor civic business.

VALUE CHOICES AND CONFLICTS

If the student is confused and astounded by the intergovernmental maze, then perhaps he or she is beginning to understand the unique nature and special problems of American public administration. Experts devote entire careers to the issues raised by administrative federalism. The student, however, should not assume that administrative service readjustments required by changing societal needs, population movements and rigid political boundaries are arrived at on purely technical grounds.

The facts are quite the opposite. Conflicting political interests, incompatible philosophies, mutual suspicions and much emotional irrationalism have caused many efforts to founder or ultimately be abandoned. Any change in administrative service area boundaries is consequential for existing economic and political interests. Both individuals and organized groups will react to such proposals from the standpoint of their own perceptions of their self-interests.

Public employees and their organizations are neither silent nor passive in administrative boundary adjustments that affect their jobs. Many proposals for consolidation of governments or the transfer of service functions have foundered in the face of vigorous and collective public employee opposition. This is especially true where public employee organizations are vigorous and have large war chests in order to lobby local legislative bodies or even the state legislature. Moreover, they frequently are able to gain the support of other labor organizations and launch quite effective campaigns to reflect their views.

The movement toward "administrative regionalism" is opposed by many persons and organizations on the ground that it is precisely the opposite direction needed for satisfying community needs. Rather, it is urged, services and authority over programs should not be centralized at higher and more remote levels but, on the contrary, should be "decentralized" to neighborhood groups, thereby allowing citizens more instead of less participation in services and public policies affecting them.

The significance of decentralization pressures in many metropolitan areas ranging from police functions to education should not be underestimated. A potent movement, it is increasingly the rallying cry of the discontented. The pressures come from both the extreme right and extreme left which have in common a negative view of expanding and remote bureaucracies at distant capitals or civic centers. On this issue citizen community groups may conflict with established public bureaucracies and their employee organizations which may oppose decentralization plans as "inefficient" and contrary to criteria of administrative competence and professional expertise. In many instances it comes down to those in control not wishing to share power with others seeking it.[23]   More and more pressures are centered on planning commissions, zoning boards, school boards and park and recreation commissions for, if not decentralization, then at least increased community input in long-range planning, selection of priorities and the allocation of fiscal resources.

The conservation–ecology movement, comprising a broad alliance of related interests, has greatly modified policy making at all levels of government.   State planning codes, along with county and municipal ordinances, have allowed homeowner groups, mountain-park-beach enthusiasts and desert devotees to vigorously express their aspirations as well as misgivings in the development of plans.   Even national planning agencies have been visibly affected.   See, for example, the accompanying chart (Figure 9–18) depicting the projected public role in the development of a master plan for Yosemite National Park.   Of the seven successive stages necessary to develop the master plan and environmental impact statements for Yosemite, the public is directly involved in four.   The future uses to which this national park will be put have already caused the commercial concessionaires and "nature purists" to clash on numerous occasions.   The ultimate Yosemite plan may serve as a harbinger of future land-use in other national parks as congressmen are increasingly drawn into the fray.

For many persons sympathetic to "true" community participation, mere "agency decentralization" is nothing but a "sop."   Agency field offices and suboffices are viewed as "window dressing" while significant policy decisions continue to be made wholly within the agency itself. Even public hearings or the device of community advisory boards are held to be inadequate.   Here, decentralization pressures merge with a political radicalism that views anything less than "all power to the people" as merely reinforcing an existing bureaucratic-dominant community power structure alliance.   It is this alliance that many critics feel must eventually be brought down if the "true interests" of the "people" are to be met.

More realistically, there are a number of public functions and services of such a technical nature as to be quite inappropriate for neighborhood or community decision making on a

The Planning Process / YOSEMITE MASTER PLAN / United States Department of the Interior / National Park Service

This chart shows the major steps in the preparation of a master plan for Yosemite National Park, and the dates by which each step is to be accomplished.

The process involves you from the earliest stage through the development of a final plan.

In the first step, data is compiled on the park's resources and your views are collected through workshops and letters. The opinions we hear from you will help to define planning issues and concerns, visitor experiences that should be available in the park, and the direction of the park's management in the future.

Utilizing resource data along with your opinions gathered during the first step, the planning team, with assistance from the public, will develop various alternative plans for the park.

These alternatives will be compiled in a report entitled "The Environmental Assessment on Alternatives." Public meetings will then be held at which we hope to hear your reactions to the alternatives.

The opinions expressed in these meetings will help narrow down the alternatives to shape the Draft Master Plan—the proposed plan for the park—and the Draft Environmental Impact Statement, which describes the plan's impacts on park resources.

After giving the public a chance to digest these drafts, open meetings will be held to obtain your reactions to the drafts of the master plan and environmental statement. Then the draft documents, including your suggestions and opinions, are submitted to the Western Regional Director of the National Park Service, and if approved become the final master plan for Yosemite.

Your participation is an important and integral part of this process. We urge your continuing involvement.

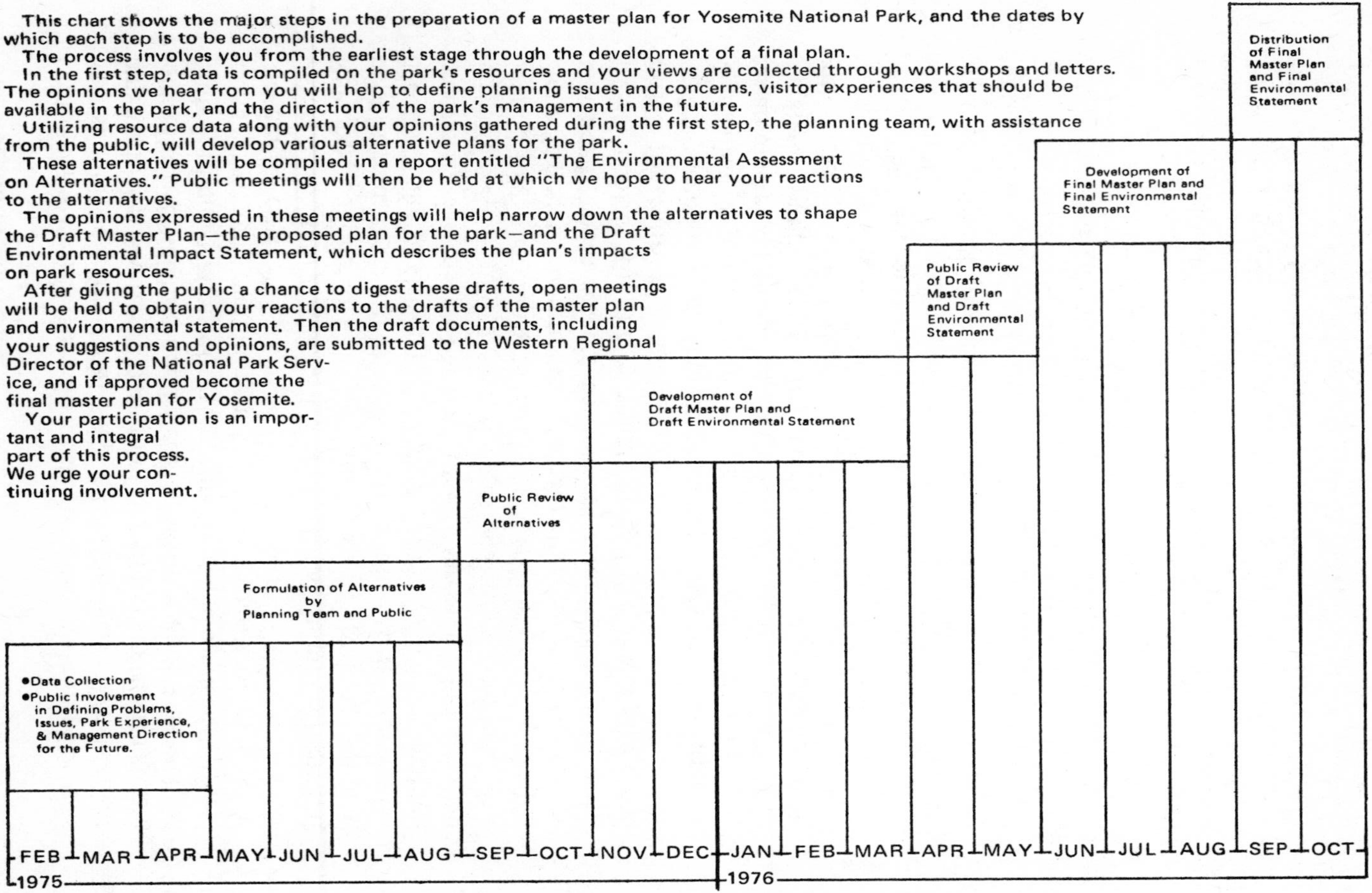

- Data Collection
- Public Involvement in Defining Problems, Issues, Park Experience, & Management Direction for the Future.

Formulation of Alternatives by Planning Team and Public

Public Review of Alternatives

Development of Draft Master Plan and Draft Environmental Statement

Public Review of Draft Master Plan and Draft Environmental Statement

Development of Final Master Plan and Final Environmental Statement

Distribution of Final Master Plan and Final Environmental Statement

FEB MAR APR MAY JUN JUL AUG SEP OCT NOV DEC JAN FEB MAR APR MAY JUN JUL AUG SEP OCT

1975 — 1976

SOURCE: United States Department of the Interior/National Park Service

Figure 9-18. PROJECTED PUBLIC ROLE IN THE DEVELOPMENT OF A MASTER PLAN

continuing basis. These obviously have city-wide implications and should be carried out on a city-wide level. What might emerge is the two-tiered pattern of decision making with strong and effective neighborhood decision-making bodies as well as central administration of certain functions and services. Efforts along these lines would result, in one expert's opinion, in a "federated city."[24]

In 1972 the Advisory Commission on Intergovernmental Relations conducted a detailed survey of nearly 1,000 municipalities and over 1,000 counties regarding their progress in decentralizing services and involving citizens in decision-making processes. The results showed some progress in administrative decentralization among several cities and a few counties. But beyond that, the data was hardly encouraging for those sympathetic to greater community participation. In fact, the report concluded, "With respect to political decentralization or community control, the survey results suggest that it will take quite a while for reality to catch up with rhetoric."[25]

The seemingly inexorable tendency toward administrative regionalism is producing in its wake a discernible countertrend toward increased pressures for grass-roots participation in the shaping of public policy. It is evident that conflicting interests with differing conceptions of their own and the "public" interest are gravitating toward essentially contradictory value-poles. The intergovernmental maze is characterized by generous proportions of cooperation and conflict; it is within this framework of contradictory tendencies that value choices affecting administrative federalism must be made.

NOTES

1. For general discussions of federalism in the United States and abroad, see William H. Riker, *Federalism: Origin, Operation, Significance.* Boston: Little, Brown, 1964; Aaron Wildavsky, *American Federalism in Perspective,* Boston: Little, Brown, 1967, Trends in the U.S. are presented in W. Brooke Graves, *American Intergovernmental Relations: Their Origins, Historical Development and Current Status,* New York: Charles Scribner's Sons, 1964; "Intergovernmental Relations in the United States," *Annals of the American Academy of Political and Social Science,* 359

(May 1965); Morton Grodzins, *The American System: A New View of Government in the United States,* Chicago: Rand McNally, 1966; Daniel J. Elezar, *American Federalism: A View from the States,* 2d ed., New York: Thomas Y. Crowell, 1972. Useful readings are found in Richard D. Feld and Carl Grafton, *The Uneasy Partnership. The Dynamics of Federal, State and Urban Relations,* Palo Alto: National Press Books, 1973.

2. Richard H. Leach, *American Federalism,* New York: W. W. Norton, 1970, chap. 1, "Federalism and Theory."

3. U.S., *Constitution,* Art. I, Secs. 9-10.

4. U.S., *Constitution,* Amendments 5 and 14.

5. See, for example, *U.S. v. Maine,* 43 L. ed. 363 (1975).

6. *Train v. City of New York,* 43 L. ed. 1 (1975).

7. *Ibid.*

8. *U.S. v. State Tax Commission of Mississippi,* 412 U.S. 363 (1973).

9. *Los Angeles Times,* April 25, 1975.

10. See Eugene P. Dvorin, "Foreign Aid by States," *National Civic Review* 53, no. 11 (December 1964): 585-90, 622.

11. See Rexford Tugwell, *A Model Constitution for a United Republics of America,* Santa Barbara: Center for the Study of Democratic Institutions and James E. Freel and Associates, 1970; C. Etzel Pearcy, *A Thirty-Eight State U.S.A.,* Fullerton, Calif.: Plycron Press, 1973; Leland D. Baldwin, *Reframing the Constitution. An Imperative for Modern America,* Santa Barbara: American Bibliographical Center; Oxford, England: Clio Press, 1972; Dwight Macdonald, "Updating the Constitution of the United States," *Esquire,* May 1974, pp. 100-116.

12. See *Multistate Regionalism,* Washington, D.C.: Advisory Commission on Intergovernmental Relations, April 1972.

13. For a detailed analysis of the work of both commissions, see Robert H. Pealy, *Organization for Comprehensive River Basin Planning. The Texas and Southeast Experiences,* Ann Arbor: Institute of Public Administration, University of Michigan, 1964.

14. *Ibid.,* p. 164.

15. *Green v. Biddle,* 8 Wheat. 1.

16. 148 U.S. 503.

17. See Frank P. Grad, "Federal-State Compact: A New Experiment in Co-operative Federalism," 63 *Columbia Law Review* 825-55.

18. For an excellent discussion of the "political" side of compacts, see Weldon V. Barton, *Interstate Compacts in the Political Process,* Chapel Hill: University of North Carolina Press, 1967.

19. For a general background to compacts, see M. Wendell, *The Interstate Compact Since 1925*, Chicago: Council of State Governments, 1951; Arthur W. Macmahon, "Interstate Compacts," *Encyclopedia of the Social Sciences*, vol. 4, p. 109 (1931); V. V. Thursby, *Interstate Cooperation: A Study of the Interstate Compact*, Washington, D.C.: Public Affairs Press, 1953; F. L. Zimmerman, "New Experience with Interstate Compacts," *The Western Political Quarterly*, 5, no. 2 (June 1952); Richard H. Leach and Redding S. Sugg, Jr., *The Administration of Interstate Compacts*, Baton Rouge: Louisiana State University Press, 1959; *Multistate Regionalism*, Washington, D.C.: Advisory Commission on Intergovernmental Relations, 1972, chap. 5. The biennial editions of the *Book of the States*, published by the Council of State Governments, describes the most recently negotiated compacts and is an excellent source of up-to-date developments in the compact field.

Reference to the *Congressional Record* rewards the reader with the reproduction of texts of those compacts assented to by Congress as well as modifications insisted upon as a condition for assent. In addition, the *Record* also reproduces modifications to existing compacts sponsored by either national or state initiative.

20. For comprehensive analysis of substate regionalism, see *Regional Decision Making: New Strategies for Substate Districts*, vol. 1, and *Regional Governance: Promise and Performance*, vol. 2. Case Studies. Washington, D.C.: Advisory Commission on Intergovernmental Relations, vol. 1, May 1973, vol. 2, October 1973. A pioneering work of continuing usefulness on the problem of governmental services and geographic boundaries is James W. Fesler, *Area and Administration*, Birmingham, Alabama: University of Alabama Press, 1949.

21. See *A Handbook for Interlocal Agreements and Contracts*, Washington, D.C.: Advisory Commission on Intergovernmental Relations, March 1967.

22. *City of Burbank v. Lockheed Air Terminal*, 411 U.S. 624 (1973).

23. See "Curriculum Essays on Citizens, Politics and Administration in Urban Neighborhoods," Special Issue, *Public Administration Review*, 32 (October 1972); Mario Fantini and Marilyn Gittell, *Decentralization: Achieving Reform*, New York and Washington: Praeger Publishers, 1973; Milton Kitler, *Neighborhood Government: The Local Foundations of Political Life*, Indianapolis and New York: Bobbs-Merril, 1969; Norman Furniss, "The Practical Significance of Decentralization," *The Journal of Politics*, 36, no. 4 (November 1974): 958–82; James Fesler, "Approaches to Understanding Decentralization," *The Journal of Politics*, 27, (August 1965); H. Paul Friesema, "Black Control of Central Cities: The Hollow

Prize," *Journal of the American Institute of Planners,* 35, no. 2 (March 1969); 75-79.

24. Joseph F. Zimmerman, *The Federated City: Community Control in Large Cities,* New York: St. Martin's Press, 1972; Herbert Kaufman presents the interesting thesis that the greater the degree of political decentralization, the greater the pressures for centralization. See his "Administrative Decentralization and Political Power," *Public Administration Review,* 29, no. 1 (January/February 1969): 3-15.

25. *The New Grass Roots Government? Decentralization and Citizen Participation in Urban Areas,* Washington, D.C.: Advisory Commission on Intergovernmental Relations, 1972, p. 21.

10

THE INTERGOVERNMENTAL MAZE: FISCAL FEDERALISM

The complexities of administrative federalism, especially the issues of boundary adjustment, are paralleled by "fiscal federalism"—no less complex and equally essential to intergovernmental administrative relations. A detailed description and analysis of the field of "public finance" is beyond the scope of this text. Instead, the authors choose to focus upon "grants-in-aid" and "revenue sharing"—two devices through which intergovernmental boundary adjustments are carried out by the use of fiscal incentives.

GRANTS-IN-AID: BACKGROUND

Revenue sharing is of quite recent origin, having been enacted into law in 1972. In contrast, grants-in-aid have evolved over a long period of time; the roots of the concept antedate the Civil War. The grant-in-aid is based upon a value assumption: federal aid to the states for a wide range of purposes strengthens rather than weakens the total governmental system. The concept of limited national powers under a written constitution was, no doubt, conducive to development of aid to the states insofar as specific objectives could be accomplished by a combination of

339

federal resources and the centering of administrative responsibilities in the states. The issue of federal authority to directly administer aid programs, aside from the question of feasibility, was therefore circumvented. From the beginning boundary adjustment took place, i.e., a growing federal interest in the affairs of the states, with the states carrying out programs for furthering the objectives of federal policy.

The Ordinance of 1785, drafted by the Congress of the Confederation prior to the adoption of the Constitution itself, set aside land in every township in the federal domain for public schools. After the United States Constitution went into effect, the federal government assumed state debts incurred during the Revolutionary War. In 1836 a surplus in the U.S. Treasury was apportioned among the states, with no expectation or requirement of repayment. Prior to the Civil War federal engineers and other specialists were assigned to aiding the states in developing roads and canal systems. The federal government had armed and equipped the state militias and upon entry into the union new states were given endowments or grants of federal land to be used for various public purposes (flood control, railroads, wagon roads, and other internal improvements), including higher education. None of these forms of aid required any significant federal control or supervision.

With the precedent of federal aid to the states already well-established, the Morrill Act of 1862 inaugurated a turning point in the aid concept. In return for grants of land for each state to be used for agriculture and mechanical arts colleges, certain preconditions were set forth by Congress. The Morrill Act therefore established the notion of "conditional grants," i.e., based upon the willingness of the recipient states to abide by the federally established conditions. Among the specific conditions in the Act were:

1. A requirement that each governor report annually to Congress concerning the uses of or disposition of the lands.

2. Funds received from the disposition of lands were required to be invested in safe securities.

3. Only the interest from these investments could be spent; the principal was to remain as a permanent endowment fund.

4. The progress of the A & M colleges established on such lands was to be the subject of annual reports to Congress.

5. No portion of funds emanating from federal sources could be utilized for construction. Instead, the buildings and equipment were to be a direct state responsibility.

In 1890 the second Morrill Act added some other significant features: annual federal grants for instructional purposes and the authorization for federal officials to withhold grants from any institution not fulfilling its obligations in a satisfactory manner. In 1895 Congress enacted legislation to provide for a federal audit of the states' use of federal funds. By 1914 various Congressional acts had introduced apportionment formulas for the distribution of funds to states, the requirement of "matching" federal funds with state funds and the necessity for advance approval by national officials of state plans to expend the monies.

By 1918 many grant programs had been utilized to stimulate state action in fields where the state might not otherwise be active or state action be too narrowly circumscribed by limited state resources. Such fields included highways, forestry, vocational education and rehabilitation, and public health.

During the depression of the 1930's, federal grants went directly to financially hard-pressed cities whereas previously virtually all had been paid directly to the states. New grant programs were oriented towards social welfare, unemployment, health and unemployment relief.

By 1970 there were over 1300 aid programs according to a survey published by the House of Representatives.[1] In 1973 some 1649 programs were listed by the Federal Office of Management and Budget.[2] Each program had been the subject of separate legislation and there had been no general grants for unspecified purposes. Rather, the grants fell within certain categories differing by objective or purpose. In fact, the term "categorical grants-in-aid" came into common usage and emphasizes the specificity of purposes. Figure 10-1 indicates the extensiveness of grant categories.

GRANTS-IN-AID: CHARACTERISTICS

Grants-in-aid should be understood as existing apart from all other national-state-local fiscal relationships. Consequently,

341

Individual	Human Needs	Food and Clothing Job Opportunity and Placement Financial Assistance Legal Assistance Child Care Social Guidance Physical Health Mental Health Aids to Handicapped
	Human Skills	General Education Basic Education for Youths and Adults Vocation and Job Training Training of Handicapped
Environmental	Physical	Housing Transportation Health Facilities Educational Facilities General Community Facilities Recreational and Cultural Facilities Land Planning and Use
	Natural	Air Pollution Water Resources Parks and Forests Agriculture Fish and Game Minerals and Energy Sources
	Social	Social Rehabilitation Recreation and Culture Local Government Support Law Enforcement Emergencies and Disasters Civil Defense
	Economic	Regional Planning and Development Community and Metropolitan Planning and Development Business, Industry, and Agriculture

ADAPTED FROM: Catalog of Federal Assistance Programs. Executive Office of the President.

Figure 10-1. THE EXTENSIVENESS OF GRANT CATEGORIES

they should not be confused with federal loans or repayable advances, surplus property or surplus commodities turned over to state or local governments, payments under federal research grants or development contracts, payments of taxes, shared revenues or federal payments to state or local governments as reimbursements for costs incurred in providing benefits or furnishing services to persons entitled to them under federal laws.

Instead, grants-in-aid should be understood as federal money authorized to be paid to state or local governments (including special districts) under the following conditions:

1. For Congressionally determined purposes;

2. According to specific formulas for the allocation of grant funds;

3. Under the supervision of a designated federal agency;

4. The recipient government(s) must expend or "match" federal funds with non-federal funds in such proportions as determined by Congress;

5. The legislative bodies of recipient governments must enact legislation declaring both willingness to participate in the specific program(s) and that sufficient non-federal funds will be budgeted to meet the "matching formula" as set forth in federal law;

6. State or local governments must designate a counterpart executive agency responsible for the actual administration of the program to the clientele or service recipients. Such agency must also be designated to work with the federal agency having supervisory responsibility for the grant program;

7. State or local officials administering grant programs are subject to such conditions and supervision as deemed appropriate by Congress, including audit of expenditures, reports to federal authorities and adherence to federal rules and regulations;

8. State or local "plans of action" must be developed to inform appropriate federal authorities as to how the recipient government(s) intends to carry out the program and assign resources, including personnel and facilities;

9. State plans must be approved prior to receipt of federal grant funds;

10. If any of the above conditions is not met, the grant-in-aid may not be forthcoming. Or, if the program has been approved and is operative, federal authorities may withdraw funding, in whole or in part, in the event of any violation of federal laws or any failure to conform to federal requirements and standards.

In summary, a grant-in-aid may be described as congressionally authorized payment of money to state or local governments for purposes and under conditions determined by Congress with the administration of the program as the responsibility of the recipient government. Grants-in-aid are for continuing longterm, non-emergency purposes and exist apart from federal disaster aid programs, which are for temporary emergency needs only.[3]

SCOPE OF FEDERAL AID

The fiscal consequences of grants-in-aid have been profound for all American governments. In 1902 federal aid comprised only 2.6% of federal domestic expenditures; by 1970 the percentage was 30.4%.[4] In 1902 federal aid comprised 0.7% of state and local revenue; in 1950 it was 11.9% and by 1970 the percentage was 18.8%.[5] The states with the highest percentages of total revenue from federal sources were Alaska (33.6%), New Mexico (29.7%), West Virginia (28.8%), Arkansas (27.5%), Mississippi (27.3%) and Wyoming (27.1%).[6] Prior to 1935 highway grants-in-aid comprised the largest single aid expenditure. In 1935 social welfare programs (including public assistance, health and education) comprised only 1.3% of all grants to state and local governments. But by 1970 the social welfare program figure had jumped to 70.1%, while highways dropped to 21.1% of all grants.[7] Agricultural conservation (including extension work and research), anti-poverty programs and public health research and services follow in that order.[8]

FISCAL LEVERAGE

The purposes of grants-in-aid are to utilize fiscal leverage to either "induce" or "assist" state and local governments to carry out certain programs. The inducement or assistance centers on efforts to:

1. Bring about institutional reform where the institution is resistant to change and therefore capable of undercutting the intent of the program;

2. Provide the conditions for state or local governments to undertake general governmental functions of benefit to the public (e.g., preservation of open space);

3. Provide the conditions for state or local governments to serve a particular constituency (the poor, the unemployed, or minorities).

Programs oriented to attain the above objectives were inaugurated where constituencies did not have sufficient strength to induce a state or local government to reform existing institutions, assume new beneficial functions or to serve a specific beneficiary class. It should be noted, however, that programs that might originally have lacked a constituency may have gained one as a consequence of a federal grant program being carried out over a period of years.[9]

Fiscal leverage to bring about or support institutional change, public policy priorities and further the interests of some groups is the key to understanding the consequences of grant programs. In fact, the varieties of apportionment formulas were designed to accomplish these specific ends. In the passage of separate legislative authorizations for new grant programs, Congress was able to pattern the apportionment formulas to the unique needs of each situation. In short, each grant formula was "custom-designed" to bring about certain predetermined consequences.

The potential fiscal leverage inherent in the grant-in-aid concept was recognized by Massachusetts when that state brought suit challenging congressional appropriations for the Maternity Act of 1921. The legislation was enacted to aid in the reduction of maternal and infant mortality and to protect the health of mothers and infants. In *Massachusetts vs. Mellon*,[10] the state challenged the Act on the ground that its purposes, centering around maternity, were not within national authority but were local, i.e., within the authority of the states. Hence, argued Massachusetts, Congress was usurping a function that was outside its constitutional powers through the grant-in-aid device and that such grant programs were forcing the states to yield a portion of their sovereignty.

The U.S. Supreme Court noted that there was not a real case or controversy as required by Article III of the Constitution, inasmuch as Massachusetts, not entering the program, lacked sufficient interest in the matter to entitle it to sue. Massachusetts, observed the Court, is merely given an option, which it is free to accept or reject. Should that state decide not to yield to alleged federal blandishments, it is "free not to yield." In other words, the state is not required to do anything. Consequently, the Court concluded that state powers had not been invaded, as nothing could be done in furthering grant programs without the consent of the states themselves.

In a companion case decided at the same time, *Frothingham vs. Mellon*, the Court dealt with the allegations of a single taxpayer—a citizen of Massachusetts—that the appropriations under the Maternity Act would increase the future burden of taxation and take her property without due process of law. Here the Court was faced with an issue never decided previously: Could a single taxpayer challenge a grant-in-aid program by attacking the appropriation act as invalid and resulting in taxation for illegal purposes? In holding that the suit could not be maintained, the Supreme Court avoided technical legalities but stressed that the single taxpayer's contribution to the federal Treasury was shared with millions of others and that the Treasury also received revenues from non-tax sources. As a result, a single taxpayer's contribution was comparatively minimal and so indeterminable that there could be no attempt to even compute it. In addition, the Court declared the act's impact on future taxation was uncertain, remote and fluctuating and was a matter of public rather than individual concern. The Court also noted that if one taxpayer could challenge an appropriation act of Congress then so could every other taxpayer, leading inevitably to chaos.

The significance of both cases is clear: There is no means of judicially challenging the purposes of a grant-in-aid program. This applies to allegations by states and by individuals as taxpayers. The grant-in-aid concept was therefore placed upon a firm constitutional foundation. Nevertheless, even as grant programs proliferated over the years and the states became increasingly involved, there were still indications of unease and discontent with the fiscal implications of grant programs, especially in the real or potential "leverage" exerted upon the states.

As individual grant programs were enacted, Congress developed widely variant formulas for determining the amounts received by recipient state and local governments. For example, grants for civil defense training, vocational education, aid to state maritime colleges and urban mass transportation technical studies are based upon a "50-50" matching formula, i.e., recipient governments must match every federal dollar received with a dollar of their own. This is the most common formula. However, wide variations do occur in some grant-in-aid programs. Thus, in venereal disease control programs, the federal government will pay 100% of the cost. In grants for local enforcement of building codes, the federal government will provide up to 2/3 of program costs for communities of 50,000 or more and up to 3/4 of costs for communities under 50,000 population. The grants for economic development planning assistance programs carried out by states, multi-county agencies or private non-profit organizations are limited to not more than 75% of the costs, while grants for state meat and poultry inspection programs may be financed up to 50% of the cost but, in addition, technical assistance may be provided by the federal government. In the Urban Beautification and Improvement grant programs, federal funds cannot exceed 50% of the costs beyond the usual local government expenditures for these activities. In other words, no federal financial aid is forthcoming until the local budgets exceed their usual allotments for beautification and improvement.

Another approach is utilized in federal grants for public airports: 75% of the grant is based upon state population and land area. In certain programs aimed at a state's rural population, federal funding is based upon the rural population under 18 years of age. More complex formulas exist for water pollution control grants, where factors to be weighted are population, extent of the water problem and financial need, and the proportion of "matching" funds is based on per capita income within the state. The ability to pay matching funds is given great weight in grants for library services to rural areas.

"EQUALIZATION"

In the past several decades the increasing use of an "equalization factor" in grant disbursement formulas has created a significant amount of controversy. Congress may desire to "equalize" the ability of the poorer, low per capita income states to receive federal grants-in-aid where they would otherwise receive few grants in comparison to the wealthier states, especially under the most common "50-50" matching formula. Consequently, many grant programs have introduced eligibility for federal dollars on an inverse proportion basis, i.e., the lower the per capita income, the greater the amounts received. Here a philosophic issue emerges: Is it morally right for states which have contributed more to the federal treasury through taxation to receive a smaller amount of money in the form of grants-in-aid than states which have contributed less?

This argument is the familiar "rob Peter to pay Paul" one. Should the citizens of one state be taxed to support public services in other states? Objections center on the allegation that the wealthier states will eventually be reduced to lower levels of public services despite their greater financial contributions to the federal treasury. Consequently, grants as a device of fiscal leverage to produce injustices are emphasized. The equalization factor in some grant programs is illustrated in Figure 10-2.

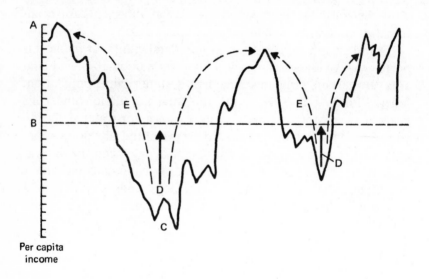

Per capita
income

Figure 10-2. GRANT "EQUALIZATION"

In Figure 10-2 the lines labeled "A" represent the per capita income of the wealthier states, identified as those above level "B." The dotted line "B" represents a theoretical minimal standard of living or level of public services below which no citizen of any state should be forced to exist. Yet, as "C" reveals, a number of states with particularly low per capita incomes are incapable of providing the theoretically desirable level if left to their own resources. However, the impact of equalization factors in grant formulas will serve, in effect, to lift the per capita income of the poorer states by the infusion of federal funds beyond what might be otherwise received. Hence, these states will be "uplifted" (see "D"—solid arrow) and begin to approach "B," the minimal desirable level.

However, assuming that the so-called "unearned increment" of grant funds is not forthcoming, the impact of conditions in the low per capita income states will, in fact, become crucial problems for the wealthier states. The dotted arrows (E) indicate the inevitable resultant population migrations from the poorer states, unable to provide their citizens with the desirable minimal level of services and standard of living, to the wealthier states.

The great migration of "Okies" and "Arkies" from the economically depressed midwestern and "dust bowl" states to California—the land of milk and honey—during the 1930's is regarded as ample demonstration of this consequence. California sent both state and local police forces to its borders to turn the human flood away until the U.S. Supreme Court later declared the movement of citizens across state lines could not be so impaired. Thus the impact of the poor-white migration was felt in California's health and welfare agencies as well as in its schools. In short, even the wealthiest states cannot escape involvement. The motion picture *The Grapes of Wrath* visually portrays the human tragedy of the poor, the ill and the dispossessed as they cross through state after state on the way to a "better life."

Similarly, the Black exodus in the 1960's from the poor states of the South to the great industrialized-urbanized areas of Chicago and Detroit, with another arm of the migration headed toward Oakland in the San Francisco Bay area and Los Angeles County in southern California, was but a Black reaction to the same bleak prospects that had triggered the earlier white migration westward. Many Blacks settling in other states along the way similarly affected state and local budgets, housing patterns and housing resources, school systems, health and welfare agencies. The problems are further compounded as those reared in rural areas find themselves crowded into central cities and forced to readjust to urbanism's most serious psychological, economic and social problems. Through "equalization" grants, the poorer states will be better able to upgrade their own public services and environments so that population migration will lose much of its justification. In other words, the wealthier states can either have the problem of the poorer states brought home directly to them or they can, through equalization formulas, attempt to have the problems solved where they originate. In either case, they cannot be unaffected, nor can they stand aloof. The impact of equalization is reflected in Figure 10-3.[11]

State	Federal Income Tax per capita	Federal Aid* per capita
California	$369	$131
New York	407	120
Utah	207	165
Michigan	366	86
Mississippi	131	192
Alaska	325	433
New Mexico	200	228
Arkansas	155	185
South Dakota	169	266

*To State-local governments and individuals

Figure 10-3. THE IMPACT OF EQUALIZATION.

Statistics alone do not always reveal a complete picture. Thus California gains in national defense contracts more than it "loses" in grants-in-aid, while Alaska, due to its unique problems and environment, has always required copious infusions of federal aid despite the fact it ranks second in personal income among the states.[12] Nevertheless, equalization as a device to redistribute wealth among states is an integral part of the value priorities reflected in Congressional decision-making.

The grant-in-aid as a fiscal leverage device is the alleged cause for competition and jockeying among the states for maximum federal funds. The well-known competition for defense and other governmental contracts is paralleled by lesser known but no less vigorous rivalries for grants-in-aid. Critics of the grant system point to interstate animosities as the end result. The spectacle of larger American cities, as well as states, having permanent representatives in the nation's capital to engage in on-the-scene "grantsmanship" is reflective of the intensity of the competition. The result may be an inequitable distribution of federal funds in which those governments with the most effective "sales pitch" gain the bulk of available money. A large number of mayors and city managers have added to their staffs individuals who are adept at writing applications for federal grant programs. In a few cases large staffs have emerged for this purpose and their activities are carefully coordinated with those of the municipality's lobbyists in Washington.

The impact of fiscal leverage is further emphasized in criticisms of grants-in-aid as a prime cause for distortions of state and local budgetary processes. The criticisms center upon two consequences: the setting of state-local value priorities toward grant programs and away from non-grant programs to the greatest extent possible. The rationale is to derive a federal dollar for every state or local dollar that is matched (in the 50-50 matching grants, for example) in preference to the expenditure of state or local dollars with little or no "return" from federal sources. Thus non-grant programs, though needed, may be starved of state-local funds, while grant programs are using up limited state-local fiscal resources for matching purposes.

ADMINISTRATIVE LEVERAGE

The first Hatch Act was passed by Congress in 1939. It prohibited federal employees in the executive branch from engaging in political activity, including political campaigning, political management, or utilizing official office to interfere with or influence any partisan election. The second Hatch Act, passed in 1940, extended the same prohibitions to state or local employees whose salaries are provided wholly, or in part, by federal funds. The Acts also confirmed previous rulings of the United States Civil Service Commission regarding prohibited political activity under previous legislation and presidential executive orders. In 1939 Congress, by an amendment to the Social Security Act, greatly influenced intergovernmental administrative relations by requiring that state and local employees whose salaries were paid wholly or in part by federal funds were to be recruited and retained according to merit principles. Implied by a "merit system" are open and competitive examinations for original appointment, a system of position classification with equitable pay plans, limited political activity, promotions based upon demonstrated competence and experience, security of tenure, prohibition of discrimination and separation only for cause.

Consequently, the impact of grants-in-aid has proceeded far beyond the attainment of congressionally induced grant objectives. The political sterilization of state and local administrative systems has been partially accomplished; although with the decentralized nature of the American political system, large numbers of state and local employees still are the products of "patronage" rather than merit selection or retention. Yet where merit principles did not exist in agencies receiving federal funds, steps had to be taken to meet federal criteria and, despite initial resistance, recipient agencies (or those portions directly connected with federal funds) were reorganized.[13]

In 1973 the Hatch Act prohibitions on political activities at national, state and local levels were challenged. However, the United States Supreme Court, emphasizing the need for "efficient public service," "good administration," and "meritorious performance," upheld the first and second Hatch Acts.[14] In a vigorous dissent, Justice William O. Douglas emphasized the "chilling effect" of vague prohibitions and expressed the belief that on their free time career public employees could, if they desired, engage in political activities provided that their job efficiency remained unimpaired.

A partial loosening of political prohibitions more in line with the views of Justice Douglas was approved by Congress in

1974 through revision of the second Hatch Act. State and local employees whose activities are funded wholly or in part by federal funds may now serve as officers or members of political organizations, form political organizations, participate in fund-raising activities for a political candidate or organization and manage the campaign of a candidate. In addition, they may solicit votes for or against a candidate, act as a recorder, watcher, challenger or similar officer at the polls on behalf of a political party or candidate and endorse or oppose a candidate in a political advertisement, broadcast, campaign literature or similar material. Also, they may serve as a delegate, alternate or proxy to a political party convention, address a convention, caucus, rally or similar gathering of a political party in support of or in opposition to a candidate, and may initiate or circulate a partisan nominating petition.

Some remaining prohibitions are the use of official influence to affect the results of an election or nomination for office; attempts to influence state or local employees to contribute anything of value for political purposes; running for office in a partisan election (although the public servant is not prohibited from being a candidate in a non-partisan election).

Some states have enacted "little Hatch Acts" which largely reflect the prohibitions formerly imposed upon federal employees and make these prohibitions applicable to state employees. Such state legislation remains effective despite congressional liberalization of the second Hatch Act. There may in time, however, be a trend toward loosening state political restrictions upon their own employees. At least, Congress has provided a significant precedent. Until that time such comprehensive "little Hatch Acts" as that of Oklahoma will bar effective political participation or activity beyond voting.

Specific congressional authorization to depart from merit principles in selected urban programs has been forthcoming where the purpose is to enlist participation and employment of minority group personnel who may lack the requisite education and/or experience requirements set forth in detailed Civil Service specifications. One of the crucial issues for the immediate future is the extent to which traditional merit system principles and the rise of professionalism within the public service for recruitment, retention and promotion are to be modified in order to allow other criteria to be given the greatest weight.[15]

Some governors have been critical of their weakened control over state agencies administering federal grant programs. Most state governments, as a heritage of nineteenth century attempts to fragment executive authority, have large numbers of official independent boards and commissions directly responsible to the voters and outside effective gubernatorial control. With the rise of grant programs some of those agencies under direct executive authority have, it is asserted, developed strong psychological ties and close relationships with their counterpart federal supervisory agencies. The result may be, in some instances, the emergence of "autonomous islands" within the executive branch characterized by divided loyalties and often resisting gubernatorial control and direction.

Since the late 1960's, newer-type grant programs have developed close fiscal and administrative links with non-public agencies. Some grants oriented to urban problems no longer are limited to local governments but have made funds available to private associations, such as private developers, citizen advisory groups, Indian tribes, municipal and civic leagues, associations of counties, commercial or industrial concerns "qualified by virtue of past experience, professional manpower and/or specialized facilities" and non-profit corporations. In these programs there is generally no matching requirement, as the objective is to stimulate experimentation and novel approaches to problems which would otherwise not be undertaken by public jurisdictions. Often the funds are to be used for demonstration purposes, e.g., a limited project to demonstrate the feasibility of non-customary methods or of new technology.

In addition, newer programs have stressed regional approaches to problems in place of traditional adherence to existing political boundaries. Some grants are available only to interstate regional agencies directly established by federal authority or created by interstate compacts. For example, several grant programs are directed specifically to the Appalachian Regional Commission, while other grants are available specifically to intercounty councils of governments. Consequently, a significant "opening up" of the grant-in-aid system has developed with much wider participation in geographical, political and economic terms. As pointed out earlier, many federal grant applications require certification by federally designated regional agencies or associations.

A degree of administrative leverage is reflected in the Intergovernmental Personnel Act of 1970. In that act Congress authorized the U.S. Civil Service Commission to make grants to state and local governments to strengthen their personnel systems "in such a manner as to encourage innovation and allow for diversity." The act also provided for the temporary assignment of federal personnel to state and local governments (including special districts) and institutions of higher education. The thrust of the act was to strengthen the personnel resources of state and local governments through grant incentives and in various ways to improve the quality, technical efficiency and training of state and local employees. The act also provided, on a shared-costs basis, for cooperative federal-state-local recruitment and examination procedures and activities as well as for federal technical assistance to state and local governments seeking to improve their systems of personnel administration. The provision authorizing the U.S. Civil Service Commission to waive payments for such assistance was clearly a means of exerting leverage. The legislative history of the act made clear that congressional intentions were not merely to upgrade administrative quality and performance in those state and local agencies engaged in federal grant programs, but to encourage an across-the-board uplifting of administrative standards.

EMERGING PROBLEMS

Both proponents and critics of the grant-in-aid system find ample ammunition to sustain their respective positions. The health of that system has undergone intense congressional scrutiny. By 1960 Congress was increasingly aware that the proliferation of grant programs was creating serious problems at all levels of government. Many grant programs had not been systematically reviewed by Congress. Consequently, some programs continued to be funded long after the need for the program had passed. Also, even when Congress had attempted to redirect or terminate grant programs the effort was often not successful. Despite the long history of federal aid to state and local government, by the mid-1960's only fourteen federal grant-in-aid programs had been terminated.[16] Also, allocation formulas were sometimes in need of revision or modification in the light of changing conditions and experiences with these programs.

Some specific grant programs had a single distribution or allocation formula; other programs employed two basic grant formulas; another group of grant programs utilized three methods; and others distributed their funds on the basis of four methods. Such variations caused many headaches for state and local budget analysts and other officials.

There were often inadequate procedures and techniques for the federal review of state and local administration of grant programs. Occasionally federal funds were not distributed according to the published allocation formulas as the governing statutes sometimes vested federal grant program administrators with extremely wide discretion.

Once a grant program had been established, a constellation of status quo forces worked to impede either termination or redirection. Hence "politics" rather than technical considerations was often the crucial determinant of the fate of reform efforts. Procedures for coordinating the large number of grant programs were breaking down. Some grant programs overlapped or duplicated others as they were passed by Congress at different times and under differing conditions. Consequently, state and local officials were often mystified as to which specific federal agencies had jurisdiction over particular grant programs. Different federal agencies sometimes were responsible for similar grants.

The use of per capita personal income as an accurate indication of relative fiscal capabilities of the states to raise revenues needed thorough reinvestigation.

Where Congress had established termination dates for grant programs (generally one to five years) state and local governments were reluctant to enter such programs and assign highly trained personnel to administer them. Also, due to the fact that the federal funding cycle was often not coordinated with state and local "budget seasons" many of these governments had to develop two budgets—one on the basis of federal approval of pending grant applications, the other on the basis of rejection of the requested funds. Hence, state and local legislative bodies and fiscal planners were faced with the problem of an inability to accurately project incoming revenues. Consequently, not only public officials but the recipients of government services were uncertain of the scope and level of services to be provided in the ensuing fiscal year. Growing "red tape" increasingly discouraged many potential applicants for federal grants, thus undercutting the purposes of the grant system itself.

Successive questionnaires to state and local officials confirmed the problem of growing bureaucratic obstacles and "red tape" in grant programs. Congressmen themselves regarded this as perhaps the number one issue—one that, unless resolved, threatened to topple the whole jerry-built grant system.

REVENUE SHARING: BACKGROUND

The concept of "revenue sharing" represents a fundamental shift in values from grants-in-aid. The roots of revenue sharing are found in dissatisfactions over the grants-in-aid system, some of which have already been mentioned. In addition, the shift from an agricultural to an urban society compounded the deficiencies of traditional fiscal relationships as exemplified by the grant system. At the beginning of the seventh decade of the twentieth century the most pressing domestic problems are urban-industrial in nature and intertwined with economic issues.

With more and more persons residing in urban areas the pressures for new services and higher levels of existing services are unrelenting. Yet, depending primarily upon the property tax, local governments face an increasingly bleak future as vast central city areas become aesthetically unattractive, congested, crime-ridden and inhabited by racial minorities and poor whites with quite limited skills and low incomes. Vast numbers of whites who can afford to do so have abandoned the central cities and have been followed by a similar exodus of manufacturing and commercial concerns, including those which had previously located their corporate headquarters in the downtown areas of central cities. The result has been increasing deterioration of central city environments as well as rapidly decreasing assessed valuations of property.

Consequently, a fiscal crisis has emerged at a time when those in the central cities are the ones least able to finance the services they require. In response to this emerging problem, which has been steadily growing in seriousness since the early 1960's, Congress has added new categorical grant programs so that in the period between 1945 and 1972 grants-in-aid have increased fourfold. In the 1960's new grant authorizations nearly tripled (see Figure 10-4). Also, in the decade 1961-1970 federal aid as a percentage of state-local revenue climbed from 12% to over 18% (see Figure 10-5). The implications are aptly described by one close observer:

> . . . the fiscal results of such sweeping initiatives by the Federal government have modified the legal concept that the states are the source of all governmental powers. The original thirteen states created the national government, assigning it certain functions and granting it essential powers. Realistically, however, adequate financial resources and the capability to respond to public desires take precedence over legal theory. The states seem less "sovereign" when 20% of their total annual revenues are drawn from the Federal treasury.
>
> Local governments have been weakened to an even greater degree. Although their expenditures have been rising sharply since 1945, local governments (many of which are creatures of their states) have not been able to deal effectively with crime, transportation and various social problems. Moreover, they have been increasingly unable to raise the funds required to provide even basic, traditional services. So the Federal government has stepped in and many localities have become administrative mechanisms for implementation of national policies rather than dynamic centers of authority and creative problem-solving.[17]

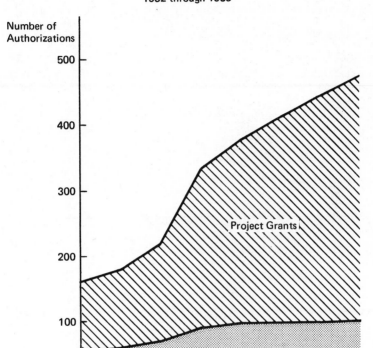

Number of Grant-in-Aid Authorizations,
1962 through 1969

SOURCE: *Advisory Commission on Intergovernmental Relations, Fiscal Balance in the American Federal System, Vol. 1; and Library of Congress, Legislative Reference service.*

Figure 10-4. PROLIFERATION OF FEDERAL
CONDITIONAL AIDS.

In addition, the bulk of categorical grants had traditionally gone to state governments which might or might not disperse a portion of these funds to their local governments. In the words of one official of the National League of Cities in 1969:

Federal Aid in Relation to State-Local Revenue, 1961 through 1970

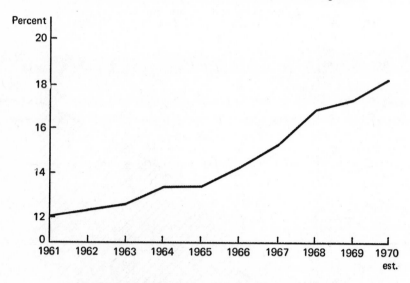

SOURCE: *Special Analysis O, Budget of the United States, Fiscal Year 1971.*

Figure 10-5. INCREASING DEPENDENCE OF STATE AND LOCAL GOVERNMENTS ON FEDERAL CONDITIONAL AIDS.

In terms of the revenue directly available to the three levels of government, the federal and—to the lesser extent—the state governments are the "haves" and local governments are rapidly becoming the "have-nots." And the haves are not sharing their resources with the have-nots in relation to the magnitude of local problems and responsibilities.[18]

President Dwight D. Eisenhower had as one of the most important objectives of his administration the "reversal" of power from federal authorities in Washington back to state and local governments. He attempted to "unscramble the egg" of American federalism by appointing a presidential commission to determine what functions exercised by the national government could best be carried out by the states. He frequently expressed concern with the debilitating effects of growing federal power

THE INTERGOVERNMENTAL MAZE: FISCAL FEDERALISM

on other American governments, presaging what he believed to be a centralization of public power in Washington with state and local governments losing their vigor, independence and sense of responsibility. The problem, however, of identifying which functions the federal government might divest itself of was extremely complex and his commission could reach no agreement on the issue, much less hope to convince Congress of the benefits of this approach. The egg simply could not be unscrambled and the notion of an intergovernmental readjustment on a functional basis was too simplistic and utopian an approach.

While supporters of the grant-in-aid system could argue that state and local governments were stimulated and reinvigorated by responsibilities for the execution of grant programs and that some had been forced to raise their levels of professionalism and expertise in order to meet federal standards, the growing ranks of the disillusioned stressed that the very success of the grant system was also its major deficiency. In other words, the proliferation of categorical grant programs served only to handcuff state and local governments as they could no longer determine their own priorities in the vast areas of public policy. Restricted by often rigid and arbitrary political boundary lines, they were also faced with the absence of financial assistance for the increasing costs of those fundamental public responsibilities outside of the federally aided categories.

A number of urbanologists and economists pushing for a new method by which to attack the growing ills of intergovernmental fiscal relations had developed some theories of "revenue sharing" in the 1960's.[19] The movement gained adherents at all levels of government, including the prestigious Advisory Commission on Intergovernmental Relations.[20] In the Ninetieth Congress some 300 bills were introduced to bring about some form of revenue sharing. Yet it was not until 1968 that a bill was finally introduced that featured revenue sharing directly with cities. The other bills had emphasized the traditional reliance upon national-state revenue sharing with "pass through" provisions for local governments—they would receive their funds after they had passed through the hands of state governments. At the same time, many states remained under the control of rural elements with little sympathy or sensitivity to the pressing problems of the urban areas. In fact, the states had provided little positive leadership in the resolution of urban ills, with the inevitable consequence of urban officials looking to Washington, D.C., for positive action and fiscal aid.

The election of Richard Nixon to the presidency was a key factor in the development of revenue sharing, for he had served as vice-president under Dwight Eisenhower and reflected the same misgivings of concentrated federal power. Congress itself had grown increasingly disenchanted with the problems of categorical grants and its own apparent inability to bring about a systematic coordination and tightening up of the whole system. At the state level at least one governor proposed a National Constitutional Convention in order, if necessary, to redraft that document so as to meet the problems of redressing the fiscal balance in favor of state and local governments. Such influential organizations as the National Conference of State Legislative Leaders and the National League of Cities added their voices to the growing tumult—the latter organization providing significant leadership and revenue sharing proposals that were largely reflected in the law that was finally passed.

In 1969 President Nixon, advocating a "new federalism," recommended legislation meant to accomplish the following:

1. Federal funding for grants, the objectives or goals of which would be determined largely by state or local governments rather than by federal authorities. This represented a significant departure from the previous concept of narrowly defined categorical grants.

2. A certain percentage of federal income tax revenues would be set aside annually for revenue sharing purposes. Thus, as federal receipts increased in a burgeoning national economy, the state and local governments would increase their share of the federal revenues accordingly.

3. Matching funds would not be required nor would the vast array of complex and confusing conditions and administrative requirements be applicable.

4. A "no strings attached" approach would be inaugurated in which the objectives would be increased flexibility and discretion, allowing experimentation with program design and execution by state and local governments.

5. State and local governments would assume the major responsibilities for value priorities as they identified their most pressing needs, be responsible for allocating available resources and would themselves control the expenditure of funds.

In 1971, in his State of the Union message, President Nixon's views were driven home with a special note of urgency:

> All across America today, states and cities are confronted with financial crisis. Some have already been cutting back on essential services. . . . Most are caught between the prospects of bankruptcy on the one hand and adding to the already crushing tax burden on the other. . . .
>
> Now the time has come to take a new direction and once again to introduce a new and creative balance to our approach to government.
>
> So let us put the money where the needs are. And let us put the power to spend it where the people are. . . .
>
> The fact is that we have made the federal government so strong it grows muscle-bound and the states and localities so weak they approach impotence.
>
> If we put more power in more places, we can make government more creative in more places. That way we multiply the number of people with the ability to make things happen—and we can open the way to a new burst of creative energy throughout America.[21]

The final measure that emerged from Congress was signed by the president in October, 1972. It was the result of extensive compromises and marked a turning point in intergovernmental administrative and fiscal relations.

THE REVENUE SHARING ACT OF 1972

Officially known as the State and Local Fiscal Assistance Act of 1972, though commonly labeled merely the Revenue Sharing Act, the legislation inaugurating revenue sharing was hailed as the "New American Revolution." In time, however, its strengths and inevitable weaknesses appeared to be balanced and this caused the initial euphoria to be diluted as the system became operational. Despite conflicting evaluations at the time of writing, there is little doubt that revenue sharing did attempt "something new under the sun." The act provided for a five-year program to share 30 billion dollars in federal revenues with state and local governments. A compromise was made in the allocation of funds. The House of Representatives proposed a formula favoring the more populous and industrial states, while the Senate favored the less populous states. The compromise allows each state to choose between a "three-factor formula" or a "five-factor formula" (see Figure 10-6). Actually, computers take both formulas into account and use that formula yielding the highest amount for each state.

The three-factor formula allocates funds on the basis of state population, per capita income, and tax effort in relation to that of other states. In the first several years of the program the three-factor formula was utilized for thirty-one states, including Alabama, Georgia, Maine, South Dakota and West Virginia. This formula tends to result in high allocations to those states with low per capita income and a high tax effort in relation to other states.

The five-factor formula allocates funds to the states on the basis of state population, urbanized population, population weighted inversely for per capita income, state individual income tax collections, and general tax effort. The first three factors are designed to take need into account. Population is used because it often tends to be directly related to fiscal need. Urbanized population is used, since the cost of providing services is generally higher in urbanized areas. The factor of population is inversely weighted for per capita income because poorer areas generally have greater financial difficulty in providing government services. These three factors are given equal weight in allocating two-thirds of the available funds.

The remaining two factors are intended to provide incentives for state and local governments to meet their financial needs with their own tax resources. The factor of state income tax collections was made separate in order to encourage this form of taxation. The factor of general tax effort takes into account all taxes collected by state and local governments.

FORMULAS FOR REVENUE SHARING
(utilizing 5.3 Billion Dollars—the first year's allocation for computational purposes)*

The 3-factor formula

Each State's share =

$$\$5.3 \text{ billion } \times \frac{\text{(Population) (GTEF)}\dagger \text{ (RIF)}\dagger\dagger \text{ of a State}}{\text{Sum of products of (population) (GTEF)}\dagger \text{ (RIF)}\dagger\dagger \text{ of all the States.}}$$

Key:

   †GTEF = General tax effort factor

           = $\dfrac{\text{Net taxes collected (State and local)}}{\text{Aggregate personal income}}$

   ††RIF = Relative income factor

           = $\dfrac{\text{Per capita income of United States}}{\text{Per capita income of that State}}$

The 5-factor formula

The 5-factor formula divides the total Revenue Sharing fund of $5.3 billion (for 1972) into five parts and each part is determined on the basis of a different factor, as shown below:

	ON BASIS OF	
1. $1/3$ of $3.5 billion		1. Population
2. $1/3$ of $3.5 billion		2. Urbanized population
3. $1/3$ of $3.5 billion		3. Population weighted Inversely for per capita Income
4. $1/2$ of $1.8 billion		4. Income tax collections
5. $1/2$ of $1.8 billion		5. General tax effort

The State's share of each part is determined, as follows:

First part: Each State's share =

$$1/3 \,(\$3.5 \text{ billion}) \times \frac{\text{Population of State}}{\text{Population of All States}}$$

Second part: Each State's share =

$$1/3 \,(\$3.5 \text{ billion}) \times \frac{\text{Urban population of State}}{\text{Urban population of all States}}$$

Third part: Each State's share equals $1/3$ of $3.5 billion on the basis of population inversely weighted for per capita income.

More specifically,
Each State's share =

$$1/3 \,(\$3.5 \text{ billion}) \times \text{ the fraction of } \frac{(\text{State population}) \times \frac{(\text{National per capita income})}{(\text{State per capita income})}}{\frac{\text{Sum of products of}}{}}$$

$$\frac{\text{(State population) (national per capita income)}}{\text{(State per capita income of all States)}}$$

Fourth part: Each State's share =

$$1/2 \,(\$1.8 \text{ billion}) \times \left(\frac{\text{State income tax}}{\text{All States' income tax}} \right)$$

Fifth part: Each State's share =

$$1/2 \,(\$1.8 \text{ billion}) \times \frac{\text{General tax effort of State}}{\text{General tax effort of all States}}$$

*SOURCE: Office of Revenue Sharing, U.S. Treasury Dept.

Figure 10-6. FORMULAS FOR REVENUE SHARING.

FORMULAS FOR DETERMINATION OF FUNDS FOR
LOCAL GOVERNMENTS WITHIN EACH COUNTY

1. *County area.* The 3-factor formula method is used:
County area's share = $2/3$ (State share) $\times$
$$\frac{\text{County population (GTEF)* (RIF)**}}{\text{Sum of products of (population) (GTEF) (RIF) for all counties}}$$

2. *Share for Indians in county* =
$$\text{Total county area share} \times \frac{\text{Indian population}}{\text{County population}}$$

3. *County government's share* = Remaining total $\times$
$$\frac{\text{Adjusted taxes of county government}}{\text{Adjusted taxes of all local government units in county, including county government*}}$$

*Adjusted taxes=local tax revenues adjusted by excluding an amount equal to revenues used for financing education.

4. *Township government's share* = Remaining total $\times$
$$\frac{\text{Sum of all adjusted taxes of such township governments}}{\text{Aggregate adjusted taxes of county, township, local units of government in county area}}$$

5. *Individual township government's share* = Amount under paragraph 4 $\times$
$$\frac{\text{(population) (GTEF)* (RIF)**}}{\text{Sum of products of (population) (GTEF) (RIF) for all townships}}$$

6. *All others* =
$$\text{Remaining total} \times \frac{\text{(population) (GTEF) (RIF)}}{\text{Sum of products of all (population) (GTEF) (RIF)}}$$

Figure 10-6. (CONT.)

Both of these factors are given equal weight in allocating the remaining one-third of the funds. The five-factor formula was initially utilized for nineteen states and the District of Columbia and included California, Connecticut, Hawaii, Illinois, Maryland and New York.

Approximately one-third of the revenue sharing funds are distributed among the states, with the remaining two-thirds

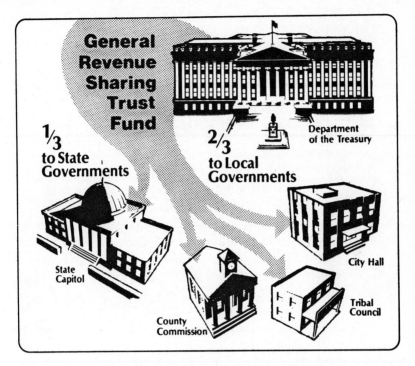

SOURCE: Office of Revenue Sharing. U.S. Treasury Dept.

Figure 10-7. GENERAL REVENUE SHARING TRUST
FUND

allocated to local governments. (See Figure 10-7). This represents a significant reversal of national policy. Under categorical grants-in-aid the states received the overwhelming amount of funds and President Nixon had proposed an allocation of two-thirds to the states and one-third to local governments. The adopted policy change is a clear indication of the significance of urban priorities in contemporary national decision-making.

State governments are permitted to spend general revenue sharing funds for any purpose or activity in which they may spend their own funds. However, local governments may utilize revenue sharing funds for capital expenditures,[22] or for maintenance and operating costs in any of eight priority expenditure areas. These are:

1. Public safety (including law enforcement, fire protection and enforcement of building codes).

2. Environmental protection (including pollution abatement, sewage disposal and sanitation).

3. Public transportation (including streets, roads and transit systems).

4. Health.

5. Recreation.

6. Libraries.

7. Social services for the poor or aged.

8. Financial administration.

One of the strategies of revenue sharing is not to allow the states to reduce or abandon their traditional support of certain functions, such as education, as a consequence of local funding through revenue sharing. A glance at the formulas applicable to local governments reveals "adjusted taxes" used for local allocational computations. Any amounts expended by local governments for education purposes are deducted from taxes used in the formula in order that local receipts would thereby be diminished. Also, education is conspicuous by its absence in the eight allowable local expenditure areas. The federal government did not desire local governments to assume the educational burden through revenue sharing. Hence, local general-purpose governments would be urged to stress urban-type services rather than to assume state-wide responsibilities. State leadership and dominance in the education field would therefore be continued. Both state and local governments are prohibited from using revenue sharing funds for the "matching" requirements of grant-in-aid programs.

State and local governments are required to report periodically to the Office of Revenue Sharing of the U.S. Treasury Department on the amounts and purposes the recipient government plans to spend or obligate. The so-called "planned use reports" are prerequisites to receiving revenue sharing funds. Planned use reports are required to be published in newspapers of general circulation in the geographic area in which the recipient government operates. News media, including bilingual media, must be advised of the publication of the report. (See Figure 10-8)

GENERAL REVENUE SHARING PLANNED USE REPORT ⑥

General Revenue Sharing provides federal funds directly to local and state governments. This report of your government's plan is published to encourage citizen participation in determining your government's decision on how the money will be spent. Note: Any complaints of discrimination in the use of these funds may be sent to the Office of Revenue Sharing, Wash., D.C. 20226.

PLANNED EXPENDITURES		
(A) CATEGORIES	(B) CAPITAL	(C) OPERATING / MAINTENANCE
1 PUBLIC SAFETY	$	$
2 ENVIRONMENTAL PROTECTION	$	$
3 PUBLIC TRANSPORTATION	$	$
4 HEALTH	$	$
5 RECREATION	$	$
6 LIBRARIES	$	$
7 SOCIAL SERVICES FOR AGED OR POOR	$	$
8 FINANCIAL ADMINISTRATION	$	$
9 MULTIPURPOSE AND GENERAL GOVT	$	
10 EDUCATION	$	
11 SOCIAL DEVELOPMENT	$	
12 HOUSING & COMMUNITY DEVELOPMENT	$	
13 ECONOMIC DEVELOPMENT	$	
14 OTHER (Specify)	$	
	$	
15 TOTALS	$	$

THE GOVERNMENT
OF

ANTICIPATING A GENERAL REVENUE SHARING PAYMENT OF

FOR THE SIXTH ENTITLEMENT PERIOD, JULY 1, 1975 THROUGH JUNE 30, 1976, PLANS TO SPEND THESE FUNDS FOR THE PURPOSES SHOWN

✓ ACCOUNT NO

(D) Submit proposals for their consideration by
to _____ A copy of this report and supporting documents are open for public scrutiny
at

(E) ASSURANCES (Refer to instruction E) I assure the Secretary of the Treasury that the non-discrimination and other statutory requirements listed in Part E of the instructions accompanying this report will be complied with by this recipient government with respect to the entitlement funds reported hereon.

Signature of Chief Executive Officer

Name & Title — Please Print   Date

IMPORTANT: THE UPPER HALF OF THIS PAGE MUST BE PUBLISHED (SEE INSTRUCTION I-8). It is not required that the lower half of this form be published.

(F) AUDIT (refer to instruction F)

1. Are your General Revenue Sharing (GRS) funds audited?
☐ yes   ☐ no

2. If 'yes', how often?
☐ every year   ☐ every two years   ☐ less than every 2 years

(H) CIVIL RIGHTS (refer to instruction H)
1. Does your government file the "EEOC State and Local Government Information" form (EEO-4) with the U.S. Equal Employment Opportunity Commission? _____ Yes _____ No

2. If "yes", what was the date of the last report? _____
If "no", answer the following questions.
3. How many persons were on your government's payroll on

March 31, 1975? _____

(G) PUBLIC PARTICIPATION (refer to instruction G) In planning for the use of GRS funds, does your government:
☐ Hold special public hearings on Revenue Sharing?
☐ Take local opinion polls?
☐ Solicit requests for funding of projects using revenue sharing funds from outside your government administration?
☐ Discuss revenue sharing at regular public meetings?
☐ Appoint advisory groups of local citizens?

DO NOT WRITE IN THIS SPACE
FOR REVENUE SHARING USE ONLY

1	2	3	4	5	6	7	8	9	10	11	12	13	14	15	16	17	18
2	1																
2	2																
2	3																
2	4																

(I) PUBLICATION (Refer to instruction I)
The upper part of this report was published in the following newspaper on the stated date at a cost of — $

✓ Name of Newspaper _____   Date Published _____

(J) PERSON COMPLETING THIS REPORT (PLEASE PRINT)

✓ _____
Name   Title   (Area code) Telephone Number

THIS REPORT MUST BE RECEIVED BEFORE JUNE 24, 1975 BY THE OFFICE OF REVENUE SHARING
2401 E STREET, N.W.
WASHINGTON, D.C. 20226

SOURCE: Office of Revenue Sharing U.S. Treasury Department.

Figure 10-8

Revenue sharing funds will be expended from the federal government's general fund, but must be deposited by the recipient governments into special trust funds from which they will disperse monies for spending purposes. The only permissible commingling of revenue sharing funds with other income of state and local governments is when revenue sharing funds are utilized for investment purposes. Revenue sharing funds must not be used in any manner which discriminates on the basis of race, color, sex or national origin.

Governments receiving revenue sharing money must use it only in accordance with the same rules and procedures that regulate the expenditure of their own money. For example, if state and local laws prohibit the use of public monies to operate an ambulance service, the use of revenue sharing funds to operate an ambulance service is likewise prohibited even though such a program would fall into the priority category of "health."

Revenue sharing funds are not available directly to unifunctional or special purpose units of government such as school districts, utility districts or library districts. The recipient government must be a general or multi-functional unit of government (comprising state governments, counties, townships, villages, boroughs and municipalities). However, special districts are not completely cut off from participation in the revenue sharing program, as recipient general governments may transfer funds to them to perform services included within the priority expenditure categories. The special districts become "secondary recipients."

Non-public, non-profit organizations or private associations may likewise become "secondary recipients" by virtue of having shared revenues received by general governments transferred to them. Their use of such revenues is limited to the expenditures allowed under law. Many Indian tribes and Alaskan native villages, although not true general-purpose local governments, are recognized as having rather unique status and structures and are eligible for the direct receipt of revenue sharing funds.[23]

Some general observations on revenue sharing are appropriate at this point. Basic to revenue sharing is the intention that it remain highly experimental. After several years of experience, there is mounting evidence that significant modifications will be made in the future as a degree of disillusionment, perhaps inevitable in a program of this magnitude and complexity, is discernible among Congressmen as well as recipient governments. While the allocation formulas are both complex and quite specific, the degree of discretion allowed to state and local governments goes far beyond that under categorical grant-in-aid programs. Even the eight areas of permissible local expenditures with revenue sharing funds are quite broad and subject to varying interpretations that might well include general administrative purposes, although this is not included specifically among the eight areas.

Reviewing the extensive congressional debates on revenue sharing, one is struck by the oft-repeated theme that the greatest degree of community input is essential to the success of the program. In particular, many Congressmen expressed concern that spending priorities, now to be determined by the recipient governments rather than Congress, be the subject of extensive and intensive community discussion and deliberation. In a very real sense, revenue sharing is a "smack" against existing community power structures which have traditionally determined who the beneficiaries of local privilege and rewards would be. The required publication of planned use reports is an attempt to "crack" the existing power structures and encourage public inputs at city council and county board meetings. Racial minority groups and others, such as the elderly and poor whites, are to be heard in the process of hammering out a schedule of priorities. In fact, following initial submission of planned use reports so as to inform the community and stimulate discussion, it is assumed by U.S. Treasury officials that modifications may follow prior to the actual appropriation, obligation or spending of revenue sharing funds. It is evident, however, that many communities not familiar with the theories or provisions underlying revenue sharing have not been active participants in the setting of priorities or goal identification.

A number of organizations, including the Urban Coalition and the Movement for Economic Justice as well as the Office of Revenue Sharing, U.S. Treasury Department, have published materials to guide citizens of local communities in demanding a voice in determining how revenue sharing funds are to be spent. Citizen participation can take many forms:

1. *Polls*: To determine how citizens think the revenue sharing should be spent.

2. *Advisory Boards*: For both short- and long-range priorities.

3. *Public Hearings*: Including special sessions of local legislative bodies.

4. *Monitoring*: Citizen groups monitor the use and impact of revenue sharing funds.

5. *Litigation*: The filing of lawsuits against responsible public officials to stop illegal expenditures of revenue sharing funds.

6. *Alternative Citizen's Budgets*: Developed by citizen groups and publicized so comparisons can be made with drafts of city council or county board budgets.

7. *Making revenue sharing priorities a major election issue*: Applicable to contests for councilmanic or county board seats.[24]

Some cogent questions are raised in a revenue sharing checklist directed to citizens of local communities by the Movement for Economic Justice:

> How much money is directly allocated to your city or town?
> How much additional money does your city or town get from your state's share of revenue sharing funds?
> Were any federal categorical grant programs to your city or county cut or eliminated this year?
> What local plans have been announced for revenue sharing funds?
> To what extent has the actual use of funds followed the announced plans?
> How much revenue sharing money has been spent on capital expenditures?
> Where was construction located?
> Are locations accessible to various constituencies?
> How much revenue sharing money was spent on social services in comparison to other uses?
> Is the priority-setting process being publicized?
> Is involvement in this process the result of community pressure or by invitation of your local government?
> What is the extent of debate and deliberation within your local government?

> What constituencies have benefited most from the revenue
> sharing program?
> What constituencies have benefited the least?
> Were there any priority areas that received revenue sharing
> funds but did not reveal increased level of effort, activity
> or performance?
> Has there been any scandal, corruption or illegality in the
> use of revenue sharing funds?
> Are revenue sharing funds reinforcing existing priorities?
> Are revenue sharing funds enabling your local government
> to begin to move into new priority areas?
> Can revenue sharing funds be better used to meet com-
> munity-determined priorities and needs?[25]

Community reactions to proposed uses vary widely. In one
large city the mayor announced that the largest portion of the
revenue sharing funds would be utilized to convert the old train
depot to a municipal parking lot and corporation yard for the
maintenance and storage of municipal vehicles and equipment.
This elicited strong vocal outrage from citizens in both the
minority-dominated central portion of the city and the white
suburbs. The residents of the central city demanded that social
welfare programs and the meeting of other human needs have
top priority. The suburban constituency insisted that their
streets be renovated to prevent the usual extensive winter flood-
ing from heavy rains. Suffice to note that the old depot is still
the old depot. In contrast, the planned use in another community over a thousand miles away of revenue sharing funds for
the purpose of carrying out a census of the local dog population
provoked little community reaction but did spark considerable
outrage on the floors of Congress, as did the construction of a
public golf course with revenue sharing funds.

REVENUE SHARING AND CIVIL RIGHTS

The non-discrimination provisions of the Revenue Sharing Act
are extremely important, as units of local government not
directly affected by previous legislation toward this end (including the Civil Rights Act of 1964 and the Equal Employment

Opportunity Act of 1972) are now subject to federal prohibitions and guidelines. It has been estimated that only about 10,000 of the 38,000 local governments receiving revenue sharing funds were involved in the requirements of previous legislation. The non-discrimination provisions of the Revenue Sharing Act combined the most important elements of the Civil Rights and Equal Employment Opportunity Acts, Consequently, about 28,000 additional local units of government are now subject to the jurisdiction of civil rights compliance specialists in the Federal Office of Revenue Sharing.[26]

Certain "rules of thumb" have been announced by the Office of Revenue Sharing:

1. All recipient governments must now be conscious of the percentage of minorities and women in their work force as compared to the percentage of minorities and women in their population. It is presumed that, in the absence of discrimination, an employer's work force will generally reflect the minority and female composition of the area from which the work force is drawn.

2. Word of mouth recruiting is insufficient to correct a minority imbalance. Affirmative action to redress the balance is required through active recruiting.

3. Utilization of revenue sharing funds for capital expenditures does not relieve recipient governments from civil rights jurisdiction of the Office of Revenue Sharing. For example, the purchase of a police vehicle would allow ORS evaluation of the employment policies of the entire police department to ensure compliance with the equal opportunity and non-discrimination requirements. Also, the determination of sites or locations for public facilities cannot have the effect of discrimination in benefits or activities, i.e., be inconvenient to concentrations of minorities in a community.

4. Where contractors or "sub-contractors" are hired to perform work involving revenue sharing funds, a non-discrimination clause should be included in the contract and, where possible, some of the contract work should be done by minority firms.

5. All neighborhoods should receive comparable services in such areas as road maintenance, public transportation, bookmobiles, etc.

6. Where possible a portion of revenue sharing funds should be deposited in minority banks.

7. The Office of Revenue Sharing will not investigate complaints that revenue sharing funds could have been better used by the recipient government as long as the expenditure was in accordance with the requirements of the Revenue Sharing Act. This is a problem to be dealt with at the local policy-making level.

The Office of Revenue Sharing has developed a complaint review process which may be used in civil rights and other matters. (See Figure 10-9.) Should the alleged violation require an adjudicatory hearing before an administrative law judge, there are steps to follow preceding and subsequent to such hearing (outlined in Figure 10-10). The student should be able to relate both charts concerning the complaint-hearing processes to the materials presented in the previous chapter on Administrative Law.

THE "FISCAL SQUEEZE"

By 1975 it was clearly evident that revenue sharing was the subject of considerable misgivings. Originally the program was understood by recipient state and local officials to provide an increase in existing revenues that would be in addition to categorical grant-in-aid funds. In practice, however, as revenue sharing funds were distributed there was a parallel decrease in categorical grants on a large enough scale to convince state and local officials that they might be hardly better off financially than before. As national economic conditions worsened in 1973 and 1974, it became apparent that federal grant-in-aid programs would not be carried out at the same expenditure level as previously. From state and local perspectives, their financial squeeze was hardly eased. From the federal perspective, state and local officials had been granted more discretionary power to determine their own program priorities with relatively few restrictive regulations. In short, the decision-making center of gravity had shifted to the lower levels of government. Also, the argument proceeded along the lines that more effective and

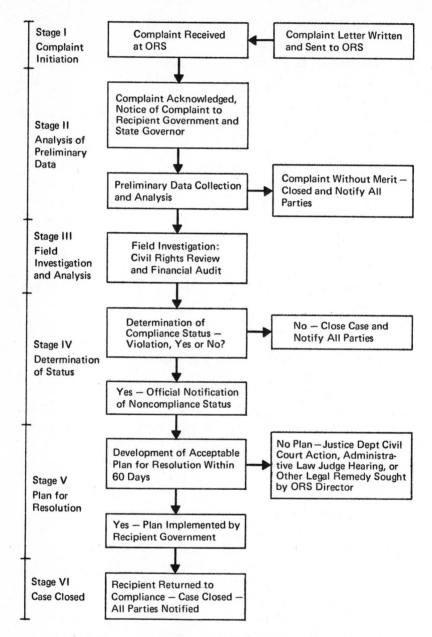

Stage I Complaint Initiation	Complaint Received at ORS	←	Complaint Letter Written and Sent to ORS
Stage II Analysis of Preliminary Data	Complaint Acknowledged, Notice of Complaint to Recipient Government and State Governor		
	Preliminary Data Collection and Analysis	→	Complaint Without Merit — Closed and Notify All Parties
Stage III Field Investigation and Analysis	Field Investigation: Civil Rights Review and Financial Audit		
Stage IV Determination of Status	Determination of Compliance Status — Violation, Yes or No?	→	No — Close Case and Notify All Parties
	Yes — Official Notification of Noncompliance Status		
Stage V Plan for Resolution	Development of Acceptable Plan for Resolution Within 60 Days	→	No Plan—Justice Dept Civil Court Action, Administra- tive Law Judge Hearing, or Other Legal Remedy Sought by ORS Director
	Yes — Plan Implemented by Recipient Government		
Stage VI Case Closed	Recipient Returned to Compliance — Case Closed — All Parties Notified		

SOURCE: *General Revenue Sharing and Civil Rights, Office of Revenue Sharing, U.S. Treasury Department.*

Figure 10-9. THE ORS COMPLAINT REVIEW PROCESS

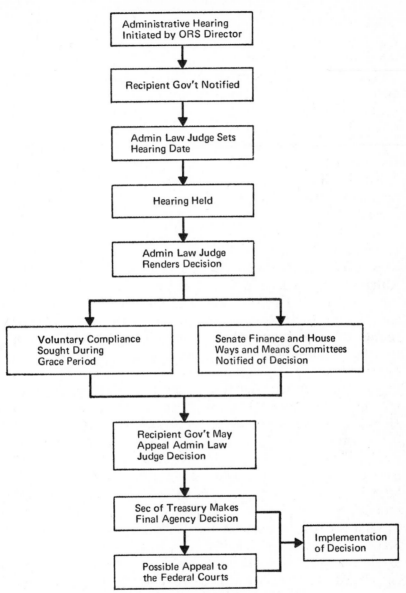

NOTE: At any time during this procedure the recipient
government and ORS may reach agreement and terminate
the proceedings.

*SOURCE: General Revenue Sharing and Civil Rights, Office
of Revenue Sharing, U.S. Treasury Department.*

Figure 10-10. ADMINISTRATIVE LAW JUDGE
HEARING STEPS

efficient use of federal money was assured by the simple fact that state and local spending could be directed precisely where the communities themselves felt there was the most need. It was obvious, however, that hat-in-hand mayors would still be frequent visitors to Washington, D.C.

In 1975 New York's Governor Hugh Carey and New York City's Mayor Abraham D. Beame went to the White House seeking emergency financial aid. New York City's financial debt had skyrocketed at the same time that confidence in the security of its municipal bonds declined precipitously. New York City was reported to be directly facing financial disaster.[27] Both U.S. Treasury Secretary William Simon and Chairman of the Federal Reserve Board Arthur Burns offered little solace. This was soon followed by President Gerald Ford's declaration that federal aid to New York in its attempt to balance its budget would not be within existing federal authority and would not, in any event, solve that city's long-term financial problem. President Ford and his fiscal advisors were, no doubt, influenced by the potential specter of other municipalities lining up behind New York as they faced increasingly difficult times in balancing income and expenditures. In the background, of course, was the rising national debt, which itself had begun to increase prodigiously through federal attempts to meet the economic recession of 1974–75 and serious industrial slowdown and growing unemployment throughout the nation. The message from Washington, D.C., was loud and clear: state and municipal governments will have to adopt a regimen of drastic fiscal belt-tightening with little hope of supplementary funds beyond grants-in-aid and revenue sharing.

The issue flared anew at the 1975 meeting of the United States Conference of Mayors. The chief executives of the nation's largest cities, those hardest hit by unemployment, announced they would favor a reduction in federal defense spending, with the funds going instead to an increased share of revenue sharing money for their cities. They had perhaps been indirectly encouraged by earlier proposals, drafted by a joint team of the U.S. Treasury, the Domestic Council and the Office of Budget and Management, which had been submitted to President Ford. The proposals were in favor of extension by Congress, with presidential support, of Revenue Sharing to 1982; increasing the funds available by about 15% in the annual pay-out and modifying the distribution formula to the extent that cities with high poverty populations and high tax efforts would receive a 30% bonus compared to more affluent jurisdictions in their own states. Eliminating the eight federal priorities for local spending was also recommended.

President Ford, however, rejected many of the proposals, including the most far reaching recommendations, i.e., to modify the distribution formula for the larger and economically more distressed cities at the expense of the smaller and more affluent ones. He also opposed the "bonus" concept. His arguments centered upon the potential for "fueling inflation."

USES OF REVENUE SHARING FUNDS

Figures released in 1975 by the Office of Revenue Sharing revealed that *combined* state and local government expenditures were:

Public Safety. 23%
Educational Services and Facilities 21%
Public Transportation 15%
Multi-Purpose and General Government 10%
Environmental Protection 7%
Recreation and Cultural Programs. 5%
Social Services for Poor or Aged 4%
Finance Administration, Libraries,
Housing and Community Development,
Corrections, Economic Development . . . . 15%[28]

These national averages for combined state and local expenditures are somewhat misleading. For example, the states spent over one-half (52%) for education purposes, while local governments expended only 1% on capital projects related to education; yet the national average computes to 21%. Obversely, local governments expended 36% of their available revenue sharing funds for public safety, while state governments expended only 1% in the public safety area, resulting in a national average of 23%. Local expenditures (exclusive of state governments) were:

Public Safety. 36%
Public Transportation 19%
Environmental Protection 11%
General Government 11%
Health. 7%
Recreation. 7%
Other Uses. 9%

Despite broadened discretion under revenue sharing, state and local governments have become increasingly dependent upon federal aid. In 1974 federal aid (including revenue sharing) exceeded 25% of all state-local revenue sources (see Figure 10-11). In 1974 revenue sharing comprised nearly 4% of state-local revenue sources. Without the usual matching requirements, however, the fiscal impact is considerably more significant than that figure alone would suggest. The point to be made is that policy discretion must be differentiated from fiscal dependence; while revenue sharing encourages the former, it does not diminish the latter. This problem, for those who regard it as a problem, has yet to be satisfactorily resolved.

ATTITUDES TOWARD REVENUE SHARING

Congressional perceptions of revenue sharing are important. A number of specific problems have been cause for concern among congressmen. In 1974 a questionnaire on revenue sharing was distributed to both houses of Congress by a subcommittee of the House of Representatives.[29] The survey revealed several problems.

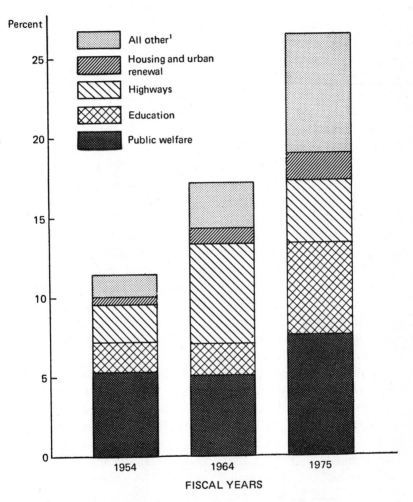

Percent

- All other[1]
- Housing and urban renewal
- Highways
- Education
- Public welfare

FISCAL YEARS

[1] Includes general revenue sharing payments in 1974 (3.7 percent of state-local revenue)

SOURCE: Trends in Fiscal Federalism 1954–1974, Washington, D.C.: Advisory Commission on Intergovernmental Relations, February 1975.

Figure 10-11. INCREASE IN FEDERAL AID IN RELATION TO STATE-LOCAL OWN SOURCE REVENUE: 1954–1974 (Federal Aid as a Percent of State-Local General Revenue From Own Sources)

The cutback in numerous federal social grant-in-aid programs made the "promises" of revenue sharing meaningless. Because of this, revenue sharing can no longer be considered as additonal relief and is, in fact, now inadequate to accomplish its original purposes.

Revenue sharing money is provided to more than 39,000 governmental jurisdictions. Many of these have not demonstrated a need for such funds. Yet in order to get revenue sharing legislation through Congress, broad compromises had to be made so that virtually every local government in the nation—regardless of size, function, or relative need—shared in the largess. Also, the formulas require significant modification so that non-viable governments are not sustained past their useful life nor are defunct units of government resurrected to an ailing life.

Civil rights groups have raised charges of serious discrimination. The charges are of several types. It is alleged that the Office of Revenue Sharing in the Treasury Department has one of the most poorly staffed and funded Civil Rights compliance programs in the entire federal establishment. Further, charges have been made that revenue sharing funds have been used to free local money, which may be used for discriminatory purposes. In addition, many citizen groups testified in Congressional hearings of their frustrated attempts to gain more impact on local governmental budget-making.

While data reflect the role of revenue sharing in helping to hold down state and local taxes, there has been little or no impact on efforts to make those taxes more progressive or more efficient. It has not significantly alleviated the financial plight of many of the nation's larger cities. While Republicans held by a 3 to 1 margin that tax reduction was a desirable use, Democrats indicated by a narrow margin that such use was undesirable.

Few guidelines have emerged by which to determine what is or is not a frivolous or undesirable expenditure. One of the key problems is congressional concern that with Congress and the administration attempting to hold down governmental spending at the national level, many state and local governments are expending revenue sharing funds on unnecessary projects and services. On the other hand, if enough regulations are promulgated to prevent abuse, then the discretionary emphasis of the revenue sharing program is undercut and the ensuing red tape will approach that characteristic of categorical grants.

Revenue sharing receives less congressional scrutiny than it deserves. While professing to grant power to the people, it locks them into the status quo. All it offers is money and in so doing breaks down accountability at all levels of government.

Smaller recipient governments find administration of the program to be costly. They must spend a disproportionate share for published planned use reports and actual use reports.

Local government reorganization, consolidation and reform are hindered or at least not aided by revenue sharing.

Congressional Republicans favor elimination of the eight high-priority functional expenditure areas for local governments, while congressional Democrats oppose any such elimination. Democrats favor specifying high-priority uses for revenue sharing funds for the states, while Republicans oppose it.

Congressional sentiment is largely in favor of continuing the prohibition against using revenue sharing money for matching federal dollars in some federal grant programs.

The increasing pace of criticism of revenue sharing as well as the emergence of some fundamental differences between the Republicans and Democrats promises that continuance of revenue sharing in its existing form is somewhat problematical. While Republicans tend to be heavily supportive, the Democrats are increasingly skeptical. Political party fortunes in congressional elections may consequently be a crucial factor in the evolution or eventual abandonment of revenue sharing as it is known today. In fiscal federalism, no less than administrative federalism, value choices must be made among conflicting alternatives and technical considerations must be tempered by the ebb and flow of political forces. There is little doubt, however, that federal funding is now a permanent feature of state and local finances and, regardless of the processes by which such funds are allocated, the national government retains the strength to establish guidelines for local programs and practices.

Public attitudes toward revenue sharing are also a factor in the dynamic interplay of political forces shaping intergovernmental fiscal policies. In 1973 a survey of over 2,000 private householders on this subject was undertaken by the Opinion

Research Corporation of Princeton, New Jersey, under the auspices of the Advisory Commission on Intergovernmental Relations. The results revealed that 56% of the American public favored revenue sharing, with 18% opposed and 26% having no opinion. On the question of whether or not expenditure "strings" should be attached to revenue sharing funds, the public sentiment favored funding for specific purposes (48%), while 30% felt the funds should be expended as those governments thought best and 22% had no opinion. On the question of which government (national, state or local) was felt to give citizens the most for their money, the national government was favored by 35%, state governments by 18% and local governments by 25%, with 22% in the "don't know" category.[30] These conclusions would tend to support the main national-urban thrust of revenue sharing and also Democratic party inclinations toward more specificity at the state level of government.

THE BLOCK GRANT

In 1974, with the revenue sharing program well under way, Congress enacted legislation of great significance for fiscal federalism. The "block grant" concept is designed to consolidate previously fragmented, though functionally related, categorical grants into larger block grants. The major piece of legislation inaugurating this concept was the Housing and Community Development Act of 1974. The act consolidated ten categorical urban development programs. The merged categorical grants were the previously separate urban renewal, model cities, neighborhood development, land acquisition, open space land, public facility loan, basic water and sewer facilities, advanced planning grant, code enforcement and neighborhood facility programs. At the same time the act did, like revenue sharing, delegate substantial program and priority direction to local communities.

The three-year program of block grants does impose some federal requirements, including community identification of community development needs, the formulation of a plan to meet those needs, the preparation of a housing assistance plan, demonstrated conformity with federal civil rights laws and citizen opportunities to participate in formulating funding applications. This act represented the largest consolidation of related but separately administered federal categorical grant programs up to that time.[31] The law may be described as perhaps a compromise between the categorical approach and revenue sharing. It does represent a movement under way in Congress to eliminate many of the problems in the grant-in-aid system.

STATE-LOCAL FISCAL FEDERALISM

The vast area of national-state-local fiscal federalism is paralleled by equally significant state-local fiscal relationships. Despite the contemporary impact of national financial aid to state and local governments, it is still true that the administrative and fiscal relationships between the states and their local governments far outbalance in scope and importance their fiscal relations with national authorities. The place of local governments in the American system is quite clear. Pronouncements of state legislatures, commentators on municipal law and a long line of judicial decisions have made local governments the "creatures" of state will. Local governments comprised of counties, municipalities (incorporated communities), special districts, townships, villages, boroughs and parishes are brought into existence by state authority and remain subject to the will of their creator. Even where "home rule" is pronounced (for example, entrenched in state constitutions) local governments are still subject to general state law in matters of statewide concern, while their own authority is limited to "municipal affairs."

Home rule in the United States is quite spotty. Most local governments are limited to specific or directly implied powers reflected in state laws and by judicial tradition of narrowly interpreting local powers vis-à-vis state authority.

The state limits the fiscal powers of local governments in various ways. For instance, local taxation may be allowed only for purposes and upon objects specified in state law. There may be state-determined maximum tax ceilings beyond which local governments cannot legally proceed. Some states may provide for "tax overrides," i.e., a referendum on the issue of whether or not local taxation may exceed state imposed tax ceilings. The decision is consequently out of the hands of local officials and vested in the local electorate.

Authority to issue bonds (borrowing money on the public credit) is restricted only to those local governments specifically vested with this authority. Further, maximum interest rates and the maximum time period for bond maturity is usually set forth in state law.

Periodic reporting of local government financial transactions to state authorities may be required. The state may have the power to audit the books and accounts of local governments. A uniform system of accounting for local governments or, alternatively, for selected local governmental agencies may be imposed.

The state may mandate certain public activities carried out at the local level which are to be financed wholly, or in part, by local governments. Common examples are the mandatory setting aside of a portion of local tax revenues for the maintenance of local courts, planning commissions and planning departments.

State fiscal services and technical advice are often rendered to local governments. The state, by marketing or certification of local government bonds, makes them more attractive in the municipal bond market. The state, in effect, by implication guarantees the reliability of the bonds by utilizing its own credit rating as an inducement to potential investors.

The state exercises a clearing house function by collecting financial data on a statewide basis through mandatory reporting and then collating and publishing the figures. Thus, statewide data and trends are available to local governments as well as interested citizens and organizations.

The state may establish standards and training for local government fiscal officers. For example, some states provide annual institutes or training conferences for local tax assessors so that intercounty variations in assessment for similar type properties are minimized.

The collection of certain revenues by the state and the return of a percentage of these revenues to counties or cities of origin are frequently referred to as "in lieu tax collection" and emphasize the often superior taxing and collecting abilities of state governments. Common examples are cigarette taxes, gasoline taxes and alcoholic beverage taxes. Where the revenues returned to the local governments are not "earmarked" or "segregated" for specific uses, this technique bears the essential characteristics of "revenue sharing." Frequently, the apportionments are made on the bases specified in state law and do not require an application by the local governmental unit.

Grants-in-aid have long been a common feature of state-local fiscal relations. The rationale and requirements are often similar to those of federal grants. In this manner, state governments are able to "encourage" local governments to enter into fields of activity deemed by the state to be of importance. An example is a state department of public health encouraging local authorities to provide specialized diagnostic services for physically handicapped children whose parents are unable to provide all or a portion of their care. The state agency may maintain statewide responsibility for financial as well as medical eligibility standards. Administration of the program would be a local responsibility (albeit under state administrative standards) with perhaps three-quarters of the costs of the program provided by the state and one-quarter of the cost by each county. The term "grant-in-aid" is not commonly used in state-local fiscal relations; the more common term is "subvention."

A number of factors have served to make local governments increasingly dependent fiscally upon the states. Perhaps the most important is the tendency of state governments to mandate additional functions and responsibilities to local governments. One exhaustive study of county government in New Jersey revealed 62.4% of total county functional expenditures were mandated by the state and that 42.8% of county employees were engaged in the administration of these mandated programs.[32] In addition, county Boards of Freeholders have little or no control over some of the largest state-mandated and locally oriented county programs. When this is combined with the fact that many local salaries may be state-determined, Boards of Freeholders in New Jersey do not have sufficient control over the administration of county affairs. Consequently, the study estimated that freeholders did not have control of 79.2% of county functional expenditures and also could not control 68.4% of county employees.[33] Extreme though this case may be, the same characteristics are repeated in state-local relations in many other states.

In such situations the combination of rigid state controls over municipal taxing and other revenue sources, local fiscal inadequacy and large numbers of state-mandated functions, together with state-imposed minimal levels and standards of local services, create an intensified dependence upon state fiscal aid. Most American local governments are dependent upon local property taxes for the bulk of their revenues. However, over a period of time many American communities have experienced close to intolerable pressures upon the local property tax base and, consequently, local officials are looking to state authorities for increased fiscal sustenance. In the period 1954–1974 state aid as a percentage of local revenue sources increased from about 40% to about 60% (see Figure 10-12).

A few large-city mayors have raised the issue of state-local revenue sharing programs paralleling the concepts of the federal approach. The problem, as viewed by the mayors, is the rising pressure upon the local property tax (perhaps the most hated of all taxes), since very few cities are authorized by the state to enact municipal progressive income taxes. These mayors take the position that if the prohibitions of municipal income taxation continues, the states should share their income tax revenues with the cities in order to prevent local property "taxpayer revolts." As the fiscal plight of many local communities worsens the issue could be one of the liveliest in state-local relations during the '70's.

In conclusion, fiscal federalism operating between the levels of American governments, just as administrative federalism, tends to break down the significance of political boundaries. Local officials in particular are subjected to the supervisory authority, administrative standards and fiscal guidelines of both national and state governments. In this perspective the broadened movement for more local "home rule" may be more than counterbalanced by increasing fiscal dependence. Once again, much of the rhetoric and symbolism of American government may be, in fact, deceptive insofar as they inaccurately reflect reality.

If some of the dominant theories of American government are to be even approximately congruent to the existing state of affairs, it is evident that extensive modification of contemporary fiscal relationships must be undertaken. Further, they must be based upon assumptions best designed to meet those dissatisfactions which are so pronounced as we gaze out upon the immediate horizon.

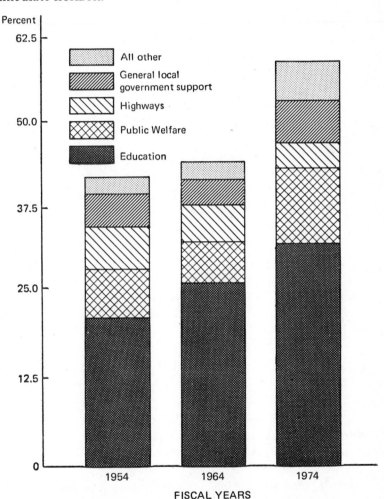

SOURCE: *Trends in Fiscal Federalism 1954-1975. Advisory Commission on Intergovernmental Relations, February 1975.*

Figure 10-12. INCREASE IN STATE AID IN RELATION TO LOCAL OWN SOURCE REVENUE: 1954–1974 (State Aid as a Percent of Local General Revenue From Own Sources)

389

NOTES

NOTES

1. See *1969 Listing of Operating Federal Assistance Programs Compiled During the Roth Study*. 91st Congress, 1st Session. House of Representatives. Document No. 91-177. Washington, D.C.: U.S. Government Printing Office.

2. *Catalog of Federal Domestic Assistance*. Washington, D.C.: Office of Management and Budget, 1973.

3. For a background to federal disaster aid, see "Disasters and Disaster Relief," *The Annals of the American Academy of Political and Social Science*, Vol. 309 (January 1957); also *Response to Disaster. Report of the Federal Reconstruction and Development Planning Commission for Alaska*, Washington, D.C.: Government Printing Office, September 1964.

4. Thomas H. Kiefer, *The Political Impact of Federal Aid to State and Local Governments*. Morristown, New Jersey: General Learning Press, 1974, p. 9.

5. U.S. Bureau of the Census. *Statistical Abstract of the United States: 1974* (95th edition). Washington, D.C.: Government Printing Office, 1974, Table No. 409, p. 252.

6. *Ibid.*, Table No. 411, p. 253.

7. *Statistical Abstract of the United States: 1970*, Table No. 418, p. 278.

8. *Loc. cit.*

9. George Williams, "Federal Objectives and Local Accountability," in Joseph D. Sneed and Steven A. Waldhorn (eds.), *Restructuring the Federal System. Approaches to Accountability in Post-Categorical Programs*. New York: Crane, Russak, 1975, pp. 129-130.

10. 262 U.S. 447 (1923).

11. *Statistical Abstract of the United States: 1970*, Tables No. 571, p. 384 and Table No. 578, p. 388.

12. *Ibid.*, Table No. 483, p. 320.

13. See Harry W. Reynolds, Jr., "Merit Controls, the Hatch Acts, and Personnel Standards in Intergovernmental Relations," in *The Annals of the American Academy of Political and Social Science*, Vol. 359 (May 1965), pp. 81-93.

14. *U.S. Civil Service Commission v. National Association of Letter Carriers*, 413 U.S. 548.

15. For an excellent discussion see Frederick C. Mosher, *Democracy and the Public Service*, New York: Oxford University Press, 1968, chapters 4-7.

16. Statement of Senator Edmund S. Muskie in *Periodic Congressional Review of Federal Grants-in-aid*. Hearings before the Subcommittee on Intergovernmental Relations of the Committee on Government Operations. U.S. Senate, 88th Congress, 2nd Session. January 14, 15 and 16, 1964, p. 4.

17. Richard E. Thompson, *Revenue Sharing: A New Era in Federalism*. Washington, D.C.: Revenue Sharing Advisory Service, 1973, pp. vi–vii.

18. Peter B. Harkins, "Would Revenue Sharing Work?" *Nation's Cities*, Vol. 7 (March 1, 1969), p. 8.

19. See, for example, Walter Heller, *New Dimensions of Political Economy*. Cambridge, Mass.: Harvard University Press, 1966.

20. See *Revenue Sharing—An Idea Whose Time Has Come*. Washington, D.C.: Advisory Commission on Intergovernmental Relations, 1970.

21. *Congressional Record – House* (January 22, 1971) pp. H 93–94.

22. "Capital" expenditures generally comprise acquisition of, or addition to, fixed assets. Examples are the purchase of land or facilities, construction projects and the repair and replacement of equipment. Specific examples are public transportation (including transit systems), purchase of fire-fighting equipment and ambulances, cars, tractors, library bookmobiles, snowplows, highway maintenance equipment, purchase of park and recreational land and construction or structural repair to school buildings (but not operating or maintenance costs of schools). Generally, the Office of Revenue Sharing accepts as permissible capital expenditures those which are determined by state and local law. If state or local law defines capital expenditure in a stricter or narrower way than does the Office of Revenue Sharing, then the state and local law must be followed.

23. *Regulations Governing the Payment of Entitlements Under Title I of the State and Local Fiscal Assistance Act of 1972*. Office of Revenue Sharing, Department of the Treasury, August 1973. See also *Native American Governments and the General Revenue Sharing Program*. Washington, D.C.: Office of Revenue Sharing, Department of the Treasury, 1975.

24. See *Revenue Sharing—Citizen Action*, Council for Economic Justice, Washington, D.C. n.d.; also *Getting Involved, Your Guide to General Revenue Sharing*, Washington, D.C.: Office of Sharing, Department of the Treasury, 1974.

25. See *Your Fair Share of Revenue Sharing. A Community Guide to General Revenue Sharing*. Washington, D.C.: Movement for Economic Justice, February 1973.

26. See *General Revenue Sharing and Civil Rights*. Washington, D.C.: Office of Revenue Sharing, n.d.

27. For an interesting account of these events, see Andy Logan, "Around City Hall: Crisis and Credibility," *The New Yorker*, Vol. LI, No. 17 (June 16, 1975), pp. 110-120.

28. "Where Have All the $$ Gone?" *ReveNews* (Office of Revenue Sharing), Vol. 3, No. 2 (April 1975), p. 2. See also *Revenue Sharing: Its Use by and Impact on State Governments*. Report to the Congress by the Comptroller General of the United States, August, 1973; *Revenue Sharing Bulletin*, Vol. 1, No. 11 (September 1973).

29. *Replies by Members of Congress to a Questionnaire on General Revenue Sharing*. 93rd Congress, 2nd Session. Intergovernmental Relations Subcommittee of the Committee on Government Operations, April 1974.

30. *Revenue Sharing and Taxes: A Survey of Public Attitude*. Washington, D.C.: Advisory Commission on Intergovernmental Relations, August, 1973.

31. "Changes in Federal Aid," in *Federalism 1974: The Tension of Interdependence*. Washington, D.C.: Advisory Commission on Intergovernmental Relations, February 1975, pp. 16-17.

32. *County Government: Challenge and Change*. Trenton: County and Municipal Study Commission, 1969, Second Report, p. 52.

33. *Ibid.*, pp. 34-35.

PART IV

NEW HORIZONS

11

THE PUBLIC
POLICY
PROCESS

Concern for the processes of policy-making signals a reawakened awareness and sensitivity to the importance of those value choices shaping public priorities and commitments to governmental action. The conduct of contemporary public affairs is partially dependent upon science and technology. Science articulates a coherent, systematic explanation of the world and the solar system in which we live. Technology is concerned with the application of science to productive techniques. Technology demands expertise, specialization and coordination. The technological revolution has deeply affected the processes by which societal values are determined and how these values are to be implemented.

THE EMERGING CONCERN WITH POLICY MAKING

The traditional approaches to the understanding of public administration encompass descriptive studies of the machinery of government, legal description and analysis centering upon the powers and legal competence of public officials and agencies, as well as studies which attempted to reform existing administrative processes based upon *a priori* and universal principles of "good management." Such principles were conceived as moral imperatives which, when applied to any situation, would result in virtuous reform. These principles rested upon the separation of policy from administration, centralization of authority and the establishment of an effective and pyramidal administrative hierarchy.

Overwhelming technological developments in recent decades and newer behavioral approaches to the understanding of human beings and the managing of human affairs belie such traditional perceptions. Administrative orthodoxy has occasionally done much mischief and is of minimal usefulness today in understanding the nature of public administration in the techno-culture of the post-industrial state.

Orthodox models are of limited utility in developing deeper insights into administrative behavior, the value dilemmas facing public agencies or the impact of administrative policy upon the social and governmental systems. It was reaction to the limitations of orthodoxy that has led to intellectual ferment within public administration and gives promise of spawning even greater advances in understanding the administration of public affairs.

It is useful to turn to the social sciences and examine developments which directly aid in understanding the administered society. Sociology, social psychology, psychology and anthropology have contributed much. Many of these concepts, assumptions and inferences (some verified and some still tentative) cut across traditional disciplinary boundaries and enhance our knowledge and understanding of modern administrative systems. General systems theory, structural-functional analysis, group behavior theory, social psychology and psychiatry have also expanded and deepened our perceptions, insights and knowledge of the complex interworkings of industrial society.

It is important to consider some of these recent efforts and explore some of the theoretical frames of reference to enable the perceptive observer to view public administrative activity as involving dynamic and complex interrelationships among given groups and actors. Hopefully, a framework will be provided which will aid students and practitioners in examining in a systematic way many of the significant case studies, empirical observations, studies of bureaucracy, data of communications research, small group experiments, decision-making analyses and other recent advances making up so much of the current literature and concerns of the field.

It is helpful to focus upon the links between public administration activity and the making of public policy. The vital requirements of a society are provided through administrative
processes. Professor Morton Kroll notes:

> A policy and its structures are wholly enmeshed. Institu-
> tions provide the broad framework within which the
> policy is operative. Organizations, which operate at a more
> immediate range within the social scale, may develop as
> entities of their own with identifications and value systems
> not necessarily related to the policy which brought them
> into being.[1]

He proceeds to observe that organizations may be "creatures
of policy" and its formulators as well. He notes they have "on
occasion . . . been known to outlive their policy rationale."
Making and implementing public policy are intimately related
to the processes not only within the public organization charged
with fulfilling that policy but with the processes that link that
organization to the broader social framework within which it
is set.[2]

PUBLIC NEEDS AND PUBLIC POLICY

Public administration involves both identifying and satisfying
public policy. This is accomplished by a variety of public
officials who are in some way accountable for their decisions
and actions through procedures established by the community.[3]
In general terms the concept of "public" encompasses the idea
of proceeding from, relating to or affecting the whole community. Specific administrative processes proceeding from,
relating to or affecting a whole community are "public."[4]

John Dewey stated, ". . . the line between private and public is
to be drawn on the basis of the extent and scope of the consequences of acts which are so important as to need control,
whether by inhibition or promotion. . . ." Dewey continues, ". . .
the state is the organization of the public effected through officials for the protection of interests shared by its members. . . ."[5]

Paul Appleby has observed that "a public" comes into being where a shared need is recognized and there seems to be no satisfactory private means for meeting such needs.[6] What processes and forces identify and determine the acts which are so important as to need control whether by inhibition or promotion?

There is a public policy-making process which identifies crucial problems, shared needs and common interests. This process is also concerned with determining the means to satisfy them. Community activities so important as to require promotion or inhibition are manifested as needs or demands. As such, they usually imply or express underlying value premises. The identification and definition of these problems and needs may involve formal and informal administrative, legislative and judicial processes which operate within a specific legal jurisdiction and social environment. These diverse processes are crucial to the effective satisfaction of such problems and needs. The accountability processes discussed in Chapter 2 are designed to encourage the integrity of the administrative processes involved even though they may operate inadequately at times. Accountability processes are distributed throughout the administrative, legislative and judicial processes. Such combinations of these processes as operate to identify and satisfy the *shared* needs might well be conceived as the crucial elements of *public* administrative activity. Shipman has described this as the "policy process." He describes it in part as:

> . . . a continuing process of social interaction, of personalities, groups, and social systems, oriented toward realization of some set of goals or, more broadly, some pattern of satisfactions. It is distinctive in that it moves ultimately through the channels provided by political institutions, it is confined and regulated by the value system implicit in the institutional system, and it accepts the sanctions of public responsibility. A capacity is thus acquired to invoke the authority of the state chiefly with respect to taxation and regulation that re-enforces value seeking drives. . . ."[7]

PREVAILING APPROACHES TO POLICY FORMATION

Past attempts to unravel the complex web of public policy-making have centered largely on the policy process itself. Here, thinking has remained relatively static in seeking universal principles which will lead to superior policy. This approach is akin to the early gropings of the scientific management school of organization theorists. Attention was focused on the sequential flow of information in a rigidly formalized organizational setting without adequate consideration of sociological factors such as roles, values and group interactions. In recent years there has been more explicit recognition of the feedback mechanism and gradual acceptance that special-interest groups may markedly influence policy formation. But overall, the policy process remained primarily centered on the linear progression of data and opinion from both bureaucrats and public towards community decision-centers such as legislative and executive branches.

Substantive Approaches

Until recently, public studies centering on the making of policy have been unstructured, lacking in analytical rigor and generally reportorially or descriptively historical. They have not been related to any theoretical or conceptual frame of reference. Newer efforts have centered upon descriptive and analytical models and may be identified as falling into five distinct substantive categories.

First are the *descriptive studies*, which focus upon the "story" and the "object lesson" about how public policy is made within a particular environment. Case studies are the most familiar representative of this category. Here events, value commitments and actors within organizations are described and analyzed by identifying a key actor or an important event or a set of circumstances which define public policy in that specific instance.

Second are those *prescriptive analytical studies* which focus upon economic choices and the logic of such choices. This approach is amenable to the use of elaborate computer game models and assumes that if you want to achieve specific outcomes, i.e., societal consequences, all that need be done is to alter the incentives and deterrents involved and adjust the cost and liabilities. It involves some mix of coercion and persuasion to achieve its end and assumes the predictability of the results. Increasing the penalities and giving tax incentives for pollution control efforts would be an example of this approach.[8]

Third are those efforts which are merely explanatory of the public policy process, i.e., they seek to identify the major determinants of public policy choices. No specific consideration is given to what policy "ought to be" or the relationship of policy to a given set of values. The focus is upon describing and accounting for differences in policy outcomes as they relate to the socioeconomic and political variables within a particular political system. If understanding the determinants of public policy contributes to a more rational policy process, this is simply a by-product. These may also be identified as *explanatory study models.*[9]

Fourth are *normative studies*, which concern definitions of the "good life." They are concerned with what "ought to be." These would include a variety of utopian models as well as those efforts which attempt to delineate models of "good government," "good welfare programs," "effective crime prevention," "good educational system," "sound tax programs," "good public transportation," and a variety of other topics about which an ideal type of design is suggested that will eliminate existing difficulties and achieve a virtuous and better life.[10]

Fifth are those *evaluation studies* which focus upon the direct impact of an ongoing program within an organization upon the environment. Here, a variety of review procedures and analyses are used to derive some basis for program evaluation in relation to the values sought. The primary concern is on assessment of people, organizational efforts and policy goals and outcomes within a public administrative setting.[11]

DECISION-MAKING APPROACHES

Theories of decision-making are eminently suitable for important insights into the infrastructure of an organization but have been of little aid in understanding the complex public policy-making processes. In a careful analysis of the "state of the art," Yehezkel Dror identifies seven decision-making models:

1. *Pure-Rationality*: This approach centers upon developing "a universally ideal pattern for decision making" which should be approximated as closely as possible.
2. *Economically Rational Model*: This is the same as the first except that efficiency and economy would be maximized.
3. *Sequential-Decision Model*: This focuses upon experimentation among a variety of alternatives in order to determine and adopt the most effective policy.
4. *Incremental Model*: This is Lindblom's well-known "muddling-through" explanation as to how policy is made. That is, there is no planning. You just, "come hell and high water," somehow muddle through.
5. *Satsifying Model*: Built upon Herbert Simon's "satisficing" approach to decision-making. It focuses upon choosing the first satisfactory alternative without exhaustively examining all possibilities.
6. *Extra-Rational Model*: Based upon extra-rational processes for arriving at the most optimal methods of decision-making and policy-making.
7. *Optimal Model*: This is an integrative approach which focuses identifying values, practicalities and problems. These are integrated into the resolution of the problems and then focus upon resource allocation, goal-setting, program alternatives, predictability of results and evaluation of the "best" alternatives. Then the decision is made as to which are acceptable options.[12]

These approaches are representative of the efforts to better understand how public policy is determined and realized. The processes involved in making public policy comprise a set of interactions among concerned persons and groups where explicit and implicit value selection occurs. The phrase "policy flow" might be more helpful to describe the policy milieu. This phrase reflects the dynamic evolution and ebb and flow of policy formation. It also expresses the point that policy emerges from the sometimes intentional or haphazard impact and coalescence of numerous factors, not all of which are readily identifiable or measurable. A multidimensional picture is required, as distinct from a one-dimensional perspective, with which to view the flow of public policy-making. Within the framework of policy flow there is no question of defining the "one best method" of policy formation, for none may exist.

In summary, policy flow involves more than mere organizational process; it involves complex social interaction. Its focus is activity which ranges beyond rigid institutional boundaries into the broader environment. It is issue-oriented and does not abandon the organizational setting entirely, but rather uses formal institutionalization as a starting point for more intensive probing of roles, values and group interactions. More specifically and importantly, it recognizes the implicit personal values of the observer and attempts to screen the relevant data to reveal the value content, role behavior and interactions.

A SYSTEMS APPROACH TO POLICY-MAKING

The systems model developed by David Easton and discussed in Chapter 3 is useful in developing conceptual "handles" to gain further understanding of the dynamics of public policy implementation. It was suggested there are specific social processes which have as their purpose the identification of shared community needs. An expression of needed action may be stated as a demand or an urgent request or a problem that requires solution. These requests have the contingent possibility of widely affecting the quality of life of a significant number of persons. In addition, in a governmental system there are processes which identify and respond to these needs in ways that are expected to eliminate or resolve them as significant social concerns.

Any system may be conceived as involving *inputs* which may be identified as needs and demands encompassing important values. This same social system (i.e., some number of its members) supplies the energy resources, financial supports and competence for the resolution of the identified concerns. Specialized institutions in this social system are concerned with performing activities resulting in diminution or elimination of those concerns. Finally, in the *output* phases the activities designed to effect the desired differences are carried out. Identified goals are hopefully achieved. Change may occur from adaptations made or the *status quo* may be maintained. The values of concern to society are consequently deemed to be implemented. The processes involved may or may not achieve the earlier stated concerns and purposes. Unanticipated results may occur. These results may be evaluated and changes in the ongoing processes be affected through *feedback*. Graphically, this is represented in Figure 11-1. It is possible to adapt the Easton model to public policy-making.

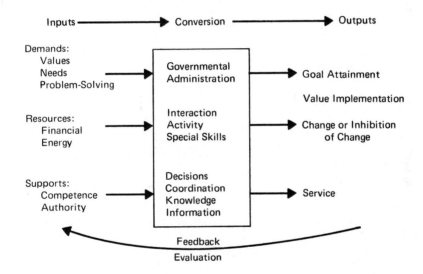

Figure 11-1. A GOVERNMENTAL POLICY PROCESS

The public policy process may then be conceived as a specialized *system* of interrelated activities which occur among specialized interacting groups and individuals. Once the foregoing assumptions are made certain consequences follow concerning the way in which public policy-making may be analyzed. First, it is a subsystem within a larger system which consists also of other interacting subsystems. Second, once the idea of a system is assumed it suggests that groups and actors in the specific system may be identifiable. Third, these groups exist in a relatively definable environment. Fourth, activity exists which results from *inputs* into the system and causes tasks to be performed which are converted into *outputs* that have consequences for both the system and the social-physical-cultural-psychological-economic environment in which it operates. These outputs may also be inputs into other systems. Fifth, the activity of the system may be characterized as essentially processes of interaction which occur among the components of the system. Sixth, such interaction occurs as patterned and regularized activities, continuous in operation and conducing toward an end. Such interaction is patterned because it follows a relatively definable course among the various groups and actors. It is regularized in that these patterns of interaction are recurrent. These regularized processes may, to a degree, be demarcated and identified.

These processes of interaction and the other components of the system may be viewed as varying in form as they relate to specific public administrative systems. Thus it is possible to utilize the idea of the *variable* within the individual system. A *variable* may be considered to be any aspect of the processes of interaction which has varying effects within the system upon other variables or upon the organizational units themselves. The particular form a variable takes within the system may be thought of as a *force* which has a specific effect upon other variables, upon specific individuals or groups within the system or upon the system as a whole. For example, the budgetary process may be considered as a variable because the specific budgeting pattern varies within a specific policy setting and within a particular administrative system. The specific form the budget takes relative to an agency or a group or unit in the sytem is a specific force with a specific impact upon the structure and functions of the system and the subsystem with which it is linked. These variables may sometimes exist as operating subsystems of a superordinate system. These subsystems perform a specific function (which varies in impact) for the larger system into which they are linked. Some of these aspects of the system will be more fully explored in later chapters.

The policy process is generally goal-oriented and intimately concerned with the implementation of social values. It is concerned with the authoritative allocation of resources and energy utilization through the application of power, human activity and personal effort. It is essentially concerned with the processes by which significant public decisions are made. The power which is available within a public administrative setting may be authoritative in that it is accepted voluntarily by those upon whom it is used. Alternatively, it may be persuasive, manipulative or coercive. In any case, it results in social and/or individual differences or the inhibition of social and/or individual differences. Public policy emerges from this setting as a result of these interactions, which involve a number of specific participants and groups from the executive, legislative, judicial and concerned clientele sectors. The development of public policy is a process of selecting the values which will guide administrative efforts.

Traditionally, public policy is seen as emerging from the legislative process, then applied by the executive and disciplined by the judiciary. In a modern technological society the process of making public policy may occur in quite a different manner. Public policy-making may be more easily understood as emerging from networks of interaction processes within a political-administrative system and embracing the formal and informal aspects of the legislature, the executive, the judiciary, independent agencies, interested pressure groups, individuals or the mass character of the larger community. Each of these exist within their own subsystems and any one of these subsystems may provide an avenue of appeal should the effort in one arena meet with failure. As is true of the larger system, each is characterized by a more or less stable power equation which exists among the participants. Each is set in an historical dimension which affects perceptions and procedures with consequential impact upon the processes of the system. Significant personalities and the nature of leadership affect the emergent nature of the policy choices. The organizations which exist within the system or subsystem have competence, authority and power to carry out activity which can have an impact in the specific environment in which they exist.[13]

The processes of public policy definition and the activities of its implementation are wholly intertwined and provide a broad network within which policy-making occurs. The *public policy process* is thus seen as:

> A sequential flow of interactions between governmental participants who discuss, argue about, and find common grounds for agreeing on the scope and types of governmental actions appropriate in dealing with a particular societal problem. This process includes: (1) seeking information to define the societal problem, (2) developing alternative solutions and (3) reaching agreement upon which alternative will best solve the problem. In short, the public policy process is a decision making process.[14]

Public policy involves value choices which may be expressed as demands, needs, wants or priorities and culminates in activity calculated to satisfy these wants. It involves mobilization of energy and resources designed to achieve a purpose through the use of administrative effort. This process occurs in a dynamic and changing setting. This policy setting is affected by exchanges from other subsystems, technological advances or declines, the existence of stability or crisis within the system as well as the nature of power transitions among the participants.

The patterns of values and behavior which characterize a public policy change continually in content and process. It obtains specificity within the setting where a governmental organization performs its functions. Administrative agencies are paramount both in shaping the content and the nature of public policy flow and subsequently in implementing policy decisions. Public policy cannot be separated from the milieu in which it evolves. Analysis of a specific policy environment would center upon identifying the component features and the dynamic characteristics of such an environment, particularly those which have a direct bearing upon the policy itself.

The power arrangements, history and tradition, kind and quality of leadership and followership, the formal and informal parameters and constraints, the institutional arrangements and competencies available and functioning, patterns of values, ethical systems and value alternatives are all important to understand the policy which eventually emerges. Each may serve as a complex influence or even be determinative of eventual public policy articulated through the administrative program within a particular setting. Each affects the nature of the boundaries and determines who will be affected. They are in a process of continuous flux and change.

The component parts may alter, be abandoned, be deleted, and shift in relation to each other. Specific administrative program activities may have a varying impact, as will specific projects and decisions, all of which combine to form a pattern of values and policies within the concerned and specific policy issue environment. It is a methodological challenge to both the practitioner and the scholar to identify these elements and weigh them on the basis of the extent to which they account for or influence policies. Nor are these forces particularly static. They may vary in impact and influence at one time or another in making and shaping policy. Professor Yehezkel Dror observed:

> Public policymaking is a very complex, dynamic process whose various components make different contributions to it. It decides major guidelines for action directed at the future, mainly by governmental organs. These guidelines (policies) formally aim at achieving what is in the public interest by the best possible means.[15]

Dror issues a call for the development of a *policy science* which could improve the design and operations of policy-making systems. He identifies the need for improved understanding and knowledge about policy-making. He focuses upon the need to integrate new knowledge and new analytical techniques into the policy-making process. Dror adds:

> The development of policy science must be speeded up, and this advanced science put to the fullest use, if critical problems are to be adequately solved. But the many changes that will have to be made in the structure and process of public policymaking in order to use this new knowledge

will involve rather substantial departures from present working methods, assumptions and cultural biases.[16]

Our technology is generating increasingly difficult, more complex and critical problems. These problems seem to defy our capacity to achieve mastery over them before they fulfill their potential threats of the destruction of man. Dror asserts that it is our "moral duty" and our "best bet" to increase our skills and understandings about policy-making and raise it to the level of a crucial science. He urges that we do it with exceptional care and humility but "without giving in to the conservative biases so deeply rooted in most individuals and social institutions." He urges us on to consider the implications, no matter how "bizarre" they might seem to us. Survival, he asserts, requires that, "We must not be distracted from carefully considering those implications on their own merits."

A FOCUS ON VALUES

Professor Alfred de Grazia has suggested:

If applied administration is to be taught at all without destructive effects upon creativity, it must be taught as an exercise in the postulation of values (often of opposites) in the systematic assessment of conditions affecting a given value system and in the prescription of preferred action for those who accept those values.[17]

The belief patterns determine how the energy and resources available in a social system shall be used. These are usually articulated as values and may be stated as needs, wants, demands or imperatives. These values provide individuals and groups with, as Kroll observes, "ways of identifying and responding to needs as well as with standards of expectation concerning the methods and mechanisms appropriate to dealing with them."[18] Values are conditioned by experience and thus influence anticipations and expectations which may be irrationally derived. Values are held implicitly and explicitly by the persons and groups involved in the policy process and thus can be hidden, explicit, amorphous, unplanned and disorganized. Values can be inconsistent, supportive or disintegrative of a social-political system. The values which determine action are conditioned by the shared and competing perceptions the participants have about the nature of our complex society. These images may be reasoned or visceral, and they relate to the expectations which citizens have for governmental activity and behavior of the public's servants. Most public policy in the United States is conceived from diverse sources pragmatically derived and ideologically biased.

Values derive from beliefs, aspirations and the requirements for sustenance and physical and psychological well-being. The emotive content may reflect anger, fear, love or joy and be born of a sense of well-being and trust, or a sense of cynicism, despair, fatalism and doom. They may reflect a vision of "The Good Life," the hope and purpose of a bright future based upon cooperative constructive action. Likewise they may reflect fatalistic, gloomy, despairing outlooks which find expression in withdrawal or destructive modes of action. Alternatively, they may be an admixture of some combination of these. Such combinations may combine with sufficient emotive force to lead to demands for action through administrative responses reflecting a broad spectrum of administrative options. These are frequently stated as needs. Values may manifest themselves concretely in the ways in which people talk and act, especially in how they choose to spend their time. Values function both as a limit upon or a stimulus to action.

Inquiry into value choices is, at most, difficult and tentative. Yet significant efforts have been made. Professor Nicholas Rescher has noted that the tools of inquiry into values can relate to the two ways that values manifest themselves.

Content analysis can be used to gain insights about values articulated through talk and the written word. Budget analysis might be used as well as observations of behavioral incidents to assess the actions in which value content may be expressed. Both methods are tentative and must be used with care, yet they are a beginning in a very difficult subject.[19] Herbert Simon, in writing of the relationships of values, experience and behavior and the linkage which takes a value from its articulation in public policy to its expression through program impact, noted that this chain "is a series of anticipations that connect a value with the situations realizing it and these situations, in turn, with the behaviors that produce them."[20]

One example might be a welfare policy which sets support for unwed dependent mothers so low that she and the child cannot get adequate nutrition or sufficient health care. The consequences of this policy will continue the cycle of dependence through another generation and frustrate the original purpose of the financial aid. Government is often required to maintain a number of programs which may be conflictive but which, nevertheless, are socially legitimate public policy. Full employment, public order, public health, standards of living, equal opportunity and a host of program areas reflect the essential value choices of governmental policy-making. Public choices contain the possibility of anticipated consequences but also of some which are unanticipated. Yet public choices will have implicit and explicit value implications.

Sir Geoffrey Vickers has observed that all public decisions are "multi-valued choices" and they involve "different ways of *seeing* the same situation, ways to which different values are attached."[21] Thus a policy-maker is vitally concerned with identifying and analyzing the multiple values which are relevant to a particular problem and engage in the controversies concerning them. Discussions and debates about policy assume that the values of those immediately concerned and of those who may be the ultimate recipients of that policy do have the capacity to change it; and further, that such change may take place through the processes of communication. Vickers notes there are three basic elements in the administrative policy-maker's tasks:

1. He must define the problem;

2. he must conceive programs leading to solution of the defined problem; and

3. he must articulate and analyze the conflicting values that appear in any solution and assess their relationship to the values sought.

A policy-maker is not only concerned with "muddling through" or balancing interests, but he or she is a "valuer" as well. He or she sets the norms through the use of information, insight and expertise which rest upon rational judgments. He or she is concerned with optimizing results. The policy-maker may become a potent advocate of the norms and values he or she sets, yet should be cautious and modest in such advocacy unless humanity itself weighs in the balance. For as Vickers observes, "The present does indeed belong to the living but only as a trust property belongs to trustees, even where the trustees are tenants for life."[22]

Throughout the administrative process, the program budgeter, cost-benefit analyst, program planner, computer specialist and policy analyst should be concerned with values, yet the task is not an easy one. What will more patience accomplish? More care? More altruism? What human values are modified or lost in this computer program? What are the human impacts of the transition to this or that policy, program or routine? It is time that considerations of value be consciously integrated throughout the entire administrative process.

Values are thus an important element in political decisions and are crucial to the administrative processes of choice and action. They are reflected in the complexities of the administrative process and are effected through either coercive or non-coercive measures.

The coercive measures would reflect the processes and procedures utilizing power and authority, manipulation, control, and generally reflect authoritarian methods or hierarchical decision and enforcement processes. The program areas most appropriate to these administrative orientations are more often those concerned with public safety, military operations, correctional and prison management, regulatory arbitration functions.

The non-coercive administrative measures, where power is not so punitive and visible, are more appropriate to the provisioning and broadening of social choices and opportunities. They are generally related to more effective personal survival and self-development. Program areas such as public health, welfare, rehabilitation, transportation, labor mediation, agriculture, commerce and education reflect these more positive administrative orientations. Yet, in either case, program activities, procedures, policy directives and program impacts may be contaminated with a number of conflicting value orientations, with the consequence of mixed administrative results. The public schools are one example. Compulsory school attendance is a coercive measure made more onerous because public budgets are tied to restrictive budgetary devices such as "full time equivalent student" or to "average daily attendance" of the client, i.e., the pupil. Yet education freed of coercive restraints may be an exhilarating and liberating experience.

PUBLIC ORGANIZATION

The primary device by which the responsibilities and tasks of public administration are performed is the public organization. Public administration is concerned with organizations which exist within particular environments and are charged with fulfilling specific public policy.

Public administration subsystems may be conceived as assemblages of public organizational units functioning according to more or less regularized patterns of interaction and interdependence. These organizations develop patterned responses to inputs and feedbacks from the sociocultural environment in which they exist. They respond through decisions and activities calculated to affect social relationships and maintain or modify institutional and systemic processes and relationships; in summary, to affect the environment. These processes of interaction and interdependence can be demarcated and identified. It is this combination of dynamic interacting forces through which the vital executive and administrative functions in public jurisdictions are performed.[23]

Administrative processes focusing on the organization are concerned with identification and definition of community problems and actions which may resolve these problems. Administrative processes involve, among other things, identification of values and the planning, design and development of policies. Another concern is the continuing operation and maintenance of programs fulfilling the stated policy. The satisfaction of the identified needs may result in differences in the environment and changes within and upon groups and individuals affected by the administrative activity. Administrative processes may be considered to be narrower and more specialized aspects of the larger political processes. Consequently, they may be considered as specialized processes within the *flow of policy*. Herbert Spiro observes that between the public recognition of a problem and the solution of such a problem there occurs a series of stages, namely: 1) formulation of the issue, 2) deliberation, 3) resolution and 4) solution.[24] Many groups within any political community may have varying needs and values which are often conflictive, yet each seeks expression through administrative effort. Such conflict may range from mild inconsistency to violent differences. The groups which espouse these needs and values may place demands against specific administrative processes.

Satisfaction of these needs or demands will occur within the value context of the community and may even give rise to new values which will control the administrative choices. Thus problems may be formulated which must be solved. This may be considered as the first phase of the administrative processes. In this phase, issues are formulated which identify conflicting demands as various groups desire to satisfy their own needs through administrative activity, even if this requires the diversion of existing goals.

The second phase of the administrative processes may be thought of as primarily concerned with selecting identifying values and developing policies which will direct administrative activity. These policies may be legislatively, judicially or administratively determined. The announcement of a guiding policy signifies the conclusion of this phase except where continuing negotiation modifies such policy guidelines. Within this phase the various alternatives available for adoption may or may not be explored. Accommodation and negotiation are primary characteristics of this phase of the administrative processes.

The third phase centers upon implementing such policy through the skilled activities of public servants in the public organization involved. It is specific program activity that will eliminate the particular problems. Program activity is conducted within the policies established in earlier phases but more often than not, such program efforts themselves will modify policies

413

due to the very nature of their operation. The executive is considerably involved in all phases of the policy flow. Administrators are thoroughly and significantly involved in formulating issues, identifying the significant values, deliberating the alternative responses and conducting programs which will modify or eliminate these issues.

The final phase of the administrative effort is concerned with the impact and evaluation of the specific administrative effort on the individual and the society. The administrative effort is designed to solve particular problems to the degree that the causes of the particular issues are modified or eliminated. It also is concerned with developing ongoing responses by routines and procedures which will abate problems, reduce incident causes, maintain a desirable, continuous effort or respond to constantly recurring needs. The achievement of significant change or establishment of routines or the maintenance of the status quo may be end results of the administrative process. These impacts may affect the evolution of the community. The activities of the program and resolution phases occur within the short-run and within a definable period of time.

If the primary elements of a system are set alongside the phases of the administrative effort, the outlines of a conceptual view of a public administration system emerge. The inputs are the demands, supports and resources of various groups and individuals and they do affect the administrative effort. Through administrative activity these inputs are converted into outputs which are designed to satisfy the demands placed against the administrative effort. The outputs of the system which become inputs into a larger system may be considered to be the actual change brought in the social or physical environment in which the administrative activity takes place. Output may also contain varieties of *feedback* which change and modify the system itself. Feedback consists of signals which return to the system and cause modifications within the system. Output and feedback exchanges occur at all phases of the administrative process and thus affect all of these phases. These modifications occur because groups will alter their demands, needs, supports, tactics or strategy in order to maximize what they expect to receive from the output.

These administrative processes can occur within a brief time span only moments in duration or stretch out over an exceptionally long period of time. Again, there is no clear-cut distinction among these various phases of the administrative processes. Each phase merges indistinguishably into the next, and the solution phase gives rise to new demands which start the cycle again. Decisions made in earlier phases may be modified by decisions made in the later phases. Every group affected by administrative effort tends to become involved in all phases of the effort. Implicit and explicit within these processes are values which are either brought to the administrative effort by a concerned group, exist within the cultural context of the effort or are generated within the administrative system itself. Such values sustain or modify administrative activity depending on the arrangement of power among the various groups, traditional historical relationships, quality of leadership and the nature of the administrative responses as well as administrative competence. The uncertainty concerning which values or norms apply to a given situation creates tensions and problems within the administrative processes as individuals and groups struggle to dominate administrative decisions. Figure 11-2 is a graphic summary representing these administrative policy processes.

To summarize, administrative processes may be thought of as concerned with: 1) the identification of wants, needs, demands, supports, resources and values to which administrative response is required; 2) the definition of policy which translates the values sought into objectives or goals to be achieved; 3) the development and conduct of programs which perform the specific activity designed to achieve the goals and objectives; 4) the accomplishment of the environmental effect which will satisfy or attempt to satisfy the requisite purpose.

Administrative activity is activity which is supported by "sustained collective action" considered to be an "integral part of a larger system," is characterized by "determined goals" and is dependent upon interchange with the larger system.[25] Figure 11-3 represents these relationships.

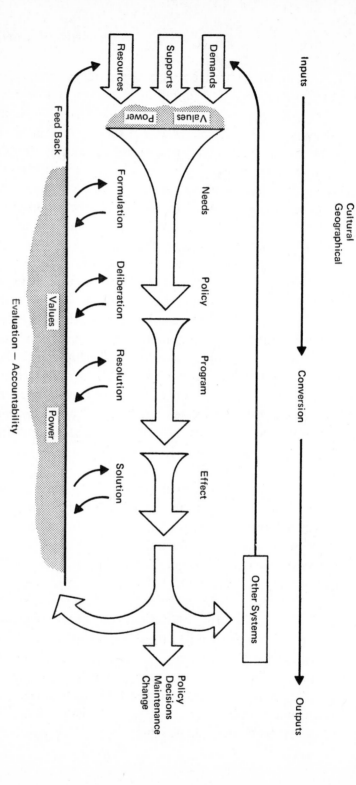

Figure 11-2. THE POLICY MAKING PROCESS OF PUBLIC ADMINISTRATION

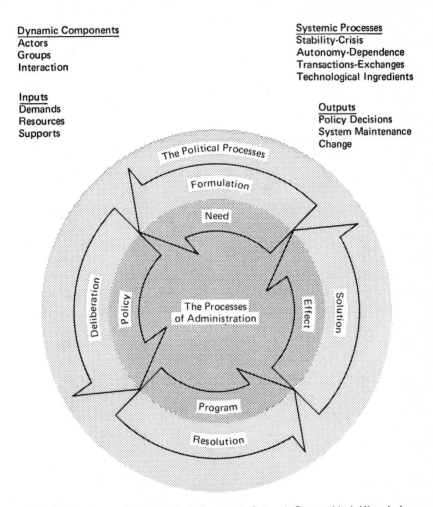

Dynamic Components
Actors
Groups
Interaction

Systemic Processes
Stability-Crisis
Autonomy-Dependence
Transactions-Exchanges
Technological Ingredients

Inputs
Demands
Resources
Supports

Outputs
Policy Decisions
System Maintenance
Change

The Political Processes

Formulation

Need

Deliberation

Policy

The Processes
of Administration

Effect

Solution

Program

Resolution

The Environment: Social, Political, Economic, Cultural, Geographical, Historical

Figure 11-3. THE POLICY FLOW ENVIRONMENT

A PUBLIC ADMINISTRATIVE SUBSYSTEM
AS "FLOW OF POLICY"

It is possible to present a generalized public administrative subsystem utilizing materials presented to this point. Take as an
example a subsystem involving the construction and maintenance

of a state highway network. The "flow of policy" (Figure 11-3) points up some primary aspects of the various phases of the system. The input demands come from a variety of groups and individuals. They are concerned with the extent, quality, variety, financing and placement of roads, streets and bridges. The supports which flow into the system come from both regular and incidental sources which are concerned with the operation of the system and its ultimate output. Most highway construction and maintenance are supported in numerous ways by a variety of legislative, governmental, trucking, automobile, commercial and tourist interests. The gasoline taxes may be collected specifically for highway purposes. The resources drawn upon for the accomplishment of the effort are not only economic but legal and technological in nature. These involve the legal authority of a highway department; the economic supports, e.g., tax base, revenue sources, etc., and the technical supports, e.g., the engineering know-how and other technical aspects of human activity which bear upon the efforts of the highway program.

These inputs merge into the first phase of the administrative effort. Specific and often conflicting demands are made by a variety of concerned persons and groups. In this phase, such conflicting needs, values and goals are identified and assessed. This assessment and identification occur with the highway department playing a central part in formulating problems concerning the placement of highways, timing, priority, feasibility and financing. Each of these problems involves conflicting and inconsistent values, needs, goals and demands. When various alternatives are identified, negotiation and accommodation occur among the concerned groups in order to arrive at policy decisions which will guide highway construction and maintenance programs. This is the policy-deliberation phase of the administrative processes.

The policy-deliberation phase merges into the next, in which the full range of activity is performed that utilizes the special skills of the public organization (bureaucracy) central to the administrative system. This is where the activity of the public agency is heavily committed. It has the legal competence to perform the tasks. This is merely the starting point. It also has those special skills requisite to conducting the activities of the specific programs, i.e., it builds bridges, streets and highways according to the established policies. Such activities are designed to resolve the problem identified in the earlier stages and satisfy the needs and demands of the larger system of administration of which it is a part. In addition, they satisfy or modify the demands of the concerned groups both inside and outside the organization.

Finally, as the program efforts proceed or near completion, there are outputs having a variety of effects. First, the required roads or bridges are constructed; hence, the needs of a variety of groups for more adequate roads are met. In this case, recreational, military, commercial interests have been, to a degree, satisfied. The physical environment is changed and social and economic relations are affected. Thus the demands and needs of the input stage are solved by the conversion processes (activity) of the system. In addition, "feedback" occurs which affects all phases of the operation and results in modifications and readjustments at all levels. This could affect placement, quality, timing, feasibility or financing. In the background, of course, lurks the possibility of difficulties encountered on the job, modified demands on the part of the concerned groups or catastrophe of one variety or another.

Figure 11-4 summarizes this simplified version of a state highway administrative system. The system can be observed as an arena of constant and dynamic activity undergoing continuous change and experiencing unceasing modification in response to new inputs, unsatisfied demands and endless feedback.

A PUBLIC POLICY FLOW MODEL

A public policy model has been developed which is based on the assumption that policy-making is linked with the question of values and places great emphasis upon the role that groups, individuals and agencies play in relation to policy formation. The authors identify this process as a "flow of policy" based upon a concept of policy-making which finds it insufficient that public policy is the end result of a rational consideration of alternatives.

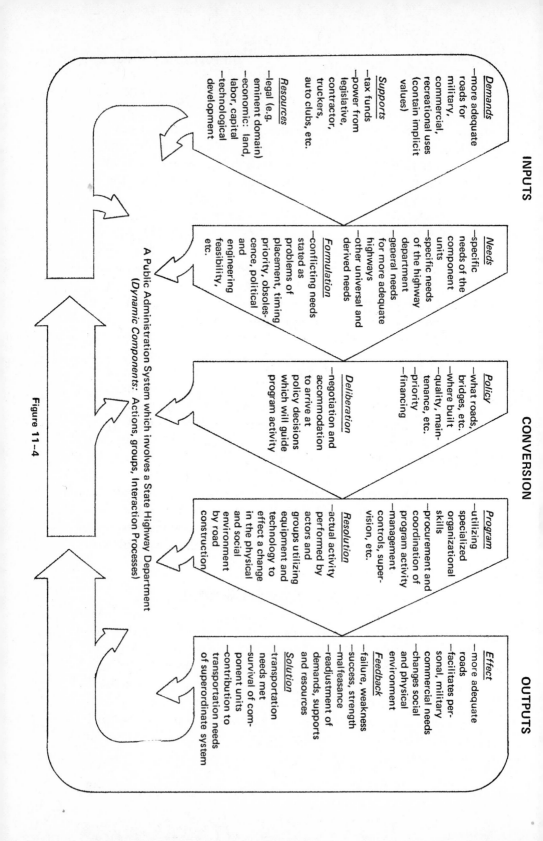

INPUTS

CONVERSION

OUTPUTS

Demands
—more adequate roads for military, commercial, recreational uses (contain implicit values)

Supports
—tax funds
—power from legislative, contractor, truckers, auto clubs, etc.

Resources
—legal (e.g. eminent domain)
—economic: land, labor, capital
—technological development

Needs
—specific needs of the component units
—specific needs of the highway department
—general needs for more adequate highways
—other universal and derived needs

Formulation
—conflicting needs stated as problems of placement, timing priority, obsolescence, political and engineering feasibility, etc.

Policy
—what roads, bridges, etc.
—where built
—quality, maintenance, etc.
—priority
—financing

Deliberation
—negotiation and accommodation to arrive at policy decisions which will guide program activity

Program
—utilizing specialized organizational skills
—procurement and coordination of program activity
—changes social and physical environment
—management controls, supervision, etc.

Resolution
—actual activity performed by actors and groups utilizing equipment and technology to effect a change in the physical and social environment by road construction

Effect
—more adequate roads
—facilitates personal, military commercial needs

Feedback
—failure, weakness
—success, strength
—malfeasance
—readjustment of demands, supports and resources

Solution
—transportation needs met
—survival of component units
—contribution to transportation needs of superordinate system

A Public Administration System which involves a State Highway Department
(Dynamic Components: Actions, groups, Interaction Processes)

Figure 11–4

. . . the outcome of the *policy flow* is the formulation of a *policy decision*, the focus of the model is on the activities which lead to that end point; including *feedback* from previous policy decisions. It is these activities which ultimately shape final choice. Accumulation of material about a particular policy issue is only one part of the task of the administrator in a technological, complex situation—it is not necessarily the most important part. Creation of public policy involves a *large number of random contributing forces* which are not easily identified.[26]

The essential elements of the model are these:

1. *Policy* is regarded as an indication of intention, a guide to action encompassing values which set social priorities in relations between government and society.

2. *Policy issues* are identified as such by interested and concerned actors, organizations and publics seeking a desired change, benefit, regulation, inhibition or prohibition. Thus policy issues—and policy issue agendas—are behaviorly, rather than morally or absolutely, determined.

3. *Policy flow* refers to the evolution of a policy issue and encompasses the total milieu of policy formation in which the random impact and coalescence of numerous factors, participants and interactions result in the dynamic ebb and flow of policy issues.

4. *Policy decisions* are specific events reflecting a confluence of values and behavior which guide administrative action and are expressed as legislation, judicial decisions, executive orders or administrative rules and regulations.

5. *Policy environment* includes as a minimum public and private agencies and key persons therein; clientele, pressure and other interest groups; and involves social processes, e.g., cooperation, accommodation, competition and conflict. The technological, cultural and physical settings are also relevant.

6. *Policy feedback* operates within the policy flow, affects interaction among the participants and modifies policy issues by altering inputs.[27]

The model is distinctive in its appreciation of the random and multi-channeled aspects of policy coalescence and in its recognition that policy issues change over time. It emphasizes the need for orderly research which might enable the policy analyst to identify and chart the critical paths leading to specific public policies.[28]

The behaviors and actions of the concerned groups and individuals develop, over a period of time, a distinctive style, a special tradition and a history which "constrains and refines" their actions and concerns. This involves:

Communication: Key actors within the policy environment often have preferred access to communication nets. This may occur, for example, when agency leadership utilizes more or less formal and informal clientele consultation processes which have developed over a period of time as a means of shaping policy alternatives.

Commitment: Intensely involved actors able to commit and obtain resources can effectively influence the evolution of policy.

Leadership: A special set of actors is crucial in the policy environment. These actors are agency heads and others who perform formal leadership roles. They have a particular set of characteristics which profoundly affect policy choices and value determinations. These leaders are respected, sometimes feared, and have prerogatives as well as varying degrees of charisma, all of which can have important consequences for policy choices.

Group Dynamics: A variety of formal and informal groups function within the *policy flow*. Actors will coalesce into temporary or sustained interaction clusters based on individual perceptions of other actors' credibility and intention in the policy environment. The effects of these alliances on the group process may be creative, spontaneous, flexible, rigid or ritualized and accordingly will alter choices as they evolve within the policy environment.[29]

There is a *policy environment* which embraces a *power configuration* and relates to the availability and nature of resources. The power configuration involves an array of clientele, pressure and legislative groups, constitutional and statutory provisions, professional staff, financial and funding arrangements and historical traditions. Resource inputs from the policy environment are classified under the following headings:

1. *Intersocietal inputs* stemming from social and technological innovation alter the perceptions of what is possible. Often these are derived from other social systems not directly impinging upon the specific social system concerned.

2. *Technological advances* which contribute to altering, modifying, elaborating and defining policy alternatives.

3. The *generational dialectic*, which is the struggle among the generations. This may involve conflict and often modifies prevailing values which results in the redirection of social energy and purpose.[30]

The value network within the policy flow is affected by the social and cultural norms which overlay the social system involved. The process of reconciling goal conflict also may affect policy options. Interpersonal and intergroup alliances or antagonisms involving common value systems, likes and antipathies and value clusters may aggregate and affect policy choices.

The existence of crisis or stability, their intensity and precariousness, vitally affects the policy process within any *policy arena*. The capacity of a public official or participant person or group to introduce crisis may alter significantly the policy options available. The degree of criticality of crisis, the capacity to generate crisis, the nature of the responses to effect change or protect the status quo, the integrative or debilitating nature of the interaction processes will have significant effects upon policy options and choices.[31]

Interaction within this process includes points where the policy becomes more specific and more articulated within the language and terms relevant to the specific policy setting concerned. This process, in which a policy becomes at once more specific, more elaborate and more clearly articulated is identified as *policy coalescence*.[32]

Struggle and bargaining occur within the interaction processes of the policy milieu. This frequently involves struggle concerning status, rule changes and power and resource utilization which affect policy decisions. The specific patterns of coalescence and points of interfacing where the policy is more clearly defined and articulated detail a *policy trail* which identifies the interaction pathway through which a specific policy has traveled during its emergence.[33]

This model has been developed as a comparative public policy research tool and can be adapted to analyze the emergence of public policy in both the presidential and parliamentary administrative systems as well as the jurisdictional and federal divisions of each where appropriate. Figure 11-5 is a summary of this model.

THE POLICY FLOW MODEL APPLIED

Understanding concerning emergence of public policy can be gained by adapting this model to a brief study of the efforts within a medium-sized city to cope with the growing demands for an affirmative action program. The city is located in the southwestern United States and significant segments of its population are Mexican-American and Black. In addition, at the time women's groups were becoming more politically active within the city. It is governed by an elected five-member city council and an appointive city manager who is the city's executive officer. The city manager has been in office for more than seven years. He is considered highly successful and has survived many crises. For the first time in council history there were two minority members in its ranks, one Mexican-American and the other a Black. All the council members were men. For decades prior to this the oil, natural gas and shipping interests dominated council-manager policy choices. This was the first time they were having to consider public policy choices responsive to a different set of "public" demands. There was a well-established city administrative structure protected by a strong civil service tradition and proud of its record of competence and accomplishment over the years.

The older, established interests resisted initiating and implementing an affirmative action program. Some of these interests went so far as to urge rejecting federal funds to avoid having to implement such a program. City professional and technical administrative personnel, clerical and blue-collar personnel as well (most of whom were civil service career persons) resisted and resented affirmative action efforts. It was seen as a threat to orderly promotion and advancement on merit and a genuine attack upon the merit principle. It was feared that standards

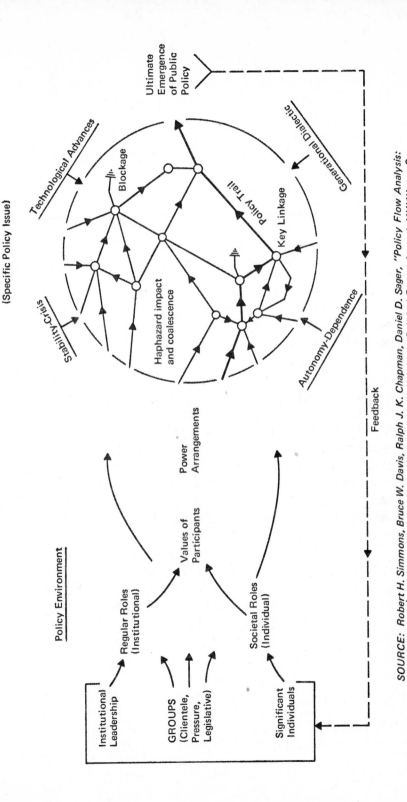

Interaction Milieu
(Specific Policy Issue)

Technological Advances

Blockage

Policy Trail

Key Linkage

Generational Dialectic

Ultimate
Emergence
of Public
Policy

Stability-Crisis

Haphazard impact
and coalescence

Autonomy-Dependence

Feedback

Policy Environment

Institutional
Leadership

Regular Roles
(Institutional)

GROUPS
(Clientele,
Pressure,
Legislative)

Values of
Participants

Power
Arrangements

Significant
Individuals

Societal Roles
(Individual)

SOURCE: *Robert H. Simmons, Bruce W. Davis, Ralph J. K. Chapman, Daniel D. Sager, "Policy Flow Analysis: A Conceptual Model For Comparative Public Policy Research," Western Political Quarterly, vol. XXVII, no. 3, September 1974, p. 467.*

Figure 11-5. PUBLIC POLICY FLOW MODEL.

would be lowered and the quality of job performance would deteriorate. The vociferous minority members on the council and their supporters were vigorous in their support of affirmative action and were not to be denied.

The various components of the policy flow model suggested above are present:

Policy Issue: This involved establishing and implementing an affirmative action.

Policy Flow: The development on the part of the concerned persons of "policy issue agendas." Each developed his own strategies and tactics to achieve the sought after outcome.

Policy Decision Process: This was under way and involved many formal and informal meetings with clientele and pressure group interests, councilmen, administrators and staff concerned.

Policy Environment: There were key actors, concerned groups, groups which were affected by the policy outcomes—all of which existed within that specific social-political-administrative environment.

Policy Feedback: This emerged as the process unfolded.

Elements of the Power System: All were present in varying degrees of involvement. The clientele, pressure, legislative and administrative interests were established and ranged around the issue with varying degrees of intensity, support and opposition. The constitutional requirements and statutory provisions and the legal and administrative consequences of non-compliance were well-known and understood, as was the historical setting in which the struggle occurred. It was understood that serious losses in federal funding would occur should the affirmative action guidelines fail of implementation. The capacity to alter the stability or spawn some degree of crisis were available to a number of the participants as well.

The Interaction Milieu

This milieu involved many sessions on the part of many groups and participants to develop their particular goals, plans, strategies and tactics while in pursuit of their policy objectives. All of these efforts and meetings, formal and informal, were important aspects of the policy flow too detailed and numerous to trace here. Our brief story takes up about one month after the city manager had appointed a young Mexican-American to head an affirmative action program. The council approved the unbudgeted position and failed at that time to supply any program funds. The hope was that the intensity of the pressure for affirmative action would recede and the demands for it would abate. The effort to implement affirmative action then would not have to be taken too seriously.

The young man, however, had some interpersonal skills and competence and he took his job very seriously. He was well aware of the unfriendly reception he would find and was fully equipped to work persuasively and directly with the situation as he found it. He was moderate, patient and persevering. After interviewing each of the administrative heads of the city departments, including the personnel department, he presented a modest budget to the city manager.

The city manager found it very difficult to schedule a meeting with the young, new director but finally managed to work him in between two other appointments, which provided him about fifteen minutes for his entire presentation. It was rushed (one budget analyst present) and both he and the city manager seemed harried and preoccupied. No answer on his program proposal and budget was forthcoming, nor were there any searching questions. They indicated to the young director that they would consider it soon. This was on a Monday. Thursday of that week was a scheduled city council meeting. Neither the affirmative action director nor the city manager was able to do much in the two and one-half days which intervened and, besides, affirmative action was not on the published agenda.

Much to the surprise of the city manager, city council, the minority members of the council and the affirmative action director, the local membership of the National Organization of Women (NOW) appeared at this meeting in full force. They demanded time and requested the agenda be altered. This was done. They had prepared and presented a full departmental organizational scheme for the new affirmative action department (not yet approved) and, in addition, they had developed

427

a supporting budget. The city manager, city council, council leadership and even the affirmative action director were all caught unawares.

An acrimonious and prolonged debate was likely to ensue and the pressing agenda of the meeting abandoned. The nimble city manager quickly announced that he had only this week approved a budget submitted to him by the new director and that the organizational arrangement suggested by him had been approved as well. Its implementation was already under way. The tension was reduced, the women had been outmaneuvered (yet had played a vital role in the establishment of an affirmative action program in the city), and the council then proceeded to other matters.

The feedback for the director had occurred at the council meeting and had come from two sources, the manager and the women. That was the first time that he had even received a hint that the budget and program which had been submitted had been considered, let alone favorably approved. It was also the first time that a women's group had taken an interest in affirmative action in that jurisdiction. He had not known of their interest, nor had they apprised him of their intended action at the council meeting. Soon after the meeting the surprised director, who learns quickly, appointed a *woman* as his deputy director.

This new director still had the problem of implementing his program among the city departments, including personnel where he would find considerable resistance to his efforts. Thus even at this stage the policy flow was still under way and the policy outcome incomplete.

This brief presentation provides a glimpse into a flow of policy which involved a specific *policy trail*. Careful investigation and analysis could identify such a pathway. Key linkages could be noted and points of policy coalescence and convergence determined after suitable investigation. In other policy situations other aspects of the policy flow process might be critical in the emerging policy outcome. The same problem in a different political-social and administrative setting would bring different factors together within the concerned setting and produce different outcomes. A court order, a legislative investigation, or a hostile yet powerful administrative opponent or a vigorous and powerful proponent could well alter the outcome. Viewing the policy process from this perspective is a most helpful way of understanding the emergence of policy in public jurisdictions and in gaining better understanding of the shape and nature of the ultimate policy outcomes.

When, in regard to a particular policy issue, policy coalesces after much struggling, negotiating and bargaining, these struggles and bargaining efforts may include judicial processes, legislative committee review or informal conferences, formal or informal administrative hearings, meetings with concerned clientele or a whole variety of other formal and informal sessions which affect the definition of policy ultimately to emerge from the process. The actors and groups who struggle in the policy arena will utilize the judicial process, or the threat of it, to affect restraint or performance of particular administrative activity. Legislative review and investigation (or the threat of them) may also be significant factors in the efforts to arrive at policy outcomes. From the political sector will come pressure and support for the goals sought by the concerned clientele. The administrative agencies concerned have their own special concerns and goals in addition to the competence, capacity and skills to effect the decision and action sought by those concerned enough to try and effect administrative activity and outcomes.

Each of these areas supplies important value constraints and imperatives to the policy struggle which affect the ultimate outcome of public policy within the administrative effort. Each may be an area of appeal when failure to achieve objectives in the processes of another occurs. In other words, the struggle to effect policy outcomes is rarely definitive. Figure 11-6 is a simplified visual presentation of the policy arena. Some mix of these aspects of a policy arena is always present in greater or lesser intensity in the policy process and underlies the actions of the actors, groups and institutions involved to achieve their sought-after ends.

Administrative processes, whether initial responses or routines, are constantly interacting within value-laden and dynamic political, legislative and judicial settings. Careful examination of an administrative organization may also reveal an environment in which administrative activity occurs where the defined limits of the consciously conceived organizations may be vague and obscure, e.g., the activity of the professional worker gives way to part-time worker, part-time worker gives way to volunteer, volunteer gives way to client-participant.

The public administrator now must be concerned that the special knowledge and information he possesses be used to further the public interest. If the public manager is to be responsive to the societal and ecological problems identified in the opening chapter, it requires him to communicate the urgency of these policy options to the public. This is necessary in order to make the public aware of the necessity for formulating a public policy responsive to the specific issue. The public administrator who has been merely reactive to policy formulated elsewhere in the private sector now must become conscientiously involved in social planning and the policy-making process. Planning which is responsive to broader social concerns and environmental needs and program action which reflects those concerns are now essential components of public administration's agenda. In the past complex systems which have been unable to adapt to changing environmental and social needs have perished. We may well be at one of those crucial forks in the road. Responsiveness, flexibility and humaneness must be the qualities of public administration.

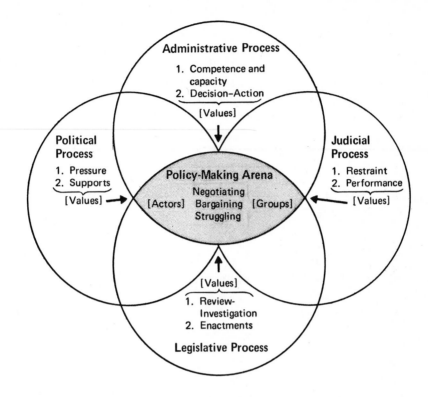

Figure 11-6. THE POLICY ARENA

NOTES

1. Morton Kroll, "Policy and Administration," in Fremont J. Lyden, George A. Shipman and Morton Kroll, *Policies, Decisions and Organizations*. New York: Appleton-Century-Crofts, 1969, p. 3, reprinted from Morton Kroll, "Hypotheses and Designs for the Study of Public Policies in the United States," *Midwest Journal of Political Science*, Wayne State University, Vol. 6, No. 4, 1962.

2. Kroll, in Lyden, Shipman, and Kroll, *op. cit.*, p. 25.

3. Leonard D. White, *Introduction to the Study of Public Administration*, 4th ed. New York: Macmillan, 1955, p. 1.

4. Herbert A. Simon, Donald W. Smithburg, Victor A. Thomson, *Public Administration*. New York: Alfred A. Knopf, 1950, p. 7.

5. John Dewey, *The Public and its Problems*. New York: Holt, 1927, p. 33.

6. Paul Appleby, *Morality and Administration in Democratic Government*. Baton Rouge, La.: Louisiana State University Press, 1952, p. 21; see also Emmette S. Redford, *Ideal and Practice in Public Administration*. University, Ala.: University of Alabama Press, 1958, pp. 108-109.

7. George A. Shipman, "The Policy Process," *Western Political Quarterly*, Vol. 12 (June 1959) p. 544.

8. Important examples of this approach are: L. L. Wade and R. L. Curry, Jr., *A Logic of Public Policy: Aspects of Political Economy*. Belmont, Calif.: Wadsworth Publishing Co., 1970; Anthony Downs, *An Economic Theory of Democracy*. New York: Harper & Row, 1957; James M. Buchanan and Gordon Tullock, *The Calculus of Consent: Logical Foundations of Constitutional Democracy*. Ann Arbor, Mich.: University of Michigan Press, 1962; Robert L. Bish, *The Public Economy of Metropolitan Areas*. Chicago: Markham Publishing Co., 1971; Mancur Olson, *The Logic of Collective Action*. Cambridge, Mass.: Harvard University Press, 1965; the landmark effort was Daniel Lerner and Harold D. Lasswell (eds.), *The Policy Sciences*. Stanford, Calif.: Stanford University Press, 1960.

9. See particularly Thomas R. Dye, *Understanding Public Policy*. Englewood Cliffs, N.J.: Prentice-Hall, 1972, and *Politics, Economics, and the Public: Policy Outcomes in the American States*. Chicago, Ill.: Rand McNally & Co., 1966.

10. B. F. Skinner, *Walden II*. New York: Macmillan, 1962; Norbert Weiner, *Cybernetics*. New York: John Wiley and Sons, 1948; and *The Human Use of Human Beings*. New York: Doubleday & Co., 1954; William Irwin Thompson, *Passages About Earth*. New York: Harper & Row, 1973; Alvin Toffler, *Future Shock*. New York: Random House, 1970; David Lilienthal, *TVA–Democracy on the March*. New York: Harper & Row, 1953; Donald N. Michael, *The Unprepared Society: Planning for a Precarious Future*. New York: Basic Books, 1968.

11. Joseph S. Wholey, John W. Scanlon, Hugh G. Duffy, James S. Fudumoto, and Leona M. Vogt, *Federal Evaluation Policy: Analyzing the Effects of Public Programs*. Washington, D.C.: Urban Institute, 1970; E. J. Mishan, *Economics for Social Decisions: Elements of Cost Benefit Analysis*. New York: Praeger Publishers, 1972; see Nicholas Henry, *Public Administration and Public Affairs*. Englewood Cliffs, N.J.: Prentice-Hall, 1975, chap. 9, pp. 222-246.

12. Yehezkel Dror, *Public Policymaking Reexamined*. Scranton, Pa.: Chandler Publishing Co., 1968, pp. 12-17.

13. Kroll, in Lyden, Shipman, and Kroll, *op. cit.*, p. 19.

14. F. J. Lyden, G. A. Shipman and R. J. Wilkinson, "Decision Flow Analysis: A Methodology for Studying the Policy Making Process," in LeBreton, *Comparative Administrative Theory*. Seattle: University of Washington Press, 1968, pp. 155-56.

15. Dror, *op. cit.*, pp. 129-196.

16. Dror, *op. cit.*, pp. 9-11 and pp. 217-304. The paragraph which follows relies on material drawn from these pages.

17. Alfred de Grazia, "The Science and Values of Administration II," *Administrative Science Quarterly*, Vol. 5, Part II (March 1961) p. 583.

18. Kroll, "Policy and Administration," *op. cit.*, pp. 12-13.

19. Nicholas Rescher, *Introduction to Value Theory*. Englewood Cliffs, N.J.: Prentice-Hall, Inc., 1969 (contains a superb bibliography); see also Moshe F. Rubinstein, *Patterns of Problem Solving*. Englewood Cliffs, N.J.: Prentice-Hall, Inc., 1975.

20. Herbert Simon, *Administrative Behavior*. New York: Macmillan, 1948, p. 74.

21. Geoffrey Vickers, *Value Systems and Social Process*. New York: Basic Books, 1968, pp. 112-132.

22. Vickers, *op. cit.*, p. 110.

23. Kroll, "Policy and Administration," *op. cit.*, pp. 26-34.

24. Herbert J. Spiro, "Comparative Politics: A Comparative Approach," *American Political Science Review* (Sept. 1962) pp. 577-583; see also his *Government by Constitution: The Political Systems of Democracy*. New York: Random House, 1959.

25. James D. Thompson, Peter B. Hammond, Robert W. Hawkes, Buford H. Junker, Arthur Tuden, *Comparative Studies in Administration*. Pittsburgh, Pa.: University of Pittsburgh Press, 1959, pp. 5-6, and chap. 1 generally.

26. Robert H. Simmons, Bruce W. Davis, Ralph J. K. Chapman, Daniel D. Sager, "Policy Flow Analysis: A Conceptual Model for Comparative Public Policy Research," *Western Political Quarterly*, Vol. XXVII, No. 3, (Sept. 1974) p. 466.

27. *Ibid.*, pp. 460-461.

28. *Ibid.*, pp. 461-462.

29. *Ibid.*, pp. 463-464.

30. *Ibid.*, p. 464.

31. *Ibid.*, p. 465.

32. *Ibid.*, pp. 465-466.

33. *Loc. cit.*

12

POLICY,
PROGRAM
AND THE
PUBLIC INTEREST

The core of the administrative processes are the public agencies, their satellite groups and those persons who interact through processes responsive to the needs and demands of an identifiable community. These demands and needs are refined by the policy-making processes. Further, they are ultimately fulfilled through program activity conducted through organizational action designed to perform the specific activities necessary to achieve satisfaction. The program context provides the framework within which a given combination of groups and individuals interact toward the accomplishment of a specific result. Central to this effort is the administered organization.

Talcott Parsons has observed that a "concrete" action system integrates the action elements in relation to a specific situation. He observes, "A value pattern . . . is always institutionalized in an *inter*action context."[1] Public policy within the administrative setting may be expressed through a course of action centered in the program activity of the concerned organization. It may be assumed that there can be no separation between policy and administration in the operational setting.

Policy defined through the planning processes within the organization contains the express value elements of the administrative environment. It cannot be separated from the specific administrative activites designed to have a particular impact (i.e., arrive at a designated goal or achieve a specific purpose) in the community.[2] Public policy achieves expression through the program activity of a public organization and is inherent in the social impact of such activity. This conception of policy is essentially the outcome of the policy process.

Policy promulgated by legislation may or may not be public policy within the meaning used here. Legislation usually overlays a set of formal values, attributed to constitutional or other philosophical sources, but these are not inevitably the values conveyed to the society by subsequent administrative action. What the legislation does do is authorize and legitimize a search, as Philip Selznick has observed, through administrative activity, for a set of impacts agreeable to interested groups in the society. In other words, legislation is more often a charter for undertaking policy formation activities. It may not be policy-making in any conclusive sense.[3]

The component groups of the administrative process are those groups implicated in any way in the program context. These may be agency groups engaged in program performance; clientele groups affected by the impacts of the program; other governmental groups that participate in some manner within the relevant program processes. These might include federal agencies, legislative committees, state agencies or local governmental groups. Their relationship may range from intensive involvement to that of superficial or sporadic participation. Such interrelationships may involve well-established, semi-autonomous administrative patterns of interaction, or it may involve a transient assemblage of concerned groups brought together only for a fleeting purpose. A program effort, whatever its substance, sustains or creates a complex of groups and brings them into conflictive, although sometimes cooperative, interdependent contact in the program setting.

ADMINISTRATIVE ACTION

A specific program focus spawns or sustains the unique composite of groups and individuals concerned with particular administrative action. This combination of program, individuals, groups and administrative action articulates an identifiable public administrative subsystem. The character and nature of such a subsystem may be illustrated by centering attention upon an example. The United States Forest Service may be viewed not only as a subsystem itself but also as embracing a number of such administrative subsystems within and impinging upon its extensive operations.

The physical environment of the Forest Service is definable as those areas of the federal lands containing vast forested areas over which the Forest Service has jurisdiction and control and, in addition, areas that are not located on forest lands but are incidental to their administration and management. This definition is only approximate, as the service may or may not control the subsoil minerals and it may purchase land or sell or trade land to the states or to private interests where consistent with its mission. The social environment is perhaps more difficult to identify. It is roughly inclusive of all those individuals and groups affected by, or who seek to affect, the operations of the Forest Service. This relationship may be quite transient or consistent and sustained, depending upon a variety of factors.

These external interests include conservation groups, sportsmen's associations, commercial interests, industrial concerns, recreational groups or other governmental organizations at the local, state, regional or national levels. In addition, many individuals acting in their private capacities become involved with the Forest Service in a great variety of ways. These large numbers of groups and persons may be considered among the important components of the public administrative subsystem of which the Forest Service is the central unit.

The inputs into this system derive from these diverse groups and include many conflicting demands placed against the administrative operations either directly through the administrative processes or through legislative or judicial action. The supports may be considered to be the financial basis which sustains the operations of the Forest Service. Supports also include the kinds of relationships with the individuals and groups which are a part of the system and enable the service to effectively fend off or modify serious attack. In addition, such support becomes a social resource which can be tapped whenever the Forest Service needs to fend off attack, resolve problems or define and establish new programs perceived by its leadership to be consistent with its mission.

The resources of the system include physical resources as well as those that can be called sociocultural resources. The physical resources derive from the controls that the Forest Service has over federal timber lands. Its sociocultural resources derive from the value commitment that the American public has concerning conservation of its natural resources and the mission assigned to the Forest Service for the accomplishment of such conservation. This discussion is obviously not a complete description of the great number of demands, supports and resources which feed into this system. Yet it does serve to identify the nature of the *inputs* which provide the starting point and justification for the administrative activity performed by the Forest Service.

The next phase of the system involves the converting of these demands, supports and resources into outputs that satisfy the demands, resolve problems, minimize conflict and thus maintain the survival of the system. Conflicting demands are often made upon the Forest Service. Conservation groups, commercial logging companies and cattlemen's associations each differ in their perceptions of their own interests and each tends to describe the "public interest" in these terms. The emerging and variant demands are perceived as problems which *need* resolution within the value context of the Forest Service mission. It is necessary (i.e., becomes a *need*) for the Forest Service to resolve these conflicting interests in such a way as to avoid destructive conflict, yet maximize support of all the groups involved for the service and maintain its "commitment to its mission." In the process the original commitment or the service may, of necessity, undergo modification.

In the initial stages of this phase, the inputs may be formulated as problems to be resolved. Still, they must be resolved in such a manner that the specialized needs of the concerned groups will be satisfied to the maximum extent. Also, the effort must be made to avoid all unnecessary potential conflict. Among the demands of conservation groups is to preserve the nation's natural resources in order to "meet the needs of future generations." Such a demand is conflictive with the desire of the commercial logger to cut timber for the nation's needs at the least possible cost and for the greatest profit. Likewise, the conflicting interests of the cattlemen and the sportsmen necessarily have to be resolved, the former intending to protect their cattle and expand their feeding ranges and the latter demanding more access to forest lands in order to expand their activities. The Forest Service must respond effectively to these conflicting demands lest its own survival be threatened.

In one case in which the Forest Service was heavily involved there were conflicting demands from the sawmill companies, which sustained a large payroll in the community and from the smaller, less economically sound operations which were sustained by only a marginal profit. *The Flagstaff Sustained Yield Unit Case* involved a perceived *need* for the community of Flagstaff, Arizona, to survive economically. Since the perceived livelihood of this community depended primarily upon forestry utilization, it was necessary, in the view of the community leaders, to manage the nearby federal forests in such a way that a sustained yield of timber would be available.[4] This would encourage the continuous operation of community sawmills and assure the stabilization of employment in Flagstaff.

The case also involved conflicting demands among national lumber purchasers whose operations were not centered in Flagstaff but who wanted access to the Flagstaff operations. The larger local sawmill companies within the community wanted a protected and continuous logging source; smaller and more itinerant sawmill companies located on the outskirts of town felt their survival was threatened by the larger local sawmills. Also, local business interests sought a sustained year-round income. The field staff of the Forest Service had its own stakes in an economically thriving community. The Washington office of the Forest Service made some attempt to protect national values and define national needs. All of these myriad interests were involved. There were, of course, many other groups which might have become involved but, in this instance, only these played crucial roles in determining the outcome.

The need for economic survival of the community was formulated as the essential problem which was to be solved. This would also meet the needs of various groups involved with the possible exception of the national lumbering groups. Various alternatives were examined and the policy which eventually evolved was the establishment of the sustained yield forest in the Coconino Forest surrounding Flagstaff. To arrive at this policy, and in order to implement it, accommodations had to be made which involved the negotiating and resolution of conflicting interests, needs and demands among the involved groups. This process of accommodation is continuous but is most essential when needs are being defined and policy established.

Here the more powerful groups were able to demand a solution more favorable to their "needs." The less powerful had to be satisfied with less. The more favorable arrangements involved the larger and more established sawmills within the city of Flagstaff. Placed in the position of less favorable arrangements were the smaller sawmill operations and the larger lumbering companies which took timber out of the area but did not provide an established payroll in the community. Among the key actors involved in negotiating these arrangements were the local personnel of the Forest Service whose role went significantly beyond forest management and ranged into the development of land-use policy with important national, as well as local, implications.

Thus the resolution of the problem was the establishment of a sustained yield forestry program which was to be administered by the Forest Service. The operation of this program was to satisfy the articulated needs of the involved groups. This program was to have the effect of solving the crucial economic needs of the community. In addition, the conservation values of the Forest Service were to be served, the local unit sustained and their efforts considerably expanded to administer the new experimental program. The local loggers were provided with a sustained supply of timber under a negotiated formula which favored the bigger mills but did not foreclose the smaller mills from some benefits. The settlement reflected the equation of political and economic power in that community at that time. It is open to challenge at any time through a variety of avenues including appeals to other arenas, such as the courts or political process.

In summary, the administrative system involved here included more than just the maintenance of conservation values, but also many other competing values were involved which had to be assessed and resolved within the operations of the system. The officials of the Forest Service found themselves deeply involved in a community survival program. The situation involved the satisfactory resolution of the conflicting needs of a number of organizations. Thus the Forest Service, in this instance, became involved in a role which ranged far beyond its formal legislatively determined mission. This was done with the encouragement and support of the community groups involved and the support requirements of its own survival.

The output of the system was the effect or impact of the changes that occurred to the groups involved as a result of the program operation. The effect of this program operation may be not only to resolve a number of problems and meet a variety of needs, but to create new problems and, therefore, additional needs. In this instance, economic survival of a local community transcended the values of a free, competitive marketplace. Yet the value content of the alternative selected within the context of this administrative system was consistent with federal policy since 1932, i.e., that government should assist in stabilizing and aiding the economic health of a community. Here, then, older values which have been carried over from the greater political system gave way to newer values generated by the system as the changing survival needs of the political community were met and resolved. This is only the barest of outlines concerning a specific instance of policy-making and need-satisfaction within a public administrative system. It serves to point up the usefulness of this perspective in examining the administrative process.

It can be seen that specific organizational arrangements are simply a part, albeit a very important part, of a broader administrative context. Likewise, this case demonstrates that *policy* and *administration* are indissolubly intertwined. It is necessary to develop even more sophisticated conceptual tools so the variety, form and nature of the interaction processes may be more fully explored and analyzed. This will help explain why, in some cases, decisions are more favorable to some interests than others. It will help assess the negotiation and accommodation processes that occur in specific systems, particularly program action systems. It may help also to account for the tendencies to seek avoidance of conflicts on the part of those whose interests are least advantageously resolved. These are only a few of the areas where insights may be expanded considerably by developing more advanced conceptual devices.

PUBLIC ADMINISTRATION SUBSYSTEMS: STRUCTURAL-FUNCTIONAL ANALYSIS

The social anthropologists and sociologists, particularly Robert Merton and Talcott Parsons, have fashioned an analytical tool that is of considerable help.[5] It is usually referred to as *structural-functional analysis.* Functional analysis depends upon a compatible and reciprocal interdependence among theory, methodology and data. Methodology is the crucial link between theory and data. Structural-functional analysis is a specialized and complex tool. Yet at present, it is still a very imprecise tool. The fundamental concepts of structural-functional analysis are essential to an understanding of public administration conceived as an operating system. It is this type of analysis which is basic to the identification of the important structural and functional elements operating within the system and it gives definition and meaning to the interaction occurring within the system.

Structure refers to the formal and informal relationships within a system and is inclusive also of the set of needs and modes of satisfaction which characterize a particular system.[6] *Function* is performed by a wide range of patterned activities, including, for example, social processes, social roles, controls, patterned emotional responses, cultural patterns and belief systems. In addition, functions are performed by occupants of designated positions.[7]

A function results from the performance of activity and is not the actual activity itself. Functions are outputs which result from and affect the active forces of the system. The processes of the system, as well as the actors, are the vehicles for the expression of these active forces. Thus a budgetary process may exert particular force in a specific system which has profound effects on other system processes, on the actors and groups in the system and on the budgetary process. These actors occupy specific positions, hold specific status and perform specific tasks and roles. In this instance, status refers to the position held by the individual actor in the system. This status results not only from his formal position, but, in addition, is affected by many informal aspects of the position and the man. Such subjective factors as skill, experience and personality play a significant part in defining status. Role, in this instance, refers to the behavior and activity expected of a person occupying a particular position in the system. Such a role may be formally and legally defined. Alternatively, it may have informal accretions which become an expected part of the role a specific actor plays. Merton, in establishing a model for functional analysis observes that *functions* are those "observed consequences" which encourage adaptation or adjustment in a given system. *Dysfunctions* are those "observed consequences" which interfere with adaptation or adjustment in a given system. In addition, functions may be *manifest* or *latent*. *Manifest functions* are those which are overt and intended by the members of the system; *latent functions* are consequences neither intended nor perceived. Such "unanticipated consequences" may be functional or dysfunctional for a specific system.[8]

The interdependent variables may be functional or dysfunctional for any one or a variety of the individuals and groups which make up a specific system. Further, what may be functional to one may be dysfunctional to another, and the reverse would also be possible. One other conceptual device may be identified and that is the operation of *mechanisms* which occur in a system. These operate not only as variables but are essential to the performance of a particular function. Thus the merit system operates as a mechanism which fulfills the function of dividing labor among a variety of groups and persons. Such a division of labor is absolutely essential to the fulfillment of organizational tasks.

The merit system has been identified as a mechanism, the manifest function of which is the division of labor. An additional function of the merit system is the maintenance of properly qualified workers for the given tasks required to be performed to accomplish the mission of the public administrative unit. These may be important functions to the system as a whole.

Thus the merit system satisfies the demands of the superordinate political system for honest and capable job performance. It becomes functional for the survival of the specific public administrative system involved, always remaining subject to change should the demands of the superordinate system for a merit system change. However, a centrally administered merit system, which is responsible for recruitment and promotion of personnel for a number of organizational units, might well be dysfunctional to a variety of separate units since it imposes a measure of outside control over personnel which may inhibit the performance of the organization or group at crucial times because of delay and inflexibility.

Many administrative organizations seek to establish their own separate personnel merit systems. At the national level there are separate merit systems for the Forest Service, T.V.A., F.B.I., the Foreign Service and the various military services. This maintains the merit system principle and encourages more autonomy for the specific system utilizing the specialized merit system. Thus these separately administered merit systems may be dysfunctional to the larger governmental system in that they encourage and promote the development of a more isolated and autonomous administrative operation.[9]

Any of the component parts of the public administrative system may, in its turn, be conceived as a functioning system containing a complex of intermeshing groups, needs, structures, functions and processes of interaction. The needs do not necessarily have to be stable or consistent and may well vary among a broad range of physiological, psychological and systematic requirements which may conflict one with another. Thus the actors, constituent groups, small formal and informal groups, formal hierarchical divisions, non-hierarchical organizational units, informal organizations, and concerned legislative groups may all be thought of as functioning systems, each with particular goals and derived needs, and involving functional interaction among a definable structure of relationships. A functional imperative for any system is its own survival. Although this is not articulated in its legislative charter, it is, nevertheless, an important, usually implicit, concomitant of any set of decisions an agency makes. Consequently, particular satisfaction or attempted satisfaction of the derived needs may be functional as regards one component part or actor and be dysfunctional as to another component part or actor. In addition, a particular pattern of self-satisfaction may be functional or dysfunctional in the manner it affects the survival of the larger system. The accommodation, resolution and solution of these conflicting needs provide the vital drama of the administrative effort.

The structural-functional approach, when utilized together with the systems approach, becomes a unique and special tool with which to study public administration. Not all of the elements essential to functional analysis of any given administrative system are identified or explored here. Rather, some of the key concepts are presented. These are basic to an understanding of public administration conceived as a pattern aggregation of processes operating to satisfy a variety of determined needs. The difficulties in determining *public policy* were examined earlier. It need be noted here that the public administrative organization which is a central component in any public policy process may play a significant role in defining those needs, as the Flagstaff case illustrated.

The utility of the approach is simply that it helps account for many of the dynamic features of administration in a systematic way and, uniquely, it provides a perception of administration that is often consistent with that of the sensitive practitioner. There is one question that is now pertinent. What is the relationship of these public administrative subsystems to the larger governmental systems in which they function?

PUBLIC ADMINISTRATIVE SYSTEMS AS SUBSYSTEMS OF A LARGER GOVERNMENTAL SYSTEM

The system described to this point may be considered as a subsystem of larger governmental systems which exist in international, national, state, regional or local arenas.[10] The Department of State, the Federal Power Commission, the Sandia Flood Control District (New Mexico), the Chicago Transit Authority or the Washington (state) Toll Bridge Authority are at once functional units required to perform a variety of activities to satisfy specifically defined needs of the larger system. Still, at the same moment, they exist within their own systems and are a part of larger political settings which sustain them and from which they were created.

Talcott Parsons has been concerned with developing a theoretical context for the broader social-economic-cultural system, and his contributions are both significant and controversial as well as difficult and complex.[11] His contributions concerning general systems theory are not the specific concern of the chapter. Instead, attention centers upon those contributions affecting the theoretical basis of public administrative systems and their interrelationships with the superordinate political systems. He has made several important contributions, two of which will be examined here. First, his concept of dynamic equilibrium; second, his formula for dynamic structural-functional analysis.

Dynamic Equilibrium

Given a functioning system of interrelated groups and actors, there must exist a relatively "stable" order so that output may be accomplished. That is, relatively sustained activity must exist conducing toward an end to be reached at some point in the future. Thus Parsons postulates, for any system there is a tendency toward seeking equilibrium. This tendency is not automatic or necessarily predictable. Rather, he views a system as containing multitudes of conflicting forces each deriving from sources seeking to satisfy their own needs. Equilibrium becomes, in one sense, the antithesis of disintegration. Yet equilibrium is not essentially stability and disequilibrium is not essentially instability, for no "static" state or mechanical state of relationships is posited by Parsons.[12] No particular pattern of interaction can simultaneously satisfy all the needs of all the individuals and groups involved. Hence, where needs remain unsatisfied, they become sources of tension and possible conflict within the given system. Often a variety of mechanisms develop which provide accommodation of conflict or potential conflict. Such accommodation may be temporary, while the lines of struggle are redrawn or the arena for the struggle changes; or it may be relatively permanent, establishing, in effect, a normative arrangement within the system which establishes accepted ways of behaving for the participants. Such activity is continuous and recurrent. Thus a dynamic equilibrium involves continuous accommodation and conflict avoidance responses from the component groups and actors which are calculated to maximize their anticipated returns. Stability and instability are deviations of these continuous processes.

An excellent example of this characteristic may be found in the system which includes the Washington State Insurance Department. The department is administered by an independently elected commissioner. His job, among other things, is to establish fair insurance rates for insurance companies and their clients operating within Washington State. His legal authority allows him to hold hearings and promulgate rules and orders. No significant hearings have been held within recent years. Instead, the commissioner has used a different device to indicate how he will interpret particular sections of the insurance code. After informal consultation with the concerned members of the insurance industry in the state, the commissioner will issue a *bulletin* which contains the interpretation of the Washington Legal Code approved by the commissioner. This bulletin has no legal standing and is not provided in the code. All members of the industry will adhere and conform to the interpretation of the bulletin. They abide by its pronouncements *as if* they were law. The prior consultation serves the purpose of accommodating any potential conflict among the members of the industry themselves or with the commissioner.[13]

Another example involves the institutions of higher education in New Mexico. The seven institutions of higher education in that state used to battle bitterly with one another for the meager financial support such a small state can provide. These struggles became seriously dysfunctional, both as to their impact upon the overall financial position of the state and the general program of higher education in New Mexico. Consequently, those groups and persons involved, which included among others legislators, college boards and alumni associations, and the college presidents themselves, perceived that it was necessary to resolve these deteriorating biennial struggles. It became necessary to arrive at an accommodative device which would avoid or mitigate the destructive competition. The instrument selected was the establishment of a Board of Educational

447

Finance. The operations of this board include the resolution of individual college budgets prior to their presentation to the legislature. The presentation to the legislature of the college budgets is unified in an overall budget document for all of higher education and presented in that manner to the legislature. Thus the Board of Educational Finance was established to mask disintegrative conflict and prevent the head-on clashes which had been so damaging in the past. With the establishment of this instrument, correlative, informal developments occurred among the college presidents. These informal arrangements established a variety of norms to which the college presidents adhere when seeking to increase their budgets before the legislature. Among these norms were those which precluded destructive criticism of college programs and thus prevented any attempts to capture funds from the similarly operating programs in other institutions.

Where stakes are exceptionally high, accommodative mechanisms may be impossible to establish or be very temporary while the groups whose needs are unsatisfied or their demands unmet seek to renew attack through some other means. Such a case may be found by examining some of the problems in regulating interstate transportation of natural gas.[14] The struggle involves billions of dollars in costs or profits, depending upon the outcome. The participants are the private producers and public regulatory bodies in the specific states which produce natural gas: Texas, Louisiana, Oklahoma, Kansas, Mississippi, Arkansas and New Mexico on the one hand, and the Federal Power Commission and the consuming states of the Northwest, Midwest and East on the other. One of the significant questions involved is whether the Federal Power Commission had authority to regulate the price of natural gas sold to interstate pipeline companies by independent producers not associated directly with the pipeline companies. With billions of dollars at stake, any accommodation or resolution of the conflict is considered to be temporary. A victory by one side in one area, as in the courts, Congress or administration, is regarded by the loser as something to seek undoing in the next year by utilizing another offensive in a different arena. This struggle still continues today.

It is possible now to view a number of systems in operation as they develop equilibrium mechanisms of accommodation and conflict, the purpose of which is to maximize the expected re-turns to the specific groups and avoid destruction which may threaten these groups. All of these public administrative systems operate within the larger political system, which Parsons calls the *Polity*, and produce outputs that have a variety of impacts upon the larger system. Each subsystem performs a function for the greater system.

Dynamic Structural-Functional Analysis

Parsons, Merton, Selznick and others have contributed signifi-cantly to the methodology underpinning structural-functional analysis. Parsons established some major perspectives in his approach which are extremely useful to the student of public administration. First, he reinforces the usefulness of needs as the starting point of any system. He postulates a variety of needs that occur in any given system which, if they remain unmet, are dysfunctional to that system. Perhaps the universal need of any system, biological or social, is its own survival. In addition to the required satisfaction of this need, each system develops particular needs relative to its own functions which are essential to its own particular survival. It must be remembered that a need in one system might well be articulated as a demand input to another system. In addition to these universal and derived needs, Parsons explains, are those needs which are related to the compatibility of a number of systems which exist together and interact. Any of these derived needs are necessary to the survival of the particular system to which they are related. They may or may not be necessarily involved in the society as a whole.

Any need which is not a universal—the need to survive is indeed a universal—may be thought of as a derived or contingent imperative. These stem from the particular characteristics of a given system. An example may be posed as follows. The pueblo peoples of the Southwest may be identified historically as a relatively self-contained social system. To survive, it must provide adequate food. Thus these separate societies depended upon beans and corn to sate this universal need. Given the arid environment and the limited technology, they responded to this need by dividing labor among males and females for growing, gathering and preparing food. In addition, the land on which they grew their corn had to be irrigated and protected against marauders. Not only was a division of labor necessary but techniques of leadership, coordination of activities and stabilized systems of making decisions were necessary. This proliferation of needs required social structure, status systems and an elaboration of roles in order that the universal need for food be satisfied. The stability of such a system was often reinforced through religious ritual and sanction. The similarity to an administrative system is apparent.

It hardly need be observed that this way of viewing public administration adds a dynamic quality ordinarily lacking in the more traditional approaches. It poses an immensely complex system of interacting groups, structures and functions which exist to satisfy a variety of universal and derived needs.

Parsons also develops a number of specific functional problems which all systems must solve in order to survive. Before identifying these, it is useful to note that Parsons sees all human activity as essentially related to a variety of operating systems. Consequently, the functional problems of survival which he poses become essential for all systems to resolve either rationally or accidentally if they are to assure their own continuance. These four problems are as follows:

1. The problems involved in *goal attainment*. This poses a means-end perspective and involves coordination of activities toward the end which the system is manifestly designed to serve.

2. The problems of *adaptation* to the external situation. This includes meeting and manipulating the environment in order to permit survival.

3. The problems of *integration*. This emphasizes the relations of the components in the system with one another, such as accommodating conflict in such a way as to enable the system to function and satisfy a requisite number of needs for the system itself and its component subsystems so as to assure survival.

4. The problems of *pattern maintenance* and *tension management*. Pattern maintenance exists where an actor (or group) reconciles the great variety of inconsistent demands and norms

imposed upon him (or the group) by his participation in the system with those in other systems where he (or the group) is also a participant.

Serious conflicting demands made on a person or group may be dysfunctional to person, group and system. Tension management is the problem of maintaining a sufficient commitment on the part of the actors sufficient for their necessary fulfillment of their tasks.

The first two of these functional problems concern the relationship of the system to its external environment. The latter two are concerned with the internal problems of the particular system. All systems must continuously solve and resolve these problems (Figure 12-1 is a graphic of this conception). In addition, a subsystem itself may fulfill one or more of these functions for the larger system in which it is located. Thus the economic institutions are primarily adaptive, whereas the diverse systems of education are in part integrative. Public administration, as defined here, falls primarily within the adaptive and goal attainment functions as a subsystem of the larger governmental system or *polity* when society as a whole is the system of reference. The courts would be found to be integrative institutions when the referent system is society as a whole.

[A] Adaptation	[G] Goal Attainment
[L] Pattern–Maintenance and Tension Management	[I] Integration

Figure 12-1. PARSONIAN PARADIGM OF A SOCIAL
SYSTEM

William Mitchell identifies the polity as the subsystem of the larger social system which deals with the authoritative allocation of system goals, mobilization of system resources and the legitimation of the processes involved in goal establishment and resource mobilization.[15] The *polity* is the *political system* and Figure 12-2 is Mitchell's graphic of the internal structure of the polity using the Parsonian schema. Adapting the Parsonian concept to the specialized social system which characterizes an administered organization, it would be possible to conceive that the adaptive functions are satisfied by the policy planning functions of the organization. The goal attainment functions would then be satisfied by the organizing and management activities; the integrative functions would be met by the implementation of the administrative activities themselves; and pattern maintenance requisites would be met through the operation of the routines and procedures established. Figure 12-3 is a graphic of this concept as applied to the organization.

A	Administrative Functions and Roles	Executive Functions and Roles	G
	Judicial Functions and Roles	Party & Legislative Functions and Roles	
L			I

SOURCE: William C. Mitchell, "The Polity and Society: A Structural-Functional Analysis." *Midwest Journal of Political Science*, vol. 2, no. 4, 1958, reprinted in Lyden, et. al., *Policies, Decisions and Organizations*, op. cit., p. 53.

Figure 12-2. PARSONIAN PARADIGM ADAPTED TO THE POLITY

The administrative system undergirding a state highway system may be examined from the standpoint of the four functional problems of survival. Such a system might be resolved as summarized in Figure 12-4. Goal attainment consists of successfully coordinating all those tasks necessary to "get the highway built" to the extent that enough are completed to ensure the continuance of the Highway Department and the other component units. Adaptation problems concern not only those relevant to mobilizing the resources necessary to the actual building of highways over a variety of terrain, but also the

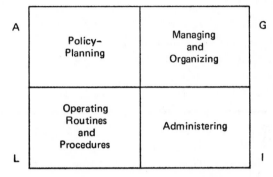

A		G
Policy– Planning	Managing and Organizing	
Operating Routines and Procedures	Administering	
L		I

Figure 12-3. THE PARSONIAN PARADIGM APPLIED
TO AN ADMINISTERED SYSTEM

External	Adaptation A. Mobilizing the necessary resources to actually construct the highway system. B. Satisfying the demands placed upon the highway system by the polity.	Goal Attainment A. Successful performance of all those tasks necessary to the fulfillment of constructing and maintaining the highway system. B. Departmental and system survival maintained. Outputs create significant functional impacts on superordinate system.
Internal	Pattern Maintenance and Tension Management A. Utilization of personnel programs, training, traditions, formal and informal group norms, ethical codes to maintain sustained performance of the actors and groups. B. The utilization of administrative, judicial and informal sanctions to achieve commitment to the necessary tasks.	Integration A. Accommodation and coordination of system components to enable the highways to be built. B. Satisfaction of a requisite number of needs of the system components to assure the avoidance of destructive conflict and survival of the components so they may render support when needed.

Figure 12-4. SOLUTION OF THE FOUR FUNCTIONAL PROBLEMS
OF SURVIVAL IN A SYSTEM INVOLVING A STATE
HIGHWAY DEPARTMENT.

economic and technical problems attendant on highway construction and maintenance.

Integration involves the satisfactory resolution of conflicts among the various units of the system, i.e., the contractors, the good roads associations, the farmers' groups, the automobile organizations, the trucking associations, other governmental units and the Highway Department itself. This would allow the successful completion of road construction and contribute to the survival of the system components. Pattern maintenance and tension management involve the utilization of personnel programs, the establishment of traditions and the creation of formal and informal group norms to achieve the sustained performance of the involved persons and groups. In addition, they involve the utilization of administrative and judicial sanctions to achieve a commitment to the necessary tasks to accomplish the goals.

Parsons asserts that each subsystem within a system must successfully resolve, accidentally or intentionally, each of these four functional problems to survive. Indeed, they receive attention in every phase of the administrative process and are often sources of tension among systems and subsystems. This theoretical framework furnishes a number of very important points of departure which lend a depth and a perspective concerning public administration, and particularly organizational activity not generally available in the more traditional approaches. An observer of the administrative process using these perspectives is not apt to suggest crucial changes in structure or function without carefully analyzing all the consequences of any suggested changes to the existing arrangements. Thus he would identify the functions and the dysfunctions of the variety of systems involved and end up with some sort of assessment of the changes relative to the needs and values of the specific system involved.

The public agency is the primary instrument selected by the polity for the fulfillment of the goals articulated through the policy process. The central concern of the organization is the program activity which it performs to accomplish the demands made of it. It is the activity of the program effort which gets the job done.

THE PROGRAM CONTEXT

Program administration lies at the core of the organizational processes. It is exceptionally complex, as it involves an intricate coordination of a vast variety of skills and specializations which must be related to available resources in order to accomplish a specifically designed outcome. There is an understandable and inherent tendency to become preoccupied with the parts and thus fail to comprehend the overall program process. For administrative practitioners these details are more concrete and more easily capture his attention. This is demonstrated in a variety of ways: the increasing mass of agency technical, administrative and operating manuals; the increasing emphasis on more specialized techniques of planning; programming, budgeting and methods analysis and design; the specialized language emergent around on-going particular administrative activities, i.e., computer programming sections, working relationships and values in what approximates a closed system. Groups not original parties will probably be excluded, unless they can bring significant power to bear into the program context to alter in some way the distribution of program benefits. Conflict and confrontation may be avenues utilized to achieve such a change. In this case, a new equilibrium has to be achieved which requires new negotiations and accommodation. Even top agency management influence may have difficulty penetrating an established system; or, on the contrary, top management commitment to powerful groups with which significant accommodations have been reached may interfere with suggestions from the field which are responsive to changing conditions in the field. The program context acquires a stubborn self-sufficiency.

Budget formulation is another occasion in-program administration that can be regarded as a turning point in policy formulation. Budgeting is conceived here as the distribution of available resources among the services carried by a given jurisdiction. The budget process varies significantly according to the program context from which the estimate is drawn. Estimates originating in contexts characterized by clearly developed, long-term programs, to which all affected groups are solidly committed, may be regarded as advanced billings for commitments that none of the groups care to reconsider. This is often the case in such areas as highway building, natural resource management, insurance regulation, etc. The long-term program is for the most part negotiated by groups dominating the program: personnel administration, budgeting, administrative accounting and the technical concerns of the program specialists.

Leadership, quality, motivational and incentive considerations influence group behavior within the program context, as do self-identification, morale, internal and external conflict. No description is particularly accurate or captures what is sensed as the *feel* of the organization. The more important ingredients of agency élan are subtle and intangible. The activities of the public agency are the central concern of agency management and the manifest expression of its capacity and competence. Shipman notes that "The program context has a nucleus of capacity, a center of legal competence and special skills assembled in a formal institution adapted to their application. This institution-bureau, service, agency . . . offers a developed capacity to instruct children, build and maintain public works, or forecast the weather. . . ."[16] Agency responses to its operating environment emerge over time as reliable, stable and predictable. These program responses reflect agency capacity to produce, provide satisfactions to the involved groups and guarantee agency survival. The flux of interacting forces tend to be stabilized, routinized and disciplined by the necessities of institutional preservation and individual role satisfaction. Whether or not the administrative institution justifies itself over a period of time depends upon how acceptably it provides program channels for the expression of individual group satisfactions.

The adjustment of intergroup relationships in a program context is essentially a gradual and evolutionary process, yet occasionally may result from crisis resolution. Sharp issues may be drawn when groups with competing purposes collide head on. The tendency is to avoid such crises as threaten established patterns through which personal and agency satisfactions are derived and institutional survival needs met. Generally, there is an inclination to seek and use recurrent occasions to renegotiate new patterns of accommodation and equilibrium. Once settlement is reached, stability is reestablished and the pattern is maintained unless conditions underlying it change. Then all questions may be reopened. These occasions for reconsidering and renegotiating settled relationships constitute a series of turning points in policy development. They are indicative of the fluidity and tentativeness of the policy process examined in the previous chapter. The planning of future programs, budget formulation, programming of operations and personnel projections are in many program areas the primary occasions for fashioning group adjustments. Policy, the value context of the administrative process, interlaces all of these organizational activities and processes.

Effective program planning, effective in the sense that it actually works to commit the allied groups to a set of projected working relationships, expresses a cooperative interdependent social structuring in the program context. This may be regarded as an established *program action system*. The value context of the plans to which these interacting groups are committed can be expected to be durable and highly resistant to external change except under serious threat. This may be considered public policy for as long as the particular equation of power persists. Well-executed planning produces a set of contexts. Budget review may bring external pressure to bear upon a developed program. However, by that time agency resources are effectively mobilized to protect the integrity of the agency mission as defined by its prior accommodations. The likelihood is that basic policy values will be sustained and ultimately ratified and altered little by legislative appropriation. Thus the budget process can be seen as an effort to mobilize strengths by devising a budget proposal calculated to appeal most strongly to the primary interacting groups capable of delivering political support in other critical arenas. The value content, or public policy, of such a legislative formulation is less an end product of deliberation than it is of an adroitly designed, carefully orchestrated and negotiated, widely accepted set of "understandings." The budget process can be regarded as the critical engagement in the struggle for agency survival. An occasion of equal importance may be where an agency operating under temporary legislation must seek legislative renewal of its charter to prevent automatic expiration of the program, i.e., it must meet the needs of the significant groups concerned with the agency mission. The ability to offer desired satisfactions as evidenced by tangible external support and buttressed by demonstrated capacity to produce results is probably the best assurance to maintain program continuity and agency survival. These settled commitments sustain the flow of public policy. They reflect great tenacity and lasting effects.

The turning points discussed so far are not the only occasions in program administration that produce significant policy impacts. Administrative audits, reorganization efforts and status drives within the system are just a few of the areas where renegotiation and readjustment of intergroup relations may be affected and public policy significantly modified. Once it is accepted that important sources of public policy are found within the program context, then these sources may be centered within the dynamic interplay of the primary groups involved. The interaction of these groups generates energies producing policy that defines the impact of administrative activity upon society.[17]

To this point our concern has been with the program focus of a specific organization. Agency program activity interfaces with the groups, individuals and environment in order to alter or maintain some aspect of the environment and the relationships or behaviors of individuals. If the energy supporting the organizational activity is insufficient and the organization and/ or the system of which it is a part cannot thereby maintain its vitality, it will tend to deteriorate and ultimately disintegrate. This might oe the case today with some inner city ghetto schools. This condition or tendency may be identified as *entropy*. An organization tends to seek and maintain its own survival and, therefore, its members tend to constantly seek a balance between the organization and the constituent support and dependency groups within the environment. This is accomplished by settled, yet evolving, sets of *quids pro quo* or *trade-offs* between these groups and what the organization delivers in return for support. This phenomenon may be identified as *homeostasis*. A tendency in any organization or system to give way to the dominance of any part of the agency or system to the disadvantage of the remaining parts may lead ultimately to the organization's demise or seriously distort systematic decisions, because it inhibits the capacity of the whole organization to respond flexibly to the total environment and develop these trade-offs, or even technological responses, necessary for survival. Adapting a word from anthropology and biology where the overdevelopment of a particular part of a species leads to its inability to adapt to environmental change and thus leads to its demise, it is possible to identify this tendency as *hypertrophy*.

PROGRAM ACTION SYSTEMS

There is an emerging awareness that the single organization, even if imbued with more than a single mission, may sometimes not be able to respond effectively to a multi-dimensional and deeply rooted social problem which requires effective governmental action. Such may be the case with adult crime, juvenile delinquency or urban poverty. In cases such as these a *program action system* may emerge which is multi-faceted in its approach to problem resolution. Interagency committees and planning groups may be utilized. Links to the private and voluntary sections may be developed. One agency may dominate the design and coordinate the responses, but all are involved in a comprehensive social action program. An action program may develop as a result of task force recommendations involving representatives from the public, private and voluntary sectors sponsored by a legislative enactment or private foundation establishing such a task force effort. From this emerges a strategy of intervention in which all concerned participate in utilizing their distinctive skills to alleviate or eliminate the causes of the problems. A design for an administrative action system might encompass the following activities:

1. Defining the problem:
   a. Identifying the context of the problem.
   b. Identifying the causes of the problem.
   c. Identifying the desirable state of affairs, i.e., what ought the situation to be?
2. Identifying the strategies of action which would alter the conditions spawning the problem:

a. Identifying the values and priorities which will guide action.

b. Identifying the alternatives which will achieve the desired results.

c. Planning the varieties of strategies to be used, time frames within which results might be anticipated, availabilities of resources and supports, and identification of the results sought, the institutions primarily concerned and the links into the environment through which the changes will be effected.

d. Identification of some tentative measures relating to the rate and levels of accomplishments involved in the effort.

3. Designing program action:

a. Participating organizations relate their capabilities to the actions deemed essential to achievement of desired results.

b. Coordination of program activity and resources, information channels established.

c. Periodic assessment and continuing policy assessment.

4. Implementing program action:

a. Implementation of the activities designed to alter the causes.

b. Program activities would be conducted through the appropriate program areas.

c. Feedback would be utilized to alter the on-going program in order to enhance effectiveness.

5. Evaluation and accountability procedures would be implemented:

a. Identification of program impacts.

b. Attributing of changes to the relevant program activity.

c. Utilization of control group comparisons where appropriate.[18]

Figure 12-5 is a model of a program action system which is designed to intervene in the social and cultural causes of poverty. It draws on skills in the public, private and voluntary sectors and relates these skills to the conditions and factors generating poverty in a technological urban environment.

A program action system draws upon a great variety of supporting activities involved in the development of the program itself. Technical support systems are utilized involving information, professional skills, technological supports and

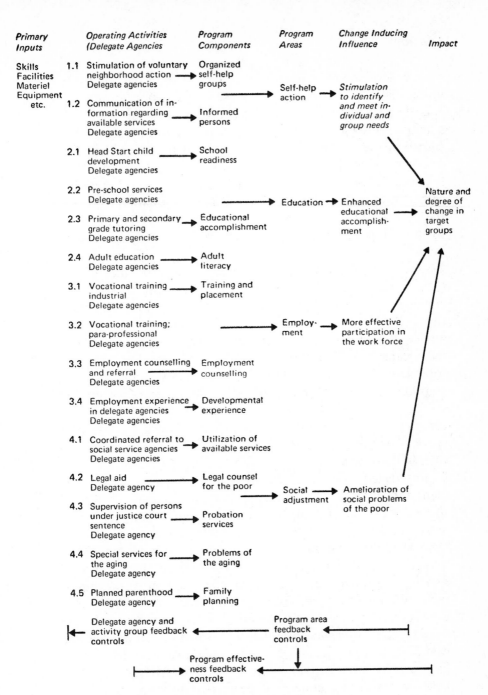

Primary Inputs	Operating Activities (Delegate Agencies	Program Components	Program Areas	Change Inducing Influence	Impact
Skills Facilities Materiel Equipment etc.	1.1 Stimulation of voluntary neighborhood action Delegate agencies	Organized self-help groups	Self-help action	*Stimulation to identify and meet individual and group needs*	Nature and degree of change in target groups
	1.2 Communication of information regarding available services Delegate agencies	Informed persons			
	2.1 Head Start child development Delegate agencies	School readiness			
	2.2 Pre-school services Delegate agencies		Education	Enhanced educational accomplishment	
	2.3 Primary and secondary grade tutoring Delegate agencies	Educational accomplishment			
	2.4 Adult education Delegate agencies	Adult literacy			
	3.1 Vocational training industrial Delegate agencies	Training and placement			
	3.2 Vocational training; para-professional Delegate agencies		Employment	More effective participation in the work force	
	3.3 Employment counselling and referral Delegate agencies	Employment counselling			
	3.4 Employment experience in delegate agencies Delegate agencies	Developmental experience			
	4.1 Coordinated referral to social service agencies Delegate agencies	Utilization of available services			
	4.2 Legal aid Delegate agency	Legal counsel for the poor	Social adjustment	Amelioration of social problems of the poor	
	4.3 Supervision of persons under justice court sentence Delegate agency	Probation services			
	4.4 Special services for the aging Delegate agency	Problems of the aging			
	4.5 Planned parenthood Delegate agency	Family planning			

Delegate agency and activity group feedback controls ← Program area feedback controls ←

Program effectiveness feedback controls ←

SOURCE: George A. Shipman, Designing Program Action, University of Alabama Press, University, Ala., 1971, p. 79.

Figure 12–5. SIMPLIFIED MODEL OF A PROGRAM ACTION SYSTEM

related legal and economic analytical skills. Communication links, shared resources and effective coordination of activities and decisions are an essential aspect of such an effort. An administrative support system is required involving the concerned agencies and groups which supply budgetary supports, personnel supports, and organization and method techniques required for on-going activities. A liaison system is designed to gather, interpret and evaluate significant information related to the conduct of the program. This information is communicated to those appropriate and concerned groups and persons able to modify program activities where necessary.

A program action system involves one or a number of program contexts containing specific capacities, special skills, legal competence and available resources assembled in formal organizations. This organization, whatever its form (i.e., bureau, service, department, agency or public corporation), maintains a ready capacity to perform action tasks such as building highways, forecasting weather, providing recreation, instructing children and adults, relocating populations or administering some other service or productive processes demanded by the public. This capacity can be directed wherever there is a demand for its special competencies and the resources are made available for their underlying support.

Interested groups in the society may be drawn into involvement and interaction with this program effort as it is perceived to be essential to the satisfaction and accomplishment of group aims. Such groups probably will seek goals, values and satisfactions that may or may not be harmonious or consistent. They may be in actual or potential conflict. Such groups may be seeking adjustment, elimination or continuation of conditions perceived as advantageous or disadvantageous to them. Defenses against existing or potential threats may also be sought.

The term *satisfaction* is helpful to denote anticipated and desired consequences of the administrative program effort. Satisfaction is the articulation of some specific values either held or sought by concerned groups to produce differences within the environment. The value itself may be nothing more than the reduction of some intense fear or anxiety, or it may be the accomplishment of an effective transportation program of speed, ease and comfort for the citizen traveler.

The satisfactions desired by these groups may have wide ranges of focus and concern. Administrative groups seek first to survive and maximize their status and power. They also pursue greater utilization of their special skills and competencies. Groups within and without the administered process may be concerned with maintaining public expenditures at a certain level or reducing them. Groups brought together in the program context may desire reciprocal benefits although the ultimate satisfactions sought may be quite different.

Whatever the goals and motivations may be, all the groups are concerned with the productive capacity of the program action system, and they seek to utilize that capacity for their own maximum satisfaction. Consequently, conflicting goals are rarely pushed to the position of checkmate where anticipated accommodation may be perceived and some goals achieved. Even if conflict may not be resolved, it may be contained. Thus the action content of the program system is encouraged and production achieved. Through this process the interacting groups may develop mutual defenses against external attack threatening or altering the arrangements deemed to be satisfactory in producing desired objectives.

Through these processes public policy may be achieved by a collectivity of organizations providing capabilities for activities that achieve specific results. These results provide satisfactions which may alter conditions, realize values, and resolve important social, economic or political problems. This is accomplished through the administrative process utilizing a program action system to accomplish such objectives. Figure 12-6 portrays this process.

This action system translates the values sought through the policy process into social reality. In this process they may undergo significant alteration. It is this sometimes subtle process in the public sector which must always be related to the public interest.

How may the public interest be maintained throughout the entire process? Is efficiency always the best measure of the public's interest being met? The public interest encompasses both program processes and the ultimate impact of the program itself.

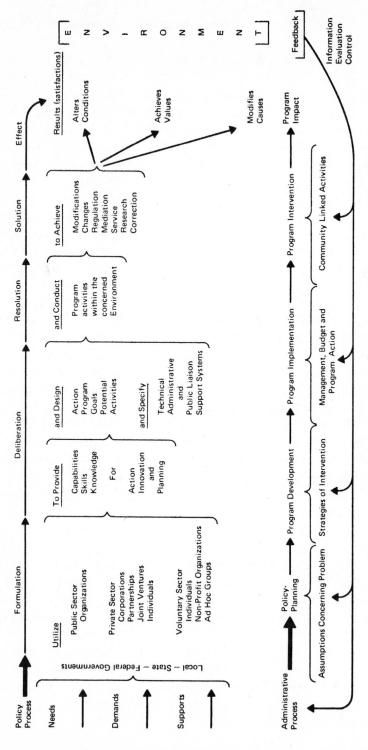

Figure 12-6. A PROGRAM DEVELOPMENT AND INTERVENTION FLOW DESIGN

PROGRAM ACTION AND THE PUBLIC INTEREST

For years scholars and practitioners have given lip service to the imagery of the "public interest" while avoiding acceptance of it as the distinctive feature of public administrative activity. The divorce of policy from organization seemed to suggest implicitly that public interest concerns would be adequately protected within those political processes defining agency mission and activities. With the realization that public administrative process is wholly within the broader policy process and that the policy process is intimately involved in the evaluation of public concerns, the problems of defining the public interest content of public administration can no longer be treated so cavalierly. The program activity of public administration translates desired values into explicit social meaning which impacts upon and within the specific environment where such action takes place.

The extensive administrative literature on the public interest reveals a vague and sometimes cynical orientation toward the problem.[19] Some commentators find it to be synonymous with the popular will. Others identify it with some "higher, truer" interests of the public without reference to majoritarian theory. Still others identify it with the results of an effective exercise of political power. In the latter instance, if a particular group succeeds in obtaining legislative and administrative support of its program, the result is in the public interest. This leads to spurious thinking represented by Charles Wilson's (former president of General Motors) famous quip, "What is good for General Motors is good for the country."

Efforts to develop an operational definition of the public interest helpful to those involved in policy-making, administrative decision-making or program planning have met with little success.[20] Nevertheless, some tentative, if timid, beginnings have been suggested. Sorauf has described the present state of affairs:

> Clearly, no scholarly consensus exists on the public interest, nor does agreement appear in the offing. Not only do scholars disagree on the defining of the public interest, they disagree as well about what they are trying to define: A goal, a process, or a myth. . . .[21]

There are some scholars who perfunctorily dismiss the idea that "in contemporary democracy the public interest—or its equivalent—is the process of group accommodation. . . ."[22] Others suggest that it cannot be ". . . determined by a mechanical counting of private interests. . . ." Nor can it be identified with the ". . . policy decisions of the public authorities. . . ."[23]

It has been suggested in this chapter that there is a value content to public policy which is developed within the matrix of administrative program activity. Gerhard Colm supports this position:

> . . . value systems and the related concepts of the public interest become manifest only through sociological articulations—the expressions of individuals and groups. . . .[24]

Utilizing a discussion of Norton Long as a reference point, Glendon Shubert suggests that "administrative due process theorists" supply a possible point of departure which might lend itself to empirical investigation:

> If we assume that the peaceful adjustment of conflicting interests is not only the consummate art of the politician, but that it is also the fundamental task of all policy processes in a democratic polity, then a model of administrative due process would be empirically verified, if in practice, the decisions actually made resulted in the maximal accommodation of the affected interests, in comparison with the relative capacities of alternative structures for making the same decisions, and measured by a reciprocally minimal recourse to other centers for public policy change (i.e., the legislature, the chief executive, courts, etc.). . . .[25]

Here, then, is a suggested tentative model that would provide a pragmatic test of public interest. An administrative decision would be in the public interest if it achieved maximal accommodation of the affected interests with minimal recourse to other centers available to reverse administrative policy. It suggests a correlative device which would involve a comparison of one administrative decisional process with another. This might involve, for example, a comparison of the capacity of the Bureau of Reclamation with the Department of Army Engineers in resolving a river basin developmental problem. Such a comparative model would be exceedingly difficult to construct. The work of Wayne Leys develops this opening edge a little further:

> But the rival claims of public interests in various activities do not demonstrate the folly or the impossibility of articulating those interests. Nor does the improbability of complete agreement on specific public policies disprove the possibility of general criteria or standards, which are properly called "the public interest." . . . There are three meanings which can be reasonably attributed to "the public interest" as a set of criteria for judging proposed governmental actions. Ideally, governmental actions will
> 1. maximize interest satisfactions (utility);
> 2. be determined by due process;
> 3. be motivated by a desire to avoid destructive social conflict (good faith).[26]

It may even be possible to utilize empirical analysis using these three criteria.

Maximizing Interest Satisfactions

This is the essence of the systems approach. At least two aspects of that process may be suggested as rewarding avenues to pursue, namely, the budget process and the program planning development and implementation process. Within such a context it would be entirely possible using empirical investigating techniques to develop meaningful insights regarding accommodation of group interests and whether they were maximal or whether one group was ascendant to the detriment of another. There would be, of course, no compromise with corruption. Due process discourages that eventuality. A starting point might be to evaluate both quality and effect of the disaffection resulting from a particular administrative act or decision.

Determination by Administrative Due Process

Norton Long supports one approach to this problem of administrative due process:

> An organization in its routines and its personnel—their training and values, professional and political—can be so structured as to maximize the likelihood that decisions will be made as a result of full consideration of the relevant facts, hypotheses, and values involved. . . .[27]

Dickinson observed in 1929 that:

> One of the valuable features of governmental control is its ability to cooperate with forces of change and development which meets obstacles in the form of established customs. Government often serves as a liberating agency through such forces. . . .[28]

Redford suggests the public interest, ". . . *may be defined as the best response to a situation in terms of all the interests and of the concepts of value which are generally accepted in our society.* . . ."[29] In other words, administrators must and should actively seek creative responses which will accommodate and ameliorate conflict and maximize satisfactions. Such creative leadership, he asserts, must be supplied at all levels of administrative activity. In considering the development of a due process conceptual model, the foregoing considerations are relevant to an identification of the *public interest* within the administrative process.

Avoidance of Destructive Social Conflict

This aspect of the problem may be examined in a number of ways. Here, too, the extent and quality of the engendered disaffection might be measured. Relevant, too, would be the extent of the appeal to legitimate and non-legitimate devices to overturn the administrative policy. These and other factors are capable of being developed as applicable criteria.

Conflict and the threat of conflict are not always dysfunctional to the administrative process. Very often important and effective changes are preceded by threats of conflict. Conflict avoidance and conflict resolution are crucial aspects of the administrative system about which much has yet to be learned. Destructive conflict is especially difficult to comprehend and assess in the administrative context. Harm to person and property would be a violation of due process considerations. Thus administrators involved in sterilizing non-consenting young, black women in Alabama and California were certainly not acting in the public interest. On the other hand, public officials in Wisconsin authorizing the use of public funds for a young, consenting woman to receive silicone breast implants to help her become more attractive and, therefore, more employable, might well be acting in the public interest though those officials were charged with the misappropriation of public funds. The confrontation between the National Guard and the students at Kent State University in Ohio presents a different problem. The seeming threat of violence at Kent by student anti-war activists following the bombing of Cambodia brought an administrative response which was swift and inappropriate under the circumstances. All available administrative means to avoid conflict were never effectively utilized.

Important educational reforms followed those difficult days on America's campuses despite heavy community pressures to "clamp down hard" on the "ungrateful students." Curriculum revision, student participation in academic policy-making, expanded programs of financial and tutorial support for deserving minority students, to identify only a few. The maintenance of public peace at Kent State demanded a full measure of attention to all the public interest issues involved. The avoidance of destructive conflict may occur by effective and swift shifting of priorities to the problems of disaffection before the flash point of discontent is reached. The style, character and behavior of the administration in the decision and policy processes is an essential component in the outcomes of those processes.

It is the administrator's task to be concerned, to design and to implement procedures which will raise the problems of public interest to the highest level of administrative consciousness.

Michael Mont Harmon of the Agency for International Development has made a most significant contribution in relating the public interest to administrative policy formulation.[30] He observes that the public interest is said to be "(1) unitary or individualistic, (2) prescriptive or descriptive, (3) substantive or procedural, and (4) ultimate (static) or dynamic." It is Harmon's position that the public interest is individualistic, descriptive, procedural, and dynamic. It is, he observes, ". . . the continually changing outcome of political activity among individuals and groups within a democratic political system." He notes that administrators are rarely concerned or do not have any, or "little conscious knowledge" of a theory of the public interest. Yet the manner in which they perform their activities does reflect the fact that they are vitally concerned. They are advocates and implementors committed to the essential correctness of the policies or programs they are administering. Harmon is concerned with the style of an administrator who is an essential and intimate part of the policy formulation process as his role vitally affects ultimate policy outcomes.

He suggests a *policy formulation grid* as a method of classifying and conceptualizing an administrator's role in policy-making. This will reflect and indicate an administrator's explicit or implicit commitment to policy choices. He suggests administrators with a high degree of certainty about the correctness of a given policy may reflect a fundamentally settled substantive view of the public interest. Those administrators who have an overwhelming concern for efficiency would harbor views of the public interest that are static, unyielding and unchanging. This, Harmon believes, is not adequate for a healthy organization or governmental system. A "healthy" system is one which can successfully respond on a continuing basis to the changing needs and demands within its environment. Figure 12-7 is a grid developed by Harmon to reflect these observations. The vertical axis on the grid represents responsiveness to the problems, needs and demands presented in the concerned environment. The horizontal axis represents policy advocacy, i.e., an administration committed to developing and supporting policies which are responsive to the problems and needs of that environment. One depicts minimal activity and 9 indicates maximum activity

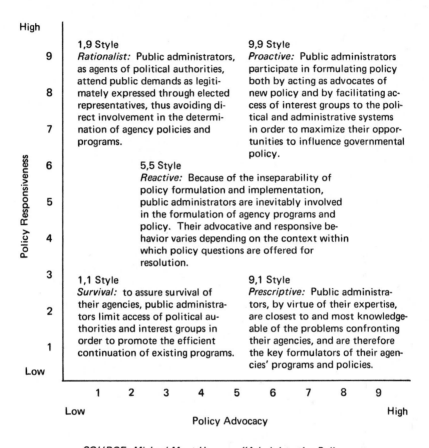

High

9   **1,9 Style**
    Rationalist: Public administrators, as agents of political authorities, attend public demands as legitimately expressed through elected representatives, thus avoiding direct involvement in the determination of agency policies and programs.

8

7

9,9 Style
Proactive: Public administrators participate in formulating policy both by acting as advocates of new policy and by facilitating access of interest groups to the political and administrative systems in order to maximize their opportunities to influence governmental policy.

6   **5,5 Style**
    Reactive: Because of the inseparability of policy formulation and implementation, public administrators are inevitably involved in the formulation of agency programs and policy. Their advocative and responsive behavior varies depending on the context within which policy questions are offered for resolution.

5

4

3

2   **1,1 Style**
    Survival: to assure survival of their agencies, public administrators limit access of political authorities and interest groups in order to promote the efficient continuation of existing programs.

1

9,1 Style
Prescriptive: Public administrators, by virtue of their expertise, are closest to and most knowledgeable of the problems confronting their agencies, and are therefore the key formulators of their agencies' programs and policies.

Policy Responsiveness

Low

          1   2   3   4   5   6   7   8   9

Low   High

                    Policy Advocacy

SOURCE: Michael Mont Harmon, "Administrative Policy Formation and the Public Interest," Public Administration Review, Sept./Oct., 1969, p. 486.

Figure 12-7. POLICY FORMULATION GRID

on the part of the specific administrator. Thus, 1 would represent low advocacy and low responsiveness and suggest a primary concern with survival alone. On the other hand, 9 would represent an administrative style which is highly responsive to needs and demands emanating from an operating environment and that the administrator's style embraces effective advocacy of appropriate solutions and programs toward resolution of the problems. Harmon concludes his effort with the following comment:

In each of the styles on the Policy Formulation Grid are assumptions about the public interest, some of which are simply illogical and others destructive of democractic values.[31]

He is most sympathetic to the "proactive" administrator because he fuses responsibility with advocacy and, therefore, is most responsive to the kind of problems which are facing the technological urban society. The responsiveness reflects ethical commitments to a humane and democratic manner of conducting public business. These are important steps toward a reemergent concern with the distinctive interest of public administration— the *public interest*.

Professor Nicholas Henry, in writing of public administration and public affairs, has reviewed "public administration's ethical evolvement." He notices three developments of significance to the emergence of the concept that ethics is pertinent to public administration. First, he cites the abandonment of the politics-administration dichotomy which forced the administrator to make decisions on bases other than efficiency, economy and principles. Second was the development of decision-theory, which introduced social and psychological factors into the decisions of decision makers. Finally, he asserts that the charge of young people of the "counterculture"—that bureaucracy is amoral—challenged the technocratic, impersonal, faceless, harsh and inhumane bureaucracy. Professor Henry observes:

The counterculture critique of the moral dilemma of the public administrator (i.e., that he is amoral because of the obfuscation of his language and symbols and the fractionalization of his sense of identity) is a profound one. Public administrationists, while increasingly concerned with administrative ethics and decision making, have not yet addressed themselves to the necessary chore of defining a workable framework of moral choice for the public administrator.[32]

The public interest which implies an ethical content must be fundamentally responsive to the human as a human. The central concern of the administrator is his contributions to policies and programs treating the human in humane ways. A remaining consideration is achieving the humane, both within the administrative system as well as at those boundaries where it faces its constituency.

NOTES

1. Talcott Parsons, *The Social System*. Glencoe, Ill.: The Free Press, 1951, p. 38.

2. Paul H. Appleby, *Morality and Administration in Democratic Government*. Baton Rouge, La.: Louisiana State University Press, 1952, p. 21; see also Emmette S. Redford, *Ideal and Practice in Public Administration*. Birmingham: University of Alabama Press, 1958, pp. 108-109; George A. Shipman, "The Policy Process," 12 *Western Political Quarterly*, 535-547, June, 1959; Herbert A. Simon, *Administrative Behavior*. New York: Macmillan, 1948, pp. 52-60.

3. Philip Selznick, *T.V.A. and the Grass Roots*. Berkeley and Los Angeles: University of California Press, 1953, *passim*.

4. Paul W. Bedard and Paul N. Ylvisaker, *Flagstaff Federal Sustained Yield Unit*. University, Alabama: University of Alabama Press, 1957.

5. Robert K. Merton, *Social Theory and Social Structure*, revised ed. Glencoe, Ill.: The Free Press, 1957, esp. pp. 19-102. For Talcott Parsons' materials, see footnote 11 below.

6. Philip Selznick, "Foundations of the Theory of Organization," *American Sociological Review*, Vol. 13, Feb., 1958, pp. 25-35.

7. Merton, *op. cit.*, p. 22.

8. Merton, *op. cit.*, p. 52.

9. For an excellent structural-functional study see Philip Selznick, *T.V.A. and the Grass Roots*. Berkeley and Los Angeles: University of California Press, 1953.

10. William O. Mitchell, *The American Polity*. Glencoe, Ill.: The Free Press, 1962, chap. 1.

11. Among the publications of Talcott Parsons, the following will be found to be quite helpful in exploring his point of view and his theories: *Toward a General Theory of Action*. Cambridge: Harvard University Press, 1951; *Working Papers in the Theory of Action*. Glencoe, Ill.: The Free

Press, 1953; "General Theory in Sociology," in Robert K. Merton, *et al.*, *Sociology Today*. New York: Basic Books, 1959, pp. 3-38; "A Sociological Approach to the Theory of Organizations," *Administrative Science Quarterly*, Vol. I, June, 1956, pp. 63-85, and Vol. II, Sept. 1956, pp. 225-239.

12. Edward C. Devereux, Jr., "Parsons' Sociological Theory," in Max Black (ed.), *The Sociological Theories of Talcott Parsons*. Englewood Cliffs, N.J.: Prentice-Hall, 1961, pp. 33-38.

13. Robert H. Simmons, "The Washington State Plural Executive: An Initial Effort in Interaction Analysis," *The Western Political Quarterly*, June, 1965, pp. 363-381.

14. Edith T. Carper, *Lobbying and the Natural Gas Bill*. University, Alabama: University of Alabama Press, 1962.

15. William C. Mitchell, "The Polity and Society: A Structural-Functional Analysis," *Midwest Journal of Political Science*, Vol. 2, No. 4, 1958, reprinted in Lyden, Shipman, and Kroll, as "The Structural Characteristics of Policymaking," *op. cit.*, pp. 45-59.

16. George A. Shipman, "Role of the Administration—Policymaking As Part of the Administering Process," in Fremont J. Lyden, George A. Shipman, Morton Kroll, *Policies, Decision and Organization*. New York: Appleton-Century-Crofts, 1969, p. 123.

17. For an exceptionally cogent demonstration of this, read George A. Shipman, "Revising Operating Policy," in Lyden, Shipman and Kroll, *op. cit.*, pp. 367-379.

18. This outline draws heavily from the following work, which is an excellent demonstration of a coordinated program action system: George A. Shipman, *Designing Program Action Against Urban Poverty*. University, Alabama: University of Alabama Press, 1971.

19. To identify only a few of the studies concerned with the problem: E. Pendleton Herring, *Public Administration and the Public Interest*. New York: McGraw-Hill Book Company, 1936; Glendon Shubert, *The Public Interest*. Glencoe, Ill.: The Free Press, 1960; Wayne A. R. Leys, "Ethics and Administrative Discretion," *Public Administration Review*, Vol. III, No. 1, Winter, 1943, pp. 10-23; Herman Finer, "Administrative Responsibility in Democratic Government," *Public Administration Review*, Vol. I, No. 4, Summer, 1941, pp. 335-350; Frank J. Sorauf, "The Public Interest Reconsidered," *The Journal of Politics*, Vol. 9, No. 4, November, 1957, pp. 616-639; C. W. Cassinelli, "Comments on Frank J. Sorauf's 'The Public Interest Reconsidered,'" *Journal of Politics*, Vol. 20, No. 3, August, 1958, pp. 553-556; C. W. Cassinelli, "Some Reflection on the Concept of the Public Interest," *Ethics*, Vol. LXIX, No. 1, October, 1958, pp. 48-61;

Carl J. Friedrich (ed.), *The Public Interest*. New York: Atherton Press, 1962, *passim*; Emmette S. Redford, "The Never Ending Search for the Public Interest," chap. 5 in his *Ideal and Practice in Public Administration*. University, Alabama: University of Alabama Press, 1958, pp. 107-137.

20. See Stephen K. Baily, "The Public Interest: Some Operative Dilemmas," in C. J. Friedrich, *op. cit.*, p. 106; see also Shubert, *op. cit., passim*.

21. Frank J. Sorauf, "The Conceptual Muddle," in Friedrich, *op. cit.*, pp. 183-190.

22. C. W. Cassinelli, "The Public Interest in Political Ethics," in Friedrich, *op. cit.*, pp. 47-48.

23. Edgar Bodenheimer, "Prolegomena to a Theory of the Public Interest," in Friedrich, *op. cit.*, p. 209.

24. Gerhard Colm, "The Public Interest: Essential Key to Public Policy," in Friedrich, *op. cit.*, p. 121.

25. Glendon A. Shubert, Jr., " 'The Public Interest' in Administrative Decision-Making," *American Political Science Review*, Vol. LI, June, 1957, p. 368.

26. Wayne A. R. Leys, "The Relevance and Generally of the 'The Public Interest'," in Friedrich, *op. cit.*, p. 256; Redford, *op. cit.*, p. 144.

27. Norton Long, *The Polity*. Chicago: Rand McNally, 1962, pp. 83-86; from "Policy and Administration, thru Goals of Rationality and Responsibility," *Public Administration Review*, Vol. 14, pp. 26.

28. John Dickinson, "Social Order and Political Authority," *American Political Science Review*, XXIXI, No. 3, August, 1929, p. 611.

29. Emmette Redford, "The Protection of the Public Interest with Special Reference to Administrative Regulation," XLVIII, *American Political Science Review*, No. 4, Dec., 1954, p. 1106.

30. Michael Mont Harmon, "Administrative Policy Formulation and the Public Interest," *Public Administration Review*, September/October, 1969, pp. 483-491.

31. *Ibid.*, p. 491.

32. Nicholas Henry, *Public Administration and Public Affairs*. Englewood Cliffs, N.J.: Prentice-Hall, 1975, p. 37.

13

BUREAUCRACY: HIERARCHY AND BEYOND

Administrative agencies are paramount in shaping the content and characteristics of public policy-making and in the subsequent implementation of policy decisions. They have their own internal policy processes interconnecting with those outside their organizational confines. Administrative influence and participation in policy-making derive from expertise, ability to command the resources within bureaucracy, individual capacities for leadership and historical traditions supporting perceptions of those persons external to the agency in a position to either block or facilitate the agency mission.

Bureaucracy is the primary device by which society orders specialized capacities of men and women toward cooperative and productive ends. With little hope of eliminating it, there are perhaps some opportunities to modify and enhance its effectiveness in the course of humane administration. Bureaucracy mobilizes physical, technical and human resources for approved social ends as determined through the policy process, a process in which managers of the great bureaucracies are significant participants. Inevitably it concentrates great power in few hands, sometimes with selfish and destructive and sometimes with constructive consequences. Historical bureaucratic societies emerged from strong feudal or patriarchal societies. The growth of American bureaucracy at all levels paralleled the growth of presidential power. A centralizing trend toward national policy dominance has been reinforced through grants-in-aid and revenue sharing, which links state and local bureaucracies into the federal administrative system. Yet it is certainly much too early to describe the diverse American administrative system as centralized. While policy at all levels is tending toward national norms, the administration of services remains highly fragmented.

The fragmented American bureaucracy evolved in response to a wide range of societal demands, needs reflecting diverse social settings and a constitutional theory rejecting enthronement of a monarch but prescribing the concept of diffused powers. The emergence of American bureaucracy is an exception to the world's past historical trends.

Historically, centralized bureaucracies have been characterized by administrative organization distinctive from political institutions, although not unaffected by them. Centralization emerges through a system of recruitment resting upon skill, wealth, achievement and political loyalty. The development of internal organizational autonomy, growing staff specialization, the introduction of salaried personnel and a distinctive professional ideology abetted the significance of bureaucratic power. Coordination of effort was provided by a hierarchy of authority; and a system of abstract rules and established routines dominated work and ordered the pattern of human relationships.[1] Throughout bureaucratic history hierarchy has been the preferred form for the accomplishment of cooperative work. Until very recently it has been heresy to view hierarchy as anything but an inseparable part of bureaucracy. Its benefits are clearly demonstrable under some conditions but under other conditions may contribute to slavery and human abuse. The great pyramids of Egypt and the Roman roads, culverts and bridges are monuments to the toil and abuse of men and women. They are also manifestations of the accomplishments of complex bureaucratic processes. It is well to remember that the Nazi solution to the "Jewish Problem" was efficiently carried out through well-planned and coordinated processes of hierarchical organization. The degree to which the administrators as participants had been morally culpable of crimes against society and of the genocide of a people is a separate issue from the effectiveness of the processes by which the goals were accomplished.

Are there alternative patterns for organizing human effort? Perhaps in the United States an alternate answer might emerge. Before dealing with this question it is useful to briefly examine the traditional context of hierarchical bureaucracy within the framework of urban-technological societies. Such societies with their rising standards of living and life expectancies have produced a "mega-scale" of organization, i.e., more and more experts mandated to accomplish a wider range of goals through increasingly specific skills. The wedding of bureaucracy to technology has achieved unprecedented gains in material wealth in the developed world. It has also created organizations surpassing the size of many modern nation-states. International Telephone and Telegraph and General Motors control the lives of more people, property and assets than the majority of members in the United Nations. All of the world's great civilizations have been characterized by vast and complex administered systems. The great armies, the great churches, the great governments, the great empires of the world, and today the great multinational corporations have been erected upon the foundations of specialization and coordination of effort to accomplish predetermined objectives. The management of these vast organized efforts is without doubt a most singular accomplishment in the evolution of the human species.

HIERARCHY, EFFICIENCY AND MANAGEMENT PRINCIPLES

On the continent Henri Fayol (1841–1925) and Max Weber (1864–1920) developed special approaches to the problems of managing large, complex organizations. Fayol, a Frenchman, was an engineer with a wide reputation and an outstanding record. His observations resulted from his experiences in the French coal mining industry and became the foundation for his outlook upon the broader aspects of administration. Fayol was concerned with the total operation at the upper administrative levels. In contrast, Frederick W. Taylor (1856–1915), an American engineer, was concerned with the minute day-to-day

activities of individual workers. Fayol observed and then identified successive elements in administration. These consisted of
forecasting, planning, organizing, commanding, coordinating
and controlling. He concentrated upon his "scalar principle."
This principle holds that the importance of administrative
responsibility increases as administrative ability increases. Fayol
also observed that administration was but one part of the
broader problem of governing an organization. From his work
and that of others in Europe and the United States there
emerged a belief in general principles of administration. These
were to become the "gospel of efficiency" discussed earlier.[2]

These principles centered upon the *division of work*, the
division of authority, the *unity of command, unity of direction*,
and the *subordination of individual interests to the general
interests* of the organization. They were basic to the traditional
outlook meant to be operative in a society dominated by
technology. Students of administration blithely assumed that
the worker is naturally lazy and must be subjected to vigorous
discipline. He must also be constantly and carefully observed
and surrounded and hedged in with a wide variety of disciplinary
threats as well as rewards.

Fayol, despite some sensitivity to the problems of human
relations (as was Taylor in the United States), nevertheless was
negatively oriented toward human nature. This outlook and its
consequent impact within public and private organizational
structure led to a succession of serious problems. Fayol was
unique at the time, however, as he understood the necessity of
building a sense of harmony among workers. He did not view
unionism as a particular threat but instead welcomed it as a
basis for creating more friendly relations and the settling of
common concerns between labor and management.

Max Weber, whose seminal contributions were reviewed
earlier, was a contemporary of Fayol and Taylor. His emphasis
on the sociology of administration is a benchmark contribution
to the understanding of organization in society. He was interested
in the nature of authority within organizations and propounded
three bases: traditional, charismatic and legal. Traditional
authority he found rooted in a council of elders; charismatic
authority was inherent in a leader's supernatural and superhuman

qualities, allowing him to exercise power and legitimacy only through his personal charisma; legal authority, for Weber, rested upon a set of normative rules and legal patterns established to control individual behavior and activities. Obedience is neither owed to elders nor to a charismatic leader but only to a legally established and impersonal order.

Weber found the most rational form of administration in bureaucracy. He described three primary characteristics of bureaucracy. First, the division of labor into offices based upon competence and responsibility. Determination of the characteristics of these offices is defined by law and administrative regulation. Second was the development of a hierarchical structure comprising superior and subordinate offices. Each office had carefully delineated characteristics and authority flowed downward in ever diminishing amounts to the lowest levels. Salaries were graded in accordance with responsibility and promotion rested upon seniority and achievement. Third, the bureaucracy operated through general and accepted rules to provide systematic internal control and order, i.e., authority. In hierarchies based upon Weber's model, authority is synonymous with "command." This combination in an extreme form may produce fear within the hierarchy, thereby contributing to worker alienation. The failure to adhere to such "orders" may trigger a range of consequences from mild reprimand to, in some military bureaucracies, death by firing squad.

The scientific management movement based on Taylor's work paralleled the rise of large public and private organizations. It focused primarily on the mechanistic characteristics of administration and the criterion for proper mechanical functioning was efficiency. Taylor's ultimate goal was the conversion of the management process to a system of "scientific laws." His was the vision of the factory, a primary corporate unit of the national economy, being operated on the principles of scientific management toward the single goal of efficiency. Armed with his stopwatch and carefully prepared schedules, he studied the physical movements of workers. The "one best way" could only be accomplished by the "one best worker." Output was to be raised by the standardization of tools and each worker was trained for those tasks for which he was best suited.[3]

His "time and motion" studies and their inherent mechanistic view of human labor generated a deep reaction and resentment because of the failure to comprehend human aspects of production processes. Today the same approach controls many public and private administrative choices. Taylorism, with its stress upon high productivity and disciplined labor, spread to the European continent and Russia. The "gospel of efficiency" generated considerable attention among foreign scholars.

Scientific management supported the use of objective criteria developed by carefully gathered empirical evidence in order to resolve industrial and public administrative problems. "Efficiency" was the new conceptual bridge spanning both continents—the answer for unending progress and bountiful production for the least cost in resources. It became the cardinal value of the emerging industrial society.

In the background public administration was "splitting away" from its political setting. The final consequence was not merely separation but the total alienation of politics and administration.[4] Because of this the overriding concern on the part of public administration scholars for decades was the bureaucratic organization. In this manner any notions of the "public interest" were irrelevant to the proper study of administration and the emerging discipline lacked a conceptual counterbalance to "efficiency." Not only did the concept of efficiency as an input-output relationship escape the external discipline of political forces, but it contained the seeds for grievous potential abuses to persons within and outside the organization.

PRINCIPLES OF FORMAL ORGANIZATION

The development of principles concerning formal organization and the concern with the internalities of organizations reached its high point in the *Papers on the Science of Administration* (1937), edited by Luther Gulick and L. Urwick, and in the efforts of J. D. Mooney and Alan C. Reiley in their *Principles of Organization* (1939).[5] Fayol's earlier work became the basis for Gulick's famous POSDCORB, which became a byword representing the golden age of orthodoxy for students of business and public administration and a central concern for managers. Planning, organizing, staffing, directing, coordinating, reporting and budgeting thus encompassed all the significant types of formal organizational activity. POSDCORB became a compass for the activities of administration and their use would, it was thought, lead "automatically" to "good" administration.

These principles underlying the basis of the classical model of administration that were so widely adopted with so little challenge are summarized below:

1. *Unity of Command.* Gulick, drawing on Fayol, stated the rule, "a man cannot serve two masters." The only exception to the unity of command comes when a person in the field must be subject to both administrative supervision and technical supervision if his task is of a technical nature. This was an attempt by Gulick to moderate the growing tendency to establish boards and commissions with administrative authority.

2. *Principle of Specialization.* After an organizational structure is developed, individuals are assigned to fit into the organization on the basis of skills.

3. *Responsibility Should Be Commensurate With Authority.* Urwick observed that in administration, ". . . all levels of authority and responsibility should be co-terminous and co-equal."

4. *Span of Control.* Urwick observed that no supervisor could supervise more than five men, although Gulick suggests that the span of control may vary depending upon a variety of circumstances.

5. The basis of the subdivision of an organization depends upon four primary factors: the *purpose* served; the *process* used; the *persons* or *things* served; or the *place* in which located. The situation itself must determine whether persons, purpose, process or place should be the guiding basis for organizational subdivision.

These principles, Taylorism and scientific management supported a simplistic, mechanistic view of public and private organizations. To this day the administrative efforts of the public sector in many countries refer to the activities of public administration as the "machinery of government." Amorality, efficiency and smooth operations are the hallmarks of this approach. Administrative operations are viewed as a machine to be "oiled properly" and "kept running smoothly." The reality of human beings performing within such administrative structures on the basis of complex psychological drives was simply ignored.

In 1947 Herbert Simon described these principles as "proverbs" and seriously questioned their validity.[6] He observed that more often than not principles came in pairs. For every principle, he wrote, "one can find an equally plausible and acceptable contradictory principle." In any particular situation there is nothing to indicate which is the appropriate "proverb" or principle to apply. He also challenged the notion that administrative efficiency was to be achieved by the implementation of these principles. He attacked each principle, revealing crucial weaknesses in support of his contention that they were, in fact, little more than proverbs:

1. *Specialization.* Administrative efficiency was presumed to increase with an increase in specialization. Simon asked, "Is this intended that *any* increase in specialization will increase efficiency?" He observed that specialization could be by *place* or by *function* and that the principle of specialization does not help at all in choosing between the two. Specialization, he noted, is not an aspect of efficient administration but rather "an inevitable characteristic of all group effort, however efficient or inefficient that effort may be."

2. *Unity of Command.* Simon found this principle to conflict with the principle of specialization. It conflicts in the sense that the specialized activities of an organization such as the accounting division or the personnel division cannot issue direct orders to a line employee. Simon observes that it is not "too far to say that unity of command . . . never has existed in any administrative organization."

3. *Span of Control.* This principle, too, conflicts with the principle of *unity of command* and the *principle of specialization*. In a large, complex organization whether the span of control is increased or decreased will under certain circumstances have either desirable or undesirable consequences. Thus Simon tells us to ask, ". . . what is the optimum point?" This crucial question is not answered by the principle of *span of control*. There are, he feels, many other considerations which must apply before

a final decision on this question can be made. This principle also throws no light on the problem of whether an organization should be centralized or decentralized.

4. *Organization, Purpose, Process, Clientele, Place.* Simon points out that any one of these may compete with the other as an organizing device. Consequently, the one selected as the basis for establishing organization may be in conflict with one of the others. Thus, he explains, public health administration might be organized on the basis of purpose, particular clientele served or place located. Which one would be the most effective is not explained by the principle. He concludes, ". . . the dilemma of choosing between alternative, equally plausible, administrative principles" is not answered by a "principle of administration" because indeed any, or none or all, may apply.

Simon leveled a devastatingly effective attack on these "principles of administration." He then suggested that organizations are primarily *processes* of decision-making. To understand organizations it was therefore necessary to understand the various elements and factors involved in making decisions. He exposed competing and conflicting influences inside the administration process.

Simon's contributions are lineal descendents of the work of Mary Parker Follett. She gained her insights from observation of business organizations and their administrative processes. She never fully accepted the findings of earlier writers on the psychological bases of administration. Follett was fascinated with the dynamics of interpersonal psychological processes.[7] In one of her first works she focused on the problem of administrative conflict. Traditionally, it has been viewed as wasteful and harmful. She described it as a process in which important differences do occur but the resolution of these differences might contribute in a constructive way toward attainment of organizational goals.

Follett suggested three ways of dealing with conflict. One is by providing a victory for one side or the other and by the consequent domination of one side by the other. The second is by accommodation and compromise. The third is "integration" by finding common ground. Here each side gives up little and both sides gain as a result of the conflict. Integration, she felt, was the most difficult to achieve. The process requires conflict to be brought into the open followed by careful examination of both symbols and realities of the situation. The next stage is analysis and evaluation of interests and desires revealed by the situation. This is followed by development of alternatives to resolve the conflict.

The major preoccupation of Taylor, Gulick, Urwick, Fayol and others "in getting things done" had led to concentration on command or direction, i.e., the transfer of orders from one to another within the hierarchy of authority for the purpose of achieving a particular end of action. This tacitly accepted organizational hierarchy is one in which, as Weber observed, power, prestige and remuneration flow in ever-diminishing amounts downward through a pyramidally shaped system. The objective was to achieve specific action by command and allow for consistent transfer of orders from one person to another. In contrast, Mary Parker Follett focused on the psychological characteristics involved in *motivating* an employee. She was more concerned with getting him involved through persuasion than in "bossing him around."

Mary Parker Follett was a pioneer far ahead of her time in her observations on the relationships surrounding power and authority. She viewed power as something that could not be delegated or conferred but rather something to be sought by self-developing managers or workers. In short, one must develop one's own powers before one could effectively exercise power. Much of the later work challenging hierarchy as the key to administration was seeded in the contributions of Mary Parker Follett. She saw authority as flowing from the function within the job performed and not as a concomitant of a specific location on a hierarchical or triangular structure. Authority was related more to an individual's expertise than to a grant of formal power delegated in an organizational framework.

At the time Follett was actively writing the Western Electric Company in Chicago was carrying out the famed "Hawthorne Studies." These comprised a series of worker control experiments lasting more than five years. The Hawthorne Studies have become a highwater mark in the "human relations" approach to administration. Attention turned from the physical environment emphasized by Taylor to the relations between the women workers and management. Still, increased production, i.e., efficiency, was the primary concern.

The studies revealed that output changed radically, not from changes in the physical environment, but with the nature of supervision and the status and prestige involved in each job. It was discovered that the causative factor in increased output was that the women had become imbued with the idea that they were a "special" group. Consequently, they sought to increase their output. That they were being studied became a source of pride and raised their status in their own eyes as well as in the eyes of fellow workers. They became a very closely knit group *cooperating* effectively with experimenters and each other. This program led to new group loyalties and solidarities. These developments emerged independently of comforts or discomforts introduced into the physical environment. At least as important as physical surroundings and monetary incentives were the psychological needs of the workers. The "gospel of efficiency" when centered only upon the physical surroundings actually inhibited the capacity of workers to function. It ignored the importance of the workers' motivational characteristics.

Chester I. Barnard's *The Functions of the Executive* was published in 1938. A former president of the New Jersey Bell Telephone Company, his many years as an executive had left him profoundly aware of both the scientific management approach and the human relations approach. He is consequently an important transitional figure. He attempted to bridge the two by a total abandonment of neither. Barnard articulated the idea there are informal processes that are operative within the formal structure of organizations and that these informal processes arise from the unconscious and serve a vital function in accomplishment of the organizational task. Further, he felt that these informal processes are crucial to the operation of the more formal organization. He conceived of administration as a "consciously coordinated, cooperative system for the accomplishment of a particular task."[8] Barnard also suggested that individuals who cannot maintain their sense of identity and the ability to make choices cannot function effectively within a cooperative system.

Both Barnard and Follett observed that authority within an organization rested on "acceptance" by the employees concerned. Whether or not an order or decision carries "authority" with it is not a function of the persons' position in the hierarchy that issues that particular order or reaches a particular decision. Authority rests upon the capacity of the recipient to accept the order. Consequently, it is related to the acceptance or the consent of the *individual actor* in the organization.

Barnard also noted a range within which all individuals accept orders willingly, but there are limits. If an order goes beyond these limits, according to Barnard, then it will not be obeyed and the administrators are open to the charge that they do not know how to use authority or that they are abusing such authority. Barnard labeled this range within which orders would be accepted the "zone of indifference."

For an inept administrator the zone of indifference is very narrow. In contrast, for an administrator who has earned employee confidence and respect, the employees' zone of indifference will be far wider. Due to his leadership qualities the administrator will be able to issue a much broader range of orders to employees with the expectation that they will be followed. The word "indifference" was probably not a happy choice by Barnard; "acceptance" might have been more descriptive and paralleled Follett's terminology more closely.

Follett and Barnard drove a spike into the comfortable illusions that men and women could be managed by "principles" that merely were to be correctly applied. Yet bureaucracy even today often operates on the assumption that it can "manage," i.e., manipulate in order to achieve more productive efforts. The results may be a deadening boredom on the assembly line or behind the sheaf of papers on the desk with little increase in productivity—not to mention the basic condition for a destructive alienation. The process is essentially circular, for alienation may lead to wasteful action, which, in turn, triggers the organization's authority system. Once brought into play, the authority system forces compliance without resolving resentments, produces a "masking role" during working hours or outright confrontation.

HIERARCHY AS AN ALIENATING FORCE

The alienating potential of hierarchy is not disputed by most modern authorities. Weber, Follett and Barnard were merely forerunners in recognizing this. Follett saw conflict as an inherent part of the organizational process, while it was traditionally viewed as interruptive, something to be avoided and repressed within the hierarchy. Barnard noticed that work was best accomplished sometimes through "informal processes." Even Weber, for all his traditional views, found alienation a product of hierarchy.

The linking of person to person within the organization causes overt and covert interactions. These imply transactions involving exchanges of power, commitment and meaning which sometimes facilitate and sometimes hinder organizational processes. They may have as their goal individual or group protection or survival in the organization. They may, alternatively, be efforts to gain power over or to "destroy" or neutralize a member of the organization.

One consequence of alienation within hierarchy is the individual resisting involvement in the task because it has no meaning, taking no risks because of the danger to his security or succumbing to mandated procedures in a ritualistic and rote manner. Eventually a pathological condition may emerge where the person may lose sight of his own humanness and his identity may be overwhelmed by the unrelenting and intimidating values of the organization. Within such an environment the individual has little choice but to seek to get job done and still "survive."

The alienating dynamic of hierarchy has given rise to a number of informal "rules" which are usually passed along the "underground" communication networks of the organization. They are universal enough to apply to most organizations. They reflect the personalization of task demands and survival goals. They generally are humorous if quite cynical in their thrust. Containing a type of "gallows" humor, they set the "hierarchical noose" more tightly around the employees' "neck." They include "conventional wisdom" which rationalizes the continuation of unfairness in the name of fairness. They encourage continued participation in the system, as the "little good" the person may do is seen to alleviate some of the pain and despair so often meted out in the name of "goodness" at the "output" (bottom) level of the hierarchy. Thus the alienated employee performs his work and rationalizes his despair through this device.

In the final analysis these survival rules for hierarchical living reinforce the alienating nature of hierarchy. They may be destructive to the individuals succumbing to their use. Practitioners who have been students in our courses have developed a number of these "rules" which have appeared in the "underground" communication nets of their organizations. Figure 13-1 is a summary of a few of these sometimes familiar spurious "rules." They reinforce the hierarchical principles because they avoid challenging its inappropriate and inhumane nature and they also reinforce role dependency. Later materials suggest more effective and humane ways of organizational participation.

Hierarchy implies formal organization, formal exercise of authority and formal institutionalized arrangements. It implies superior and subordinate human relationships which are vertical in direction. This is a situation of unequal power where the superior is "one up" and the subordinate is "one down." The superior has "more" authority, "more" power and the subordinate person has "less" power, "less" authority. The superior must "evaluate" the subordinate, must decide upon the person's competence, must decide upon retention or upon firing. Hierarchy was considered essential to coordinating work effort. Yet Barnard and Follett noticed that work is accomplished primarily because of the horizontal "informal" linkages among the employees rather than because of orders coming down vertically from higher authority.

ALTERNATIVES TO HIERARCHY

Frederick C. Thayer has asked a significant question: "Is it possible that the effective conduct of social business occurs *in spite of* hierarchy, not because of it?"[9] Until recently this question never occurred to students and practitioners of

Role	Hidden Meaning	Seeming Function	Actual Alienating Dysfunction
Don't Plan, Scheme.	Look out for your own welfare.	Personal survival. Task performance	Encourages one to be manipulative
Information is Power. Dispense it Sparingly.	Information is crucial to the organization. Use it in your own interest.	Personal survival	Encourages one to play power games.
Tell the Whole Truth One-half at a Time.	Be careful what you say. Know how it will be received.	Personal survival.	Encourages participation in power game.
Nice Guys Finish Last.	Being loving and humane is costly because other people are out to get you.	Personal survival.	Degrades humane feelings.
Quit While You're Ahead.	Losers never make it.	Personal survival.	Encourages deceptiveness.
Don't Stick Around Long Enough to Clean Up Your Mistakes.	Avoids bad personnel evaluation. Always look like a winner. (Everybody "screws up")	Personal survival.	Don't take responsibility for your actions.
When in Doubt — Mumble.	Never admit you don't know the answer.	Personal survival.	Encourages deception.
Always Guard Your Flank.	When you have "hurt" someone, he will be out to get you.	Personal survival.	Don't trust anyone.
Keep Your Guard Up At All Times.	Don't trust anyone.	Personal survival.	Don't trust anyone.
The Squeaky Wheel Gets the Grease.	Know what you need to get your job done. Then ask for it in a manner as to get it.	Personal survival. Task performance	Encourages power play.
Don't Rock the Boat.	Don't threaten your peer-task or support group.	Personal survival.	Encourages no taking of responsibility.
Don't Make Waves.	Know the unwritten "expected" organizational norms of behavior. Troublemakers are bad news.	Personal survival.	Discourages creativity and innovation.
Keep Your Nose Clean.	Behave according to organizational ethical practice.	Personal survival.	Discourages straightforward communication.
All Good Ideas Are Yours.	It's important to get and keep a good reputation for excellent contributions.	Personal survival.	Encourages deception.
Don't Get Caught.	When you feather your own nest, the price may be high.	Personal survival.	Encourages deception.

Figure 13-1. "INFORMAL" SURVIVAL RULES FOR HIERARCHICAL LIVING

organizational management. One of the major factors interfering with the conduct of an organization's mission is that one of its primary goals is simply its own survival. Thayer, in noting that this observation holds true for "corporations, nation-states, and public agencies," comments:

> This is why welfare agencies behave in ways which perpetuate poverty instead of removing it, and why the Federal Bureau of Investigation pours money and people into the Communist Party. To ensure survival (boundary maintenance in the jargon of administration, security in that of the nation-state. . . .[10]

He suggests that hierarchical leaders are always involved in a competitive struggle for scarce resources in order to assure survival, "corporations for markets, universities and public agencies for funds, armies for territory." Discipline, order, rewards and punishment are all required to keep the organization functioning. Survival of the agency and employee security are indissolubly linked together. The fate of the employee always hangs in the balance.

Thayer contends that "vertical theory" either creates or exacerbates problems and that solutions to problems do not emerge from the formal organizational setting. Problem-solving appears to be an integral part of human interaction. Face-to-face relationships often involve "fronting up" to conflict and resolving it. John Dewey observed:

> In its deepest and richest sense, a community must always remain a matter of face-to-face intercourse.[11]

The sense of identity which exists beyond the rationalizing process is found in the "feeling side" of men and women. Hence these links with other human beings in small face-to-face work groups may become a possible explanation for work accomplishment "in spite of hierarchy." This reflects Dewey's reference to a deeper, richer sense of community. The alienating characteristics of hierarchy may themselves, under such conditions, be completely overwhelmed. The dynamics of the small group may so effectively counter alienation that "the work gets done—authority be damned!"

Today autonomous organizations, whether powerful nation-states or single American governments, can accomplish little of importance by themselves. They are increasingly dependent upon cooperative relationships. Thayer identifies four organizational trends which focus upon these relationships:

1. *Transorganizational Processes*: These processes derive from the middle ranges of the hierarchical pyramid, cutting across established organizational boundaries and organizing skills, information and work in significant but non-hierarchical ways.

2. *Organizational Development*: This seeks to introduce democratic processes involving employees and work groups into those decision processes affecting them where their work is designed and defined.

3. *Citizen Participation*: Clients, customers, those who are affected by organizational decisions seek effective participation in the organizational processes of decision-making.

4. *Worker-Employee Participation*: Boreaom and monotony have significant organizational and social costs including alienation. This is now forcing the "redesign of industrial technology."

These trends, with their underlying theme of broadened participation, comprise a frontal assault upon the traditional authority structure. Centralized authority when combined with the Protestant work ethic and the urge toward efficiency in totality becomes oppressive, often arbitrary and inhumane. Equally significant, it encourages an amoral framework for organization decisions.

THE POSITIVE SIDE OF CONFLICT

Lewis Coser, in a study of conflict, writes:

> . . . conflict tends to be dysfunctional for a social structure in which there is no or insufficient toleration and institutionalization of conflict. The intensity of a conflict which threatens to "tear apart," which attacks the consensual basis of a social system, is related to the rigidity of the

structure. What threatens the equilibrium of such a structure is not conflict as such but the rigidity itself which permits hostilities to accumulate and to be channeled along one major line of cleavage when they break out in conflict.[12]

Conflict may be essential to the maintenance and survival of organizations. Katz and Kahn observe that organizations function through adjustments and compromises which occur among their competitive and conflicting elements. Competition between different subsystems within a system (horizontal strain) and conflict between the various levels of the hierarchy of privilege, reward and power (vertical strain) derive from our democratic ethos, specifically, e.g., equality of opportunity and equality of treatment. They observe that the conflict evoked by the distinctions of rewards and power between hierarchical ranks is magnified if:

. . . the different levels in the organization are defined more in terms of ascribed than achieved status.[13]

Hence conflict may well be an endemic part of hierarchy. Kenneth Boulding notes that changes in the top leadership may lead to unstable and conflictive responses at the subordinate levels of the hierarchy since power tends to be concentrated disproportionately in a few key roles near the apex of the organizational pyramid. The ways in which these roles are performed during the transfer of power have serious consequences for the entire interlinked hierarchical organization.[14] Anthony Downs advances the notion that the greater the instability of an agency's internal and external environment the greater the likelihood that major conflict and changes may occur when changes in major personnel occur. On the other hand, where there is great consensus among the agents within the power setting of the agency, it is less likely to incur conflict and resistance when major personnel changes occur.[15]

The cooperative effort required to accomplish work within the organization may be fostered, as Coser suggests, by conflict and threats of conflict from the external environment. However, the situation may also be dysfunctional to the system and possibly threaten organizational survival. This is especially so if there is no effective institution for provision of flexible responses. The impact of conflict upon the alienating character of hierarchy is apparent. Cooperative effort, mature and supportive of human concerns, does not *need* to arise only in response to external threats to security and survival. Yet hierarchy appears to be a formidable barrier to the achievement of cooperative possibilities.

Professor James D. Carroll takes to task these strict hierarchical rules, rigid pay schedules, restrictive personnel recruitment procedures and time attendance requirements which do not relate to creative mental efforts. He believes they will become increasingly dysfunctional to the conduct of satisfying, productive work and accomplishment. Carroll concludes:

> Authority, the willingness and capacity of individuals to function in cooperative systems, needs to be reconstructed through open political processes of inquiry and search, to direct constructively the growing tension between individual freedom and public order in a changing environment.[16]

Carroll forges another important thrust toward loosening the iron grasp of hierarchy on visions of the "ideal of organization." Administrative theorists seem to be cautiously edging up to a direct challenge.

NON-STATIC ORGANIZATIONS

More and more attention is being given to alternatives to the hierarchical organization. Viewing the organization not as monolithic but as flexible and open in its responses is an important step along the road to non-hierarchical organization. James D. Thompson in *Organizations in Action* states:

> The organization must find and maintain a viable technology and it must have some capacity to satisfy demands of a task environment . . . these demands may be

changing . . . a technology . . . effective yesterday may be
inadequate today.[17]

Morley Segal, building on the work of Thompson, focuses
upon the relationships between the organization and the environment in which it functions. He developed a typology of
organizational structures which may be used in response to a
turbulent environment. The three typologies he develops are
viewed as a "defense" of the organization against the vagaries
and uncertainties of environment. They are not fully alternative
views of hierarchy, yet they still serve primary organizational
survival needs. Organizations should center more attention on
how their environmental setting links up with the internal structure of the organization, how organizational decision processes
relate to the environment and how organizational boundaries
with the environment are spanned. Segal suggests an organization's broader response to its environment is based upon its own
selective perceptions. Differing perceptions lead to variations in
responses. He identifies three alternative perceptions:

1. *Chain Structured*: These "organizations perceive their
environment as static and homogeneous." The response is
narrow and limited. This, Segal suggests, is closest to the classical
model. The manner in which the units of the organization are
arranged reflect best how the organization can function, e.g., a
sewage treatment plant or a military induction center may be
considered chain structured organizations.

2. *Mediatively Structured*: The environment is perceived as
discrete, definable and comprehensible within understandable
processes and units. The organization arranges itself so that it
can respond and mediate "between a world of diversity and uniform organizational process." Anguishing difficulties may arise
because the need of a client may not fit the defined categories
available within the organizational responses. Departments of
Welfare, Police and Employment Security are examples of
mediatively structured organizations.

3. *Adaptively Structured*: This responds not selectively but
rather to the full turbulence of its environment. It is comprehensive and adaptive to the problem of the client and does
not attempt to fit the client's problem into predetermined

organizational categories. These organizations rearrange structure and role within the agency to adapt to the new situation. Segal suggests the adaptively structured organization "is fully responsive to its environment, for environmental change does not always take place in terms of fixed categories."[18]

This represents a flexible response to deliver a number of services coherently in an environment where value outcomes need to be consistent in their results. Thus a welfare program designed to deliver effective financial aid to an eligible recipient should not at the same time drive the father out of the house. Some overly stringent requirements force fathers, unable to find employment, out of the home. Should he remain at home, the amount of aid the mother might otherwise be eligible for is reduced. An adaptive organization could respond in amounts which preserve the home and still deliver the needed aid. The center of Segal's efforts is still the organization. The survival of the organization remains paramount. Yet his work suggests the development of organizations along non-hierarchical, non-traditional lines.

Some scholars suggest that organizations be only "task" centered. The life of the organization should only be temporary and related to the fulfillment of its task, at which time it would be disbanded. Bennis has observed:

> "Hierarchical bureaucracy" is becoming less and less effective . . . hopelessly out of joint with contemporary realities, and . . . new shapes, patterns, and mottos—currently recessive—are merging which promise drastic changes in the conduct of the corporation and managerial practices in general. So, within the next 20–50 years we should all be witness to, and participate in, the end of bureaucracy and the rise of new social systems better able to cope with the twentieth century demands.[19]

Bennis regards the decline of bureaucratic hierarchy as necessary to the accomplishment of social purpose. The traditional model of an organization, with its narrow orientation toward human psychology and motivation and its concern for routinization, specialization, hierarchical structure, has become rigid and unresponsive. In the thrust to define a more meaningful and more effective organizational context, the search for open models and experimental orientations toward organizations occurred. Bennis predicts the emergence of "temporary organizations" which will accomplish these social needs.

Alvin Toffler, in his book *Future Shock*, wrote of the coming "adhocracy." Toffler proposes an alternate possibility to a future in which the worker is a "helpless cog in some vast organizational machine" and "frozen into a narrow, unchanging niche in a rabbit-warren bureaucracy;" a future which will "squeeze his individuality out of him, smash his personality and compel him, in effect, to conform or die." Toffler suggests as bureaucracy becomes more rigid another future will emerge marked by the "breakdown of bureaucracy"—not its "triumph." He suggests we are witnessing a new form of organization which

> increasingly challenges and ultimately will supplant bureaucracy. Hierarchy will collapse and the new organizations will be temporary, fluid, and varied. A person's organizational ties with people, things and places will be mobile and alternating, turning over at rapid rates. Permanence, routine and deadening ritual will be gone. Turbulence and change become the rule.
>
> In this setting a new kind of "organization man" will emerge. One who, having no commitment to any organizational form, will be willing to use his or her skills and creative energy to solve problems with equipment provided by the organization and within the temporary groups established by it. This the employee will do as long as he or she determines the time frames in which the work is done and as long as interest in the problem is maintained. More and more the worker will be primarily committed to his or her own fulfillment.[20]

Obviously, there is a need for some continuing organizational efforts to perform on-going functions such as collecting taxes and providing law enforcement. Yet non-hierarchical temporary organizational forms might well conduct the public's business without that alienation so frequently marking much of the interfacing of the agency with its clientele, as well as with its own personnel. When public social policy and service are delivered in an inhumane, undignified, denigrating way, the impact counteracts the desired results of the policy and militates against restoration of effective citizen participation in the broader political community. It is the nature of hierarchy under such conditions to produce these results.

If hierarchy were to recede or disappear, organization would still remain. However, the demise of hierarchy should not be celebrated too soon. It is as tenacious as it may be unworthy. It enjoys time-honored use and recognition. It is comfortable for those at the top and for those who rely upon its activities and services. People will endure and suffer the known and accept its burdens before risking adventure into the unknown. So the mystique and promise of sharing the scarcity of power, prestige and remuneration within hierarchy continues to maintain the personal commitments of the employed to hierarchy and, in the process, perpetuate its alienating influences. Today the requirements of our society reflect needs and demands far different from the maintenance of centralized hierarchical systems. Myriad problems cry for resolution. Adequate recreation, full employment, environmental protection, adequate provisioning of health needs, revitalized regulation of many segments of the economy, mediation of conflict and disputes and more effective education stand upon the nation's uncompleted agenda.

INTERACTION PROCESSES AND ORGANIZATIONS

Administration is a social process. It is best understood as the interaction of persons and groups in a specific and defined physical setting involving communication and emotional transactions which center upon processes involving cooperation, accommodation, competition and conflict. Individuals and groups utilize interaction processes to affect organizational choices to achieve goals which they determine are important. Interaction implies a transaction which has consequences for the persons involved in the exchange as well as those who are or could be affected. The goals may be quite specific or very vague and ill-defined. They may be compatible or conflicted and diverse. Figure 13-2 is a graphic of this observation.

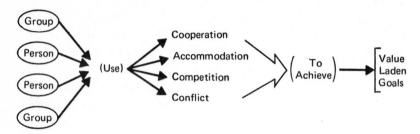

Figure 13-2. GOAL SEEKING INTERACTION

The functional and dysfunctional consequences of conflict to the administrative process have been suggested. When conflict occurs, there is always the possibility of trauma to the administrative effort and its threat cannot be ignored. The use of actual force or violence, legitimate or otherwise, would, of course, result in some impact ranging across a continuum from mild to severe. Such violence may involve harm to person or property by individuals or groups organized or spontaneous. This would result in heavy-handed, forceful responses. It may be preceded or accompanied by many kinds of demonstrations. Occasionally, a legitimate strike may even erupt into violence.

The responses to threatened or overt violence will vary and depend upon the particular situation. Some situations may call for avoidance of force, some for the use of great "shows of force." A show of force may inflame an already difficult situation. Negotiations involving compromise and accommodations may follow. Appeals to the judicial process, writs of mandamus and specific cease and desist injunctions may be sought. Occasionally, martial law may be utilized, although its appropriateness might be later questioned. Events at Kent State University are a case in point.

A wide variety of administrative sanctions may be sought and utilized. These may involve lease withdrawal, suspension of existing privileges, contract recision, program cutbacks and budget reductions. Economic sanctions utilizing the boycott, penalty tariffs and taxation may also be used. Social sanctions such as formal ostracism, threats, and formal and informal organizational penalties are included in the arsenal. Violence is not a frequent concomitant of conflict. Its absence is more the rule. Conflict is related to change and is an important element in it. Groups within the program context do not have necessarily identical goals and may be in actual or potential conflict. Where this occurs adjustment, elimination or continuation of a situation may be sought on the basis of what is perceived as advantageous or disadvantageous to the group. Defenses are often constructed against actual or perceived threats.

Competition is a muted form of the struggle by methods other than confrontation and conflict. The forms of competition within an organization may assume varied patterns. Legitimate procedures may be used to thwart or veto the goals of competitive groups and individuals. Economic, social and judicial means may also be used. Norms, understandings and informal processes may block or undercut a perceived or potential competitor. Political devices might also be utilized to thwart, restrain or neutralize an opponent or threat. This might involve lobbying, garnering votes, seeking financial contributions and voluntary efforts to achieve the desired influence. Access to key legislative groups and appeals to political party organizational officials are useful if sources are available to alter or frustrate a perceived threat.

Accommodation is a crucial process for the survival of the concerned groups and the accomplishment of goals. This involves the bargaining which is essential to the accommodative process. It is a series of agreements, tolerations or response patterns signaling diverse and often opposing groups to work together toward the accomplishment of specific administrative results. A special form of accommodation may be identified as cooptation, where individuals or groups previously hostile or unfriendly are, through an exchange transaction, brought into a supportive and cooperative relationship. The reciprocity patterns may be quite varied: an act for a promise; an exchange of spoken or unspoken acts and promises, overtly or implicitly understood.

Sometimes modification of role relationships among individuals and groups may be involved. Temporary coalitions for realizing similar ends may emerge among usually hostile groups.

Cooperative groups and individuals work together toward a shared goal. They are usually friendly, equal and harbor no pay-off expectations within the interaction processes. Cooperative efforts may be dominant in an organization though hierarchy itself may be dysfunctional to this process. In summary, cooperation emerges from concerned groups and individuals seeking similar goals through mutually compatible means.

These interaction processes are essential to administration. They are utilized by all persons for the accomplishment of individual and group objectives. These processes are at the heart of the communication system and in any specific situation they will be manifested in a variety of arrangements. Policy definition, program implementation and articulation of needs or demands are dependent upon these mechanisms. Levels of support, quality of response to needs, defensive strategies, and commitment to program implementation result from interaction processes. They are channels through which information and signals flow.

These interaction processes are modified by technological developments, scientific advances, geographical considerations and physical characteristics. The links may be person to person, within the group involved, among the groups concerned, peer to peer, expert to layman, superior to subordinate. They may be undistorted and uncontaminated with value overlays or they may involve overt and covert personal agenda and power plays. They may involve a whole panorama of communication methods utilizing such specifics as the electronic media, visual or spoken, the printed word, rules and orders, face-to-face, public or private, procedures, routines. Figure 13-3 summarizes these observations.

These processes form a network through which the business of the organization is conducted. They are a functional part of the administrative process. Most frequently they are discernible, patterned and comprehensible. However, they may occur in random and unintentional ways if the organization is under stress or in the throes of conflict. Their uses by actors in the administrative system in furtherance of goals may be overt or covert or buried within the subconscious of each participant.

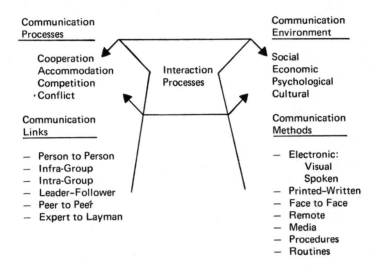

Figure 13-3. COMMUNICATION AND INTERACTION

These networks provide the linkages so important for the conduct of administrative business. Definition of need, policy planning and program implementation are accomplished through these networks. The interaction which occurs across these processes sets the level, quality, integrity, authenticity, credibility, supports, defenses, intensity and variety of administrative activity which occurs within the setting concerned. This network is embedded within the organizational processes and interlinks with the associated environment.

FROM CLOSED TO OPEN ORGANIZATIONS

The earlier monolithic perceptions of organization now need to give way to understanding organization as a collection of dynamic interacting activities. Today a vast literature exists using behavioral models, simulation, decisional analysis, case studies and role analysis to better understand the internal dynamics of organizations. Professor Nicholas Henry suggests traditional organizational theory as representing "closed" models and the newer perspectives as embracing "open" models of organizational theory. He asserts:

503

1. Organizations and their environments can and do change.

2. Organizations and the people in them act to survive.

3. Organizations and the people in them can and do learn from their mistakes.[21]

This is an organic, non-mechanistic view of organizations, where hierarchy recedes into the background as the emerging nature of the organization comes more to the fore. He perceives the organization as non-static, open and changing.

Viewing the organization as open and flexible moves in the direction of a more complete understanding of organizational dynamics and away from the rigidities of the closed model. Henry has observed four ways of looking at models of organization. In contrasting closed and open models, he notes that there are four fundamental differences: (1) perceptions of the organizational environment; (2) perceptions of the nature of man; (3) perceptions of the use of manipulation in organizations; and (4) perceptions of the role and significance of organizations in society.[22]

The environmental setting in the open models is viewed as dynamic, changing and complex. In the open model human beings are seen as in charge of their own personal goals and their own personal ways of achieving their goals. In the closed organization power is oriented toward the manipulation of people to achieve organizational ends. In the open model manipulation is seen as dehumanizing. The closed organization is more authoritarian, more rigid and more narrow. Open model methods are related to achieving humanness, openness and more effective communication and innovation. The major features of "open" organizational models are:

1. Tasks are organized in non-routine ways which respond to situational needs.

2. Specialized knowledge is not the possession of any one member but rather is to be shared and utilized to accomplish the organizational efforts.

3. Individual job orientation gives way to teamwork in getting the job done.

4. Conflict is resolved within the interaction processes, particularly at the level at which the conflict occurs.

5. The organization is perceived as fluid rather than rigid and routinized in structure.

504

6. Knowledge is available anywhere in the organization and each person in the organization knows something relevant and important to the accomplishment of organizational tasks.

7. Interaction between people and among people is more significant than interaction with hierarchical authority.

8. Interaction is concerned with accomplishment, not the maintenance of the command hierarchy.

9. Accomplishment and high-quality performance are emphasized rather than rigid conformity to routine.

10. Prestige and respect are related not to role dependence or credentials but to the capacity of a person to do what he or she does well.[23]

The closed system is concerned with the constant search for certainty. The open system is involved with the continuous expectation of uncertainty. Thompson notes, ". . . complex organizations as open systems [are] indeterminate and faced with uncertainty, but at the same time . . . subject to criteria of rationality and hence needing determinateness and certainty."[24]

TWO OPEN SYSTEM ORGANIZATIONAL MODELS

Two significant organization theorists, Rensis Likert and the late Douglas McGregor, have focused their concerns on the open system organization. Each has developed models which contrast remarkably with the closed hierarchical model.

Rensis Likert has developed four models of organization. He identifies them as the exploitative-authoritative model (system 1), the benevolent-authoritative model (system 2), the consultative model (system 3) and the participative group model (system 4). Likert utilizes seven key organizational variables in his models. Summarized, they are:

1. The leadership processes.
2. The nature of management motivation used.
3. The character of communication processes.
4. The nature of the interaction process.
5. The character of the decision process.
6. The character of how goals are set and ordered.
7. The nature of the organizational control process.

Each of these ranges across the four systems from a point where management has total domination of the process in System 1, to System 4, which is an open systems model where the employee has full participation in the nature of the organizational process.

A System 4 organization is one in which the members of the organization have confidence and trust in management and in one another. The subordinates feel free to risk without retribution discussion about their jobs and careers with their superiors. They feel free to contribute and obtain ideas from the organization processes. Economic rewards and compensation are developed through group participation, through goal-setting, improving methods and participation in evaluation processes. Communication with the members of the interfacing groups within the organization is extensive and complete. Information and communication is accurate, without risk and candid. Feedback without defensiveness is encouraged and welcomed. Friendly interaction with a high degree of self-confidence and trust occurs and teamwork is very substantial throughout the organization. There is wide employee participation in the decision-making processes as well as in problem-solving processes of the organization. Goals are established, emergencies excepted, through group participation and individual and group resistance resolved. There is widespread responsibility to review the total organizational process from top to bottom in a safe, risk-free, formal and informal way.

The System 4 organization reflects the participative group model Likert developed in research on productivity and morale. His data indicated the importance of the face-to-face work unit as the key element in the organization's functioning. Likert discerned that adequate development of the individual within his or her own face-to-face groups is not only an aid to the productivity and morale of the individual but also to organizational problem-solving.[25]

Douglas McGregor's theories of organization are based upon alternative perceptions of human beings. His two alternative models are identified as Theory X and Theory Y. Theory X is a closed-systems and Theory Y an open-systems model. McGregor stated the underlying assumptions of Theory X:

1. *The average human being has an inherent dislike of work and will avoid it if he can.*

2. *Because of this human characteristic of dislike of work, most people must be coerced, controlled, directed, threatened with punishment to get them to put forth adequate effort toward the achievement of organizational objectives.*

3. *The average human being prefers to be directed, wishes to avoid responsibility, has relatively little ambition, wants security above all.*[26]

McGregor asserts that so long as these Theory X assumptions are the primary influence upon managerial strategy there will be no capacity to discover or utilize the potentialities of the average person.

Theory Y is based firmly upon a considerable body of evidence, both clinical and experimental, that: "*The emotional and rational aspects of man are inextricably interwoven; it is an illusion to believe they can be separated.*"[27]

He based Theory Y upon the following assumption:

1. *The expenditure of physical and mental effort in work is as natural as play or rest.* The average human being does not inherently dislike work . . . work may be a source of satisfaction. . . .

2. *External control and the threat of punishment are not the only means of bringing about the effort toward organizational objectives . . . self-direction and self-control* (may be used) *in the service of objectives. . . .*

3. *Commitment to objectives is a function of the rewards associated with their achievement.* The most significant of such rewards, e.g., the satisfaction of ego and self-actualization needs, can be direct products of effort directed toward organizational objectives.

4. *The average human being learns, under proper conditions, not only to accept but to seek responsibility.* Avoidance of responsibility, lack of ambition and emphasis on security are generally consequences of experience, not inherent human characteristics.

5. *The capacity to exercise a relatively high degree of imagination, ingenuity and creativity in the solution of organizational problems is widely, not narrowly, distributed in the population.*

6. *Under conditions of modern industrial life, the intellectual potentialities of the average human being are only partially utilized.* [28]

The Theory Y organization is closely related to an open, flexible and spontaneous environment and requires a humane orientation to organizational development. The Theory X organization is closely related to a tighter, more rigid, hierarchical, authoritarian organizational climate and requires mechanistic models of organizational development. McGregor observed the assumptions underlying Theory Y are far more consistent with the existing knowledge in the social sciences than is Theory X. Theory X, he suggests, rests upon control and authority, i.e., "the scalar principle." Theory Y rests upon "integration," viz., the creation of conditions that encourage organizational members to achieve their own goals through directing their efforts toward effective conduct of the organizational effort.

BEYOND HIERARCHY: A TRANSITIONAL VIEW

The organization today is in flux and transition. McGregor's Theory Y and Likert's System 4 are indicative of the directions in which internal organizational efforts and arrangements are moving. The information developed up to now provides the basis for a transitional view of the public organization. It is a specialized social system consisting of interlinking subsystems comprising individuals and informal work groups within a framework of formal organization. The organization operates in an environment which is a more complex social system and has significant exchanges with that environment.

The organization functions to achieve value-laden goals which the public through the policy process has determined to be desirable. Figure 13-4 is a conceptual pictograph of this transitional organization. It is a subculture with its own value net, language forms and ritualized expectations around behavior and dress. It reflects the culture surrounding it, yet the organization molds such mores, behavior and cultural components to its own indigenous patterns.

A variety of specialized activities is performed inside the organization and is essential to its productive efforts. Such activities include keeping of records, hiring of personnel and maintaining personnel files, purchasing of equipment and supplies necessary for organizational effort, receiving and ordering them and a budget process.

Agencies must maintain a variety of technical services supportive of total organizational efforts. Specialized activities may include auditing, the use of library and research services and the development of personnel appeals and review procedures. A university, for example, would be concerned with setting up procedures for making curricular decisions, instruction, counseling, library services, employment assistance and the registration of students. These activities are organized as subsystems and subsequently divide into further subsystems to accomplish the effort required. A library, for example, may contain a vast number of specialized services: research services, book purchasing, cataloging, bookmobiles, lending services, book recovery programs, a specialized government documents section, technical supports, storage, microfilm, reserve services, community services and information resources programs.

Formal authority throughout the organization is invested in administrators who generally are ordered in an hierarchical way. Tasks are performed by workers. The administrators are responsible for organizing, directing, controlling, establishing decision-making procedures, planning, implementing programs, reviewing, coordinating and supervising the organizational effort. The workers are concerned with the continuing performance of organizational efforts and have the knowledge, competence and skills to perform those tasks.

Managers and workers participate in determining objectives, planning and staffing, developing of safety procedures, data collection and processing, establishing and using decision criteria and procedures, budgeting and financing procedures, program development and implementation, program impact concerns and program review. The manager is ultimately responsible for these activities while the worker and manager are both involved with the technical and administrative support systems. Each is concerned with the public liaison system so vital to survival and to understanding the tasks that organizations perform. Both managers and workers are concerned with information, evaluation of the total effort and evaluation of each individual effort as well.

These characteristics more clearly conform to current understanding of the nature of modern organizations. Hierarchy and its accompanying rigidities are found to seriously interfere with the accomplishment of organizational tasks and purposes. The transitional organization finds hierarchy hanging on tenaciously while heavy inroads upon it are made from the newer systems and humanistic approaches. Alternative modes of organization and coordination are required. Hierarchy, once thought to be a divinely originated rule of organizational behavior, need no longer dominate organization rationale in light of what we know about human nature and human needs.

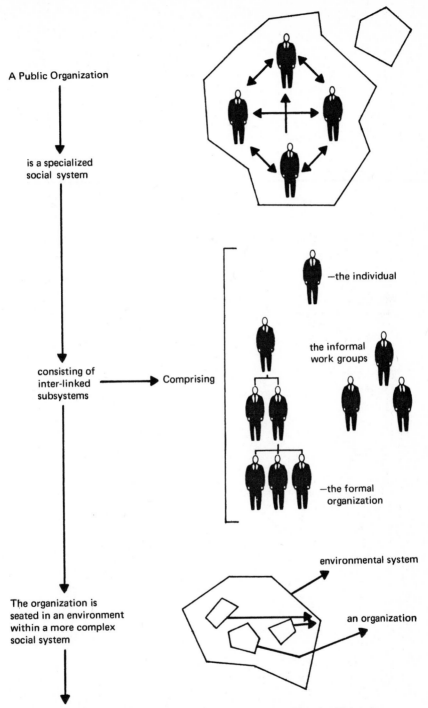

A Public Organization

is a specialized
social system

consisting of
inter-linked
subsystems

Comprising

—the individual

the informal
work groups

—the formal
organization

environmental system

an organization

The organization is
seated in an environment
within a more complex
social system

ADAPTED FROM: Le Breton, Comparative Administrative Theories, University of Washington Press, 1968, pp. 198-200

Figure 13-4. CONCEPTUAL PICTOGRAPH OF A PUBLIC ORGANIZATION

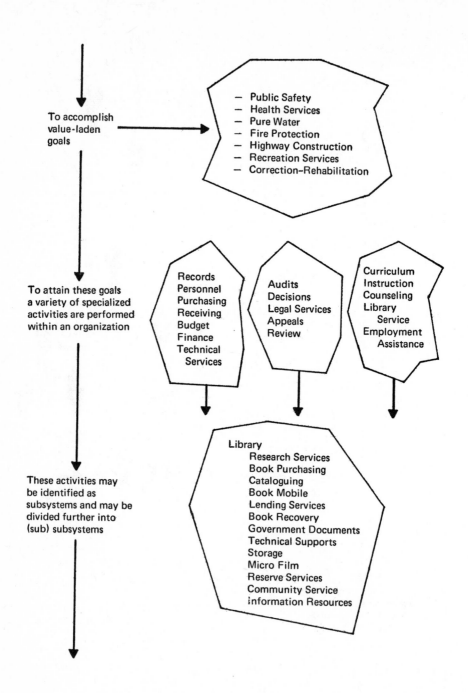

To accomplish
value-laden
goals

- Public Safety
- Health Services
- Pure Water
- Fire Protection
- Highway Construction
- Recreation Services
- Correction–Rehabilitation

To attain these goals
a variety of specialized
activities are performed
within an organization

Records
Personnel
Purchasing
Receiving
Budget
Finance
Technical
   Services

Audits
Decisions
Legal Services
Appeals
Review

Curriculum
Instruction
Counseling
Library
   Service
Employment
   Assistance

These activities may
be identified as
subsystems and may be
divided further into
(sub) subsystems

Library
   Research Services
   Book Purchasing
   Cataloguing
   Book Mobile
   Lending Services
   Book Recovery
   Government Documents
   Technical Supports
   Storage
   Micro Film
   Reserve Services
   Community Service
   information Resources

Figure 13–4. (CONT.)

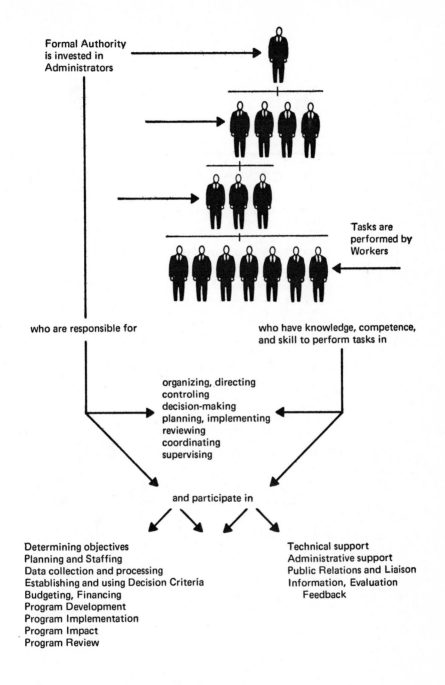

Formal Authority is invested in Administrators

Tasks are performed by Workers

who are responsible for

who have knowledge, competence, and skill to perform tasks in

organizing, directing
controling
decision-making
planning, implementing
reviewing
coordinating
supervising

and participate in

Determining objectives
Planning and Staffing
Data collection and processing
Establishing and using Decision Criteria
Budgeting, Financing
Program Development
Program Implementation
Program Impact
Program Review

Technical support
Administrative support
Public Relations and Liaison
Information, Evaluation
    Feedback

Figure 13–4. (CONT.)

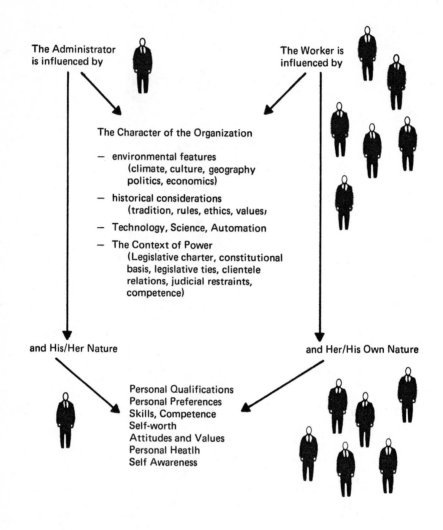

The Administrator is influenced by

The Worker is influenced by

The Character of the Organization

— environmental features
  (climate, culture, geography
  politics, economics)
— historical considerations
  (tradition, rules, ethics, values)
— Technology, Science, Automation
— The Context of Power
  (Legislative charter, constitutional
  basis, legislative ties, clientele
  relations, judicial restraints,
  competence)

and His/Her Nature

and Her/His Own Nature

Personal Qualifications
Personal Preferences
Skills, Competence
Self-worth
Attitudes and Values
Personal Heatlh
Self Awareness

Figure 13-4. (CONT.)

514

NOTES

1. S. N. Eisenstadt, *The Political Systems of Empires*. Glencoe, Ill.: The Free Press, 1963, pp. 21-22.

2. Henri Fayol, *General and Industrial Management*. London: Pitman, 1930; James D. Mooney and Alan C. Reiley, *Onward Industry*. New York and London: Harper Bros., 1931; see also their *The Principles of Organization*. New York: Harper and Row, 1939.

3. Frederick W. Taylor, *Scientific Management*. New York: Harper, 1947.

4. Woodrow Wilson, *Political Science Quarterly*, reprinted in Vol. LVI, December, 1941, pp. 493-494.

5. Luther Gulick and L. Urwick, *Papers on the Science of Administration*. New York: Institute of Public Administration, 1937; Mooney and Reiley, *op. cit.*

6. Herbert A. Simon, *Administrative Behavior*. New York: Macmillan, 1948, pp. 20-45.

7. Mary Parker Follett, *Dynamic Administration, The Collected Papers of Mary Parker Follett*. Henry C. Metcalf and L. Urwick (eds.). New York: Harper and Row, 1942.

8. Chester I. Barnard, *The Functions of the Executive*. Cambridge, Mass.: Harvard University Press, 1938.

9. Frederick C. Thayer, *An End to Hierarchy! An End to Competition!* New York: New Viewpoints, A division of Franklin Watts, 1973, p. 9.

10. Ibid.

11. John Dewey, *The Public and Its Problems*. New York: Henry Holt, 1927, reissued by the Swallow Press, Chicago, p. 211.

12. Lewis Coser, *The Functions of Social Conflict*. London: Routledge & Kegan Paul, Ltd., 1956, p. 157.

13. Daniel Katz and Robert L. Kahn, *The Social Psychology of Organizations*. New York: John Wiley & Sons, 1966, pp. 447-449.

14. Kenneth E. Boulding, *Conflict and Defense: A General Theory*. New York: Harper, 1963, pp. 156-157.

15. Anthony Downs, *Inside Bureaucracy*. Boston: Little, Brown & Co., 1967, pp. 191-192, 217, 263, 276.

16. James D. Carroll, "Noetic Authority," *Public Administration Review*, September/October, 1969, p. 499.

17. James D. Thompson, *Organizations in Action*. New York: McGraw-Hill Book Company, p. 145.

18. Morley Segal, "Organization and Environment: A Typology of Adaptability and Structure," *Public Administration Review*, May/June, 1974, pp. 212-220.

19. Warren G. Bennis, *Changing Organization*. New York: McGraw-Hill Book Company, 1966, p. 4.

20. Alvin Toffler, *Future Shock*. New York: Random House, Inc., 1971, pp. 124-151. See also "Symposium on Organizations for the Future," ed. Dwight Waldo, *Public Administration Review*, Vol. 33, No. 4., July/Aug., 1973, pp. 299-335.

21. Nicholas Henry, *Public Administration and Public Affairs*. Englewood Cliffs, N.J.: Prentice-Hall, 1975, p. 79.

22. *Ibid.*, pp. 55-82.

23. *Cf*. Tom Burns and G. M. Stalker, *The Management of Innovation*. London: Tavistock Publications, 1961.

24. James D. Thompson, *op. cit.*, p. 16.

25. Rensis Likert, *The Human Organization*. New York: McGraw-Hill Book Company, 1967, pp. 3-46.

26. Douglas McGregor, *The Human Side of Enterprise*. New York: McGraw-Hill Book Company, 1960, pp. 33-49.

27. Douglas McGregor, *The Professional Manager*. New York: McGraw-Hill Book Company, 1967, p. 18.

28. Douglas McGregor, *The Human Side of Enterprise*, pp. 45-76.

14

PUBLIC MANAGEMENT: PERSPECTIVES, CONCERNS AND PRACTICES

Management practice draws on the theoretical resources available in philosophy and humanities, the social sciences, mathematics, statistics and the physical and behavioral sciences. These ideas are refined, tested and applied through the disciplines of law, engineering, economics, political and social science and computer technology. Information from these fields of knowledge flows into the applications of management in the context of organizational dynamics. Management practice likewise draws on ever changing and evolving organizational theory.

Organizational theory is concerned with the arrangements within the boundaries of an organization and the techniques for managing the human effort within those boundaries. Organizational theory is concerned with the application of social and individual values. Earlier we observed that policy is the value content of the administrative process and program activity encompasses the organizational expression of those values. Groups and individuals interacting in a program context are seeking a variety of purposes which may not at all be harmonious and consistent. Indeed, they may be related to inhibiting the organizational activity, resisting change or seeking more rapid change; they may be concerned with survival. In short, it is a conflicted setting. The manager, then, deals continuously with contradictory values. Management choices have important consequences for the persons and environments affected. Figure 14-1 is a graphic summary of how the value demands

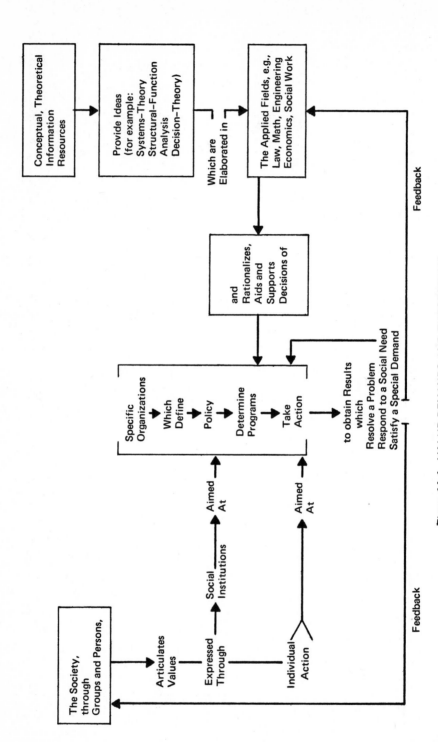

Figure 14-1. VALUE DEMANDS AND THEORETICAL RESOURCES OF AN ADMINISTERED ORGANIZATION

and the theoretical resources affect the organization. The manager must effectively integrate these diverse inputs into the organizational purpose and effort.

Management techniques may range from autocratic to collegial and include mediational and democratic techniques. Autocratic techniques of management rest precisely on authority and a chain of command which is represented in the more authoritarian organizations, such as the military or domestic police agencies in the urban setting. Mediational techniques of management suggest that decision, conflict, design and tasks may be mediated between worker and management or between manager and manager to accomplish the efforts required. Democratic techniques rest upon a decision process which is defined by majority rule, where the majority requires those who dissent from that view to conform to it. In the management context, however, it is considered to be participatory leadership where the worker is involved in management tasks in a variety of ways. Collegial management rests upon equality of power and mutuality of respect for the accomplishment of its purpose. It may be linked with democratic decision-making through majority rule or it may relate to a consensual decision-making, where no decision is made unless all are generally committed to that decision.

MANAGEMENT CONCERNS

Psychological transactions, social dynamics, the nature of due process, the problems involved in individual motivation, the structural formal and informal power arrangements, the nature of legitimate authority, the quality of formal and informal leadership and the nature of role structure and relationships in an organization are fundamental problems of concern to managers. Scientific knowledge and the evolving techniques of technology linking the organization to its environment are vital management concerns. The manager is concerned with decision-making, organization and task design and the utilization of energy and resources. The manager is concerned with welding these together within the dynamic organizational context to accomplish the purposes of the organization. Decision-making systems are involved in the planning, coordinating, programming, evaluation, organizational modifications and innovations, budgeting and research functions. Organizational task designs are concerned with how authority is organized within the agency, the structure of the agency itself and how they relate both horizontally and vertically each to the other. Organizational task designs focus upon how responsibility and accountability are designed and applied within the organization, the specific hierarchical design, the nature of departmental organization, both vertical and horizontal, the design of teams to accomplish the tasks which have to be coordinated to accomplish the organizational effort.

The problem of selecting and supervising personnel to accomplish the effort is a vital management concern. The communication processes of concern to the manager are both overt and covert and overlie organizational interaction. The use, storage and recall of information are essential to management practice. Management is concerned with quality of supervision, nature of supervisory leadership, computational techniques and strategies and data processing systems used. He or she is vitally interested in the decision systems used within the organization. These primary concerns are the vital core of management-practice.

The crucial problems with which the manager is concerned relate to the accomplishment of the specific tasks required to accomplish a coordinated effort. The goals towards which these efforts must be focused must be identified. The organizational effort must be accomplished efficiently and effectively, with dignity and within humane treatment.

Management effort increasingly must be conducted within value constraints that are related to the preservation of the planetary life cycle. Change, problem solving and conflict resolution oriented to the survival of his agency occupy the manager's attention ever more frequently. Figure 14-2 is a summary of the relationships between management concerns and practices, organizational theory and the underlying theoretical resources.

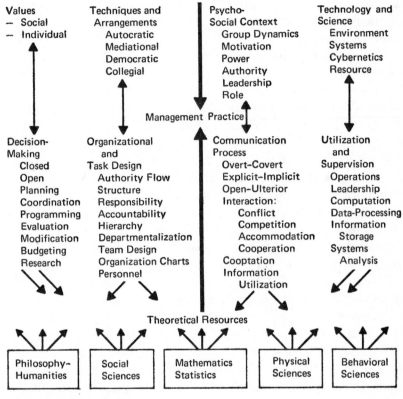

| Values
— Social
— Individual | Techniques and
Arrangements
Autocratic
Mediational
Democratic
Collegial | Psycho-
Social Context
Group Dynamics
Motivation
Power
Authority
Leadership
Role | Technology and
Science
Environment
Systems
Cybernetics
Resource |

Management Practice

| Decision-
Making
Closed
Open
Planning
Coordination
Programming
Evaluation
Modification
Budgeting
Research | Organizational
and
Task Design
Authority Flow
Structure
Responsibility
Accountability
Hierarchy
Departmentalization
Team Design
Organization Charts
Personnel | Communication
Process
Overt-Covert
Explicit-Implicit
Open-Ulterior
Interaction:
Conflict
Competition
Accommodation
Cooperation
Cooptation
Information
Utilization | Utilization
and
Supervision
Operations
Leadership
Computation
Data-Processing
Information
Storage
Systems
Analysis |

Theoretical Resources

| Philosophy–
Humanities | Social
Sciences | Mathematics
Statistics | Physical
Sciences | Behavioral
Sciences |

Crucial Problems:
- Task Accomplishment-Goal Achievement
- Efficiency-Effectiveness
- Dignity and Humane Treatment
- Preservation of the Planetary Life-Cycle
- Values and Change
- Problem Solving
- Conflict Resolution

Figure 14-2. ORGANIZATION THEORY

MANAGEMENT PERSPECTIVES

The manager today is concerned with two alternative orientations toward management methods. The first grows out of the scientific management approaches and is identified as Operations

Research (OR). The other grows out of the human relations approaches and is identified as Organizational Development (OD). Both are concerned with effective delivery of the organizational mission.

Operations Research is concerned with the systematic approaches to problem-solving and the application of the scientific method within the organization. The manager is involved with the evaluation of the processes through which the work of the organization is accomplished. The manager must constantly relate the whole problem of evaluation to analytical techniques, strategic designs and the operational context.

The manager's primary attention, then, is focused on decision-making, supervision and evaluation, and overlaid on this are analytical, strategic, operational and coordinating concerns. Now it is possible to adapt the Parsonian construct to this model of managerial functions. Adaptive needs of the organizational social system require attention to policy, planning, values and goals which adapt the organization to its environment. These are primarily the analytical and strategic concerns of the manager. Once policy is determined, the planning is done, the values and the goals identified, the manager must exercise "strategic" concern for their implementation. This involves goal attainment. Goal attainment encompasses program development, program implementation and program intervention, which are then designed to accomplish what has been planned.

Once the goals are designated and the strategies concerning their implementation conceived, the organizational task must be set in motion. Management must integrate the various specializations within the organization and amass the energy required to accomplish the effort. These integrative activities involve the technical, administrative, budgetary and personnel functions. These vital subsystems of the organizational social system, which appear so concrete, reflect the hierarchical aspects of the organization. Application of humanistic psychological techniques within the context of the organization are all utilized in a variety of ways and characterize an aspect of organizational development. These resource experiences are utilized within the more open and dynamic organizational systems.

MANAGEMENT TASKS

The manager is always vitally concerned with analytical, strategic, operational and coordinative tasks required to accomplish the organization's purpose. These tasks are an important segment of the manager's job. Organization analysis and reanalysis are continuously required. Strategic planning, which relates capabilities to performance, is of continuous concern to the management, who must also coordinate through a variety of supervisory techniques work activity to accomplish what the organization must do.

The manager, then, is constantly concerned with decision-making, viz., the variety of decisions, the nature of the decision process and the interlinking of the decision process to overall organizational performance. Supervision which relates the organization to the specific capabilities of the worker requires special management attention. Supervision is management's effort to relate material resources to the human effort which accomplishes the total organizational effort. Supervision concerns the use of mathematical models, both in decision-making and understanding organizational processes, the application of quantification and the utilization of mathematical and statistical procedures and an emphasis on economic and technical concerns rather than the psychosocial aspects of the organization. Electronic computers are fundamental tools of supervision. Supervision emphasizes the total systems approach to the nature of the organization and seeks "optimal" decisions generally within a closed system. Assumptions about supervision are related to normative models, that is, "what ought to be," rather than descriptive models, which are concerned with "what is."

Organization development is primarily concerned with enhancing the individual interaction among the members of the organization. Organizational development is concerned with the satisfaction of legitimate human concerns and of attention to valid human emotions within the context of the organization. It focuses, as well, on increased understanding among the membership, reducing tensions by *fronting up* to emotions in a manner that enhances the nature of team orientation and intergroup cooperation. It focuses on developing more effective techniques for conflict resolution in non-authoritarian management methods. It is less structured and more related to a positive orientation toward the human being, both within the context of the organization and the contact nexus the organization has with its environment as it meets the needs of its clientele. It is this integrative function in which the "daily tasks" of the organization are performed. Figure 14-3 is a Parsonian paradigm illustrative of these concepts. The analytical and operational functions of the manager may be placed on an horizontal axis with the strategic and coordinative activities of the manager established as a vertical coordinate. Thus through the Parsonian paradigm it is possible to obtain a view of the totality of the managerial function.

It is important to remember when looking at Parsons' Paradigm that the organization is essentially a "contrived" social system. Katz and Kahn observed:

> Social structures are essentially contrived systems. They are made of men and are imperfect systems. They can come apart at the seam overnight, but they can also outlast by centuries the biological organisms which originally created them. The cement which holds them together is essentially psychological rather than biological. Social systems are anchored in the attitudes, perceptions, beliefs, motivations, habits, and expectations of human beings.[1]

ANALYTICAL CONCERNS

The manager's analytical concerns must focus upon organizational purposes as they relate to power available to an organization. The nature of power and the power overlay which characterizes the environment are of vital concern, because the survival of the organization hangs in the balance. The capacity, effort and ability of those in the organization to perform their tasks, their capacity to fend off threats, facilitate and implement their competencies and draw upon necessary resources are vitally linked to the nature of the power concept.

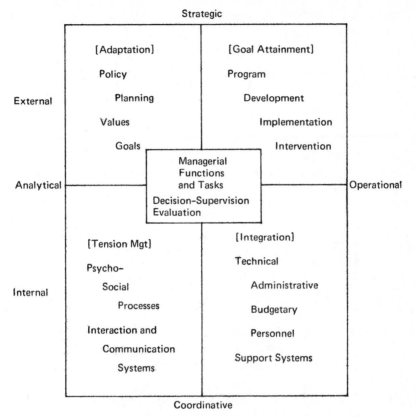

Figure 14-3. PARSONIAN PARADIGM OF
ORGANIZATIONAL DEVELOPMENT CONCEPTS

Management analysis must be concerned with time perspectives—the time frames within which each task must be accomplished, the timing and coordinating of individual and team efforts, long-run and short-run considerations and how these interrelate. The analytical functions of management concern the kind of tasks needed, how they may be organized, the specializations that can be developed or aggregated within the organization and the technical and organizational methods that can be related usefully to the organization's efforts. Managerial analytical concerns focus upon the nature of the environment, the input and support systems that come from the environment and the variations that are occurring in the everchanging environment in which it is located. Management analysis involves constant reevaluation of the entire organizational effort. These analytical concerns then must be integrated into the strategic, coordinative and operational activities of the manager. This requires decision and implementation through task activity.

Coordinating Concerns

The problems involved in coordinating the organizational effort require management attention to be given to the decision and implementation processes which are involved in middle-range supervision.

Operational Concerns

The operational concerns of management must be responsive to the analytical needs and this again requires decision and implementation. The focus here is on task performance, i.e., carrying it out efficiently and effectively. Here the manager must be attentive to the accomplishment of the organizational purpose in a humane way, both on the part of the worker and in the context of the organization's environment. Figure 14-4 is a graphic summary of these management perspectives which comprehend all the concerns of an effective manager.

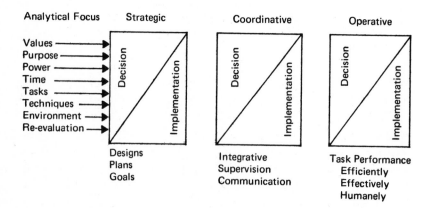

Figure 14-4. MANAGEMENT PERSPECTIVES: ANALYTICAL, STRATEGIC, COORDINATION AND OPERATIONAL CONCERNS

These analytical and strategic functions found in an hierarchical organization are generally performed at the upper levels of the hierarchy. Coordinative functions are performed by middle-range managers. In a traditional organization these may be superintendents and department heads. In a university organization these generally are the deans and department chairmen. In the traditional public organization strategic and analytical concerns are performed by staff attached to the agency head or secretary and the assistants immediately under the agency head or the undersecretaries. The coordinating activities are performed by middle-range management.

Specialized public agencies may participate in overall strategic planning that involves more than one agency through the use of interagency policy committees. William Morrow has observed a tremendous growth in these policy ties among federal executive agencies. Morrow observes, for example, significant policy interaction among a number of federal executive agencies and the Council of Economic Advisors.[2] He identifies significant policy ties to the Council of Economic Advisors from the Departments of Treasury, Labor, Commerce, Housing and Urban Development (HUD), Health, Education and Welfare (HEW), as well as with the Federal Reserve Board. The Office of Consumer Affairs, formed in 1971, has significant policy ties with the Departments of Labor, Commerce, Agriculture, HEW and subsidiary ties to the Federal Trade Commission.

Operational functions are performed at the lowest level of management and by the workers. Ideally, in a university setting, for example, the college professor in the classroom is the major operational focus of the university. The support of the professor in the classroom with the technical, clerical and material support systems becomes an essential part of the quality of teaching that is delivered in the classroom. Class size, classroom technology, lighting and resources are important aspects of the classroom situation which affect the quality of instruction. The time a professor is able to spend with any particular student and the qualitative nature of that interaction are vitally linked to the analytical, strategic, coordinative processes.

THE TASK ENVIRONMENT

The manager must know what specific tasks are required to get the mission of the agency performed. These tasks must be identified and defined. Management is concerned with identifying the kinds of materiel and resources needed, the human and physical energy required, and the information required and supplied within that environment. The task environment involves the most specific forces relevant to the conversion processes by which the organization responds to the requirements of achieving its mission.

Sometimes the broader social context may impinge on the narrow task environment of an organization. Thus in the late '60's the turmoil involved in conscription and dissent relative to the Viet Nam War interrupted the narrower concerns of the educational process in many universities across the land so that the task environment was interrupted and new concerns, new strategies, were required to respond to the changing social needs.

The organizational task environment may be fundamentally affected by the nature of crisis and change within a broader social environment. Alvin Toffler notes in *Future Shock* the impact of increasing turbulence in a modern technological society. He observes:

> The acceleration of change in our time is, itself, an elemental force. This accelerated thrust has personal and psychological, as well as sociological consequences. . . .[3]

Toffler suggests *Future Shock* is a time phenomenon and can be equated to a kind of culture shock in one's own social system. This has a way of disorienting individuals because the change is so rapid that the traditional landmarks recede from view and the feelings of insecurity tend to be overwhelming. Under this impact the distinction between the general environment and the task environment is constantly changing. There are continually new technological breakthroughs to which task environment must be responsive if organizational performance is to be continuous.

The environmental turbulence which characterizes the more advanced techological societies today creates many problems for the rigid, static and closed organization. The creative manager must be adaptive and responsive to the changing environment. In the turbulent, constantly changing environment the organizational goals are continuously renegotiated. The support systems are in constant flux. Management response and leadership in task environment, thus, must be specific but flexible, constantly responsive to the requirements of the organization itself. Routinization and stability are perhaps desirable because they encourage a sense of security and predictability, yet may, if too intense and tenacious, be dysfunctional to managerial requirements.

Change is not only characteristic of an external environment but responsive change within the organization itself is a requirement in the modern public agency. Hierarchy which is rigid, routinized and unchanging tends to be dysfunctional and often inhibits the capacity of a manager to respond effectively to the altering needs required in a sociopolitical system wherein it functions. Figure 14-5 is a summary of these relationships between task environment and goal achievement.

MANAGEMENT BY OBJECTIVES (MBO)

There have been many approaches utilized by management to integrate individual and group goals with overall organizational goals. Operations research and organizational development are two separate avenues serving this function. One of the more recent and most comprehensive of these approaches is "Management by Objectives" (MBO). Management by objectives seeks to organize individuals and groups within the context of the total organization in a goal-setting process.

Management by objectives focuses on the problems of fulfilling the mutual expectations and needs of both the overall organization and the individual workers and managers who are the participants in the organizational processes. It is a reciprocal relationship between management and the individual. Sometimes

529

General Environment

Cultural →Social →Economic →Scientific →Political →Physical →Demographic →Legal

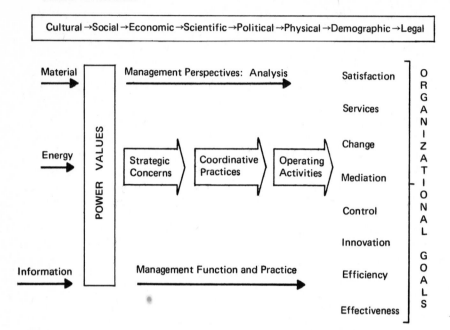

Figure 14-5. TASK ENVIRONMENT AND GOAL
ACHIEVEMENT

this relationship is obscure and "muddy," sometimes this relationship is clear and easily perceived. When it is clear, there is little room for misunderstanding. When there are hidden expectations and these expectations are diffuse, there is a great deal of room for misunderstanding, out of which conflict and disappointment occur. This may spawn activity falling short of, not only organizational goals, but individual goals as well. Clarity around expectations and clarity around organizational and personal goals are essential concomitants of organizational life and a central concern to management.[4]

The alienating influence of role dependence is still a characteristic of hierarchical management, indicating that human activity inside an organization is subject to influence and manipulation. The manager must be concerned with the evoking of appropriate action from a participant. March and Simon suggest that influence over the motivation to produce particular activity from the worker is a function of influencing three basic categories.

(a) The evoking of action alternatives for the individual; (b) the consequences of evoked alternatives anticipated by the individuals; and (c) the values attached to consequences by the individual. Each of these aspects is partly under the control of the organization but partly also determined by extraorganizational factors.[5]

This focus on organizational needs detracts from the nature of the individual and his need to participate creatively in choices around his own activities. It also created a context which was productive of what William H. White called "the organization man," an upwardly mobile, role-dependent personality, totally out of touch with his own autonomy and his own independence, for his success was wedded to his survival and success on the organizational hierarchical ladder. The problems of morality and misuse and abuse of subordinates became visible, paramount concerns with the unfolding of the Watergate incident.

It is the manipulative quality in MBO which is indicative that it is a lineal descendent of scientific management. Where its primary concern is the achievement of efficiency over effectiveness it is simply Taylorism in modern guise. Management by objectives is a program usually initiated and sometimes imposed by managerial performance appraisal procedures. Yet more recently it has encompassed the long-range planning control systems and strategic planning systems within an organization. It is a primary way of integrating the goals of the individual participant with the goals of the organization. It is reflective of the continuous effort to relate the distinct autonomous individual needs to the overall needs of an organization and to coordinate specialized human activity to attain specific organizational purposes.

In implementing a management by objectives program, one of the concerns is whether such implementation should be imposed by management or articulated up from the bottom of the hierarchy through participation of lower level personnel who are closer to the actual operation of the agency. Those who support the top-down approach indicate that it has the advantage of providing clearer guidelines for lower level participants. On the other hand, it inhibits effective participation and causes loss of motivation. Management by objective programs are not usually effective when autocratically imposed. Successful management by objective programs stress collaboration, cooperative effort, team building and communication planning. A management by objective program is a participatory one involving real choices by both management and the participant worker. Studies of MBO programs where implemented suggest that such programs do improve communications, increase understanding, improve planning, create more effective and positive attitudes toward the organization as a whole and in the evaluation of processes.

MBO may be utilized as a planning strategy which seeks to influence results toward ends that management wishes. It attempts to blend individual needs and plans of managers toward the accomplishment of organizational purpose over a specific time. The goal is to reconcile and integrate human effort, resources and facilities toward common goals while at the same time avoiding discord and discontent. Generally, the implementation of an MBO program involves the whole organization, i.e., management, leadership, individual unit supervisors, subsection supervisors and the individual participants, each developing goals and aggregating these goals into a total organizational effort. Paul Mali suggests that management by objectives is a five-phased process. He notes:

> An organization accomplishes a total mission by breaking it up into several phases, developing operating plans for each phase, involving managers to implement each phase, and setting a time scale for each phase's completion. Managing by objectives is a five-phased process; . . . It is an activity carried out in a sequence of steps taken in a certain order.[6]

Adopting Mali's overall categories with some modification, we can project basically five stages to an MBO program. These encompass the following:

Stage 1–Determining the objective.

Stage 2–Articulating the objective.

Stage 3–Investing the objective.

Stage 4–Implementing the objective.

Stage 5–Evaluating consequences and utilizing feedback.

Stage 1: Determining the Objective

This first stage is concerned with determining organizational objectives and breaking down these overall objectives into ones that are specifically relevant to each section and each worker inside the organization. It requires policy inputs from top management, supervisory and peer inputs, as well as individual inputs. This particular stage is concerned with analyzing the various alternative goals and defining specific overall organizational objectives.

Effective organizational techniques for obtaining feedback about the needs of individuals is necessary at this stage. Here, too, systematic identification of results needed by the organization for survival, growth, improvement and problem-solving occur. It is at this stage, as well, that the individuals themselves focus on what their concerns and needs are inside the organization.

Important analytical questions are raised: Where is the organization now? How did it arrive at this place? What is the nature of the situation? What are some of the problems that need to be confronted? What are the causes of these problems? What are the trends, projections and indicators concerning the future course of action of the organization? The goal of Stage 1 is to identify a list of important and needed potential objectives.

Stage 2: Articulating the Objective

Stage 2 is concerned with defining specific objectives within the agency and establishing objectives for each unit and person. This process involves a management team as well as participation from the workers. A proposal is developed which includes intended commitments by the individuals, groups, departments and the entire organization concerning the identified goals and objectives.

This proposal is generally written and communicated through the hierarchy, interlocks with other subunits horizontally and moves upward into the strategic planning section. The purpose of this stage is to identify important goals about which people can become excited and to stimulate them to deliver results. The assumption here is that if effective work is to be obtained from the participants, it is important to get them involved in making important choices early on in the process. The ultimate objective of this phase is a formal, written statement of objectives.

Stage 3: Investing the Objective

Here the written statement of objectives is submitted to the organization for validation. This procedure requires the individual department and the overall organization to commit themselves to the various goals. This procedure translates the objectives into commitments. It involves conferences, negotiation, informal discussions, modification, integration, trade-off arrangements, timing, links into the budgeting structure, as well as identifying a range of possibilities within the budgeting structure. It is here in the overall MBO process that many objectives are discarded as unattainable and not particularly useful, and new ones may be developed. These are renegotiated and reevaluated in a process that recapitulates Stages 1 and 2. The goal of this phase is to invest the chosen objectives with personal commitments. It is important to note that through all of these stages so far, as in the next two, management leadership and employee participation are essential to the process.

Stage 4: Implementing the Objective

Once a valid statement of objectives is accepted, a system which implements it in the organizational context is initiated. This generally relates to the kinds of activity encompassed in Organizational Development (OD). It involves due process, motivation, concern with specific tasks designed by individual workers in specific sections or specific departments. It involves task planning. It may involve encounter groups and T groups, sensitivity training, problem-solving groups, etc. It focuses the "zone of acceptance" and "non-acceptance" of authority by the worker. It involves the complex communication processes in the agency. The objective of this stage is to implement the articulated goals into the context of organizational activity. It is a process in the sense of effective listening, i.e., not only listening to words, but listening to the vital concerns of the manager and of the worker. It must be reciprocal in order that meaningful involvement in the task and the organizational purpose can occur.

Stage 5: Evaluating Consequences and Utilizing Feedback

This stage is concerned with revising the total management by objectives program. It is a reevaluation of organizational structure, decision-making processes, techniques of leadership and followership. It is a reevaluation of the communication and interaction processes. It involves a careful look at the totality of the atmosphere of the agency and the nature of the tasks performed. This stage involves evaluation, which utilizes feedback. It may involve measurement of past progress and the development of expectations around future progress. It involves concepts of reporting and analysis that involve both the worker participant and the manager. The goal of this stage is to develop reporting concerning task accomplishment as it relates to established targets.

Here, too, the managerial functions and tasks concerned with decision, supervision and evaluation are crucial yet inadequate without effective employee participation. Management skills involving analytical capacities, strategic design, operational supervision and coordinative efforts are essential to the implementation of the management by objectives program.

It is management responsibility to implement the MBO program across a series of time frames in which the first stage of analysis occurs within the first time frame, and the second stage, where the specific outcomes are determined, is accomplished within a second time frame, which then moves to Stage 3, where task implementation is designed. Subsequently, the MBO program moves into a fourth time frame, where task performance is articulated and, finally, a fifth time frame in which evaluation and feedback occur. Figure 14-6 presents management by objectives as a design for revitalizing an organization through management leadership and employee participation.

PERFORMANCE MEASUREMENT AND EVALUATION

Performance measurement is a significant part of a manager's task. It is very difficult because organizations have a wide variety of goals, using multiple criteria in the measurement of those performances. A university may measure its own perform- ance in terms of number of students graduated, the status of some of the graduates, the quality of its faculty as determined by community participation and publication through research and the services provided the community. Business organization, of course, rests upon profit maximization. Performance meas- urements involve *effectiveness*, which is particularly concerned with the achievement of the goals that the organization has—how well the values and the goals of the organization have been met. Performance measurement is also concerned with *efficiency*, i.e., the use of as few resources as possible in attaining the organizational goals.

One group of writers has suggested that in the area of public health, a more systematic and comprehensive approach to evaluating the effectiveness and efficiency of programs is needed. These observers note that all programs in public health may be viewed as collections of combinations of resources, activities and objectives to achieve desired results which are the objectives of program activities. Each objective implies one or more neces- sary conditions which give rise to that objective. Relating to this the concept of *effectiveness*, they observe:

> Programs may differ in their effectiveness; that is, in the extent to which pre-established objectives are attained as a result of activity. Effectiveness in attaining objectives is distinct from program appropriateness and adequacy.

These same observers proceed to define the program context of efficiency. Program efficiency, they observe, is defined:

. . . as the cost in resources of attaining objectives. The efficiency of a program may be unrelated to its effectiveness, adequacy, and appropriateness.[7]

These observers indicate the necessity of developing two other evaluative categories, namely, *appropriateness* and *adequacy*. Appropriateness responds to the need to relate the program objectives to a priority network of choices and values within the organization and within the program focus. Adequacy relates to whether the specific program activity will result in a complete solution of the problem or in a more modest reduction of the problem by a specific amount, or limiting the objective. As such, then, appropriateness, adequacy, effectiveness and efficiency within the context of a public organization, as applied to program action systems, become very helpful measures for management to use.

Organization system goals pertain to the purposes and desired conditions which the organization seeks as a distinct entity. Continuing existence, growth and stability are examples of organization goals. In contrast to this, a program action system focuses on desired values and results that characterize the inputs from the environment, which act as demands on the organization. It is possible to conceive, then, that a program action system could be linked into public organizational activity through MBO. This could render a more elaborate and explicit definition of the multiple goals characteristic both of the organization and the program. Interlinking both the program action system and the management by objectives, organizational activity would move from the strategic phase through a coordinative phase to the operational level, and the goals and the means for the accomplishment would become more specific, more short-range; consequently, more measurable.

The tendency for an organization to exist for its own sake tends to be reflected within the management by objectives context, but when related to program action it could more thoroughly relate to the goals and values required of the organization. The implementation and evaluation of these goals and values is the particular concern of the public manager.

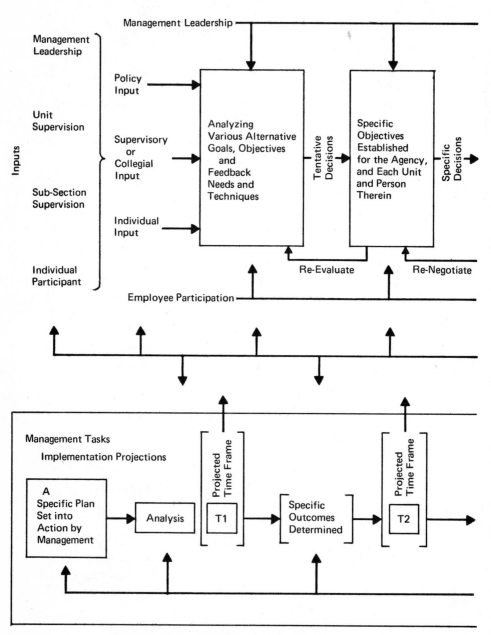

Figure 14-6. MANAGEMENT BY OBJECTIVES

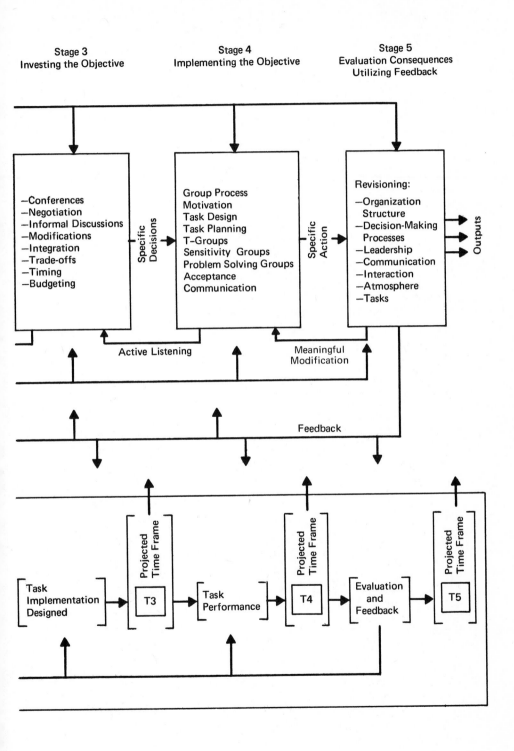

MANAGEMENT, TECHNOLOGY, AND HUMAN BEINGS

Another dimension of the organization which vitally concerns management is the link between the technological system and the human beings who function inside an organization. The manager today must deal with uncertainties and ambiguities. He must be concerned with adapting the organization to the new and changing requirements within the context of the environment. Management is a process which spans and links the various subsystems of the organization in order that the organizational mission be fulfilled. But more than that, the public manager must reach beyond his organization and participate in the policy process, a process which is dynamic, uncertain, ambiguous, in which the manager is not in full control but attempting to assess the nature of the problem to which effective response must be made. Thus management must not only be aware of the dynamic interplay of the technical, structural and psychosocial forces in the environment but within the dynamic context of the organization as well.

The organization is more than a social system. It is a social system which integrates human activities in relation to a variety of technologies. The technical system within an organization is determined by the task requirements of the organization and shaped by the nature of specialized knowledge and skills required, the types of machinery and equipment involved and the nature and variety of facilities available. The technical subsystems have major impacts on the structure of the organization, the quality of the human relationships and the kind of management response that is required. Any alteration of the technical system has a fundamental impact on the organization. Technology has the capacity to convert spontaneous and unreflective human behavior to stable, deliberate, controlled and routinized behavior. Jacques Ellul has observed:

> In our technological society, *technique* is the *totality of method rationally arrived at and having absolute efficiency* in *every* field of human activity.[8]

Technology and the urge to be efficient have come to dominate every field of human endeavor. Technology is used in translating the inputs into the organization into the outputs from the organization into the environment. This conversion process utilizes men and women adapted to machines supported by specialized technology. Computer systems are used not only for purposes of finance and accounting, but they can be adapted to record-keeping, information services, inventory information and a variety of other uses which require information storage.

Jacques Ellul suggests in his *Technological Society* that technology has become an end in and of itself which, if unabated and unconstrained by humane considerations, will become an engine that dominates the totality of society itself, negating the individual and permeating all aspects of life on the planet. He has stated his case most dramatically in a variety of ways. For example:

> What yet remains of private life must be forced into line by invisible techniques, which are also implacable because they are derived from personal convictions. Reintegration involves man's covert spiritual activities as well as his overt actions. Amusements, friendships, art—all must be compelled toward a new integration, thanks to which there is to be no more social maladjustment or neurosis. Man is to be smoothed out, like a pair of pants under a steam iron.[9]

The technical system within an organization can so dominate that the human beings become no more or no less than automated extensions of the machine. Yet it has sometimes released human beings in the organization to perform more creative and more humane activities. The interaction between the technical and psychosocial systems is an important reflection of the nature of technology within society itself.

The development of large organizations is closely tied to the emergence of industrial society and the accompanying technological changes. These large organizations that interlink vast complexes of specialized technological systems can produce astounding results. The successful placing of a man on the moon and subsequent space research required vast networks of human and technological interactions involving a great number of organizations interwoven in complex interdependent and supportive ways to successfully accomplish such a mission. These

541

immense technological organizations, public and private, are the primary users of the earth's resources and are creators of the technology utilized. They are, in fact, a social "machine" utilizing and developing the information and knowledge from science for their own purposes. Universities, of course, are a fundamental part of this process. Technology has transformed the infrastructure of the social and managerial systems within large-scale organization and has altered the goals of the industrial society itself. This is because of the capacity of these technological giants to deliver a seemingly increasingly safe, healthier and more comfortable quality of life for a tremendous number of human beings on the planet. By adapting and utilizing technology undergirded by science, large-scale organizations developed the means for growth and diversification and expanded their role in the whole of society. Large organizations implement these developments by absorbing into their operations highly trained scientists, professionals, technical personnel whose loyalty runs primarily to the organization in unquestioning devotion.

ORGANIZATIONAL TECHNOLOGY

Studying organizational technologies is a helpful way to understand the problems and differences which occur in a variety of organizations where technology is a significant concomitant.

Technology within an organization can range along the highly specialized, single action oriented assembly line to the most complex technological operation; i.e., it may range from a uniform and relatively simple technology such as craft production to a non-uniform, complex technology such as that utilized in a research laboratory of a university general hospital or aerospace complex.[10] Managers may use a mixed variety of these technologies for the accomplishment of organizational purposes.

Electronic Data Processing

Perhaps the most dramatic advance in technological contributions to organizational processes is the rapidly increasing utilization of computer and electronic data processing. Electronic data processing (EDP) is also known as automatic data processing (ADP). It is the application of the computer to the organizational context. It is a profoundly important addition to management science. Every state government has at least one computer and state governments alone, having integrated computers into their public services, spent in 1967 more than 107.5 million dollars for their utilization.

In 1967 the federal government utilized over 3,000 computers to accomplish the purposes of record keeping and information services. They are of great importance in operations research and are particularly useful to the Internal Revenue Service (IRS). Twenty-seven computers worth over 12 million dollars were utilized by the IRS in 1966. These computers did work that would ordinarily have taken 12,000 employees to do and, as a result of their precision, additional revenues were generated in excess of 27 million dollars; sixty-one million dollars in refunds were withheld to cover debts owed from back taxes and over 700,000 missing income tax returns were identified which, at that time, might have yielded an additional 156 million dollars in federal revenue. Skillful use of the computer identified over 19 million dollars in errors in arithmetic and identified 416,000 duplicate refund claims.[11]

There is a tendency in the adaptation of computers to the organizational context to strive for utopian perfection. Robert Boguslaw, in an important study entitled *The New Utopians*, examined the dangers. The earlier utopians embraced theories that created imaginary societies free from human imperfection. They populated these societies and their social systems with perfect human beings, a perfect social structure and perfect principles. They imposed goodness from without and thereby derived a good and perfect society. Their concern was on creating a good life focused primarily on filling stomachs. In contrast, Boguslaw has suggested:

New Utopians are concerned with non-people and with people-substitutes. Though planning is done with computer hardware, system procedures, functional analysis, and heuristics. . . . It begins with an acceptance of the status quo in such areas as the facts of our physical environment, human physiology, and the state or projected state of machine technology. It considers the requirements for food, shelter, reproduction, and recreation in the light of this status quo and proceeds to explain how human groups can and do adapt to the world in which they find themselves. The principles, empirical conclusions, theory, hypotheses, and notions that then appear are post hoc. The world of physical reality becomes the constant to which social theory must adapt. Social science becomes . . . a very conservative intellectual force. . . . [I]n a world of rapid changes in the technology and utilization [of] high-speed computers, this conservatism takes the form of a concern with the *consequences* that advances in automation will have for such things as family life, planet, juvenile delinquency, community organization, leisure, and educational practice.[12]

The social consequences of introducing automated equipment into a specific organizational setting may be very significant. Large social dislocations occur, ranging from mass unemployment to problems involved in returned workers whose skills are reduced to obsolescence by automatic equipment. These are among the first serious questions causing great social concern today. Questions concerning these kinds of problems rarely surface prior to the introduction of automation, because they are outside the social consciousness of the manager in the private sector, nor are they within the relevant purview of the manager in the public sector.

The public manager is woefully deficient in the kinds of long-range planning that is required to adapt technological components into the social system and respond to the consequences that flow from such an introduction. The introduction of machine systems into a social setting results in profound dislocation of human beings, unemployment and short- and long-run social problems which have not as yet been responded to effectively.

Boguslaw observes that the new technicians concerned with the introduction of these computer technologies into the social system are concerned neither for "souls nor stomachs." "People problems" are left as afterthoughts to be dealt with by those social scientists and public officials in other facets of the social system that are concerned when such social disruption occurs, e.g., the welfare worker, the policeman, the rehabilitation counselor. Boguslaw observes that these efforts simply parallel the social consequences and the really serious questions about the technological status quo are seldom, if ever, raised. He suggests in *The New Utopians*:

> System engineers and system designers characteristically address themselves to a quite different set of problems. Their concern is with "hardware," "equipment," and "equipment systems." Their task is characteristically pictured as the making of decisions involving alternate choices of equipment or the optimum use of equipment that has already been installed. Their tasks revolve about these choices. Their world is the world of automated equipment.[13]

Designing a System with an ADP Component

Boguslaw identifies four different approaches to systems design which managers may use. Each rests on differences in methodology and technique. Summarized, they are:

1. *The Formalist Approach*. The formalist approach uses explicit or implicit models. It rests on the basis of two models, replica and symbolic. Replica models are pictorial presentations and symbolic models are intangible. They use ideas, concepts and abstract symbols to represent objects. Arrows and symbols are used to represent flow and the nature of the information flow and are diagrammatic in form. These symbolize the major aspects of the system. Mathematical models are a subclass of these symbolic systems. In these models the system must be closed and formal and encounter no unpredictable, improbable situations.

2. *The Heuristic Approach*. The heuristic approach is open-ended and uses principles as guides to action. It is not bound by

preconceptions about systems or what the system will encounter. The guides to action are utilizable even in the face of completely unanticipated situations and in situations for which no formal model or analytic solution is presently available.

3. *The Operating Unit Approach.* This approach rests neither on models nor on selected principles. It begins rather with people or machines selected or modified to possess certain preconceived performance characteristics. As the system or organization ultimately unfolds it will reflect and incorporate the design that these units provide. One or the other may be flexible or inflexible, i.e., the machine may be flexible and the human component inflexible or the other way around. The system rests on a range of choices about how the operating components will be integrated.

The effectiveness of central control is reduced so that this particular model, as the others previously, poses the dilemma of freedom vs. control.

4. *The Ad Hoc Approach.* This approach "involves no models, no principles or operating units." It proceeds on the basis of a perceived here-and-now reality as the only constant. The designing begins with an analysis of the existing state of affairs. It varies under different conditions requiring different purposes. It may be adapted to a system where a future system is more or less clearly perceived by the designer. It is open, flexible and responsive to the ever-changing needs in a turbulent environment. This approach is responsive to simulation programs.[14]

In those areas where a computer is introduced the implications for management are significant. Low-skilled workers are virtually eliminated except for those in the service areas. The middle manager whose value consists of a kind of psychological "know-how" to get the job done within the context of specific bureaucracy gives way to the routinization of decision-making and information flow. The kind of data for which the middle manager was prized and the significant suggestions or implementation that were part of his skill and expertise can be identified more effectively by data analysis supplied through the computer memory bank. The analysis required can be speedy, more complete and more elaborate as prescribed by predetermined coherent analytical schemes.

Also, in those organizations where computers have been utilized the more highly skilled, psychologically demanding positions are those involved in adapting the computer to the organization itself as well as those involved in designing and formulating effective computer programs to meet organizational needs. This contributes to shaking foundations since previously safe "expertise" and "status" positions are often eliminated from the organization of hierarchy. Even though computer-related systems and program designs may have profound impacts in the organizational context, they cannot resolve problems of conflict, consensus and decision. These activities of management simply do not fade away. Environments and conditions change. The contradictions and conflicts which occur when people have different sets of values and ideologies, different role orientations and different group identity, nevertheless still occur within an organization and these human vagaries are an ever present part of organizational life.

Organizations with stable and routinized procedures tend to adapt computational approaches to their problems. Other organizations that are dynamic with more complex technical needs require a more innovative, reflective adaptation of the computer to decision-making processes. Organizations with a more routinized and stable technological infrastructure emphasize performance goals and accomplishment. Management by objectives would be more compatible with this kind of organization. Organizations with a more dynamic technology, however, tend to relate more to problem solving and program action.[15]

VALUES AND COMPUTERS

There exists a pervasive suspicion that computers will somehow dominate and control human beings and thus contribute to the continuing alienation that occurs within the organization. Management must, therefore, focus upon obtaining and maintaining humane values within the organization as technology becomes ever more a concomitant of the organizational life. Values are not scientifically, logically or intellectually derived. They are needs, vague sometimes, specific at others. They relate to physical needs and the psychological well-being of human beings. The process of identifying values which the public seeks to implement is a function of the policy process.

Computer-based systems become increasingly more significant in shaping contemporary society and, therefore, it becomes important to pursue the implications of the adaptation of the computer and technology to individual values. The major difficulty in accomplishing this and linking the computer into the process is a lack of clarity involved in the efforts to specify values in clear and exact terms. Value differences sometimes are just different perspectives of the same phenomenon. There may be honest differences of opinion about the most effective way to achieve mutually agreed upon goals. They also may reflect fundamental differences in primary orientations toward the world in which we live.

The tremendous tenacity of the value of efficiency has been previously noted. It is a concept which underpins our contemporary Western civilization. It is more efficient to ride in an automobile than to walk. It is more efficient to fly than to drive a car or take a bus or a train. It is more efficient to use a guided missile than a manned bomber. We can now destroy all of mankind efficiently! We have developed efficient ways to utilize the earth's resources, but at this point in time efficient utilization of the earth's resources promises to deplete them more rapidly. Although we may go faster and farther and arrive sooner, we may end the life support system on planet Earth. Consequently, what is efficient in one sense may be inefficient in another. Stated another way we need to become efficient in replenishing the earth's finite energy and resources as effectively as we utilize them so they will be continuously available to future generations. Human beings within the policy process provide choices and energize those choices through organizational commitment that will make the difference. Boguslaw concludes his insightful book with the observation that the computer's greatest threat "consists precisely in its potential as a means for extending control over man."[16] A humane technological system integrates men and women in the performance of tasks by identifying their needs, analyzing the tasks and designing jobs which take cognizance of human needs. Men and women must be related in a humane way to the machine. The design, development and implementation of the technical processes inside the organization must be responsive to humane values and the machines must be designed and modified accordingly, not *vice versa*.

MANAGEMENT PROCESSES AND ORGANIZATIONAL STRUCTURE

Much has already been said in this and other chapters on the nature of organizational structure where hierarchy is involved. Formal and informal organization has been noted. The arrangement of authority within hierarchy has been observed. The use of organization charts to obtain a simplified picture of the organization has been noted. Reference has been made to the traditional concepts of organizational structure which involve the scalar principle, the utilization of authority, responsibility and accountability which rest upon concepts of rights and duties, and the idea of span of control, the concepts of line and staff (staff persons providing knowledge and analysis and the line persons actually carrying out the organizational mission).

Perhaps an additional word is needed concerning the concept of differentiation as it concerns management. Differentiation within the context of an organization is the division of the organization into subsystems, i.e., departments and sections. Differentiation can occur, of course, along many functional lines, e.g., separating the legal, library and engineering activities into separate units.

There are two primary ways that differentiation occurs within the context of an organization. Hierarchy is established by vertical differentiation, i.e., there is a division of labor at a number of levels within the organization, and this reflects a different responsibility and authority. Thus vertical differentiation involves formal hierarchy, problems of coordination, supervision and commands. Earlier it was suggested that hierarchy involves authority, prestige and remuneration which diminish downward through hierarchy, or the other way around—it increases upward toward the apex of the pyramid. Horizontal differentiation or departmentalization occurs differently. It may be related to specialized functions, technical activities or geographical location. Those are the three primary ways that horizontal differentiation may occur. Figure 14-7 is a graphic of these observations.

Integration and linkage of a variety of activities, however, is not satisfied by the simple exigencies of hierarchical organization; other kinds of linkage are required. An integration of all organizational activities must occur. Operations Research and Organizational Development referred to earlier are part of the means utilized by management to integrate the human effort within the organization for the accomplishment of its purposes. Several ways are being developed and tried within the organization to accomplish such coordination and integration. One, for example, centers upon the establishment of a particular program with the designation of a principle program manager responsible for coordinating the diverse organizational activities to accomplish the objectives of a particular program. A program manager is responsible for organizing, negotiating and achieving all the activities required in accomplishing the ultimate objective of the program. He may be given full authority, but full authority is not enough. He must exercise influence and be effective through the use of his own personal abilities. Another example is the use of committees within an organization and across organizational lines to focus on policy and coordination problems. These may be formalized procedures established through a variety of organizational links.

Currently there is an immense thrust for a more flexible posture and away from rigid bureaucratic forms. Management goals are more and more to pursue adaptive, organic, less structured, flexible organization with temporary positions and roles, which allow more dynamic and equal interplay among functional parts and persons involved in the organization. This is in marked contrast to the permanent structure characteristic of more mechanistic organizational systems or the "permanent" semi-feudal system of a university. Warren G. Bennis, in his important book *Changing Organizations*, has observed that in the more flexible, dynamic organizations it is the function of the executive to become a coordinator or

"Linking pin" between various project groups. He must be a man who can speak the diverse languages of research and

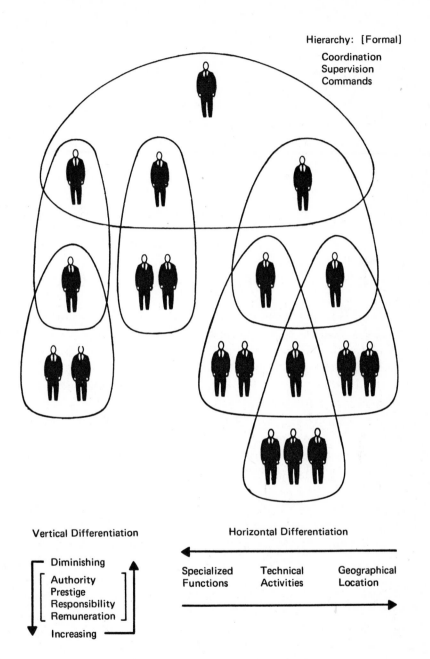

Figure 14-7. ORGANIZATION STRUCTURE:
LINKAGE FUNCTIONS

who can relay information and mediate among the groups. *People will be differentiated not vertically according to rank and role but flexibly according to skill and professional training.*[17]

Organization charts do not reflect the essential dynamics of the organization. The manager must provide the decision, supervision and evaluation which adapts the organization to the policy requirements and establishes goals for the organization to accomplish. It is the manager's responsibility to integrate the technical, administrative, budgetary and personnel support systems into a melange of service processes which accomplish the work of the organization.

THE MANAGER AND THE ORGANIZATION: A SUMMARY

Kast and Rosenzweig have a graphic which summarizes managerial tasks we have presented in this chapter. This is reproduced as Figure 14-8.[18] They note that a manager must be constantly concerned with maintaining a dynamic equilibrium which is responsive to the total system, concerned with external conditions and trends, aware of the internal subsystems, both the technical and psychosocial structure, their limitations and their strengths. The manager must develop objectives, strategies and tactics for the organization as a whole which include short-, medium- and long-range plans. The manager must be concerned with coordinating and organizing the technical substructures, task specialization, methods of coordinating, differentiation, integration and supervision. The manager must be concerned with information decision systems, operational research and organizational development, data retrieval and how to get effective coordinating and strategic decisions. The manager is further involved in the shaping of influence and the emergence of leadership as well as the reward and remuneration systems within the agency. The manager is concerned with the agency as a system which includes operations, feedback, management, development and organization analysis and research. The manager is a key actor in the design and accomplishment of the organizational mission.

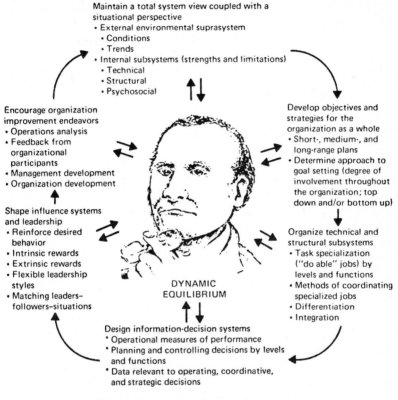

Maintain a total system view coupled with a
situational perspective
• External environmental suprasystem
  • Conditions
  • Trends
• Internal subsystems (strengths and limitations)
  • Technical
  • Structural
  • Psychosocial

Encourage organization
improvement endeavors
• Operations analysis
• Feedback from
  organizational
  participants
• Management development
• Organization development

Shape influence systems
and leadership
• Reinforce desired
  behavior
• Intrinsic rewards
• Extrinsic rewards
• Flexible leadership
  styles
• Matching leaders-
  followers–situations

Develop objectives and
strategies for the
organization as a whole
• Short-, medium-, and
  long-range plans
• Determine approach to
  goal setting (degree of
  involvement throughout
  the organization; top
  down and/or bottom up)

Organize technical and
structural subsystems
• Task specialization
  ("do able" jobs) by
  levels and functions
• Methods of coordinating
  specialized jobs
• Differentiation
• Integration

DYNAMIC
EQUILIBRIUM

Design information-decision systems
* Operational measures of performance
* Planning and controlling decisions by levels
  and functions
* Data relevant to operating, coordinative,
  and strategic decisions

SOURCE: Fremont E. Kast and James E. Rosenzweig,
Organization and Management: A Systems Approach, 2nd
ed., McGraw Hill, Inc., 1974, p. 516.

Figure 14-8. THE MANAGERIAL TASK

The material presented here generally reflects that organizations with concomitant authoritarian, supervisory practices are
dysfunctional to the accomplishment of agency mission because
they inhibit the commitment that the worker is able to make to
the organization. Effective management supervision requires
humane responses and leadership which ranges beyond the
narrow limits of authority rooted in the formal hierarchy.

The successful supervisor and manager has to do more than
maintain discipline and compliance with official orders, which
themselves may be antithetical to the accomplishment of the
desired effort. The manager must encourage subordinates to
exert effort and to assume responsibility and to exercise creative
initiative and make it possible for them to do so.

It is these abilities, the broader perspectives and interpersonal skills, that the manager must bring together to become an effective participant in the organizational process. The manager must do this in the public service through the decision, planning and budgetary processes that are a part of the context of the public agency.

NOTES

1. Daniel Katz and Robert L. Kahn, *The Social Psychology of Organizations*. New York: John Wiley and Sons, Inc., 1966, p. 33.

2. William L. Morrow, *Public Administration Politics and the Political System*. New York: Random House, 1975, pp. 70-72.

3. Alvin Toffler, *Future Shock*. New York: Random House, 1971, p. 2.

4. Herbert Simon, *Administrative Behavior* (2nd ed.). New York: Macmillan Co., 1959, p. 198.

5. James G. March and Herbert A. Simon, *Organizations*. New York: John Wiley and Sons, Inc., 1958, p. 82.

6. Paul Mali, *Managing by Objectives*. New York: John Wiley and Sons, Inc., 1972, p. 12.

7. O. Lynn Deniston, Irwin M. Rosenstock, William Welch, V. A. Getting, "Evaluation of Program Effectiveness and Program Efficiency," in Fremont J. Lyden and Ernest G. Miller, *Planning, Programming, Budgeting: A Systems Approach to Management*. Chicago, Ill.: Markham Publishing Co., 1972; this and the quote preceding are found in pp. 142-143.

8. Jacques Ellul, *The Technological Society*, translated by John Wilkinson. New York: Alfred A. Knopf, Inc., 1964, p. xxv.

9. *Ibid.*, p. 411.

10. James D. Thompson, *Organizations in Action*. New York: McGraw-Hill Book Company, 1967, pp. 15-19.

11. Frederich G. Withington, *The Real Computer: Its Influence, Uses, and Effects*. Reading, Mass.: Addison-Wesley, 1969.

12. Robert Boguslaw, *The New Utopians, a Study of System Design and Social Change*. Englewood Cliffs, N.J.: Prentice-Hall, 1965, pp. 2-3.

13. *Ibid.*, p. 4.

14. *Ibid.*, pp. 9-25 and 41-161.

15. Fremont E. Kast and James E. Rosenzweig, *Organization and Management, a Systems Approach*. New York: McGraw-Hill Book Company (2nd ed.), 1974, pp. 195–205.

16. Boguslaw, *op. cit.*, p. 204.

17. Warren G. Bennis, *Changing Organizations*. New York: McGraw-Hill Book Company, 1966, p. 12.

18. Kast and Rosenzweig, *op. cit.*, p. 516.

PART V

THE ADMINISTERED WORLD

15

DECISION,
PLANNING AND
BUDGET PROCESSES

The public manager is concerned with making decisions and evaluating the impact of those decisions. Policies, planning and program development decisions link the agency to its environment and overlay the dynamic organizational processes. The manager must translate the decisions made at the strategic organizational level into the middle range and operational levels. Finally, the manager, through the decision process, must coordinate the technical, administrative, budgetary and personnel support systems. In the pages which follow we will examine the relationships between the operative and strategic levels, and we will discuss how the manager uses those relationships to achieve coordination of the various support systems.

THE DECISION PROCESS

Strategic Level Decisions

Strategic decisions by upper management focus upon key issues and problems. Management must use agency information sources to identify and bring into focus the value framework, needs, demands and problems which are relevant to organizational activities. These information sources may be formal or informal meetings, conferences or a series of task forces that concentrate on particular concerns. Additional information may flow from legislative committee activity, legislative debates, legislative budget documents, as well as legislative enactments, including appropriations. Queries from legislators, complaints, requests for relevant information concerning legislative decisions, press and media commentary, advisory board discussions and decisions, consultant reports and feedback on agency activity in publications are all useful sources for information. Inputs from other governmental agencies and from the private and voluntary sectors also are important information sources providing data for the analytical process at the strategic level of management concern.

Strategic decision-making involves the identification of policies and programs that relate organizational performance to the information received. Value networks are considered within the strategic, analytical process, as are public interest factors, participant group attitudes, alternatives and options relevant to the fulfillment of organizational purposes. Liaison relationships with other agencies of the federal, state and local governments and legal requirements and constraints lie within the analytical processes at the strategic level.

The information sources supply the expectations and the hopes from the variety of groups and interests affected by organizational activity. Strategic analysis matches these expectations to capacities within the organization capable of fulfilling those expectations. This is followed by decisions about the specific strategies to be utilized in organizing these activities.

The strategies developed from such analysis rest upon the organization's capacity to maximize support, identify required programs and initiate program development. Budget estimates must be related realistically to the possible program alternatives. Program evaluation systems must be designed. Administrative operations and technical supports are identified. Careful attention is given to the timing of these interrelated processes.

When this mass of information is evaluated and the strategic decisions made, management concern moves to the middle ranges of the organization which are linked to the strategic level through information and supervision processes. The impact of strategic decisions at the middle-range and operational levels relates to the nature and quality of program impacts, results, supports and the nature of the interaction with the client system. These are important to the evaluation of strategic decisions. Important feedback for change and modification of decisions generate from this level. Figure 15-1 is a summary of these strategic decision concerns.

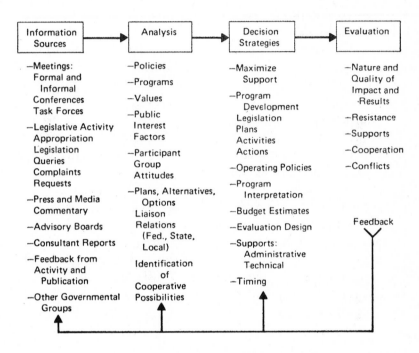

Figure 15-1. MANAGERIAL DECISIONS:
STRATEGIC LEVEL

Middle-Range Decisions

Middle-range decisions include the kinds of internal organizational consultation and supervision required for the implementation procedures necessary to carry out program design. These decisions must be responsive to the nature and quality of coordination required within the organization.

When narrowly conceived, the budget system involves the rate and levels of organizational expenditures, program costs

and projected costs required to sustain organizational performance. Once these are determined through the decision process,
the budget process is concerned with allocations and allotments.
The budget process relates useful data to the decision system to
discover whether the anticipations have been met. Data processing and computational analysis are often used here. The budget
is concerned with program financial obligation rates and financial
procedures and the providing at the operational level of fiscal
services which would include record keeping, accounts payable,
accounts receivable and payroll processing. The budgetary
decision process relates to program evaluation and analysis of
the costing methods used, evaluation of the computational
techniques and the expenditure controls used.

The personnel decision system identifies work force projections, personnel, staffing and training programs needed. Once
the program is operational the personnel management system
must involve linking the worker and the manager into a classification and compensation pattern and must be concerned with
recruitment and replacement as well. It also involves establishing
and operating promotion and supervision procedures. The
personnel decisions must be concerned with motivation, staffing,
training and performance evaluation. In the public sector this
function is often circumscribed by legislation involving civil
service, affirmative action and collective bargaining prescriptions
and prohibitions.

Operational Level Decisions

The technical, administrative and operational decision systems
range through program development, program operations and
program evaluation. Technical decision-making relates the
technology required in the particular organization to the program requirements, priorities and projections. The technical
decision system includes programming, scheduling, work performance and work evaluations. Program operations are evaluated by management and these evaluation decisions link back
into modifications of the technical program to more effectively
support the organizational processes.

The technical support system includes the professional and technical disciplines used within a variety of organizations. These include economics, law, forest technology, geology, biology, oceanography, astrophysics and other technical capabilities which may be utilized within an agency as it identifies a specific mission for which these resources and expertise are needed.

The administrative support decisions involve organization and management activities (O & M), i.e., budget and financial routines, organizational methods and personnel service functions. The administrative system supports and supplies administrative activity such as clerical supports, storage, messenger service, mail services and record maintenance which underpin the related program action systems.

The operations decision system is concerned with analyzing, projecting and supplying requirements in advance of program needs. It relates physical and space needs to program requirements and links in materiel and equipment needs to all other systems which require such support. Operations decisions relate also to production and delivery of services and materiel needs to both headquarters and field units and are usually subject to rigorous audit procedures.

Evaluation here consists of analyzing utilization, distribution, storage, scheduling and delivery services and requirements. These administrative services have a time phasing of their own and run through their own cycle of planning, programming and evaluation, which integrates generally with the overall organizational programs. Figure 15-2 is a summary graphic of managerial decisions as they relate to the technical, administrative and operational needs.

Decision-Flow Methodology

Managerial decision-making is broad-ranging and may include computational techniques, although these may apply primarily to a relatively narrow range of well-defined quantifiable problems at the middle and lower ranges of management. Nevertheless, it may generate important data which public management

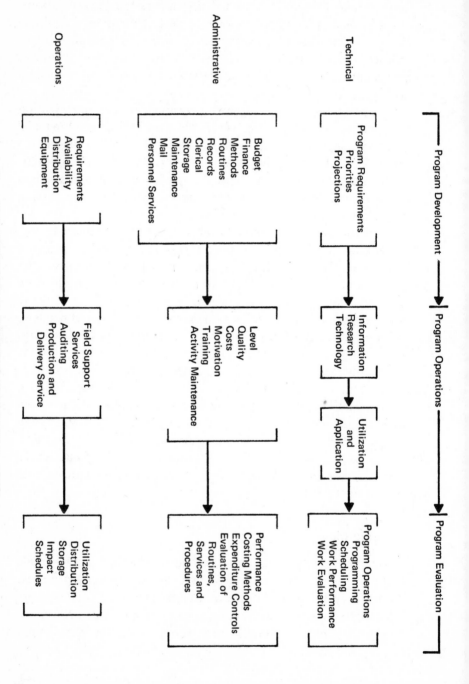

Figure 15-2. MANAGERIAL DECISIONS: OPERATIONAL LEVEL

can use at the strategic level. Problem solving in the strategic, operational, technical and administrative subsystems often involves mediation and compromise.

Psychological, social, political and philosophical considerations become important judgments in the context of decision-making. Value nets, both of the individual participants and the organization, are important concomitants of the decision process.

In a public organization the decision process is generally complex, especially at the strategic level. It may emphasize solutions which satisfy the overwhelming majority of participants rather than the best solution in light of all the considerations, for the "best" solution may sometimes be unacceptable to an important segment of a participant group. Figure 15-3 is a summary graphic of the over-all agency decision process. It is distinctive because it ranges beyond the organization and links into the organizational environment.

The cognitive components of decision-making are knowledge, information and analysis. The bahavioral components of decision-making involve a stimulus which evokes response, which, in turn, evokes a consequence. Lyden, Shipman and Wilkinson developed a working model which assumed that a public decision is an amalgam of a number of contributions, of which public values and attitudes are a part. The interaction pattern which involves the agency and its "publics" is not constant or unchanging. Rather, they suggest, it develops, evolves and changes shape and form over time. They suggest:

> One of the primary reasons why the public policy process has always appeared to be such a mystery to many people is this fluidity, this refusal to remain in the confines of the institutional structures designed to deal with public issues.[1]

They have suggested that a systematic way of representing this dynamic interaction is by identifying the nature of the processes through which the decision is reached. They suggest three major stages in the public decision process. The first they identify as a pre-decision stage, where there is the recognition of a problem and underlying predispositions concerning that problem. A particular event or condition may have precipitated the recognition of the need for a solution of the problem. It is initiated by a particular actor or persons in the environment where the problem is felt to be of significance. The second stage is the transaction stage between the persons concerned in the environment and the agency personnel responsive to those persons. At this stage alternatives are delineated and defined, information which is relevant is sought and analyzed, mechanisms for resolving the problem within the organizational context and through organizational activity are identified. These may involve budgets, contracts, executive orders and needed legislative action. The final aspect of the public decision process relates

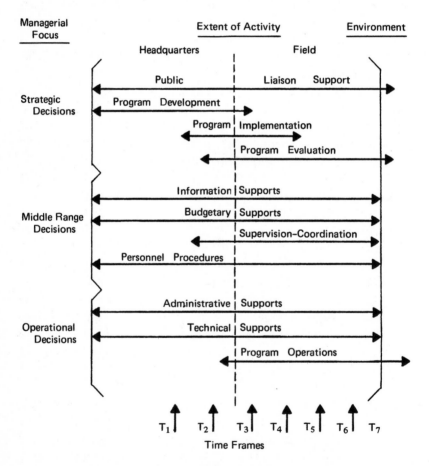

Figure 15-3. ORGANIZATIONAL DECISION CONTEXT

to the responses to the particular decisions taken, the way the decision impacts in the environment and how it is received.

They suggest beginning with an overt action which occurred within a specific decision chain and then organizing that process sequentially, identifying the overt actions in the order of their appearance. Each action may be analyzed individually by identifying the stimulus occasioning the reaction and then analyzing the reaction and the consequences resulting from the action in relation to the decision reached. Thus they suggest a decision-flow methodology which identifies a stimulus, which produces a response, which leads to a consequence, which itself becomes a response. Such a decision-flow is overlaid by a network of values, individual and social, and is vitally affected by the context of power involved in that decision process. A simplified example illustrates this approach. A group of persons within a small community seeks more tennis courts because of the long waiting lines and the inadequate number of courts presently available. They approach the park director with their request. The park director analyzes the information, reviews the conflicted value context (perhaps a municipal swimming pool would serve more of the public and be a more suitable expenditure for the limited funds available), and decides to submit a new proposal to the park commission for additional courts. The park director reports to the park commission, which analyzes the need and examines the variety of options available. They determine a course of action which provides for a variety of new courts in several areas of the city to be financed through new recreation bonds supported by a property tax referendum. This recommendation is forwarded to the mayor, who responds favorably, calls a meeting of the council and asks them to place the bond on the next ballot. The council meets and at that meeting representatives from recreation interests, the taxpayers association and business interests attend. These represent the various participant groups that reflect value concerns and power relationships within the community.

The council proceeds to a decision to place the bond issue on a forthcoming election ballot. Figure 15-4 is a summary of this suggested decision-flow methodology. The manager of a public agency dealing with problems at the strategic level could

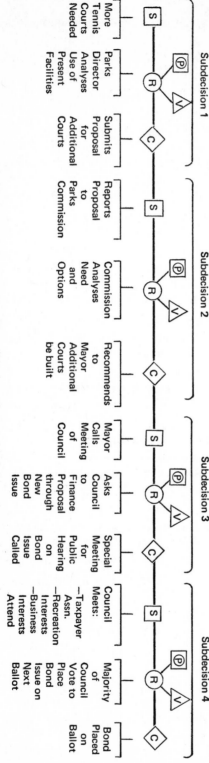

ADAPTED FROM: Fremont Lyden et. al., "Decision-Flow Analysis," in Lebreton, Comparative Administrative Theory, U. of Wash. Press, p. 161.

Figure 15–4. DECISION CHAIN METHODOLOGY

be much more specific and much more informed in relating organizational capabilities to environmental needs if this kind of decision-flow analysis were used. Lyden, Shipman and Wilkinson suggest this decision-flow methodology is developmental and encourage the continued development of more refined ways of studying the decision-making process in the policy-making field.

Computer-Assisted Decision Systems

Decisions at the strategic level tend to be different and unique each time they occur. Within the middle-range and operational decision levels, decisions are more repetitive and routine, reflecting a definite procedure worked out for handling them, including even the exceptional cases and the appeals and reviews from decisions already taken.

Decision-making inside an organization is susceptible to more precision and is now even programmed within the context of computational and computer technology. Such program decisions are amenable to decision-flow analysis. It is possible to introduce more precision routinization of organizational decisions. It is possible to implement an information decision system which is assisted by automatic data processing and computer programs. This would entail, first, the identification of the system design suitable for the particular organizational needs and would supply the kinds of information that the users need at the decision points to assist them in making their decision. A second phase in the implementation of a program such as this would be to translate the kind of data sought into the data processing techniques already available to the organization. Once these are designed and determined the third task is to implement such information systems through the organizational processes. A successful computer-assisted information decision system would require the persons who will use the system to specify the nature of the information needed and participate in the designation of the information flow process. Once that occurs the electronic data processing people can then respond to the kind of implementation required to fulfill such information needs.

Computer programming generally is centralized in most agencies for reasons of economy, because of the specialized skills and knowledge required to implement and conduct computer-related activities. When these information decision flow techniques are utilized to enhance the capacity of management to make decisions, quantification, computation and statistical decision theory become relevant skills and specializations within the organization. They relate to the flow of information, the quality of the decision and to the process of evaluating the potential outcomes of alternative courses of action.

One perspective on decision-making by management is that such a process needs to be systematic, logical and reasoned, i.e., *rational*. When considered from the perspective of the decision-maker and at the time of the decision, the choice within this context always seems rational because it moves the decision-maker toward his goal as he perceives it. Mathematical models are a fundamental part of the science of management and the relationship of management decision-making to problem solving. Yet computation and statistics alone are not enough. Values and power must always be in the conscious mind of the decision-maker. There can be no responsible decisions if this is not the case. The behavior of components and elements within the working environment as well as the organization infrastructure are vital concomitants of the decision-making process.

Decision Strategies

Thompson and Tuden have observed several types of decisions that occur within an organization. Each type of decision calls for a different strategy. They suggest these various strategies relate to a variety of organizational structures which facilitate those strategies.[2] They identify three strategies, to which two others may be added:

1. Decision by computation
2. Decision by majority rule
3. Decision by inspiration
4. Decision by consensus (our own)
5. Decision by individual judgement (our own)

Each of these may be supported by a requisite structure. Decision by computation can be programmed within the electronic data processing equipment. Decision by majority rule is utilized in a committee decision system. It is a structure of compromise. Decision by inspiration reflects a state of anomie, i.e., it is distinctive and unique, where no restraints or constraints exist for the decision maker. Decision by apparent consensus occurs within the structure of a small face-to-face group where no action is taken unless all are in agreement intellectually and emotionally with the course of action chosen. Finally, decision by individual judgment is related to bureaucratic command and authority and reflects an individual decision that may be made without reference to any particular source. Thus a dynamic and complex organization involves a range of outcomes in which a great variety of decision techniques may be found.

A number of persons involved in decisions within the organization may respond to the very same stimulus in a variety of ways, some perceiving it as a matter for computational analysis, others seeing it as a matter of judgment, still others suggesting that it needs to be facilitated through the bargaining structures available within the organization, and others still suggesting that it be responsive to the collegial decision procedures which may characterize the professional relationships within the organization. Thus there may be a number of decision strategies suggested within the same organization and related to the same problem.

Thompson and Tuden conclude their essay with the suggestion that:

> . . . for organizational decisions to be implemented effectively both consensus and choice are necessary. If for reasons of expediency, choice is made *before* consensus is achieved, the burden of achieving consensus *following* choice remains.[3]

Their use of consensus here applies to adapting a decision to become accepted within an organization by all who will be affected by it. Thus they see it as "needed" even if "persuasion" is required. We, however, see consensus as a possible decision process and separate from implementation and acceptance of a decision.

It is useful to think of inspirational decision strategy as akin to intuiting, feeling a way into a decision rather than being inspired by some "divine" revelation. Intuitive decision strategy in a *de novo* situation may be as valid as majority rule or computational decision strategy. Figure 15-5 is a summary graphic of the application of decision strategy to organizational information flow and decision flow. It focuses on problem identification, noting the substantive and value alternatives available and moves through announcing or communicating the results of the decision process. The subsequent context of the decision process may be summarized to include the identification of changes desired, focusing on the effects resulting and locating or identifying the causes that engendered the problem. This leads to an elaboration of the available possibilities, the assessment of the value net and the identification of the power context affecting the problem. A variety of decision strategies may impinge upon a problem. Finally, after the decision has been made, value priorities are identified. The power context is either altered, maintained or modified in some way and the course of action determined.

In summary, decision flow involves the accumulation of information, subjects this information to analysis and relates this to a variety of decision strategies. These decision strategies may involve command, judgment, decision by majority, intuitive judgment, computational programmed decision or consensual decisions. These are not available as effective decision patterns within an organization until those persons who are the decision-receivers as well as those persons who are the decision-makers arrive at a clear understanding concerning the decision. At that time it is a viable decision. Still the problem of determining a valid decision remains, for a valid decision must be responsive to the problem. This, in the long run, can only be determined by an ongoing evaluation process.

THE POWER CONTEXT

The growing recognition of the importance of power in administration encourages greater attention to the resources and sources of power that an organization may draw on for its supports. It has been easier to deal with power in its narrower hierarchical

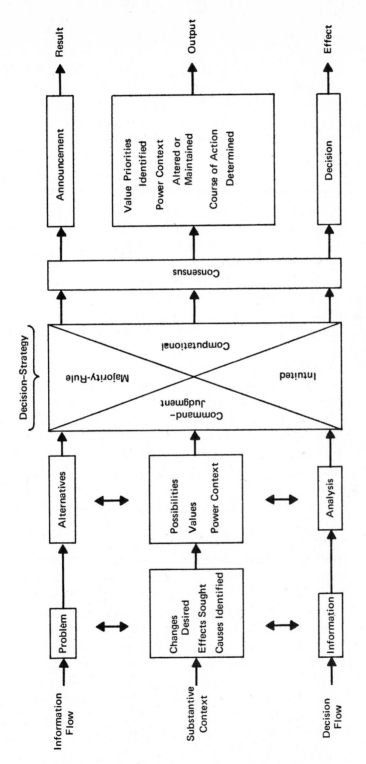

Figure 15-5. DECISION STRATEGY

content as a distribution of information, influence, income and prestige in diminishing amounts downward through a pyramidal structure. Study and research have been centered on the nature of power within a hierarchy as formal authority and also as an "informal flow" among the participants in the hierarchical process.[4]

The organization is viewed as a system for the conversion of social demands into social change by using human energy skills, physical resources and information. Agency leadership then must be concerned with the organizational mission and attentive to the power context in which it functions. The power context varies from agency to agency and relates to the unique characteristics of the jurisdiction in which it is set and from which it draws its resources. One useful way of examining organizational power is to examine organizational characteristics in the following eight categories:

1. The nature of executive leadership.
2. The fiscal and budgeting relationships.
3. The context of program activity.
4. The federal, legislative, judicial and clientele relationships.
5. Traditional, historical patterns.
6. The nature of the social system within the agency and the nature of the social system into which the agency is linked in its environment.
7. The nature of the personnel systems or patterns within the agency.
8. The nature of expertise available in the agency.

The nature and activities in each of these categories within a public organization may serve as resources of power on which the agency may draw to better effect its survival and its mission. Likewise, forces within these categories may also impede, diminish or inhibit the agency's capacity to survive and to perform its mission. The accumulation of power which can be drawn upon by an agency at any given moment varies through time but can be conceived as the *power configuration* of the agency. The forces which can be utilized by the agency to obtain desired ends or to defend against forces which threaten depends upon an accurate assessment of the resources of power by management.

Power tends to become institutionalized within the public organization. Agency subsystems develop entrenched program commitments which affect in fundamental ways the nature of the policy choices, expenditures, fiscal patterns and the taxation policies that affect the organization.

A study of Washington State government centering attention on the executive branch examined the relationship between the governor and a number of state agencies. It was observed that some state agencies were more autonomous and independent and other state agencies were more dependent and less autonomous in relation to the governor. An examination of these categories generated an understanding about the nature of power that could be utilized by participant agencies within a state executive system to more effectively control the definition of their own mission, to fend off interference from the legislature, the governor, or from the clientele or, alternatively, to create effective ties to the legislature, clientele and governor. They could also fend off one or the other of these and keep interference at a minimum. They could gain more autonomy over their operations and more control of their budget.

In the Washington State study the dilemma of the governor was perplexing. The governor is theoretically and often held publicly responsible for the exercise of effective leadership, yet he is often without adequate tools for such exercise because key agencies are able to fend off gubernatorial influence over key agency decisions concerning programs and budget. The Washington State Departments of Insurance, Education and Natural Resources have important ties with clientele groups, cooptive in nature, which created an interdependency and operated as an effective restraint and inhibition to gubernatorial interference. The Department of Highways had conclusive relationships that were close, formal and informal, with a joint interim legislative committee, and the Department of Employment Security had crucial ties and formal administrative and legal requirements imposed on it by the federal government. In all of these situations the relationships circumjacent to the agency, whether legislative, clientele or federal, were significant and determinative influences in fending off the governor's participation in their policy process. Likewise, they created dependencies with those circumjacent subsystem units. Where the agency head was a constitutionally established independently elected executive, this too, restrained the governor's access to the agency policy system.

In the case of the Insurance Department, Natural Resources Department and Education Department, a legally separate executive supported independence from the governor in developing a more autonomous organizational system. The existence of effective professional staff within an agency tended to lend high status to the agency and reinforce the capacity of the agency's executive to fend off threats and behave autonomously. This is because of the nature of information, technical expertise and knowledge to which the agency's top executive has access.

Within the state of Washington the nature of the budgetary process was an important determining factor in the relationship of these agencies to the governor and in their capacity to control their own programs more effectively and independently. Some agencies, such as the Insurance Department, the Department of Natural Resources, and the Education Department, obtained statutory exceptions from the governor's quarterly budgetary review. Consultation with the central budget agency, a significant part of the governor's management arm, was avoided. At the time of the study, the Department of Education, Department of Employment Security and the Department of Highways were not involved in significant consultation. In contrast, the Department of Natural Resources and the Department of Insurance involved significant cooperation and consultation in the preparation of the budget with the central budget agency.

The governor's control over man hours and allotments was considerably diluted as supervisory devices over agencies headed by independently elected officials and institutions of higher learning and was not important where the Department of Employment Security and the Highway Department were concerned.

In regard to biennial budgetary review, the Department of Natural Resources and the Department of Insurance were in some degrees subject to the governor's supervision. Education, Highways, and Employment Security always independently developed their own budget. The Employment Security budget heavily reflected federal requirements and was generally modified by rewriting the budget according to approved congressional and presidential directives.

Two agencies involving appointed executives, viz., the Department of Highways and Employment Security, although not specifically exempted from the budget and accounting act, nevertheless, in practice, were exempted from such supervision. Every agency either had or was in the process of developing significant dedicated funding which encouraged fiscal independence from gubernatorial supervision because the agencies related to this dedicated funding as if it "owned" such funding.

Two of the agencies, the Insurance Department and the Education Department, had strong traditions of autonomy, even though this implied strong ties with the clientele groups or legislative committees. It implied the existence of strong dependencies. This interfered with and inhibited the governor's capacity to exercise a stronger influence on strategic agency decisions. Figure 15-6 summarizes the relationship of these power resources to the five agencies on which the study centered attention. The study found that Washington State's executive system was an interlinked, operating and functioning arrangement of more or less autonomous subsystems. These autonomous subsystems performed activity designed to satisfy the needs of the clientele which they served and were calculated to make a difference in their operating environment. The power resources on which they drew assured some autonomy and self-sufficiency and operated to encourage the agencies' survival and growth. These agency subsystems were a definite part of the Washington executive, functioning according to regularized yet gradually changing patterns of interaction and interdependence. The executive function in the state of Washington was diffused among these more or less self-sufficient systems.

The governor, although the transcendent figure in the larger administrative system, was inhibited in a variety of ways from full control over these systems. He was able to gain access in times of crisis or extreme public need but quite remote from the more determinative, regularized policy-making processes which characterized the agencies' subsystems and their linkages with their environment. He had few administrative controls over these agencies and he was not able to effectively *manage* the totality of executive process. Thus power, responsibility and authority were diffused and divided throughout Washington State's executive system.[5]

The Power Dimension: Crucial Centrifugal Forces

FORCES

Agencies	1 Strong Circumjacent Ties	2 Legal Separation of Executive	3 Effective Professional Staff in Agency	4 Statutory Exception from Gov. Budgetary Quart. Review	5 Practiced Exception from Gov. Biennial Review	6 Significant Dedicated Funding	7 Strong Tradition of Autonomy in System
Insurance Department	XC	XC	X	X	X	XC	X
Employment Security......	XC		X			D	D
Natural Resources	XD	XC	XC	X	X	X	D
Education Department......	XC	XC	X	XC		X	X
Highway Department	XC	X	X		X	XC	D
	Supports independence from governor Creates dependency on tie	Supports independence from governor Restrains governor	Reciprocal relation of head and staff Reinforces executive independence High agency status	Restrains Governor Sustains fiscal independence	Restrains Governor Sustains fiscal independence	Guaranteed survival Fiscal independence Budget entire amount Distorts plural executive fiscal system	Restrains Governor Sustains independence and circumjacent ties

KEY: X—Force exists and is operative concerning agency.
C—Critical determinative force.
D—Developing but not yet mature and effective.

SOURCE: Robert H. Simmons, "The Washington State Plural Executive: An Initial Effort in Interaction Analysis," Western Political Quarterly, vol. XVIII, no. 2, part 1, June, 1965, p. 374.

Figure 15-6. THE WASHINGTON STATE EXECUTIVE SYSTEM

In each agency, management was vitally concerned with nuturing more autonomy and developing more power resources in order to advance the agency mission, goals and objectives and fend off interference from the governor, where the threats of budget reduction would most likely emanate. The agency heads were most attentive to the nature of power affecting the agency. The ties with various clientele, legislative or federal support groups, even though creating dependent and at the time cooptive, mutually supportive relationships, served to enhance their capacity to draw support and defend their agency programs when threatened. Each state differs, of course, from this pattern. In some states the governor has an item veto which considerably enhances his power. It can be observed from this study, however, that the nature of the power relationships within public jurisdiction is of considerable importance in understanding an agency decision process.

THE PLANNING PROCESS

Planning is a word which has been anathema to the public administrator; yet planning is essential if the conduct of the affairs of government are to proceed adequately, effectively and economically. What is planning? Robert Lee and Ronald Johnson suggest planning involves:

1. Emphasis upon rationality and choice selection.
2. Attention to goals and objectives of society and/or organizations.
3. Focus upon deriving means for the attainment of these goals and objectives.
4. Orientation toward the future.[6]

There is much confusion about the meaning and definition of planning. There are a great many varieties of plans, planning and planners. It can encompass long-use planning, project or capital planning, planning highways, urban renewal, weapon systems. It can involve urban and regional planning. When it involves land use it may be very narrow and center upon physical and economic considerations rather than overall social factors and values.

Economic planning is still another facet which focuses on guiding the national economy to achieve its full potential. In American society economic planning has been condemned as "socialistic" and an interference with the free marketplace, or even an attempt to gain authoritarian control over the lives of people.

Bertram Gross makes the case that we are emerging into a post-service society or civilization. We must, he suggests, "escape the icy grip of technocratic planning," and he firmly encourages the development of ". . . a humanist style of *learning through planning* and a theory of planning as widespread *social learning*." He suggests that this is a fundamental requirement if we are to "escape the new superhighways to post-industrial serfdom and begin to release the vast potentials for humanist reconstruction." The humanist yearnings, he suggests, cannot be vague nor incremental:

> Post-industrial humanism . . . does imply a certain measure of idealistic specificity. The new ideals of power, values, and rationality must be idealistic enough to cope with the survival and aspiration crises, with societal and personal fragmentation, with the erosion of authority. They must be specific enough to sustain a rising level of hope, confidence, and personal commitment.[7]

Planning is an essential tool in the transition from the service society to post-industrial humanism. Without planning we may well be overwhelmed by our own disarray and our incapacity, thus paralyzing us from "fronting up" to our survival needs. Benveniste suggests four varieties of planning: trivial, utopian, imperative and intentional. He suggests that the primary difference between the first two and the latter two are that the former simply legitimate the status quo and the latter are intended to shift the course of events. If we are to assure that *trend is not destiny*, social planning must be used and it must be of the kind, quality and variety that will enable us to move successfully into the post-industrial humanist society. Benveniste's classifications considerably help to assess the kind of planning which must be addressed and used.

Trivial Planning. This kind of planning does not alter present trends or respond to future uncertainty. It simply reinforces present activities, i.e., "it is more of the same." It is "window dressing," safe in form and threatening to no one. It may be a handsomely prepared document or statement of absolute trivia. It could be a program budget all dressed up but simply restating the old-line items in a new bottle. It could be a plan to respond to unemployment needs which simply extends benefits and takes half-measures to alleviate the basic causes. Nothing is done nor intended about the problem. Trivial planning tends to be associated with well-entrenched bureaucracies.

Utopian Planning. This is a set of visionary goals which no one expects to be achieved. No one takes them seriously and they are usually announced as "cure alls" to problems such as poverty, illiteracy and housing. They are simply "good intentions." They are plans for an event that will never happen. Yet utopian plans offer new perspectives and help to alter predominant values and build receptivity to planned future interventions.

Imperative Planning. This planning is done in a "command" economy. It is a plan wherein norms and goals are established and the means of production are managed in a comprehensive and coordinated manner. Incentives and disincentives are used and political and managerial authority are used to carry out the policy decisions to the level of control necessary to fulfill the planned production schedules. Imperative planning is both political and technical and is legitimized through the political and technical processes.

Intentional Planning. The implementation of the plan depends upon the intentional support of those committed to the plan. It requires strategies and tactics within the political sector to develop support. It may not be fully revealed to all involved and, in contrast to the imperative plan where the power is present to mandate the plan, the intentional plan must combine technical capability with political support. Benveniste suggests that it is rooted in the experts' capacity and abilities. Intentional planning may be utilized to reduce uncertainty in situations which are complex and involve a number of organizations or jurisdictions pursuing diverse and conflicting goals. It is an essential aspect of a program action system.[8]

Benveniste suggests that most planning contains all the elements of these four model types. Even in the most closed system political leadership cannot control or command the experts' actions all of the time. Generally, the planner and the expert are more or less free agents to encourage the adoption, rejection or modification of any plan. Certainly they are in a position to obstruct the implementation programs. Under such conditions the experts' goal is not to support or to find the best solution; rather it is to support and develop a plan which, both politically and technically, has a chance of being adopted and implemented.

PLANNING AND THE FRAGMENTED ADMINISTRATIVE SYSTEM

It has been suggested that planning is not possible in the American political system because power is dispersed among a variety of governmental sources already described. The reasoning goes that political power is dispersed and efforts at overall planning will always fail.

The opponents of planning indicate planning cannot occur in a dispersed governmental situation because centralization of power and authority is needed to implement the plan. Politicians generally are assumed to be opposed to planning because it imposes constraints on their powers to make decisions. Many administrators, too, oppose planning because it may move in the face of survival of the organization and require the dismantling of an organization or the posture of seeing an organization as temporary and subordinate to the purposes of achieving the program mission.

Planning, it is suggested by some, is destructive and stands in the way of achieving what the public wishes. Others see it only for dreamers and not suitable for practical affairs. These approaches see the public interest as multi-faceted and planning as an attempt to determine public priorities on the basis of a single hierarchy of values to be imposed upon all. Budget costs are seen as uncontrollable. The existence of the possibility of sudden crisis is said to fundamentally interfere with the capacity to develop long-range plans. Thus Lee and Johnson observe:

Decision making, then, is concentrated upon finding resources to meet these needs, with little available time or money for more deliberate planning.[9]

Even the maintenance of present programs becomes a frantic search which deliberate planning seemingly cannot avoid. Those opposing the possibility of long-range planning indicate that the ability of predicting the future is so limited and so vague that to determine plans around a future course of events is an exercise in unrealistic fantasy. This approach suggests that even if the problems of forecasting and causal relationships could be resolved, planning would be excessively burdensome for decision-makers. Yet planning is fundamental if public management is to face and solve the problems which confront them, develop the means of overcoming their complexity, identify social goals, relate the utilization of human and physical energy resources to overall socially desirable results and government is to be held accountable. It is no longer sufficient to just "muddle through," as Charles Lindblom suggests.[10]

The value net which commits energy resources for the accomplishment of human purpose must be articulated within a planning and program context underpinned by a budget system which encourages and assesses each commitment so that the problems identified and the qualitative results sought for human existence can be achieved. If this is done, planning is an essential ingredient in that task.

Thus if human energy and planetary resources are to be utilized efficiently, effectively, without waste and in a manner which preserves the possibility of their use for future generations, we must accept a utilization process responsive to planning and action programs which respond to specific planning and include effective evaluation of such a process. Such evaluation must be responsive to the values sought and the results actually achieved.

Management at the strategic levels of the organization interacting within the policy context of the organization is concerned with the planning effort as it relates to policy, programming and implementation of such policy and program. Planning involves an overall system of policy planning, programming, implementation and evaluation. Implementation and evaluation cannot occur without adequate measures being developed and derived at the planning stage.

Policy planning within an organization is concerned with:

1. The development of policy, including the identification of the values sought;

2. defining of purposes and objectives; and

3. the identification of resources required.

Implementation plans are concerned with the articulation of program action. Finally, when designing evaluation activities, the planners must be concerned with the values and objectives sought, the quality and nature of their impact, the utilization rate of resources, the environmental impact of the utilization of those resources, i.e., whether they are finite and exhaustible or replenishable and their relationship to the life cycle of the planet and the life support systems of the planet. Figure 15-7 is a summary graphic of the planning perspective.

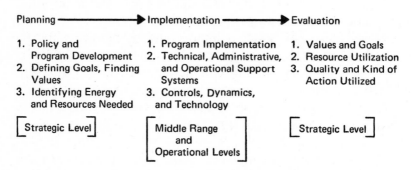

Figure 15-7. THE PLANNING PERSPECTIVE

The manager, through the planning staff, is in a position to identify the kind of governmental action required in designing a program and furthermore can relate the budgetary estimates realistically to the effort. According to Shipman there are three major forms of governmental action which are appropriate to a public organization. First, self-help, which is intended to provide public reinforcement for private action; two, coercive action employing publicly sanctioned force; and three, non-coercive action. Figure 15-8 indicates the major forms of governmental action, the sources of the standards which relate to their application and who initiates the kind of action that can obtain. In addition, Figure 15-8 indicates the administrative responsibility and activity which are relevant to each form of action. Judicial involvement, as well, is identified. Finally, the consequences which the particular form of action engenders are identified in Figure 15-8. Thus it provides a summary of the legitimate forms of governmental action which in some combination may be available for a public agency to use.

Planning, Program and Implementation

A future crisis, the utilization of natural resources, and a varity of other concerns pose a unique concern and a central responsibility on the stewardship of the public manager. It essentially rests upon management diagnostic and planning skills. A manager must be able to visualize the needs of the future, identify the key issues and problems which may arise, initiate timely and appropriate courses of action and identify alternatives which keep the risk of unpreparedness to a minimum. The essential tool for this is planning. The managers at the strategic levels of the organization are concerned with detecting the issues and problems which will arise in the future and developing an effort within the organization which is responsive to those issues and problems. Management is responsible for identifying available resources and contingencies that may change the course of action designated. Management must prepare for these contingencies long enough in advance to allow the necessary time to prepare, to maneuver and to act. Accurate information, effective analysis and resourceful understanding are required guides for the contemplated steps into the future. Charles M. Mottley suggests:

> The specialized branch of the planning activity which is concerned with anticipating events, making diagnoses and shaping appropriate courses of action, so that an organization can be in the best position, ready and capable, to respond effectively to contingencies, is called *strategic planning*.[11]

Form	Source of Standard	Initiation
I. *Self-help.* Civil action.	Statutes, customary and case law.	By aggrieved party.
II. *Coercive; A. Non-determinative.* Criminal law enforcement.	Criminal law. Failure to obey an administrative order often an offense.	Law enforcement agency.
B. Determinative.	Conclusive administrative action (note A).	
1. Prior Restraint. Specific privilege authorized.	Specific exemption from general prohibition.	Applicant for license or permit.
2. Corrective Intervention. Persons ordered to "cease and desist."	Statutory provisions forbid certain practices.	By administering agency; complaint alleges illegal practices.
III. *Non-Coercive.* No restraints or penalties imposed. Services or other supports provided (note B).		
A. Service. Generally available, no specific charges or eligibility standards applied.	Statutory standard authorizes objective. Substantial administrative discretion.	In the administering agency.
B. Assistance. Money grants or other benefits.	Statutes specify objectives, basis of eligibility and nature of benefits. Substantial administrative discretion.	Eligible persons apply.
C. Proprietary. Activity conducted on a self-supporting basis.	Statutes authorize the activity and specify general methods of operation.	In the administering agency.

A. Determinative administrative action means that the action process is complete at the administrative level although judicial proceedings may be used to obtain compliance.

SOURCE: *Adapted from "Public Policy Issues Raised by Weather Modification:" A Strategy for Governmental Involvement," in W. R. Derrick Sewell, ed., Human Dimensions of Weather Modification, Research Paper No. 105, Univ. of Chicago, Dept. of Geography, 1966, pp. 289–303.*

Figure 15–8. MAJOR FORMS OF GOVERNMENTAL ACTION

Administration	Judiciary	Consequences
Rarely involved.	Determination of rights of parties.	Resolution of immediate issue; legal precedent.
Customary "enforcement level." No formal adjudication; investigation and prosecution.	Determination of degree of guilt.	Upon conviction assessment of penalty.
Rule-making controlling applicants and licensees; determination of eligibility of applicants, discipline of licensees; investigation	Mainly judicial review of discipline.	Authorization to exercise privilege.
Rule-making interprets statues. Policy sets "enforcement level." Formal adjudication. Research, investigation, prosecution, supervision of violators.	Judicial review applies to procedure and interpretation of law. Also to compel compliance.	Persons may carry on regulated activity subject to "cease and desist" order.
Agency sets quality level and activity rate on basis of need and feasibility. Operates the activity.	Rarely involved except for public liability and eminent domain.	Service provided to meet a defined need.
Agency sets eligibility standards and level of entitlement. Adjudication rare. Operates the activity.	Rarely involved except for special statutory remedies.	Specific support or assistance provided.
Agency determines specifics of service. Operates the activity.	Rarely involved except for public liability and eminent domain.	Specific service provided for purchase by consuming public.

B. Policy results are obtained by direct action rather than by regulation or restraint. However, regulation may be used to protect against fraud, etc. but such remedies only protect against abuse. All non-coercive action is determinative.

Mottley suggests that policy is an essential agreement with regard to the objectives of action and the ways and means of achieving those objectives. It implies, he suggests, "an accurate diagnosis of the needs of future situations, a definition of the issues involved, a capability to act, the will to act, and timeliness of the action."[12] Figure 15-9 shows schematically the organizational strategic planning concepts suggested by Mottley.

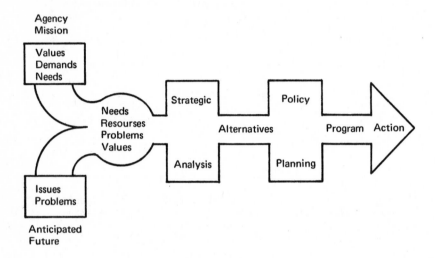

Figure 15-9. STRATEGIC PLANNING WITHIN AN ORGANIZATION

LeBreton suggests a day in the life of an organization never passes where there is not a need for the participants within management to be accurately concerned with some phase of planning and suggests that the problems and opportunities may vary across the lines and levels of responsibilities within the organization.

He suggests a planning-implementation process which involves fourteen steps.[13] LeBreton's implementation model is summarized in Figure 15-10.

Drawing upon LeBreton and Mottley, it can be suggested that strategic planning involves analytical considerations focusing on the suitability, feasibility and acceptability of possible courses of action.

PLANNING-IMPLEMENTATION MODEL

The Modified process or planning-implementation model has three significant components:
1. The planning-implementation process,
2. Dimensions,
3. The relationship of dimensions to the planning-implementation process.

PLANNING PROCESS

1. Becoming aware of a possible need for formulating a plan
2. Formulating a precise statement of the objective of the plan to be prepared
3. Preparing a broad outline of the proposal or plan
4. Obtaining approval of the proposal
5. Organizing planning staff and assigning responsibility
6. Determining the specific outline of the plan
7. Establishing contact with all cooperating units
8. Obtaining necessary data
9. Evaluating data
10. Formulating tentative conclusions and preparing tentative plans
11. Testing components of tentative plans and making adjustments where appropriate
12. Preparing the final plan
13. Testing the plan and making adjustments where necessary
14. Submitting plan for approval

IMPLEMENTATION PROCESS

1. Receipt of approved plan
2. Obtaining an understanding of the technical components of the plan
3. Interpretation of ramifications of plans
4. Determination of role of implementor
5. Organizing implementation staff and assigning responsibility
6. Preparation of an implementation plan
7. Taking action and making necessary commitments
8. Notifying organization members of the new program
9. Interpretation of operational plans to subordinates
10. Instruction of subordinates in their control assignments
11. Gathering data on progress of plan
12. Review and evaluation of plan
13. Taking corrective action when necessary
14. Report of progress to authorized personnel

ADAPTED FROM: LeBreton, Comparative Administrative Theory, Seattle, University of Washington, 1968. p. 169-173.

Figure 15-10. A PLANNING-IMPLEMENTATION MODEL

Suitability. Suitability analysis identifies possible alternatives and choices of action which will be in accord with established policy guidelines. Mission responsibilities, assumptions and applicable criteria which aid in determining suitable or unsuitable courses of action must be identified. Most courses of action that remain after being sifted at this stage would then move on to analysis which focuses on feasibility.

589

Feasibility. Feasibility studies center on appraising the effects of a number of vital factors. These include application of required standards, the relationship of the potential courses of action to the conditions in the environment, the restrictions imposed by the technological constraints, limitations on alternative courses of action through such things as funding, facilities, skills and capabilities. The courses of action which remain from this stage would then move on to studies which center on their acceptability.

Acceptability. Those courses of action which have been sifted and judged to be suitable and feasible are then subjected to analytical evaluations which provide the basis for defining acceptable courses of action. At this stage, too, the nature of the organizational social system into which the action alternatives will impact also need to be assessed and analyzed. Inappropriate alternatives would be discarded and set aside and a judgement made as to the acceptable alternatives to be utilized and implemented.

Strategic planning provides conceptual access into possible future situations. It encourages the application of social concerns about the future to discern what may be encountered on the way to the desired goals. Varieties and techniques of mission analysis and strategic analysis provide important insights and foresights which are applicable to the planning process. The kinds of decisions which grow out of a systematic identification of the issues, definitions and selection of alternatives and the evaluation of alternatives is a helpful way to meet the strategic planning needs of management.[14]

Strategic planning focuses on diagnosing the nature and character of the demands, problems and needs presented through the policy process. It is concerned with delineating problem causes, specifying the issues and formulating a program or series of programs which are responsive to the situation as diagnosed and delineated. Strategic analysis leads to an examination and elimination of proposals which are inappropriate by examining their suitability, feasibility and acceptability. Possible programs of action which are found suitable, feasible and acceptable are retained as policy options for management choice. Figure 15-11 is illustrative of this process.

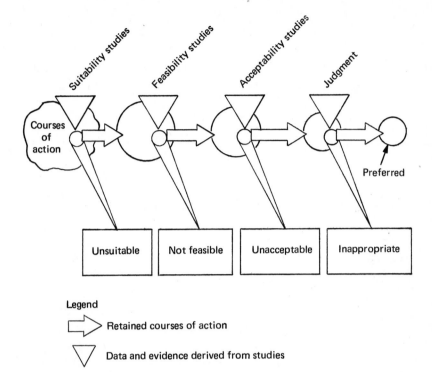

Legend

⇨ Retained courses of action

▽ Data and evidence derived from studies

◯ Sorting gate controlled by selection criteria

SOURCE: Charles M. Mottley, "Strategic Planning" in
Fremont J. Lyden and Ernest G. Miller (editors) Planning,
Programming, Budgeting: A Systems Approach to Management, Chicago, Markham Publishing Co., 1972, reprinted
from Management Highlights, release No. 56, Office of
Management Research, U.S. Dept. of the Interior, (Sept.
1967) by permission of the author, p. 135.

Figure 15-11. THE SELECTION PROCESS FOR DERIVING
A PREFERRED COURSE OF ACTION.

Once the management decision is reached and the program
or series of programs is to be implemented, the plan moves to
the development stage, where it is translated into specific
objectives and there the operational ways and means of implementing the program are developed. This strategic policy planning process designates a preferred plan and supportive program actions which are responsive to the needs, demands and

problems faced by the agency and forms the basis of program and budget planning.

A plan, then, is a predetermined course of action taken after careful analysis. It is comprehensive and established at the strategic level, which provides a framework for decision-making and action at other levels in the organization and within the subsystems of the overall operations. Managerial planning provides a framework for political decision-making across a diverse collectivity of activities over a relatively long period of time. It is an effective means of coping with the uncertainty of the future and the temporariness of the present. It facilitates creative innovation and adaptation. The essential link between planning, action and control is the budgetary process.

THE BUDGETING PROCESS

Budgeting links the financial resources of a public jurisdiction to human energy and physical resources in a coordinated effort to accomplish policy objectives. Systematic budgeting did not begin to enter the literature of bureaucracy and administration until the late nineteenth century, with the emergence of large, complex, technological government. Paradoxically, it was state and local government in the United States which preceded the federal government in establishing systematic budgetary practices. No formal executive budget was established until 1921. Since that time the federal government has led in developing budgeting systems. A budget, in modern administration today, is at the heart of the administrative process. The budget process is to the public manager what profit maximization is to the manager in the private sector.

The budget is a document containing words and figures which propose specific expenditures for particular items related to designated purposes. Generally, the words describe the item and expenditure, such as salary, equipment and travel. This may then be linked into purposes such as improving mental health, juvenile delinquency control or public education, and the figures are attached to each item in the budget. There is an assumption of a direct connection between what is written and what will unfold in the future. The budget in this sense is an articulation

592

of intended future behavior. Wildavsky observes that where funds are limited a division must be made and the budget often becomes the process for making such choices among a variety of alternatives. In this sense it is a political process. Wildavsky notes:

> Although the language of a budget calls for the achievement of certain goals through planned expenditures, investigation may reveal that no funds have been spent for these purposes, that no money has been used for other purposes, that quite different goals have been achieved, or that the same goals have been gained in different ways.[15]

Wildavsky observes that a budget is a web of social and legal relationships in which commitments and trade-offs are made by all concerned and where a variety of sanctions may be invoked. The budget is a network of communication in which information is generated and fed back to participants. Once a budget is enacted it becomes a precedent which is a powerful force for the continuation of specific kinds of activity and increases the probability that the activitiy will be continued. Thus Wildavsky states that a budget is "unequivocally . . . an expectation, an aspiration, a strategy, a communications network, [and] a precedent."[16]

THE VARIETY OF BUDGETS USED IN THE UNITED STATES

Line-item budgeting was established roughly between 1915 and 1935, when the federal system was established under the procedures of the Budget and Accounting Act of 1921, which established the Bureau of the Budget and the General Accounting Office as congressional checks on federal expenditures. The emphasis was on the basis of control and review of expenditures. It reflected the scientific management's school of thought and emphasized honesty, efficiency and inflexibility.

Performance budgeting came into existence roughly between 1935 and 1960. With the rapid increase in federal spending that occurred in the post-Depression years and responsive to the income tax law passed in 1913, the President's Committee on Administrative Management recommended in 1937 that the Bureau of the Budget change its orientation from control and review to utilizing the budget as a management tool.

The growing prominence of management concepts within public administration became known during this period as "Operations and Management" (O & M). In 1949 the Hoover Commission recommended that the entire budgetary concept of the federal government be refashioned into a budget based upon functions, activities and projects. The commission suggested that it be designated a "Performance Budget." Actually from 1939 through 1946, under the leadership of BOB Director Harold D. Smith, the federal government had actually been practicing performance budgeting. The Hoover Commission underlined the inadequacy of line-item budgeting, and their recommendations became law with amendments to the National Security Act of 1949 and the Budget and Accounting Procedures Act of 1950.[17]

Line-Item Budgeting

Line-item budgets have several key features. First, the budgetary division is listed by organization unit, i.e., department or agency, and under this the type of expenditures by category, i.e., salaries, purchases, supplies. The purpose of this budget, as indicated before, is expenditure control and the safeguarding of funds for use. It focuses on the concept of a balanced budget and regular review of expenditure activities. The primary disadvantage of a line-item budget is that it emphasizes the increase or decrease of expenditures rather than focusing on the problem of relating administrative effort to public policy goals. Once an expenditure program is established in a line-item budget, there is little examination of the policy and goals and much examination of expenditure patterns.

There is no effective link between the line-item budget and governmental objectives, nor is it possible to relate actual expenditures to the accomplishment or output of governmental activity. It funds activities that have developed through time and does not encourage questioning concerning these activities and their relationship to overall public policy values. Activities are easily concealed and interdepartmental comparisons and reorganizations are generally impossible. Duplication of effort may be present and remain undetected because the control focuses on expenditures rather than planning and evaluation.

The line-item budget controls the maximization of funds by each administrator and therefore encourages destructive competition among agency heads for the scarce funds available. Each department prepares its own budget requests and comprehensive budgeting is well nigh impossible. Interdepartmental collaboration is thereby discouraged and coordination rendered ineffective.

Performance Budgeting

Performance budgeting, sometimes called the Program Budget, is concerned with inputs and outputs. Budget analysis and budget officers within agencies found their concern focused upon control and precision accounting rather than on the development of performance activity within an agency's program. The emphasis was on work-cost measurements and a variety of these devices was explored. Under the performance budget, administrative and managerial skills tended to dominate administrative decision-making, in contrast to line-item budgeting, where accounting and finance took precedence within the context of organizational decision-making. Management's concern was directed away from how many typewriters and paper clips were purchased and attention was focused upon the efficiency with which an activity was being accomplished. The central questions of whether there was a need for the activity and how that activity might relate to overall governmental goals were ignored. The primary goal of the performance budget was, in a word, efficiency. The maintenance of efficiency and economy in government was the primary focus and not whether that government effectively responded to public need.

Planning-Programming-Budgeting Systems (PPBS)

Performance budgeting represented an important advance in budgetary theory. Yet its emphasis upon performance ignored the overall commitment of governmental resources to the accomplishment of desired values and the articulated needs and demands. Significant strides in performance measurement were made, but it related little to how funds should be allocated, to what programs and for what reason. In addition, performance budgeting became subjected to effective administrative and legislative power maneuvers. The emphasis upon efficient performance impeded effective public planning at a time when vast special problems were beginning to emerge to which effective long-range policy responses were needed. Performance budgeting tended to increase incrementally the costs of an agency's program. The central question, "Why is this program needed?" rarely got asked. In performance budgeting as in line-item budgeting, once the program was established it was only a matter as to what level it would be funded. These kinds of concerns eventually encouraged the development of new concepts in budgeting.[18]

Bell Telephone Laboratories and General Motors began as early as the 1920's to integrate systems analysis and program budgeting. Yet it remained, for the Rand Corporation, in the post-World War II years, to articulate a distinctive advance in the budgetary process that would relate evaluation and control to long-range planning. Although the Rand concern related to weapons system analysis, it has in the decades of the 1960's and 1970's been adapted into long-range civilian programs at all levels of government.

The Rand program, articulated in 1960, came to the attention of the Kennedy administration, which implemented it in the Department of Defense in 1961 under the direction of Robert McNamara.[19] The DOD was fraught with cutthroat competition among the services. Each vying for control over a particular weapons system, each viewed its own particular program as essential to defense. There was no overall coordinated policy view, no relating of the defensive potential of the U.S. to the programs of intricate nuclear war.

PPBS was introduced into the defense establishment in an attempt to get overall coordination of defense policy and effective linking of the efforts of the various services. PPBS worked so well for the Department of Defense that it was adopted in all federal departments in 1965 by President Lyndon B. Johnson. By 1967 the Bureau of the Budget had implemented the use of PPBS in twenty-one agencies and looked toward its implementation in many others.

In 1970, under the Nixon administration, the Bureau of the Budget was retitled Office of Management and Budget (OMB), which emphasized a new managerial orientation. Efficiency and effectiveness were emphasized. Overall planning under this concept tended to fade and many programs that linked public need to operational programs were retrenched or phased out totally. In addition, increased layers of authority between budgeters and policy-makers occurred.

In 1971 the OMB issued a memorandum to all agencies indicating that they were no longer required to submit a budget under the multi-year program or to submit financing plans, program memoranda and analytical studies and schedules. Information classified according to program and appropriation was no longer required by the agencies. The goal of the Nixon administration was to limit PPB considerably. Concern with social needs and planning faded and efficiency moved to the center of primary concern again, this time in the guise of management by objectives (MBO).

A CLOSER LOOK AT PROGRAM BUDGETING

It is probably premature to lay PPBS to rest because governmental operations at all levels are becoming exceedingly complex and difficult to describe and understand satisfactorily. Mayor Pete Wilson of San Diego, California, feels that San Diego has saved multi-millions of dollars annually and has developed a program budgeting system which provides a ". . . backbone on which to build an organized and systematic means of implementing stated objectives. The budgetary process should be involved with more than historically allocating the revenue pie from year to year. . . ." Mayor Wilson is very supportive of the adaptation of program budget and budget analysis to the budgeting process of San Diego.[20]

Program, i.e., governmental, outputs must more effectively meet public demands. The electorate is becoming ever more sensitive as to who, how and where public tax dollars are spent. Government programs must be stated and justified effectively and convincingly and output options related to effective program criteria. Program evaluation and priority ranking must be effective as well as efficient. In the public sector the decision, planning and budget processes are intimately and intricately interrelated. In contrast to the private sector, the public manager must be constantly attentive to the public values which are being implemented. The whole development of program action systems, advanced particularly by Shipman, grows out of the primary concern with the implementation of programs to effect the delivery of essential public values as determined by the policy process.

Considerations of efficiency must relate primarily to the accomplishment of those program efforts which fulfill those desirable values. In the private sector, on the other hand, the concept of efficiency is primarily related to profit maximization and, therefore, is more narrowly conceived. Effectiveness is a more useful and helpful concept. Public managers need to hesitate before they tortuously apply concepts of efficiency borrowed from the private sector without fully subjecting them to humane criteria and measures which modify the harshness which would otherwise overlay such adaptation. Figure 15-12 shows the policy decision areas, the corresponding type of budget and the administrative information and action sources which support a variety of governmental budgets and the policy decisions to which those budgets relate.

The emerging nature of the governmental budgeting process renders obsolete the incremental approach to budgeting. Doing what we have done before and adjusting it to inflationary and deflationary trends would give way in the Shipman schema to relating effective public policy-planning decisions to appropriate support budgets and program action systems which will considerably encourage more effective relationships between the goals

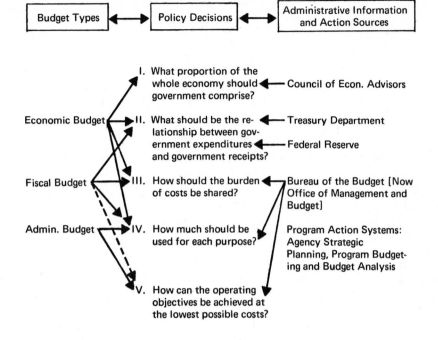

| Budget Types | ⟷ | Policy Decisions | ⟷ | Administrative Information and Action Sources |

I. What proportion of the whole economy should government comprise? ◄─── Council of Econ. Advisors

Economic Budget

II. What should be the relationship between government expenditures and government receipts? ◄─── Treasury Department
◄─── Federal Reserve

Fiscal Budget

III. How should the burden of costs be shared? ◄─── Bureau of the Budget [Now Office of Management and Budget]

Admin. Budget

IV. How much should be used for each purpose? ── Program Action Systems: Agency Strategic Planning, Program Budgeting and Budget Analysis

V. How can the operating objectives be achieved at the lowest possible costs?

SOURCE: Unpublished biographical sketch of George A. Shipman by Fremont J. Lyden. Univ. of Washington School of Public Affairs.

Figure 15-12. SHIPMAN'S POLICY–BUDGET–ACTION LINKAGE FORMAT

sought within the polity and the output activities delivered by public agencies.

The implications of this three-fold budgetary model are only now beginning to be researched and considered by scholars and practitioners in their efforts to develop effective "cross-walks" and "matrices" as a way of linking public intention to administrative activity in a comprehensive manner.

The key building block in this process is the program budget. This budget system is a systematic method of linking long-range planning with multi-year budgeting systems and more effective evaluation. It rests on defining public needs, establishing action programs with objectives responding to those needs and developing and implementing programs by the most effective and efficient means available.

Some Advantages of PPBS

Budget Analysis. The accumulation of the program budget documents within a particular jurisdiction makes possible the *budget analysis.* Budget analysis focuses on the allocations within the program budget through an evaluation of the programs made independently from departmental and agency as well as executive controls and reviews. A broad and effective data base underpinning program budgeting is required, not only to enhance the capacity of management to better coordinate and effect their own programs, but department and agency management need information and facts to justify requests for funds which underpin the agency programs, operations and existence.

Program deficiencies and areas where improved performance can occur may be identified with the vastly improved information data base. Computer data processing is an essential requirement within the context of the program budget. The computer is able to sort and arrange the tremendous volumes of data not only economically but in a fashion which is readable and systematic in an almost instantaneous manner. Accounting within this context becomes more than a bookkeeping and storage function. It becomes an important information resource for program management.

The county of San Diego uses the Accounting and Resources Management System (ARMS). This is a computer application which integrates financial data, personnel and equipment utilization, work load statistics and other vital data into one system for improved financial management. The inputs are sorted, classified and stored in the appropriate memory location in the computer. The impact of each transaction within the jurisdiction is updated concurrently and the system provides meaningful output data while immensely reducing the number of man hours required to provide these data. Electronic data processing can underpin in a very helpful way the requirement for increased data which is inherent in the program budget process.

One general by-product in utilizing program budgeting is the reorganization of administrative units within a jurisdiction along more functional lines. Combined with such reorganization management planners and legislative bodies are better able to link priorities into the operating program areas, and management improvement programs which increase effectiveness and coordination also are achieved. Capital improvements are integrated into the operating budget, which enhances long-range planning capabilities of those jurisdictions utilizing program budgeting by linking expenditures directly to the operational requirements which utilize capital improvement. Within the framework of a program budget, management programs can be introduced to improve the level of service provided, enhance management's capabilities to effectively meet program needs and stimulate a desire to provide better service.

Program budgeting and program analysis underpin effective administrative decision-making. They enhance and specify the issue. They relate annual review of the program context to long-range planned goals within the jurisdiction. They provide more information, encourage more objective decision-making, allow priorities to be set among competing alternatives more effectively, make evaluation easier and provide for the layman more understandable and comprehensible information about public expenditures.

The program budget formula includes references on operating expenditures for the past fiscal year, the current expenditures and the projected expenditures for the oncoming fiscal year. It provides systems information for an annual review of programs and links these to the long-range planned goals.

PPBS Applied: The San Diego Experience

In San Diego, annual *budget analysis* of the proposed budget for the oncoming fiscal year occurs and is supported by continuous evaluation and feedback as to how effective these programs are in meeting the defined public needs. Thus the evaluation cycle becomes an integral part of the budgetary process. Multi-year projections based on past expenditures which are measured against program goals are being developed. The impact of current operations can be assessed against current expenditures, which then can be used to support effective long-range planning. A study by Michael Babunakis suggests a series of policy guidelines which are required of San Diego's PPBS experience for effective transition and implementation of a program budget and budget analysis system. They include:

1. A strong, high-level commitment.
2. The legislative body must be involved in implementation.
3. Political power realities cannot be ignored.
4. The implementation effort must be strong and determined.
5. There must be a complete, overall plan for implementation.
6. The initial efforts should be centralized as much as possible.
7. Expectations of what the system can do must be realistic.
8. The person in charge of the implementation must have well-defined authority and must be an expert in the field.
9. The support of department or agency personnel is necessary.
10. Implementation should be carried out from within the government. The use of outside consultants needs to be avoided whenever possible.
11. Those involved must feel they will benefit.
12. Good communication at all levels is imperative.
13. Enthusiasm for and confidence in the system is necessary.[21]

The entire San Diego city budget is divided among various individual departments. Each departmental budget contains a summary which lists expenditures for operating programs and capital improvements. The operating program is further divided into staffing, inclusive of either position or man-years requirements plus personnel and non-personnel expenses for past, present and future fiscal years. Thus multi-year comparisons and projections are possible. Non-personnel expenditures, inclusive of supplies, services and equipment, are also identified at this point. This is followed by a fund-source analysis which identifies the revenue sources for the operating and capital improvement programs. This is followed by a statement of departmental goals and the operating program summary.

A program budget contains an overall program category such as control and reduction of crime, maintenance of public works and the protection of public health. A program is a collectivity of independent, closely related services and activities which contribute toward a common objective. Within the program activity are a series of objectives which may be divided or identified as *program elements*, each with its own objectives. A program element is a subdivision of a program with a specific objective within the program. Thus there are programs, sub-programs and program elements. This is represented in Figure 15-13. These are then followed by a broad statement of intended accomplishment of the program element and linked into the overall goals for the sub-programs and the program itself that identify major goals to accomplish. These goals and objectives are formulated on the basis of identified need articulated into fairly specific objectives and qualitative and quantitative accomplishments of what and how much is to be done.

The program document contains the authority on which the program or program element rests and is generally cited with a general description of the overall program or program element stated in non-professional, understandable language. It contains a general description easily accessible to a lay person who wants to understand the relationship of expenditures to activity. This is followed by an input description of the manpower and resources used by the program with personnel expenses subdivided into program activities generally on position or man-year basis. The input represents the program's or program elements' actual cost. This is followed by output, which is a designation of the measurement, degree and achievement of objectives focusing, in the case of San Diego, on three items: (1) effectiveness, which centers on how well objectives are accomplished without regard to cost; (2) efficiency, which measures how economically input is converted into output by examining costs and years; and (3) basic work load analysis, through measurement of activity level, magnitude of work and a variety of other indicators.

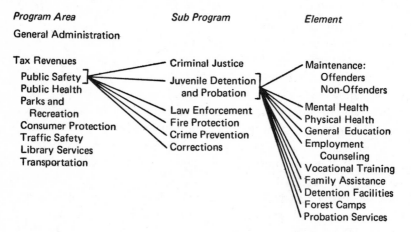

Figure 15-13. A POSSIBLE PROGRAM BUDGET STRUCTURE

Program budgeting components contain some combination of the following:
1. Program
2. Program Element
3. Goals and Objectives
4. Need
5. Authority
6. General Description
7. Input
8. Output

The city of San Diego meets the public's need for information resources by establishing a program which includes a variety of supports. One is the Central Library (program).

A sub-program is the Central Library Program (program element). Figure 15-14 presents the San Diego program as an example to enable the reader to observe the ease with which a program budget can be comprehended.

San Diego began to implement a program budget in fiscal year 1972-73. Prior to this time the performance budget was used. The city of San Diego has greatly improved the efficiency of operations, with major tax savings. It has related governmental allocations to operations more effectively. It has provided decision-makers at the administrative and legislative levels with more adequate information with which to make decisions and more comprehensive analysis of all possible alternatives. It has achieved better planning and more effectively coordinated operational supervision. San Diego has increased public awareness via its program budget documents and suggests that greater understanding and, therefore, greater accountability of expenditures will follow through the legislative process. PPBS within this city has become an effective management tool.

Evaluation of the Budget

A program budget creates a favorable environment for comprehensive analysis and evaluation of programs. A program budget and budget analysis are responsive to the need in public administration for more effective evaluation of public administration outcomes. Concern with assessment and outcomes which center attention on the evaluation of administrative routines and policy outcome is not popular, nor does it gain much attention within public administration. Consequently, it is fairly formative and not fully developed to any degree. San Diego is experimenting with a concept of budget analysis. In San Diego the responsibilities for budget analysis rest with legislative analysis.

Budget analysis is independent of executive program budget responsibility. It is functionally separated from program administrative responsibilities, budgetary policy and preparation of the budget document. The analysis process itself centers on the systematic posing of incisive and important questions about program alternatives, program costs, magnitude of the services performed and is inclusive not only of qualitative analysis but

Central Library Program (20.20)

Need — A comprehensive collection of research and information resources is needed by the community to facilitate the pursuit of information. The effectiveness and efficiency of such a program is maximized by a centralized facility.

Objectives — To achieve a higher per capita attendance figure; to initiate the recording of patron unfilled needs and complaints per capita; to maintain the amount of library materials available per capita; to increase the circulation of library materials per capita; to initiate the recording of materials used in the library besides those circulated in order to gauge collection use; and to increase the answering of information, reference and research questions.

Authority — Municipal Code, Chapter II, Article 2, Division 2, Section 22.0201; Article 2, Division 18, Section 22.1801.

General Description — The Central Library includes five adult-oriented sections, a children's section, a young adults' collection, a rare books collection (Wangenheim Room), and supportive services, supplemented by a full depository of United States and State of California documents. The staff selects materials in anticipation of public use, and assists the public in obtaining the most benefit from these resources. The proposed budget includes the addition of 4.17 position-years to continue the Directory and Information Service, and to handle the increased workload for the Art, Music, and Recreation Section. The increase in Non-Personnel Expense for FY 1975 reflects price increases for books, periodicals, and binding.

	Actual FY 1973	Current FY 1974	Proposed FY 1975	Final FY 1975
Input				
Staffing (Position–Years)	79.12	70.61	74.78	
Personnel Expense	$ 831,470	$ 769,322	$ 819,432	
Non-Personnel Expense	278,608	333,901	376,869	
TOTAL	$1,110,078	$1,103,223	$1,196,301	
Output				
Attendance, per capita	NA	NA	NA	
Patron unfilled needs and complaints, per capita	NA	NA	NA	
Library materials available, per capita	2.02	2.05	2.05	
Total circulation	790,543	806,392	812,198	
Materials circulated, per capita	1.06	1.07	1.08	
Materials used in the library besides those circulated, per capita	NA	NA	NA	
Information, reference and research questions, per capita	1.06	1.07	1.08	

SOURCE: Michael Babunakis (Project Director), *Recasting The Budgetary Process*, Urban Observatory of San Diego, Calif. (Zip 92101), Aug. 1974, pp. 224–225.

Figure 15-14.

qualitative evaluation as well. Computer technology is utilized as an aid to problem solving. Specific problems are systematically examined and possible solutions and their costs and benefits are evaluated.

The focus of budget analysis is to provide meaningful alternatives and priorities within the decision process for the legislature and more effectively informs the council or the legislature when the budget moves to that stage. Analysis focuses on program modification, expansion, curtailment, continuation and termination and relates revenue sources to administrative expenditures through continuous review.

Quantification requires that costs and benefits be identified and related. *Cost-benefit analysis* focuses on dollars and their relationship to expenditures. *Cost-effectiveness* relates qualitative data to program expenditures and becomes a systematic examination of alternatives as they relate to a fixed level and quality of outcome. Both the advantages and disadvantages and variations in a program can be related to costs and program quality with effectiveness altered accordingly. In a word, cost-effectiveness looks at desirability; cost-benefit looks at direct cost according to dollar value.

The Changing Uses of Budgeting

The budget process which has emerged to date projects a continuation of present trends, suggesting that government is action-oriented and interventionist in its role in the social system. Administrative organizations are seen as possessing the confidence to solve major problems within the context of the definable public interest. These organizations depend on an appropriate coordination of adequate funding among a variety of agencies, are charged with program action to implement and fulfill values determined through the public policy process.

The public manager is the responsible initiating agent in the process. It has been suggested by some policy-makers that full employment is no longer essential for survival of growth and abundance and that a new economics predicated not on full employment but on freeing men and women from work and guaranteeing adequate income is required. Such a new economics needs to assure an abundance of nature's wealth, and a high quality of physical and psychological existence delivered in a humane way needs to be the focus of the concern of the policy-maker.

This view suggests that the techniques and analysis of program budgeting which center on economic efficiency alone as the primary criterion for evaluating public programs are inconsistent with the newer requirements placed on administrative action. The post-industrial state, it is asserted, must be concerned less with increasing gross national product and standards of economic progress and more with the delivery of humane treatment and a high quality of existence so that men and women can reach toward greater self-fulfillment.

NOTES

1. Fremont J. Lyden, George A. Shipman, Robert W. Wilkinson, Jr., "Decision-Flow Analysis, A Methodology for Studying the Public Policy-Making Process," in Preston P. LeBreton (ed.), *Comparative Administrative Theory*. Seattle: University of Washington Press, 1968, pp. 156-157; see also pp. 158-168.

2. James D. Thompson and Arthur Tuden, "Strategies in Decision-Making," in Fremont J. Lyden, George A Shipman and Morton Kroll, *Policies, Decisions and Organization*. New York: Appleton-Century-Crofts, 1969, pp. 310-330.

3. *Ibid*., p. 330.

4. Anthony Downs, *Inside Bureaucracy*. Boston: Little, Brown & Company, 1967, p. 58.

5. Robert H. Simmons, "The Washington State Plural Executive," *Western Political Quarterly*, June, 1965, 363-381.

6. Robert D. Lee, Jr., and Ronald W. Johnson, *Public Budgeting Systems*. Baltimore: University Park Press, 1973, p. 150;*cf.* Yehezkel Dror, *Ventures in Policy Sciences*. New York: American Elsevier, 1971, p. 106.

7. Bertram M. Gross, "Planning in an Era of Social Revolution," *Public Administration Review*, May/June, 1971, p. 287.

8. Guy Benveniste, *The Politics of Expertise*. Berkeley, Calif.: The Glendessary Press, 1972, pp. 105-118.

9. Lee and Johnson, *op. cit.*, pp. 153-154.

10. Charles E. Lindblom, "The Science of Muddling Through," *Public Administration Review*, Vol. 19, 1959, pp. 79-88.

11. Charles M. Mottley, in *Management Highlights*, release No. 56, Office of Management Research, U.S. Dept. of Interior, Sept. 1967, reprinted in Fremont J. Lyden and Ernest G. Miller, *Planning, Programming, Budgeting*. Chicago: Markham Publishing Co., 1972, p. 125.

12. *Ibid.*, p. 126.

13. Preston P. LeBreton (ed.), *Comparative Administrative Theory.* Seattle: University of Washington Press, 1968, pp. 169-178.

14. Mottley, *op. cit.*, pp. 134-140.

15. Aaron Wildavsky, *The Politics of the Budgeting Process*. Boston: Little, Brown and Co., 1964, p. 2.

16. *Ibid.*, pp. 3-4.

17. Arthur Smithies, "Conceptual Framework for the Program Budget," in David Novilk, *Program Budgeting, Program Analysis and the Federal Budget*. Cambridge, Mass.: Harvard University Press, 1965, p. 31.

18. Allen Schick, *Budgetary Innovation in the States*. Washington, D.C.: The Brookings Institution, 1971, pp. 15-16.

19. Charles J. Hitch and Roland McKean, *The Economics of Defense in the Nuclear Age*. Cambridge, Mass.: Harvard University Press, 1960.

20. Michael Babunakis (Project Director, Legislative Analyst, City of San Diego), *Recasting the Budgetary Process*. Urban Observatory of San Diego, Calif., 1974, pp. 1-3. Much of what follows on program budgeting draws on the information in this study.

21. *Ibid.*, pp. 56-87.

16

TOWARD A HUMANE BUREAUCRACY

A HUMANISTIC APPROACH

The pervasive view of bureaucracy, until quite recently, has been that it is value-free and simply a set of interrelationships to be overseen and guided to work smoothly as some well-oiled machine. The overlays of administrative rules, orders, routines and precedents, as well as published scholarly research, are communicated in the third person ("he," "she," "it," "they") and drain from the vital and dynamic human interplay the drama, the tragedy and the accomplishments which are so much a part of bureaucracy each day.

In contrast, the "humanistic" approach to bureaucracy is not value-free and emphasizes the impact of bureaucratic procedures, attitudes and values. The first concern is the overall societal consequences of bureaucratic decisions. The results of particular administrative policy decisions upon the well-being of society are regarded as important elements to be considered. An administrative action system can inaugurate or sustain a reign of terror, with its coercive power, penalties and techniques. Conversely, it is capable of producing an environment nurturing many joyful experiences and supportive of human accomplishments.

A second concern of the humanistic approach is the point at which the individual bureaucrat and the recipient, or "client" of the agency, face each other. This is the real testing ground of any democratic society. The most familiar bureaucrat-client link is that involving an exchange between strangers—the bureaucrat behind his or her desk at the motor vehicle department, the traffic officer querying the driver through the window of the auto or the citizen speaking to his property tax appeal board. The one on the governmental side realistically has more power and is on the "one up" side of the desk. The applicant, detainee or appellee on the other side is in the "one down" position. If not exactly a supplicant, he or she is still, generally, in the less favored position. The resources, available time, crucial information and benefits to be conferred or withheld and assessment of penalties are on the bureaucratic side. Although democratic theory advances the notion of societal control of bureaucracy, the individual *per se* is less a ruler and more a subject.

The humane approach stresses that this interfacing may in most situations be positive rather than negative, rewarding rather than debilitating and personal rather than disinterested, as more and more citizens look to more and more bureaucrats for vital resources, requests and information ranging from medical care to retirement benefits.

Weber and Thayer: Power and Alienation

Many aspects of Weber's theory of bureaucracy have been frighteningly accurate. The bureaucracy he presents is an "iron cage" from which a successful escape may be possible but only by first carefully examining its nature. Weber insisted that bureaucracy inevitably accompanies modern mass democracy. The demand for "equality before the law" causes the leveling of social differences and replaces avocational administration by permanent "privileged" notables with paid professional labor. Where the bureaucratization of administration has been completely carried through, a form of power relations is established that is practically unshatterable. The decisive reason for the advance of bureaucratic organization as democracy matures is purely technical superiority over other forms of organization.

Weber was concerned with the problem of individual autonomy in a world that was increasingly subjected to the inexorable machinery of bureaucratic administration. Weber states:

> It is horrible to think that the world could one day be filled with nothing but those little cogs, little men clinging to little jobs and striving towards bigger ones . . . . This passion for bureaucracy . . . is enough to drive one to despair. It is as if in politics . . . we were deliberately to become men who need "order" and nothing but order, who become nervous and cowardly if for one moment this order wavers, and helpless if they are torn away from their total incorporation in it.[1]

Everyone becomes caught in the machine. The individual bureaucrat cannot squirm or wiggle out of the apparatus in which he is harnessed. It seems that only the person at the top "can arrest or change in any way the direction of the mechanism; all others seem and feel powerless." He suggests, furthermore, that the material fate of the masses becomes totally dependent on the efficient functioning of the bureaucratic apparatus once it is established. This is because its authority rests on expertise and functional specialization of tasks which cannot be easily replaced or substituted. Furthermore, once the apparatus has become indispensable, due to its "impersonal" character, it is easily made to work for anybody who knows how to gain control over it.

Weber points out, too, that "every bureaucracy seeks to increase the superiority of the professionally informed by keeping their knowledge and intentions secret." The "official secret" is an essential and specific component of power plays, which are reviewed later. Weber indicates this is basically a self-destructive phenomenon because it jeopardizes the legal authority on which bureaucratic authority rests by spawning suspicion and mistrust.[2]

Weber suggests the modern state comes to control the means of administration, warfare and financial organization. Essentially a separation is established between the political leader and the civil servant or official. The civil official, he notes, should remove himself totally from the arena of politics and engage in impartial administration:

> . . . the honor of the civil servant is vested in his ability to execute conscientiously the order of the superior

> authorities, exactly as if the order agreed with his own conviction. This holds even if the order appears wrong to him and if, despite the civil servant's remonstrances, the authority insists on the order. Without this moral discipline and self-denial, in the highest sense, the whole apparatus would fall to pieces. The honor of the political leader, of the leading statesman, however, lies precisely in an exclusive personal responsibility for what he does, a responsibility he cannot and must not transfer.[3]

Weber is suggesting that there should be a separation of the civil servant not only from politics but also from power and responsibility.

One of the striking contradictions in Weber's work stresses the need for a social science free of value judgments, yet the implications of his ideal-type analysis led him to introduce value judgments about bureaucracy. Carl Friedrich observes:

> . . . [Weber's] very words vibrate with something of the Prussian enthusiasm for the military type of organization, and the way seems barred to any kind of consultative, let alone cooperative, pattern. That the latter kind of pattern may be a higher type, that it may represent a "more fully developed" form of administrative organization, not only in terms of humanitarian values, but also in terms of results, is all but excluded as a possibility.[4]

Reinhard Bendix suggests that the Weberian model of bureaucracy presents the dilemma of contradictory tendencies. Through specialization and concentration of skills the bureaucracy carries out its mission superbly. Yet, on the other hand, professionalization and concern with administrative efficiency impel the bureaucracy toward a monopoly of power while "at the same time it becomes incapable of determining how its power should be used."[5] Having gained societal dominance, each bureaucrat ends up in an "iron cage" from which no escape is possible. He becomes, in reality, the most tragic victim of his own success.

Another problem with Weber's model is that the weakest point, the "Achilles heel," of his hierarchy is at the very top. If the top is captured by *coup d'état*, subversion or occupation by a victorious army, the entire structure is captured intact. Bureaucracy cannot be overthrown by mass revolutionary movements or frontal assault. The bureaucratic apparatus, whether good or evil, gains absolute power over the entire society. Power is rarely neutral and once the fact of bureaucratic power is accepted the moral consequences of the exercise of that power must then be directly faced!

The popular belief that the career bureaucracy merely carries out the will of the people through their elected representatives is deceptive. We observed elsewhere, "Power which is transitory can seldom control power which is continuous."[6] Elected officials no less than monarchs become more and more dependent on bureaucratic expertise. In more contemporary parlance career bureaucrats are heavily involved in daily policy-making.

When the chief of police in one of America's largest cities urges citizens to arm themselves because the police force is no longer able to provide security against criminal assaults but that same weekend deploys over 100 policemen to randomly search and harass teenagers attending a rock concert, he is both determining policy on the basis of his own value judgments and determining significant moral priorities. Even lower-level bureaucrats have very formidable powers of decision-making with great value implications, as Lieutenant William Calley's actions at My Lai and Daniel Ellsberg's exposure of the previously secret Pentagon Papers demonstrate.

Frederick Thayer in his *An End to Hierarchy! An End to Competition!* suggests that all "democratic" governments have been designed to preserve hierarchy.

> Even at its best, "democracy" had tended only to *limit* the power of the rulers, without changing the fundamental *relationship* between those who rule and those who are ruled. This is because all theories of "democracy" contain within them the pervasive assumption that hierarchy is

inevitable, desirable and necessary, the assumption that no organization (*family, church, corporation, public agency, nation-state*) can achieve its social purpose other than through *the interaction of those designated "superiors"* and those labeled "subordinates."[7]

In contrast to Weber, Thayer raises the possibility that the fundamental causes of our work and interpersonal alienation are deeply embedded in our traditional dedication to the values of hierarchy and competition. For Thayer, the necessity for hierarchy flows from the negative Hobbesian view of human nature, which views men as having no objectives other than to acquire as much material goods as possible at the expense of others. Under such conditions only absolute authority backed with physical force is capable of establishing or maintaining a secure social world. Hence, Thayer asserts, the formal structure of all modern organization is Hobbesian and similarly reflects belief in the danger of free human behavior.[8]

Weber proposes the ideal pyramidal bureaucracy as the highest manifestation of rationality and efficiency and is willing to accept the price of everyone being confined to narrowly defined roles from which no deviation can be tolerated. Thayer suggests that this uncritical acceptance of hierarchy has prevented us from seeking deeper explanations. "Most theorists still feel that they must question and resist the involvement of middle-level administrators, employees or citizens in public decision-making—not only because it violates conventional political theory, but also because it violates the 'ideal' bureaucratic model they (ironically) know to be intolerable anyway."[9]

Thayer proposes "the transformation of superior-subordinate relationships into non-hierarchical small-group processes in which no single individual can impose his style on another."[10] In the face of conventional wisdom, this proposal seemed rather startling, but Thayer suggests ways in which it might be implemented without a total restructuring of the existing social-bureaucratic organizations. The starting point would be a revisualization of group participation without the blinders of traditional authority relations. Thayer proposes a network of small groups with adequate links capable of *confronting conflict* in healthy ways rather than concealing it in order to arrive at consensus collectively. To cries, "But that's not efficient!" Thayer argues:

> Most of the time, the unintended consequences affect individuals and groups who were not consulted before decisions were made. There could be no better way of discovering as many such problems as possible than to include in decision processes those individuals most likely to be affected by them. Although this would slow down the process, it would produce more effective decisions which, because hidden consequences had been discovered in advance, would become cost-effective through cost-avoidance.[11]

Thayer suggests the shift away from rigid, permanent lines to fluid, temporary networks expresses the reality of the functions and interactions in which individuals are engaged. Meanwhile, "the permanent vertical structure churns out efficiency reports, related more to its view of discipline than to what actually goes on."[12]

Power Plays in Bureaucracy: Family Origins

Weber calls the household the most "natural" of the closed types of social action, and suggests that "the earliest substantial inroads into unmitigated . . . authority proceed not directly from economic motives but apparently from the development of exclusive sexual claims of the male over women subjected to their authority."[13] He states:

> The domestic household is the fundamental basis of loyalty and authority, which in turn is the basis of many other groups. This "authority" is of two kinds: (1) the authority derived from superior strength and (2) the authority derived from practical knowledge and experience. It is, thus, the authority of men as against women and children; of the able-bodied as against those of lesser capacity; of the adult as against the child; of the old as against the young . . . it

617

becomes a part of the relationships originally having a domestic character.[14]

Ronald Sampson suggests in *The Psychology of Power* that Freud's inability to see any possibilities for human development in the direction of cooperative equality and peace was due to his inability to challenge the accepted view of the relations which ought to obtain between men and women. For Freud, the social relationship between man and woman was inevitably one of dominance and subjection. Freud's view that equality between the sexes was impossible and undesirable, while purporting to be a scientific hypothesis, was actually, Sampson suggests, little more than the contemporary prejudice of his class and time.[15]

Sampson verifies the prevailing climate of opinion by printing some of the outraged reviews found in daily newspapers at the time of the publication of John Stuart Mill's essay *The Subjection of Women*. Mill observed in this work that particularly in the conjugal family, the dominance of men over women had anti-social consequences not only for women, but also for men and for the children of such a union. He suggested that the power to hold others in servitude was essentially morally corrupting for men; that the powerlessness engendered in women created frustration and resentment; and that such a family became a "school of despotism" in which children learned the weapons of the struggle for power. Sampson observes that the weapons of self-deception, repression and evasion, although morally debilitating, are often the only recourse available to children in their weakness. But "the price paid by constant efforts to appease the power of others is a gradual erosion of the ability to formulate and live with a truthful picture of reality."[16]

The work of Claude Steiner is based on the thesis that the family teaches both powerfulness and powerlessness. He identifies the technique in this process as "the Rescue Game." Children are forced into a *Victim* role, while the roles of *Rescuer* and *Persecutor* are taught by the example of the parents. Thus the classic family script:

Father is the Persecutor. Mother is the Rescuer, and the Kids are the Victims. In a situation like this the roles switch around so that Father becomes Mother's Victim when she Persecutes him for hurting her children, and then Mother becomes the children's Victim when they take advantage of her kindness. Later the children may Rescue Mother when Father attempts to beat her up while she passively submits, and so on. As the Children grow up and begin to acquire some power independent of the Parents, they begin to cash in on the long-time resentment for having become Victimized, and thus become the Parents' Persecutors.[17]

In organizations this drama is acted out in many ways and many times with varying participants. Each person may play one of these roles at one time or another as it relates to peers or subordinates, supervisors or themselves. This is the "Drama Triangle," i.e., there are the three basic game roles (Victim, Persecutor, Rescuer) arranged in a triangle in a way which shows how a person may switch from one role to another in relation to one's self or to another.[18]

Steiner suggests that within the family most human beings are "scripted" to be comfortable in relationships where they are either "one-up" or "one-down" to another human being. In short, the family teaches powerlessness to some, powerfulness to others.

All children are taught that one must obey certain persons of authority and relate to them from a one-down position. Children are also *taught* that human beings of the female sex are appropriately, naturally one-down to human beings of the male sex, that workers are one-down to bosses, Blacks are one-down to Whites, and so on. The effect of such intense scripting into acceptance of unequal distribution of power between human beings is that people continue to seek and expect inequality in their relationships.[19]

The destructive consequences of these processes are repeated infinitely within the organization. Steiner suggests that most of

the "games" people play comprise the bulk of their daily transactions with each other and are simply "power plays." Furthermore, the particular type of power plays continually engaged in
by an individual are pathetic repetitions by adults of the games
they learned and were forced to use as children in the arena of
family power struggles. If the unequal relationships and competitive behavior of both family and the organization are viewed
not as biologically inherent but as socially conditioned, it
may be possible to construct new models of social order based
on Thayer's non-competitive, non-hierarchical cooperative
relationships.

POWER PLAYS: SOME SOCIAL AND
ORGANIZATIONAL CONSEQUENCES

John Stuart Mill revealed insight into this problem. He observed
the shrinking liberty of the individual in emerging "democratic"
societies. He argued from a purely utilitarian point of view for
open and free discussion of all opinions, no matter how much
they were at variance with conventional wisdom on any subject.
He found the growing social conformity of great numbers of
people profoundly disturbing. He was deeply concerned that
"Individual spontaneity is hardly recognized by the common
modes of thinking as having any intrinsic worth, or deserving
any regard of its own account."[20]

More than a century later contemporary organization
theorists are still grappling with this problem. Mill insisted that
in order to have geniuses in any society, "It is necessary to preserve the soil in which they grow. Genius can only nurture and
develop in an atmosphere of freedom."[21] A damning antithesis
to the organizational context.

Weber stood powerless in the face of the "ideal" bureaucracy he had constructed. Mill, on the other hand, reflected on
the potential freedom for men and women once freed from
organizational constraints:

> Supposing it were possible to get houses built, corn grown,
> battles fought, causes tried, and even churches erected and

prayers said, by machinery—by automatons in human form—it would be a considerable loss to exchange for these automatons even the men and women who at present inhabit the more civilized parts of the world . . . . Human Nature is not a machine to be built after a model and set to do exactly the work prescribed for it, but a tree which requires to grow and develop itself on all sides, according to the inward forces which make it a living thing.[22]

One exciting contemporary writer, sociologist Lewis Yablonsky, has identified "Robopathology" as the classic disease of organizational life in modern times. "Robopaths are efficient functionaries and bureaucrats."[23] They have become so cut off from their feelings that they exhibit robot-like behavior. "This dehumanized level of existence places people in roles where they are actors mouthing irrelevant platitudes, experiencing programmed emotions with little or no compassion or sympathy for other people."[24] Herbert Marcuse has called this condition one of "perfect alienation" in a one-dimensional society.[25] Both Yablonsky and Marcuse warn that in this state of affairs violence reaches monstrous proportions. Only completely compartmentalized, powerless people could accept such things as doomsday buttons and automated battlefields.

Rollo May, in *Power and Innocence*, cites Hannah Arendt's statement that "Violence is the expression of impotence."[26] May suggests that our survival depends on whether human consciousness can be asserted, and with sufficient strength, to stand against the stultifying pressures of technological progress. "Ideally," he warns, "we must find ways of sharing and distributing power so that every person, in whatever realm of our bureaucratic society, can feel that he too counts, that he too makes a difference to his fellows and is not cast out on the dunghill of indifference as a non-person."[27]

American political and organizational theorists have not fully confronted the full implications of the issues raised here. Democratic society has yet to deal effectively with the relationships between the bureaucratic order and the theory of democracy. Bensman and Vidich suggest the difficulty of the problem:

> Bureaucracy must always be something more than a technical system of administration. It is also a system for the organization and distribution of power and the formulation of policy within institutions, between institutions, and within societies. From this perspective, bureaucracy in its full form is diametrically opposed to the Jeffersonian and Jacksonian image of a viable democracy.[28]

They suggest that the American bureaucrat masks the authoritarian style of bureaucracy with friendly, equalitarian euphemisms. They suggest that the "breezy, friendly, personal, and non-officious" style stems from the American frontier influence characteristic of the Jacksonian period. "This causes the power holder to conceal his power in proportion to its growth." They further suggest this has resulted in the masking of the true nature of American bureaucratic practice:

> As a result of this mask, the subordinate in any organization has at subliminal levels the ability to make precise estimates of the actual power positions of each office-holder in the organization. With this as his framework, the formal, equalitarian, personal, and friendly responses of co-workers are based on these estimates. In the American system the official knows how to be informal and friendly without ever intruding into the office of the superior, and the superior knows how to be equalitarian without ever losing his authority. Thus *bureaucracy functions in the classical Weberian way while retaining an air of American friendliness and informality.* (Italics supplied)
>
> This special bureaucratic by-product of Jeffersonian and Jacksonian democracy creates a bureaucratic style in which it becomes a major requirement to mask authority relations. As a result, very substantial changes have taken place in the ideology of the social worker, the human relations specialist, the psychological counselor, the personnel officer, and in interpersonal relations in almost all bureaucratic job situations.[29]

American bureaucracy carries the "face" of democracy by virtue of the words and symbols used, but not its "heart." Weber's proposition that "bureaucratization" results from "democratization" comes to full fruition. The language of equal rights and the friendly smile mask the harsh power of bureaucracy in a democratic society. Modern democracy, which nurtured technological bureaucracy, is itself captured and made a prisoner of that same bureaucracy. That varieties of societal alienation are emerging need not be too surprising. A special kind of invidious bureaucratic hypocrisy is nurtured and becomes S.O.P.—Standard Operating Procedure. Bensman and Vidich continue:

> In actual bureaucratic practice the subordinate is expected to agree voluntarily with his superior and to suggest the conditions for his subordination without ever openly acknowledging the fact of his subordination. The rhetoric of democracy has become the *sine qua non* of bureaucratic authoritarianism.[30]

They suggest that democracy's substance is, in fact, being replaced with "bureaucratic authoritarianism." Gradually, even imperceptively, the harsh image and language of the bureaucratic characteristic of the Weberian model is being replaced by the friendly, personal equalitarian image and language of Jacksonian democracy. This development conceals the harsh, authoritarian nature of bureaucracy while maintaining a facade of near joviality and friendly concern. The straight talk and clear meanings, the honest, direct language so characteristic of the American heartland and exemplified by President Truman fade away. Distorted imagery takes its place and what one hears bears a diminishing relationship to reality. These writers have developed a table which illustrates some of these euphemisms and the "messages" they actually convey *if* candor were used (see Figure 16-1).

Men and women give up their power in a bureaucracy to roles but people can only play roles by detaching themselves from their real feelings. The ability to do this is another

Euphemism	Real Meaning
Obedience:	
We expect your cooperation.	Obey.
I'd like to have consensus on this issue.	I expect you to repress all differences.
Obligation and duty require this.	My job and responsibilities require your obedience.
Being reminded of one's place:	
It's a wonderful idea, but at the present we don't have the time to give your idea the attention and consideration it needs.	Drop it.
You're kidding, aren't you.	You're out of line.
That's an interesting idea that needs further developing.	Let's not discuss it now.
We must respect the autonomy and individual rights of others.	You're overstepping your authority.
You can do that if you want to, but I'll take no responsibility for it if it gets out of hand.	You do it at your own risk, but I'll take the credit for it if it's successful.
With some development and elaboration, the germ of your idea could be useful.	I'm stealing your idea; forget it, the idea is no longer yours.
That was a good idea you had at our meeting yesterday.	I'm giving it back to you.
Ways to get fired:	
You've been late three times in the past month.	Warning of forthcoming dismissal.
Your work is not up to your usual standards.	Warning of forthcoming dismissal.
You haven't reached your full potential in this job.	You're not fired, but don't expect a raise or promotion.
We feel that this organization can do no more to further your career.	You're fired.

Euphemism	Real Meaning
We can't stand in the way of your growth.	You're fired.
You're too well trained for this job.	You're fired.
We'll give you excellent references.	Please leave without making a scene.
We'll give you an extra month's severance pay.	Please leave and forget you ever worked here.
At other levels:	
Free lunch.	A small, somewhat ambiguous bribe setting the stage for bigger bribery.
Fringe benefits.	Fairly serious bribery.
Hanky-panky.	Serious bribery.
A preliminary meeting.	Setting out to rig a forthcoming meeting.
A well-organized meeting.	A rigged meeting.
An informal coffee meeting.	An incipient plot.
A private meeting.	A plot.

SOURCE: Joseph Bensman, Arthur J. Vidich, *The New American Society: The Revolution of the Middle Class*, Chicago, Quadrangle Books, 1971, pp. 24-25.

Figure 16-1. THE LANGUAGE MASKS OF BUREAUCRACY

dysfunctional aspect of sex-role scripting. As children we are whole people capable of thinking, intuiting, doing and feeling. Male-female roles are learned well in early life. Steiner observes that role scripting penalizes boys for *feeling* and *intuiting*, while girls are penalized for *doing* and *thinking*. When these penalties occur, children are taught to ignore and often deny the feelings, i.e., discount the reality of what, *in fact*, is felt.

As adults in bureaucratic settings the splitting off from real feelings continues. Thus the ideal bureaucrat is born. There is no need to face one's own emotions or feelings of sympathy or regret. The bureaucrat now becomes an "actor" and finds a degree of "safety" in role dependency. In this process formal authority is protected from challenge and "freedom" is conditional and based upon powerlessness. The work situation is joyless, mindless and loveless; hence nearly everyone *feels* anger. Cumulatively, the real emotions might be powerful, even explosive, enough to force a change in the situation. However, the anger is usually repressed and negated rather than safely released by the individual experiencing it. It is, consequently, projected on to someone else in the organization who is too impotent to effectively deal with it. As a result, the destructive network continues to be woven strand by strand, individual by individual, into the oppressive bureaucratic fabric.

Occasionally, real emotions are split off and projected into a safe repository, e.g., someone takes on the "clown role" to act out the group's joy or relieve tensions through laughter. A "crazy one" may arise to safely absorb the fears of the group members. Individuals within the group almost always collude in the process of role differentiation by selecting roles for themselves which are comfortable and reinforce their personal robopathic ways of behaving. The end of the process is truly tragic— for innumerable individuals who refuse to *own* their innermost feelings and give up their only source of real power to effect change. Formal authority remains intact.[31]

THE BANAL WORK GROUP

Most persons in American society spend the greater part of their waking day within the confines of a "work group." This small group, usually about five in number, is where the organizational work "gets done." Borrowing a term, it is useful to call these groups "banal work groups." They are the "everyday garden variety" of group. It is helpful to examine some of their characteristics. They are developed for the purpose of conducting organizational tasks and reflect the power setting in which each individual was socialized. Thus the mood and spirit of the group reflect the lovelessness, mindlessness, joylessness, powerlessness and unequal interpersonal relationships characteristic of human relations in an industrial culture.

The interpersonal transactions of group members are generally competitive and laden with the drama of power plays. Authority transactions are characterized by criticism (usually identified by the term "evaluation"), controls, organizational management rules and orders which reinforce the alienating nature of the work environment.[32] The groups are subject to more or less rigid controls relating to monitoring standards, job performance and evaluation, and personal reviews. Competition which pits co-worker against co-worker precludes the intimacy and closeness which are required if people are to feel good about themselves and perform tasks in which they take pride. Discounting may range from gentle teasing to dripping sarcasm—all delivered with the personable smile. If the power contest occurs among players who perceive themselves as equal, it may be a "pitched battle," with important ramifications for the organization. Factions develop and organizational programs with attendant problems of budget, resources and human energy weigh in the balance.

POWER PLAYS IN THE ORGANIZATION

A power relationship involves two or more persons and is the essential characteristic of interpersonal relations in organizational life. There is, in fact, no equality, there is no satisfaction, and the power game may increase or recede in intensity over time. The reward in winning a power game is the seeming appearance of security and control. Yet it is not intrinsically satisfying to the human being who plays it or is caught up in it. The pay-offs for the one-up players (supervisors, experts, etc.) are status, comfort, privilege, and the benefits for the one-down players are seemingly fewer, or no, cares, responsibilities and worries. There are many forms these games may take.

The most characteristic game within the banal work groups is the drama-triangle, i.e., the rescuer-victim-persecutor game alluded to earlier. It is important for students to understand the "game" is real! People win, people lose, people get hurt! Someone gets ahead while many more stay behind. It can be as vicious as it can be sweet. Power is the "name of the game" within the bureaucracy. The traditional goal of management has been to control, manipulate and manage in order to obtain a high-performing, steady worker who "cares not" and "wants not." Dissatisfaction and discontent stem from the worker's alienation from his own inherent humanness. To achieve a reversal of the situation is the fundamental challenge of the future.

VALUES, ORGANIZATIONS AND POWER PLAYS

Harold Lasswell developed the hypothesis that one who seeks power often does so "as a means of compensation against deprivation." The accumulation of "power is expected to overcome low estimates of the self."[33] This is a compensatory personal posture and often the drive for power is hidden from the consciousness of the person who seeks it. Lasswell argued in 1948 that unless we increase our efforts to understand personality development within a culture and unless we come to some agreement as to which personality components of potential leaders are conducive to the maintenance of democratic equilibrium, we will find ourselves under some form of totalitarian state. He proposed the development of a social psychiatry in conjunction with the development of a science of democratic policy-making. This would accomplish, he suggested, a general raising of the level of social health and consciousness, which would enable the citizenry to reimpower themselves through the selection of leaders capable of commitment to democratic values. An effective starting point would be to take on the task of demystifying power relations and hierarchy within organization in order to nurture and release the full potential of the humans working within its confines.

627

ORGANIZATIONAL DEVELOPMENT

"Organizational Development" is a relatively new body of organizational theory and practice. It has grown, within the last
decade and a half, out of an awareness that the development
and evolution of an individual within an organization are a
separate concern and activity from the development of the organization itself. The maximization of individual effort is a phenomenon distinct from organizational effectiveness.

In the immediate post-World War II years training within an
organization was simply the conveying of information and
learning skills. It was neither related to the total needs of the
organization nor to a fuller understanding of the psychological
processes enveloping workers within the organization.

In the post-World War II years new developments in interpersonal experiences such as sensitivity training and T-groups
began to have important impacts within organizations which
were experimenting with new approaches to training activities
and employee relations. T-groups and sensitivity training are
sharing groups based upon intimacy and trust. The former
adapts psychological therapy techniques into the group situation and the latter emphasizes direct feedback about how a person's interpersonal transactions are being perceived by others in
the group. Both use skilled facilitators to lead them.

These activities were initially quite successful and feedback
concerning personal interactions within the group provided significant data and insights. The T-group and related experiences
became new and important tools in training and education. In
addition, the groups themselves experienced increased effectiveness and potential. Organizational knowledge and activity that
were both diagnostic and therapeutic for individuals and the organization began to emerge on a broadened scale.

An almost explosive expansion of interest in these awareness groups occurred in the late 1960's, leading to a great variety of experience groups including psychodrama, Synanon
games, encounter group experiences, transactional analysis,
radical therapy problem-solving groups and Tavistock group
relations events. Psychodrama, developed by J. L. Moreno, emphasizes role-playing. Synanon games are a special encounter

emphasizing direct expression of one's own feelings to others in the group. Encounter group experiences generally center upon honest verbal interpersonal exchanges. Transactional analysis, developed by Eric Berne, focuses upon the nature of early childhood scripting and how that relates to current interpersonal transactions. Radical therapy problem-solving groups use specially developed group methods to aid a group member in solving personal problems. The Tavistock group relations events emphasize intergroup experiences with a special attention given to intergroup dynamics and authority relationships. There are, of course, many others. Some of these recorded spectacular and significant results, while others have been less successful.

LEARNING AND ORGANIZATIONAL DEVELOPMENT

This movement reflecting increased interest in organizational interpersonal transactions led to an increased concern with "Human Resources Development." Malcolm Knowles declares:

> One of the misconceptions of our cultural heritage is the notion that organizations exist solely to get work done. This is only one of their purposes; it is their *work* purpose. But every organization is also a social system that serves as an instrumentality for helping people meet human needs and achieve human goals . . . this is the primary purpose for which people themselves take part in them—to meet *their* needs and achieve *their* goals.[34]

Basing his work on the "Theory Y" model of Douglas McGregor, Knowles suggests a procedure which will be responsive to the psychological needs of persons within organizations as well as meeting the organizational needs. He suggests a process model which focuses on a set of seven steps involving learners and the elements of the learning situation:

1. Establish a climate conducive to learning;
2. create a mechanism for mutual planning;
3. diagnose the needs for learning;
4. formulate program objectives;

5. design a pattern of learning experiences;

6. conduct these learning experiences with suitable techniques and materials;

7. evaluate the learning outcomes and rediagnose learning needs.

He is concerned with the procedures and resources for helping learners acquire information, understanding, skills, attitudes and values. These stand in contrast to the "content model," which is simply concerned with transference of information and skills.[35] Knowles' model is "andragogical" (adult centered) and includes not only the "open system" theories of organization but also the concept of modern economics that human input is a more critcal determinant of organizational output than the material capital within that organization. He parallels the nuclear physicist's concept that an energy system is more expansive and more amplifiable through the release of energy than by the control of energy. Hence the "human resources developer" is the most crucial performer in determining which organizations will survive in the future.

TEAM DEVELOPMENT

Team Development is also an outgrowth of the new interest in organizational development. The nature of group interaction and the observation that organizational work assigned to groups is accomplished has brought a new awareness of the importance of teamwork, team building and team development. The emphasis is primarily on the organizational task, yet clearly the nature of the transactions within the team and across team lines which are supportive and crucial to the team effort are also of concern. The goal is to enhance team stability by organizing tasks on a work team basis. This is seen as an effective way of producing organizational activity in a creative and helpful way.[36]

DILEMMAS IN ORGANIZATIONAL DEVELOPMENT

Five significant problems in the future of organizational development may be identified:

1. If an open organization is to be truly constructive, what will be the theoretical information needed, the value overlays and change methodology?

2. The essence of the modern organization is the alienating concept of evaluation often taking place in an effort to achieve "efficiency." Yet organizational development has not yet transcended the evaluation and efficiency measures of the scientific management era.

3. The problem of creating a non-manipulative and more trusting and open world as a part of the organization environment is an important aspect of achieving effective personal growth in organizational development.

4. The system of punishment and rewards within the organization is now so pervasive and powerful that it severely constrains the OD process.

5. The relationship between the organization and its environment is a contradictory one. Organizational development seeks non-competitive cooperative behavior. Yet in the private sector the organization is designed to compete in its environment. The public sector may be more compatible to cooperative behavior between the organization and the client the organization serves.

Organizational development is concerned with applying the group skills and enhanced communication processes, group process experiences and techniques to the action system of the organization. Consequently, we may well be at the threshold of some phenomenal changes. Organizational development promises to proceed in far different directions than routinized, systematic, ordered, mechanical relationships. It is open-ended. It is situational and keyed into the evolutionary and emergent nature of the organization. It relates to exploring the variety of possibilities for action, developing new support and communication patterns and softening the nature of hierarchy that might otherwise burden this process.[37]

OD could well become a force for social evolution and change of major social importance. Charles Hampden-Turner seeks to arrive at some understanding of what type of psychosocial development would encourage the creative development of the individual in an organizational setting and interrupt the trend toward *robopathic* alienation.[38] Hampden-Turner notices that what human beings regard as important and salient in their

631

lives are "their novel and *non-repetitive* activities . . . ." But what organizational specialists and social investigators do is focus on the precise and invariable patterns of behavior that are already fixed. This is directly counter to what human beings seek. These unchanging patterns give social investigators and organizational specialists handles and hooks on which to attach their expertise. Kahn perceives:

> The organization is an open system, a system of roles; it consists of continuing, interdependent cycles of behavior, related in terms of their contribution to a joint product.[39]

He believes these role linkages are the fundamental social units of an organization. It is these linkages to which organizational specialists and social investigators must shift their attention.

Clark and Krone observed that a truly effective organization is one that can integrate "pro-actively" with its psychosocial and biophysical environments. This, they suggest, can be most effectively accomplished through the small group, i.e., the primary way a person performs tasks and links up persons in the organization. Clarke and Krone focus on several crucial areas. First, the communication linkages, task group team meetings and linkages, development laboratories and informal face-to-face exchanges. Second, they focus on the person and his individual world, what Vickers has called the "appreciative system." This helps identify the relations he or she has with persons of different age, sex, color, religion, political persuasion and hierarchical position which will help identify how he or she perceives others and how he or she relates adaptively or resistively to others in work and life situations.

They suggest four systems of intervention which organizational development can draw upon. First, the communication system, which involves the individual in his small group; second, the appreciative system, the individual and his world; third, the organization and its future in a turbulent environment, which requires open-systems planning; and four, the organization and its present turbulent environment, which means open systems designing.

Such intervention must proceed from an opening process around communication interaction to a broader appreciation of the context of the worker and the setting in which he or she works into a link with the organization through open-systems planning and finally the integration of this open system into the internal structure which they call open-systems designing. The perspectives of a new manager, they maintain, is larger "only to the extent that he appreciates those aspects of this world that have to do with the growth of people and the growth of his own capacity to facilitate the growth of people.[40] This supports the work of psychologist Abraham Maslow.

Maslow observed that the most effective and best managers increase the health of the workers whom they manage. He suggests:

> They do this in two ways: One is via the gratification of basic needs for safety, for belongingness, for affectionate relationships and friendly relationships with their informal groups, prestige needs, needs for self-respect . . . the other is via the gratification of the metamotivations or the meta-needs for truth and beauty and goodness and justice and perfection and law. . . .[41]

However, the manager cannot provide these things in a paternal way. He must sincerely and believingly encourage the possibility of attaining them within the organization. The danger involved in the infragroup process is identified by Irving Janis as "groupthink." He suggests that this is a quick and easy way to:

> Refer to a mold of thinking that people engage in, when they are deeply involved in cohesive in-group, when the members' strivings for unanimity override their motivation to realistically appraise alternative courses of action.[42]

Janis equates "groupthink" with deterioration of mental efficiency, escape from reality and faulty moral judgment. These result from in-group pressures.

Creativity and communication are mediated by codes of values and it is important to be concerned with values which facilitate successful, creative and humane interactions and those which impede this process. The values we urge upon one another each day can be fashioned, exchanged and translated into action if those same values are affirmed and reaffirmed by the organization.

Carl Rogers stands in sharp contrast to Hobbes' view of human nature. Rogers believes:

> That given an adequate human climate, man chooses to develop in ways that are both personally and socially enhancing, that move him in directions constructive for himself and for others.[43]

He suggests that if we are to avoid catastrophies threatening the modern world, this capacity for freely constructive functioning on the part of all persons must be released in personal relationships, within the educational processes and within work organizations. Human communication is the principal vehicle to change the appreciative systems of each person. Trend need not be destiny. Planned change is possible. Humane bureaucracy is attainable, embracing organizations and workers and their clientele. A new awareness of organizational interpersonal processes could make life more meaningful and contribute to the elimination of destructive alienation so much a part of contemporary life. "Humane bureaucracy," like "democracy," defies precise definition. This does not, however, deny our knowledge of the conditions necessary for its existence.

NOTES

1. Quoted in Reinhard Bendix, *Max Weber, An Intellectual Portrait*. New York: Doubleday & Co., Inc., 1960, pp. 455–456.

2. H. H. Gerth and C. Wright Mills (eds.), *From Max Weber: Essays in Sociology*. New York: Oxford University Press, 1946, pp. 223–228.

3. *Ibid.*, p. 95.

4. Carl J. Friedrich, "Some Observations on Weber's Analysis of Bureaucracy," in Robert K. Merton, Ailsa P. Gray, Barbara Hockey, Hanan C. Selvin (eds.), *Reader in Bureaucracy*. Glencoe, Ill.: The Free Press, 1952, p. 31.

5. Reinhard Bendix, "Bureaucracy and the Problem of Power," in Robert K. Merton, et al., *op. cit.*, p. 129.

6. Eugene P. Dvorin and Robert H. Simmons, *From Amoral to Humane Bureaucracy*. San Francisco: Canfield Press, 1972, p. 38.

7. Frederick C. Thayer, *An End to Hierarchy! An End to Competition!* New York: New Viewpoints, 1973, p. 44.

8. *Ibid.*, p. 62.

9. *Ibid.*, p. 118.

10. *Ibid.*, p. 140.

11. *Ibid.*, p. 39.

12. *Ibid.*, p. 13.

13. Max Weber, *Economy and Society*, edited by Guenther Roth and Claus Wittich. New York: Bedminster Press, 1968, p. 363–364.

14. *Ibid.*, p. 359.

15. Ronald V. Sampson, *The Psychology of Power*. New York: Vintage Books, 1965, p. 29.

16. *Ibid.*, p. 117.

17. Claude Steiner, *Scripts People Live*. New York: Grove Press, Inc., 1974, p. 151.

18. Stephen B. Karpman, "Script Drama Analysis," *Transactions Analysis Bulletin*, 7, 26, 1968, pp. 39–43.

19. Steiner, *op. cit.*, pp. 213–214.

20. John Stuart Mill, *On Liberty (1859)*, edited by Alburey Castell. Northbrook, Ill.: A. H. M. Publishing Co., 1947, p. 56.

21. *Ibid.*, p. 64.

22. *Ibid.*

23. Lewis Yablonsky, *Robopaths*. Baltimore: Penguin Books, 1972, p. 15.

24. *Ibid.*, p. 6.

25. Herbert Marcuse, *One-Dimensional Man*. Boston: Beacon Press, 1964.

26. Rollo May, *Power and Innocence*. New York: W. W. Norton & Co., 1972, p. 23.

27. *Ibid.*, p. 243.

28. Joseph Bensman and Arthur J. Vidich, *The New American Society*. Chicago: Quadrangle Books, 1971, p. 22.

29. *Ibid.*, p. 23.

30. *Ibid.*

31. W. R. Bion, *Experiences in Groups*. New York: Basic Books, 1959; Isabel E. P. Menzies, *The Functioning of Social Systems as a Defense Against Anxiety. A Report on the Study of Nursing Service of a General Hospital*. Tavistock Pamphlet No. 3., London, 1967; Margaret J. Rioch, "All We Like Sheep . . . (Isaish 53:6) Followers and Leaders," *Psychiatry*, Vol. 34, 1971, pp. 258-273.

32. Steiner, *op. cit.*, pp. 49-163, 293-319; see also generally Eric Berne, *What Do You Say After You Say Hello?* New York: Grove Press, 1972.

33. Harold D. Lasswell, *Power and Personality*. New York: The Viking Press, 1948, p. 39.

34. Malcolm S. Knowles, "Human Resources Development in OD," *Public Administration Review*, March/April, 1974, p. 115.

35. *Ibid.*, p. 117 and generally pp. 115-123.

36. See F. J. Lyden, "Project Management: Beyond Bureaucracy," *Public Administration Review*, July/August, 1970, pp. 435-436, and George F. S. Lehner, "Team Development Trainer's Workshop," *Public Administration Review*, March/April, 1974, pp. 124-129.

37. Larry Kirkhart and Brian F. White, Jr., "The Future of Organization Development," *Public Administration Review*, March/April, 1974, pp. 129-140.

38. Charles Hampden-Turner, *Radical Man*. New York: Anchor Books, 1971.

39. R. L. Kahn, *et al.*, *Organizational Stress*. New York: John Wiley and Sons, 1964, pp. 375-398.

40. J. V. Clark and C. G. Krone, "Towards an Overall View of Organizational Development in the Early Seventies," in John M. Thomas and Warren G. Bennis, *Management of Change and Conflict*. Baltimore: Penguin Books, Inc., 1972, pp. 284-303.

41. Abraham H. Maslow, *Eupsychian Management*. Homewood, Ill.: Richard D. Irwin and the Dorsey Press, 1965, p. 75.

42. Irving L. Janis, *Groupthink*. Boston: Houghton Mifflin Co., 1972, p. 9.

43. Carl R. Rogers, "A Humanistic Conception of Man," in R. E. Farson (ed.), *Science and Human Affairs*. Palo Alto, Calif.: Science and Behavior Books.

17

CONCLUSION: PERILS OF ORTHODOXY

It is fitting that this volume conclude on a note of controversy. No book enhancing the crucial role of value choices in administrative decision-making can shrink from controversial issues. To the extent that administrative processes are part of a much broader societal environment, the dilemmas and crises in which the society is embroiled provide the stage upon which the administrative "actor" plays his role. That role is often creative, often negative and restricting, but always consequential. The subtitle "Values, Policy and Change" reflects belief in their interlinkages and interdependence. We recognize our fundamental commitment to John Stuart Mill's interpretation of true democracy as being open-ended, in conflict with itself and never settling down. Like Mill, we have a deep and abiding faith in the progressive perfectability of most humankind and the necessity of human diversity, autonomy and individual responsibility.

Within this belief framework we hold that the most effective administrative system is that which does not oppose or even tolerate these values but, quite differently, nurtures them. Intellectually and emotionally our sympathies lie with the "new" public administration, despite our awareness of a number of serious issues it raises. However, its emphasis upon attempting to modify the existing economic and political power structure, the potential for greatly expanded individual fulfillment in the face of an increasingly administered society and its insistence upon social justice rather than due process as the ultimate goal of public policy appear to us to be rational prescriptions for ills traceable to administrative orthodoxy.

Yet today "system maintainers" within public administration hold the new public administration at arm's length and view it with deep suspicion, if not profound revulsion, under the illusion that both agency and personal survival are assured by continuance of the existing order of things. Safety from the unknown and untried is identified with the status quo. The lessons of history, however, demonstrate time and again that this is not only illusory but is, in fact, an invitation to disaster. This peculiar form of self-deception either fails to take into account the inevitability of change or seeks to accord it a peripheral rather than a central role.

VICTOR A. THOMPSON: POST-INDUSTRIAL NEO-WEBERISM

We have been awaiting for some time a major and well-reasoned counterattack upon the general thrust of the new public administration. The publication of Victor A. Thompson's *Without Sympathy or Enthusiasm. The Problem of Administrative Compassion*[1] is the most significant critique of newer trends in public administration and deserves to be carefully read by students of administration alongside Frank Marini's *Toward a New Public Administration. The Minnowbrook Perspective*,[2] which is possibly the best volume expounding the new public administration. It is beyond the scope of this concluding chapter to delve deeply into the richness afforded by exposure to these divergent approaches. We merely note that this should be an integral part of public administration education. No student should be denied this worthwhile and exhilarating experience.

We do feel that Thompson's general theme deserves our own comments, leaving to more detailed reviews many of the secondary issues he raises. Thompson's volume expands upon a theme in Richard N. Goodwin's *The American Condition*.[3]

Thompson reveals his basic congruence with the assumptions in Goodwin's volume.

The organization-tool is a consciously adapted design for goal accomplishment. It is a system . . . it is a hundred percent prescription. It is a system of roles and rules. It does not describe behavior; it prescribes it. . . . In the artificial system, all relationships are impersonal and abstract. There is not only no compassion; there is no way that compassion can be included. . . . In the final analysis, compassion is an individual gift, not an organizational one.[4]

In a similar vein,

The client becomes part of a problem category, not a historical person: He becomes an applicant for welfare, a speeder, a cardiac case, etc. In this transaction, he is not a person. The transaction is impersonal and this fact actually facilitates the expert solution of his problem. Interpersonal emotions do not interfere with the instrumental application of the specialist's expertise. . . . His [the client's] individuality, which is his identity, is ignored.[5]

Further,

Good service is professional, impersonal and equal—that is universalistic and non-compassionate.[6]

Finally,

The modern administrative norm, which made efficient administration possible, was the rule that everyone in the same problem category should be treated equally. The result of the norm was to strip away the uniqueness of individuals and to turn administration into an efficient business of mass processing of cases within each problem category. This resulted in an enormous lowering of unit costs, plus other valuable consequences, such as predictability. Thus, the norm was a necessary pre-requisite of modern mass democratic government. . . . The rule of law in this sense is an administrative necessity in an industrial country. Industrialism is impossible without the lowered costs and increased predictability that results.[7]

For Thompson administrative efficiency is the highest value to be preserved and the organization is a tool, nothing more, to accomplish this end. Administrative efficiency is the key concern of the bureaucratic "functionary." The goals toward which such efficiency may be applied are not the proper concern of the members of the organization. In Thompson's words:

> A functionary does his duty, applies his skills, performs his practiced routines, regardless of what goal or whose goal is involved. A screwdriver does not choose among goals or among owners. It does what it is told.[8]

The "rule of law," like efficiency, is viewed as incompatible with deviation from universalistic rules and regulations. Thompson observes:

> Administrative "compassion" can be thought of as special treatment, as "stretching" the rules, as the pre-modern "rule of men" rather than the "rule of law."[9]

Thompson insists that administration must be impersonal, abstract and oblivious to "special treatment" or compassion. He cites, among others, the example of "a speeder" and advances the proposition that "interpersonal emotions do not interfere with the instrumental application of the specialist's expertise . . . [the client's] unique individuality, which is his identity, is ignored."[10] To which we reply that there is a wide range of variables in the policeman's internal mental "set," in addition to a staggering number of variables in the immediate external environment surrounding him. Let us assume possibly the *simplest* situation, i.e., a "speeder" apprehended by a traffic officer. Dr. Karl Menninger lists a *few* of the many intangible variables which the mere apprehension of a violator may call into play.

1. The intelligence and experience of the police officer who observes the offense or to whom it is reported.

2. His emotional state at the time of observing the offense and attempting to follow up on his observation.

3. The moral philosophy or code of this officer and his department.

4. His susceptibility to dissuasion or corruption and the current police practice in that community at that time.

5. The demeanor, clothing, general appearance, hair grooming and speech of the suspect.

6. The color of his skin: white, yellow, brown, red, or black.

7. The reaction of the accosted offender to the encounter, including the verbal facility and clarity with which he explains or defends his action or predicament.

8. Inferences or evidence regarding the arrested man's connections—social, financial, political.

9. The time of day, the place, the surroundings, the witnesses, the availability of help for either party.

10. The wisdom and the state of mind of the police court judge or other authority before whom the offender is taken by the arresting officer.

11. The availability of space for detaining the suspect.

12. The general state of mind of the people everywhere at the time of this arrest.

13. The stage of the sin-into-crime shift, and the degree of zeal of coercion-to-virtue prevalent in that area at that time. These vary greatly from city to city, from precinct to precinct, from city to country, from agricultural to industrial communities, and from year to year.[11]

As if this weren't enough, Menninger emphasizes the complexity of the situation as the officer "must decide in a few minutes whether to take an offender in charge or release him, where to take him or send him, and how to get him there, and what to accuse him of."[12] In point of fact, in this simple confrontation of public servant and private citizen, interpersonal emotions *do* shape the application of the specialist's expertise and, despite Professor Thompson's protestations to the contrary, the unique individuality and identity of the "violator" is not only *not* ignored but may be the crucial elements in the shaping of a final decision. Expertise here becomes relative, as it is possible, or perhaps even probable, that different traffic officers confronted with the identical situation might arrive at opposite conclusions. To what is this owing? Certainly not to any impersonal involvement, but rather to a highly personal or even subconscious involvement and resolution of the problem based upon evaluation of the unique circumstances surrounding it. The officer may find any doctrine of deterministic and impersonal universalism in conflict with the realities of day-to-day administration.

The authors take exception to the doctrine that bureaucratic roles are non-creative and that conscience, emotion and compassion must be abandoned. According to Thompson, the modern bureaucrat can offer only impersonal and non-compassionate treatment as the artifically prescribed roles and rules "are bundles of duties (and powers). They do not care; they have no feelings."[13] This position overlooks the great mass of data leading to the conclusion that artificially prescribed roles are, in fact, shaped by incumbents themselves and their interactions with colleagues, subordinates and, often, their clients.

The validity of the organization chart as a true reflection of agency decision-making has long been rejected. The externally and artificially determined roles of bureaucrats are developed in conjunction with the agency's organization chart; otherwise it would have to be assumed that externally determined roles may conflict with formal superior-subordinate or central-field relationships—a clearly untenable proposition.

The nub of the matter is simply that being "artificial" by definition, "artificially prescribed roles" cannot reflect the operative and often determinative human elements in administrative settings. The works of many psychologists, psychiatrists, sociologists and political scientists as well as common experience should warn us against an easy acceptance of non-emotional, purely rationalistic-mechanistic modes of administrative behavior in "lock-step" with artificially determined and preconceived bundles of duties and powers. This is oversimplication *in extremis*. Conscience and emotion are central to understanding administrative decision-making. In fact, the crucial contemporary question is simply under what *conditions* and to *what degree* they are compatible with the broader "public interest." In 1974 the National Academy of Public

Administration published a tentative draft of ethical guidelines for public administrators. The statement, in part, reads:

> Where there is discretion, there is uncertainty, and there may be conflicting obligations and loyalties. In dealing with this situation, the administrator is subject to a double hierarchy of authority, one impersonal and one personal, which defines his obligations. The hierarchy of law (constitutional, statutory, administrative) is impersonal. The chain of direction or command, into which he fits somewhere, is quite personal. The law in its various forms frequently is stated in general terms, which must be interpreted, and the courts, which formally and potentially have the last word in interpretation, never get around to definitive interpretations on the vast majority of issues that arise administratively. It thus falls to the administrative authorities to interpret and delineate the law through policies, programs, instructions, rules, procedures, and an infinity of decisions. Neither the formal law nor the administrative law is always internally consistent; and public officials, both political executives and professional administrators, do not always agree in their interpretation of the law and its implementation through policies and programs. They can and do disagree about what is wise or in the public interest. Disagreements grow out of different values, out of different degrees of ignorance or understanding, and out of different purposes. Here is where the most difficult ethical issues arise for administrators. They are not mindless minions of the organization, but are pledged by the system to employ their brains, not just their brawn in the public service. They are pledged to think and be honest in their thoughts.[14]

The position of the individual is clear—he is central to much of his own decision-making on behalf of his organization. More simplistic interpretations of administrative behavior may relieve us of many of the dilemmas we might otherwise face, but they are simply not persuasive descriptions of reality.

645

Thompson emphasizes the "rule of law" as incompatible with administrative compassion. Yet there is much in the law that reflects compassion. The abandonment of torture in most civilized countries, the privilege against self-incrimination, trial by jury and, significantly, a jury of one's peers, the right to defense counsel, the legislative "private bill" granting individual relief, the executive powers of "clemency" (pardon, commutation of sentence, reprieve), parole, probation, the suspended sentence, the right of appeal and many others reflect the emergence of a legal system permeated with regard for compassion. The great English constitutional authority A. V. Dicey, who coined the term "rule of law," contends that it implies the predominance of regular law as opposed to the use of arbitrary power; that all officials are, like other citizens, subject to the ordinary laws; and that persons can be punished or tried for crimes only in the courts of law.

Yet the rule of law never meant the absence of compassion. In fact, Dicey points out with great detail the rejection by Englishmen of the continental practice of administrative law courts. He insists that civil servants are subject to the ordinary courts. This, in itself, reflects not merely the limitation of executive authority but a compassionate concern for the citizens of the realm affected by such authority. The "rule of law" is not incompatible with the great "rights" of personal freedom, freedom of speech and public meetings. It is described by Dicey as excluding "arbitrariness, of prerogative, or even of wide discretionary authority on the part of government."[15] But the emphasis was on prevention of arbitrariness or discretion in punishment for other than breaches of the law. Certainly, it is difficult to advance the proposition that the rule of law implies that the civil servant is to ignore mitigating circumstances or special appeals or pleas.

To turn a deaf ear to mitigating circumstances or entreaties in favor of "going by the book" is to assume first that all contingencies are covered by the "book," which they are not, and secondly, to assume that the rule is always a good one, which it may not be. Should the civil servant continue to enforce a rule felt by his or her own conscience to be a "bad" rule and, on the basis of evidence presented by a special plea, to be unjust? We do not believe so. The draft statement of ethical guidelines by the National Academy of Public Administration allows for a number of sequential actions short of resignation in order to influence changes of policy. Modern administrators initiate and shape policy. The need is not to deny this discretion but to assure that whenever possible it is channeled toward humane ends and in a compassionate manner.

The agency without compassion probably does not exist—the question is simply *whose* special pleas are to be recognized in public policy. What Thompson really suggests is that the claims of those outside the existing power structure should fall on deaf ears in the name of "efficiency" and the "rule of law." Thompson insists that the rules of the game be followed, i.e., by negotiation or, as he terms it, the "politics of contract"–by negotiation, compromise and bargaining by interested parties."[16] Yet, as Duane Lockard has convincingly demonstrated in *The Perverted Priorities of American Politics*, the rules themselves determine who has and who will maintain power. Thompson assumes the rules of the game are neutral; Lockard shows they are not. Lockard notes:

> The rules that prescribe the way politics are to be conducted are never neutral; inevitably they give advantages to some and place handicaps on others . . . the rules are never the product of purely objective contemplation (even though that is certainly involved too) but of calculations about the self-interest of any change . . . they facilitate participation in determining policy for certain elements or prevent others from participating. . . .
>
> Unhappily one of the fundamental consequences of the rules, as they now exist and tend to be interpreted, is that those without prestige and power tend to be even more pushed outside the comfortable gambits of American life by the character of those rules and their interpretation.[17]

Some of the consequences of policy-making by these rules are increasing alienation, maldistribution of tax responsibility, social injustice, continuing poverty, non-fulfilling labor and maldistribution of the benefits of public policy.[18] Participation in the governmental process becomes less meaningful and public agencies are viewed as "the enemy" by significant segments of the population.

Thompson's view of bureaucracy as little more than a conduit between external policy-making and the final delivery of services or enforcement of regulations flies full in the face of the latest findings of public policy analysis. Increasingly, public agencies will, of necessity, have to be concerned with causes and goals aside from their primary ones. Public employees, providing essential services over which government has a monopoly, such as police and fire, or near monopoly, such as sanitation, social welfare and education, may simply refuse to play by the traditional rules of the game—preferring, instead, to strike or withhold services by becoming victims of rather selective forms of the flu. Under these conditions talk of organizations as machine-like instruments or tools reacting only to externally imposed stimuli does little to ameliorate the emerging problems of a transitional society. Militant and assertive public employees themselves give the lie to the "conduit-screwdriver" theory. They have emerged as a major political, economic and social force, whose proportion in the working population is rapidly increasing, and, it should be noted, this force is neither value-neutral nor value-free. Under such conditions the primacy accorded to organizational efficiency becomes suspect. As Orville Poland notes in his discussion of program evaluation and administrative theory:

> Most evaluations are undertaken in terms of the achievement of objectives—emphasizing the value, efficiency. Yet public administration is entering an era in which other values are being pressed. Some of these values are incompatible with or irrelevant to efficiency. The growth of collective bargaining has made bargaining a way of decision-making. A decision made by compromise through the bargaining process is not one made rationally and scientifically.[19]

Thompson holds that an agency's single externally determined goal is its sole concern. Yet numerous commentators have observed that survival may be its most basic instinct and, in that process, externally mandated goals have often been compromised. Further, career development programs, community public relations, employee welfare and the establishment of non-discriminatory personnel policies have become, in fact, "givens" on agency priority agendas. The pressures in these directions are simply overwhelming. This is reality.

Thompson's fears that "equality" may be a harbinger of the collapse of the merit system are shared by many concerned persons. Yet we believe that "merit" has been a highly relative concept. The techniques for widespread abuse of that system are well-known: local residence requirements, "loaded" appointments to civil service commissions, oral "examinations" designed to assure the appointment of preselected choices (with virtual impossibility of effectual appeal), and examinations constructed to effectively screen out ethnic and cultural minorities. Veterans' preference, while laudable, may have little relationship to merit. In some state and local jurisdictions veterans' preference may, under certain conditions, be extended to a mother or wife. The disabled veteran is usually accorded more preference "points" than a non-disabled veteran while the non-veteran, despite possibly greater "merit," is allocated no points. The same preference may also apply to promotions or reductions-in-force. To equate, as Thompson does, the thrust of the new public administration with the dilution of the "merit" system is to close one's eyes to the fact that a diluted system has been acceptable from the beginning.

Curiously, Professor Thompson's neo-Weberism is a complete reversal of his earlier views. In his *Public Administration*, co-authored with Professors Herbert Simon and Donald Smithburg, the following crucial passage appears:

> We have now canvassed and attempted to evaluate the accountability procedures and forces in America which enforce responsiveness upon our bureaucracy and thus determine the values and goals reflected in administrative decisions. With regard to these controls *we can safely say that a bureaucracy is always to some extent free from them, and the bigger and more complex it is, the more it is free. The administrator is always to some extent an*

649

initiator of values, partly as a representative of some interest group or groups, but also independently, in his own right. He can never be completely governed by others, and, as a matter of fact, he has considerable latitude of choice before the consequences of his decisions will bring reactions that threaten survival . . . .

The administrators are not insulated from society like Plato's guardians. They are tied to society by all the formal procedures of accountability, by the need to satisfy politically powerful clientele groups and *by their own social training and identifications.*[20]

His administrator of the '50's bears little resemblance to his "functionary" of the mid-'70's. Where extensive research and observation have since confirmed his earlier views, he now resurrects the discarded notion of Weber's "harnessed" bureaucrat—the most tragic figure in all of administrative literature. He also attempts to reinvigorate the defunct Wilsonian dichotomy between the making of policy and its execution.

We do not quarrel with Thompson's goal of critically analyzing the new public administration. Indeed, we share some of his concerns for potential abuses. We are concerned, however, that the conditions and bases for his singular conceptual reversal were not included as a requisite preamble to his latest conclusions.

Professor Thompson's post-industrial neo-Weberism is little more than an illusory image of what can never be—a bureaucracy of childlike simplicity where, devoid of emotions or conscience, the ends of public policy are of no consequence to the administrators of public authority. The organization is now man's natural state. Rather than depending upon outmoded and negativistic orthodoxy, the task of public administration is to unceasingly probe the outer circumference of existing knowledge and develop new hypotheses and models more consistent with an attitude of attempting to understand than to believe that we know—and thereby foreclose all further knowledge. Public administration has probed far beyond the old orthodoxy and, as in Victor Herbert's *Toyland*, "once you've passed its borders you can ne'er return again."

Professor Emmette S. Redford articulates a radical departure from traditional political theories. He states:

> Man . . . is subordinate to decisions made in and action taken through institutions. He is not born in a natural state subject to nature alone, but in an administered society where numerous organizations allocate advantages and disadvantages to him.[21]

This is precisely why in a democratic society human dignity and compassion are so essential. Neither administrative nor social stability are assured by denying this proposition. Very simply put, man's institutions are too important to be left to the "professionals" and "experts." "Efficiency," in its orthodox formulation as a relationship of input resources to output, is inadequate as the ultimate criterion of organizational effectiveness.

PROBLEMS OF HUMAN DIGNITY

To set forth the proposition that there is a necessity for moral concern and personal responsibility by those exercising the great regulative and coercive powers of the modern state is not to deny the existence of difficult problems and dilemmas. It merely shifts the controversy to a more meaningful level. Some problems inherent in administrative doctrines of human dignity are:

1. Their application to specific situations may be very difficult. How to weigh one man's dignity over another's?

2. If human dignity is applicable, as it apparently is, to both administrators and citizens, how are potential conflicts to be resolved?

3. Are there conditions under which the "public interest" may conflict with the doctrine of human dignity?

4. What is the role of administrators with a commitment to human dignity working within traditional hierarchical organizations?

5. How does moral concern relate to the systems approach? What is the meaning of human dignity in this context?

6. Can the value of a human being be measured or computed? If so, how? If not, how can it realistically be utilized as a criterion for organizational design or administrative decision-making?[22] What are alternative guidelines?

THE "NEW" ORTHODOXY

All of the perils are not in the heavy hand of the past. Some are already discernible in the more immediate future. The trend toward "professional" imagery in public administration may be little more than personal "puffery"—an effort to redress the past abysmal societal perceptions of the public employee. Often the "professional" outlook has led to status quoism and to serving self-interest rather than public interest.

The movement to introduce a uniform approach to the content of public administration programs in colleges and universities despite our highly diverse governmental system appears to be making significant headway. The rise of national organizations and associations, some of a surprisingly élitist nature, purporting to speak for "standards" and "quality" of public administration education raises crucial issues. The accreditation movement in other academic fields (engineering, architecture, law, medicine, etc.) is now spilling over into public administration. Accreditation is a two-edged sword. Where it might stimulate the raising of standards in academic programs, it might also impose a deadening conformity—a situation to be avoided in a period of unease and social and economic transition.

The greatest strength of public administration today is its ideological diversity and the diffusion of leadership between practitioners and theoreticians, system maintainers and humanistic radicals, behaviorists and philosophers. No one single figure has dominated the field since Woodrow Wilson, and while some major figures have many disciples, the diffusion of intellectual leadership has, on the whole, been a healthy influence.

Perhaps the most important quality to be maintained as we join the uncertain future is a healthy scepticism so that the freedom from orthodoxies of the past is not exchanged for the fetters of new orthodoxy. The nature of truth is anything but settled.

The story is told of an ancient and far-away king who wished to find the wisest man in all the land. The three men deemed to be the wisest were brought before him. To each he asked, "Why are you the wisest?" The first replied, "I am the wisest, Your Highness, because the truth comes to me from contemplation of my inner self. I climb to the mountain top and the eternal truths are to be found there as I ponder the meaning of life in deep introspection. These truths I then carry back to the valleys below so they shall govern the affairs of all humankind."

The second replied, "I am the wisest, Your Highness, because I do not deal with introspection, for to know only oneself is to know only the fool. I see and I experience. I have traveled to the furthest reaches of the furthest horizons through strange lands and across vast oceans and past mighty rivers. I have seen and experienced most of what there is to see and experience."

The third replied, "I do not climb the high mountain peaks, Your Highness, nor have I traveled beyond my little village. I spend my days in the marketplace and listen very carefully. I certainly cannot be wise because each time I have heard the truth another argument sounds the truer. Each argument has its own grain of truth." Whereupon the King turned on his heels and retreated to ponder which of the three was truly the wisest.

NOTES

1. Victor A. Thompson, *Without Sympathy or Enthusiasm. The Problem of Administrative Compassion*. University, Alabama: University of Alabama Press, 1975.

2. Frank Marini (ed.), *Toward a New Public Administration. The Minnowbrook Perspective*. Scranton: Chandler, 1971.

3. Richard N. Goodwin, *The American Condition*. Garden City: Doubleday, 1974.

4. Thompson, *op. cit.*, p. 13.

5. *Ibid.*, p. 9.

6. *Ibid.*, p. 58.

7. *Ibid.*, p. 41.

8. *Ibid.*, p. 10.

9. *Ibid.*, p. 21.

10. *Ibid.*, p. 9.

11. Karl Menninger, M. D., *Whatever Became of Sin*? New York: Hawthorne Books, 1973, pp. 54-55. Footnotes omitted.

12. *Ibid.*, p. 55.

13. Thompson, *op. cit.*, p. 17.

14. George A. Graham, "Ethical Guidelines for Public Administrators: Observations on Rules of the Game," *Public Administration Review*, Vol. 34, No. 1 (Jan.-Feb., 1974), p. 90.

15. A. V. Dicey, *Introduction to the Study of Law and the Constitution*, 8th edition. London: Macmillan, 1927, p. 198.

16. Thompson, *op. cit.*, p. 67.

17. Duane Lockard, *The Perverted Priorities of American Politics*. New York: Macmillan, 1971, pp. 28, 39, 43.

18. See Edward S. Greenberg, *Serving the Few. Corporate Capitalism and the Bias of Government Policy*. New York: John Wiley & Sons, 1974.

19. Orville F. Poland, "Program Evaluation and Administrative Theory," *Public Administration Review*, Vol. 34, No. 4 (July-August, 1974), p. 337.

20. Herbert A. Simon, Donald W. Smithburg and Victor A. Thompson, *Public Administration*. New York: Alfred A. Knopf, 1950, pp. 554-555. Italics supplied.

21. Emmette S. Redford, *Democracy in the Administrative State*. New York: Oxford University Press, 1969, p. 179.

22. For an interesting development of this theme and one approach to the value of a human life see J. E. Hayzelden, "The Value of Human Life," *Public Administration* London, Vol. 46 (Winter, 1968), pp. 427–441.

BIBLIOGRAPHY

CHALLENGES AND ISSUES IN PUBLIC ADMINISTRATION

Books

Barkun, Michael. *Disaster and the Millennium*. New Haven, Conn.: Yale University Press, 1974.

Barnet, Richard J., and Muller, Ronald E., *Global Reach: The Power of the Multinational Corporations*. New York: Simon & Schuster, 1974.

Birnbaum, Norman. *The Crisis of Industrial Society*. New York: Oxford University Press, 1969.

Boulding, Kenneth E., *The Meaning of the 20th Century: The Great Transition*. New York: Harper Colophon, 1964.

Christoffel, Tom, et al., *Up Against the American Myth*. New York: Holt Rinehart Winston, 1970.

Chester, Daniel N. and Bowring, Nona, *Questions in Parliament*. Oxford: The Clarendon Press, 1962.

Dahl, Robert A., *A Preface to Democratic Theory*. Chicago: University of Chicago Press, Phoenix Books, 1956.

Davis, John P., *Corporations*. New York: Capricorn Books, 1961.

Domhoff, G. William, *The Higher Circles*. New York: Random House, 1970.

——*Who Rules America?* Englewood Cliffs, New Jersey: Prentice Hall, 1967.

Dvorin, Eugene P. and Simmons, Robert H., *From Amoral to Humane Bureaucracy*. San Francisco: Canfield Press, 1972.

Eisenhower, Milton, and U. S. Commission on the Causes and Prevention of Violence. *To Establish Justice, To Insure Domestic Tranquility: The Final Report of the National Commission on the Causes and Prevention of Violence*. New York: Bantam, 1970.

Ellul, Jacques, *The Technological Society*. New York: A. A. Knopf, 1965.

Eells, Richard, *The Government of Corporations*. New York: Free Press, 1962.

Engler, Robert, *The Politics of Oil: Private Power & Democratic Directions*. Chicago: University of Chicago Press, 1961.

Epstein, Edwin M., *The Corporation in American Politics*. Englewood Cliffs, N.J.: Prentice-Hall, 1969.

Ehrlich, Paul R., *The End of Affluence*. New York: Ballantine, 1974.

Facts and Figures on Government Finance (17th ed.). Tax Foundation, New York, 1973.

Fantini, Mario and Gittel, Marilyn, *Decentralization: Achieving Reform*. New York: Praeger Publishers, 1973.

Fesler, James W., *The Independence of State Regulatory Agencies*. Chicago: Public Administration Service, 1942.

Fuller, R. Buckminster, *Utopia or Oblivion: The Prospects for Humanity*. New York: Bantam Paperback, 1969.

Galbraith, John Kenneth, *The Affluent Society*. Boston: Houghton Mifflin Company, 1958.

Gaus, John, *Reflections on Public Administration*. Alabama: University of Alabama Press, 1974.

Greenberg, Edward S., *Serving the Few: Corporate Capitalism and the Bias of Government Policy*. New York: John Wiley & Sons, 1974.

Green, Mark J., et al., *The Closed Enterprise System*. New York: Grossman, 1972.

Griffith, Ernest S., *Congress: Its Contemporary Role*. New York: New York University Press, 1961.

Heilbroner, Robert L., *An Inquiry into the Human Prospect*. New York: W. W. Norton & Co., 1974.

Hamilton, Alexander, et al., *The Federalist*, No. 51, New York: Modern Library.

Howarth, Patrick, *Questions in the House*. London: William Clowes, 1956.

Kohlmeier, Louis M., Jr., *The Regulators: Watchdog Agencies and the Public Interest*. New York: Harper & Row, 1969.

Krueger, Robert B., et al., *The United States and International Oil*. New York: Praeger, 1975.

Lewis, Richard, *The Nuclear Power Rebellion*. New York: Viking, 1972.

Lipson, Leslie, *The American Governor*. Chicago: University of Chicago Press, 1939.

Long, Norton E., *The Polity*. Chicago: Rand McNally, 1962.

MacIver, R. M., *The Web of Government*. New York: Free Press, 1965.

Marchetti, Victor and Marks, John D., *The C. I. A. and the Cult of Intelligence*. New York: Alfred A. Knopf, Inc., 1974.

Meadows, Donella H., et al., *The Limits to Growth*. New York: Universe Books, 1972.

Mitford, Jessica, *Kind and Usual Punishment*. New York: Knopf, 1973.

Muller, Herbert J., *Uses of the Future*. Bloomington: Indiana University Press, 1974.

Neustadt, Richard E., *Presidential Power*. New York: Wiley, 1960.

Nieburg, H. L., *Culture Storm: Politics and the Ritual Order*. New York: St. Martin's Press, 1973.

Nossiter, Bernard D., *The Mythmakers*. Boston: Beacon Press, 1964.

Peabody, Robert L. and Polsby, Nelson W. (eds.), *New Perspectives on the House of Representatives*. Chicago: Rand McNally, 1963.

Prewitt, Kenneth and Stone, Alan. *The Ruling Elites: Elite Theory, Power, and American Democracy*. New York: Harper & Row, 1973.

Raskin, Marcus, *Notes on the Old System*. New York: David McKay Company, 1974.

Redford, Emmette S., *Ideal and Practice in Public Administration*. University, Alabama: University of Alabama Press, 1958.

——*The Regulatory Process*. Austin: University of Texas, 1969.

Robbins, William, *The American Food Scandal*. New York: William Morrow, 1974.

Roszak, Theodore, *The Making of a Counter Culture*. Garden City: Doubleday & Co., 1969.

——*Where the Wasteland Ends: Politics and Transcendence in Postindustrial Society*. Garden City: Anchor, 1973.

Rossiter, Clinton, *The American Presidency* (rev. ed.). New York: Harcourt Brace, Harvest Book, 1960.

Rourke, Francis E., *Bureaucracy, Politics and Public Policy*. Boston: Little Brown Company, 1969.

Said, Abdul A. and Simmons, Luiz R. (eds.), *The New Sovereigns: Multinational Corporations as World Powers*. Englewood Cliffs, N.J.: Prentice-Hall, 1975.

Schwartz, Eugene S., *Overskill*. Chicago: Quandrangle Books, 1971.

Selznick, Philip, *Leadership in Administration*. New York: Row, Peterson, 1957.

——*TVA and the Grassroots*. Berkeley and Los Angeles, California: University of California Press, 1953.

Smith, Bruce L. R. and Hague, D. C., *The Dilemma of Accountability in Modern Government: Independence vs. Control*. London: MacMillan, 1971.

Spiro, Herbert J., *Responsibility in Government: Theory & Practice*. New York: Van Nostrand Reinhold, 1969.

Tawney, R. H., *The Acquisitive Society*. New York: Harcourt, Brace & World, 1920.

Toffler, Alvin, *Future Shock*. New York: Bantam Books, 1971.

Tussman, Joseph, *Obligation and the Body Politic*. New York: Oxford University Press, 1960.

Weisband, Edward and Franck, Thomas M. *Resignation in Protest*. New York: Grossman Publishers, A Division of Viking Press, 1975.

Wildavsky, Aaron, *The Politics of the Budgetary Process*. Boston: Little Brown & Co., 1964.

Willbern, York, *The Withering Away of the City*. Birmingham: University of Alabama Press, 1964.

Winslow, John F., *Conglomerates Unlimited: The Failure of Regulation*. Bloomington: Indiana University Press, 1973.

Wise, David and Ross, Thomas B., *The Invisible Government*. New York: Bantam, 1965.

Woll, Peter, *American Bureaucracy*. New York: W. W. Norton, 1962.

Articles, Government Documents, Occasional Papers

ACIR Report, M-86, *Trends in Fiscal Federalism 1954-1974*. Advisory Commission on Intergovernmental Relations, Washington, D.C., February, 1975.

Appleby, Paul H., "Public Administration and Democracy," in Martin, Roscoe C., *Public Administration and Democracy*. Syracuse, N.Y.: Syracuse University Press, 1965.

Ervin Committee, *The Senate Watergate Report: The Final Report of the Senate Select Committee on Presidential Campaign Activities*. New York: Dell, 1974. Volume 1.

——*The Senate Watergate Report: The Final Report of the Senate Select Committee on Presidential Activities*. New York: Dell, 1974. Volume 2.

Finer, Herman, "Administrative Responsibility in Democratic Government," *Public Administration Review*, Vol. I, No. 4, Summer 1941, pp. 336-337.

Friedrich, Carl J., "Public Policy and the Nature of Administrative Responsibility," in Friedrich, C. J. and Mason, Edward S. (eds.), *Public Policy*. Cambridge: Harvard University Press, 1940.

Fusfeld, Daniel R., "The Rise of the Corporate State in America," *Journal of Economic Issues*, Vol. VI, No. 1, March, 1972, pp. 1-22.

Galbraith, John Kenneth, "What Comes After General Motors?" *The New Republic*, November 2, 1974.

Huitt, Ralph K., "The Congressional Committee: A Case Study," *American Political Science Review*, Vol. XLVIII, No. 2, June, 1954.

Kaufman, Herbert, "Emerging Conflicts in the Doctrines of Public Administration," *American Political Science Review*, Vol. L, December, 1956.

Lalonde, Marc, *A New Perspective on the Health of Canadians*. Ottawa: Ministry of National Health and Welfare, 1974.

Martinson, Robert, "The Paradox of Prison Reform," *The New Republic*, Vol. 166, April 1, 1972.

Masters, Nicholas A., "House Committee Assignments," *American Political Science Review*, Vol. LV, No. 2, June, 1961.

Parker, Richard, *The Myth of the Middle Class*. New York: Harper Colophon, 1972.

Paulsen, David F., and Denhardt, Robert B. (eds.), *Pollution and Public Policy*. New York: Dodd, Mead, and Co., 1973.

Redford, Emmette, "The Protection of the Public Interest with Special Reference to Administrative Regulation," *American Political Science Review*, XLVIII, No. 4, December, 1954.

Rose, D. J., "Energy Policy in the U. S.," *Scientific American*, January, 1974.

Ray, Dennis M., "Corporations and Academic Foreign Relations," *The Annals of the American Academy of Political Science*, Philadelphia, September, 1972.

Shipman, George A., "The Pacific Northwest States," *The States of the Pacific Northwest*, American Assembly, The Washington Research Council, Seattle, 1957.

Simmons, Robert H., "American State Executive Studies: *A Suggested New Departure*," Western Political Quarterly, December, 1964.

Snell, Bradford, *American Ground Transport,* Subcommittee Anti-Trust and Monopoly, California State Judiciary Committee, February 26, 1974, pp. 23-26.

Stone, Christopher D., "Should Trees Have Legal Standing? Toward Legal Rights for Natural Objects," 45, *So. Cal. Law Review*, pp. 450-501.

U. S. Bureau of Census, *Historical Statistics of the United States, Colonial Times to 1957,* Washington, D. C., U. S. Government Printing Office, 1960.

——*Statistical Abstract of the United States: 1974* (95th ed.). Washington, D. C., U. S. Government Printing Office, 1974.

Willbern, York, "Administrative Control of Petroleum Production in Texas," in Redford, Emmette S. (ed.), *Public Administration and Policy Formation*. Austin: University of Texas Press, 1956.

——"Administration in State Government," American Assembly, *The Forty-Eight States: Their Tasks as Policy Makers and Administrators*. New York: Columbia University Press, 1955.

Wiltse, Charles M., "The Representative Function of Bureaucracy," *American Political Science Review*, Vol. XXXV, June 1941.

HISTORY AND PHILOSOPHY OF PUBLIC ADMINISTRATION

Books

Adams, Henry (ed.), *Documents Relating to New England Federalism 1800-1815*. New York: Burt Franklin, 1877.

Barber, James David, *Power in Committees: An Experiment in the Governmental Process*. Chicago: Rand McNally and Co., 1966.

Barnard, Chester I., *The Functions of the Executive*. Cambridge: Harvard University Press, 1938.

Bell, Daniel, *The Coming of Post-Industrial Society: A Venture in Social Forecasting*. New York: Basic Books, 1973.

Bernstein, Marver, *Regulating Business by Independent Commissions*. Princeton: Princeton University Press, 1955.

Burnham, James, *The Managerial Revolution. What is Happening in the World*. New York: John Day Co., 1941.

Clough, Wilson Ober (ed.), *Intellectual Origins of American National Thought* (second ed.). New York: Corinth Books, 1955.

Cox, Edward F., Fellmuth, Robert C. and Schulz, John E., *The Nader Report on the Federal Trade Commission*. New York: Grove Press, 1969.

Cunningham, Raymond J. (ed.), *The Populists in Historical Perspective*. Boston: D. C. Heath, 1968.

Dahlberg, Jane S., *The New York Bureau of Municipal Research. Pioneer in Government Administration*. New York: New York University Press, 1966.

Easton, David, *A Framework for Political Analysis*. Englewood Cliffs, N.J.: Prentice-Hall, 1965.

—— *A Systems Analysis of Political Life*. New York: Wiley, 1965.

Eisenstadt, S.N., *The Political Systems of Empires*. New York: The Free Press, 1963.

Foulke, William Dudley, *Fighting the Spoilsmen Reminiscences of the Civil Service Reform Movement*. New York and London: G. P. Putnam's Sons, 1919.

Friederich, Carl J. (ed.), *Nomos V. The Public Interest*. New York: Atherton Press, 1962.

Friendly, Henry J., *The Federal Administrative Agencies: The Need for Better Definition of Standards*. Cambridge: Harvard University Press, 1962.

Frost, Richard T., *Cases in State and Local Government*. Englewood Cliffs, N.J.: Prentice-Hall, 1962.

Gerth, H. H. and Mills, C. Wright (eds.), *From Max Weber: Essays in Sociology*. New York: Oxford University Press, 1958.

Golembiewski, Robert T. and White, Michael, *Cases in Public Management*. Chicago: Rand McNally, 1973.

Goodnow, Frank J., *Municipal Home Rule. A Study in Administration*. New York: Macmillan, 1895.

Gulick, Luther and Urwick L. (eds.), *Papers on the Science of Administration*. New York: Institute of Public Administration, 1937.

Hackney, Sheldon, *Populism: The Critical Issues*. Boston: Little Brown, 1971.

Hall, Calvin S., *A Primer of Freudian Psychology*. New York: Mentor Books, 1960.

Harvey, Donald R., *The Civil Service Commission*. New York: Praeger Publishers, 1970.

Heady, Ferrel, *Public Administration: A Comparative Perspective*. Englewood Cliffs, N.J.: Prentice-Hall, 1966.

Herring, E. Pendleton, *Public Administration and the Public Interest*. New York and London: McGraw-Hill Book Co., 1936.

Hyneman, Charles S., *Bureaucracy in a Democracy*. New York: Harper and Row, 1950.

James, William, *Pragmatism and Other Essays*. New York: Washington Square Press, 1963. paperback.

Janis, Irving, *Victims of Group Think*. Boston: Houghton Mifflin, 1972.

Karl, Barry Dean, *Executive Reorganization and Reform in the New Deal. The Genesis of Administrative Management, 1900-1939*. Cambridge: Harvard University Press, 1963.

Krislov, Samuel, *The Negro in Federal Employment. The Quest for Equal Opportunity*. Minneapolis: University of Minnesota Press, 1967.

Lasswell, Harold D., *Psychopathology and Politics*. Chicago: University of Chicago Press, 1930.

Leach, Richard H., *American Federalism*. New York: W. W. Norton, 1970.

Lockard, Duane, *The Perverted Priorities of American Politics*. New York: Macmillan, 1971.

MacAvoy, Paul W., *The Crisis of the Regulatory Commissions An Introduction to a Current Issue of Public Policy*. New York: W. W. Norton, 1970.

Mandelker, Daniel R., *Managing Our Urban Environment Cases, Text, and Problems*. Indianapolis: Bobbs-Merrill, 1971.

Marini, Frank (ed.), *Toward a New Public Administration. The Minnowbrook Perspective*. Scranton: Chandler Publishing Co., 1971.

Martin, Roscoe C. (ed.), *Public Administration & Democracy*. Syracuse: Syracuse University Press, 1965.

Mills, Warner E. Jr., and Davis, Harry R. *Small City Government. Seven Cases in Decision Making*. New York: Random House, 1962.

Mosher, Frederick, *Democracy and the Public Service*. New York: Oxford University Press, 1968.

Nelson, Dalmas, *Administrative Agencies of the U.S.A., Their Decisions and Authority*. Detroit: Wayne State University Press, 1964.

Noll, Roger G., *Reforming Regulation, An Evaluation of the Ash Council Proposals. A Staff Paper*. Washington, D.C.: The Brookings Institute, 1971.

Ostrom, Vincent, *The Intellectual Crisis in American Public Administration*. University, Alabama: University of Alabama Press, 1973.

Presthus, Robert, *Behavioral Approaches to Public Administration*. University, Alabama: University of Alabama Press, 1965.

Redford, Emmette S., *Democracy in the Administrative State*. New York: Oxford University Press, 1969.

Revel, Jean-Francois, *Without Marx or Jesus The New American Revolution Has Begun*. New York: Delta Publishing Co., 1972.

Rheinstein, Max (ed.), *Max Weber on Law in Economy and Society*. New York: Simon and Schuster/Clarion Books, 1954.

Russell, Bertrand, *Power: A New Social Analysis*. New York: Barnes & Noble, 1962.

Sadler, William A., *Existence and Love: A New Approach in Existential Phenomenology*. New York: Charles Scribner's Sons, 1969.

Schwartz, Bernard, *The Professor and the Commissions*. New York: Alfred A. Knopf, 1959.

Simon, Herbert A., *Administrative Behavior: A Study of Decision-Making Processes in Administrative Organization*. New York: Macmillan, 1948.

Smith, Darrell Hevenor, *The United States Civil Service Commission: Its History, Activities and Organization*. Baltimore: The Johns Hopkins University Press, 1928.

Syed, Anwar, *The Political Theory of American Local Government*. New York: Random House, 1966.

Stewart, Frank Mann, *The National Civil Service Reform League–History, Activities and Problems*. Austin: University of Texas Press, 1929.

Stockfish, J. A., *The Political Economy of Bureaucracy*. New York: General Learning Press, 1972.

Van Riper, Paul, *History of the United States Civil Service*. Evanston, Illinois: Row, Peterson, 1958.

Waldo, Dwight, *The Administrative State: A Study of the Political Theory of American Public Administration*. New York: The Ronald Press, 1948.

Waldo, Dwight. *Perspectives on Administration*. University, Alabama: University of Alabama Press, 1956.

Waldo, Dwight (ed.), *Public Administration in a Time of Turbulence*. Scranton: Chandler Publishing Co., 1971.

Weber, Max, *Politics as a Vocation*. Philadelphia: Fortress Press, 1965.

White, Leonard D., *Introduction to the Study of Public Administration*. New York: Macmillan, 1955.

——*The Federalists: A Study in Administrative History*. New York: Macmillan Co., 1961.

——*The Jacksonians: A Study in Administrative History–1829–1861*. New York: Macmillan Co., 1963.

665

────── *The Jeffersonians: A Study in Administrative History—1801-1829*. New York: Macmillan Co., 1961.

──────*The Republican Era 1869-1901*. New York: Macmillan Co., 1963.

Wilson, Woodrow, *Congressional Government: A Study in American Politics*. New York: Meridian Books, 1965.

Articles, Government Documents, Occasional Papers

Advisory Council on Intergovernmental Personnel Policy. *More Effective Public Service. The First Report of the President and the Congress by the Advisory Council on Intergovernmental Personnel Policy— January 1973*. Subcommittee on Intergovernmental Relations of the Committee on Government Operations, U.S. Senate, 93rd Congress, 2nd Session, March 1974, pp. 19-20.

Advisory Council on Intergovernmental Personnel Policy. *More Effective Public Service Supplementary Report to the President and the Congress*. Prepared by the Advisory Council of Intergovernmental Personnel Policy—July 1974. Subcommittee on Intergovernmental Relations of the Committee on Government Operations, U.S. Senate, 93rd Congress, 2nd Session, October 1974.

Brownlow, Louis, "A General View in the Executive Office of the President: A Symposium," in *Public Administration Review*, Vol. I, No. 2 (Winter 1941), pp. 103-104.

Carey, William D., "Central Field Relationships in the War Production Board," *Public Administration Review*, Vol. 4, No. 1 (Winter 1944), p. 31.

Dahl, Robert A., "The Science of Administration: Three Problems," *Public Administration Review*, Vol. VII, No. 1 (Winter 1947), p. 3.

Easton, David, "An Approach to the Analysis of Political Systems,", *World Politics*, Vol IX, April, 1957.

Emmerich, Herbert, "Administrative Normalcy Impedes Defense," *Public Administration Review*, Vol. 1, No. 4, (Summer 1941), p. 318.

Federal Women's Program: *A Study of Women in the Federal Government 1970*. Prepared for the Federal Women's Program (Washington, D.C.: U.S. Civil Service Commission, Manpower Statistics Division, December 1971), p. 7.

Freeman, J. Leiper, "Bureaucracy in Pressure Politics," *Annals of the American Academy of Political and Social Science* (September 1958), pp. 11-19.

Harris, Joseph P., "The Emergency National Defense Organization," *Public Administration Review*, Vol. I, No. 1, (Autumn 1940), p. 21.

Henderson, L. J., Whitehead, T. N., and Mayo, Elton, "The Effects of Social Environment," in *Papers on the Science of Administration*, edited by Luther Gulick and L. Urwick. New York: Institute of Public Administration, 1937.

Holden, Mathew Jr., "Imperalism in Bureaucracy," *American Political Science Review*, Vol. LX, No. 4, (December 1966), pp. 943-951.

Huntington, Samuel P., "The Marasmus of the I.C.C.," 61 *Yale Law Journal*, pp. 467-509.

Huntley, Robert J. and MacDonald, Robert J., "Urban Managers: Organizational Preferences, Managerial Styles and Social Policy Roles," *The Municipal Yearbook 1975*. Washington, D.C.: International City Management Association, 1975.

Kaufman, Herbert, "Organization Theory and Political Theory," *American Political Science Review*, Vol. LVIII, No. 1 (March 1964).

Long, Norton E., "Power and Administration," *Public Administration Review*, Vol. 9, No. 4 (Autumn 1949), pp. 257-264.

MacIntyre, Alastair, "Existentialism," *Encyclopedia of Philosophy*. New York: Macmillan and the Free Press, 1972, Vol. 3, pp. 147-154.

Report on Regulatory Agencies to the President-Elect. Committee on the Judiciary, 86th Congress, 2nd Session December, 1960.

Sayre, Wallace S., "Trends of a Decade in Administrative Values," *Public Administration Review*, Vol. XI, No. 1 (Winter 1951), p. 5.

Stillman, Richard J. II, "Woodrow Wilson and the Study of Administration: A New Look at an Old Essay," *The American Political Science Review*, Vol. 67, No. 2 (June 1973), pp. 582-588.

Thompson, Proctor, "Size and Effectiveness in the Federal System," in *Essays in Federalism*. Claremont, Calif.: Institute for Studies in Federalism, 1961.

U.S. Code annotated, Title 50, War and National Defense, Ch. 15, Sect. 403.

Wilbern, York, "Professionalization in the Public Service: Too Little or Too Much?" *Public Administration Review*, Vol. XIV, No. 1 (Winter 1954), pp. 3-21.

Wilson, Woodrow, "The Study of Administration," *Political Science Quarterly*, Vol. 2 (June 1887), pp. 197-222.

—— "The Study of Administration," (reprint) *Political Science Quarterly*, vol. LVI, no. 4 (December 1941), p. 482.

Wynia, Bob L., "Federal Bureaucrats' Attitudes Toward a Democratic Ideology," *Public Administration Review,* Vol. 34, No. 2 (March April 1974), pp. 156-162.

ADMINISTRATIVE LAW AND FEDERALISM

Books

Baldwin, Leland D., *Reframing the Constitution. An Imperative for Modern America.* Santa Barbara: Oxford, England: American Bibliographical Center, Clio Press, 1972.

Barton, Weldon V., *Interstate Compacts in the Political Process.* Chapel Hill: University of North Carolina Press, 1967.

Dvorin, Eugene P., *The Senate's War Powers, Debate on Cambodia from the Congressional Record.* Markham Publishing Co., 1971.

Elezar, Daniel J., *American Federalism: A View From the States*, 2nd ed. New York: Thomas Y. Crowell, 1972.

Fantini, Mario and Gittell, Marilyn, *Decentralization: Achieving Reform.* New York and Washington: Praeger Publishers, 1973.

Feld, Richard D. and Grafton, Carl, *The Uneasy Partnership: The Dynamics of Federal, State and Urban Relations.* Palo Alto: National Press Books, 1973.

Fesler, James W., *Area and Administration.* University, Alabama: University of Alabama Press, 1949.

Freund, Ernest, *Administrative Powers Over Persons and Property.* Chicago: University of Chicago Press, 1928.

Graves, W. Brooks, *American Intergovernmental Relations: Their Origins, Historical Development and Current Status.* New York: Charles Scribner & Sons, 1964.

Grodzins, Morton, *The American System: A New View of Government in The United States.* Chicago: Rand McNally, 1966.

Heller, Walter, *New Dimensions of Political Economy.* Cambridge: Harvard University Press, 1966.

Kiefer, Thomas H., *The Political Impact of Federal Aid to State and Local Governments.* Morristown, New Jersey: General Learning Press, 1974.

Kotler, Milton, *Neighborhood Government: The Local Foundations of Political Life.* Indianapolis and New York: Bobbs-Merrill, 1969.

Landis, James M., *The Administrative Process*. New Haven: Yale University Press, 1947.

Leach, Richard H., *American Federalism*. New York: W. W. Norton, 1970.

Leach, Richard H. and Sugg, Redding S. Jr., *The Administration of Interstate Compacts*. Baton Rouge: Louisiana State University Press, 1959.

Pealy, Robert H., *Organization for Comprehensive River Basin Planning: The Texas and Southeast Experiences*. Ann Arbor: Institute of Public Administration, University of Michigan, 1964.

Pearcy, C. Etzel, *A Thirty-Eight State U.S.A.* Fullerton, Calif.: Plycron Press, 1973.

Pritchett, Herman C., *The Roosevelt Court*. New York: Macmillan, 1948.

Riker, William H., *Federalism: Origin, Operation. Significance*. Boston: Little, Brown, 1964.

Thursby, V. V., *Interstate Cooperation: A Study of the Interstate Compact*. Washington, D.C.: Public Affairs Press, 1953.

Tugwell, Rexford, *A Model Constitution for a United Republics of America*. Santa Barbara: Center for the Study of Democratic Institutions and James E. Freel and Associates, 1970.

Wendell, M., *The Interstate Compact Since 1925*. Chicago: Council of State Governments, 1951.

Wildavsky, Aaron, *American Federalism in Perspective*. Boston: Little, Brown, 1967.

Williams, George, "Federal Objectives and Local Accountability," in Joseph D. Sneed and Steven A. Waldhorn (eds.) *Restructuring the Federal System Approaches to Accountability in Post-Categorical Programs*. New York: Crane, Russak, 1975.

Zimmerman, Joseph F., *The Federated City: Community Control in Large Cities*. New York: St. Martin's Press, 1972.

Articles, Government Documents, Occasional Papers

"Curriculum Essays on Citizens, Politics and Administration in Urban Neighborhoods," Special Issue, *Public Administration Review*, Vol. XXXII (October 1972).

Dvorin, Eugene P., "Foreign Aid by States," *National Civic Review*, Vol. LIII, No. 11 (December 1964), pp. 585–590, 622.

Fesler, James, "Approaches to Understanding Decentralization," *The Journal of Politics*, Vol. 27 (August 1965).

Friesema, H. Paul, "Black Control of Central Cities: The Hollow Prize," *Journal of the American Institute of Planners*, Vol. XXXV, No. 2 (March 1969), pp. 75-79.

Furniss, Norman, "The Practical Significance of Decentralization," *The Journal of Politics*, Vol. 36, No. 4 (November 1974), pp. 958-982.

"Intergovernmental Relations in the United States," *Annals of the American Academy of Political and Social Science*, Vol. 359 (May 1965).

Kaufman, Herbert, "Administrative Decentralization and Political Power," *Public Administration Review*, Vol. 29, No. 1 (January/February 1969), pp. 3-15.

Macmahon, Arthur W., "Interstate Compacts," 4 *Encyclopedia of the Social Sciences*, 109 (1931).

Reynolds, Harry W. Jr., "Merit Controls, the Hatch Acts, and Personal Standards in Intergovernmental Relations," in *The Annals of the American Academy of Political and Social Science*, Vol. 359 (May 1965).

The New Grass Roots Government? Decentralization and Citizen Participation in Urban Areas. Washington, D.C.: Advisory Commission on Intergovernmental Relations, 1972.

Zimmerman, F. L., "New Experience with Interstate Compacts," *The Western Political Quarterly*, Vol. V., No. 2, (June 1952).

THE PUBLIC POLICY PROCESS AND PROGRAM ACTION SYSTEMS

Books

Bedard, Paul W. and Ylvisker, Paul N., *Flagstaff Federal Sustained Yield Unit*. University, Alabama: University of Alabama Press, 1957.

Bish, Robert L., *The Public Economy of Metropolitan Areas*. Chicago: Markham Publishing Co., 1971.

Buchanan, James M. and Tullock, Gordon, *The Calculus of Consent: Logical Foundations of Constitutional Democracy*. Ann Arbor: University of Michigan Press, 1962.

Carper, Edith T., *Lobbying and the Natural Gas Bill*. University, Alabama: University of Alabama Press, 1962.

Devereux, Edward C. Jr., "Parsons' Sociological Theory," in Max Black (ed.) *The Sociological Theories of Talcott Parsons*. Englewood Cliffs, N.J.: Prentice-Hall, 1961.

Dewey, John, *The Public and its Problems*. New York: Holt, 1927.

Downs, Anthony, *An Economic Theory of Democracy*. New York: Harper & Row, 1957.

Dror, Yehezkel, *Public Policymaking Reexamined*. Scranton, Pa.: Chandler Publishing Co., 1968.

Dye, Thomas R., *Politics, Economics, and the Public: Policy Outcomes in the American States*. Chicago: Rand McNally & Co., 1966.

—— *Understanding Public Policy,* Englewood Cliffs, N.J.: Prentice-Hall, 1972.

Fayol, Henri, *General and Industrial Management*. London: Pitman, 1930.

Gross, Bertram M., *The Managing of Organizations,* Vols. I and II, Glencoe, Ill.: The Free Press, 1964.

Henry, Nicholas, *Public Administration and Public Affairs*. Englewood Cliffs, N.J.: Prentice-Hall, 1975.

Lerner, Daniel and Lasswell, Harold D. (eds.) *The Policy Sciences*. Stanford, Calif.: Stanford University Press, 1960.

Lilienthal, David, *TVA—Democracy on the March*. New York: Harper & Row, 1953.

Lindbloom, Charles E., *The Policy-Making Process*. Englewood Cliffs, N.J.: Prentice-Hall, 1968.

Lyden, Fremont J., Shipman, George A. and Kroll, Morton, *Policies, Decisions and Organizations*. New York: Appleton-Century-Crofts, 1969.

Merton, Robert K., *Social Theory and Social Structure*. revised ed. Glencoe, Ill.: The Free Press, 1957.

Michael, Donald N., *The Unprepared Society: Planning for a Precarious Future*. New York: Basic Books, 1968.

Mitchell, William O., *The American Polity*. Glencoe, Ill.: The Free Press, 1962.

Mishan, E. J., *Economics for Social Decisions: Elements of Cost Benefit Analysis*. New York: Praeger Publishers, 1972.

Olson, Mancur, *The Logic of Collective Action*. Cambridge: Harvard University Press, 1965.

Parsons, Talcott, *Toward A General Theory of Action*. Cambridge: Harvard University Press, 1951.

—— *The Social System*. Glencoe, Ill.: The Free Press, 1951.

—— *Working Papers in the Theory of Action*. Glencoe, Ill.: The Free Press, 1953.

Rescher, Nicholas, *Introduction to Value Theory*. Englewood Cliffs, N.J.: Prentice-Hall, 1969.

Rubinstein, Moshe F., *Patterns of Problem Solving*. Englewood Cliffs, N.J.: Prentice-Hall, 1975.

Schiff, Ashley L., *Fire and Water: Scientific Heresy in the Forest Service*. Cambridge: Harvard University Press, 1962.

Shipman, George A., *Designing Program Action Against Urban Poverty*. University: University of Alabama Press, 1971.

Shubert, Glendon, *The Public Interest*. Glencoe, Ill.: The Free Press, 1960.

Simon, Herbert, *Administrative Behavior*. New York: Macmillan, 1948.

Simon, Herbert, Smithburg, Donald W. and Thomson, Victor A., *Public Administration*. New York: Alfred A. Knopf, 1950.

Skinner, B. F., *Walden II*. New York: Macmillan, 1962.

Spiro, Herbert J., *Government by Constitution: The Political Systems of Democracy*. New York: Random House, 1959.

Thompson, James D., Hammond, Peter B., Hawkes, Robert W., Juner, Buford H., Tuden, Arthur, *Comparative Studies in Administration*. Pittsburgh: University of Pittsburgh Press, 1959.

Thompson, William Irwin, *Passages About Earth*. New York: Harper & Row, 1973.

Toffler, Alvin, *Future Shock*. New York: Random House, 1970.

Vickers, Geoffrey, *Value Systems and Social Process*. New York: Basic Books, 1968.

Wade, L. L. and Curry, R. L. Jr., *A Logic of Public Policy: Aspects of Political Economy*. Belmont, Calif.: Wadsworth Publishing Co., 1970.

Wholey, Joseph S. Scanion, John W., Duffy, Hugh G., Fudumoto, James S., and Vogt, Leona M., *Federal Evaluation Policy: Analyzing the Effects of Public Programs*. Washington, D.C.: Urban Institute, 1970.

Wiener, Norbert, *Cybernetics*. New York: John Wiley and Sons, 1948.

—— *The Human Use of Human Beings*. New York: Doubleday & Co., 1954.

Articles, Government Documents, Occasional Papers

Cassinelli, C. W., "Comments on Frank J. Sorauf's 'The Public Interest Reconsidered', " *Journal of Politics*, Vol. 20, No. 3, August 1958.

——"Some Reflection on the Concept of the Public Interest," *Ethica*, Vol. LXIX, No. 1, October, 1958.

Dickinson, John, "Social Order and Political Authority," *American Political Science Review*, Vol. XXIXI, No. 3, August, 1929.

deGrazia, Alfred, "The Science and Values of Administration II," *Administrative Science Quarterly,* Vol. 5, Part II, March, 1961.

Harmon, Michael Mont, "Administrative Policy Formulation and the Public Interest," *Public Administration Review*, Sept./Oct. 1969.

Hinderaken, Ivan, "The Study of Administration: Inter-disciplinary Dimensions," *Summary of Proceedings of the Western Political Science Association*, supplement to the *Western Political Quarterly* 16 (September 1963), pp. 5-12.

Leys, Wayne A. R., "Ethics and Administrative Discretion," *Public Administration Review*, Vol. III, No. 1, Winter 1943.

Lyden, F. J., Shipman, G. and Wilkinson, R. J., "Decision Flow Analysis: A Methodology for Studying the Policy Making Process," in LeBreton, *Comparative Administrative Theory*. Seattle: University of Washington Press, 1968.

Mitchell, William C., "The Polity and Society: A Structural-Functional Analysis," *Midwest Journal of Political Science*, Vol. 2, No. 4, 1958.

Parsons, Talcott, "A Sociological Approach to the Theory of Organizations," *Administrative Science Quarterly*, Vol. 1, June, 1956, and Vol. II, Sept. 1956.

——"General Theory in Sociology," in Robert K. Merton, et al., *Sociology Today*. New York: Basic Books, 1959.

Sorauf, Frank J., "The Public Interest Reconsidered," *The Journal of Politics*, Vol. 9, No. 4, November 1957.

Selznick, Phillip, "Foundations of the Theory of Organization," *American Sociological Review*, Vol. 13, Feb. 1958.

Shipman, George A., "The Policy Process," *Western Political Quarterly*, Vol. 12, June 1959, p. 544.

Shubert, Glendon A. Jr., "'The Public Interest' in Administrative Decision-Making," *American Political Science Review*, Vol. LI, June 1957.

Simmons, Robert H., Davis, Bruce W., Chapman, Ralph J. K., Sager, Daniel D., "Policy Flow Analysis: A Conceptual Model for Comparative Public Policy Research," *Western Political Quarterly*, Vol. XXVII, No. 3, Sept. 1974.

Spiro, Herbert J., "Comparative Politics: A Comparative Approach," *American Political Science Review*, Sept. 1962.

PUBLIC MANAGEMENT

Books

Argyvis, Chris, *Interpersonal Competence and Organizational Effectiveness*. Homewood, Ill.: Dorsey Press, 1962.

—— *Organization and Innovation*. Homewood, Ill.: Richard D. Irwin, Inc., 1965.

Bakke, E. Wight, *Bonds of Organization*. New York: Harper, 1950.

Bennis, Warren G., *Changing Organization*. New York: McGraw-Hill Book Co., 1966.

Benveniste, Guy, *The Politics of Expertise*. Berkeley, Calif.: Glendessary Press, 1972.

Boguslow, Robert, *The New Utopians: A Study of System Design and Social Change*. Englewood Cliffs, N.J.: Prentice-Hall, 1965.

Boulding, Kenneth E., *Conflict and Defense: A General Theory*. New York: Harper, 1963.

Boulding, Kenneth E., *The Organizational Revolution*. New York: Harper & Row, 1953.

Buchanan, J. M., *Public Finance in Democratic Process*. Chapel Hill: University of North Carolina Press, 1967.

Burkhead, Jesse, *Government Budgeting*. New York: Wiley, 1956.

Burns, Tom and Stalker, G. M., *The Management of Innovation*. London: Tavistock Publications, 1961.

Caiden, Gerald, *Administrative Reform*. Chicago: Aldine, 1969.

Coser, Lewis, *The Functions of Social Conflict*. London: Routledge & Kegan Paul, Ltd., 1956.

Crozier, Michel, *The Bureaucratic Phenomenon*. Chicago: The University of Chicago Press, 1964.

Downs, Anthony, *Inside Bureaucracy*. Boston: Little, Brown, 1967.

Dror, Yehezkel, *Ventures in Policy Sciences*. American Elsevier, 1971.

Ellul, Jacques, *The Technological Society*. Translated by John Wilkinson. New York: Alfred A. Knopf, 1964.

Follett, Mary Parker, *Creative Experience*. New York: P. Smith, 1951 (1924).

—— *Dynamic Administration. The Collected Papers of Mary Parker Follett*. Henry C. Metcalf and L. Urwick (eds.). New York: Harper & Row, 1942.

Golembiewski, Robert T., *Men, Management and Morality: Toward a New Organizational Ethic* New York: McGraw-Hill, 1965.

Golembiewski, Robert T. (ed.), *Public Budgeting and Finance, Readings in Theory and Practice*. Itasca, Ill.: F. E. Peacock, 1968.

Gore, William J., *Administrative Decision–Making: A Heuristic Model*. New York: Wiley, 1964.

Gouldner, Alvin W., *Patterns of Industrial Bureaucracy*. New York: The Free Press of Glencoe, 1954.

Haveman, Robert N. and Julius Margolis (eds.) *Public Expenditures and Policy Analysis*. Chicago: Markham Publishing, 1970.

Hitch, Charles J. and McKean, Roland, *The Economics of Defense in the Nuclear Age*. Cambridge: Harvard University Press, 1960.

Kast, Fremont E. and Rosenzweig, James E., *Organization and Management: A Systems Approach*. New York: McGraw-Hill Book Co. (2nd ed.), 1974.

Katz, Daniel and Kahn, Robert L., *The Social Psychology of Organizations*. New York: John Wiley & Sons, 1966.

Krupp, Sherman, *Patterns in Organizational Analysis: A Critical Analysis*. Philadelphia: Chilton Publishing Co., 1961.

Lee, Robert D. Jr., and Johnson, Ronald W., *Public Budgeting Systems*. Baltimore: University Park Press, 1973.

Likert, Rensis, *The Human Organization*. New York: McGraw-Hill Book Co., 1960.

——*New Patterns of Management*. New York: McGraw-Hill, 1961.

Lyden, F. J. and E. G. Miller, *Planning–Programming–Budgeting: A Systems Approach to Management*. Chicago: Markham Publishing Co., 1972.

McGregor, Douglas, *The Human Side of Enterprise*. New York: McGraw-Hill Book Co., 1960.

—— *The Professional Manager*. New York: McGraw-Hill Book Co., 1967.

Mali, Paul, *Managing by Objectives*. New York: John Wiley and Sons, 1972.

Malick, Sidney and Edward H. Van Ness (eds.), *Concepts and Issues in Administrative Behavior*. Englewood Cliffs, N.J.: Prentice-Hall, Inc., 1962.

March, James G. (ed.), *Handbook of Organizations*. Chicago: Rand McNally and Co., 1965.

March, James G. and Simon, Herbert A., *Organizations*. New York: John Wiley and Sons, 1958.

Merton, Robert K., Gray, Aïlsa P., Hockey, Barbara, Selvin, Hanan C. (eds.), *Reader in Bureaucracy*. Glencoe, Ill.: The Free Press, 1952.

Mooney, James D. and Reiley, Alan C., *Onward Industry*. New York and London: Harper Bros., 1931.

——*The Principles of Organization*. New York: Harper and Bros., 1939.

Morrow, William L., *Public Administration Politics and the Political System*. New York: Random House, 1975.

Perrow, Charles, *Organizational Analysis: A Sociological View*. Belmont, Calif.: Wadsworth, 1970.

Schick, Allen, *Budgetary Innovation in the States*. Washington, D.C.: The Brookings Institute, 1971.

Sharkansky, Iva, *The Politics of Taxing and Spending*. Indianapolis: Bobbs-Merrill, 1970.

Sherman, Harvey, *It All Depends: A Pragmatic Approach to Organization*. University, Alabama: University of Alabama Press, 1966.

Taylor, Frederick W., *Scientific Management*. New York: Harper, 1947 (first published in 1911).

Thompson, James D., *Organizations in Action*. New York: McGraw-Hill, 1967.

Thayer, Frederick C., *An End to Hierarchy! An End to Competition!* New York: New Viewpoints, 1973.

Withington, Frederich G., *The Real Computer: Its Influence, Uses, and Effects*. Reading, Massachusetts: Addison-Wesley, 1969.

Articles, Government Documents, Occasional Papers

Babunakis, Michael, *Recasting the Budgetary Process*. Urban Observatory of San Diego, Calif., 1974.

Carroll, James D., "Noetic Authority," *Public Administration Review*, Sept/Oct. 1969.

Council of State Governments, *Budgeting by the States*. Lexington, Ky. Council of State Governments, 1967.

Deniston, O. Lynn, Rosenstock, Irwin M., Welch, William, Getting, V. A., "Evaluation of Program Effectiveness and Program Efficiency," in Fremont J. Lyden and Ernest G. Miller, *Planning, Programming, Budgeting: A Systems Approach to Management*. Chicago: Markham Publishing Co., 1972.

Fite, Harry H., "Administrative Evaluation of ADP in State Government," *Public Administration Review*. 21 (Winter, 1961), pp. 1–7.

Goffman, Erving, "The Characteristics of Total Institutions," in *Walter Reed Institute of Research, Symposium on Preventive and Social Psychiatry.* Washington, D.C.: U.S. Government Printing Office, 1957, pp. 43-84.

Gouldner, Alvin W., "Cosmopolitans and Locals: Toward an Analysis of Latent Social Roles," *Administrative Science Quarterly*, 2 (Dec., 1957 and March, 1958), pp. 231-306, 440-480.

Gouldner, Alvin, "Organizational Analysis," in *Sociology Today*, edited by Robert K. Merton, Leonard Broom, and Leonard S. Cottrell, Jr., New York: Basic Books, Inc., pp. 400-428.

Gross, Bertram M., "Planning in an Era of Social Revolution," *Public Administration Review*, May/June, 1971.

Landau, Martin, "The Concepts of Decision-Making in the Field of Public Administration," in *Concepts and Issues in Administrative Behavior*, Sidney Malick and Edward H. Van Ness (eds.). Englewood Cliffs, N.J.: Prentice-Hall, 1962.

Lindbloom, Charles E., "The Science of Muddling Through," *Public Administration Review*, Vol. 19, 1959.

Luther, Robert A., "PPBS in Fairfax County: A Practical Experience," *Municipal Finance* (August 1968), pp. 34-42.

McGregor, Douglas, "Theory X and Theory Y," in *People in Public Service: A Reader in Public Personnel Administration*, edited by Robert T. Golembiewski and Michael Cohen, Itasca, Ill.: F. E. Peacock Publishing, 1970.

Merton, Robert K., "Bureaucratic Structure and Personality," *Social Forces*, 18 (1940), pp. 560-568.

Public Automated Systems Service. *Automated Data Processing in Municipal Government.* Chicago, Public Administration Service, 1966.

——*Automation in State Government, 1966-67: A Second Report on Status and Trends.* Chicago: Public Administration Service, 1967.

Quade, E. S., "Systems Analysis Techniques for Planning-Programming-Budgeting," in *Planning-Programming-Budgeting: A Systems Approach to Management.* Edited by Fremont J. Lyden and Ernest G. Miller. Chicago: Markham Publishing Company, 1972.

Schick, Allen, "The Road to PPB, the Stages of Budget Reform," *Public Administration Review*, Vol. 26 (Dec. 1966), pp. 243-258.

Segal, Morley, "Organization and Environment: A Typology of Adaptability and Structure," *Public Administration Review*, May/June 1974.

Smithies, Arthur, "Conceptual Framework for the Program Budget," in David Novilk, *Program Budgeting, Program Analysis and the Federal Budget*. Cambridge: Harvard University Press, 1965.

Simmons, Robert H., "The Washington State Plural Executive: An Initial Effort in Interaction Analysis," *The Western Political Quarterly*, Vol. XVIII, No. 2, June 1965.

Waldo, Dwight (ed.), "Planning-Programming-Budgeting System: A Symposium," *Public Administration Review*, Vol. 26 (December 1966), pp. 243-310.

Waldo, Dwight (ed.), Planning-Programming-Budgeting System Re-Examined: Development, Analysis and Criticism, A Symposium," *Public Administration Review* 29 (March–April 1969), pp. 111-202.

HUMANE BUREAUCRACY

Books

Bennis, Warren G., *Organizational Development: Its Nature, Origins and Prospects*. Reading, Massachusetts: Addison-Wesley Publishing Co., 1969.

Bensman, Joseph and Vidich, Arthur J., *The New American Society: The Revolution of the Middle Class*. Chicago: Quadrangle Books, 1971.

Berne, Eric, *What Do You Say After You Say Hello?* New York: Grove Press, 1972.

Bion, W. R., *Experiences in Groups*. New York: Basic Books, 1959.

Bendix, Reinhard, *Max Weber, An Intellectual Portrait*. New York: Doubleday and Co., 1960.

Dicey, A. V., *Introduction to the Study of Law and the Constitution*, 8th edition. London: Macmillan, 1927.

Gerth, H. H. and Mills, C. Wright (eds.), *From Max Weber: Essays in Sociology*. New York: Oxford University Press, 1946.

Goodwin, Richard N., *The American Condition*. Garden City, New York: Doubleday, 1974.

Hampden–Turner, Charles, *Radical Man*. New York: Anchor Books, 1971.

Hoffer, Eric, *The True Believer*. New York: Harper & Row, 1951.

Kahn, R. L., et al., *Organizational Stress*. New York: John Wiley and Sons, 1964.

Knowles, Malcolm S., *The Modern Practice of Adult Education*. New York: Association Press, 1970.

Lasswell, Harold D., *Power and Personality*. New York: The Viking Press, 1948.

Lewin, Kurt, *Resolving Social Conflicts*. New York: Harper & Row, 1948.

Lockard, Duane, *The Perverted Priorities of American Politics*. New York: Macmillan, 1971.

Marcuse, Herbert, *One-Dimensional Man*. Boston: Beacon Press, 1964.

——*Eupsychian Management*. Homewood, Ill.: Richard D. Irwin and the Dorsey Press, 1965.

——*Motivation and Personality*. New York: Harper & Row, 1970.

May, Rollo, *Power and Innocence*. New York: W. W. Norton & Co., 1972.

Menninger, Karl, *Whatever Became of Sin?* New York: Hawthorne Books, 1973.

Menzies, Isabel E. P., *The Functioning of Social Systems as a Defense Against Anxiety. A Report on the Study of Nursing Service of a General Hospital*. London: Tavistock Pamphlet No. 3, 1967.

Mill, John Stuart, *On Liberty (1859)*, edited by Alburey Castell. Northbrook, Illinois: A. H. M. Publishing Co., 1947.

Sampson, Ronald V., *The Psychology of Power*. New York: Vintage Books, 1965.

Schutz, William, *FIRO: A Three Dimensional Theory of Interpersonal Behavior*, Holt Rinehart, 1958, published later as *The Interpersonal Underworld*, Science and Behavior Books, 1960.

Steiner, Claude, *Scripts People Live*. New York: Grove Press, 1974.

Thomas, John M. and Bennis, Warren G., *Management of Change and Conflict*. Baltimore, Md.: Penguin Books, 1972.

Thompson, Victor Alexander, *Modern Organization*. New York: Alfred A. Knopf, 1961.

—— *Without Sympathy or Enthusiasm: The Problem of Administrative Compassion*. University, Ala.: University of Alabama Press, 1975.

Tullock, Gordon, *The Politics of Bureaucracy*. Washington, D.C.: Public Affairs Press, 1965.

Weber, Max, *Economy and Society*. Guenther Roth and Claus Wittich (eds.). New York: Bedminster Press, 1968.

Whyte, William H., *The Organization Man*. New York: Simon and Schuster, 1956.

Yablonsky, Lewis, *Robopaths*. Baltimore: Penguin Books, 1972.

BIBLIOGRAPHY

Articles, Government Documents, Occasional Papers

Graham, George A., "Ethical Guidelines for Public Administrators: Observations on Rules of the Game," *Public Administration Review,* Vol. 34, No. 1 (Jan/Feb 1974).

Hayzelden, J. E., "The Value of Human Life," *Public Administration.* London, Vol. 46, Winter, 1968.

Karpman, Stephen B., "Script Drama Analysis," *Transactions Analysis Bulletin* 7, 26, 1968.

Kirkhart, Larry and White, Brian F. Jr., "The Future of Organization Development," *Public Administration Review,* March/April, 1974.

Knowles, Malcolm S., "Human Resources Development in OD," *Public Administration Review,* March/April, 1974.

Lehner, George F. S., "Team Development Trainer's Workshop," *Public Administration Review,* March/April, 1974.

Lyden, F. J., "Project Management: Beyond Bureaucracy," *Public Administration Review,* July/August, 1970.

Platt, C. Spencer, "Humanizing Public Administration," *Public Administration Review,* Vol. VII, No. 3 (Summer 1947), pp. 193-199.

Poland, Orville F., "Program Evaluation and Administrative Theory," *Public Administration Review,* Vol. 34, No. 4 (July/August 1974).

Rioch, Margaret J., "All We Like Sheep . . . (Isiah 53:6) Followers and Leaders," *Psychiatry,* Vol. 34, 1971.

Rogers, Carl R., "A Humanistic Conception of Man," in R. E. Farson (ed.), *Science and Human Affairs.* Palto Alto, California: Science and Behavior Books.

INDEX

democratization of bureaucracy, 200-208

Without Sympathy or Enthusiasm. The Problem of Administrative Compassion, 640

Woll, Peter, 59

Women in public employment, 174-175

Work group, 625-626

Worker-employee participation, 493

Yablonsky, Lewis, 621